R. Gupta's®

POPULAR MASTER GUIDE

DSSSB–TEACHERS

PGT

PHYSICS

Recruitment Exam

by

RPH Editorial Board

RAMESH PUBLISHING HOUSE, NEW DELHI

Published by
O.P. Gupta *for* Ramesh Publishing House

Admin. Office
12-H, New Daryaganj Road, Opp. Officers' Mess,
New Delhi-110002 ✆ 23275224, 23245124

E-mail: info@rameshpublishinghouse.com
For Online Shopping: www.rameshpublishinghouse.com

Showroom
• Balaji Market, Nai Sarak, Delhi-110006 ✆ 23282525 📱 9354373464
• 4457, Nai Sarak, Delhi-110006

Book Code: R-1313

ISBN: 978-93-5012-012-5

Price: ₹ 320

Printed at: Deepak Offset, Delhi

CONTENTS

❑❑❑

Scheme of Examination

DSSSB will conduct **One Tier Exam** for PGT posts having two section:

Section-I

S.No.	Subject	Questions	Marks
1.	Mental Ability and Reasoning Ability	20	20
2.	General Awareness	20	20
3.	English Language & Comprehension	20	20
4.	Hindi Language & Comprehension	20	20
5.	Numerical Aptitude & Data Interpretation	20	20
	Total	**100**	**100**

Section-II

S.No.	Subject	Questions	Marks
1.	MCQs pertaining to Post-Graduation qualification and teaching methodology required for the post.	**200**	**200**

Previous Years' Paper

Delhi Subordinate Services Selection Board (DSSSB)

PGT–PHYSICS, RECRUITMENT EXAM, 2025

(Exam held on 30-07-2025)

Subject Knowledge – Physics & Teaching Methodology

1. A cell of emf 12 V and internal resistance 1 Ω is connected to an external resistor of 5 Ω. What is the current drawn from the cell?

1. 4 A
2. 3 A
3. 2 A
4. 1.5 A

2. Given the electron mobility $\mu_e = 1500$ cm²/V·s and effective mass $m_e = 9.11 \times 10^{-31}$ kg, what is the relaxation time τ of electrons?

1. 8.5×10^{-13} s
2. 6.5×10^{-12} s
3. 4.5×10^{-14} s
4. 8.5×10^{-9} s

3. Which of the following is a use of ultraviolet rays?

(*i*) They are used for water purification.
(*ii*) They are used in radar systems for aircraft navigation.
(*iii*) They are used for radio and television communication systems.
(*iv*) They are used in high precision eye surgery.

1. Both (*i*) and (*iv*)
2. Both (*ii*) and (*iv*)
3. Both (*i*) and (*iii*)
4. Both (*ii*) and (*iii*)

4. Which of the following materials has the LOWEST electrical resistivity at 0°C?

1. Iron
2. Tungsten
3. Aluminium
4. Platinum

5. A power line has a resistance of 0.1 Ω per kilometre. If a current of 500 A flows through a 50 km long power line, then what is the power loss in the line?

1. 2500 W
2. 1250 kW
3. 125 MW
4. 1250 W

6. Which of the following statements about eddy currents in transformer is true?

1. Laminating the core increases the effect of eddy currents.
2. Eddy currents are induced by direct current (DC) flux.
3. Eddy currents reduce the heating effect in the iron core.
4. Eddy currents are induced by alternating magnetic flux.

7. Which of the following is the typical wavelength spectrum of X-rays?

1. 0.1 m to 1 mm
2. $< 10^{-3}$ nm
3. 400 nm to 1 nm
4. 1 nm to 10^{-3} nm

8. Which of the following devices DOES NOT utilise the effect of eddy currents in its primary operation?

1. Magnetic braking in trains
2. Electric fan
3. Electric power meters
4. Induction furnace

9. Which of the following statements is true for electromagnetic waves?

1. They need a material medium to propagate.
2. They carry energy and momentum.
3. They are composed of particles only.
4. They transport charge from one place to another.

10. The electrostatic potential at any point in a region with electrostatic field is _____.

1. the work done to move a unit positive charge from infinity to that point
2. the product of electric field and charge
3. the rate of change of electric field
4. the electric field strength at that point

11. If three resistors $R_1 = 0.1\ \Omega$, $R_2 = 0.01\ \Omega$ and $R_3 = 0.001\ \Omega$ are connected in parallel, what is the equivalent resistance of the combination?

1. 0.09 MΩ 2. 0.09 kΩ
3. 9 Ω 4. 0.9 mΩ

12. What happens when multiple cells are connected in series?

1. The total emf is the average of all emf values
2. The total internal resistance is reduced while emf remains the same
3. Both the total emf and total internal resistance decrease
4. The total emf and total internal resistance are equal to the sum of each cell's emf and resistance respectively

13. A metallic wire has a resistance of 20 Ω at 20 °C. If its temperature co-efficient of resistivity is 0.005 $°C^{-1}$, at what temperature would its resistance increases to 30 Ω?

1. 100°C 2. 120°C
3. 90°C 4. 80°C

14. Which phenomenon allows microwaves to efficiently transfer energy to water molecules in food?

1. Doppler effect 2. Resonance
3. Refraction 4. Interference

15. Two coils, A and B, have mutual inductance of 'X' H. If the current in A increases uniformly from 0 to 30 A in 2 s, causing a flux linkage change of 90 Wb in B, find X (assume perfect coupling).

1. 3 H 2. 1/3 H
3. 1/30 H 4. 30 H

16. What is the dimensional formula for the EMF of a cell?

1. $M L^2 T^{-3} A^1$ 2. $M L^{-2} T^{-3} A^{-1}$
3. $M^2 L^3 T^3 A^{-1}$ 4. $M L^2 T^{-3} A^{-1}$

17. A bar magnet is dropped such that its North pole points downwards, falling through the centre of a horizontal conducting ring. The ring is initially at rest. As the North pole of the magnet approaches the ring from above, then passes through it, and finally moves away below it, what is the direction of the induced current in the ring (as seen from above) and the nature of the force exerted by the ring on the magnet?

1. When approaching, the current is anti-clockwise and force is repulsive; when moving away, the current is clockwise and force is attractive.
2. When approaching, the current is anti-clockwise and force is attractive; when moving away, the current is clockwise and force is repulsive.
3. The current is always clockwise, and the force is always attractive.
4. When approaching, the current is clockwise and force is attractive; when moving away, the current is anti-clockwise and force is repulsive.

18. What does the mobility (μ) of a charge carrier represent in an electric field?

1. The magnitude of drift velocity per unit electric field
2. The number of electrons moving per second
3. The rate at which charge carriers accelerate in a magnetic field
4. The amount of charge per unit voltage

19. Which of the following statements is true about the polarisation of electromagnetic waves?

1. Only radio waves can be polarised.
2. Every electromagnetic wave can be polarised.
3. Only microwaves can be polarised.
4. Only visible light can be polarised.

20. A copper wire of cross-section 1 mm^2 is carrying a current of 2 A. The density of conduction electrons in copper is 8.5 $\times 10^{28}$ m^{-3}. What is the drift velocity of copper electrons?

1. 1.4×10^{-3} m/s
2. 0.14×10^{-3} m/s
3. 14×10^{-3} m/s
4. 0.014×10^{-3} m/s

21. In a non-polar molecule, the centres of positive and negative charges lie at the same point. What does this imply about the molecule?

1. The molecule behaves like a small magnet.
2. The molecule always gets attracted to a charged object.
3. The molecule has a strong permanent dipole moment.
4. The molecule has no permanent dipole moment.

22. What will be the value of electric potential at a point located 0.1 m away from a point charge of 10^{-7} C? (Take $k = 1/4\pi\varepsilon_0 = 9 \times 10^9$ Nm^2/C^2)

1. 9 V
2. 900 V
3. 90 V
4. 9000 V

23. How does an intrinsic semiconductor behave at absolute zero temperature (0 K)?

1. Like a perfect conductor
2. Like a superconductor
3. Like a metal with high conductivity
4. Like an insulator with no free charge carriers

24. An electric dipole with dipole moment 8×10^{-9} C m is aligned at 60° with the direction of a uniform electric field of magnitude 4×10^4 NC^{-1}. What will be the magnitude of the torque acting on the dipole?

1. $16\sqrt{3} \times 10^{-5}$ Nm
2. 16×10^{-5} Nm
3. 8×10^{-5} Nm
4. $8\sqrt{3} \times 10^{-5}$ Nm

25. If three capacitors with capacitances, 5 μF, 8 μF and 10 μF are connected in parallel, then what is the effective capacitance (C_{eff})?

1. 0.425 μF
2. 0.85 μF
3. 23 μF
4. 11.5 μF

26. An earth satellite is orbiting at a height such that the radius of its orbit from the centre of the earth is R. If the acceleration due to gravity at this orbital height is g', what is the orbital velocity of the satellite?

1. $\sqrt{2g'R}$
2. $\sqrt{g'R}$
3. $g'R$
4. $\sqrt{\frac{g'}{R}}$

27. If three capacitors with capacitances $C_1 = 1$ μF, $C_2 = 1$ *n*F and $C_3 = 1$ *m*F are connected in series, then what is the effective capacitance (C_{eff}) approximately?

1. 1 *n*F
2. 0.33 μF
3. 0.5 *n*F
4. 1.5 μF

28. Which of the following correctly gives the function of a full wave rectifier?

1. It is a device that converts direct current to alternating current.
2. It is a device that converts alternating current to direct current.
3. It is a device that converts high voltage at low current to low voltage at high current.
4. It is a device that converts low voltage at high current to high voltage at low current.

29. A Zener diode with a Zener breakdown voltage Vz of 6.0 volt is used in a voltage regulator circuit. Suppose that, this Zener diode is connected in parallel with a load/external resistor, what will be the voltage across the load resistor when Zener diode is operating in its breakdown region?

1. Depends on the input voltage
2. Less than 6.0 volts
3. More than 6.0 volts
4. 6.0 volts

30. Which quantity changes with time during uniformly accelerated motion?

1. Only Acceleration
2. Only Velocity
3. Only Displacement
4. Both Displacement and Velocity

31. Which component is commonly used with the load R_L in parallel connection to filter the output of a full-wave rectifier to smooth the DC signal?

1. Diode
2. Inductor
3. Capacitor
4. Resistor

32. What is the output of a NOR gate when both inputs are 0?

1. 0
2. 1
3. Depends on previous inputs
4. Undefined

33. If the orbital period of a planet is doubled, then by what factor does it Third Law of Planetary Motion?

1. $\sqrt[3]{4}$
2. $\sqrt[3]{10}$
3. $\sqrt[3]{12}$
4. $\sqrt[3]{6}$

34. According to the energy band model, which type of material possesses a very wide energy band gap, typically greater than 3 eV, making it a very poor conductor of electricity at room temperature?

1. Superconductors
2. Insulators
3. Conductors
4. Semiconductors

35. Why is the I–V characteristic curve of a solar cell plotted in the fourth quadrant?

1. Because the solar cell only works in reverse bias
2. Because the solar cell supplies current instead of drawing it
3. Because voltage and current are both negative in a solar cell
4. Because the solar cell absorbs current from the load

36. At large distances, the electric field of a dipole is strongest ______.

1. when it is perpendicular to the axis of the dipole
2. when it is at a 45° angle to the axis of the dipole
3. when it is along the axis of the dipole
4. when the field is uniform in all directions

37. A 5 μF air-filled capacitor is inserted with a dielectric of constant 4. What is the new capacitance?

1. 1.25 μF
2. 20 μF
3. 5 μF
4. 4 μF

38. According to the concept of electric field, a charge Q creates an electric field in the space around it. When another infinitesimally small charge *q* is brought near it and placed at a point P, what happens?

1. Both charges remain unaffected unless connected by a wire.
2. The electric field due to Q exerts a force on *q* placed at point P.
3. Charge *q* feels no force unless it is in motion.
4. The charge *q* creates a force field that pushes Q away.

39. If no electric charge is enclosed inside a closed surface, what can we say about the total electric flux through that surface?

1. It is always positive.
2. It is equal to the charge placed outside the surface.
3. It depends on the shape and size of the surface.
4. It is zero, because no charge is inside the surface.

40. Which of the following statements about equipotential surfaces is always true?

1. The electric potential is zero everywhere on an equipotential surface.
2. Two equipotential surfaces can intersect each other.

3. Work done in moving a charge along an equipotential surface is always non-zero.
4. Electric fields are always perpendicular to equipotential surfaces.

41. Which of the following statements about a bar magnet and an equivalent solenoid is true?

1. A bar magnet and an equivalent solenoid both have a magnetic field only inside their bodies.
2. A bar magnet and an equivalent solenoid both have a magnetic field both inside and outside.
3. A bar magnet has a magnetic field both inside and outside, whereas a solenoid has a magnetic field only inside.
4. A bar magnet has a magnetic field only inside its body, whereas a solenoid has a magnetic field both inside and outside.

42. For photo-electric emission to occur from a metal surface, the energy of the incident photon must be _____.

1. less than the work function of the metal
2. independent of the work function of the metal
3. equal to the kinetic energy of the emitted electron
4. greater than or equal to the work function of the metal

43. Polar satellites typically have _____.

1. medium altitude and long period
2. low altitude and short period
3. high altitude and short period
4. very high altitude and long period

44. A system of three particles with masses 2 kg, 3 kg, and 5 kg are located at (1, 0), (2, 0) and (3, 0) respectively. The *x*-coordinate of CM is _____.

1. 2.5   2. 2.3
3. 2.0   4. 3.0

45. A straight wire of mass 325 g and length 3 m carries a current of 4.5 A. It is suspended in mid-air by a uniform horizontal magnetic field B. What is the magnitude of the magnetic field (Take $g = 10\ \text{m/s}^2$)?

1. 0.240 T   2. 0.120 T
3. 0.440 T   4. 0 T

46. Two equal masses attract each other with the gravitational force 'X' N at distance *d*. If each mass is tripled and the distance is reduced to *d*/6, what is the new force in terms of X?

1. X/324 N   2. X/36 N
3. 36X N   4. 324X N

47. A bar magnet has a magnetic moment M. Consider the two points P and Q. Point P is located on the axial line of the magnet at a distance (*d*) form its centre. Point Q is located on the equatorial line of the magnet at the same distance (*d*) from its center. What is the ratio of the magnitude of the magnetic field strength at point P to the magnetic field strength at point Q?

1. 2 : 1   2. 4 : 1
3. 1 : 1   4. 1 : 2

48. Let $\vec{a}$ and $\vec{b}$ be two vectors, and let θ be the smaller angle between them. Which of the following is true?

1. $|\vec{a} \times \vec{b}| = ab \cos \theta$
2. $\vec{a} \times \vec{b} = ab$
3. $\vec{a} \cdot \vec{b} = ab \cos \theta$
4. $\vec{a} \cdot \vec{b} = ab \sin \theta$

49. Magnetic susceptibility (χ) of a paramagnetic material is _____.

1. negative
2. zero
3. positive and large
4. positive and small

50. A circular disc has moment of inertia I_{cm} about its center and perpendicular to its plane. What is its moment of inertia about a tangent perpendicular to its plane?

1. $I_{cm} + MR^2/2$ 2. $I_{cm} + 2MR^2$
3. $I_{cm} + MR^2/4$ 4. $I_{cm} + MR^2$

51. A current carrying loop with magnetic dipole moment; ($\vec{m}$) is placed in a magnetic field ($\vec{B}$) such that a torque ($\vec{\tau}$) acts on the loop. Which of the following is the correct mathematical relation for torque in terms of magnetic moment and magnetic field?

1. $\vec{\tau} = \vec{m} \times \vec{B}$ 2. $\vec{\tau} = \vec{m} + \vec{B}$
3. $\vec{\tau} = \vec{m}/\vec{B}$ 4. $\tau = \vec{m} \cdot \vec{B}$

52. The magnitude of the moment of force (torque) produced by a force about a given axis depends on which of the following factors?

1. Both the magnitude of the force and the perpendicular distance from the axis of rotation to the line of action of the force
2. Only the magnitude of the force
3. Only the direction of the force
4. The mass of the object

53. Which of these is NOT a common application of the parallel axis theorem?

1. Determining the moment of inertia of a flywheel
2. Calculating the moment of inertia of a compound pendulum
3. Finding the moment of inertia of a sphere about its diameter
4. Computing the moment of inertia of a planet about its rotational axis which is not at the centre

54. Two musical tuning forks are struck simultaneously. One fork vibrates at a frequency of X Hz and the other at Y Hz. A listener hears a fluctuating sound due to the interference of the two waves. Which of the following correctly represents the beat frequency ν, heard by the listener? (Assume X is greater than Y.)

1. $\nu = X - Y$ 2. $\nu = X/Y$
3. $\nu = X + Y$ 4. $\nu = X\,Y$

55. A ball is thrown vertically upwards at a velocity of 20 m/s from the top of a building. The height of the point from where the ball is thrown is 25 m from the ground. How high will the ball rise from the top of a building? [Take $g = 10$ m/s^2]

1. 25 m 2. 20 m
3. 30 m 4. 45 m

56. In the alpha scattering experiment, a very small fraction of alpha particles were deflected by large angles. What does this imply?

1. Alpha particles are unstable
2. Electrons are massive
3. Nucleus is small and dense
4. Nucleus is negatively charged

57. For a source moving at 30 m/s towards an observer moving at 20 m/s towards the source, with the speed of sound being 340 m/s and the emitted frequency being 500 Hz, the observed frequency is approximately ________.

1. 485 Hz 2. 430 Hz
3. 580 Hz 4. 515 Hz

58. A point on the rim of a wheel moves a linear distance of 5.0 m. If the radius of the wheel is 0.5 m, what is the angular displacement of the wheel in radians?

1. 5.0 rad 2. 10.0 rad
3. 2.5 rad 4. 0.1 rad

59. According to Kepler's third law ($T^2 \alpha R^3$); if earth's orbital period is approximately 1 earth year and its average distance from the sun is R_E, what would be the approximate orbital period of a hypothetical planet whose average distance from the sun is $4R_E$?

1. 16 earth years 2. 4 earth years
3. 64 earth years 4. 8 earth years

60. The angular speed of a motor wheel is decreased from 3120 rpm to 1200 rpm in X seconds. If the angular deceleration of the motor wheel is 4π rad/s^2, then what is the value of X?

1. 1.6 s 2. 16 s
3. 4800 s 4. 480 s

61. If a wave has a frequency of 50 Hz, what is its angular frequency (ω) and time period (T)?

1. 100.0 π rad/s; 0.02 s
2. 25.0 π rad/s; 0.005 s
3. 50.0 π rad/s; 0.01 s
4. 125.0 π rad/s; 0.03 s

62. A particle performing SHM has an amplitude of 3 cm and an angular frequency of 2 rad/s. What is its maximum acceleration?

1. 12 m/s^2 2. 0.18 m/s^2
3. 18 m/s^2 4. 0.12 m/s^2

63. The direction of particle vibration is perpendicular to wave motion in _____.

1. longitudinal waves
2. sound in air
3. light
4. pressure wave in liquid

64. The pressure of an ideal gas is due to _____.

1. weight of gas molecules
2. intermolecular forces
3. repulsive forces
4. collision of molecules with walls

65. According to the kinetic theory of an ideal gas, which of the following correctly gives the relation between pressure P, number density *n*, mass of a molecule *m* and mean of squared speed $\overline{v^2}$?

1. $P = \frac{1}{2}nm\overline{v^2}$ 2. $P = \frac{1}{3}nm\overline{v^2}$

3. $P = \frac{1}{3}nm\overline{v}$ 4. $P = \frac{3}{2}nm\overline{v^2}$

66. According to the Second Law of Thermodynamics, which of the following statements is true?

1. The efficiency of a heat engine can be equal to unity and the refrigerator's coefficient of performance always be infinite.
2. The efficiency of a heat engine can be unity but the refrigerator's coefficient of performance is always infinite.
3. The efficiency of a heat engine can never be unity and the refrigerator's coefficient of performance can never be infinite.
4. Both efficiency and coefficient of performance can never be determined.

67. A fluid has a bulk modulus of 2.0×10^9 N/m^2. If the fluid undergoes a fractional decrease in volume of 0.001, what is the increase in pressure required to achieve this change?

1. 2.0×10^6 N/m^2
2. 0.001 N/m^2
3. 2.0×10^{12} N/m^2
4. 2.0×10^9 N/m^2

68. Which of the following is necessary for lift generation in aerofoils?

1. Rotation of the wing
2. Faster air flow above
3. Equal path principle
4. Increase in air density

69. When light of the right frequency shines on a metal surface, tiny particles called electrons are released from the surface. What are these electrons called?

1. Free electrons 2. Valence electrons
3. Photoelectrons 4. Thermo particles

70. What do we call the average distance a gas molecule travels before it hits another molecule?

1. Drift velocity
2. Mean free path
3. Rotational distance
4. Kinetic range

71. What do we call the ratio of shearing stress to shearing strain in a material?

1. Elastic limit 2. Modulus of rigidity
3. Bulk modulus 4. Young's modulus

72. Which of the following correctly represents the relation between the de Broglie wavelength (λ) of a particle of mass *m*, speed *v* and Planck's constant (*h*)?

1. $\lambda = h \times mv$ 2. $\lambda = h/mv$
3. $\lambda = mv/h$ 4. $\lambda = mv$

73. A metal rod has an original length of 1.5 m at 20°C. If its temperature is raised to 120°C, what is the increase in its length? (Coefficient of linear expansion α for the metal is 1.2×10^{-5} °C^{-1}.)

1. 1.8×10^{-2} m 2. 1.8×10^{-3} m
3. 1.5×10^{-3} m 4. 1.2×10^{-3} m

74. According to Bohr's second postulate, an electron can revolve around the nucleus only in certain allowed orbits. What condition must its angular momentum satisfy in these orbits?

1. It increases with the electron's distance from the nucleus, without a specific rule
2. It must be equal to $nh/2\pi$, where *n* is a whole number
3. It must be equal to *nh*, where *h* is Planck's constant
4. It can take any continuous value depending on speed

75. The Poisson's ratio for a given material is 0.5. If a uniform rod made of this material suffers a longitudinal strain of 4×10^{-3}, then what is the value of the lateral strain experienced by the rod?

1. -4×10^{-3} 2. -2×10^{-3}
3. -12.5×10^{-3} 4. -0.5×10^{-3}

76. Which of the following statements are true about the property of elasticity of a material?

(*i*) A material that is able to regain its original shape and size after the removal of the deforming force is said to be elastic.
(*ii*) Rubber is more elastic than iron.
(*iii*) Within the elastic limit, the stress applied on a body is directly proportional to the strain produced in a body.
(*iv*) The modulus of elasticity of a body has the same units as energy.

1. (*ii*) and (*iv*) 2. (*ii*) and (*iii*)
3. (*i*) and (*iv*) 4. (*i*) and (*iii*)

77. Which of the following is a correct definition of Simple Harmonic Motion (SHM)?

1. A motion where restoring force is proportional to velocity.
2. A periodic motion in which acceleration is proportional to displacement and directed opposite to it.
3. A motion with constant speed in a straight line.
4. A random motion that repeats.

78. A Carnot heat engine operates between a hot reservoir at 300 K and a cold reservoir. The engine is currently 30% efficient. If the temperature of the cold reservoir remains unchanged, what should be the temperature of the hot reservoir to increase the engine's efficiency to 50%?

1. 210 K 2. 21 K
3. 42 K 4. 420 K

79. In a wave equation, $y = A \sin(kx - \omega t + \phi)$. What is the expression $(kx - \omega t + \phi)$ called?

1. Amplitude of the wave
2. Frequency of the wave
3. Wavelength of the wave
4. Phase of the wave

80. The Zeroth Law allows us to ______.

1. define entropy
2. define energy
3. calculate work done
4. define temperature

81. In the following relation, $P = a\sqrt{x}/(b + t^2)$, P represents pressure, *x* represents distance, and *t* represents time. For the equation to be dimensionally correct, what will be the dimensions of *a* and *b*, respectively?

1. $[M^{-1}L^{3/2}]$; $[T^2]$ 2. $[T^2]$; $[M^1L^{-3/2}]$
3. $[M^1L^{-3/2}]$; $[T^2]$ 4. $[T^2]$; $[M^{-1}L^{3/2}]$

82. Coherence length (L_c) is inversely proportional to _____.
1. the frequency of the light
2. the wavelength of the light
3. the speed of light
4. the bandwidth of the light source

83. Which factor DOES NOT significantly affect fluorescence quantum yield?
1. Molecular structure
2. Planck's constant
3. Solvent polarity
4. Room temperature

84. Which of the following is NOT a derived unit in the SI system?
1. Candela (cd) 2. Radian (rad)
3. Newton (N) 4. Hertz (Hz)

85. Which of the following is a fundamental quantity?
1. Electric potential
2. Magnetic flux
3. Torque
4. Amount of substance

86. A spring requires a force of 20 N to stretch it by 0.1 m. What is the potential energy stored in the spring when it is stretched by 0.2 m from its equilibrium state or position?
1. 8 J 2. 0.5 J
3. 4 J 4. 2 J

87. A constant force of 25 N acts on an object causing it to move a distance of 2.0 m in the direction of the force. How much work is done by the force?
1. 0.5 J 2. 2 J
3. 15 J 4. 50 J

88. A 2 kg mass is released from a height of 5 m above the ground. Calculate its speed just before it hits the ground.

[Assume no air resistance and that all potential energy converts into kinetic energy. Take $g = 10 \text{ m/s}^2$]
1. 15 m/s 2. 7.5 m/s
3. 10 m/s 4. 5 m/s

89. In a frictionless roller coaster, which point has maximum kinetic energy?
1. Lowest point
2. Middle point
3. All points have equal kinetic energy
4. Highest point

90. Which of the following components is essential for focusing the electron beam in a Scanning Electron Microscope (SEM)?
1. Optical lens
2. Crystal monochromator
3. Aperture diaphragm
4. Magnetic lens

91. In measurements, what does 'accuracy' primarily refer to?
1. How close repeated measurements are to each other.
2. The smallest unit that can be measured by an instrument.
3. How close a measured value is to the true or accepted value.
4. The number of significant figures in a measurement.

92. The power P delivered to a moving particle varies with time t according to the equation: $P = (9t^2 + 2t - 1)$ watt, where t is in seconds. What will be the change in the kinetic energy of the particle between t = 2s and t = 4s?
1. 38 J 2. 40 J
3. 178 J 4. 180 J

93. Which of the following statements is true for a conservative force?
1. It is always a frictional force.
2. It always leads to a loss of mechanical energy.
3. The work done by the force depends on the path taken.
4. The work done by the force in a closed loop is zero.

94. Which of the following expressions is NOT dimensionally consistent for energy?
1. Pressure × volume

2. Mass × velocity
3. Power × time
4. Force × distance

95. A cyclist comes to a stop by skidding over a distance of 4 metres. The force exerted by the road on the cycle is 300 N and acts opposite to the motion. How much work does the road do on the cycle?

1. −1200 J   2. 0 J
3. +300 J   4. +1200 J

96. Which of the following best explains the transition from the Zeeman effect to the Paschen-Back effect?

1. The transition occurs as the magnetic field strength increases
2. The transition occurs with the introduction of an electric field
3. The transition occurs in presence of both electric and magnetic field
4. The transition occurs as the magnetic field strength decreases

97. In the normal Zeeman effect, how many components does a single spectral line split into?

1. 2   2. 4
3. 3   4. 5

98. Which of the following statements about significant figures is NOT true?

1. All the zeros between two non-zero digits are not significant, no matter where the decimal point is, if at all.
2. All the non-zero digits are significant.
3. The terminal or trailing zero(s) in a number without a decimal point are not significant.
4. If the number is less than 1, the zero(s) on the right of the decimal point but to the left of the first non-zero digit are not significant.

99. Which of the following physical quantities is dimensionless?

1. Density   2. Work
3. Refractive Index   4. Pressure

100. Dimensional analysis CANNOT be used to ______.

1. ensure homogeneity of various mathematical expressions
2. determine the numerical values of physical quantities
3. understand the relation among different physical quantities
4. check the derivation, accuracy and dimensional consistency

101. What is the physical significance of the electromagnetic current density J^{μ}?

1. It represents the distribution of electric and magnetic fields.
2. It is a measure of the potential energy in the field.
3. It describes the flow of charge and current in spacetime.
4. It denotes the velocity of charged particles.

102. Which of the following statements is true regarding gauge invariance?

1. The scalar potential ϕ is gauge invariant.
2. Different gauge choices can lead to different predictions for physical observables.
3. Gauge invariance ensures that physical quantities like the electric and magnetic fields are unaffected by the choice of gauge.
4. The choice of gauge affects the physical electromagnetic fields.

103. A long cylindrical shell with inner radius *a* and outer radius *b* carries a uniform volume charge density ρ. What is the electric field at a distance *r* from the axis of the cylinder where $a < r < b$?

1. $\frac{\rho r}{2\varepsilon_0}\left(1-\frac{a^2}{b^2}\right)$ 2. $\frac{\rho r}{2\varepsilon_0}\left(1+\frac{r^2}{b^2}\right)$
3. $\frac{\rho r}{2\varepsilon_0}\left(1-\frac{r^2}{b^2}\right)$ 4. $\frac{\rho r}{2\varepsilon_0}\left(1-\frac{a^2}{r^2}\right)$

104. In thermogravimetric analysis, what does the onset temperature of a decomposition process indicate?

1. The temperature at which weight gain begins
2. The temperature at which the sample completely decomposes
3. The temperature at which the sample melts
4. The temperature at which weight loss begins

105. In transmission electron microscopy, what does the term 'bright-field imaging' refer to?

1. Imaging the electrons transmitted through the specimen
2. Imaging the secondary electrons emitted from the specimen
3. Imaging the X-rays emitted by the specimen
4. Imaging the electrons scattered by the specimen

106. What is a soliton in the context of classical field theory?

1. A stable, localised wave packet that maintains its shape while propagating at constant speed
2. A solution to the Schrödinger equation with non-linear potential
3. A type of particle with zero rest mass
4. A field configuration that decays exponentially at large distances

107. In field theory, the Lagrangian density L for a scalar field ϕ is invariant under translations in space and time. According to Noether's theorem, what quantity is the conserved current?

1. Stress-energy tensor
2. Noether's current
3. Probability current
4. Electric current

108. In Yang-Mills theory, what does the gauge field A^a_μ represent?

1. A tensor field associated with general relativity
2. A vector field associated with local U(1) symmetry
3. A vector field associated with a non-Abelian gauge group
4. A scalar field with local U(1) symmetry

109. What does the energy-momentum tensor $T^{\mu\nu}$ represent in classical field theory?

1. The potential energy and kinetic energy of particles
2. The stress, energy density and flux of the fields
3. The curvature of spacetime
4. The distribution of electric and magnetic fields

110. A change in magnetic flux through a loop induces _____.

1. a change in electric flux through the loop
2. an electromotive force (EMF) in the loop
3. a constant magnetic field through the loop
4. a current in the loop only if the loop is a closed circuit

111. The Larmor formula gives the power radiated by a _____.

1. Moving neutral particle
2. Uniformly charged conductor
3. Charge at rest in a field
4. Non-relativistic accelerated point charge

112. What does a depolarisation ratio close to zero indicate about a Raman band in Raman spectroscopy?

1. The Raman band is depolarised.
2. The Raman band is from a rotational transition.
3. The Raman band is non-symmetric.
4. The Raman band is completely polarised.

113. What principle does Differential Thermal Analysis primarily rely on for measuring temperature differences between a sample and a reference?

1. Heat flow difference
2. Heat capacity variation
3. Mass change
4. Entropy generation

114. The Euler-Lagrange equations are applicable when the system's _____.

1. Constraints are non-holonomic
2. Constraints are holonomic and scleronomic
3. Coordinates are non-generalised
4. Motion is dissipative

115. What is the standard form of the Lagrangian density for a real scalar field ϕ?

1. $\frac{1}{2}\partial_\mu\varphi\partial^\mu\varphi + \frac{1}{2}m^2\varphi^2$
2. $\frac{1}{2}\partial_\mu\varphi\partial^\mu\varphi + m^2\varphi^2$
3. $\frac{1}{2}\partial_\mu\varphi\partial^\mu\varphi - m^2\varphi^2$
4. $\frac{1}{2}\partial_\mu\varphi\partial^\mu\varphi - \frac{1}{2}m^2\varphi^2$

116. In classical field theory, the principle of locality asserts that:

1. fields must have identical values at all spatial points simultaneously
2. fields at different spatial points can influence each other instantaneously
3. interactions between fields are limited to neighbouring points in space and time
4. time evolution of fields is independent of their spatial distribution

117. The monochromator in X-Ray Diffraction (XRD) is primarily used to _____.

1. split the X-ray beam
2. increase the intensity of X-rays
3. select a single wavelength of X-rays
4. accelerate X-rays

118. Which of the following detectors is typically used in Transmission Electron Microscopy (TEM) for diffraction pattern acquisition?

1. X-ray energy dispersive detector
2. Backscattered electron detector
3. Fluorescent screen
4. Secondary electron detector

119. In the Coulomb gauge, the divergence of the vector potential A is _____.

1. equal to the scalar potential
2. equal to the charge density
3. zero
4. equal to the magnetic field

120. What does the intensity of a peak in an X-ray diffraction pattern indicate?

1. The wavelength of the X-rays used
2. The type of atoms in the crystal structure
3. The angle of incidence
4. The number of diffracting planes

121. Quantum dots behave like atoms because:

1. they have continuous electronic states
2. they have a nucleus same as in atoms
3. they have discrete electronic states
4. of the presence of free electrons

122. Which of the following materials can be considered a two-dimensional (2D) nanostructure?

1. Carbon nanotube 2. Fullerene
3. Quantum wire 4. Graphene

123. What is the relationship between the Einstein coefficients B_{21} and B_{12} in thermal equilibrium for a system at temperature T?

1. $B_{21} < B_{12}$ 2. $B_{21} = B_{12}$
3. $B_{21} > B_{12}$ 4. $B_{21} \neq B_{12}$

124. In spontaneous emission, an excited atom returns to a lower energy state _____.

1. only in presence of external radiation
2. without any external influence
3. only under thermal equilibrium
4. only if stimulated by another atom

125. The Yukawa potential was introduced to describe the nuclear force as a result of _____.

1. pion exchange
2. photon exchange
3. gluon confinement
4. electromagnetic interaction

126. Which of the following is NOT an example of a point defect?

1. Dislocation
2. Interstitial impurity
3. Vacancy
4. Substitutional impurity

127. In the Raman spectrum of carbon nanotubes, what does the G-band represent?

1. Defects in the nanotube structure
2. Radial breathing mode of the nanotubes
3. Graphitic-like tangential stretching mode of the C-C bonds
4. The electronic transitions within the nanotube

128. Which of the following nanostructures exhibits piezoelectric properties, contributing to its mechanical strength?

1. Gold nanoparticles
2. Zinc oxide nanowires
3. Carbon nanotubes
4. Graphene

129. Which of the following synthesis methods is commonly used to prepare Metal Organic Framework (MOF) nanostructures?

1. Thermal evaporation under high vacuum
2. Flame spray pyrolysis
3. Solvothermal
4. Laser ablation in liquid

130. Time resolved spectroscopy is done using lasers because of the property that laser beams:

1. travel with the speed of light
2. are highly divergent in nature
3. can have very long duration pulses
4. can have very short duration pulses

131. Which of the following is NOT a method of characterisation of nanoparticles?

1. X-ray diffraction 2. Microscopy
3. Chromatography 4. Spectroscopy

132. In fibre-optic communication, lasers are primarily used because they provide _____.

1. broad spectrum and low coherence
2. high bandwidth and directionality
3. pulsed incoherent light
4. low-frequency emissions

133. Which of the following is NOT necessarily a requisite for a laser action?

1. Resonator 2. Optical fibre
3. Active medium 4. Energy source

134. Which of the following best describes the principle of optical cooling (laser cooling)?

1. Exciting atoms to metastable states
2. Using red-detuned light to reduce atomic momentum
3. Heating atoms with infrared lasers
4. Compressing atomic wavefunctions with microwaves

135. Which of the following is a primary application of CO_2 lasers?

1. Tattoo removal 2. Metal cutting
3. Hair removal 4. Ophthalmic surgery

136. Which of the following is NOT true for laser-induced fluorescence spectroscopy?

1. Fluorescence probes are the basis of many very sensitive assays developed for biological molecules of interest.
2. Fluorescence probes are highly fluorescent reagents that are designed to bind strongly and specifically to certain targets.
3. Emission usually occurs at energies that are less than the energies of excitation.
4. Emission usually occurs at energies that are greater than the energies of excitation.

137. Drift velocity is _____.

1. inversely proportional to the force on an electron due to applied electric field
2. directly proportional to the mass of an electron
3. inversely proportional to the strength of applied electric field
4. directly proportional to the mobility of an electron

138. What is the primary and major role of surfactants in the synthesis of nanostructures?

1. To enhance the optical properties
2. To increase the reaction temperature
3. To control the growth and prevent aggregation of nanostructures
4. To act as reducing agents

139. What does 'coherence' refer to in the context of lasers?

1. The property of a laser beam to have a well-defined phase relationship over time and space
2. The degree of spatial concentration of a laser beam
3. The ability of a laser beam to travel long distances without divergence
4. The ability of a laser to produce high power output

140. Among the following dimensional types of nanostructures, which one has the highest surface-to-volume ratio?

1. It is the same in all dimensions.
2. One-dimensional (1 D) nanostructure
3. Two-dimensional (2 D) nanostructure
4. Zero-dimensional (0 D) nanostructure

141. What is the main purpose of declaring a variable?

1. To display output to the user
2. To perform mathematical calculations
3. To store data that can be used and modified by the program
4. To read input from the user

142. In quantum theory, a composite system of two subsystems A and B is described by _____.

1. The product of the probability distributions
2. A classical mixture of their wavefunctions
3. The sum of Hilbert spaces of A and B
4. The tensor product of their Hilbert spaces

143. In a combined quantum system, if the total wave function is given by $\psi_{AB} = \psi_A \otimes \psi_B$, which statement is true?

1. Subsystems A and B are combined to form an entangled state.
2. The total wave function ψ_{AB} cannot be a valid quantum state.
3. Subsystems A and B are combined to form a superposition state.
4. Subsystems A and B are combined to form a separable state

144. The charge distribution of a nucleus can be approximated by _____.

1. Gaussian distribution
2. Woods–Saxon distribution
3. Step function
4. Parabolic distribution

145. The multipolarity of a gamma transition is defined by _____.

1. energy of emitted photon
2. change in angular momentum and parity of the nucleus
3. type of daughter nucleus formed
4. lifetime of the parent nucleus

146. Which of the following is a possible spin-parity (I^{π}) state for a nucleus with an unpaired $p_{3/2}$ neutron?

1. $5/2^+$
2. $3/2^+$
3. $1/2^+$
4. $3/2^-$

147. In time-dependent perturbation theory, the perturbation is usually treated as _____.

1. A function of momentum
2. A constant potential
3. A small time-varying term in the Hamiltonian
4. A wavefunction correction

148. The radius of the uranium-238 nucleus is approximately _____. (Assume: Nuclear radius constant $R_0 = 1.2$ fm)

1. 2.5 fm
2. 4.8 fm
3. 7.4 fm
4. 10.0 fm

149. What is a supernova?

1. A dying planet
2. A newly formed star

3. A star expanding into a red giant
4. The explosion of a massive star

150. What will be the value of the following expression in C?

```
int a = 5, b = 10;
!(a > b)
```

1. 0 2. Undefined
3. -1 4. 1

151. In the context of numerical methods, which of the following is a primary advantage of the Runge-Kutta methods over the Euler method?

1. Simplicity of implementation
2. Ability to handle stiff equations
3. Lower computational cost
4. Higher accuracy for a given step size

152. Given the following code, what will be the output?

```
int arr[] = {10, 20, 30, 40, 50};
int *p = arr;
printf("%d\n", *(p + 2));
```

1. 20 2. 10
3. 30 4. 40

153. The liquid drop model is particularly useful for explaining _____.

1. magic numbers in nuclei
2. average binding energy trends
3. fine structure in nuclear energy levels
4. spin and parity of nuclear states

154. The central difference approximation for the first derivative $f'(x)$ has an error term that depends on the _____.

1. fourth derivative of the function
2. third derivative of the function
3. second derivative of the function
4. first derivative of the function

155. What is the range of values that can be stored in an unsigned char in C?

1. −32768 to 32767
2. −128 to 127
3. 0 to 255
4. 0 to 32767

156. The force responsible for the exchange of gluons between quarks within hadrons (such as protons and neutrons) is _____.

1. weak nuclear force
2. electromagnetic force
3. gravitational force
4. strong nuclear force

157. The central difference approximation is often preferred over forward and backward difference approximations because _____.

1. it is simpler to compute
2. it requires fewer data points
3. it has a higher accuracy for a given step size
4. it can be used for nonuniform grids

158. The Runge-Kutta method is classified as _____.

1. multi-step, explicit method
2. predictor-corrector method
3. single-step, explicit method
4. multi-step, implicit method

159. In a magnetically confined plasma, a Tokamak is an example of which type of system?

1. Electrostatic confinement
2. Closed system
3. Mirror confinement
4. Open system

160. The ratio of gravitational mass to inertial mass is equal to:

1. 1/2 2. 1
3. 2 4. 0.1

161. For a three-dimensional Fermi gas, the density of states g(E) near the Fermi energy E_F is proportional to _____.

1. E 2. E^3
3. $E^{1/2}$ 4. E^2

162. Which of the following statements is true regarding Feynman diagrams?

1. They are used to compute probabilities of interactions.
2. They represent physical paths taken by particles.

3. They describe only classical phenomena.
4. They are solutions of the Schrödinger equation.

163. What is the primary purpose of the LSZ reduction formula in quantum field theory?

1. To derive the equations of motion for quantum fields
2. To establish the commutation relations for field operators
3. To determine the propagators for virtual particles
4. To calculate scattering amplitudes from time-ordered correlation functions

164. Which of the following is a necessary condition for a gas to behave as a plasma?

1. The mean free path of electrons must be zero
2. The density of electrons must be lower than that of ions
3. The temperature must exceed 1000 K
4. The Debye length must be much smaller than the system size

165. In the context of squeezed states, what does a negative Mandel Q parameter indicate?

1. Poissonian statistics
2. Super-Poissonian statistics
3. Sub-Poissonian statistics
4. Undefined statistics

166. What is the main effect of decoherence on a quantum superposition state?

1. It has no effect on the superposition state.
2. It converts the superposition into a statistical mixture of states.
3. It amplifies the superposition.
4. It stabilises the superposition.

167. In quantum optics, the master equation approach is particularly useful for analysing ______.

1. hydrogen atom spectrum
2. particle in a box
3. spontaneous emission and cavity damping
4. free particle motion

168. The frequency of small amplitude plasma oscillations in a cold, collision less plasma is called ______.

1. plasma frequency
2. drift frequency
3. larmor frequency
4. cyclotron frequency

169. The critical temperature T_c for Bose-Einstein condensation in a dilute gas of non-interacting bosons with number density n, is given by ______.

1. $T_c = \frac{h^2}{40k_B m} n^{2/3}$
2. $T_c = \frac{h^2}{2\pi k_B m} n^{1/3}$
3. $T_c = \frac{h^2}{4k_B m} n^{3/2}$
4. $T_c = \frac{h^2}{2\pi k_B m} n^{2/3}$

170. The ultraviolet catastrophe refers to the failure of which theory to explain blackbody radiation?

1. Special relativity
2. Classical electrodynamics
3. Planck's theory
4. Quantum mechanics

171. Which of the following is the principal advantage of using polarised light microscopy?

1. To view fluorescent specimens
2. To measure the refractive index of the specimen
3. To enhance contrast in birefringent materials
4. To increase the numerical aperture

172. In the Breit-Wigner formula, what does the width Γ of the resonance represent?

1. The amplitude of the scattering process
2. The mass of the resonant particle
3. The energy of the resonance
4. The total decay rate of the resonant state

173. In quantum computing, what is the purpose of the Toffoli gate?

1. It performs a controlled-NOT operation on two qubits.

2. It performs a NOT operation on a single qubit.
3. It performs a controlled-controlled-NOT operation (CCNOT).
4. It swaps the states of two qubits.

174. Which of the following transitions can be observed in the Raman spectrum of a diatomic molecule?
1. Rotational transitions only
2. Vibrational transitions only
3. Electronic transitions only
4. Both rotational and vibrational transitions

175. With ∇ as the derivative, the equation of state of plasma fluid can be expressed as _____.
1. $P/\nabla P = \gamma n$ 2. $P/\nabla P = \gamma n/\nabla n$
3. $\nabla P/P = \gamma \nabla n$ 4. $\nabla P/P = \gamma \nabla n/n$

176. The responsivity (R) of a photodetector is given by _____.
1. R = Photon energy/Charge
2. R = Voltage/Power
3. R = Photocurrent/Incident Optical Power
4. R = Power/Voltage

177. In cosmology, which constant of motion is directly associated with the conservation of energy in a homogeneous and isotropic universe?
1. Scale factor
2. Hubble constant
3. Total energy per unit mass
4. Redshift

78. The standard Gibbs free energy change is related to the equilibrium constant K by _____.
1. $\Delta G° = RT \ln K$
2. $\Delta G° = -RT \ln K$
3. $\Delta G° = -T\Delta S$
4. $\Delta G° = \Delta H - RT$

79. At which of the following temperatures does Planck's distribution law apply?
1. Only room temperature
2. Absolute zero
3. Only high temperatures
4. Any temperature above absolute zero

180. What is the primary goal of renormalisation in quantum field theory?
1. To regularise and absorb infinities into redefined physical parameters
2. To ensure that the theory remains classical at high energies
3. To determine the exact solutions of the field equations
4. To eliminate the need for gauge fixing

181. Immanuel Kant discussed his aesthetic theory in the book _____.
1. Aesthetica
2. Judgement of Beauty
3. Critique of Judgement
4. Teleological Judgment

182. What does 'multilingualism' refer to?
1. The ability to speak only one language fluently
2. The ability to use and understand two or more languages
3. The ability to understand multiple languages but speak only one
4. The ability to speak only in a formal setting

183. Which of the following strategies is most effective for aligning resources with learning objectives in lesson planning?
1. Choosing resources that provide multiple ways to achieve the learning objectives
2. Selecting resources based on their popularity among other teachers
3. Using digital tools for every lesson regardless of content
4. Selecting resources that match the textbook's content

184. Which of the following best describes a learning objective in a lesson plan?
1. A description of what students will be able to do by the end of the lesson
2. A list of activities the teacher will conduct during the lesson

3. A summary of the homework assignment given after the lesson
4. A reflection on how the lesson went and how to improve it

185. Which of the following theories emphasises the role of social interactions and cultural tools in cognitive development during childhood?
1. Erikson's Psychosocial Development Theory
2. Piaget's Theory of Cognitive Development
3. Bandura's Social Learning Theory
4. Vygotsky's Sociocultural Theory

186. Which of the following is NOT a characteristic of subjective type test?
1. Improvement in speaking skills
2. Consistency in the scores
3. Subjective scoring
4. Writing skills enhancement

187. The goal of quantitative content analysis is to measure textual content _____.
1. and arrive at a comprehension of social action through interpretation
2. and give a female-centered spin on the traditional quantitative approaches used by men
3. and discuss research ethics in a critical manner
4. in an objective and systematic way

188. Universal Design for Learning (UDL) emphasises which principle(s) as a means to support diverse learners?
1. Rigidity in teaching strategies
2. Exclusivity in assessment
3. Flexibility in learning environments
4. Uniformity and instructional materials

189. Which of the following is NOT the characteristic of an academic discipline?
1. It has theories and concepts.
2. It is a body of specialised knowledge.
3. It is without subjects.
4. It has specific terminology.

190. Which stage, as per NEP 2020, has multidisciplinary study, building on the subject-oriented pedagogy with greater depth, greater critical thinking, greater attention to life aspirations and greater flexibility and student choice of subjects?
1. Secondary Stage
2. Foundation Stage
3. Preparatory Stage
4. Graduation Stage

191. Which of the following is NOT an example of physical resources of educational institutions?
1. Electricity 2. Infrastructure
3. School building 4. Support staff

192. Which of the evaluations is carried along with formative evaluation?
1. Summative Evaluation
2. Diagnostic Evaluation
3. Post-active Evaluation
4. Pre-Active Evaluation

193. Logical Positivists explored the philosophical significance of the theory of _____.
1. Gravitation 2. Uniqueness
3. Relativity 4. Attraction

194. Which of the following describes gender bias in educational curricula?
1. The curriculum promotes gender equality
2. The curriculum includes diverse perspectives
3. The curriculum is developed collaboratively by all genders
4. The curriculum emphasises traditional gender roles

195. Which of the following best describes the relationship between mental abilities and cognitive development according to Jean Piaget's theory?
1. Mental abilities develop through a fixed sequence of stages that are influenced by both biological maturation and environmental interaction

2. Cognitive development happens only through formal education, not natural interactions with the environment
3. Mental abilities remain constant throughout life, unaffected by experiences or maturation
4. Cognitive development is solely determined by genetic factors, independent of experiences

196. How is gender socialisation primarily done?
1. By ensuring all individuals are treated the same regardless of gender
2. By focussing only on education within schools
3. By shaping individuals' beliefs, behaviours, and roles according to societal expectations of masculinity and femininity
4. By teaching individuals how to select their biological sex

197. The emphasis of _____ is on understanding cognitive theories of learning and their contribution to various methods of teaching.
1. system approach
2. humanistic approach
3. managerial approach
4. intellectual/academic approach

198. Which approach is essential for creating an inclusive school environment that supports children with special needs?
1. Individualised Education Programs (IEPs) tailored to meet specific student needs
2. Implementing a one-size-fits-all curriculum
3. Segregating students with special needs into separate classrooms
4. Providing minimal resources for special education teachers

199. Which of the following is a common tool used in 'Assessment for Learning' to help students reflect on their progress?
1. End-of-term exams
2. Rubrics
3. Norm-referenced grading
4. Standardised tests

200. Which teaching strategy is characterised by the gradual release of responsibility, starting with teacher-led instruction and moving towards student independence, often described by the framework 'I do, We do, You do'?
1. Scaffolding
2. Discovery learning
3. Cooperative learning
4. Flipped classroom

ANSWERS

1	**2**	**3**	**4**	**5**	**6**	**7**	**8**	**9**	**10**
3	1	1	3	2	4	4	2	2	1
11	**12**	**13**	**14**	**15**	**16**	**17**	**18**	**19**	**20**
4	4	2	2	1	4	1	1	2	2
21	**22**	**23**	**24**	**25**	**26**	**27**	**28**	**29**	**30**
4	4	4	1	3	2	1	2	4	4
31	**32**	**33**	**34**	**35**	**36**	**37**	**38**	**39**	**40**
3	2	1	2	2	3	2	2	4	4
41	**42**	**43**	**44**	**45**	**46**	**47**	**48**	**49**	**50**
2	4	2	2	1	4	1	3	4	4
51	**52**	**53**	**54**	**55**	**56**	**57**	**58**	**59**	**60**
1	1	3	1	2	3	3	2	4	2
61	**62**	**63**	**64**	**65**	**66**	**67**	**68**	**69**	**70**
1	4	3	4	2	3	1	2	3	2

71	72	73	74	75	76	77	78	79	80
2	2	2	2	2	4	2	4	4	4
81	**82**	**83**	**84**	**85**	**86**	**87**	**88**	**89**	**90**
3	4	2	1	4	3	4	3	1	4
91	**92**	**93**	**94**	**95**	**96**	**97**	**98**	**99**	**100**
3	3	4	2	1	1	3	1	3	2
101	**102**	**103**	**104**	**105**	**106**	**107**	**108**	**109**	**110**
3	3	4	4	1	1	1	3	2	2
111	**112**	**113**	**114**	**115**	**116**	**117**	**118**	**119**	**120**
4	4	1	2	4	3	3	3	3	4
121	**122**	**123**	**124**	**125**	**126**	**127**	**128**	**129**	**130**
3	4	2	2	1	1	3	2	3	4
131	**132**	**133**	**134**	**135**	**136**	**137**	**138**	**139**	**140**
3	2	2	2	2	4	4	3	1	4
141	**142**	**143**	**144**	**145**	**146**	**147**	**148**	**149**	**150**
3	4	4	2	2	4	3	3	4	4
151	**152**	**153**	**154**	**155**	**156**	**157**	**158**	**159**	**160**
4	3	2	2	3	4	3	3	2	2
161	**162**	**163**	**164**	**165**	**166**	**167**	**168**	**169**	**170**
3	1	4	4	3	2	3	1	4	2
171	**172**	**173**	**174**	**175**	**176**	**177**	**178**	**179**	**180**
3	4	3	4	4	3	3	2	4	1
181	**182**	**183**	**184**	**185**	**186**	**187**	**188**	**189**	**190**
3	2	1	1	4	2	4	3	3	1
191	**192**	**193**	**194**	**195**	**196**	**197**	**198**	**199**	**200**
4	2	3	4	1	3	4	1	2	1

EXPLANATORY ANSWERS

1. Total resistance of the series circuit:

$$R_{total} = R_{external} + r_{internal}$$
$$= 5\ \Omega + 1\ \Omega$$
$$= 6\ \Omega.$$

Current drawn from the cell (Ohm's law):

$$I = \frac{E}{R_{total}} = \frac{12\ V}{6\ \Omega} = 2\ A$$

Therefore, the current is exactly 2 A.

2. Relation between mobility and relaxation time:

$$\mu = \frac{e\tau}{m^*} \Rightarrow \tau = \frac{\mu m^*}{e}$$

Unit conversion:

$$\mu = 1500\ cm^2 = 0.15\ m^2$$

Substitution:

$$\tau = \frac{(0.15)\ (9.11 \times 10^{-31}\ kg)}{1.60 \times 10^{-19} C}$$
$$= 8.54 \times 10^{-13}\ s$$
$$\approx 8.5 \times 10^{-13}\ s$$

The listed exact choice is 8.5×10^{-13} s.

3. Ultraviolet uses:

(*i*) UV-C is germicidal ⇒ used in water purification.

(*iv*) Excimer UV lasers (e.g., 193 nm) are used in high-precision eye surgery.

(*ii*) Radar uses microwaves (not UV).

(*iii*) Radio/TV use radio waves (not UV).

Hence, only (*i*) and (*iv*) are correct.

4. Comparative electrical resistivities near 0° C (lower means better conductor):
ρ_{Al} (lowest among the given) < ρ_W < ρ_{Fe} < ρ_{Pt}.
Therefore, aluminium has the lowest resistivity among the listed materials at 0° C.

5. Total line resistance:
$$R = (0.1\ \Omega/\text{km}) \times (50\ \text{km}) = 5\ \Omega.$$
Power loss (Joule heating) in the line:
$$P_{loss} = I^2R = (500\ \text{A})^2 \times 5\ \Omega = 250{,}000 \times 5 = 1{,}250{,}000\ \text{W} = 1250\ \text{kW}.$$
Thus, the power loss is 1250 kW.

6. Eddy currents in a transformer arise only when the magnetic flux through the iron core changes with time. Since transformers operate strictly on alternating magnetic flux, the changing flux induces circulating currents in the core. These eddy currents cause heating and power loss, and to reduce them the core is laminated. Therefore, the only correct statement is that eddy currents are induced by alternating magnetic flux.

7. X-rays have wavelengths shorter than ultraviolet and longer than gamma rays. Their typical spectral range lies between 1 nm and 10^{-3} nm. This corresponds to the region where high-energy photons are produced by bremsstrahlung or inner-shell electronic transitions.
Thus, the correct wavelength range is from 1 nm down to 10^{-3} nm.

8. Magnetic braking in trains uses eddy currents generated in metallic discs or wheels. Electric power meters rely on eddy-current torque for rotation. Induction furnaces use eddy currents to heat metal. An electric fan, however, operates on the motor principle and does not rely on eddy currents for its primary function.
Hence, it is the device that does not utilise eddy currents.

9. Electromagnetic waves consist of oscillating electric and magnetic fields that propagate without the need for any material medium. They always carry energy and momentum; photons associated with the wave transport momentum $p = E/c$ though no net charge is transported. Therefore, the statement that they carry energy and momentum is the only correct one.

10. Electrostatic potential at a point is defined as the work done by an external agent in bringing a unit positive test charge from infinity to that point against the electric field, without any acceleration. This definition arises directly from the conservative nature of electrostatic fields. Thus, the correct expression relates potential to the work done in moving a unit charge from infinity.

11. For three resistors in parallel, the equivalent conductance adds:
$$\frac{1}{R_{eq}} = \frac{1}{R_1}+\frac{1}{R_2}+\frac{1}{R_3} = \frac{1}{0.1}+\frac{1}{0.01}+\frac{1}{0.001} = 10 + 100 + 1000 = 1110\ \Omega^{-1}.$$
Hence, $R_{eq} = \dfrac{1}{1110} = 9.009... \times 10^{-4}\ \Omega = 0.9009\ \text{m}\Omega$ (to 4 s.f.).
This matches 0.9 mΩ.

12. For n cells in series, voltages add and internal resistances add:
$$E_{total} = \sum_{i=1}^{n} E_i,\quad r_{total} = \sum_{i=1}^{n} r_i$$
Thus, both total emf and total internal resistance are equal to the sum of each cell's emf and resistance respectively.

13. Temperature dependence of resistance (metal):
$$R = R_0\,[1 + \alpha\,(T - T_0)]$$
Given $R_0 = 20\ \Omega$ at $T_0 = 20°$ C, $\alpha = 0.005\ °\text{C}^{-1}$
and $R = 30\ \Omega$.
$$\frac{R}{R_0} = 1 + \alpha\,(T - 20)$$
$$\Rightarrow\quad 1.5 = 1 + 0.005\,(T - 20).$$
Thus, $0.5 = 0.005\,(T - 20)$
$$\Rightarrow\quad T - 20 = \frac{0.5}{0.005} = 100$$
$$\Rightarrow\quad T = 120°\ \text{C}.$$

14. Microwave heating of water arises from rotational excitation of polar H_2O molecules: the alternating microwave field couples strongly to the molecular dipole, leading to efficient absorption (dielectric

loss) when the driving frequency matches/closely matches rotational modes (resonant coupling), converting electromagnetic energy to thermal energy.

15. For perfect coupling, flux linkage in coil B is $\lambda_B = MI_A$.

A change ΔI_A produces

$$\Delta\lambda_B = M\,\Delta I_A$$

$$\Rightarrow \quad M = \frac{\Delta\lambda_B}{\Delta I_A}$$

Given, $\Delta\lambda_B = 90$ Wb (turns)

and $\Delta I_A = 30 - 0 = 30$ A

$$M = \frac{90}{30} = 3 \text{ H.}$$

16. EMF has the same dimension as potential difference (volt).

Using $V = W/Q$ with work $W = [ML^2\,T^{-2}]$ and charge $Q = [A\,T]$, we get

$$[V] = \frac{[ML^2T^{-2}]}{[A\,T]} = M\,L^2\,T^{-3}\,A^{-1}$$

Hence the dimensional formula is $M\,L^2\,T^{-3}\,A^{-1}$.

17. **As viewed from above the ring:** Approaching (N-pole above ring, moving down): The magnetic flux through the ring (directed downward) increases. By Lenz's law, the induced current creates an upward field to oppose this increase. An upward field at the ring's center corresponds to an anti-clockwise current (right-hand rule). The interaction is therefore repulsive (magnet is pushed away).

Moving away (N-pole below ring, moving further down): The downward flux through the ring decreases. The induced current now tries to keep the flux downward, so it produces a downward field, which corresponds to a clockwise current (as seen from above). The interaction is therefore attractive (magnet is pulled back). Thus anti-clockwise & repulsive when approaching; clockwise & attractive when moving away.

18. Mobility μ is defined as drift velocity per unit electric field:

$$\mu = \frac{v_d}{E} \Rightarrow v_d = \mu E.$$

It quantifies how fast a charge carrier drifts for a given applied field.

19. Electromagnetic waves are transverse; their electric field can have a definite orientation. Hence every electromagnetic wave (radio, microwave, IR, visible, UV, X-ray, γ) can, in principle, be polarised.

20. Drift velocity from current density:

$$I = n\,q\,A\,v_d$$

$$\Rightarrow \quad v_d = \frac{I}{nqA}$$

Given, $I = 2$ A,

$n = 8.5 \times 10^{28}$ m^{-3},

$q = 1.6 \times 10^{-19}$ C,

$A = 1$ mm^2

$= 1 \times 10^{-6}$ m^2,

$$v_d = \frac{2}{(8.5\times10^{28})(1.6\times10^{-19})(1\times10^{-6})}$$

$$= \frac{2}{13.6\times10^{3}} = 1.47 \times 10^{-4} \text{ m/s}$$

$$\approx 0.14 \times 10^{-3} \text{ m/s.}$$

This exactly matches the listed value 0.14×10^{-3} m/s.

21. In a non-polar molecule, positive and negative charge centres overlap. This gives a net dipole moment of zero. So the molecule has no permanent dipole moment.

22. Use, $V = \dfrac{kq}{r}$

Substitute: $V = \dfrac{(9\times10^{9})(1\times10^{-7})}{0.1}$

$= 9 \times 10^3 = 9000$ V.

So the electric potential is 9000 V.

23. At 0 K, no electrons are thermally excited. The valence band is full and conduction band is empty. Hence the semiconductor behaves like an insulator.

24. Use, $\tau = pE \sin\theta$

Substitute: $\tau = (8 \times 10^{-9})(4 \times 10^4) \sin 60°$

$$\tau = (32\times10^{-5})\left(\frac{\sqrt{3}}{2}\right)$$

$$= 16\sqrt{3}\times10^{-5} \text{ N.m}$$

So the torque is $16\sqrt{3}\times10^{-5}$ N.m.

25. For parallel capacitors:

$$C_{eff} = C_1 + C_2 + C_3$$
$$C_{eff} = 5 + 8 + 10 = 23\ \mu F$$

So the equivalent capacitance is 23 μF.

26. For a satellite in circular orbit, the required centripetal acceleration is provided by gravity.

Use, $\frac{v^2}{R} = g'$

So the orbital velocity is

$$v = \sqrt{g'R}$$

This matches option 2 exactly.

27. For capacitors in series:

$$\frac{1}{C_{eff}} = \frac{1}{C_1} + \frac{1}{C_2} + \frac{1}{C_3}$$

Convert all to farads:

$$C_1 = 1\ \mu F = 10^{-6}\ F,$$
$$C_2 = 1\ nF = 10^{-9}\ F,$$
$$C_3 = 1\ mF = 10^{-3}\ F.$$

Now, $\frac{1}{C_{eff}} = 10^6 + 10^9 + 10^3$

Dominant term is 10^9.

So, $C_{eff} \approx \frac{1}{10^9} = 1\ nF.$

28. A full-wave rectifier converts both halves of an AC waveform into DC. So it converts alternating current to direct current.

29. When a Zener diode is in breakdown, it maintains a constant voltage equal to its Zener voltage across the load. Here, that value is 6.0 V.

30. In uniformly accelerated motion, acceleration is constant. Velocity changes with time, and displacement also changes with time. So both vary.

31. In a full-wave rectifier, the DC output still contains ripples. A capacitor connected in parallel with the load R_L charges to the peak value and discharges slowly, filling the gaps between peaks. This smooths the waveform into a more steady DC.

32. A NOR gate gives output 1 only when both inputs are 0.
For any other input combination, the output becomes 0.
Here both inputs are 0, so output = 1.

33. Kepler's Third Law gives

$$T^2 \propto R^3$$

So, $R \propto T^{2/3}$

If the period is doubled:

$$\frac{R_{new}}{R_{old}} = (2)^{2/3} = \sqrt[3]{4}$$

So the orbital radius increases by a factor of $\sqrt[3]{4}$ ·

34. In the band model, a material with a very large band gap (> 3 eV) does not allow electrons to move from the valence band to the conduction band at room temperature. This makes the material a very poor electrical conductor. Such a wide band gap is the property of insulators.

35. A solar cell delivers current to the external circuit. That means current flows out of the device, and the device supplies power. In the I – V graph convention, a device that supplies power operates in the fourth quadrant, where current is negative (outward) and voltage is positive across the load. So the correct reason is that a solar cell supplies current.

36. For large distances, the electric field of a dipole varies as:

Axial field: $E_{axial} = \frac{2p}{4\pi\varepsilon_0 r^3}$

Equatorial field: $E_{eq} = \frac{p}{4\pi\varepsilon_0 r^3}$

Thus, the field is strongest along the axis of the dipole.

37. A dielectric increases capacitance by a factor equal to its dielectric constant k:

$$C' = kC$$
$$= 4 \times 5\ \mu F = 20\ \mu F.$$

38. A charge Q creates an electric field at point P. When a small charge q is placed at P, it experiences the force

$$\vec{F} = q\vec{E}$$

Thus the field due to Q exerts a force on q.

39. Gauss's law:

$$\Phi_E = \frac{Q_{enclosed}}{\varepsilon_0}$$

If enclosed charge is zero, total flux is zero, irrespective of shape or size of the surface.

40. Electric field lines are always perpendicular to equipotential surfaces; otherwise, work would be required to move along that surface, which contradicts its definition.

41. A bar magnet has field lines that emerge from its north pole, loop through space, and enter its south pole; field exists inside and outside. An equivalent solenoid behaves similarly: strong field inside, returning field outside. Hence both have fields inside and outside.

42. Photoelectric condition: $h\nu \geq \phi$ (photon energy $\geq$ work function). If $h\nu > \phi$, surplus appears as kinetic energy.

43. Polar satellites: low Earth orbits (~ few hundred - ~1000 km) with short periods (~100 min).

44. Center of mass on x-axis:

$$x_{CM} = \frac{\sum m_i x_i}{\sum m_i}$$

$$= \frac{2(1)+3(2)+5(3)}{2+3+5}$$

$$= \frac{2+6+15}{10} = \frac{23}{10} = 2.3.$$

45. Equilibrium: magnetic force balances weight.

$$ILB = mg$$

$$\Rightarrow \quad B = \frac{mg}{IL} = \frac{0.325\times 10}{4.5\times 3} = \frac{3.25}{13.5}$$

$$\approx 0.2407 \text{ T}.$$

46. Gravitational force scales as

$$F \propto \frac{m_1 m_2}{r^2}$$

Tripling each mass

$\Rightarrow$ factor $3 \times 3 = 9$; reducing distance to $d/6$

$\Rightarrow$ factor $1/(1/6)^2 = 36$.

Net factor $9 \times 36 = 324$.

New force $= 324$ X.

47. Dipole fields at distance d:

$$\text{axial } B_{ax} = \frac{\mu_0 2M}{4\pi d^3}$$

$$\text{equatorial } B_{eq} = \frac{\mu_0 M}{4\pi d^3}$$

Ratio $B_{ax} : B_{eq} = 2 : 1$.

48. Vector identities:

$$\vec{a}\cdot\vec{b} = ab\cos\theta$$

$$\text{and } |\vec{a}\times\vec{b}| = ab\sin\theta$$

Hence only the dot-product statement with $\cos\theta$ is correct.

49. Paramagnets have $\chi > 0$ and $\chi \ll 1$.

50. For a disc, axis through center perpendicular to plane:

$$I_{cm} = \frac{1}{2}MR^2$$

Tangent axis is parallel and at distance R.

By parallel-axis theorem:

$$I = I_{cm} + MR^2.$$

51. For a magnetic dipole in a uniform magnetic field, the torque is the vector cross product of magnetic moment and field:

$$\vec{\tau} = \vec{m}\times\vec{B}$$

$$|\tau| = m\, B\sin\theta$$

Direction follows the right-hand rule.

52. Torque about a given axis depends on the applied force and its lever arm (perpendicular distance from the axis to the force's line of action):

$$\tau = F\, r_\perp = F\, r\sin\theta.$$

hus both F and $r_\perp$ matter.

53. The parallel-axis theorem shifts MOI from the centre of mass to a parallel axis:

$$I = I_{CM} + Md^2.$$

It is used for flywheels (off-centre axes), compound pendulums (pivot not at CM), and planets (rotation about axes not through CM). A sphere about its diameter is already a CM axis; no shift is needed.

54. Beat frequency equals the absolute frequency difference:

$$\nu_{beat} = |X - Y| = X - Y (X > Y).$$

55. Maximum rise (from the launch point) for vertical throw with initial speed u:

$$u^2 = 2gh_{max}$$

$$\Rightarrow \quad h_{max} = \frac{u^2}{2g} = \frac{(20)^2}{2\times 10} = \frac{400}{20}$$

$$= 20 \text{ m}.$$

Hence, the ball rises 20 m above the building top.

56. In Rutherford's experiment, large-angle deflections occurred rarely. Such strong deflection demands a very concentrated mass and charge. Hence the atom's positive charge and most of its mass are in a tiny, dense nucleus.

57. Doppler formula (both moving towards):

$$f' = f\frac{v + v_o}{v - v_s} = 500 \cdot \frac{340 + 20}{340 - 30}$$

$$= 500 \cdot \frac{360}{310} \approx 580.6 \text{ Hz.}$$

So the observed frequency is about 580 Hz.

58. Angular displacement:

$$\theta = \frac{s}{r} = \frac{5.0}{0.5} = 10 \text{ rad.}$$

59. Kepler's third law:

$$T^2 \propto R^3$$

For $R = 4\ R_E$

$$\left(\frac{T}{1}\right)^2 = 4^3 = 64 \Rightarrow T = 8 \text{ years.}$$

60. Convert to rad/s:

$$\omega_i = 3120 \text{ rpm} = 104\pi$$

$$\omega_f = 1200 \text{ rpm} = 40\pi$$

With $\alpha = -4\pi \text{ rad/s}^2$

$$\omega_f = \omega_i + \alpha t$$

$$\Rightarrow \quad t = \frac{40\pi - 104\pi}{-4\pi} = 16\,\text{s}.$$

61. For frequency, $f = 50$ Hz:
Angular frequency:

$$\omega = 2\pi f = 2\pi(50) = 100\pi \text{ rad/s}$$

Time period: $T = \frac{1}{f} = \frac{1}{50} = 0.02$ s.

62. Maximum acceleration in SHM:

$$a_{max} = \omega^2 A$$

Given, $A = 3$ cm $= 0.03$ m,

$\omega = 2$ rad/s:

$$a_{max} = (2)^2\ (0.03)$$

$$= 4 \times 0.03 = 0.12 \text{ m/s}^2.$$

63. In transverse waves, particles vibrate perpendicular to the direction of wave propagation. Light is a transverse wave.

64. Gas pressure arises from continuous elastic collisions of molecules with the container walls.

65. From the kinetic theory of gases, the pressure exerted by an ideal gas is

$$P = \frac{1}{3} nm\overline{v}^2$$

where, n = number density,

m = mass of one molecule,

$\overline{v}^2$ = mean of squared molecular speed.

This comes from averaging momentum transfer during elastic molecular collisions in all three spatial directions, giving the factor 1/3.

66. Second law forbids a perfect heat engine and a perfect refrigerator.
For an engine, some heat must be rejected $\Rightarrow$ efficiency $\eta < 1$.
For a refrigerator, finite temperature difference implies finite work input $\Rightarrow$ coefficient of performance (COP) is finite, never infinite.

67. Bulk modulus:

$$B = -\frac{\Delta p}{\delta V / V}$$

Given, $B = 2.0 \times 10^9$ N/m^2 and fractional decrease $\Delta V/V = -0.001$.

Hence, $$\Delta P = -B\left(\frac{\Delta V}{V}\right)$$

$$= 2.0 \times 10^9 \times 0.001$$

$$= 2.0 \times 10^6 \text{ N/m}^2.$$

68. Lift requires lower pressure on top than below. This is produced by faster airflow above the aerofoil (Bernoulli effect). Rotation or "equal path" are not necessary conditions.

69. Emission of electrons by light of sufficient frequency is the photoelectric effect; the emitted electrons are photoelectrons.

70. The average distance a gas molecule travels between successive collisions is the mean free path.

71. Shear stress divided by shear strain gives the modulus of rigidity (also called shear modulus).

$$G = \frac{\text{Shearing stress}}{\text{Shearing strain}}.$$

72. de Broglie wavelength is

$$\lambda = \frac{h}{mv'}$$

where h is Planck's constant, m mass, v speed.

73. Linear expansion formula:

$$\Delta L = \alpha L_0 \, \Delta T.$$

Given: $L_0 = 1.5$ m,

$$\alpha = 1.2 \times 10^{-5} \ ^\circ C^{-1}$$

$$\Delta T = 120 - 20 = 100 \ ^\circ C$$

$$\Delta L = (1.2 \times 10^{-5})(1.5)(100)$$

$$= 1.8 \times 10^{-3} \text{ m.}$$

74. Bohr's quantisation rule:

$$L = n\frac{h}{2\pi}, \quad n = 1,2,3,...$$

Angular momentum must be an integral multiple of $h/2\pi$.

75. Poisson's ratio:

$$\nu = \frac{\text{Lateral strain}}{\text{Longitudinal strain}}$$

Given, $\nu = 0.5$

$$\varepsilon_{long} = 4 \times 10^{-3}$$

$$\varepsilon_{lat} = -\nu\varepsilon_{long}$$

$$= -(0.5)(4 \times 10^{-3})$$

$$= -2 \times 10^{-3}.$$

76. (*i*) is correct (definition of elastic body).

(*ii*) is false in physics usage—steel/iron is "more elastic" (higher modulus) than rubber.

(*iii*) is correct (Hooke's law: stress $\propto$ strain within elastic limit).

(*iv*) is false (modulus has units of pressure, not energy).

Hence true statements: (*i*) and (*iii*).

77. In SHM, the acceleration is directly proportional to displacement and directed opposite to it:

$$a = -\omega^2 x.$$

78. Carnot efficiency:

$$\eta = 1 - \frac{T_c}{T_h}$$

Given, $T_h = 300$ K,

$$\eta = 0.30$$

$\Rightarrow$ $T_c = 0.70 \times 300 = 210$ K.

For $\eta = 0.50$ with same T_c:

$$0.50 = 1 - \frac{210}{T_h} \Rightarrow T_h = 420 \text{ K.}$$

79. In $y = A \sin (kx - \omega t + \phi)$,

the quantity $(kx - \omega t + \phi)$ is the phase of the wave.

80. Zeroth law enables the operational definition and measurement of temperature (transitive thermal equilibrium).

81. Given relation:

$$P = \frac{a\sqrt{x}}{b + t^2}$$

Dimensions:

$$P = [ML^{-1} T^{-2}]$$

$$\sqrt{x} = [L^{1/2}]$$

$$t^2 = [T^2]$$

$\Rightarrow$ b must also have dimension $[T^2]$.

Now, $$[a] = P.\frac{(b + t^2)}{\sqrt{x}}$$

$$= [ML^{-1}T^{-2}].\frac{[T^2]}{[L^{1/2}]}$$

$$= ML^{-3/2}.$$

So, $a = [ML^{-3/2}]$ and $b = [T^2]$.

82. Coherence length L_c varies inversely with the bandwidth $\Delta\nu$ (or $\Delta\lambda$) of the light source:

$$L_c \propto \frac{1}{\Delta\nu}$$

Thus it is controlled mainly by spectral width, not by frequency or wavelength alone.

83. Fluorescence quantum yield depends strongly on:

- Molecular structure,
- Solvent polarity,
- Temperature.

Planck's constant does not influence quantum yield.

84.
- candela (cd) $\rightarrow$ base SI unit (luminous intensity)
- radian $\rightarrow$ derived
- newton $\rightarrow$ derived
- hertz $\rightarrow$ derived

Thus candela is NOT a derived SI unit.

85. Fundamental SI quantities include: length, mass, time, electric current, temperature, luminous intensity, amount of substance.

Electric potential, magnetic flux, torque are all derived.

86. First find spring constant:

$$k = \frac{F}{x} = \frac{20}{0.1} = 200 \text{ N/m.}$$

Potential energy:

$$U = \frac{1}{2}kx^2 = \frac{1}{2}(200)(0.2^2)$$

$$= 100(0.04) = 4 \text{ J}.$$

87. Work done by a constant force:

$$W = F\,d = 25 \times 2 = 50 \text{ J}.$$

88. Use energy conservation:

$$mgh = \frac{1}{2}mv^2$$

$$\Rightarrow \quad v = \sqrt{2gh}$$

$$v = \sqrt{2(10)(5)} = \sqrt{100} = 10 \text{ m/s}.$$

89. Kinetic energy is greatest where potential energy is least. Lowest point has minimum height ⇒ maximum kinetic energy.

90. In SEM, electrons are focused using magnetic lenses, not optical lenses.

91. Accuracy refers to closeness of a measured value to the true/accepted value (not repeatability, which is precision).

92. Change in kinetic energy

$$= \int_2^4 P\,dt = \int_2^4 (9t^2 + 2t - 1)\,dt$$

$$= \left[3t^3 + t^2 - t\right]_2^4 = 204 - 26 = 178 \text{ J}.$$

93. For a conservative force, work over any closed path is zero (path – independent).

94. Dimensional check for energy:
P × V (yes), F × d (yes),
Power × time (yes);
$m \times v$ is momentum, not energy.

95. Work by road on cycle:

$$W = \vec{F}\,.\,\vec{s} = Fs \cos 180°$$

$$= 300 \times 4 \times (-1) = -1200 \text{ J}.$$

96. The Zeeman effect becomes the Paschen–Back effect when the magnetic field becomes very strong. In this regime, the magnetic interaction dominates spin–orbit coupling, causing the pattern of splitting to change.

97. In the normal Zeeman effect (when spin does not contribute), one spectral line splits into three components: one unshifted and two symmetrically shifted.

98. Statement (1) is incorrect because zeros between non-zero digits are always significant. The other three statements are true rules of significant figures.

99. Refractive index is a ratio of two speeds ⇒ no dimensions. The others all have dimensions.

100. Dimensional analysis cannot give numerical values of physical quantities; it only gives form/consistency.

101. The four-current density J^μ combines charge density and current density into a single spacetime quantity:

$$J^u = (c\rho, \vec{J})$$

It describes how charge and current flow through spacetime, which act as sources for electromagnetic fields in Maxwell's equations.

102. Gauge invariance means that changing the potentials (ϕ, $\bar{A}$) by a gauge transformation does not change the physical electric and magnetic fields. All observable predictions remain the same.

103. For a cylindrical Gaussian surface of radius r (where $a < r < b$) and length L:

Enclosed charge:

$$Q_{enc} = \rho \text{ (volume enclosed)}$$
$$= \rho[\pi r^2 L - \pi a^2 L]$$
$$= \rho\pi L(r^2 - a^2).$$

Gauss's law:

$$E(2\pi r L) = \frac{Q_{enc}}{\varepsilon_0} = \frac{\rho\pi L(r^2 - a^2)}{\varepsilon_0}$$

Solve for E:

$$E = \frac{\rho(r^2 - a^2)}{2\varepsilon_0 r} = \frac{\rho r}{2\varepsilon_0}\left(1 - \frac{a^2}{r^2}\right)$$

This expression exactly matches option 4.

104. In thermogravimetric analysis (TGA), the onset temperature is the temperature at which weight loss first begins, indicating the start of decomposition.

105. In TEM bright-field imaging, the image is formed from electrons that pass through (are transmitted through) the specimen, with darker regions corresponding to greater scattering/absorption.

106. A soliton is a stable, localised, non-dispersive wave packet that keeps its shape and speed while propagating, due to a balance between dispersion and non-linearity.

107. Translation symmetry in space and time leads, via Noether's theorem, to conservation of energy and momentum. The associated conserved object is the stress - energy tensor $T^{\mu\nu}$.

108. In Yang - Mills theory, A_{μ}^{a} is a vector gauge field corresponding to a non-Abelian gauge group (e.g., SU(2), SU(3)). The index a labels the group generators.

109. The energy - momentum tensor $T^{\mu\nu}$ contains energy density, momentum density, stresses and fluxes of the fields.

110. According to Faraday's law, a changing magnetic flux induces an EMF in the loop. A current flows only if the loop is closed, but EMF is always induced.

111. The Larmor formula gives the radiated power

$$P = \frac{q^2 a^2}{6\pi\varepsilon_0 c^3},$$

which applies only to a non-relativistic accelerated point charge.

112. A depolarisation ratio close to zero means the scattered Raman light is highly polarised. This occurs for totally symmetric vibrations.

113. Differential Thermal Analysis (DTA) measures the temperature difference between a sample and an inert reference as both are heated. This arises due to differences in heat flow during phase or chemical changes.

114. Euler - Lagrange equations apply when the system has holonomic (equation-type) and scleronomic (time-independent) constraints, allowing description via a Lagrangian.

115. For a free real scalar field ϕ, the standard Klein - Gordon Lagrangian density is:

$$L = \frac{1}{2}\partial_{\mu}\phi\, \partial^{\mu}\phi - \frac{1}{2}m^2\phi^2$$

The first term is the kinetic term and the second (negative) term is the mass term. This exactly matches option 4.

116. Locality means that a field at a point interacts only with its immediate neighbours—no instantaneous action at a distance is allowed.

117. A monochromator in XRD removes all unwanted wavelengths and passes only one wavelength so that Bragg peaks are sharp and interpretable.

118. In TEM, diffraction patterns are recorded on a fluorescent screen (or camera coupled to it).

119. The Coulomb gauge condition is: $\nabla \cdot A = 0$.

120. Peak intensity depends on how many lattice planes satisfy Bragg's condition, i.e., how many planes contribute to diffraction.

121. Quantum dots confine electrons in all three spatial dimensions. This confinement produces quantised energy levels instead of a continuous band, just like in isolated atoms. Because their electronic states become discrete, quantum dots show "artificial atom" behaviour such as sharp optical absorption and emission lines.

122. A two-dimensional nanostructure must have one dimension in the nanometre range while the other two dimensions extend much larger. Graphene is a single atomic layer of carbon atoms arranged in a honeycomb lattice. It is only one atom thick, making it a perfect 2D material.

123. Einstein coefficients describe absorption and stimulated emission. In thermal equilibrium, absorption probability and stimulated emission probability must balance, meaning that the coefficients tied to these two processes are equal for the same transition.
Therefore, $B_{21} = B_{12}$.

124. Spontaneous emission happens when an excited atom returns to a lower energy state on its own, emitting a photon without needing any external radiation. It is an inherent quantum process governed by the lifetime of the excited state.

125. Yukawa proposed that nuclear forces arise from the exchange of massive mesons, later identified as pions. The finite mass of the pion leads to a short-range potential of the form

$$V(r) \propto \frac{e^{-mr}}{r},$$

successfully explaining the strong but short-range behaviour of nuclear force.

126. Point defects involve irregularities at a single lattice point, such as missing atoms (vacancies), atoms in incorrect positions (interstitials), or impurity atoms replacing host atoms (substitutional). A dislocation, however, is a line defect extending through many lattice points, so it is not a point defect.

127. In carbon nanotubes, the G-band appears near $\sim 1580\ cm^{-1}$ and corresponds to the graphitic tangential stretching mode of sp^2-bonded carbon atoms. It represents ordered, graphitic-like vibrations along the tube wall.

128. Zinc oxide (ZnO) nanowires belong to the wurtzite crystal family, which lacks a centre of symmetry. This gives them piezoelectric properties, enabling them to generate electric charge under mechanical stress and contributing to mechanical robustness.

129. Metal – Organic Framework (MOF) nanostructures are widely synthesised using solvothermal methods, where metal ions and organic linkers react in a high-temperature solvent inside sealed vessels, allowing controlled crystal growth.

130. Time-resolved spectroscopy requires extremely fast time measurements on the order of picoseconds to femtoseconds. Only lasers can provide such ultra-short duration pulses, allowing precise tracking of fast molecular and electronic dynamics.

131. Nanoparticle characterisation involves determining structure, size, shape and composition using tools like X-ray diffraction (crystallinity), microscopy (TEM/SEM imaging), and spectroscopy (optical/electronic properties). Chromatography, however, is mainly used for chemical separation and purification, not structural characterisation of nanoparticles.

132. Lasers are used in fibre-optic communication because they produce highly directional, coherent, monochromatic beams that allow very high data-carrying bandwidth over long distances with minimal loss.

133. Laser action requires:

- active medium (where population inversion occurs),
- energy source (pump) to excite the medium,
- resonator (optical cavity) to amplify light.

An optical fibre is not required for laser formation; it is only used for communication after the laser is generated.

134. Laser cooling works by shining red-detuned light on moving atoms. When atoms absorb photons opposite their motion, their momentum decreases, effectively cooling them.

135. CO_2 lasers emit strongly in the infrared region ($\sim 10.6\ \mu m$) and provide very high power, making them ideal for industrial cutting, welding, engraving and machining metals.

136. In laser-induced fluorescence, a molecule absorbs high-energy (short-wavelength) light and re-emits lower-energy (longer-wavelength) light. This means fluorescence emission always occurs at energies less than excitation. Therefore, the statement saying emission occurs at greater energy is false.

137. Drift velocity v_d of electrons is

$$v_d = \mu E,$$

where μ is the mobility.

Hence drift velocity is directly proportional to mobility (and to the electric field).

138. Surfactants attach to surfaces of forming nanoparticles and control growth, prevent particles from sticking together and stabilise the dispersion. Their major role is to prevent aggregation and direct morphology.

139. Coherence means the laser light has a constant, well-defined phase relationship across time (temporal coherence) and across the beam (spatial coherence). This gives lasers their interference and precision properties.

140. Zero-dimensional nanostructures (e.g., nano-particles, quantum dots) have confinement in all three dimensions, giving them the maximum surface-to-volume ratio, higher than 1D or 2D structures.

141. A variable is declared so that the program can store a value in memory and later use, change, or manipulate that value during execution.

142. In quantum mechanics, a composite system is described by the tensor product of the Hilbert spaces of its subsystems, ensuring all combined states (including entangled states) are allowed.

143. A total wavefunction of the form

$$\psi_{AB} = \psi_A \otimes \psi_B$$

is a direct product of individual states. Such a state has no entanglement; subsystems remain independent.

144. Nuclear charge density is well approximated by the Woods – Saxon distribution, which accurately describes a nearly constant central density with a smooth fall-off at the edges.

145. Gamma multipolarity (E1, M1, E2, ...) is determined solely by how much angular momentum and parity the nucleus must change during the transition.

146. An unpaired neutron in a $p_{(3/2)}$ orbital has orbital angular momentum $l = 1$ (p-state) and total angular momentum $j = 3/2$.

Neutrons have positive intrinsic parity, and parity of an orbital is $(-1)^l$.

Thus: $\pi = (-1)^l = -$.

So the allowed spin – parity is

$$I^\pi = \frac{3^-}{2}$$

147. In time-dependent perturbation theory, the Hamiltonian is written as:

$$H(t) = H_0 + V(t),$$

where $V(t)$ is a small time-varying perturbation.

148. Nuclear radius formula:

$$R = R_0\, A^{(1/3)}$$

For A = 238:

$$A^{(1/3)} \approx 6.2,$$

So, $R = 1.2 \text{ fm} \times 6.2$

$$\approx 7.44 \text{ fm}.$$

149. A supernova is a violent explosion of a massive star, occurring either after core collapse or thermonuclear runaway.

150. Expression: $!(a > b)$

Given, $a = 5$, $b = 10$:

$a > b \Rightarrow 5 > 10$

$\Rightarrow$ false $\Rightarrow 0$.

Logical NOT of 0 is 1.

151. Runge – Kutta schemes attain a higher order of accuracy than Euler for the same step size h. Thus, for a fixed h, truncation error is much smaller than Euler's $O(h)$.

152. Pointer arithmetic: $*(p + 2)$ = arr[2]. With arr = {10, 20, 30, 40, 50}, we get 30.

153. The liquid drop model treats the nucleus like a fluid drop and explains global trends such as average binding energy vs. A (volume, surface, Coulomb, asymmetry terms).

154. Central difference for $f'(x)$:

$$\frac{f(x+h)-f(x-h)}{2h} = f'(x) - \frac{h^2}{6}f^{(3)}(x) + O(h^4),$$

so the leading error term depends on $f^{(3)}(x)$.

155. In C, an unsigned char stores 8-bit non-negative integers: 0 to 255.

156. Gluons are the gauge bosons of Quantum Chromodynamics (QCD) and mediate the interaction between quarks inside hadrons. This interaction is the strong nuclear force, the strongest force in nature at the subatomic scale.

157. The central difference formula has truncation error of order $O(h^2)$, whereas forward/backward differences have error $O(h)$.

Therefore central differences give higher accuracy for the same step size.

158. Runge – Kutta methods compute the next value from the current value only, without requiring several previous points.

Hence they are single-step and are usually explicit (like classic RK4).

159. A Tokamak confines plasma using strong magnetic fields arranged in a closed toroidal geometry, so particles follow closed magnetic lines and remain trapped.

160. Experiments confirm gravitational mass = inertial mass, a foundation of the equivalence principle in general relativity. So their ratio is exactly 1.

161. For a 3-dimensional free Fermi gas, the density of states varies as

$$g(E) \propto E^{1/2}$$

This comes from counting states in a spherical shell in k-space where $E \propto k^2$.

162. Feynman diagrams are a graphical shorthand for terms in the perturbation expansion of correlation functions. They are used to compute scattering amplitudes and probabilities of interactions, not literal particle paths.

163. The LSZ (Lehmann – Symanzik – Zimmermann) reduction formula connects time-ordered correlation functions of fields to physical scattering amplitudes, allowing calculation of S-matrix elements.

164. A gas behaves as a plasma if collective electrostatic effects dominate. This requires

$$\lambda_D \ll L,$$

i.e., the Debye length must be much smaller than the system size, ensuring charge shielding and collective behaviour.

165. The Mandel Q parameter indicates photon number statistics:

- $Q > 0$: super-Poissonian
- $Q = 0$: Poissonian
- $Q < 0$: sub-Poissonian (signature of nonclassical light, e.g., squeezed states)

Thus negative Q implies reduced fluctuations below shot-noise.

166. Decoherence destroys the phase relation between components of a quantum superposition. As a result, the system no longer behaves like a coherent superposition but instead becomes a statistical mixture of classical alternatives.

167. The master equation describes how the density matrix evolves when a system interacts with its environment. It is widely used in quantum optics to study lossy cavities, spontaneous emission, damping, and decoherence.

168. In a cold, collisionless plasma, electrons displaced from equilibrium oscillate collectively at a natural frequency that depends on electron density. This is called the plasma frequency.

169. For a dilute gas of non-interacting bosons, the critical temperature T_c for Bose – Einstein condensation is

$$T_c = \frac{h^2}{2\pi k_B m}\left(\frac{n}{\xi(3/2)}\right)^{2/3},$$

where $\zeta(3/2) \approx 2.612$

Since $\zeta(3/2)$ is a numerical constant, the dependence is always:

- proportional to $n^{2/3}$
- divided by $2\pi k_B\, m$

Among the options, the only one with correct power of density $n^{2/3}$, correct mass dependence, and correct Planck constant factor structure is:

$$T_c = \frac{h^2}{2\pi k_B m} n^{2/3}$$

This matches option 4.

170. The ultraviolet catastrophe refers to the failure of classical electrodynamics (Rayleigh – Jeans law) to explain the behavior of blackbody radiation at high frequencies, predicting infinite energy. Planck's quantum hypothesis resolved the issue.

171. Polarised light microscopy is used to enhance contrast in birefringent materials (e.g., crystals, fibers) via polarization-dependent intensity changes.

172. In the Breit – Wigner resonance, the width Γ relates to the lifetime τ via $\Gamma = \hbar/\tau$; thus it measures the total decay rate of the resonant state.

173. The Toffoli gate flips the target qubit only if both control qubits are 1; i.e., a controlled – controlled – NOT (CCNOT).

174. Raman spectroscopy can show rotational and vibrational transitions (often combined as ro-vibrational lines).

175. For an adiabatic plasma: $P \propto n^{\gamma}$.
Taking $\nabla \ln P = \gamma \nabla \ln n$ gives

$$\frac{\nabla P}{P} = \gamma \frac{\nabla n}{n}.$$

176. Responsivity measures how effectively a photodetector converts incoming optical power into electrical current. Its definition is:

$$R = \frac{\text{Photo-current}}{\text{Incident Optical Power}}$$

This tells how many amperes are produced per watt of input light.

177. In a homogeneous and isotropic universe (FRW cosmology), the conserved quantity associated with energy is the total energy per unit mass of a particle, derived from applying the Friedmann equation to geodesic motion.

178. The thermodynamic relation connecting standard Gibbs free energy change and equilibrium constant is:

$$\Delta G^\circ = -RT \ln K.$$

This shows that a large K (equilibrium strongly to the right) means negative ΔG°.

179. Planck's radiation law describes the spectral distribution of blackbody radiation and is valid at any temperature above absolute zero. Classical laws fail, but Planck's law works universally.

180. Renormalisation removes divergences by redefining mass, charge, and coupling constants so that physical predictions remain finite and measurable.

181. Kant presented his complete aesthetic philosophy—including judgments of beauty, the sublime, and purposiveness—in his major work Critique of Judgement (1790).

182. Multilingualism means the ability to use and understand two or more languages for communication.

183. The strongest way to align resources with objectives is to choose materials that offer multiple ways for students to reach the intended learning outcomes, giving flexibility for different learning styles.

184. A learning objective clearly states what students will be able to do at the end of instruction—observable and measurable.

185. Vygotsky emphasised social interaction, cultural tools, and language as the primary drivers of cognitive development.

186. Subjective type tests involve open-ended responses and rely on the examiner's judgement, leading to subjective scoring and improved writing or speaking skills. However, they do not guarantee consistent scoring because different examiners may score differently.
Thus, "Consistency in the scores" is not a characteristic.

187. Quantitative content analysis focuses on counting and measuring textual elements using objective, systematic, and replicable procedures.

188. Universal Design for Learning (UDL) supports diversity by allowing flexibility in methods, materials, activities, and assessments so all learners can access learning.

189. An academic discipline is defined by concepts, theories, specialised knowledge, and terminology. It is not characterised as "without subjects."

190. NEP 2020 describes the Secondary Stage (Classes 9 – 12) as multidisciplinary, with deeper critical thinking, flexibility, and student choice of subjects.

191. Physical resources include tangible facilities like buildings, electricity, classrooms, laboratories, etc. Support staff are human resources, not physical resources.

192. Formative evaluation is ongoing and helps identify learning difficulties during instruction. Diagnostic evaluation is conducted alongside or before formative processes to detect learner problems and provide corrective feedback.

193. Logical Positivists (Vienna Circle) analysed the empirical meaning and logical structure of scientific theories, especially focusing on the philosophical implications of Einstein's theory of relativity.

194. Gender bias in curriculum appears when content reinforces traditional, stereotypical gender roles, limiting perspectives and equality.

195. Piaget stated that cognitive development occurs through four fixed, universal stages, driven by biological maturation and interaction with the environment. Experiences help construct mental structures.

196. Gender socialisation happens when society shapes how individuals think, behave, and see their roles on the basis of norms of masculinity and femininity.

197. The intellectual/academic approach focuses on understanding cognitive theories of learning and how they guide effective teaching methods.

198. Inclusive education requires IEPs, which tailor instruction, goals, and support to each child with special needs.

199. Rubrics help students reflect on what they have achieved, what is expected, and how to improve—making them a key tool in Assessment for Learning.

200. The model that moves from teacher demonstration ("I do") to guided practice ("We do") to independent work ("You do") is the essence of scaffolding.

Previous Paper (Solved)

Delhi Subordinate Services Selection Board

DSSSB–PGT (Physics) Recruitment Exam, 2021*

POST SPECIFIC SUBJECT RELATED QUESTIONS

1. Action and reaction forces act on what?
A. The different bodies
B. The same body but different position
C. The same body or different body
D. The same body only

2. Find the maximum value of acceleration of the bus if a mass of 3 kg lying on the floor of the bus will remain stationary (Given the co-efficient of static friction is 0.15):
A. 0.5 ms^{-2} B. 2.0 ms^{-2}
C. 1.5 ms^{-2} D. 2.5 ms^{-2}

3. The dimension of potential energy is:
A. $M^1L^2T^{-1}$ B. $M^0L^2T^{-2}$
C. $M^1L^1T^{-2}$ D. $M^1L^2T^{-2}$

4. Impulsive force is:
A. Small force acts in a short time
B. Large force acts in a long time
C. Small force acts in a long time
D. Large force acts in a short time

5. Find the dimensional-formula of $X_0 + ut + \frac{1}{2}at^2$:
A. $M^{-1}L^1T^1$ B. $M^0L^{-1}T^0$
C. $M^0L^1T^0$ D. $M^1L^{-1}T^1$

6. If during a collision, the initial velocities and final velocities of both the bodies are along the same straight line then it is called:
A. Direct collision
B. Head on collision
C. Head to head collision
D. Natural collision

7. Gravity is an example of:
A. Kinetic force
B. Conservative energy
C. Conservation of energy
D. Conservative force

8. When spring is called hard then the value of spring constant is ______.
A. High B. Low
C. Medium D. Zero

9. Neutrino is a particle emitted in:
A. δ-decay B. α-decay
C. β-decay D. γ-decay

10. Suppose that a projectile is launched with velocity V_0 that makes an angle θ_0 with the horizontal axis. What is the time of flight of the projectile?
A. $V_o \sin\theta_0/g$ B. $2V_0 \cos\theta_0/g$
C. $g \sin\theta_0/V_0$ D. $2V_0 \sin\theta_0/g$

11. The relation between Ergs(erg) and electron volt(eV) is:
A. 1 erg = 0.625×10^{-10} eV
B. 1 erg = 0.625×10^{-12} eV
C. 1 erg = 0.625×10^{12} eV
D. 1 erg = 0.625×10^{10} eV

12. The dimensional formula of mass is:
A. $[M^1L^0T^0]$ B. $M^1L^1T^{-2}$
C. $M^1L^2T^{-1}$ D. $M^1L^1T^1$

13. Equilibrium of a particle in mechanics refers to the situation when the particles are in ______.
A. Both translational and rotational equilibrium
B. Conditional equilibrium only
C. Rotational equilibrium only
D. Translational equilibrium only

14. In β-decay, the nucleus emits:
A. proton B. neutron
C. positron D. electron

* Online exam held on 29/06/2021.

15. To measure 0.0001 m length accurately one what can be use?
A. Meter scale B. Screw gauge
C. Vernier Callipers D. Spherometer

16. A car is moving with a speed of 5 ms^{-1} on a smooth road and its mass is 10 quintal. It collides with a wall and the wall is mounted with a spring of spring constant 6.25×10^3 Nm^{-1}. Find the maximum compression of the spring.
A. 1.00 meter B. 4.00 meter
C. 3.00 meter D. 2.00 meter

17. Plane angle is defined as the ratio of:
A. Length of arc to the radius
B. Length of the arc to the square of the radius
C. The intercepted area of a spherical surface to the square of its radius
D. Area of the circle to the radius

18. The error which is associated with the resolution of the instrument is known as ______.
A. Absolute error B. Relative error
C. Random error D. Least count error

19. Voltage and current are given as V = (100 ± 9)V and I = (100 ± 0.5)A. Find the percentage error in resistance (R).
A. 5 per cent B. 14 per cent
C. 9 per cent D. 12 per cent

20. The accuracy in measurement of mass 9.89 g is ±0.01 g. Then the relative error in 9.89 g is:
A. ±10 per cent B. ±0.01 per cent
C. ±0.1 per cent D. ±1 per cent

21. Escape speed of a body is independent of ______.
A. Mass of the body
B. Gravity
C. Gravity and radius of the earth
D. Radius of the earth

22. In pure translational motion at any instant of time all particles of the body have ______.
A. Different momentum
B. Different velocity
C. Same momentum
D. Same velocity

23. If d is the depth, R_E is the radius of the earth and g is the acceleration due to gravity at earth's surface, the g at a depth d, $g(d)$ is:
A. $g(d) = g(1 - 2d/R_E)$
B. $g(d) = g(1 + 2d/R_E)$
C. $g(d) = g(1 - d/R_E)$
D. $g(d) = g(1 + d/R_E)$

24. Which of the following is a scalar quantity?
A. Angular velocity
B. Linear momentum
C. Angular momentum
D. Angular frequency

25. Find the moment of inertia of a hollow ring about its tangent.
A. $\frac{3MR^2}{4}$ B. MR^2
C. $\frac{MR^2}{4}$ D. $\frac{5MR^2}{4}$

26. Accleration due to gravity above the surface of the earth is not dependent on?
A. Radius of the earth
B. Mass of the earth
C. Height
D. Gravity of the earth

27. The relation between time period T and radius R, of the circular orbit of a planet about the sun, where gravity is G, and mass of the sun is M_S is:
A. $T = \sqrt{\frac{4\pi^2}{GM_S}R^2}$ B. $T = \sqrt{\frac{4\pi^2}{GM_S}R^3}$
C. $T^2 = \frac{4\pi^2}{GM_S}R$ D. $T = \frac{4\pi^2}{GM_S}R$

28. The centre of gravity of a body is that point where the total gravitational torque on the body is ______.
A. Infinite B. Zero
C. Maximum D. Minimum

29. A river is 1000 m wide and water flows at a speed of 50 m/min. A man can swim at a speed of $66\frac{2}{3}$ m/min in still water. What is the time needed by the man to cross the river?

A. 15 min B. 20 min
C. 10 min D. 25 min

30. Find the escape speed for moon:
A. 11.2 km/s B. 2.11 km/s
C. 3.2 km/s D. 2.3 km/s

31. We don't have to specify the direction of ______.
A. Unit vector
B. A null vector
C. Displacement vector
D. Radius vector

32. The moment of inertia of a hollow cylinder of radius R is MR^2 about:
A. Parallel axis B. Diameter
C. Perpendicular axis D. Axis of cylinder

33. What is the position of the centre of mass for two particles of equal masses?
A. It lies between any point of the masses
B. It lies near each mass
C. It lies at perpendicular distance from either of the mass
D. It lies exactly midway between the masses

34. Find the magnitude of linear velocity of a particle whose angular velocity is $7\hat{i}+3\hat{j}-5\hat{k}$ and the distance from the origin is $\hat{i}-\hat{j}+\hat{k}$.
A. 15.75 ms^{-1} B. 13.75 ms^{-1}
C. 12.35 ms^{-1} D. 14.62 ms^{-1}

35. The example of rotation where axis may not be fixed?
A. Spinning top and potters wheel
B. A ceiling fan only
C. A spinning top only
D. A potter's wheel only

36. The year of a planet is 29.5 times that of the earth. If the distance between sun and the earth is 1.50×10^8 km, then find the distance between the planet and the earth?
A. 1.43×10^{14} meter B. 1.34×10^{14} meter
C. 1.34×10^{12} meter D. 1.430×10^{12} meter

37. Which statement is false for a "rigid body"?
A. It has perfectly definite shape
B. The shape is unchangeable
C. All particles of the body are moving together
D. The rigid body is not in pure translational motion

38. A boy throws a stone at a speed of 28 ms^{-1}. The stone makes 30° angle with the horizontal surface. Find the maximum height of the stone from the ground.
A. 12.0 meter B. 6.0 meter
C. 8.0 meter D. 10.0 meter

39. A pair of forces of equal magnitude but acting in opposite direction with different lines of action is known as:
A. Moment B. Precession
C. Couple D. Centre of mass

40. Find the total energy of a circularly orbiting satellite:
A. Negative B. Zero
C. Positive D. Infinite

41. Calculate the total work done in bringing a charge of 5×10^{-7} C from infinity to a point which is 10 cm away from a charge of 3×10^{-9} C.
A. 1.6×10^{-4} J B. 1.35×10^{-4} J
C. 1.6×10^{-5} J D. 1.6×10^{-9}

42. Which of the following is not a mechanical wave?
A. Sound wave B. Seismic wave
C. Light wave D. Water wave

43. How much negative charge is present is 500 g of water?
A. 1.34×10^6 C B. 3.68×10^7 C
C. 2.68×10^7 C D. 1.34×10^7 C

44. What is the electrostatic potential energy, when two charges 5 μC and –3 μC are placed at a distance of 16 cm away from each other?
A. –0.95 J B. 0.8 J
C. 0.9 J D. –0.84 J

45. The electric field of an electric dipole at a point on the equatorial plane for $r >> a$ is ______.
A. $-\dfrac{2p}{4\pi t_0 r^3}$ B. $-\dfrac{p}{4\pi t_0 r^3}$
C. $\dfrac{2p}{4\pi t_0 r^3}$ D. $\dfrac{p}{4\pi t_0 r^3}$

46. What is the length of simple pendulum if frequency is 0.5 Hz (g = 9.8 ms^{-2})?

A. 2 meter B. 4 meter
C. 3 meter D. 1 meter

47. In a non polar molecule, the molecule has ______.

A. Intrinsic dipole moment
B. No intrinsic dipole moment
C. Week dipole moment
D. Permanent dipole moment

48. The relation between the average energy of vibrations (E) and temperature (T) is:

A. E proportional T
B. E proportional 1/T
C. E proportional T^2
D. E proportional $1/T^2$

49. Which law of Kepler can be understood as a consequence of a conservation of an angular momentum which is valid for any central force?

A. Law of orbits
B. Law of semi major axis
C. Law of areas
D. Law of periods

50. Gamma is the ratio of two specific heats. What is the value of gamma for air?

A. 2.4 B. 2
C. 1.4 D. 1

51. When the frequency of a periodic is small then it is called:

A. Repeating
B. Vibration
C. Oscillation
D. Damping

52. Which statement is false in case of Coulomb's law?

A. It is true when one charge is positive and another is negative
B. It is true when both charges are positive
C. It is true when both charges are negative
D. It is true only when both charges are positive

53. Find the amplitude for forced oscillations in case of small damping?

A. $A=\dfrac{F_0}{m(w^2+w_d^2)}$ B. $A=\dfrac{F_0}{(w^2-w_d^2)}$

C. $A=\dfrac{F_0}{(w-w_d)}$ D. $A=\dfrac{F_0}{m(w^2-w_d^2)}$

54. According to Gauss's law the electric field at a distance r from an infinitely long straight uniformly charged wire (charge density λ) is ______.

A. $\vec{E}=\dfrac{2\lambda}{\pi t_0 r}\vec{n}$ B. $\vec{E}=\dfrac{\lambda}{4\pi t_0 r}\vec{n}$

C. $\vec{E}=\dfrac{\lambda}{2\pi t_0 r}\vec{n}$ D. $\vec{E}=\dfrac{\lambda}{\pi t_0 r}\vec{n}$

55. SI unit of angular wave number is:

A. Radian
B. ms^{-1}
C. rad s^{-1}
D. rad m^{-1}

56. The SI unit of electric flux is:

A. NC^{-1}m^2 B. NCm^2
C. NC^{-1}m^{-2} D. NCm^{-1}

57. The value of the permittivity of the free space in SI unit is ______.

A. 8.854×10^{-14} c^{2}N^{-1}m^{-2}
B. 8.854×10^{-19} c^{2}Nm^{-2}
C. 7.854×10^{-12} cN^{-1}m^{-2}
D. 8.854×10^{-12} c^{2}N^{-1}m^{-2}

58. Which statement is true for electrostatics of conductors?

A. Electrostatics potential is not constant throughout
B. Inside a conductor, electrostatic field has some value
C. The interior of a conductor can have no excess charge in the static situation
D. Inside a conductor, electrostatic field is normal to the surface

59. For simple harmonic motion which of the following is true?

A. Displacement of the particle varies with velocity
B. Displacement of the particle varies with distance

C. Displacement of the particle varies with time

D. Displacement of the particle varies with amplitude

60. The phase constant of simple harmonic motion is dependent on:

A. Displacement B. Time
C. Amplitude D. Frequency

61. A wire of mass 0.4 kg and length 1.6 m carries a current of 3 A. Around the wire a uniform magnetic field is present. Find the magnitude of magnetic field.

A. 0.93 T B. 0.82 T
C. 0.74 T D. 0.65 T

62. Find the magnitude of magnetic field when an electron moves in a circular path of radius 26 cm with a speed of 3×10^7 m/s. Mass and charge of electron is 9×10^{-31} kg and 1.6×10^{-19} C respectively.

A. 6×10^{-2} T B. 6×10^{-4} T
C. 6×10^{-6} T D. 6×10^{-8} T

63. Suppose four particles of same mass, present at the vertices of a square of side "*a*", then the potential energy of the system is: (G-gravity, *m*-mass)

A. (4.2 G*m*/*a*) J B. (5.41 Gm^2/*a*) J
C. (–5.41 Gm^2/*a*) J D. (–4.2 G*m*/*a*) J

64. The range of resistivity of a material is of 10^{-8} Ωm to 10^{-6} Ωm. Find the material?

A. Insulator B. Resistor
C. Semiconductor D. Metals

65. According to Biot-Savart Law, the magnitude of the magnetic field at a distance *x* from the centre of current (I) carrying circular loop of radius R in vacuum of permeability μ_0 is:

A. $\frac{\mu_0 IR^2}{2(x^2+R^2)^{3/2}}$ B. $\frac{\mu_0 IR}{2(x^2+R^2)^{3/2}}$

C. $\frac{\mu_0 IR}{2(x^2+R^2)}$ D. $\frac{\mu_0 IR}{2(x^2+R^2)^2}$

66. The resistivity of a semiconductor ______.

A. decrease with increasing temperatures
B. increase with decreasing temperatures
C. decrease with decreasing temperatures
D. increase with increasing temperatures

67. Weber is a unit of ______.

A. Magnetic flux B. Magnetic moment
C. Magnetic induction D. Velocity

68. Which of the following called the Bohr radius?

A. $a_0 = \frac{h^2\varepsilon_0}{\pi me^2}$ B. $a_0 = \frac{h^2\varepsilon}{\pi me^2}$

C. $a_0 = \frac{h\varepsilon_0}{\pi me^2}$ D. $a_0 = \frac{h^2\varepsilon_0}{\pi me}$

69. When the magnetic force $q(\vec{V} \times \vec{B})$ not zero?

A. When velocity and magnetic field are anti parallel
B. When velocity and magnetic field are perpendicular to each other
C. When velocity and magnetic field are parallel
D. When velocity and magnetic field directions are opposite

70. In Balmer Series, line with the longest wavelength, 656.3 nm in the ______ is called H_α; the next line with wavelength 486.1 nm in the ______ is called H_β.

A. Blue-green, red B. Violet, blue-green
C. Red, blue-green D. Red, violet

71. The internal resistance of a dry cell is ______ the common electrolytic cell.

A. much higher than
B. equal
C. much less than
D. less than

72. Which instrument has the advantage that it draws no current from the voltage source being measured?

A. Potentiometer B. Galvanometer
C. Wheatstone bridge D. Meter bridge

73. If the area of the cross section of a conductor is halved then its resistance become ______.

A. two times B. infinite
C. half D. zero

74. The magnitude of the drift velocity per unit electric field is:

A. Resistivity B. Mobility
C. Electricity D. Conductivity

75. The earth's magnetic field is about:
A. 3.6×10^{-5} T B. 3.9×10^{-5} T
C. 3.6×10^{-6} T D. 3.9×10^{-6} T

76. The relation between orbital radius and the electron velocity is:
A. $r \propto \frac{1}{v^2}$ B. $r \propto v$
C. $r \propto v^3$ D. $r \propto v^2$

77. The SI unit of current density is:
A. $\frac{A}{m^2}$ B. Am^2
C. $\frac{m^2}{A}$ D. $\frac{A}{m}$

78. 1 gauss = ______ tesla:
A. 10^{-6} B. 10^{-2}
C. 10^{-3} D. 10^{-4}

79. Find the capacitance of a parallel plate capacitor when the area of the plate is 1 m^2 and the distance between them is 1 mm?
A. 8.88×10^{-9} F B. 8.85×10^{-8} F
C. 8.85×10^{-9} F D. 8.88×10^{-8} F

80. Which is not the limitation of ohm's law?
A. V depends on I non linearly
B. The relation between V and I is non unique
C. The relation between V and I depends on the sign of V for the same absolute value of V
D. The relation between V and I is dependent on R

81. The expression for zero point energy which is a consequence of the Heisenberg uncertainty principle is:
A. $E_0 = \hbar^2/4ma^2$ B. $E_0 = \hbar/ma^2$
C. $E_0 = \hbar^2/8ma^2$ D. $E_0 = \hbar/8ma^2$

82. To transmit music an approximate bandwidth of ______ is required.
A. 20 kHz B. 12 kHz
C. 18 kHz D. 26 kHz

83. What is the range of frequency band for uplink in satellite communication?
A. 6.5 – 7.642 GHz B. 4.2 – 5.6 GHz
C. 3.7 – 4.2 GHz D. 5.925 – 6.425 GHz

84. If an antenna radiates electromagnetic waves from a height 40 m then what is the range of transmission of the wave? Given radius of earth = 6.4×10^6 m.
A. 25.34 km B. 23.45 km
C. 22.63 km D. 21.59 km

85. If $L^* \simeq 2 \times 10^{10} L_\theta$ is a characteristic galaxy luminocity, then the luminosities of a giant elliptical is:
A. $L > L^*$ B. $L \leq L^*$
C. $L = L^*$ D. $L \geq L^*$

86. Find the mass of ^{12}C atom?
A. 1.99×10^{-26} kg B. 1.99×10^{-23} kg
C. 1.99×10^{-24} kg D. 1.99×10^{-25} kg

87. The element gold has ______ isotopes.
A. 36 B. 30
C. 32 D. 34

88. Which series lies in the ultraviolet region?
A. Bracket B. Pfund
C. Lyman D. Paschen

89. The surface brightness of the disk at a distance r from the centre and the disk scale length r_d, measured along the mid plane of the disk is given by:
A. $I_d(r) = I_d(0)\, e^{-r/rd}$ B. $I_d(r) = I_d(0)\, e^{r/rd}$
C. $I_d(r) = I_d(0)\, e^{-r/rd}$ D. $I_d(r) = I_d(0)\, e^{rrd}$

90. The half life of radium is 1600 years. What fractions of a sample of radium that would remain after 8000 years?
A. $\frac{1}{32}$ B. $\frac{1}{8}$
C. $\frac{1}{64}$ D. $\frac{1}{5}$

91. No electron conduction is possible between the Valence Band and Conduction band when ______.
A. $E_g < 3$ eV B. $E_g < 2$ eV
C. $E_g > 2$ eV D. $E_g > 3$ eV

92. What element will be formed if thorium-230 undergoes alpha decay?

A. Radium-234 B. Uranium-234
C. Radium-226 D. Uranium-226

93. The loss of strength of a signal while propagating through a medium is known as ______.
A. Transducer B. Modulation
C. Repeater D. Attenuation

94. For hydrogen atom the radius of innermost orbit of electron is 4.5×10^{-12} m. What is radius of $n = 4$ orbital?
A. 1.72×10^{-10} m B. 7.2×10^{-11} m
C. 4.5×10^{-10} m D. 4.5×10^{-12} m

95. What will be the angle of projection to find the maximum horizontal range by a projectile?
A. 60° B. 30°
C. 45° D. 90°

96. Which statement is false for nuclear force?
A. the nuclear force between neutron-neutron is same
B. the nuclear force between two nucleons falls rapidly to zero as their distance is more than a few femtometers
C. the nuclear force is independent on the electric charge
D. the nuclear force is much less than the coulomb force

97. Which diode is used as voltage regulator?
A. Photovoltaic devices
B. Light emitting diode
C. Photodiode
D. Zener diode

98. The absolute magnitude (M_B) of a giant galaxy as suggested by Hubble is:
A. $M_B \leq -20$ B. $M_B \geq -40$
C. $M_B \geq -20$ D. $M_B < -20$

99. One of the types of normal galaxies is:
A. septicular B. lenticular
C. ventricular D. vavioler

100. Which statement is false for LED?
A. Fast on-off switching capability
B. Fast action and no warm up time required
C. High operational voltage and less power
D. Long life and ruggedness

101. The measured latent heat of water is 2256 J/g. At atmospheric pressure, 1g of water has a volume 1 cm^3 in liquid phase and 1671 cm^3 in vapour phase. Then the value of ΔU is:
A. 2086.8 J B. 1086.8 J
C. 2069.2 J D. 1069.2 J

102. If a function $f(z)$ is analytic and its derivative is continuous at each point within a simply connected region R, then for every closed path C in R the line integral of $f(z)$ around C is zero. This sentence 3 describes:
A. Fourier's Integral Theorem
B. Contours Integral Theorem
C. Cauchy's Integral Theorem
D. Laplace's Integral Theorem

103. Which one is false for extensive variable?
A. Extensive variable indicates the size of the system.
B. The product of an intensive variable like P and an extensive quantity ΔV is extensive
C. Pressure, temperature and density are extensive variable
D. The variable whose values get halved in each part are extensive.

104. Suppose we have a spherical system consisting of N particles that are interacting gravitionally. If the position of the ith particle be r_i and its velocity V_i then total kinetic energy is:
A. $T = m\sum_{i=1}^{N} V_i^2$ B. $T = \sum_{i=1}^{N} m_i V_i^2$
C. $T = \frac{1}{2}\sum_{i=1}^{N} m_i V_i^2$ D. $T = \frac{1}{2} m\sum_{i=1}^{N} V_i^2$

105. An isotherm is:
A. The volume-temperature curve for a fixed pressure
B. Thc pressure-temperature curve for a fixed volume
C. Specific heat-pressure curve for a fixed volume
D. The pressure-volume curve for a fixed temperature

106. The real and imaginary parts $u(x, y)$ and $v(x, y)$ of an analytic function $f(z)$ separately satisfy the two dimensional Laplace equation and are known as ______.

A. Harmonic functions
B. Logarithmic function
C. Memorphic function
D. Differentiable function

107. What will be the dispersive power for wavelength 2λ, if dispersive power is 'D' for wavelength λ?

A. $\frac{D}{8}$ B. $\frac{D}{2}$

C. $\frac{D}{4}$ D. D

108. An active galaxy produces energy at the rate of ______.

A. $10^{40} - 10^{42}$ ergs S^{-1}
B. $10^{44} - 10^{47}$ ergs S^{-1}
C. $10^{42} - 10^{44}$ ergs S^{-1}
D. $10^{47} - 10^{50}$ ergs S^{-1}

109. A group of elements can be split into subsets such that all the elements are conjugate to each other, the similarity transformation being done by some element of the group itself, but no two elements belonging to two different subsets are conjugate to each other. Such subsets are called:

A. Symmetric group
B. Classes of the group
C. Cyclic group
D. Permutation group

110. Which statement is false for a quasi-static process?

A. The system remains in mechanical equilibrium with the surroundings
B. It is an infinitely slow process
C. The pressure and temperature of the process are same with the environment
D. The system remains in thermal equilibrium with surrounding

111. Laplace integral is represented as ______.

A. $e^{-px} = \frac{2p}{\pi}\int_0^\infty \frac{\cos x\, dx}{p^2+k^2}, x \geq 0, p > 0$

B. $e^{-px} = \frac{2\pi}{p}\int_0^\infty \frac{\cos kx\, dx}{p^2+k^2}, x \geq 0, p > 0$

C. $e^{-px} = \frac{2p}{\pi}\int_0^\infty \frac{\cos kx\, dx}{p^2+k^2}, x \geq 0, p > 0$

D. $e^{-px} = \frac{p}{\pi}\int_0^\infty \frac{\cos kx\, dx}{p^2+k^2}, x \geq 0, p > 0$

112. Which classification of active galaxy have no prominent emission lines and the spectrum is dominated by a continuum?

A. BL Lacertae object
B. Star Burst Galaxies
C. Optically violent variable
D. Seyferet Galaxies

113. When the value of spectral index, $\alpha \leq 0.4$, the spectrum is called ______.

A. High spectrum
B. Flat spectrum
C. Low spectrum
D. Steep spectrum

114. In complex Fourier series, the value of coefficients a_0 is:

A. $\int_{T/2}^{-T/2} f(x)dx$ B. $\frac{1}{T}\int_{-T/2}^{T/2} f(x)dx$

C. $\frac{1}{T}\int_{T/2}^{-T/2} f(x)dx$ D. $\int_{-T/2}^{T/2} f(x)dx$

115. Which statement is true for carnot engine?

A. The efficiency of carnot engine is one
B. Working between hot and cold reservoirs, other engine can have more efficiency than a carnot engine
C. The efficiency of the carnot engine is independent of the nature of the working substance
D. A carnot engine is an irreversible engine

116. In case of a refrigerator the working substance does not go through which of the following steps?

A. Heat is absorbed by the surrounding and change liquid to vapour
B. Sudden expansion of the gas from high to low pressure which cools it and converts it into a vapour-liquid mixture

C. Release of heat by the vapour to the surroundings bringing it to the initial state and completing the cycle
D. Heating up the vapour due to external work done on the system

117. Euler identity is represented as ______.
A. $i\theta = \cos\theta + i \sin\theta$
B. $e^{i\theta} = \sin\theta + i \cos\theta$
C. $e^{i\theta} = \cos\theta + i \sin\theta$
D. $e^{\theta} = \sin\theta + \cos\theta$

118. How many globuler cluster are associated within our galaxy?
A. about 100 B. about 400
C. about 1000 D. about 150

119. The complete group of symmetry for diatomic molecules do not contain the element of the following?
A. Reflection symmetry in a horizontal plane passing through the centre of the molecule.
B. The reflection symmetry in any plan other than vertical passing through the line of atoms.
C. Axial rotational symmetry about the line joining the atoms.
D. Two fold rotational symmetry about any horizontal axis passing the centre of the molecule.

120. In which process no work is done on or by the gas?
A. Isobaric process
B. Isothermal process
C. Adiabatic process
D. Isochroic process

121. The operator $\int \varphi^* (D_{op}\psi) d\tau = \int (D_{op}\ \varphi)^* \psi d\tau$ is known as:
A. Orthonormal B. Hamiltonian
C. Hermitian D. Parity

122. Which of the following is not a notable consequence of the uncertainty principle?
A. The position of particle is defined in quantum physics
B. The path of particle is not defined in quantum physics
C. Atomic oscillators pass a certain amount of energy known as Zero point energy, even at absolute zero temperature
D. Electrons do not exist inside the nucleus

123. According to the second law of thermodynamics the entropy of the universe:
A. Can decrease
B. Can never decrease
C. Can be infinity
D. Can be zero

124. The sum of the diagonal element of a matrix is called the ______ of the matrix.
A. Inverse B. Transpose
C. Trace D. Eigen value

125. The principle of relativity is:
A. The laws of physics are different in all inertial frames of reference
B. The laws of physics are the same in all inertial frames of reference
C. The speed of light should be the same in all uniformly moving systems
D. The speed of light has same constant value in all inertial frames of reference

126. The time independent Schrodinger equation is:
A. $-\dfrac{h^2}{2m}\psi''(x) + v(x)\,\psi(x) = E\psi(x)$
B. $-\dfrac{h^2}{2m}\psi(x) + v(x)\,\psi(x) = E\psi''(x)$
C. $-\dfrac{h^2}{2m}\psi''(x) + v(x)\,\psi''(x) = E\psi''(x)$
D. $\dfrac{h^2}{2m}\psi''(x) + v(x)\,\psi(x) = E\psi(x)$

127. Which statement is false for a spherically symmetric potential?
A. It depends only upon the radial coordinate r
B. It is independent of the polar coordinate *cp*
C. It depends on the polar coordinate
D. It depends only upon the radial coordinate r and it is independent of the polar coordinate *cp*

128. Which of the following is an example of a particle that travels at the speed of a light?

A. Proton B. Positron
C. Photon D. Electron

129. Which one of the following is not the boundary condition for the wave function $\psi(x)$?
A. $\psi(x)$ should be square-integrable
B. $\psi(x)$ should be single valued everywhere
C. both $\psi(x)$ and $d\psi/dx$ should be continuous everywhere
D. $\psi(x)$ should be infinite

130. The alpha radiation is not used in radiotherapy because:
A. It is unable to penetrate human skin
B. It is toxic to human tissues
C. It is not easily available
D. It is extremely costly

131. The temperature range covered by an iron-constantan thermocouple is ______ to ______.
A. –220°C to 1300°C B. –200°C to 760°C
C. 0°C to 1700°C D. 100°C to 500°C

132. Which is not a basic property of similar matrix?
A. If A is similar to B and B is similar to C then, A may not be similar to C
B. Similar matrices have the same characteristic polynomial and hence exactly the same eigen values including multiplicities
C. A matrix is similar to itself
D. A is similar to B if and only if B is similar to A

133. What is the normal frequency of L-C circuit?
A. $\frac{1}{2\pi}\sqrt{\frac{1}{C}}$ B. $\frac{1}{2\pi}\sqrt{\frac{C}{L}}$
C. $\frac{1}{2\pi}\sqrt{\frac{1}{LC}}$ D. $\frac{1}{2\pi}\sqrt{LC}$

134. If the lightest nucleus of hydrogen whose mass is 1.673×10^{-27} kg and radius is 1.2×10^{-15} m, then the density of nuclear matter is:
A. 2.3×10^{16} kg/m^3 B. 2.3×10^{17} kg/m
C. 23×10^{17} kg/m D. 2.3×10^{17} kg/m^3

135. Quasars can be observed in many parts of the electromagnetic spectrum except:
A. Visible ray B. Infrared
C. Gamma rays D. Radio

136. The relativistic linear momentum of a particle of rest mass m_0 moving with velocity V is defined by:
A. $P = m_0v/(1 + v^2/c^2)^{1/2}$
B. $P = m_0v/(1 - v^2/c^2)^{1/2}$
C. $P = m_0v/(1 - v^2/c^2)$
D. $P = -m_0v/(1 + v^2/c^2)^{1/2}$

137. Which is the frame of reference in which Newton's first law holds true?
A. Inertial frame B. Uniform frame
C. Internal frame D. Intersticial frame

138. Complete the following nuclear fission reaction:
${}^{1}_{0}n + {}^{235}_{92}U \rightarrow {}^{141}_{56}Ba + \_\_\_\_\_\_ + 3{}^{1}_{0}n + 200$ MeV.
A. Ge B. Kr
C. La D. Xe

139. An electron of mass M of the atom has an angular momentum L. Since this electron has a charge e and is moving inside the atom then the magnetic moment of the electron is:
A. $\mu_L = \frac{e}{\mu}L$ B. $\mu_L = -\frac{e}{\mu}L$
C. $\mu_L = \frac{e}{2\mu}L$ D. $\mu_L = -\frac{e}{2\mu}L$

140. When the two operations of complex conjugation and transposition are carried out one after another on a matrix, the resulting matrix is called:
A. Hermitian conjugate
B. Transposition conjugate
C. Complex conjugate
D. Simple conjugate

141. The relation between centripetal force and radius of the circle is:
A. $F_c \propto r^2$ B. $F_c \propto 1/r$
C. $F_c \propto 1/r^2$ D. $F_c \propto r$

142. The relation between number density of electron (n) and the Fermi energy (E_F) of metal at T = 0 k is given by:
A. $n = 2\pi/3\ (8m/h^2)^{3/2}\ (E_F)^{3/2}$
B. $n = \pi/3\ (8m/h^2)^{3/2}\ (E_F)^{3/2}$
C. $n = \pi/3\ (4m/h^2)^{3/2}\ (E_F)^{3/2}$
D. $n = \pi/4\ (8m/h^2)^{3/2}\ (E_F)^{3/2}$

143. The relation between air drag and velocity of the object is:
A. Air drag $\propto$ V B. Air drag $\propto \sqrt{V}$
C. Air drag $\propto V^2$ D. Air drag $\propto \frac{1}{V}$

144. Lorenz number for sodium metal is:
A. 2.34×10^{-8} W Ωk^{-2}
B. 2.25×10^{-8} W Ωk^{-2}
C. 2.17×10^{-8} W Ωk^{-2}
D. 2.37×10^{-8} W Ωk^{-2}

145. The relative strength of electromagnetic force is in the order of ______.
A. (10^{-2}) B. (10^{-3})
C. (10^{-4}) D. (10^{-5})

146. Which one is not a fundamental force in nature?
A. Electroweak force B. Strong force
C. Frictional force D. Gravitational force

147. The relative biological effectiveness (RBE) of fast neutron is ______.
A. 8 B. 10
C. 4 D. 5

148. What will be the ratio of acceleration of an electron and a proton, if they are placed in a uniform electric field?
A. In a ratio of proton and electron masses
B. One
C. Zero
D. In a ratio of electron and proton masses

149. If the eccentricity is less than one, then the conic section is:
A. Hyperbola B. Circle
C. Parabola D. Ellipse

150. Which method is particularly useful in determining the orientation of a single crystal?
A. Ewald method B. Laue method
C. Bragg method D. Powder method

151. What will happen, if proton is projected perpendicular to magnetic field?
A. It will turn in semicircle
B. No magnetic field effect on the motion of proton
C. Proton will move in same direction but will get momentum
D. Proton will continue to move in the same direction but will never gain momentum

152. AVF cyclotrons produce energies beyond ______ for protons:
A. 800 MeV B. 1000 MeV
C. 600 MeV D. 400 MeV

153. Which of the following is an example of non-ohmic resistance?
A. Copper wire B. Wire of tungsten
C. Carbon resistor D. Diode

154. Which type of crystal system is present in potassium dichromate?
A. Monoclinic B. Triclinic
C. Orthorhombic D. Trigonal

155. The relation between crystal scattering factor (f_c), geometrical structure factor (F) and lattice structure factor (S_c) is :
A. $F = f_c \times S_c$ B. $S_c = 2F/f_c$
C. $S_c = F \times f_c$ D. $F = f_c/S_c$

156. The dimension of the damping factor is:
A. $[M^1L^1T^{-1}]$
B. it's a dimensionless quantity
C. $[M^2L^1T^{-1}]$
D. $[M^1L^2T^{-1}]$

157. When an object is inverted in space with respect to a point (within it) and still remains invariant is known as ______ symmetry.
A. Reflection B. Inversion
C. Rotational D. Translational

158. At high temperatures heat capacity is independent of temperature and for all solid it is equal to: [R-equal to universal gas constant]
A. 5R B. 3R
C. 2R D. 4R

159. Which one of the following is not an assumption of Drude-Lorentz theory about metals?
A. The interaction between free electrons themselves is too small and can be ignored
B. Valance electrons behave as free electrons and can move all around the volume of the metal

C. Free electrons behave as molecules of an ideal gas and obey kinetic theory of gases and the Maxwell Baltzman distribution law
D. Negatively charged ions located at the lattice sites offers a uniform potential and influence the motion of free electrons

160. Which one is not a feature of motion under central conservative forces?
A. The particle always moves in a plane perpendicular to the direction of the angular momentum
B. The total potential energy is not constant
C. The total kinetic energy is constant
D. The angular momentum about the centre of force is constant both in magnitude and direction

161. The Michelson interferometer is used as ______.
A. Extended Monochromatic source
B. Monochromatic source
C. Light source
D. Common light source

162. The area of each Fresnel half period zone is nearly equal to ______.
A. πb B. $\pi \lambda$
C. $\pi b \lambda$ D. $b \lambda$

163. For a wave motion the relation between total energy (TE) and amplitude (a) of wave is:
A. TE $\propto a$ B. TE $\propto a^2$
C. TE $\propto 1/a^2$ D. TE $\propto 1/a$

164. Which statement is false for the sclera of the eyeball of human?
A. It is an opaque, fibro-elastic capula
B. It is soft
C. It withstands the intraocular pressure in the eye
D. It protects the inner part of the eye

165. Which one of the following is not a characteristic of IC LM 380?
A. It has internally fixed gain of 50
B. Output is also short circuit proof
C. It can work on a wide range of supply voltage from 5 to 22V
D. Total harmonic distortion is higher than 0.2%

166. What is the refractive index of cornea?
A. 1.33 B. 1.38
C. 1.4 D. 1.34

167. Resolving power of Fabry-Perot interferometer is given by:
A. $\dfrac{\lambda}{\Delta\lambda} = 4\pi \cos r\sqrt{F}/4.147\lambda$
B. $\dfrac{\lambda}{\Delta\lambda} = \pi h \cos r\sqrt{F}/4.147\lambda$
C. $\dfrac{\lambda}{\Delta\lambda} = 4\pi h \cos r\sqrt{F}/4.147\lambda$
D. $\dfrac{\lambda}{\Delta\lambda} = \pi h \cos r\sqrt{F}/4.147$

168. The differentiator circuit is obtained by replacing R_1 (Input Resistance) of an inverting amplifier by a ______.
A. Capacitor B. Transistor
C. Rectifier D. Diode

169. The intensity of the polarised light reaching the detector is given by:
A. $I(\theta) = I(0) \sin^2 \theta$ B. $I(\theta) = \cos^2 \theta$
C. $I(\theta) = I(0) \cos^2 \theta$ D. $I(\theta) = \sin^2 \theta$

170. A Lloyd's mirror produces a/an:
A. Chromatic fringe
B. Multichromatic fringe
C. Double chromatic fringe
D. Achromatic fringe

171. Which is not a suitable difference between Biprism and Lloyd's mirror fringes?
A. In biprism, the fringes are circular but in Lloyd's mirror fringes are oval in shape.
B. The central fringe in biprism is less sharp than that in Lloyd's mirror.
C. In biprism, the complete pattern of fringes is obtained. In Lloyd's mirror ordinarily, only a few fringes on one side of the central fringe are visible
D. In biprism, the central fringe is bright, while in Lloyd's mirror it is dark

172. At the very centre of the retina is a small yellowish depression, called fovea which contains ______.

A. Neither rods nor cones
B. Rods and cones both
C. Only cones
D. Only rods

173. The Hall coefficient of copper at room temperature is:
A. (-1.70 Vm^3 A^{-1} $Tesla^{-1}$)
B. ($+0.33$ Vm^3 A^{-1} $Tesla^{-1}$)
C. (-0.30 Vm^3 A^{-1} $Tesla^{-1}$)
D. (-0.55 Vm^3 A^{-1} $Tesla^{-1}$)

174. Which is not a performance parameter associated with voltage regulator?
A. Load stability
B. Temperature stability
C. Ripple rejection
D. Input regulation

175. ______ is not a type of amplifier according to circuit configuration.
A. Ground collector B. Grounded emitter
C. Base emitter D. Grounded base

176. In metal, relaxation time of electron:
A. decreases with increase in temperature
B. increases with temperature
C. suddenly changes at 400 K
D. does not depend upon temperature

177. Which of the following is not an advantage of negative feedback?
A. It reduces distortion
B. It increases the input impedence
C. It decreases the band width
D. It improves the stability of amplifier gain

178. The central maximum in double slit pattern is ______ times brighter than that in single slit pattern.
A. double B. fourth
C. fifth D. thrice

179. The diffraction pattern of a circular aperture consists of concentric rings with a central bright disc. The first dark ring appears when:
A. $\sin \theta = 2.12\ \lambda/D$ B. $\sin \theta = 1.22\ \lambda/D$
C. $\sin \theta = 1.34\ \lambda/D$ D. $\sin \theta = 2.22\ \lambda/D$

180. The diameter of the *n*th bright ring of Newton's ring is:
A. $D_n \propto \sqrt{2n - 1}$ B. $D_n \propto \sqrt{n^2 - 1}$
C. $D_n \propto \sqrt{n^2 + 1}$ D. $D_n \propto \sqrt{n - 1}$

181. Which of the following is a characteristic of Learner-centred Performance-Based Assessment?
A. Focus is on knowing learning deficit of the learner
B. Continuous and comprehensive assessment
C. Assessment of learning
D. Focus is on learning product and outcome

182. Which is not a suitable-criteria for evaluation of a physics textbook?
A. Correctness of the content
B. Paper quality should be better
C. Appropriateness of language
D. Promoting students thinking about phenomena experience and knowledge

183. Which of the following is not a technique which could be adopted for presenting and introducing of any new concept related to physics?
A. Involving students in their homework
B. Carrying out activities and experiment and raising question
C. Presenting a problem to the student
D. Narration stories incident etc

184. Which of the following is not included in Dr. Madeline Hunter's research about what effective teachers usually include in their lessons?
A. Input
B. Detailed introduction
C. Independent practice
D. Purpose

185. What is the topmost level in the Cone of Experience?
A. Watch still pictures
B. Listen to lecture
C. Participate in a hands-on workshop
D. Read text

186. ______ is known as 'father of observation astronomy'.
A. Galileo B. Aryabhatta
C. Aristotle D. Kepler

187. Which of the following is not a feature of continuous and comprehensive evaluation process in Physics?
A. It does not mean more frequent tests and examination
B. Since teaching learning in a school is a continuous process and assessment is an integral part of this process, so it is essential
C. Teacher uses only a fixed technique of evaluation
D. Teacher provides feedback on different aspect of learning

188. Which of the following work should nerver done by a teacher?
A. Maintain distance in spite friendly with his students
B. Sympathetic towards students
C. Make fun to their colleagues in the presence of your students to win the trust of your students
D. Repeated praise should be given to the student for his ability/good works

189. Which of the following is not a responsibility of physics teacher?
A. Determination and grading evaluation of students
B. To prepare inspirational lessons
C. Identify and analyse the necessities of the students
D. To notice physical power and weakness of the student

190. Which of the following is related to project method of teaching?
A. Hilda Taba
B. Ralph W. Toyler
C. Lawrence Steinhausen
D. W.H. Kilpatrick

191. A physics teacher can use audiovisual material/ additional material in the classroom. How can it help students?
1. It will increase the curiosity of the students in the subject.
2. It will divert the attention of the students from the subject.
3. It will help slow learners
A. Only 2 and 3 B. 1, 2 and 3
C. Only 1 and 3 D. Only 1 and 2

192. Keeping in view the following:
1. Collaborative learning
2. Brainstorming
3. Homework

Which of the following are teaching-learning strategies for lifelong learning?
A. Only 2 and 3 B. Only 1 and 2
C. Only 1 and 3 D. 1, 2 and 3

193. For ensure progressive learning which of the following method can adopt by physics teacher?
1. Using new edition of textbooks.
2. Participating in various seminars conducted for teachers.
A. Only 1 B. 1 and 2 both
C. Only 2 D. Neither 1 nor 2

194. Which of the following approaches is NOT adopted in taking up a project of physics?
1. Performing experiments
2. Using an interesting available data
3. Engagement in exploration
A. Only 3
B. Only 1 and 2
C. Neither 1 nor 2 nor 3
D. Only 2

195. According to the Blooms's Mastery Learning Strategy students who score ______ marks or more are considered at mastery level.
A. 0.8 B. 0.75
C. 0.85 D. 0.7

196. Which one of the following is the benefits of project work of physics?
A. They are not directly testable
B. It is more time takeable
C. Lack of rewards for teachers
D. It increases interdisciplinary activities

197. Consider the following skills:
1. Communication skills
2. Security skills
3. Sycomotor skills

Which of the above is necessary for a teacher of physics?

A. Only 1 and 3 B. 1, 2 and 3
C. Only 2 and 3 D. Only 1 and 2

198. Which of the following is not a type of project-work in Physics?
A. Fun B. Experimental
C. Survey D. Observational

199. Which one is not one of the Pillars of Learning given by the International Commission of Education?
A. learning individually
B. learning to be
C. learning to do
D. learning to know

200. Which of the following is not a quality of a good physics teacher?
A. Average knowledge of mathematics
B. Attentive to details
C. Tolerant and resourceful
D. Inventive, creative and curious

ANSWERS

1	2	3	4	5	6	7	8	9	10
A	C	D	D	C	B	D	A	C	D
11	**12**	**13**	**14**	**15**	**16**	**17**	**18**	**19**	**20**
C	A	A	D	C	D	A	D	B	C
21	**22**	**23**	**24**	**25**	**26**	**27**	**28**	**29**	**30**
A	D	C	D	A	B	B	B	A	D
31	**32**	**33**	**34**	**35**	**36**	**37**	**38**	**39**	**40**
B	D	D	A	C	D	D	D	C	A
41	**42**	**43**	**44**	**45**	**46**	**47**	**48**	**49**	**50**
B	C	C	D	B	D	B	A	C	C
51	**52**	**53**	**54**	**55**	**56**	**57**	**58**	**59**	**60**
C	D	D	C	D	A	D	C	C	B
61	**62**	**63**	**64**	**65**	**66**	**67**	**68**	**69**	**70**
B	B	C	D	A	A	A	A	B	C
71	**72**	**73**	**74**	**75**	**76**	**77**	**78**	**79**	**80**
A	A	A	B	A	A	A	D	C	D
81	**82**	**83**	**84**	**85**	**86**	**87**	**88**	**89**	**90**
C	A	D	C	D	A	C	C	C	A
91	**92**	**93**	**94**	**95**	**96**	**97**	**98**	**99**	**100**
D	C	D	B	C	D	D	A	B	C
101	**102**	**103**	**104**	**105**	**106**	**107**	**108**	**109**	**110**
A	C	C	D	D	A	A	B	B	C
111	**112**	**113**	**114**	**115**	**116**	**117**	**118**	**119**	**120**
C	A	B	B	C	A	C	D	B	D
121	**122**	**123**	**124**	**125**	**126**	**127**	**128**	**129**	**130**
C	A	B	C	B	A	C	C	D	A
131	**132**	**133**	**134**	**135**	**136**	**137**	**138**	**139**	**140**
B	A	C	D	A	B	A	B	D	A
141	**142**	**143**	**144**	**145**	**146**	**147**	**148**	**149**	**150**
C	B	C	C	D	C	B	A	D	B

151	152	153	154	155	156	157	158	159	160
A	C	D	B	D	B	B	B	D	B
161	**162**	**163**	**164**	**165**	**166**	**167**	**168**	**169**	**170**
A	C	B	B	D	B	C	A	C	D
171	**172**	**173**	**174**	**175**	**176**	**177**	**178**	**179**	**180**
A	C	D	A	C	A	C	B	B	A
181	**182**	**183**	**184**	**185**	**186**	**187**	**188**	**189**	**190**
B	B	A	B	C	A	C	C	D	D
191	**192**	**193**	**194**	**195**	**196**	**197**	**198**	**199**	**200**
C	B	B	C	C	D	B	A	A	A

Previous Paper (Solved)

Delhi Subordinate Services Selection Board

DSSSB–PGT (Physics) Recruitment Exam, 2018*

POST SPECIFIC SUBJECT RELATED QUESTIONS

1. A particle moves along a curved path, given by $y = ax^2$ and the x component of its velocity is a constant equal to 'c'. Its acceleration is equal to:

A. $\frac{1}{2}ac^2$ B. ac^2

C. $4ac^2$ D. $2ac^2$

2. The dimension of Planck's constant is same as that of:

A. Rotational kinetic energy

B. Angular momentum

C. Angular velocity

D. Linear momentum

3.

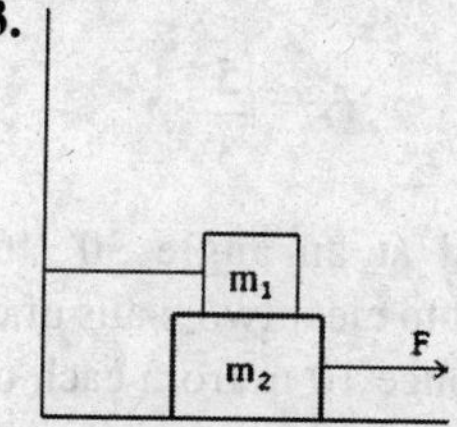

With reference to the figure shown, the force required to pull out the block having mass 'm_2' with an acceleration 'a' (coefficient of friction between the surfaces concerned = μ) is?

A. $(2\ m_1 + m_2\ )\ \mu g + m_2 a$

B. $(m_2 + m_1)\mu g + m_2 a$

C. $(2m_2 + m_1)\mu g + m_2 a$

D. $(2m_1 + m_2)\mu g + (m_1 + m_2)a$

4. 1 watt expressed in cal/sec is equal to:

A. 14.34

B. 860.42

C. 0.239

D. 0.042

5.

The velocity vs. time graph, PQ of a particle is shown in the figure for the time interval $t = 0$ sec to $t = 20$ sec. Find the displacement of the particle during this period in the length unit chosen for the above graph.

A. 144 B. 128

C. 98 D. 104

6. $kgm^2s^{-3}\ A^{-1}$ is equivalent to:

A. Watt B. Ampere

C. Henry D. volt

7. t°C is equivalent to $(t + 273.15)$ kelvin, that is TK. Then in Fahrenheit scale TK will be equivalent to:

A. $\frac{5}{9}(t + 459.67)$ B. $1.8(t + 273)$

C. $1.8(t + 290.93)$ D. $\frac{5}{9}\left(t + \frac{32}{9}\right)$

8. (farad × ohm) is equivalent to:

A. sec^2 B. sec^{-2}

C. sec D. sec^{-1}

9. The velocity of a particle in ms^{-1} is $\left(2\hat{i} - 3\hat{j} + 4\hat{k}\right)$. What is the component of this velocity along the direction of the vector $\left(\hat{i} + \hat{j} + \hat{k}\right)$?

* Online exam held on 04/07/2018.

A. $3\sqrt{3}\ ms^{-1}$ B. $\frac{\sqrt{3}}{3}\ ms^{-1}$

C. $2\sqrt{3}\ ms^{-1}$ D. $\sqrt{3}\ ms^{-1}$

10. A body of mass of 10 kg is placed on a smooth inclined plane. It is supported separately by a force acting horizontally, and then by a force acting parallel to the plane. If the normal reactions in these cases are N_1 and N_2 respectively, then ($g = 10\ m/s^2$)
A. $N_1N_2 = 10^4$ newton^2
B. $N_1N_2 = 4 \times 10^3$ newton^2
C. $N_1N_2 = 2 \times 10^4$ newton^2
D. $N_1N_2 = 5 \times 10^3$ newton^2

11. A glass plate can just support a weight of 54 kg. The plate with a body on it is raised with gradually increasing acceleration. It is found that the plate breaks when the acceleration is 8 ms^{-2}. Find the mass of the body in kg (take $g = 10\ ms^{-2}$).
A. 90 B. 60
C. 120 D. 30

12. In an experiment with a mirror and scale galvanometer, the scale used has its smallest division equal to 1 mm. For a current the direct and reverse readings were respectively 14.4 cm and 14.5 cm, the reading should be recorded as:
A. 14.5 cm B. $(14.4 \times 14.5)^{1/2}$ cm
C. 14.45 cm D. 14.4 cm

13. In a mathematical treatment the expression of a function of velocity, u, appears as e^{-bu^2}. The dimension of b is:
A. L^2T^{-2} B. ML^2T^{-2}
C. MLT^{-1} D. $L^{-2}T^2$

14. A particle moves in three dimension such that its position vs. time equations (x, y, z in metres and t in seconds) are:

$x = t^2 + t + 2,\ y = t^2 - t + 1,\ z = 2\sin\pi t$

Find the expression of the acceleration vector at $t = 1$ sec.

A. $2(\hat{i} + \hat{j})\ ms^{-2}$ B. $4(\hat{i} - 9\hat{j})\ ms^{-2}$

C. $(2\hat{i} - \hat{j} + 2\hat{k})\ ms^{-2}$ D. $(2\hat{i} + 3\hat{j} + \hat{k})\ ms^{-2}$

15. The refractive index of glass with respect to air was being determined using the paper, rectangular glass slab and pin method by applying the formula:

$\mu = \frac{p_{air}}{p_{glass}}$, where the symbols have their usual meanings. For a particular reading the data were $p_{air} = 6$ cm, $p_{glass} = 4$ cm. These were measured by a scale whose smallest division was 1 mm. Find the maximum possible percentage proportional error for the above measurement.
A. 2.83 B. 0.83
C. 4.17 D. 0.17

16. A man rows a certain distance directly across a river and downstream in time a sec and b sec respectively. If the man can row in still water at the rate of 10 ms^{-1} and the river flows at the rate of 4 ms^{-1}. Find the ratio $a : b$.

A. $\sqrt{\frac{7}{3}}$ B. $\frac{1}{2}\sqrt{7}$

C. $\frac{1}{2}\sqrt{5}$ D. $\sqrt{\frac{5}{3}}$

17. A body is projected at an angle 30° to the horizontal, so as just to clear two walls of equal height 5 m at a distance 10 m from each other. The total range of the body in meters is?
A. 10 cot 15° B. $10\sqrt{3}$
C. 20 cot 15° D. 20

18. A projectile of mass 40 kg is shot vertically upwards with a velocity 80 m/s. After 5 sec it explodes into two equal parts, and one of them travels vertically up with a velocity 100 m/s. What is the velocity of the other fragment (in magnitude and direction) at this instant? (take $g = 10\ m/s^2$)
A. 20 m/s upward
B. 20 m/s downward
C. 40 m/s downward
D. 40 m/s upward

19. Two inertial frames of reference defined by space and time co-ordinates (x, y, z, t); (x', y',

z', t') are such that the primed system moves with a uniform velocity with respect to the unprimed system. The velocity of a body measured by the two systems are u and u' respectively. Given below are four sets of equation, linking the x, y, z components of u and u' (v is directed along x, x'-axes)

(p) $u'_x = u_x - v,\ u'_y = u_y - v,\ u'_z = u_z - v$

(q) $u'_x = u_x - v,\ u'_y = u_y,\ u'_z = u_z$

(r) $u'_x = u_x + v,\ u'_y = u_y + v,\ u'_z = u_z + v$

(s) $u'_x = u_x + v,\ u'_y = u_y,\ u'_z = u_z$

Choose the correct set of equations.

A. (q) B. (s)
C. (r) D. (p)

20. The displacement (x) vs. time (t) of a particle follows the condition:

$x^2 = pt^2 + 2qt + r$

Where p, q and r are constants. It is found that the acceleration of the particle varies at x^n, then n is equal to?

A. –4 B. –2
C. –1 D. –3

21. A dice of mass 'm', which has a radius 'a' can rotate freely about a horizontal axis through 0. The distance of 0 from the centre of the dice is $r(r < a)$. If the dice is released in this position it acquires an angular acceleration arising out of the torque due to the weight of the dice. Find the value of 'r' for which this angular acceleration is maximum.

A. $\frac{a}{2\sqrt{2}}$ B. $\frac{a}{2}$

C. $\frac{a}{\sqrt{2}}$ D. $\frac{a}{4}$

22. A chord is drawn from one end of the vertical diameter to any point of a vertical circle. The inclination of the chord to the vertical is 'α'. The time taken by a particle to slide down the chord is:

A. Independent of α
B. Proportional to cot α
C. Proportional to $\sqrt{\cot\alpha}$
D. Proportional to cos α

23. A spherical shell (*i.e.* hollow sphere) is made in a steel sphere of radius 'R' such that the shell passes through the centre of the original steel sphere. The mass of the steel sphere was 'M'. It is found that the force of attraction exerted by this partly hollow sphere on a particle of mass 'm' which lies at a distance 'x' from the centre of the steel sphere on the straight line joining the centres of the sphere and the hollow is $\frac{GMm}{x^2}\left(1-\frac{1}{8y^2}\right)$. Then y is equal to:

A. $\left(1+\frac{R}{2x}\right)$ B. $\left(1-\frac{R}{2x}\right)$

C. $\left(1-\frac{R}{x}\right)$ D. $\left(1+\frac{R}{x}\right)$

24. Seven particles of equal mass are placed at the angular points of a regular octagon. The C.M. of the system is found to be at a distance n OA from O, the centre of the octagon, where A is the unoccupied angular point. Then 'n' is equal to?

A. $\frac{1}{6}$ B. $\frac{1}{7}$

C. $\frac{1}{8}$ D. $\frac{1}{14}$

25. A rod AB of length 6 m slides in the xy-plane with its end A on the y-axis which is vertical. When the rod makes an angle 45° with the vertical, the linear acceleration of A is 1 ms^{-2} down the y-axis. What is its angular acceleration at this instant in radians sec^{-2}?

A. $\left\{\frac{\sqrt{2}}{3}\left(1-\frac{\sqrt{2}}{6}\right)\right\}$ in clockwise sense

B. $\left\{\frac{\sqrt{2}}{6}\left(1-\frac{\sqrt{2}}{6}\right)\right\}$ in anticlockwise sense

C. $\left\{\frac{\sqrt{2}}{6}\left(1-\frac{\sqrt{2}}{6}\right)\right\}$ in clockwise sense

D. $\left\{\frac{\sqrt{2}}{3}\left(1-\frac{\sqrt{2}}{6}\right)\right\}$ in anticlockwise sense

26. A particle of mass 10 gm moves under the influence of a force field.

$\vec{F} = 2(\sin t\,\hat{i} + \cot\,\hat{j})$ in newton's. If the particle is initially at rest at the origin of co-ordinates, then the work on the particles upto $t = \pi$ sec is?

A. 1600 joules B. 800 joules
C. 1000 joules D. 1200 joules

27. Which among the following as/are a no-work force(s)?

(*p*) Force experienced by a charged particle moving in a uniform magnetic field.
(*q*) Normal reaction when a man is walking on a smooth road
(*r*) Tension in the string of a simple pendulum
(*s*) Viscous drag on a body moving through a fluid medium

A. Only (*q*) B. Only (*p*) and (*r*)
C. Only (*s*) D. (*p*), (*q*) and (*r*)

28. A gymnast stands on a freely rotating platform holding heavy weights in his hands. With his arms stretched parallel to the platform, his rotational speed is 1 rev per sec, whereas when he draws them down along his body, his rotational speed increases to 3 rev per sec. The ratio of his moment of inertia in the two cases is:

A. 3 : 1 B. 9 : 1
C. 9 : 2 D. $\sqrt{3}:1$

29. A ball is projected vertically upwards from a point A to reach its greatest height B. It again returns to the point B. In course of the above journey is passes through two points P and Q twice (Q is above P). Now, which among the following options is true?

A. Time of rise from P to Q is greater than Time of fall from Q to P
B. (Time of rise from P to Q) plus (Time of fall from Q to P) is equal to Half of the total time of flight.
C. Time of rise from P to Q is less than Time of fall from Q to P
D. Time of rise from P to Q is equal to the Time of fall from Q to P

30. Two bodies move under their mutual action and reaction only. No external force is acting on the system. Based on the above examine the statements given below:

(*p*) The centre of mass of the system moves with an increasing velocity.
(*q*) The centre of mass of the system moves with a decreasing velocity.
(*r*) The centre of mass moves with a uniform velocity.
(*s*) It is possible to detect a frame of reference in which the centre of mass is at rest.

A. Only (*r*) is true
B. Only (*q*) is true
C. Both (*r*) and (*s*) are true
D. Only (*p*) is true

31. Determine the moment of inertia of a uniform rod of length L and mass M about an axis passing through its C.M. and perpendicular to the rod.

A. $\frac{1}{3}$ ML^2 B. $\frac{1}{24}$ML^2
C. $\frac{1}{12}$ML^2 D. $\frac{1}{6}$ML^2

32. If a bucket weighing 1 kg is lowered at a constant acceleration 2.5 m/s^2 by a string (assumed to be massless) by a distance of 4 m, the work done by the string will be (take g = 10 m/s^2).

A. 10 J B. $\frac{160}{3}$J
C. –30 J D. $-\frac{160}{3}$J

33. A particle of mass 10 gm on a smooth horizontal table is fastened to one end of a fine string which passes through a small hole in the table. It supports at its other end a particle of mass 20 gm. Find the velocity with which the particle on the table be projected horizontally so as to describe a circle of radius 5 cm. (take g = 10 m/s^2)

A. 0.5 m/s B. 1 m/s
C. 1.5 m/s D. 1.25 m/s

34. A ball strikes another ball, having four times its mass, which is moving with one-third of its velocity in the same direction. If the impact reduces the first ball to rest, the coefficient of restitution is:

A. $\frac{3}{4}$ B. $\frac{5}{8}$

C. $\frac{3}{8}$ D. $\frac{7}{8}$

35. A car of mass m accelerates on a smooth horizontal road under the action of a driving force. In the process its speed increases from v_1 to $\left(\frac{6x}{m}+v_1^3\right)^{1/2}$ within a distance x and the engine develops a constant power output p, if all the quantities are in SI units, the value of P in watt is equal to?

A. 2.5 B. 2
C. 3 D. 4

36. Which among the Kepler's laws of planetary motion would still remain valid had the gravitational force not followed the inverse square variation?

A. Only First law
B. Only Second law
C. Only Third law
D. First and Third law

37. A particle of mass m is moving under the influence of a consecutive force field given by $\vec{F}=-kr^3\hat{r}$. Then, pick up the correct alternative from the following:

A. $\frac{1}{2}m\left(\frac{dr}{dt}\right)^2+\frac{1}{3}kr^2$ = a constant

B. $\frac{1}{2}m\left(\frac{dr}{dt}\right)^2$ = a constant

C. $\frac{1}{2}m\left(\frac{dr}{dt}\right)^2+\frac{1}{4}kr^4$ = a constant

D. $\frac{1}{2}m\left(\frac{dr}{dt}\right)^2+\frac{1}{5}kr^5$ = a constant

38. Two blocks of mass as m_1 and m_2 connected to each other by a massless inextensible string length l and these are placed along a diameter of a turn table. There is no friction between m_2 and the surface of the table whereas the friction between m_1 and the surface of the table is μ. The able is rotating with an angular velocity w about a vertical axis passing through the centre of the turn table. The masses m_1 and m_2 are lying at distances r_1 and r_2 respectively from the centre of the turntable. If the masses are observed to be at rest with respect to an observer on the turn table. Calculate the frictional force on m_1.

A. $(m_1r_1 - m_2r_2)\omega^2$ B. $m_2(r_1 - r_2)\omega^2$
C. $m_1(r_1 - r_2)\omega^2$ D. $(m_1r_1 + m_2r_2)\omega^2$

39. A block of mass 2 kg sliding on a smooth horizontal surface with a uniform speed 1 m s^{-1} is brought to rest by a spring in its path, which gets compressed by 2 m in the process. What is the spring constant is newton per meter?

A. $\sqrt{2}$ B. 1

C. $\frac{1}{2}$ D. $\frac{\sqrt{3}}{2}$

40. Two particles of masses 2 m and 3 m move under the influence of their mutual action and reaction only, no external force is acting on the system. They execute uniform circular motion about their common centre of mass, the distance between them being 'R'. If the total angular momentum of the system is L, then their angular velocities are:

A. $\frac{L}{3mR^2}$ B. $\frac{L}{2mR^2}$

C. $\frac{L}{6mR^2}$ D. $\frac{5L}{6mR^2}$

41. The elastic limit of a typical rock is 'E' in newtons/metre^2, the Bulk Modulus and mean density of the rock are B and ρ respectively in newton/metre^2 and kg/m^3. Estimate the maximum height of a mountain in earth.

A. $\frac{(E-B)}{\rho g}$ B. $\frac{E}{\rho g}$

C. $\frac{3E}{2\rho g}$ D. $\frac{B}{\rho g}$

42. The efficiency of a reversible engine is 20% on reducing the temperature of the sink by 20°C, the efficiency increases by 25%. Find the original temperature of the source in degree centigrade.

A. 127 B. 77
C. 147 D. 107

43. A body of mass 0.2 kg is suspended from a spring of force constant 1 Nm^{-1}. A damping force acts on the system such that the resistive force is 6 N corresponding to an instantaneous velocity 10 ms^{-1}. If the system is now subject to a periodic force, F = 10 cos *t*, then what would be the phase difference between the forced oscillation and the original vibration?

A. $\tan^{-1}\frac{4}{3}$ B. $\tan^{-1}\frac{2}{3}$

C. $\tan^{-1}\frac{3}{4}$ D. $\tan^{-1}\frac{1}{2}$

44. Calculate the force required to separate two glass plates of area 0.02 sq metre with a film of water 8×10^{-5} metre thick between them. Surface tension of water = 0.07 Nm^{-1}.

A. 35 N B. 40 N
C. 28 N D. 30 N

45. The base of a steel saucepan has a diameter of 24 cm at 20°C. What will be the increase in area of the base of the saucepan when it is filled with boiling water? It is given that coefficient of linear expansion of steel $= 1.2 \times 10^{-5}$ °C^{-1}.

A. $12^3 \times 8\pi \times 10^{-5}$ cm^2
B. $12^3 \times 8\pi \times 10^{-6}$ cm^2
C. $12^3 \times 16\pi \times 10^{-5}$ cm^2
D. $12^3 \times 16\pi \times 10^{-6}$ cm^2

46. There is a small hole on one side of a carton (25 cm × 10 cm × 4 cm) at a point 1 cm below the top. Juice of density 2 g cm^{-3} is leaking out through the hole at a constant rate of 10 *g*/min. What will be the pressure of the juice at the bottom of the carton 5 min after the juice started leaking through the hole? (g = 10 ms^{-2})

A. 390 N/m^2
B. 650 N/m^2
C. 780 N/m^2
D. 260 N/m^2

47. The radii of the small and large piston of a hydraulics press are respectively 6 cm and 72 cm. It is worked by a hand lever whose arms ratio is 4 : 27. If a force F newton's is applied on the handle of the lever, what is the force developed by the large piston in newton's?

A. 972 F B. 144 F

C. $\frac{64}{3}$F D. 81 F

48. A particle of mass 10 g is executing S.H.M. of amplitude 2 cm. When the particle passes through its mean position, its energy is 2×10^{-4} J. Obtain the equation of motion of the particle if its epoch is 30°. It is given that at the initial instant, its position is increasing with time. Express position (x) in metres and time (t) in sec.

A. $x = (0.01)\sin\left(20t + \frac{\pi}{6}\right)$

B. $x = (0.02)\sin\left(20t + \frac{\pi}{3}\right)$

C. $x = (0.02)\sin\left(10t + \frac{\pi}{6}\right)$

D. $x = (0.01)\sin\left(10t + \frac{\pi}{3}\right)$

49. A thermodynamic process undergone by a perfect gas is depicted in the P-V diagram as ∠MNL. It is given that $V_2 = 2V_1$. $P_2 = 2P_1$. Obtain T_M, T_N in terms of T_L (symbols have their usual meanings)

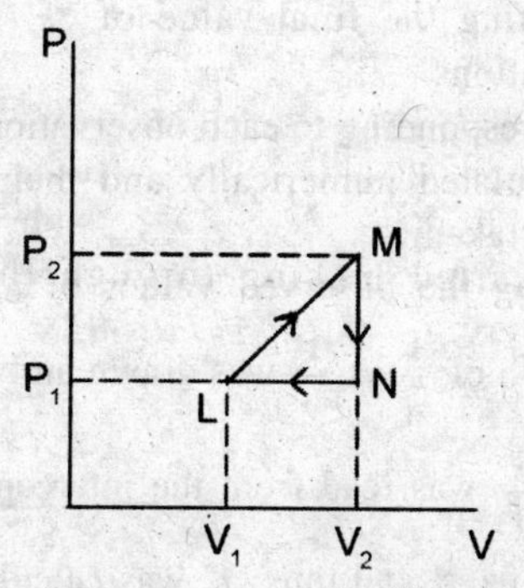

A. $4T_L, 2T_L$ B. $3T_L, (1.5)T_L$

C. $2T_L, T_L$ D. $T_L, 2T_L$

50. Find the force of attraction between a thin uniform rod of length 20 cm on a mass 1 kg located outside the rod on the same line as the rod and at a distance 10 cm from an end. The mass of the rod is 2 kg.

A. $\frac{2G}{3} \times 10^2$ N B. $\frac{3G}{4} \times 10^2$ N

C. $\frac{G}{2} \times 10^2$ N D. $\frac{G}{3} \times 10^2$ N

51. A thermodynamic system undergoes a change from a state '1' to state '2' described by the co-ordinates $(P_1V_1T_1)$ and $(P_2V_2T_2)$ respectively, where the symbols have their usual meanings. The equation of state of the system is known. Now, on the basis of above examine which one of the following can be calculated?

(p) The amount of heat added to the system

(q) The change in the internal energy of the system

(r) The total heat content of the system

(s) The work done on the system

A. (q) B. (s)

C. (p) D. (r)

52. Two spherical drops of water of the same size attain terminal velocities of magnitude 0.1 ms^{-1}. In the process of falling they coalesce to form a single drop. What will be the new terminal velocity?

A. $\frac{1}{5}2^{2/3}$ ms^{-1} B. $\frac{1}{20}2^{1/3}$ ms^{-1}

C. $\frac{1}{10}2^{1/3}$ ms^{-1} D. $\frac{1}{10}2^{2/3}$ ms^{-1}

53. When the temperature of air increases from 30°C to t °C, the velocity of sound in air (assumed to behave like a perfect gas) increases by 1.64% (apx). Find 't' (nearest to whole number).

A. 40 B. 45

C. 35 D. 48

54. The ratio of specific heats at constant pressure and constant volume of a diatomic gas is γ_1 and that for a mono atomic gas is γ_2. Then $\gamma_1 : \gamma_2$ is:

A. 24 : 25 B. 4 : 5

C. 21 : 25 D. 5 : 3

55. Argon gas at atmospheric pressure and at 27°C is kept confined in a vessel of volume 1 m^3. The effective diameter of argon atom is 3 A.U. Determine the mean free path (apx.) (1 atom pressure = 10^5 N/m^2, $k_B \cong \sqrt{2} \times 10^{-23}$ J/K)

A. $\frac{10^{-6}}{4\pi}$ m B. $\frac{10^{-6}}{2\pi}$ m

C. $\frac{10^{-6}}{3\pi}$ m D. $\frac{10^{-6}}{\pi}$ m

56. The polar equation of the orbit of a particle moving under a central force is given by $r = e^{-\theta}$. The force is:

A. attractive and varies as r^{-3}

B. attractive and varies as r^{-4}

C. repulsive and varies as r^{-4}

D. repulsive and varies as r^{-3}

57. The displacement vs. time equation of an S.H.M. is $x = \left\{5\cos\left(\frac{\pi t}{8}\right) + 12\sin\left(\frac{\pi t}{8}\right)\right\}$, where '$x$' is in cm, and '$t$' in sec. Find its amplitude.

A. 17 cm B. 13 cm

C. 17 cos $\frac{\pi}{8}$ cm D. 8.5 cm

58. Which among the following processes can never be reversible?

A. Free expansion

B. Electrolysis

C. Extension of a spring under a load

D. Isothermal compression

59. A particle of mass 'm' is subject to two forces, $F_x = -m\omega^2 x$; $F_y = -m\omega^2 y$ is two mutually perpendicular directions. It obeys the initial condition: $x = \frac{dy}{dt} = 0$. Had the forces acted individually, each would have led to SHM_S of unequal amplitudes. (The symbols have their usual meanings). What would be trajectory of the resultant motion of the particle?

A. Circle B. Hyperbola
C. Parabola D. Ellipse

60. A cylinder of length $2l$ contains a gas $1l$ is divided into two equal parts by a piston of mass 'm'. If the piston is displaced to the left through a distance 'x' and let go, then find the frequency of the oscillation of the piston if the process takes place isothermally. The volume of the cylinder is V, its cross-sectional area α. Assume that 'x' is very small, so that the terms involving x^2 and higher powers can be neglected. The original pressure applied by the piston is 'P'.

A. $\frac{1}{2\pi}\sqrt{\frac{P\alpha}{ml}}$ B. $\frac{1}{2\pi}\sqrt{\frac{2PV}{m\alpha}}$

C. $\frac{1}{2\pi}\sqrt{\frac{PV}{m\alpha}}$ D. $\frac{1}{2\pi}\sqrt{\frac{2P\alpha}{ml}}$

61. A particle is executing inform angular motion with an angular velocity $\overrightarrow{W} = (2\hat{i} - \hat{j} + 5\hat{k})$ radians sec^{-1}. (–1, 2, 3) is a position of the particle in its path (co-ordinates are in metres). Find the linear velocity of the particle in ms^{-1}.

A. $-12\hat{i} + 4\hat{j} - 9\hat{k}$ B. $-13\hat{i} - 11\hat{j} + 3\hat{k}$

C. $-11\hat{i} + 13\hat{j} - 4\hat{k}$ D. $12\hat{i} + 10\hat{j} - 3\hat{k}$

62. $A^2 s^4\ kg^{-1} m^{-2}$ is equivalent to:

A. mho B. ohm
C. farad D. $(farad)^{-1}$

63. In an experiment for the determination of focal length of a convex lens using $u - v$ method, that is applying the formula $\frac{1}{v} + \frac{1}{u} = \frac{1}{f}$, the four methods stated below were applied for calculating the final value of 'f' from ten observations.

(p) Corresponding to each observation 'f' was calculated numerically and their average was taken.

(q) Using the observed values of u and v a graph of $\frac{1}{u}$ vs $\frac{1}{v}$ was drawn and the value of $\frac{1}{f}$ was read from the intercepts on the two axes, and thus 'f' was calculated.

(r) Using the observed value a graph of u vs v was drawn and f was calculated by choosing $u - v$ values from a point on the graph.

(s) After completing the process of drawing u vs v graph as in case (r), the graph was made to intersect with the line, $u = v$. The point of intersection is $u = v = 2f$, from which f was obtained.

Which of the above methods would you prescribe as the best?

A. (q) B. (r)
C. (s) D. (p)

64. A point moves uniformly along a straight line. Its angular velocity about any point at a distance 'r' from it varies as:

A. $\frac{1}{r}$ B. r^2

C. r D. $\frac{1}{r^2}$

65. P and Q are two points, such that they are respectively 8 m and 12 m above the ground level which is horizontal. PQ = 5 m. What is the minimum velocity with which a particle must be projected from the horizontal plane as that it passes through P ad Q, ($g = 10\ ms^{-2}$)

A. $4\sqrt{5}\ ms^{-1}$ B. $5\sqrt{5}\ ms^{-1}$

C. $5\sqrt{10}\ ms^{-1}$ D. $4\sqrt{10}\ ms^{-1}$

66. $\frac{\text{ohm}}{\text{henry}} = ?$

A. s^2 B. s^{-1}
C. s D. s^{-2}

67. A particle of mass 10 g moves with a velocity 10 m/s along a straight line and collides with another particle of mass 20 g which is moving with a velocity 5 m/s along the same line. If after collision, the first particle is brought to rest, the velocity of the other particle after impact is:

A. 2.5 m/s B. 4 m/s
C. 10 m/s D. 5 m/s

68. Given below are four sets of numbers which are proportional to the magnitudes of three forces acting simultaneously at a point.

(*p*) 2, 8, 9
(*q*) 3, 7, 9
(*r*) 3, 7, 10
(*s*) 3, 7, 11

In which case equilibrium is not possible?

A. (*q*) B. (*r*)
C. (*p*) D. (*s*)

69. A particle moving in a straight line follows the equation:

$v^2 = 4x - x^2$

What is the range of motion?

A. $x \geq 4$ B. $0 < x < 4$
C. $x \leq 0$ D. $0 \leq x \leq 4$

70. Given below are four statements related to uniformly accelerated motion.

(*p*) The velocity vs. time graph is always a straight line passing through the origin.
(*q*) The square of the velocity has a linear relation with the displacement.
(*r*) The velocity has a linear relation with the square of the displacement.
(*s*) The displacement during a period of time is the arithmetic mean between the initial and final velocities.

Which among the above statement(s) is/are true?

A. only (*r*) B. (*r*) and (*s*)
C. (*p*) and (*q*) D. (*q*) and (*s*)

71. A train is approaching a massive hill with a speed of 55 km/hr. It sounds a whistle of frequency 570 Hz when it is at some distance from the hill. A wind with a speed of 45 km/hr is blowing in the direction of motion of train. Find the frequency of the whistle as heard by an observer on the hill. (velocity of sound in air = 1150 km/hr)

A. 595 Hz B. 580.5 Hz
C. 597.5 Hz D. 585 Hz

72. A steamer is going due East with a velocity 10 ms^{-1}, and wind is blowing from North. The smoke from the chimney points 30° West of South. Find the magnitude of the velocity of wind.

A. 30 ms^{-1} B. $10\sqrt{3}$ ms^{-1}
C. $30\sqrt{3}$ ms^{-1} D. $\frac{10\sqrt{3}}{3}$ ms^{-1}

73. A flexible heavy chain of length 10 m, is moving over a smooth fixed pulley. The two unequal portions of the chain are hanging vertically. The instant when the middle point of the chain is at a distance 3 m below the pulley. The acceleration with which it is moving is: (g = 10 m/s^2)

A. 2 m/s^2 B. 4 m/s^2
C. 6 m/s^2 D. 3 m/s^2

74. 1 KWh expressed in eV is:

A. 2.247×10^{25} B. 1.124×10^{25}
C. 1.124×10^{24} D. 2.247×10^{23}

75. A particle starts from rest and accelerates, where its acceleration *vs.* time equation is:

$f = p - qt$,

where p and q are positive constants. Find the distance travelled by the particle till the time it reaches its maximum velocity.

A. $\frac{p^3}{3q^2}$ B. $\frac{3p^3}{2q^2}$
C. $\frac{p^3}{q^2}$ D. $\frac{p^3}{2q^2}$

76. An open carriage is travelling at 20 m/s. A boy standing on the carriage throws a ball vertically upward with a velocity 10 m/s. The direction of motion of the carriage is along the x-axis, and the vertical dissection is along the y-axis. The frame of reference attached with a stationary observer is defined by (x, y, t) and that with the carriage is (x', y', t'). Where the symbols have their usual meanings. Wrote the displacement vs. time equations correcting (x, y): (x', y') with (t, t'). Take $g = 10$ m/s^2.

A. $x = 20t$, $y = 10t$
$x' = 0$, $y' = 10t'$

B. $x = 0$, $y = 10t - 5t^2$
$x' = 20t$, $y' = 10t' - 5t'^2$

C. $x = 0$, $y = 10t$
$x' = 0$, $y' = 10t'$

D. $x = 20t$, $y = 10t - 5t^2$
$x' = 0$, $y' = 10t' - 5t'^2$

77. Given below is the equation of radioactive decay and the expression for centrifugal force on a particle of mass 'm' moving with uniform angular velocity 'w' in a circle of radius 'r'.

$N = N_o e^{-\lambda t}$, $F = mw^2r$

(symbols have their usual meanings)

λ in the first equation has the same dimension as that of what on the right hand side of the second equation?

A. w^2 B. m
C. w D. r

78. A heavy uniform rod is in equilibrium with one and resting against a smooth vertical wall, and the other against a smooth plane included to the wall at 45°. If 'α' is the inclination of the rod to the horizon, then tan α is equal to:

A. $\frac{1}{2}$ B. $\frac{1}{6}$

C. $\frac{1}{4}$ D. $\frac{1}{3}$

79. The value of 'g' is being obtained using a simple pendulum by applying the formula, $T = 2\pi\sqrt{\frac{l}{g}}$ 'l' is measured using a metre scale having smallest division 1 mm, and 'T' is measured using a stop watch whose smallest division is 0.001 sec. For a particular measurement $l = 1$ m and T = 2 sec, obtained by way of measuring the time for 10 oscillations as 20 sec. What is the maximum possible percentage error?

A. 0.22 B. 0.11
C. 0.20 D. 0.01

80. Two wires are fixed on a sonometer. The length of the wires are in the ratio 48 : 25, their diameters are in the ratio 3 : 1. The densities of the materials of the wires are in the ratio 1 : 9. If the tensions in the wire are in the ratio 4 : 1, then find the frequency of beats produced if the note of the lower pitch is 240 Hz.

A. 12 Hz B. 5 Hz
C. 15 Hz D. 10 Hz

81. A body of mass 'm' bounces on hard ground from a height 'h_1' and after rebound rises to a height 'h_2'. Find the impulse.

A. $\left\{\sqrt{2g}\, m\left(\sqrt{h_1} - \sqrt{h_2}\right)\right\}$ in the vertically upward direction

B. $\left\{\sqrt{2g}\, m\left(\sqrt{h_1} + \sqrt{h_2}\right)\right\}$ in the vertically upward direction

C. $\left\{\sqrt{2g}\, m\left(\sqrt{h_1} + \sqrt{h_2}\right)\right\}$ in the vertically downward direction

D. $\left\{\sqrt{2g}\, m\left(\sqrt{h_1} - \sqrt{h_2}\right)\right\}$ in the vertically downward direction

82. A two dimensional co-ordinate system is so chosen that the x-axis is horizontal and y-axis points vertically downward. A particle of mass 10 g is released to have a free fall from the point (4, 0) (the figures are in metres). Its torque at any time 't' about the origin of co-ordinates is:

A. Nil
B. Not independent of t
C. $0.4\hat{k}$ Nm
D. $-0.4\hat{k}$ Nm

83. A train moving with a velocity 40 km/hr passes through a station at 9 AM. After 1.5 min a lightning bolt strikes the railway tracks 2 km from the station in the same direction as that of the motion of the train. Find the co-ordinates of the lightning flash as measured by an observer at the station.

A. $x = 2$ km, $t = 9$ h/m
B. $x = 2$ km, $t = 9$ h lm 30s
C. $x = 1$ km, $t = 9$ h
D. $x = 2$ km, $t = 9$ h 30s

84. A body of mass 2 kg is moving along a path, such that its position vector expressed as a function of time is given by,

$$\vec{r} = \left(3t^2\hat{i} + t^4\hat{j} - t^3\hat{h}\right)$$

Where 'r' is in metres and 't' is in seconds. Find the work done on the body during $t = 0$ to $t = 1$ sec.

A. 72 J   B. 52 J
C. 41 J   D. 61 J

85. Which among the following is (are) conservative force(s)?

(p) Gravitational force between two masses
(q) Force between two static charges
(r) Force between two current carrying conductors
(s) Frictional force on a rough surface

A. Only (s)
B. (p), (q) and (r)
C. Only (p)
D. Only (p) and (q)

86. 1 Mev expressed in HP-hr is equal to:

A. 5.967×10^{-20} B. 5.967×10^{-10}
C. 2.984×10^{-20} D. 2.984×10^{-10}

87. A bomb explodes in mid-air. What will be the path described by each splinter?

A. Ellipse
B. Straight line
C. Parabola
D. Rectangular hyperbola

88. For which among the following is the SI unit Nsm^{-2}?

A. Viscous drag
B. Surface tension
C. Tensile stress
D Coefficient of Viscosity

89. Kg m^2 s^{-2} A^{-2} is equivalent to:

A. Fardo   B. Ohm
C. Henry   D. Watt

90. A body is kept on a rough inclined plane (coefficient of friction between the body and the plane $= \frac{1}{3}$) and it is just prevented from sliding down by the application of a force, P_1, up the plane. It is also just made to move up the plane by the application of a force P_2 up the plane. It is found that $P_2 : P_1 = 2 : 1$. The inclination of the plane to the horizontal is:

A. $\tan^{-1}\left(2-\sqrt{3}\right)$ B. 45°
C. 60°   D. $\tan^{-1}\frac{1}{2}$

91. In the differential equation mix + $kx = 0$, where the symbols have their usual meanings, the dimension of $\frac{k}{m}$ is:

A. T^2 B. T^{-2}
C. LT^{-2} D. $L^{-1}T$

92. A two–dimensional conservative potential is given by, $V(x, y) = x^2 - xy + y^2$ (in joules)

What is the work done in taking a particle in this field from (2, 1) to (3, 2)?

A. 5 J   B. 3 J
C. 2 J   D 4 J

93. Find the moment of inertia of an annular cylinder of mass 'm' and having inner and outer radii 'r_1' and 'r_2' respectively about the axis of the cylinder.

A. $\frac{m}{6}\left(r_1^2 + r_2^2 + r_1r_2\right)$ B. $\frac{m}{4}\left(r_1^2 + r_2^2\right)$
C. $\frac{m}{4}\left(r_1^2 + r_2^2 + r_1r_2\right)$ D. $\frac{m}{2}\left(r_1^2 + r_2^2\right)$

94. A 50 g bullet is fired through a stack of fibre board sheets 10 cm thick. The velocity of the bullet at the point of approaching the stack is 500 ms^{-1}. What will be its velocity in ms^{-1} at the exit point form the stack if the average resistance offered by the stack to the bullet is 4×10^4N.

A. 400 B. 200
C. 300 D. 500

95. A uniform wire 60 cm long is bent into the shape of a triangle ABC, such that the sides BC, CA, AB are in the ratio 4 : 5 : 6. Three particles of masses x, y, z (in grams) are placed at A, B, C and it is found that the centre of gravity remains unchanged. Then, $x : y : z$ is equal to:

A. 9 : 8 : 7 B. 11 : 10 : 9
C. 6 : 5 : 4 D. 3 : 2 : 1

96. The formula used for the measurement of Young's Modules (Y) of the material of a beam by the method of flexure is obtained using the formula.

$$y = \frac{mgl^3}{4bd^2\delta}$$

Where m = the load applied to the beam whose value is supplied

l = length of the beam, measured by a metre scale having smallest division, 1 mm.

b = breath of the beam measured by a slide callipers having Vernier Constant, 0.01 mm.

d = the depth of the beam measured by a screw gauge having least count equal to 0.01 mm.

δ = the depression of the beam measured with the help of a travelling microscope, having Vernier Constant equal to 0.01 mm.

Find the maximum possible percentage error for the measurement, when it is given that the corresponding data are

$l = 1$ m, $b = 2$ cm, $d = 0.5$ cm, $\delta = 2$ mm

A. 1.9% B. 2.1%
C. 1.8% D. 2.0%

97. With the objective of minimizing personal error in measurement of diameter of a wire by a screw gauge of least count 0.001 cm, the measurement was taken thrice and the readings were 0.313 cm, 0.313 cm and 0.314 cm, what should be recorded as the average?

A. 0.31333 cm B. 0.3133 cm
C. 0.313 cm D. 0.313333 cm

98. In the case of an one-dimensional motion, the relation between to velocity (v) and position (x) is given by,

$$v = 2\sqrt{a(x\cos x - \sin x)},$$

Where 'a' is a constant. Find its acceleration

A. $2\,ax\cos x$ B. $-2\,ax\sin x$
C. $2\,ax\sin x$ D. $-2\,ax\cos x$

99. A labourer throws bricks to another labourer vertically above him by 4 m, so that each brick reaches him at a speed of 4 ms^{-1}. What proportion of his energy would be able to save if he throws the bricks, so that each of them just reaches him? (g – 10 ms^{-2})

A. $\frac{1}{6}$ B. $\frac{1}{12}$
C. $\frac{1}{8}$ D. $\frac{1}{10}$

100. A ball directly strikes another ball at rest and is itself reduced to rest by the impact. If two-third of its initial kinetic energy is lost due to collision, find the coefficient of restitution.

A. $\frac{1}{2}$ B. $\frac{1}{3}$
C. $\frac{2}{3}$ D. $\frac{1}{4}$

101. A bomb explodes in air into three parts. Two of them having masses 100 g, each move at an angle 120° with each other having equal velocity 100 m/s each. The third splinter moves in a direction opposite to the bisector of the angle between the directions of motion of the first two parts with a velocity of magnitude 25 m/s, what is the mass of the third splinter in gms.

A. 400 g B. 500 g
C. 200 g D. 250 g

102. For the same velocity of projection a projectile has got equal ranges for two angles of projection corresponding to which greatest height attained are 12 m and 27 m, what is the value of range?

A. 36 m
B. $54\sqrt{2}$ m
C. $48\sqrt{2}$ m
D. 72 m

103. A particle is moving along a straight line. It starts from rest and moves with a uniform acceleration 'a', fill if attains a velocity 'v' and then travels with uniform retardation 'b' till it again comes to rest. The total time of travel is 't'. Then,

A. $\frac{1}{a}+\frac{1}{b}=\frac{t}{v}$
B. $\frac{1}{a}+\frac{1}{b}=\frac{v}{2t}$
C. $\frac{1}{a}+\frac{1}{b}=\frac{2t}{v}$
D. $\frac{1}{a}-\frac{1}{b}=\frac{t}{v}$

104. A body of mass 'm' has been falling from rest under the action of gratuity for t seconds. Find the vertical force required to be applied in order to bring it to rest within another distance 'a'. ('m' is in kg and 'a' is in metres)

A. $Mg\left(1+\frac{gt^2}{2a}\right)$
B. $Mg\left(1+\frac{gt^2}{4a}\right)$
C. $mg^2\frac{t^2}{2a}$
D. $mg^2\frac{t^2}{4a}$

105. On a rainy day when a boy is running at a speed of 4 ms^{-1}, rain strikes him vertically at a speed of 4 ms^{-1}. For what speed of the boy will rain strike him at an angle of 45°?

A. 2 m/s
B. $8\sqrt{2}$ m/s
C. 6 m/s
D. 8 m/s

106. A ball moving on a smooth horizontal plane in a straight line with a velocity 100 cms^{-1} hit to an identical ball which is at rest. The collision is perfectly elastic and the two balls move along two straight paths after the collision. The velocity of the first ball gets reduced to 60 cms^{-1} find the angle between the direction of the ball after the collection.

A. 90°
B. 30°
C. 45°
D. 60°

107. Find the centre of mass of three equal rods each of length '$2a$' forming the consecutive sides of a square.

A. It is at a distance of $\frac{a}{2}$ from the centre of the square on the line through the centre perpendicular to the middle rod.

B. It is at a distance $\frac{a}{6}$ from the centre of the square on the line through the centre perpendicular to the middle rod.

C. It is at the centre of the middle rod.

D. It is at a distance of $\frac{a}{3}$ from the centre of the square on the line through the centre perpendicular to the middle rod.

108. A conservative force field is given by, $\vec{F}=(x+2y+4z)\hat{i}+(2x-3y-z)\hat{j}+(4x-y+2z)\hat{k}$ obtain the scalar potential function from which it has been derived.

A. $-x^2+3y^2-\frac{z^2}{2}-2xy+yz-4zx$
B. $-x^2-3y^2-\frac{z^2}{2}+xy-yz+2zx$
C. $-\frac{x^2}{2}+3y^2-\frac{z^2}{2}-xy+yz-2zx$
D. $-\frac{x^2}{2}+\frac{3}{2}y^2-z^2-2xy+yz-4zx$

109. Which among the following is/are the characteristics of a conservative force field?

(p) The force can be derived from a potential by taking its negative space gradient.

(q) The work done by the force round a closed path is zero.

(r) The total mechanical energy is a constant of time.

(s) For the motion of a particle in the field, the gain in kinetic energy is equal to the loss in potential energy.

A. Only (p) and (q)
B. (p), (q), (r) and (s)
C. Only (p)
D. Only (p), (q) and (r)

110. A particle is under the influence of a central potential, given by $V=\frac{R_o}{\tau}u_o e^{\frac{-2r}{R_o}}$, where the symbols have their usual meanings. Find the equilibrium position of the particle.

A. $\frac{R_o}{4}$ B. $2R_o$

C. $\frac{R_o}{2}$ D. R_o

111. Two boats cross a river 400 m wide. The speed of each boat in still water is 2.5 ms^{-1} and the speed of the stream is 1.5 ms^{-1}. One boat crosses the river along the shortest path and the time taken is p sec, whereas the other crosses in shortest time and the time taken is q sec, then $(p - q)$ is equal to:

A. Zero B. 40

C. 10 D. 20

112. A particle of mass 10 g moves under the influence of a force field, $\vec{F} = 2(\sin t\,\hat{i} + \cos t\,\hat{j})$ in newtons. If the particle is initially at rest at the origin of co-ordinates, then the instantaneous power in watts applied to the particle is:

A. 0 B. 400 sin t

C. 100 sin t D. 200 cos t

113. A picture frame of rectangular shape weighing 5 kg is hung from a wall by a cord 5 cm long, fastened to two rings 3 cm, apart on the top edge of the frame. Find the tension in the cord. (g = 10 ms^{-2})

A. $34\frac{1}{4}$N B. $6\frac{1}{8}$N

C. $24\frac{1}{8}$N D. $37\frac{1}{8}$N

114. ABCD is a quadrilateral. Forces represented in magnitude and direction by $\overline{AB}$, $\overline{AD}$, $\overline{BC}$, $\overline{DC}$ act simultaneously. The direction of the resultant force:

A. is along AC B. bisects BD

C. is along BD D. bisects AC

115. A load W is raised by a rope, from rest to rest, through a height 10 m. The least time in which the ascent can be made is $\sqrt{\frac{5}{2}}$ sec. It is known that the greatest tension which the rope earn safely bear is nW. 'n' is equal to:

A. 2 B. 10

C. 5 D. 3

116. A string OPQR is such that OP – PQ – QR. Masses equal to 10 g are fastened at P, Q, R and these are made to rotate on a smooth horizontal table. If the string always remains strainght and taut, them the tension in the portions OP, PQ, PR are as:

A. 6 : 5 : 3 B. 3 : 2 : 1

C. 1 : 2 : 3 D. 3 : 5 : 6

117. A body of mass 'm' rests on an inclined plane of inclination 'α' in limiting equilibrium by way of application of a force P at an angle θ with the inclined plane. The coefficient of friction between the body and the plane is μ. Then P is equal to:

A. $mg \cdot \frac{\mu\cos\alpha + \sin\alpha}{\cos\theta + \mu\sin\theta}$

B. $mg \cdot \frac{\mu\cos\alpha + \sin\alpha}{\sin\theta + \mu\cos\theta}$

C. $mg \cdot \frac{\cos\alpha + \mu\sin\alpha}{\mu\cos\theta + \sin\theta}$

D. $mg \cdot \frac{\mu\cos\alpha + \sin\alpha}{\mu\cos\theta + \sin\theta}$

118. Two balls of equal mass are moving in the same direction along the same straight time with velocities of magnitude in the ratio 2 : 1. They collide and in the process lose x% of their kinetic energy. If the coefficient of restitution is $\frac{2}{3}$, find x:

A. $5\frac{2}{9}$ B. $5\frac{1}{4}$

C. $6\frac{1}{4}$ D. $5\frac{5}{9}$

119. A bullet of mass 50 g moving with a velocity 'v' strike a block of mass 2 kg. The block is free to move in the direction of the block. In the process there is a loss of kinetic energy of 4100 J. Find u in metres per sec.

A. 205 B. 410

C. $410\sqrt{2}$ D. 820

120. For a two dimensional motion, the x and y component of velocities of the particle 1 are given by,

$$\frac{dx}{dt} = 6\pi \sin 2\pi t, \quad \frac{dy}{dt} = 3\pi \cos 2\pi t$$

It is also given that $x = 6$, $y = 0$ at $t = 0$. The equation l of the path of the particle is:

A. $(x-9)^2 + 6y^2 = 36$

B. $(x-9)^2 + 4y^2 = 9$

C. $x^2 + 4(y-3)^2 = 36$

D. $x^2 + 4y^2 = 9$

121. In the circuit shown what should be the value of the capacitance of the capacitor 'C', so that the equivalent capacitance between the points A and B is 1μF. All the capacitance values indicated are in μF?

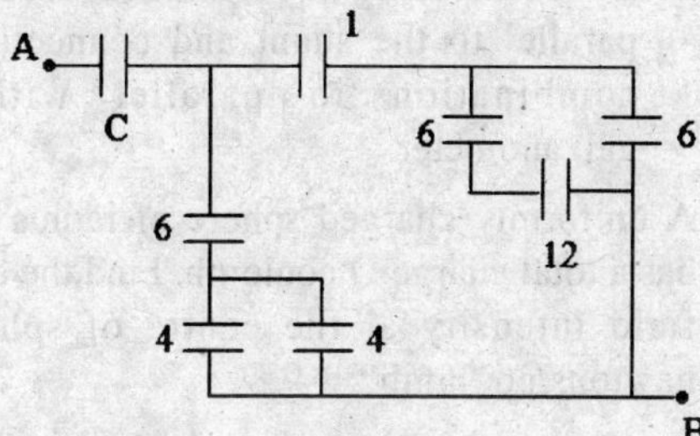

A. $\frac{24}{17}$ μF B. $\frac{156}{125}$ μF

C. $\frac{167}{105}$ μF D. $\frac{334}{257}$ μF

122. An electric motor starts from rest and on application of a torque on the shaft, that is about the axis of rotation of the motor, it acquires an angular acceleration, $\alpha = 2t - t^2$ during the first 2 seconds of its start, after which it becomes zero. What will be the total angular displacement (in terms of number of revolution) of the shaft in 5 sec?

A. $\frac{4}{3\pi}$ B. $\frac{4}{\pi}$

C. $\frac{8}{3\pi}$ D. $\frac{16}{3\pi}$

123. Three charges are located at the three corners of a square (each side – a) as shown in the figure. How much energy is required to bring another charge $+q$, from far away and place it at the vacant corner?

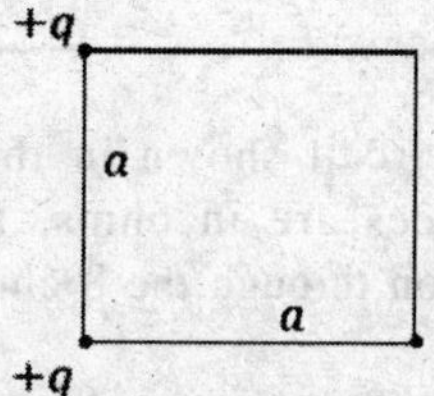

A. $\left(\frac{1}{4\pi\epsilon_0}\frac{q^2}{\sqrt{2}a}\right)$ B. $\left(\frac{1}{4\pi\epsilon_0}\frac{3q^2}{a}\right)$

C. $\left(\frac{1}{\pi\epsilon_0}\frac{q^2}{a}\right)$ D. $\left(\frac{1}{4\pi\epsilon_0}\frac{3q^2}{\sqrt{2}a}\right)$

124. A resistor has been provided in the form of a spherical shell, formed of two concentric metallic spheres of radii R_1 and R_2 ($R_2 > R_1$) and the interim space being filled with a material of resistivity δ. Find its resistance.

A. $\frac{(R_2 - R_1)\delta}{4\pi R_1 R_2}$ B. $\frac{\delta(R_2^2 - R_1^2)^{1/2}}{4\pi R_1 R_2}$

C. $\frac{\delta(R_2^2 - R_1^2)^{1/2}}{2\pi R_1 R_2}$ D. $\frac{(R_2 - R_1)\delta}{2\pi R_1 R_2}$

125. Calculate the kinetic energy attained by a charged particle of mass 'm' and charge 'q' after moving through a distance 'b' along an electric field $\vec{E}$.

A. qEb B. $\frac{1}{2}qEb$

C. $2\,qEb$ D. $\sqrt{2}\,qEb$

126. A conduction is in the form of a rod of length 'l' and cross-sectional area 'A'. Its temperature coefficient of resistance is α_R, the temperature coefficient of resistivity of its material is α_P and its coefficient of linear thermal expansion is α. Find the approximate relation between α_R, α_P and α.

A. $\alpha_P = \alpha_R - 2\alpha$ B. $\alpha_P = \alpha_R - \alpha$
C. $\alpha_R = \alpha_P - 2\alpha$ D. $\alpha_R = \alpha_P - \alpha$

127.

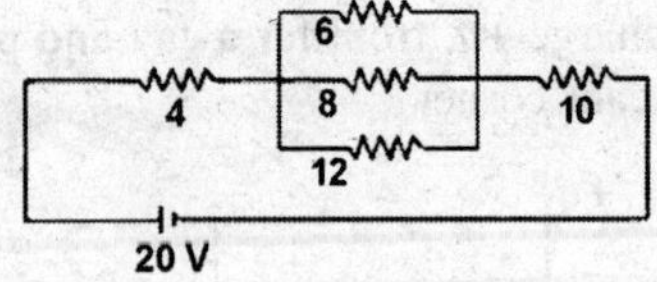

In the circuit shown in the figure all the resistances are in ohms. Find the power dissipation through the 8 ohm resistance.

A. $\frac{32}{25}$ watt B. $\frac{32}{125}$ watt

C. $\frac{64}{125}$ watt D. $\frac{64}{25}$ watt

128. An insulating disc of radius R, has a uniform surface charge density, σ. It rotates with an angular velocity ω. Find the total circulating current.

A. $\frac{1}{4}\sigma\omega R^2$ B. $\frac{1}{2}\sigma\omega R^2$

C. $\sigma\omega R^2$ D. $2\sigma\omega R^2$

129. A charge $-\frac{q}{2}$ is placed at the origin of co-ordinates and another charge $+\frac{q}{3}$ is placed at $(a, 0)$. How far from the origin is the resultant intensity due to the two charges is zero?

A. $\left(3+\sqrt{6}\right)a$ B. $\left(3+2\sqrt{6}\right)a$

C. $\left(3-2\sqrt{2}\right)a$ D. $\left(3-\sqrt{6}\right)a$

130. Two similar conducting balls of mass '*m*' and charge '*q*' hang from silk threads each of length '*l*'. Their angles of inclination with the vertical is each equal to θ, where θ is very small. In this situation the distance between the balls is '*a*' then one of the ball is discharged. Thereafter the distance between the balls become '*b*'. Then '*b*' in terms of '*a*' will be given by:

A. $\frac{a}{4}$ B. $\frac{a}{2}$

C. $\left(2^{\frac{-2}{3}}\right)a$ D. $\left(2^{\frac{-1}{3}}\right)a$

131. A galvanometer of resistance 15 Ω gives full scale deflection when a current 0.02 amp passes through it. It is to be converted into an ammeter reading 15 A in its full scale. For this purpose you have been provided with an only shunt resistance, 0.04 ohm. How will the conversion desired be achieved?

A. By connecting a resistance 0.01 Ω in parallel to the shunt and connecting the combination in parallel with the galvanometer.

B. By connecting a resistance 14.96 Ω in series with the galvanometer and combining the available shunt with the said series combination.

C. By connecting a resistance 14.58 Ω in series with the galvanometer and combining the available shunt with the said series combination.

D. By connecting a resistance 0.02 Ω in parallel to the shunt and connecting the combination in parallel with the galvanometer.

132. A uniformly charged sphere of radius 25 cm has a total charge Q coulomb. Find the electric field intensity at the centre of sphere in newtons/coulomb?

A. $\frac{2Q}{5\epsilon_0}$ B. $\frac{Q}{125\epsilon_0}$

C. Zero D. $\frac{Q}{50\epsilon_0}$

133.

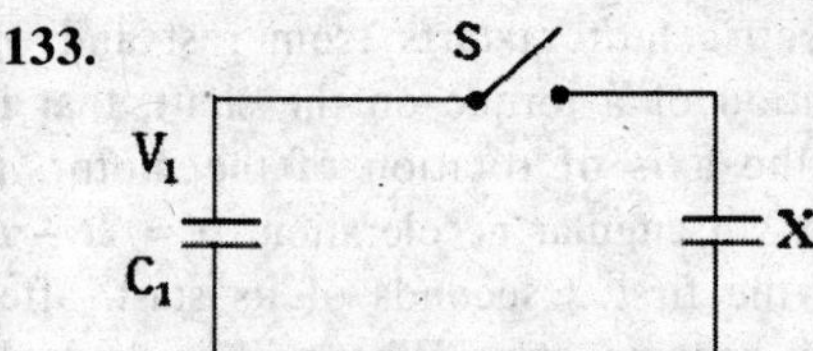

A capacitor of capacitance C_1 is charged to a potential difference V_1. The charging battery is then disconnected and C_1 is connected to a capacitor X of unknown capacitance. The potential difference across the combination is now V_2. Find the energy stored in the system after the switch S is closed.

A. $\frac{1}{2}C_1(V_1+V_2)V_1$ B. $\frac{1}{2}C_1V_1V_2$

C. $\frac{1}{2}C_1(V_1-V_2)\frac{V_2^2}{V_1}$ D. $\frac{1}{2}C_1(V_1+V_2)V_2$

134. 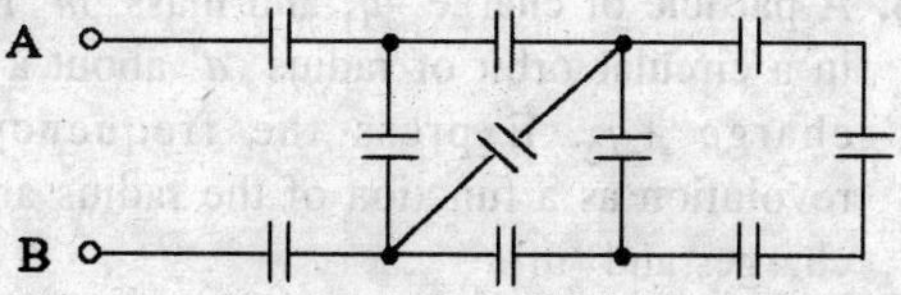 All the capacitors shown in the above network have the same value of capacitance. The equivalent capacitance between A and B turns out to be $1\frac{21}{144}$ μF. Find the capacitance of each capacitor.

A. 1 μF B. 3 μF

C. 11 μF D. 1.5 μF

135. An electric dipole of moment $\vec{p}$ is placed in a uniform electric field of $\vec{E}$, such that $\vec{p}$ makes an angle of 30° with $\vec{E}$. If the dipole has to be rotated through an angle 90° about an axis perpendicular to $\vec{p}$, what will be the work done?

A. $\frac{\sqrt{3}-1}{2}pE$ B. $\frac{\sqrt{3}+1}{2}pE$

C. $\frac{1}{2}pE$ D. $\frac{\sqrt{3}}{2}pE$

136. A uniformly charged sphere of radius 25 cm has a total charge of a Q coulombs. Find the electric field intensity at a point 5 cm from the centre of the sphere.

A. $\frac{2Q}{125\pi\epsilon_0}$ newtons/coulomb

B. $\frac{4Q}{5\pi\epsilon_0}$ newtons/coulomb

C. $\frac{Q}{125\pi\epsilon_0}$ newtons/coulomb

D. $\frac{2Q}{5\pi\epsilon_0}$ newtons/coulomb

137. A carbon resistor has the colour code as per the sequence: BROWN – ORANGE – BLUE – RED – GREEN. Its resistance is:

A. 36.8 ohm with a tolerance of ±5%

B. 1.36×10^4 ohm with a tolerance of ±0.5%

C. 4.52×10^5 ohm with a tolerance of ±10%

D. 2.58×10^3 ohm with a tolerance of ±0.5%

138. A particle of mass m is at the point (b, o) say B. The y-axis is chosen vertically downward and the particle is let fall from B parallel to the y-axis, find the angular momentum of the particle about the origin 2 sec after the ball.

A. $\frac{1}{2}mg\,b\hat{k}$

B. $-2mg\,b\hat{k}$

C. $-\frac{1}{2}mg\,b\hat{k}$

D. $2mg\,b\hat{k}$

139. A network of conductors is made in the shape of a regular octahedron by joining 12 equal conductors of same conductance (each equal to 2 mho) as shown in the figure. If the current enters through A and exits through B, then find the equivalent conductance of the network in mho.

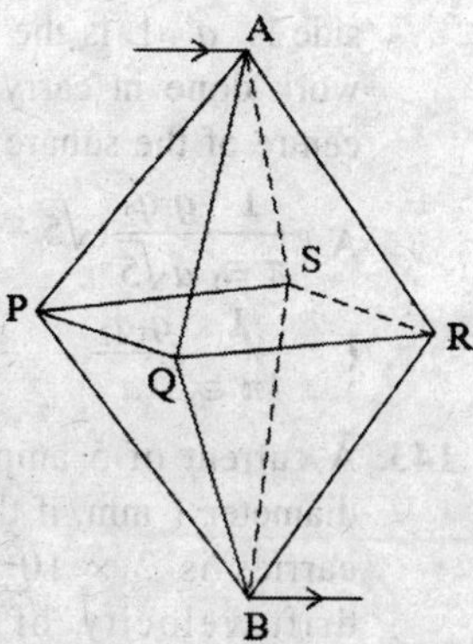

A. 8 B. 1

C. 4 D. 2

140. Two dipoles having charges $(-q, +q)$ and each of length $2a$ are placed on the x-axis, such that the distance between their centres 'b' and the co-ordinates of the charges of the left dipoles are as follow: $-q\ (0, 0)$ and $+q(2a, 0)$. Find the force of attraction extended on the left dipole by the right dipole.

A. $\left(\frac{q^2}{4\pi\epsilon_0}\right)\left[\frac{(b^2-4a^2)}{(b^2+4a^2)^2}+\frac{1}{b^2}\right]$

B. $\left(\frac{q^2}{4\pi\epsilon_0}\right)\left[\frac{(b^2+4a^2)}{(b^2-4a^2)^2}+\frac{1}{b^2}\right]$

C. $\left(\dfrac{q^2}{2\pi \epsilon_0}\right)\left[\dfrac{(b^2-4a^2)}{(b^2+4a^2)^2}-\dfrac{1}{b^2}\right]$

D. $\left(\dfrac{q^2}{2\pi \epsilon_0}\right)\left[\dfrac{(b^2+4a^2)}{(b^2-4a^2)^2}-\dfrac{1}{b^2}\right]$

141. Two identically charged spheres are suspended by strings of equal length. At the equilibrium position the strings make an angle θ with each other. Now, the metal spheres are suspended in a liquid of density 0.6 gm/ce and dielectric constant 2. Find the density of the material of the spheres if the angle between the strings remain unchanged.

A. 1.6 gm/ce B. 0.9 gm/ce
C. 0.8 gm/ce D. 1.2 gm/ce

142. Four charges $q_1, q_2, -q_1, -q_2$, are placed at the four corners A, B, C, D of a square, whose each side is 'a'. L is the midpoint of BC. Find the work done in carrying a charge q_2 from the centre of the square to L.

A. $\dfrac{1}{\pi \epsilon_0}\dfrac{q_1q_2}{a\sqrt{5}}(\sqrt{5}-1)$ B. $\dfrac{1}{4\pi \epsilon_0}\dfrac{q_1q_2}{a\sqrt{5}}(\sqrt{5}-1)$

C. $\dfrac{1}{4\pi \epsilon_0}\dfrac{q_1q_2}{a}$ D. 0

143. A current of 5 amp flows through a wire of diameter 1 mm, if the concentration of charge carries is 2×10^{27} m^{-3}. Find the average drift velocity of the electrons in cm/s ($e = 1.6 \times 10^{-19}$ C)

A. 4 B. 6
C. 2 D. 3

144. Three capacitors having capacitances C_1, C_2, C_3 are such that $C_1 : C_2 : C_3 = 2 : 3 : 4$. The difference between the in equivalent capacitances when connected in series and parallel is 35 μF. Find the value of G.

A. $\dfrac{26}{3}\pi$F B. $\dfrac{13}{3}\pi$F

C. $\dfrac{52}{9}\pi$F D. $\dfrac{39}{8}\pi$F

145. A uniformly charged sphere of radius 25 cm has a total charge of Q coulombs. Find the electric field intensity at a point on the surface of the sphere in newtons/coulomb.

A. $\dfrac{4Q}{125\pi E_0}$ B. $\dfrac{Q}{\pi E_0}\cdot\dfrac{1}{625}$

C. $\dfrac{Q}{4\pi E_0}\cdot\dfrac{1}{625}$ D. $\dfrac{4Q}{25\pi E_0}$

146. A particle of charge $-q_1$ and mass 'm' moves in a circular orbit of radius 'a' about a fixed charge $+q_2$. Express the frequency (n) revolution as a function of the radius and the charges and 'in'.

A. $2\sqrt{2}a^{3/2}\left(\dfrac{\pi m \epsilon_0}{q_1q_2}\right)^{1/2}$ B. $2a^{3/2}\left(\dfrac{\pi m \epsilon_0}{q_1q_2}\right)^{1/2}$

C. $\sqrt{2}a^{3/2}\left(\dfrac{\pi m \epsilon_0}{q_1q_2}\right)^{1/2}$ D. $a^{3/2}\left(\dfrac{\pi m \epsilon_0}{2q_1q_2}\right)^{1/2}$

147. In the circuit shown, all the resistances are in ohms. Find the power dissipation through the 6 ohm resistance.

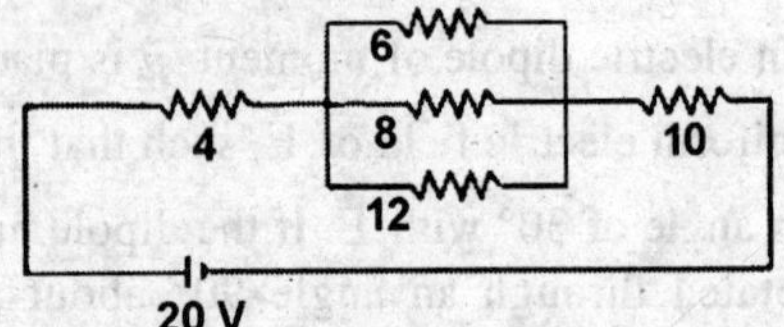

A. $\dfrac{192}{125}$ watt B. $\dfrac{384}{225}$ watt

C. $\dfrac{324}{125}$ watt D. $\dfrac{256}{225}$ watt

148. In the circuit shown all the resistances are in ohms. Find the values of i_1, i_2, i_3 in amperes.

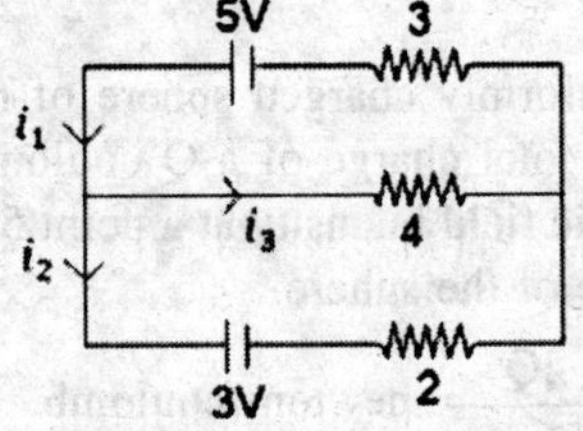

A. $\dfrac{11}{13}, \dfrac{3}{13}, \dfrac{8}{13}$ B. $\dfrac{13}{16}, \dfrac{5}{16}, \dfrac{1}{2}$

C. $\dfrac{10}{13}, \dfrac{3}{13}, \dfrac{7}{13}$ D. $\dfrac{11}{15}, \dfrac{14}{15}, \dfrac{7}{15}$

149. A series circuit consists of a copper voltmeter (internal resistance = 4 ohm), a battery of negligible internal resistance and a resistance box. By adjusting the resistance box for 4 ohm, the mass of copper deposited at the cathode in 10 minutes is 30 gm. To what value should the resistance box be adjusted to have a deposit of 40 gms of copper in 20 minutes?

A. 10 ohm B. 5 ohm
C. 6 ohm D. 8 ohm

150. A series circuit consists of a copper voltmeter, a battery of religiable box. By adjusting the resistance box for 4 ohm, the mass of copper deposited on the cathode is 30 gm in 10 minutes, and on adjusting if for 8 ohm, the mass of copper deposited is 40 gm in 20 minutes. Find the internal resistance of the voltmeter.

A. 3 ohm B. 4 ohm
C. 1 ohm D. 2 ohm

151. Four statements have been given below about Peltier Effect, Examine them:

(*p*) As a result of this effect heat is absorbed and evolved at the same time.
(*q*) The effect occurs throughout the wrap.
(*r*) If the direction of current is reversed, the hot junction becomes cold and the cold junction becomes hot.
(*s*) The heat evolved and absorbed depends linearly on the resistance of the conductors.

A. (*p*) and (*s*) are true; (*q*) and (*r*) are false
B. (*p*) and (*q*) are true; (*r*) and (*s*) are false
C. (*p*) and (*r*) are true; (*q*) and (*s*) are false
D. (*q*) and (*r*) are true; (*p*) and (*s*) are false

152. A uniformly charged sphere of radius 25 cm has a total charge of a Columbs. Find the electric field intercity at a point 75 cm from centre of the sphere in newtons/coulomb.

A. $\frac{27Q}{16\pi \epsilon_0}$ B. $\frac{25Q}{4\pi \epsilon_0}$

C. $\frac{4Q}{9\pi \epsilon_0}$ D. $\frac{4Q}{108\pi \epsilon_0}$

153. Given three resistances 2 Ω, 4 Ω and 6 Ω, suitable combinations of three cars produce all the resistance (in ohms) of which option given below?

A. $12, \frac{12}{11}, 3, \frac{8}{3}, \frac{5}{3}, \frac{22}{3}, \frac{11}{2}, \frac{22}{5}$

B. $12, \frac{12}{11}, 3, \frac{8}{5}, \frac{5}{4}, \frac{22}{3}, \frac{11}{4}, \frac{22}{5}$

C. $12, \frac{12}{11}, 3, \frac{4}{3}, \frac{5}{3}, \frac{22}{3}, \frac{11}{6}, \frac{22}{5}$

D. $12, \frac{12}{11}, 3, \frac{8}{3}, \frac{5}{4}, \frac{11}{4}, \frac{11}{6}, \frac{22}{5}$

154. Given below are four statements based on the concept of equipotentials.

(*p*) The equipotential surfaces for an infinitely long linear charge are cylindrical. The axes of the cylinders being coaxial with the line charge.
(*q*) Electric field lines intersect the equipotentials normally.
(*r*) Two equipotential surfaces may intersect.
(*s*) For an electric dipole the equipotential surface is a plane that perpendicularly bisects the line joining the charges.

Which among the above is/are true?

A. Only (*r*) B. Only (*p*)
C. (*p*) & (*q*) D. (*p*), (*q*) & (*s*)

155. A point charge $+q$ is placed at a distance 'a_2' from an earthed circular metal disc of radius 'a_1'. Find the induced charge.

A. $\left(\frac{q}{\pi}\right)\tan^{-1}\left(\frac{a_1}{a_2}\right)$ B. $-\left(\frac{q}{\pi}\right)\tan^{-1}\left(\frac{a_1}{a_2}\right)$

C. $\left(\frac{2q}{\pi}\right)\tan^{-1}\left(\frac{a_1}{a_2}\right)$ D. $-\left(\frac{2q}{\pi}\right)\tan^{-1}\left(\frac{a_1}{a_2}\right)$

156. A potentiometer wire has a total length of 1000 cm. It is driven by a cell of E.M.F 4V having a resistance 460 Ω in series. A source of potential difference, 10 mV gets balanced by a length of 60 cm, of the potential wire. Find the value of the resistance of the potentiometer wire.

A. 20 Ω B. 10 Ω
C. 30 Ω D. 15 Ω

157. A resistance network is prepared in the shape of a regular tetrahedron, the sides being four conductors each of conductance 2 mho. If current enters into the system from one of the four vertices and comes out from the opposite corner, find the effective conductance of the network.

A. 4 mho B. 8 mho
C. 2 mho D. 1 mho

158. A resistance R is connected in parallel with a bulb (0.2 W, 1 V) and the combination is connected in series with a 2 ohm resistor and 2 V battery of internal resistance 0.5 ohm. If the bulb is to operate at the designed voltage, what must be the value of R?

A. 4 ohm B. 6 ohm
C. 5 ohm D. 10 ohm

159. Four arrangements of circuits with capacitors are shown below. Each capacitors has capacitance equal to 1 μF.

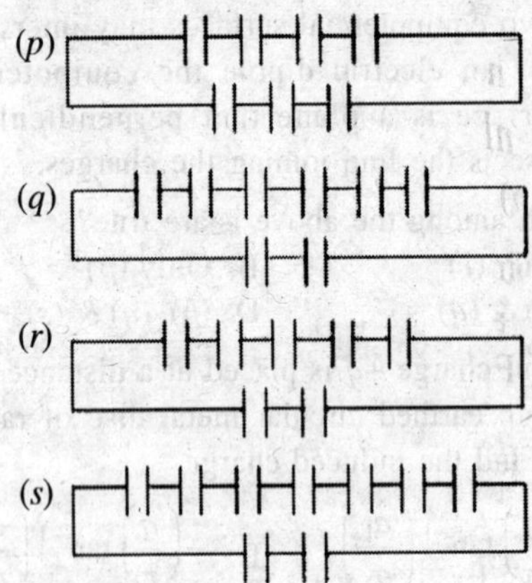

Which among the above arrangements will produce an equivalent capacitance 0.1 μF?

A. (q) B. (r)
C. (s) D. (p)

160. A metal sphere of radius R_1 carries a charge Q. It is surrounded by a spherical shall of thickness $(R_2 - R_1)$ of a linear dielectric material of permittivity $\in$. Find the potential at the centre of the sphere (relative to infinity)

A. $\frac{Q}{4\pi}\left(\frac{1}{\epsilon_0 R_1}+\frac{1}{\in R_1}-\frac{1}{\in R_2}\right)$

B. $\frac{Q}{4\pi}\left(\frac{1}{\epsilon_0 R_2}+\frac{1}{\in R_1}-\frac{1}{\in R_2}\right)$

C. $\frac{Q}{4\pi}\left(\frac{1}{\epsilon_0 R_2}-\frac{1}{\in R_1}+\frac{1}{\in R_2}\right)$

D. $\frac{Q}{4\pi}\left(\frac{1}{\epsilon_0 R_2}+\frac{1}{\in R_2}-\frac{1}{\in R_2}\right)$

161. A rod of length l is placed in a uniform magnetic field of induction B. The rod is moved with velocity V as shown. Find the e.m.f induced across the rod.

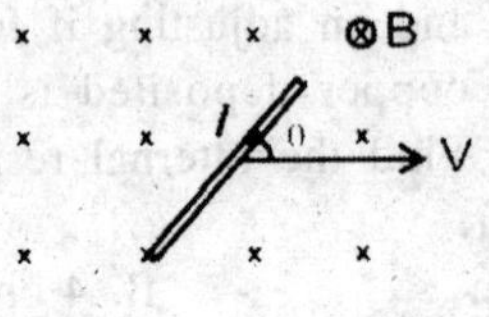

A. Zero B. BlV sin θ
C. BlV D. BlV cos θ

162. The current density in a conductor of circular cross-section of radius R varies with radius in accordance with the relation $j = kr(\pi - r)$. Where the symbols have their usual meanings. Find the total current.

A. $\frac{\pi^2 K}{6}a^3$ B. $2\pi K\left(\frac{\pi}{3}-\frac{1}{4}\right)a^3$

C. $2\pi K\left(\frac{\pi}{4}-\frac{1}{3}\right)a^3$ D. $\frac{\pi^2 K}{12}a^3$

163. In an L – C – R series circuit the voltage across the inductor, capacitor and Resistor are 80 V, 40 V, and 30 V respectively. Find the voltage applied across the L–C–R series combination.

A. 70 V B. 50 V
C. Zero D. 150 V

164. Two capacitors C_1 and C_2 ($C_1 > C_2$) are connected in series with a supply of voltage V. The total electrical energy of the capacitors in this situation is E_1. Then they are connected in parallel to the same supply voltage, and then the electrical energy of the capacitors is E_2. Find C_1 in terms of V, E_1, E_2.

A. $\frac{1}{V^2}(E_2+\sqrt{E_2^2-4E_1E_2})$

B. $\frac{1}{V^2}(E_1+\sqrt{E_2^2-4E_1E_2})$

C. $\frac{1}{V^2}(E_2-\sqrt{E_2^2-E_1E_2})$

D. $\frac{1}{V^2}(E_2+\sqrt{E_2^2-E_1E_2})$

165. Three statements are given below regarding joule heating effect—

(*p*) Heat is evolved as well as absorbed

(*q*) The effect takes place throughout the circuit

(*r*) On reversing the direction of current, cooling takes place instead of heating.

Which one(s) among is/are true?

A. Only (*p*) B. Only (*q*)
C. (*p*) & (*r*) D. (*q*) & (*r*)

166. A square loop of side *a* is placed in a uniform magnetic field of induction B such that plane of the loop is perpendicular to the magnetic field. The loop is suddenly pulled out of the field. Find the charge that flows through the loop. Resistance of the loop is R.

A. $\frac{Ba}{R^2}$ B. $\frac{Ba}{R}$
C. $\frac{Ba^2}{R}$ D. $\frac{B\cdot\pi a^2}{R}$

167. A point source is placed at the bottom of a beaker and filled with liquid of refractive index μ to a height *h*. Find the minimum radius of the disc to be placed on the surface of the liquid to stop the light emerging out of the liquid.

A. $\frac{h}{u^2}$ B. μh
C. $\frac{h}{\sqrt{u^2-1}}$ D. $\frac{h}{u}$

168. The self inductances of two coils are 2 mH and 8 mH. And assume that their coefficient of coupling is 1 then find their coefficient of mutual inductance.

A. 32 mH B. 16 mH
C. 6 mH D. 4 mH

169. In a transformer the number of terms in primary and secondary coils are 1000, and 200 respectively. A signal of 500 V is applied to the primary coil. Find the voltage across the secondary coil.

A. 100 V B. 2500 V
C. 200 V D. 1000 V

170. The self inductance of a coil is 20 mH. In one millisecond the current passing through it decreases from 2 A to zero. Find the e.m.f. indued in the coil.

A. 4 mV B. 40 V
C. 4 V D. 40 mV

171. A parallel plate capacitor has plates of area 'A' and a separation '*d*'. The plates are charged to a potential difference 'V' after which the charger is removed. A dielectric slab of thickness '*t*' and dielectric constant E is then placed symmetrically between the plates. In this situation, what is the potential difference across the plates?

A. $V_0\left[1-d\left(1-\frac{1}{E}\right)\right]$ B. $\frac{V_0}{d}\left[d-\frac{t}{E}\right]$
C. $\frac{V_0}{d}\left[t-d\left(1-\frac{1}{E}\right)\right]$ D. $\frac{V_0}{d}\left[d-t\left(1-\frac{1}{E}\right)\right]$

172. A cell consists of two parallel copper electrodes in the form of plates 4.5 cm apart and area 0.75 sq m. Find the potential difference (correct up to one place of decimal) which gets established between the plates to provide a constant current to deposit 440 g of copper on the cathode in 1 hour (Take E.C.E of copper equal to 3×10^{-7} kg C^{-1})

A. 0.3 V B. 0.6 V
C. 0.5 V D. 0.4 V

173. A cycle wheel has N spokes the radius of the cycle wheel is *r*. It is rotating with an angular frequency *w*, magnetic field of induction B is acting perpendicular to the plane of the wheel. Find the e.m.f induced between the axis and a point on rim.

A. $NB\omega r^2$ B. $\frac{B\omega r^2}{2}$
C. $NB\omega r$ D. $\frac{NB\omega r^2}{2}$

174. An inductor of inductance 2 mH and a capacitor of capacitance 2 mH and a capacitor of capacitance 8 mf are connected in parallel. Find the frequency of L-C oscillations produced.

A. $\frac{250}{\pi}$ Hz B. $\frac{500}{\pi}$ Hz

C. $\frac{125}{\pi}$ Hz D. 500π Hz

175. In the circuit shown in the figure, the internal resistance of the battery is 0.5 ohm. All the resistances shown are in ohms. Find the current in the battery.

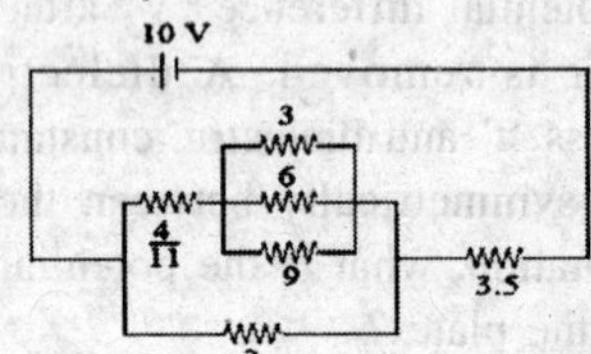

A. 2.5 amp B. 3 amp

C. 2 amp D. 1 amp

176. In an L–C–R series circuit, induction and capacitive reactances are 50 Ω and 20 Ω respectively and resistance is 40 Ω. Find the power factor of the circuit.

A. 1 B. 0.5

C. 0.6 D. 0.8

177. A coin is placed at the bottom of a beaker and the beaker is filled with water to a height of 12 cm and observed from the surface of water. Find the apparent depth of coin. Refractive index of water is $\frac{4}{3}$.

A. 16 cm B. 9 cm

C. 12 cm D. 4.8 cm

178. A potentiometer wire has a total length of 1000 cm. It is driven by a cell of E.M.F 4 V having a resistance R in series with it. A source of potential difference 10 mV gets balanced by a length of 60 cm of the potentiometer wire. Find the value of R if the resistance of the potentiometer wire is 20 ohm.

A. 640 ohm B. 440 ohm

C. 620 ohm D. 460 ohm

179. In the circuit shown all the resistances are in ohms. Find the power dissipation through the 4 ohm resistance.

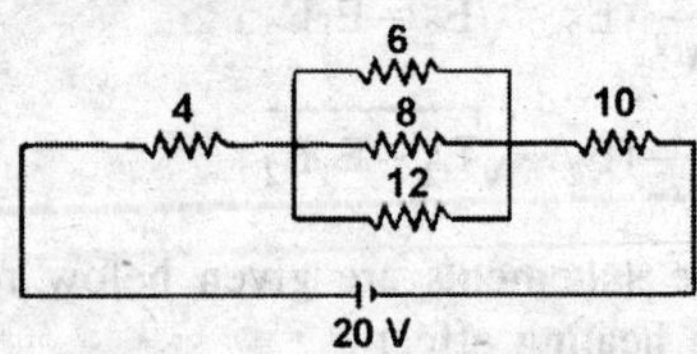

A. 1.44 W B. 2.88 W

C. 7.2 W D. 5.76 W

180. At the centre of a circular loop of radius R a square loop of side a [a << R] is placed as shown. If current is passed through circular loop find their coefficient of mutual induction.

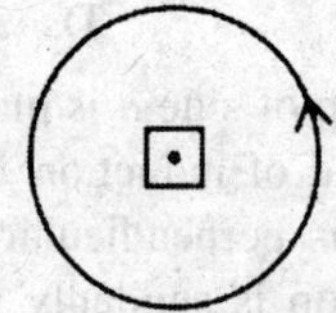

A. $\frac{\mu_0 a}{2R}$ B. $\frac{\mu_0 a^2}{2\pi R}$

C. $\frac{\mu_0 a^2}{2R}$ D. $\frac{\mu_0 a}{R}$

181. What does the acronym HTML stand for?

A. Hypertext Multiple Language

B. Hypertransfer Marking Language

C. Hypertext Marking Logic

D. Hypertext Markup Language

182. Taking feedback from children after the lessons is:

A. Assessment

B. Reporting

C. A Classroom Assessment Technique

D. Lesson planning

183. Ramesh secured 15th rank. Which type of test was this evaluation based on?

A. Standardized B. Norm referenced

C. Criterion referencing D. Diagnostic

184. In machine language, the presence of an electric pulse followed by the absence of another electric pulse is represented as:

A. (0) B. (01)

C. (10) D. (1)

185. Education of girls is seen as "Education for social cohesion rather than Social progress." In which of the following documents?
A. NPERC 1990 B. NCFSE 2000
C. NCF 1975 D. NPE 1986

186. Science teachers can enhance their proficiency through reading by:
A. Updating with latest scientific developments
B. Discussion with colleagues
C. Giving home assignments
D. Substantiating lessons with latest scientific developments

187. Story telling comes from the art of:
A. Memory B. Acting
C. Narrating D. Explaining

188. Technology aided learning can substitute a teacher effectively when we use:
A. Interactive e-lessons
B. PowerPoint presentations
C. Audio-visual aids
D. Programmed learning

189. A social science text takes the responsibility of incorporating, which one of the following value?
A. Knowledge of resource locations
B. Awareness for technology
C. Appreciation for land, culture and heritage
D. Understanding population trends

190. Which element do debate and extempore speech help to develop?
A. Reading fluency
B. Being articulate in speech
C. Writing skill
D. Emotional intelligence

191. Inclusive Education policy is an initiative to support the larger objective of _______ . *Choose the right option*
A. Special needs education
B. Girl child education
C. Minority education
D. Education for all

192. Which quality of a test reflects its desired outcome?
A. Reliability B. Validity
C. Functionality D. Feasibility

193. Constructivist development model by Vygotsky signifies:
A. Discussing with peers
B. Learning by doing
C. Working individually
D. Reading

194. Concept formation is a result of:
A. Drilling B. Memorising
C. Perceptions D. Teaching

195. Which of the following is a key mathematical skill?
A. Observing B. Drawing
C. Computing D. Illustrating

196. A class scheduled to go to a fort as an educational excursion. What best alternative plan can the teacher be made for Ashish, who uses crutches to walk?
A. Asking him to stay in the classroom and complete an assignment
B. Cinema performance
C. Give him a break
D. Friend system for mutual support

197. Poetry in languages aims to teach ....
A. Activity
B. Aesthetic and Miscellaneous Expressions
C. Rythm (Taal)
D. Song

198. Leela at 11 months looked for help from her mother to pick up a doll from the top of a table but at the age of two she pulled a chair and climbed on it to reach the doll. What development had taken place?
Complete the sentence choosing the correct option.
A. Language development
B. Physical development
C. Cognitive and physical development
D. Emotional development

199. Which of the following is the epistemological basis for scientific knowledge, according to pragmatists?
A. Opinions B. Experiments
C. Interpretations D. Problem solving

200. Special educators help teachers in:
A. Talking to students B. Remediation
C. Instructing D. Reporting

ANSWERS

1	2	3	4	5	6	7	8	9	10
D	B	A	C	D	D	C	C	D	A
11	**12**	**13**	**14**	**15**	**16**	**17**	**18**	**19**	**20**
D	A	D	A	C	A	A	C	A	D
21	**22**	**23**	**24**	**25**	**26**	**27**	**28**	**29**	**30**
C	A	B	B	B	B	D	A	D	C
31	**32**	**33**	**34**	**35**	**36**	**37**	**38**	**39**	**40**
C	C	B	D	B	B	C	A	B	D
41	**42**	**43**	**44**	**45**	**46**	**47**	**48**	**49**	**50**
B	A	C	A	C	C	A	C	A	A
51	**52**	**53**	**54**	**55**	**56**	**57**	**58**	**59**	**60**
C	D	A	C	C	A	B	A	D	A
61	**62**	**63**	**64**	**65**	**66**	**67**	**68**	**69**	**70**
B	C	A	D	C	B	C	D	D	B
71	**72**	**73**	**74**	**75**	**76**	**77**	**78**	**79**	**80**
C	B	C	A	A	D	C	A	B	D
81	**82**	**83**	**84**	**85**	**86**	**87**	**88**	**89**	**90**
B	C	B	D	D	A	C	D	C	B
91	**92**	**93**	**94**	**95**	**96**	**97**	**98**	**99**	**100**
B	D	D	C	B	A	C	B	A	B
101	**102**	**103**	**104**	**105**	**106**	**107**	**108**	**109**	**110**
A	D	A	A	D	A	B	D	B	C
111	**112**	**113**	**114**	**115**	**116**	**117**	**118**	**119**	**120**
B	B	A	B	C	A	A	D	B	B
121	**122**	**123**	**124**	**125**	**126**	**127**	**128**	**129**	**130**
D	C	A	A	A	D	A	B	A	C
131	**132**	**133**	**134**	**135**	**136**	**137**	**138**	**139**	**140**
A	C	B	B	B	B	B	D	C	D
141	**142**	**143**	**144**	**145**	**146**	**147**	**148**	**149**	**150**
D	D	C	A	C	B	B	A	D	B
151	**152**	**153**	**154**	**155**	**156**	**157**	**158**	**159**	**160**
C	C	A	D	D	A	A	C	B	B
161	**162**	**163**	**164**	**165**	**166**	**167**	**168**	**169**	**170**
B	B	B	A	B	C	C	D	A	B
171	**172**	**173**	**174**	**175**	**176**	**177**	**178**	**179**	**180**
D	A	B	C	C	D	B	D	D	C
181	**182**	**183**	**184**	**185**	**186**	**187**	**188**	**189**	**190**
D	C	B	C	B	D	C	A	C	B
191	**192**	**193**	**194**	**195**	**196**	**197**	**198**	**199**	**200**
D	B	A	C	C	D	B	C	B	B

Previous Paper (Solved)

Delhi Subordinate Services Selection Board

DSSSB–PGT (Physics) Recruitment Exam, 2015*

POST SPECIFIC SUBJECT RELATED QUESTIONS

1. Thermal expansion of materials arises from:
A. Strong bonds
B. Thermal vibrations
C. Weak bonds
D. Asymmetry of potential energy curve

2. The Compton effect tells that a photon has:
A. energy
B. momentum
C. intrinsic spin
D. angular momentum

3. In the first excited state of an one-dimensional harmonic oscillator with angular frequency ω, the energy eigenvalue is:
A. $\frac{1}{2}h\omega$ B. $\frac{3}{2}h\omega$
C. $h\omega$ D. $2h\omega$

4. A current amplifier is characterised by:
A. low input impedance and high output impedance
B. high input impedance and low output impedance
C. low impedance at both input and output terminals
D. high impedance at both input and output terminals

5. The wave function of a particle in a classically forbidden region is:
A. a sine function B. a cosine function
C. an exponential D. zero

6. The dispersion relation for electromagnetic waves in certain medium is given by $\omega^2 = ak$, where 'a' is constant, 'ω' is the frequency and 'k' is the magnitude of the wave vector. The velocity of energy propagation in this medium is:
A. $\frac{2a}{\omega}$ B. $\frac{a}{\omega}$
C. $\frac{a}{2\omega}$ D. $\frac{a}{4\omega}$

7. If the atomic mass of deuteron is 2.014102 u, then its binding energy is:
A. 4.448 MeV B. 6.663 MeV
C. 2.224 MeV D. 1.02 MeV

8. The Larmor frequency for an electron in the $n = 2$ state of hydrogen placed in a magnetic field of strength one tesla is:
A. 4.4×10^{10} rad/s B. 8.8×10^{10} rad/s
C. 1.1×10^{10} rad/s D. 5.5×10^{10} rad/s

9. The collision time for electron scattering in pure Ag ($E_F = 5.5$eV) at 300 k is 10^{-14}s. The mean free path of electron is:
A. 9.4×10^{-8} m B. 1.39×10^{-8} m
C. 3.3×10^{-8} m D. 4.2×10^{-8} m

10. The quantum mechanical operators of two observables commute. It implies that:
A. We can measure both quantities simultaneously
B. We cannot measure both quantities simultaneously
C. No conclusion can be made about their simultaneous measurement
D. These are canonically conjugate quantities

11. In a Helium-Neon laser, the laser transition takes place in:
A. He atoms only
B. Ne atoms only
C. Either He or Ne atoms
D. Both He and Ne atoms

12. In quantum mechanics, a particle is represented by a:

* Tier-I Exam

A. Wave
B. Wave packet
C. Particle
D. Nothing can be said

13. Broadening of spectral lines also occurs due to the:
A. Position – momentum uncertainty
B. Energy – time uncertainty
C. Angular momentum – angular displacement uncertainty
D. None of the above

14. In a optical fibre cable, the signal is propagated along:
A. the core
B. the cladding
C. both core and cladding
D. surface of the cladding

15. The average lifetime of an atom in metastable state is:
A. 10^{-3} sec B. 10^{-7} sec
C. 10^{-9} sec D. 10^{-12} sec

16. The units of the Planck constant h are that of:
A. energy
B. power
C. momentum
D. angular momentum

17. In a photoelectric effect experiment at a frequency above cut off, the number of electrons ejected is proportional to:
A. their kinetic energy
B. the work function
C. the frequency of the incident light
D. in intensity of light

18. Piezo-electric effect is the production of electricity by:
A. Chemical energy B. Varying field
C. Temperature D. Pressure

19. If the carbon monoxide (CO) molecule shows a strong absorption line at the frequency 6.42×10^{13} Hz then the effective force constant for this molecule is:
A. 1.86×10^3 N/m B. 5.43×10^3 N/m
C. 8.16×10^3 N/m D. 9.53×10^3 N/m

20. The de Broglie wavelength of an electron accelerated through 50 V is:
A. 3.4 Å B. 7.1 Å
C. 4.3 Å D. 1.7 Å

21. P-type and n-type semiconductors can be distinguished by measuring:
A. Temperature dependence of electrical conductivity
B. Hall coefficient
C. Resistivity
D. Photoconductivity

22. The probability that a particular state having energy E is occupied by an electron in metals is given by:

A. $f(E) = \dfrac{1}{\exp\left(\dfrac{E-E_F}{kT}\right)-1}$

B. $f(E) = \dfrac{1}{\exp\left(\dfrac{E_F-E}{kT}\right)+1}$

C. $f(E) = \dfrac{1}{\exp\left(\dfrac{E-E_F}{kT}\right)+1}$

D. $f(E) = \dfrac{1}{\exp\left(\dfrac{E_F-E}{kT}\right)-1}$

23. The average energy of a free electron in a metal at zero Kelvin is:
A. $E_{av} = \dfrac{3}{5}E_F$ B. $E_{av} = \dfrac{5}{3}E_F$
C. $E_{av} = \dfrac{1}{2}E_F$ D. $E_{av} = E_F$

24. A microchemical ensemble represents:
A. A system in contact with a heat reservoir
B. An isolated system in equilibrium
C. A system that can exchange particles with its surroundings
D. A system under constant external pressure

25. The deviation of the charge distribution of a nucleus from spherical symmetry can be estimated by measuring its:

A. electric charge
B. electric dipole moment
C. magnetic dipole moment
D. electric quadrupole moment

26. A sinusoidal voltage $V_0 \sin \omega t$ is applied across a series connection of resistor R and inductor L. The amplitude of the current in this circuit is:

A. $\frac{V_0}{\sqrt{R^2+\omega^2L^2}}$ B. $\frac{V_0}{\sqrt{R^2-\omega^2L^2}}$

C. $\frac{V_0}{\sqrt{R+\omega L}}$ D. $\frac{V_0}{R}$

27. Suppose temperature of the sun goes down by a factor of two then the total power emitted by the sun will go down by a factor of:

A. 2 B. 4
C. 16 D. 8

28. The ground state energy of a particle in an infinite square will potential of width L is E. If the width of the well is reduced to L/2, then the ground state energy becomes:

A. 2E B. E/2
C. 4E D. E/4

29. The average distance between atoms along the body diagonal of the diamond cubic crystal with cell parameter 'a' is:

A. $\frac{a\sqrt{3}}{4}$ B. $\frac{a\sqrt{3}}{8}$

C. $\frac{a\sqrt{3}}{2}$ D. $a\sqrt{3}$

30. Thermocouple consists of:

A. Two dissimilar metals
B. Two similar metals
C. Metal and a semiconductor
D. Metal and an insulator

31. A unit cell has $a = 5Å$, $b = 8Å$, $c = 3Å$, $\alpha = 90°$, $\beta = 65°$ and $\gamma = 54°$. This unit cell is called:

A. Orthorhombic B. Monoclinic
C. Triclinic D. Tetragonal

32. The probability of finding a free electron in Ag at 300 k at an energy level 1.01 E_F (for Ag E_F = 5.5 eV) is:

A. 0.5 B. 0.11
C. 0.005 D. 0

33. The SI unit of electrical conductivity is:

A. $kg^{-1}m^{-3}s^3A^2$ B. $kgm^3s^{-3}A^2$
C. ohm m D. $ohm^{-1}m^{-3}$

34. Superconductors when cooled below T_C undergo a transition to the following state:

A. Paramagnetic B. Ferromagnetic
C. Diamagnetic D. Ferrimagnetic

35. Boson is a particle with:

A. integral spin
B. half integral spin
C. zero spin
D. zero mass

36. The residue of the function of complex variable

$f(z) = \frac{5z-2}{z(z-1)}$ at $z = 1$ is:

A. 0 B. 1
C. 2 D. 3

37. The correct relation of Pauli matrices is:

A. $\sigma_x\sigma_y = \sigma_z$
B. $\sigma_y\sigma_x = \sigma_z$
C. $\sigma_x\sigma_y - \sigma_y\sigma_z = 0$
D. $\sigma_x\sigma_y + \sigma_y\sigma_z = 0$

38. The generating function of Legendre's polynomial $P_n(x)$ is $(1 - 2xt + t^2)^{-1/2}$.

Then $P_n(1)$ is:

A. 0 B. 1
C. 2 D. $\frac{1}{2}$

39. Quantum mechanical wave function of hydrogen atom contains:

A. Legendre and Hermite polynomial
B. Legendre and Associate Laguerre polynomial
C. Legendre polynomial and Bessel function
D. Associate Laguerre polynomial and Bessel function

40. In usual notations, the Laplace transform of $f(t) = e^t$ is:

A. s B. s^2

C. $\frac{1}{s-1}$ D. $\frac{1}{s}$

41. Fourier series which will represent $f(x) = x$ in the interval $-\pi < x < \pi$, then:

$$1-\frac{1}{3}+\frac{1}{5}-\frac{1}{7}+\frac{1}{9}-.... =$$

A. $\frac{\pi}{4}$ B. $\frac{\pi}{2}$

C. $\frac{\pi}{6}$ D. $\frac{\pi}{8}$

42. If A^{ij} is a contravariant tensor, then its tensor will be:

A. A_{ij} B. A_{ji}

C. $-A^{ij}$ D. A^{ji}

43. The direction of propagation of a electromagnetic wave is given by:

A. $\vec{E}\cdot\vec{B}$ B. $\vec{E}$

C. $\vec{B}\cdot\vec{E}$ D. $\vec{E}\times\vec{B}$

44. If magnetic monopole existed then which of the following Maxwell's equation will be modified?

A. Div D = ρ B. Div $\vec{B} = 0$

C. Curl $\vec{E} = \frac{-\partial\vec{B}}{\partial t}$ D. Curl $\vec{H} = \vec{J}+\frac{\partial\vec{D}}{\partial t}$

45. Eight electric dipoles of charges of magnitude 'e' are placed inside a cube. The total electric flux coming out of the cube will be:

A. $\frac{8e}{\epsilon_0}$ B. $\frac{16e}{\epsilon_0}$

C. $\frac{e}{\epsilon_0}$ D. Zero

46. $\nabla^2 V = -4\pi\rho$ represents

A. Maxwell's equation B. Laplace equation

C. Poisson's equation D. Lorentz equation

47. The potential energy of a central force is given by $V(r) = br^{n+1}$ where 'b' is a constant, 'r' is the distance from a fixed point in space. The orbit of a particle moving under the action of this central force is stable when:

A. $n = -5$ B. $n = -4$

C. $n = -3$ D. $n = -2$

48. A particle is moving in an inverse square force field. If the total energy of the particle is positive, then the trajectory of the particle is:

A. Circular B. Elliptical

C. Parabolic D. Hyperbolic

49. If the plane intercepts for a unit cell are $3a$, $2b$ and $2c$, then the Miller indices of the plane are:

A. (0 1 1) B. (3 2 2)

C. (2 3 2) D. (2 3 3)

50. The energy of lattice vibration is quantised. The quantum of energy is called:

A. Boson B. Photon

C. Phonon D. Lepton

51. Choose the correct statement:

A. Heat capacity is constant at low temperature

B. Heat capacity is constant at high temperature

C. Heat capacity is independent of temperature

D. Heat capacity decreases with increase in temperature

52. There are regions of energy for which Bloch function solutions of wave equation do not exist. These are called:

A. Conduction region B. Valence region

C. Forbidden region D. Plasma state

53. In superconductors, the energy gap is due to:

A. electron-phonon interaction

B. electron-electron interaction

C. phonon-phonon interaction

D. electron-photon interaction

54. A feature that distinguishes the J-K flip flop from S-R flip flop is the:

A. Toggle condition B. Present input

C. Type of clock D. Clear input

55. A silicon diode is in series with a 1 kΩ resistor and a 5 V battery. If the anode is connected to the positive battery terminal, the cathode voltage with respect to the negative battery terminal is:

A. 0.7 V B. 0.3 V

C. 5.7 V D. 4.3 V

56. A diode that has a negative resistance characteristic is the:

A. Schottky diode
B. Tunnel diode
C. Laser diode
D. Hot carrier diode

57. Universal gates are:
A. AND and OR
B. NAND and NOR
C. OR and NOT
D. AND and XOR

58. Practical solar cells have fill factor:
A. greater than 1
B. zero
C. 1
D. less than 1

59. In an n-type semiconductor, as temperature increases, the Fermi level:
A. move towards conduction band
B. move towards middle of forbidden-energy gap
C. does not vary
D. may or may not shift depending upon the concentration of donor atoms

60. Compared to bipolar junction transistor, a JFET has:
A. low input impedance
B. high voltage gain
C. high input impedance and high voltage gain
D. high input impedance and low voltage gain

61. Second order reflection from (1 0 0) plane should satisfy the following Bragg condition:
A. $d_{100} \sin\theta = \lambda$
B. $d_{100} \sin\theta = 2\lambda$
C. $2d_{100} \sin\theta = \lambda$
D. $d_{100} \cos\theta = \lambda$

62. The transformation $Q = q^m\cos(np)$; $P = q^m \sin(np)$ represents a canonical transformation for:
A. $m = 1, n = 2$
B. $m = \frac{1}{2}, n = 2$
C. $m = 2, n = \frac{1}{2}$
D. $m = 2, n = 1$

63. The momentum of an electron (mass = m) which has the same amount of kinetic energy as its rest energy is (c = speed of light in vacuum):
A. $\sqrt{3}$ mc
B. $\sqrt{2}$ mc
C. mc
D. $\frac{mc}{\sqrt{2}}$

64. Hamilton's canonical equations of motion are:
A. $\dot{q}_1 = \frac{\partial H}{\partial P_1}$ and $p_1 = \frac{\partial H}{\partial q}$
B. $\dot{q}_1 = \frac{\partial H}{\partial P_1}$ and $\dot{p}_1 = \frac{\partial H}{\partial q_1}$
C. $q_1 = \frac{\partial H}{\partial \dot{P}_1}$ and $\dot{p}_1 = \frac{\partial H}{\partial \dot{q}_1}$
D. $q_1 = \frac{\partial H}{\partial \dot{P}_1}$ and $p_1 = -\frac{\partial H}{\partial \dot{q}_1}$

65. The entropy of the universe tends to:
A. a minimum
B. zero
C. a maximum
D. no particular value as it remains constant

66. The particles in a system obeying the Maxwell-Boltzmann statistics are:
A. only identical
B. identical but distinguishable
C. only indistinguishable
D. identical but indistinguishable

67. If R is taken as the gas constant per mole of a gas and N as Avogadro's number, the Boltzmann's constant is correctly related as:
A. RN
B. RN^2
C. $\frac{N}{R}$
D. $\frac{R}{N}$

68. The ground state energy of a Bose-Einstein gas is zero. The number of molecules in the ground state at a finite temperature is:
A. maximum, nearly equal to the total number
B. half the total number
C. zero
D. nothing can be said since the number depends on the temperature

69. The electron in a hydrogen atom with a radius equal to first Bohr radius has a velocity equal to (c is velocity of light in vacuum):
A. $\frac{c}{5}$
B. $\frac{c}{10}$
C. $\frac{c}{137}$
D. $\frac{c}{8}$

70. The maximum number of electrons in a subshell with orbital quantum number 'l' is:
A. $(2l + 1)$
B. $(2l - 1)$
C. $2(2l + 1)$
D. $2(2l - 1)$

71. The magnetic moment associated with the first orbit in hydrogen atom is given by:

A. $\frac{h}{4\pi me}$
B. $\frac{ehm}{4\pi}$
C. $\frac{eh}{4\pi m}$
D. $\frac{4\pi m}{he}$

72. The ratio of frequencies of the first line of the Lyman series and the first line of the Balmer series is:

A. $\frac{27}{5}$
B. $\frac{27}{8}$
C. $\frac{8}{27}$
D. $\frac{4}{27}$

73. The SI unit of absorbed dose is:

A. Curie
B. Gray
C. Roentgen
D. Rad

74. The energy of a gamma photon emitted during positron-electron annihilation process is:

A. 3.82 MeV
B. 0.511 MeV
C. 1.275 MeV
D. 1.8 MeV

75. Indicate the dominant process when 1 MeV gamma ray interacts with carbon target:

A. Photoelectric effect
B. Pair-production
C. Compton effect
D. Annihilation

76. For most inert gases the average energy required to produce an electron-ion pair is about:

A. 0.3 eV
B. 30 MeV
C. 30 keV
D. 30 eV

77. A quantum mechanical operator should be a:

A. null operator
B. singular operator
C. linear operator
D. non-linear operator

78. A quantum mechanical wave function:

A. should always be a real function
B. should always be a complex function
C. can be simultaneous eigen function of two operators
D. cannot be simultaneous eigen function of two operators

79. A particle is trapped inside a three dimensional infinite deep potential well. The width of the potential well in all direction is 'L'. The energy of particle in a level is $\frac{5h^2}{8mL^2}$. The degeneracy of the level is:

A. 2
B. 4
C. 6
D. 8

80. A simple harmonic oscillator of mass m_0 and angular frequency ω is perturbed by an additional potential bx^3. The first order correction to the ground state energy of the oscillator will be:

A. $\frac{1}{2}h\omega$
B. $\frac{3bh^2}{4m^2\omega^2}$
C. $h\omega$
D. zero

81. The quantum scattering processes can be analysed by:

A. Partial wave method
B. The Born approximation
C. Both the above mentioned methods
D. The WKB method

82. The Dirac equation:

A. is valid for relativistic systems
B. is valid for fermions
C. explains intrinsic spin of electrons
D. All the above mentioned options are correct

83. Choose the incorrect statement:

A. the Klein-Gordon (KG) equation is valid for all bosons
B. the Klein-Gordon equation is valid for only spin zero particles
C. the KG equation shows emergence of negative energy eigenvalues
D. the KG equation is relativistically invariant

84. The Fermi's Golden rule is applicable to:

A. time independent harmonic perturbation potential
B. time independent anharmonic perturbation potential
C. time dependent harmonic perturbation potential
D. time dependent anharmonic perturbation potential

85. If 50 KV is the applied potential in an X-ray tube, then the minimum wavelength of X-rays produced is:

A. 0.5 nm
B. 2.5 nm
C. 0.25Å
D. 5Å

86. Multiplicity of the state $^2D_{3/2}$ is given by:
A. 1
B. 2
C. 3
D. 4

87. The normal Zeeman effect is:
A. Observed only in atoms with an even number of electrons
B. Observed only in atoms with an odd number of electrons
C. Not a confirmation of space quantization
D. A confirmation of space quantization

88. The temperature coefficient of resistivity for a semiconductor is:
A. positive
B. negative
C. zero
D. None of the above

89. The Schrodinger equation is valid for:
A. a relativistic system
B. a non-relativistic system
C. all kinds of systems
D. can not be said

90. If the probability distribution is independent of time then the state of the system is said to be:
A. constant
B. time independent
C. stationary
D. degenerate

91. Which one of the following is **not** conserved in β-decay?
A. Iso-spin
B. Parity
C. Baryon number
D. Charge

92. The energy released by the fission of Uranium atom is 200 MeV. The number of fissions per second required to produce 3.2 W of power is:
A. 10^{13}
B. 10^{15}
C. 10^{17}
D. 10^{19}

93. One Barn is:
A. 10^{-14} m^2
B. 10^{-18} m^2
C. 10^{-24} m^2
D. 10^{-28} m^2

94. The half life of Pa-218 is 3 minutes. The fraction of 10 g sample of Pa-218 left after 15 minute is:
A. $\frac{1}{32}$
B. $\frac{1}{16}$
C. $\frac{1}{64}$
D. $\frac{1}{25}$

95. $A^{ijk}_{lm}B^{m}_{l}$ is a tensor of rank:
A. 7
B. 3
C. 5
D. 6

96. For an electron in hydrogen atom, the states are characterised by the usual quantum numbers n, l, m_l. The electric dipole transition between any two states requires that:
A. $\Delta l = 0;\ \Delta m_l = 0, \pm 1$
B. $\Delta l = \pm 1;\ \Delta m_l = \pm 1, \pm 2$
C. $\Delta l = \pm 1;\ \Delta m_l = 0, \pm 1$
D. $\Delta l = \pm 1;\ \Delta m_l = 0, \pm 2$

97. An atom emits a photon of wavelength 600 nm by transition from an excited state of life time 8×10^{-9}s. If $\Delta\gamma$ represents minimum uncertainty in the frequency of the photon, the fractional width $\Delta\frac{\gamma}{\gamma}$ of the spectral line is of the order of:
A. 10^{-4}
B. 10^{-8}
C. 10^{-12}
D. 10^{-16}

98. Hall coefficient is:
A. Directly proportional to carrier concentration
B. Inversely proportional to carrier concentration
C. Independent of carrier concentration
D. Directly proportional to carrier concentration only at low temperatures

99. At room temperature, the current in an intrinsic semi-conductor is due to:
A. electrons
B. ions
C. holes
D. both electrons and holes

100. The main principle used in nuclear radiation detection used in Geiger-Muller counter is based on:
A. the detection of free charge carriers
B. light sensing
C. the visualisation of the tracks of the radiation
D. some hybrid techniques

ANSWERS

1	2	3	4	5	6	7	8	9	10
D	B	B	A	C	C	C	B	B	A
11	**12**	**13**	**14**	**15**	**16**	**17**	**18**	**19**	**20**
B	B	B	A	A	D	D	D	A	D
21	**22**	**23**	**24**	**25**	**26**	**27**	**28**	**29**	**30**
B	C	A	C	D	A	C	C	C	A
31	**32**	**33**	**34**	**35**	**36**	**37**	**38**	**39**	**40**
C	B	A	C	A	D	D	B	B	C
41	**42**	**43**	**44**	**45**	**46**	**47**	**48**	**49**	**50**
A	D	D	B	D	B	D	D	D	C
51	**52**	**53**	**54**	**55**	**56**	**57**	**58**	**59**	**60**
B	C	B	A	D	B	B	D	A	D
61	**62**	**63**	**64**	**65**	**66**	**67**	**68**	**69**	**70**
A	B	A	B	C	B	D	A	C	C
71	**72**	**73**	**74**	**75**	**76**	**77**	**78**	**79**	**80**
C	A	B	B	C	D	C	C	C	D
81	**82**	**83**	**84**	**85**	**86**	**87**	**88**	**89**	**90**
C	D	A	C	B	B	D	B	B	C
91	**92**	**93**	**94**	**95**	**96**	**97**	**98**	**99**	**100**
B	C	D	A	B	C	B	B	D	A

PHYSICS

UNIT-1

Physical World and Measurement

UNITS FOR MEASUREMENT

(i) For measurement of a physical quantity we require some standard unit of that quantity. A lion is heavier than goat. This is a well known fact but the question is, how many times? The answer to this question can be given easily if we select a standard mass calling it a **unit mass.** If the lion is 100 times the unit mass and the goat is 10 times, then we get immediately the answer that the lion is 10 times heavier than goat. Similarly, if one knows about the **unit length** and someone tells him that Railway station is 50 times the unit length from here, then one can easily decide whether to go on foot or by a bus.

(ii) The chosen standard of same kind taken as reference to measure a physical quantity, is called as the unit of that quantity. The measurement of a physical quantity means to determine the number of times, its unit is contained in the physical quantity. Hence the measurement of a physical quantity consists of two parts:

(a) first part gives how many times of the standard unit is contained in the physical quantity.

(b) the second part gives the name of the standard unit.

(iii) For example, if we are required to measure the mass of a gas cylinder, the unit selected for the measurement must be that of mass. Suppose we use kilogram as the unit. We place the weights of 1 kg or 2 kg or 5 kg one by one in the pan of the balance and find out the number of kilograms which balance the mass of cylinder. Suppose the mass of cylinder is balanced by 18 pieces of 1 kilogram each. Then, 18 is called the numerical value of the mass of cylinder. Thus we may write:

Mass of cylinder = 16 × 1 kg = 16 kg

The unit of the physical quantity has also to be written along with the result of measurement.

(iv) Hence we can write the following in a general way:

Measure of a physical quantity

= Numerical value of the quantity × size of its unit

If n represents the numerical value of the physical quantity of a unit whose size is u then measure of a physical quantity = nu

If the size of the unit chosen is small, then the numerical value of the quantity will be large and vice-versa. It is clear that measure of the physical quantity is always same i.e.

$$nu = \text{constant}$$

If n_1 is numerical value of the physical quantity for some unit u_1 and n_2 for some other unit u_2, then

$$n_1u_1 = n_2u_2$$

FUNDAMENTAL AND DERIVED UNITS

(i) Fundamental units are independent of each other and can not be further resolved into any other units. All other units can be expressed in terms of these fundamental units. The quantities mass, length and time are called fundamental quantities. For measuring these quantities, there are independent units such as kilogram, metre and second.

(ii) For other physical quantities, if a separate unit is defined for each of them, then it will become quite difficult to remember all of them because their number will be quite high. It is found that units of the other physical quantities can be expressed in terms of the fundamental units of mass, length and time. The units of all such physical quantities which can be expressed in terms of the fundamental units of mass, length and time are called derived units.

Example: The unit of area is a derived unit. The unit of area is area of a square having its length and breadth each equal to the unit length. The unit of volume is the volume of a cube having its all the sides of unit length. In fact, the unit of any physical quantity can be obtained from its definite equation, e.g., let us consider the defining equation of speed.

$$\text{Speed} = \frac{\text{Distance travelled}}{\text{time taken}}$$

$$\therefore \text{Unit of speed} = \frac{\text{unit of distance, i.e., length}}{\text{unit of time}}$$

$$= \frac{\text{metre}}{\text{second}} = \text{ms}^{-1}.$$

SYSTEMS OF UNITS

These are mainly four in number:

1. **CGS system:** This system was established in France. It is based on centimetre, gram and second as the fundamental units of length, mass and time respectively. It is a metric system of units. In this system unit of force is taken as dynes, unit of energy as ergs, unit of power as ergs/sec and so on.
2. **FPS system:** This system is called as British system of units. It is based on foot, pound and second as the fundamental units of length, mass and time respectively. In this system of units, unit of force is taken as poundal, unit of energy as foot-poundal, unit of power as foot-poundal/sec and so on.
3. **MKS system:** This system of units was also established in France. It makes use of metre, kilogram and second as the fundamental units of mass, length and time. It is also a metric system of units and closely related to cgs system of units.
4. **SI system:** The units of mass, length and time can be used to find the units of physical quantities in mechanics only. These three fundamental units are not sufficient to find the units of physical quantities which come across in other branches of physics like optics, electrodynamics, heat etc. The general conference of weights and measures held in 1971 decided a new system of units which is known as the International System of Units. It is abbreviated as SI from the French name Le Systeme International d'Unites. It is based on the following seven fundamental (or basic) and two supplementary units:

	Basic physical quantity	Name of the unit	Symbol
1.	Length	metre	m
2.	Mass	kilogram	kg
3.	Time	second	s
4.	Electric current	ampere	A
5.	Temperature	kelvin	K
6.	Luminous intensity	candela	Cd
7.	Amount of substance	mole	mol
	Supplementary physical quantity	**Unit**	**Symbol**
1.	Plane angle	radian	rad
2.	Solid angle	steradian	sr

BASIC AND SUPPLEMENTARY UNITS OF SI SYSTEM

The seven fundamental and two supplemetary units of SI system are defined as follows:

1. **Metre:** On atomic standards, metre is defined as to be equal to 1,650, 763.73 wavelengths in vacuum of the radiation emitted due to transition between the levels $2p_{10}$ and $5d_5$ of the isotope of Krypton having mass number 86.

   Krypton-86 emits light of several different wavelengths. The light emitted by Krypton-86 due to transition between the levels $2p_{10}$ and $5d_5$ is orange red in colour and has wavelength 6057.8021 Å or 6.0578021×10^{-7} m. The number of these wavelengths in 1 m can be counted by using an optical interferometer which comes out to be 1,650,763.3.
2. **Kilogram:** There is no definition of unit kilogram on atomic standards. Therefore in SI system, Kilogram is the mass of a platinum-iridium cylinder kept in the International Bureau of Weights and Measures at Paris.
3. **Second:** Unit second can be defined on atomic standards. One second is defined to be equal to

the duration of 9,192,631,770 vibrations corresponding to the transition between two hyperfine levels of Caesium-133 atom in the ground state.

4. **Kelvin:** It was adopted as the unit of temperature. The fraction 1/273.16 of the thermodynamic temperature of triple point of water is called 1 K.
5. **Ampere:** It was adopted as the unit of current. It is defined as the current generating force of 2×10^{-7} Newton per metre between two straight parallel conductors of infinite length and negligible circular cross-section, when placed at a distance of one metre in vacuum.
6. **Candela:** It was adopted as the unit of luminous intensity. One candela is the luminous intensity in perpendicular direction of a surface of 1/600,000 metre^2 of a black body at a temperature of freezing platinum (2046.65 kelvin) and under a pressure of 101,325 N/m^2.

   Candela is redefined in 1979 as

   It is the luminous intensity in a given direction due to a source which emits monochromatic radiation of frequency 540×10^{12} Hz and of which the radiant intensity in that direction is 1/683 watt per steradian.
7. **Mole:** It was adopted as the unit of amount of substance. The amount of a substance that contains as many elementary entities (molecules or atoms if the substance is monoatomic) as there are number of atoms in 0.012 kg or Carbon-12 is called a mole. This number (number of atoms in 0.012 kg of carbon-12) is called Avogadro constant and its best value available is 6.022045×10^{23}.
8. **Radian:** It was adopted as the unit of plane angle. It is the plane angle between the two radii of a circle which cut off from the circumference, an arc equal to the length of the radius.

   Plane Angle in Radian = length of arc/radius
9. **Steradian:** It was adopted as the unit of solid angle with its apex at the centre of sphere that cuts out an area on the surface of the sphere equal to the area of the square, whose sides are equal to the radius of the sphere.

   Solid angle in steradian = area cut out from the surface of sphere/radius^2

SOME PRACTICAL UNITS OF THE STANDARD OF LENGTH

1. **Parallactic second (Parsec):** It is the largest practical unit of distance. It is the distance at which an arc of length one astronomical unit ($= 1.496 \times 10^{11}$ m) subtends an angle of one second of an arc.

$$r = \frac{l}{\theta} = \frac{1.496 \times 10^{11} \text{ m}}{1 \text{ second}}$$

$$\text{or,} \quad 1 \text{ parsec} = \frac{1.496 \times 10^{11} \text{ m}}{\pi/(60 \times 60 \times 180) \text{ radian}}$$

$$= \frac{1.496 \times 10^{11} \times 60 \times 60 \times 180}{\pi}$$

$$\text{or,} \quad 1 \text{ parsec} = 3.08 \times 10^{16} \text{ m} = 4.2 \text{ light year}$$

2. **Light Year:** It is also a practical unit of distance used in astronomy to measure the distance of nearer stars. One light year is the distance travelled by the light in one year in vacuum of free space or air.

$$1 \text{ Light year} = 3 \times 10^8 \text{ m/s} \times 365 \times 24 \times 60 \times 60 \text{ s}$$

$$\text{or } 1 \text{ Light year} = 9.5 \times 10^{15} \text{ m} = 9.5 \times 10^{12} \text{ km}$$

3. **Astronomical unit:** It is defined as the average distance between sun and earth, i.e., radius of earth's orbit.

$$1 \text{ A.U.} = 1.496 \times 10^{11} \text{ m}$$
$$= 1.496 \times 10^8 \text{ km} \approx 1.5 \times 10^8 \text{ km}$$

   This unit is also used in astronomy to measure distance of planets.
4. **Microns:** It is a unit of distance defined as micrometre.

$$1 \text{ microns} = 1\ \mu\text{m} = 10^{-6} \text{ m}$$

   This units is normally used to express the wavelength. The wavelength of visible light is of the order of 4000×10^{-10} m or 0.4 microns.
5. **Angstrom:** It is also a practical unit of length used in atomic physics.

$$1 \text{ Å} = 10^{-10} \text{ m} = 10^{-8} \text{ cm}$$

The size of an atom or wavelength of gamma rays are of this order.

6. **X-ray unit:** It is an obsolete unit of distance.
   1 X-ray unit $= 10^{-13}$ m $= 10^{-11}$ cm
7. **Fermi:** It is the smallest practical unit of distance used in nuclear physics.
   1 Fermi $= 10^{-15}$ m $= 10^{-13}$ cm
   The size of the nucleus is of this order.

SOME PRACTICAL UNITS OF THE STANDARD OF MASS

1. **Chandra Shekhar limit (C.S.L.):** It is largest practical unit of mass
   1 C.S.L. = 1.4 times the mass of sun
2. **Metric Ton:** 1 Metric Ton = 1000 kg
3. **Atomic mass unit (a.m.u.):** It is not the atomic standard of mass but a practical unit of mass used in atomic and nuclear physics and is the smallest unit. It is defined at present as 1/12th of the mass of one C-12 atom, i.e.,

$$1 \text{ a.m.u.} = \frac{1}{12} \times \text{mass of one C-12 atom}$$

$$= \frac{1}{12} \times \frac{12}{N} = \frac{1}{N}$$

$$= \frac{1}{6.023 \times 10^{23}} \text{ gm}$$

i.e. 1 a.m.u. is just equal to the reciprocal of Avogadro's Number.

$$1 \text{ a.m.u.} = \frac{1}{6.023 \times 10^{23}} \text{ gm}$$

$$= 1.67 \times 10^{-24} \text{ gm}$$

$$= 1.67 \times 10^{-27} \text{ kg}$$

The mass of proton or neutron is of this order.

SOME PRACTICAL UNITS OF STANDARDS OF TIME

1. **Century:** It is the largest unit of time.
2. **Year:** It is the time taken by earth to complete one revolution around the sun in its orbit.
3. **Lunar Month:** It is the time taken by moon to complete one revolution around the earth in its orbit.
   1 L.M. = 27.3 days
4. **Solar day:** It is the time taken by earth to complete one rotation about its axis with respect to sun.
   Average solar day: It is defined as the time taken by earth to complete one rotation on its axis with respect to sun, the average being taken over a solar year. It has been found
   1 solar year = 365.25 avg. solar day

$$\text{or, avg. solar day} = \left(\frac{1}{365.25}\right) \text{th part of solar year.}$$

DIMENSIONS OF A PHYSICAL QUANTITY

(i) In all the systems of units, the derived units of all the physical quantities can be expressed in terms of the fundamental units of mass, length and time. raised to some power. The powers to which fundamental units must be raised in order to express a physical quantity, are called its dimensions. To make it clear, consider the physical quantity density which is defined as mass per unit volume.

$$\text{Hence, density} = \frac{\text{mass}}{\text{volume}} = \frac{\text{M}}{\text{L}^3} = \left[\text{M}^1\text{L}^{-3}\text{T}^0\right]$$

(ii) (a) Above expression shows that dimensions of density are 1 in mass, –3 in length and 0 in time.

(b) Dimensional formula for density is $[\text{ML}^{-3}]$ or $[\text{ML}^{-3}\text{T}^0]$

(c) Dimensional equation for density is $[d] = [\text{ML}^{-3}\text{T}^0]$

APPLICATIONS THEORY OF DIMENSIONS IN MECHANICS

(A) To find dimensions of a dimensional constant

In order to find the dimensions of a dimensional constant, we use some law or formula containing that constant and put the dimensions of all other physical quantities except the constant. Let us take few examples as given below:

(a) Planck's constant (*h*)

(i) According to Planck's equation:

$$E = h\upsilon$$

or $h = E/\upsilon$

We have $[h] = [ML^2T^{-2}]/[T^{-1}] = [ML^2T^{-1}]$

(ii) From de Broglie's equation:

We have $[h] = [LMLT^{-1}] = [ML^2T^{-1}]$

(iii) From second postulate of Bohr's theory:

$$mvr = nh/2\pi$$

or $h = (2\pi/n) \times mvr$

We have $[h] = [MLT^{-1}L] = [ML^2T^{-1}]$

(b) Gravitational constant (G)

According to Newton's law of gravitational:

$$F = Gm_1m_2/r^2$$

or $G = Fr^2/m_1m_2$

$$[G] = [MLT^{-2} \times L^2]/M^2 = [M^{-1}L^3T^{-2}]$$

(c) Coefficient of Viscosity (η)

(i) According to Newton's formula:

$$F = \eta A \frac{dv}{dx}$$

or $\eta = \dfrac{F}{A(dv/dx)}$

$\therefore$ $[\eta] = [MLT^{-2}]/([L^2] \times [LT^{-1}/L]) = [ML^{-1}T^{-1}]$

(ii) From Stoke's Law:

$$F = 6\pi \eta r v$$

or $\eta = F/6\pi r v$

$\therefore$ $[\eta] = [MLT^{-2}]/([L] \times [LT^{-1}]) = [ML^{-1}T^{-1}]$

(iii) From Poissuelle's formula:

$$\frac{dQ}{dt} = \frac{\pi p r^4}{8\eta l}$$

or $\eta = \dfrac{\pi p r^4}{8l(dQ/dt)}$,

[dQ/dt = Volume of liquid flowing per sec]

$\therefore$ $[\eta] = [ML^{-1}T^{-2}][L^4]/([L][L^3T^{-1}]) = [ML^{-1}T^{-1}]$

(B) To convert a physical quantity from one system to other (e.g., from M.K.S. to C.G.S. or C.G.S. to M.K.S.)

(a) 1 Newton = 1 kg. m/sec^2 $\{\because [F] = [MLT^{-2}]\}$

$= 1 \times (10^3 \text{ gm}) \times (10^2 \text{ cm})/\text{sec}^2$

$= 10^5 \text{ gm cm/sec}^2$

$=$ **10^5 dynes**

(b) 1 dyne $= 1 \text{ gm cm/sec}^2$

$= 10^{-3} \text{ kg} \times 10^{-2} \text{ m/sec}^2$

$= 10^{-5} \text{ kg m/s}^2$

$=$ **10^{-5} Newton**

(c) 1 Joule $= [1 \text{ kg} \times \text{m}^2]/\text{sec}^2$ $\{\because [W] = [ML^2T^{-2}]\}$

$= [10^3 \text{ gm} \times 10^4 \text{ cm}^2]/\text{sec}^2$

$= [10^7 \text{ gm} \times \text{cm}^2]/\text{sec}^2$

$=$ **10^7 ergs**

(d) $h = 6.67 \times 10^{-34}$ (MKS unit)

$= 6.67 \times 10^{-34} \times [10^3 \text{ gm} \times 10^4 \text{ cm}^2]/\text{sec}$ $\{\because [h] = [ML^2T^{-1}]\}$

$= 6.67 \times 10^{-34} \times 10^7$

$= 6.67 \times 10^{-27}$ (cgs unit)

(e) $G = 6.6 \times 10^{-8}$ (cgs unit)

$= 6.6 \times 10^{-8} \times [(10^{-2})^3 \text{ m}^3]/10^{-3} \text{ kg sec}^2$ $\{\because [G] = L^3M^{-1}T^{-2}]\}$

$= 6.6 \times 10^{-8} \times 10^{-3} \text{ m}^3/\text{kg-sec}^2$

$= 6.6 \times 10^{-11}$ (MKS unit)

(C) To check the accuracy of a given equation or formula

(i) An equation consists of various terms which are separated from each other by the symbols of equality, plus or minus. The dimensions of all the terms in an equation must be identical. This is another way of saying that one can add or subtract similar physical quantities. Thus, a velocity cannot be added to a force or an electric current cannot be subtracted from the thermodynamic temperature. This simple principle is called the **principle of homogeneity of dimensions** in an equation. It is a very useful method for checking the accuracy of a given equation. If the dimensions of all the terms are not same, the equation must be wrong.

(ii) Let us check the following equation

$$s = ut + \tfrac{1}{2} at^2$$

according to the principle of dimensional homogeneity.

Here s is the distance travelled by a particle in time t which starts at a speed u and has an acceleration a along the direction of motion.

Now $[s] = [L]$

$[ut]$ = velocity × time

= (Length/time) × time

= [L]

$[\frac{1}{2} at^2] = [at^2]$ = acceleration × (time)^2

= (velocity/time) × (time)^2

= [(length/time)/time] × (time)^2

= [L]

This shows that the equation is dimensionally correct.

(D) To deduce relation among physical quantites

This is also based on the principle of homogeneity. If one knows the quantities on which a particular physical quantity depends and if one guessess that this dependence is of product type, method of dimension may be helpful in the derivation of the relation. Let us take few examples as discussed below:

(i) Derivation of relation $E = mc^2$

If the energy depends on mass m, speed c and Planck's constant h, then

$$E = f(mch)$$

We assume that the dependence of energy on these quantities is of product type, i.e.

$$E = k\,m^x c^y h^z \qquad \ldots(1)$$

where k is a dimensionless constant and x, y and z are exponents which we want to evaluate.

Taking the dimensions of both sides,

$$[ML^2T^{-2}] = [M]^x [LT^{-1}]^y [ML^2T^{-1}]^z$$

or $[ML^2T^{-2}] = M^{x+z} L^{y+2z} T^{-y-z}$

If the equation is dimensionally correct, then

$$x + z = 1 \qquad \ldots(2)$$

$$y + 2z = 2 \qquad \ldots(3)$$

$$-y - z = -2 \qquad \ldots(4)$$

Solving, we get $z = 0$, $y = 2$, and $x = 1$

Hence, we have

$$E = km^1c^2h^0 = kmc^2$$

k is dimensionless constant and is determined experimentally. It is found to be equal to 1. Thus

$$E = mc^2$$

(ii) Derivation of Stoke's Law

Let $F = f(\eta v r)$

where η is coefficient of viscosity of medium, v is the velocity of body and r is its radius.

Suppose, $F = K\eta^x v^y r^z$

Taking dimensions of both sides, we get

$$[MLT^{-2}] = K\,[ML^{-1}T^{-1}]^x [LT^{-1}]^y [L]^z$$

$$MLT^{-2} = K\,M^x L^{-x+y+z} T^{-x-y}$$

Since dimensions on both sides must be identical, hence $x = 1$, $-x + y + z = 1$, $-x - y = -2$

Solving, we get $x = 1$, $z = 1$ and $y = 1$

Hence, we have

$$F = K\eta^1 v^1 r^1$$

K is determined experimentally. It is found to be equal to 6π. Hence

$$F = 6\pi\eta v r$$

LIMITATIONS OF THE THEORY OF DIMENSIONS

1. If a physical quantity is given, its dimensions are unique but converse may or may not be true i.e. if dimensions are given, physical quantity may or may not be unique as many physical quantities has same dimensions. e.g. physical quantity work has got the unique dimensions as $[ML^2T^{-2}]$ but if the dimensions $[ML^2T^{-2}]$ are give to us then they may represent the physical quantities like Work, Energy and Torque, i.e., physical quantity is not unique.
2. Theory of dimensions does not give any information about dimensionless constant K.
3. Theory of dimensions cannot be applied to formulae containing trigonometrical, exponential etc functions e.g. $y = a \sin \omega t$ and $N = N_0 e^{-\lambda t}$.
4. Theory of dimensions cannot be applied to derive formula containing more than three physical quantities, however, it can be used to check the formula. If a physical quantity depends upon more than three factors, then relation among them cannot

be established because we can have only three equations by equating the powers of M, L and T and only the values of three powers can be calculated.

THEORY OF DIMENSIONS APPLIED TO HEAT

1. In heat, temperature is assumed to be a fundamental quantity with dimension θ and unit K.
2. **Heat:** As Q represents energy, hence
$$[Q] = [ML^2T^{-2}]$$
and unit is calories.
3. **Sp. heat:** $Q = ms/\Delta\theta$
$$\therefore \quad L = Q/m\Delta\theta$$
Hence $[s] = [ML^2T^{-2}]/[M\theta] = [L^2T^{-2}\theta^{-1}]$
and unit is cal/gm °C
4. **Latent heat:** $Q = mL$
$$\therefore \quad L = Q/m$$
i.e. $[L] = [Q]/[m] = [ML^2T^{-2}]/[M] = [L^2T^{-2}]$
Its unit is cal/gm.
5. **Coefficient of thermal conductivity**
$$Q = K.A\,(\theta_1 - \theta_2)\,t/d$$
or $K = Qd/[A(\theta_1 - \theta_2)\,t]$
$$\therefore \quad K = \frac{(dQ/dt)}{[A(d\theta/dx)]} = \frac{[ML^2T^{-2}]/[T]}{[L^2][\theta/L]} = [MLT^{-3}\theta^{-1}]$$

THEORY OF DIMENSIONS APPLIED TO ELECTROSTATICS

1. While dealing with electrostatics or electricity normally current is treated as fundamental quantity with dimensions [A] and unit ampere.
2. **Charge:** $I = q/t$
or $q = It$
$$\therefore \quad [q] = [AT]$$
Unit of charge = Ampere × sec = coulomb.
3. **Potential:** $V = W/q$,
$$\therefore \quad [V] = \frac{[W]}{[q]} = \frac{[ML^2T^{-2}]}{[AT]} = [ML^2T^{-3}A^{-1}]$$
Its unit is joule/coulomb or Volt.
4. **Intensity of electric field:**
$$E = \frac{F}{q};$$
$$\therefore \quad [E] = \frac{[F]}{[q]} = \frac{[MLT^{-2}]}{[AT]} = [MLT^{-3}A^{-1}]$$
Its unit is $\frac{\text{newton}}{\text{culomb}}$ or $\frac{\text{Volt}}{\text{metre}}$.
5. **Capacity:** $q = CV$
or $C = \frac{q}{V} = \frac{q}{Q/q} = \frac{q^2}{W}$
$$\therefore \quad [C] = \frac{[A^2T^2]}{[ML^2T^{-2}]} = [M^{-1}L^{-2}T^4A^2]$$
Its unit is coulomb/volt or farad.

THEORY OF DIMENSIONS APPLIED TO ELECTRICITY

1. **Resistance:** $V = IR$
or $R = V/I = W/qI$
$$\therefore \quad [R] = \frac{[W]}{[q][I]} = \frac{[ML^2T^{-2}]}{[AT][A]} = [ML^2T^{-3}A^{-2}]$$
Its unit is volt/amp. or ohm.
2. **Conductance:** $C = \frac{1}{R}$
Hence, $[C] = \frac{1}{[R]} = [M^{-1}L^{-2}T^3A^2]$

Its unit is $(\text{ohm})^{-1}$ or mho.

3. **Specific resistance (r) or resistivity:**

$$R = \rho(l/A)$$

or $$\rho = RA/l$$

$$\therefore \quad [\rho] = \frac{[ML^2T^{-3}A^{-2}]\,[L^2]}{[L]}$$

$$= [ML^3T^{-3}A^{-2}]$$

Its unit is ohm × metre or ohm × cm.

4. **Conductivity or specific conductance (σ):**

It is defined as

(i) $$\sigma = 1/\rho$$

or $$[\sigma] = 1/[\rho] = [M^{-1}L^{-3}T^3A^2]$$

Its unit is $(\text{ohms} \times \text{metre})^{-1}$ or mhos/ metre

(ii) σ can also be defined as

$$J = \sigma E$$

or $$\sigma = \frac{J}{E} = \frac{I/A}{V/l} = \frac{Il}{VA}$$

As $[V] = ML^2T^{-2}]/[AT]$

$$[\sigma] = \frac{[AL][AT]}{[ML^2T^{-2}][L^2]}$$

$$= [M^{-1}L^{-3}T^3A^2]$$

5. **Coefficient of self or mutual inductance:**

$$e = L\left(\frac{dI}{dt}\right) \text{ or } M\left(\frac{dI}{dt}\right)$$

$$\therefore \quad L = e\left(\frac{dt}{dI}\right) = \frac{W}{q}\left(\frac{T}{I}\right)$$

or $$[L] = \frac{[ML^2T^{-2}][T]}{[AT][A]}$$

$$= [ML^2T^{-2}A^{-2}]$$

Its unit is volt × sec/amp or ohms × sec or henry.

DIMENSIONS OF SOME COMPOSITE QUANTITIES

1. Quantities like $\frac{1}{2}qV$ or $\frac{1}{2}cV^2$ or $\frac{1}{2}LI^2$ or VIt or I^2Rt etc. are all equivalent to work or energy. Hence the unit of all these quantities is joule (J) and dimensions are $[ML^2T^{-2}]$.

2. *(a)* Unit of the quantity (L/R) is henry/ohm

   As henry = ohms × sec

   hence, unit of L/R is = sec

   i.e. $[L/R] = [T]$

   (b) Similarly, unit of product CR is farad × ohm

   or $\frac{\text{coulomb}}{\text{volt}} \times \frac{\text{volt}}{\text{amp}}$ or sec.

   i.e. $[CR] = [T]$

   (c) Also, unit of product $\sqrt{LC}$ is

   $\sqrt{[\text{henry} \times \text{farad}]}$

   or $\sqrt{[\text{ohm} \times \text{sec} \times (\text{coulomb/volt})]}$

   or $\sqrt{[(\text{volt/amp}) \times \text{sec} \times (\text{coulomb/volt})]}$

   or $\sqrt{[\text{sec}^2]}$ or sec

   i.e. $[\sqrt{LC}] = [T]$.

MULTIPLE CHOICE QUESTIONS

1. The number of particles crossing the unit area perpendicular to the Z-axis per unit time is given by

$$N = -D\frac{N_2 - N_1}{Z_2 - Z_1}$$

where N_2 and N_1 are the number of particles per unit volume at Z_2 and Z_1 respectively. What is the dimensional formula for D?

(a) $M^0L^{-1}T^2$ (b) $M^0L^{-1}T^{-1}$
(c) $M^0L^2T^{-1}$ (d) $M^0L^2T^2$

2. The dimensional formula for change in momentum is same as that for
(a) force (b) impulse
(c) acceleration (d) velocity

3. The dimensional formula for the time rate of change of impulse is same as that for
(a) force (b) impulse
(c) power (d) energy

4. The dimensions of angular frequency are the same as that of the
(a) frequency (b) time period
(c) angle (d) angle/frequency

5. The dimensional formula for electromotive force is same as that for
(a) force (b) energy
(c) potential (d) current

6. The dimensional formula for strain is same as that for
(a) stress (b) modulus of elasticity
(c) thrust (d) angle of twist

7. The dimensional formula for angular frequency is same as that for
(a) angle (b) frequency
(c) angle × frequency (d) angle/frequency

8. What are the dimensions of force × displacement/time in length?
(a) −2 (b) 0
(c) 2 (d) none of the above

9. The Vander Waal equation is $\left(p + \frac{a}{V^2}\right)$ $(V - b) = RT$ where p is pressure, V is molar volume and T is the temperature of the given sample of gas. R is called molar gas constant, a and b are called Van der Waal constants. Which of the following does not possess the same dimensional formula as that for RT?
(a) pV (b) pb
(c) $\frac{a}{V^2}$ (d) $\frac{ab}{V^2}$

10. The Vander Waal equation is $\left(p + \frac{a}{V^2}\right)$ $(V - b) = RT$ where p is pressure, V is molar volume and T is the temperature of the given sample of gas. R is called the molar gas constant, a and b are called Vander Waal constants. The dimensional formula for a is same as that for
(a) V^2 (b) p
(c) pV^2 (d) RT

11. The Vander Waal equation is $\left(p + \frac{a}{V^2}\right)(V - b) = RT$ where p is pressure, V is molar volume and T is the temperature of the given sample of gas. R is called molar gas constant, a and b are called Van der Waal constants. The dimensional formula for b is same as that for
(a) p (b) V
(c) pV^2 (d) RT

12. Which of the following is the dimensional formula for the gravitational constant?
(a) $M^{-1}L^3T^{-2}$ (b) $M^2L^2T^{-2}$
(c) $M^0L^0T^0$ (d) $M^{-2}L^{-2}T^{-2}$

13. The dimensions of (velocity)^2/radius are the same as that of
(a) Planck's constant
(b) gravitational constant
(c) dielectric constant
(d) none of the above

14. Which of the following pairs of physical quantities does not possess same dimensional formula?
(a) impulse and momentum

(b) pressure and modulus of elasticity
(c) thrust and force
(d) work and stress

15. The Van der Waal equation is $\left(p + \frac{a}{V^2}\right)(V - b) = RT$ where p is pressure, V is molar volume and T is the temperature of the given sample of gas. R is called molar gas constant, a and b are called Vander Waal constants. The dimensional formula for RT is same as that for
(a) energy (b) force
(c) specific heat (d) latent heat

16. The Vander Waal equation is $\left(p + \frac{a}{V^2}\right)(V - b) = RT$ where p is pressure, V is molar volume and T is the temperature of the given sample of gas. R is called molar gas constant, a and b are called Van der Waal constants. The dimensional formula for $\frac{ab}{RT}$ is
(a) ML^5T^{-2} (b) $M^0L^3T^0$
(c) $ML^{-1}T^{-2}$ (d) none of the above

17. In the relation $y = a \cos(\omega t + kx)$, the dimensional formula for k is
(a) M^0LT (b) $M^0L^{-1}T^0$
(c) M^0LT^{-1} (d) $M^0L^{-1}T^{-1}$

18. Which of the following pairs does not have the same dimensions?
(a) frequency and angular frequency
(b) angular velocity and velocity gradient
(c) velocity gradient and angular frequency
(d) angular frequency and potential gradient

19. The dimensional formula for the angular momentum is same as that for
(a) Planck's constant
(b) impulse
(c) torque
(d) gravitational constant

20. Which of the following does not have same dimensions as the pressure?
(a) stress (b) thrust
(c) bulk modulus (d) radiation pressure

21. If g is the acceleration due to gravity and R is the radius of earth, then the dimensional formula for gR is
(a) ML^2T^{-2} (b) $M^0L^2T^{-2}$
(c) $M^2L^2T^{-2}$ (d) $M^0L^0T^0$

22. If m is mass and k is the force per unit length, what is the dimensional formula for m/k?
(a) $M^0L^0T^0$ (b) $M^0L^2T^0$
(c) $M^0L^0T^2$ (d) $M^2L^0T^0$

23. In the relation $dy/dt = 2\omega \sin(\omega t + \phi_0)$, the dimensional formula for $(\omega t + \phi_0)$ is
(a) MLT (b) MLT^0
(c) ML^0T^0 (d) $M^0L^0T^0$

24. In the relation $y = r \sin(\omega t + kx)$, the dimensional formula for kx is same as
(a) r/ω (b) r/y
(c) $\omega t/r$ (d) $yr/\omega t$

25. Which of the following is not a dimensionless quantity?
(a) strain
(b) solid angle
(c) dielectric constant
(d) Planck's constant

26. Which of the following pair does not possess same dimensions?
(a) impulse and momentum
(b) angular frequency and velocity gradient
(c) stress and strain
(d) surface tension and surface energy

27. Which of the following quantities does not possess the same dimensions as the other two quantities listed below?
(a) frequency (b) velocity gradient
(c) angular speed (d) potential gradient

28. Which of the following pairs of physical quantities possess same dimensions?
(a) force and surface tension
(b) frequency and velocity gradient
(c) angular speed and solid angle
(d) Stefan's constant and Planck's constant

29. The equation which depicts the relation between the basic and derived units is called
(a) defining equation
(b) dimensional equation
(c) homogeneity equation
(d) none of the above

30. Given that v is the speed, r is radius and g is acceleration due to gravity. Which of the following is dimensionless?

(a) v^2r/g (b) v^2/rg
(c) v^2g/r (d) v^2rg

31. Which of the following is dimensionless quantity?
(a) gravitational constant
(b) molar gas constant
(c) relative density
(d) relative velocity

32. Which of the following have the same dimensions as v^2/r? Where v is the speed of the particle describing a circular path of radius r
(a) acceleration (b) momentum
(c) force (d) impulse

33. Which of the following does not possess the same dimensions as pressure?
(a) bulk modulus (b) energy density
(c) stress (d) energy gradient

34. Given that M is the mass suspended from a spring of force constant k. The dimensional formula for $[M/k]^{1/2}$ is same as that for
(a) frequency (b) time period
(c) velocity (d) wavelength

35. In the relation $x = R \cos(\omega t - kx)$, the dimensional formula for ωt is same as that for
(a) x/R (b) kx/R
(c) $k\omega/xt$ (d) $\omega R/k$

36. If n is the numerical value of the physical quantity in the system in which its unit is u, then which of the following relations is correct?
(a) $\frac{n}{u}$ = constant (b) $\frac{u}{n}$ = constant
(c) nu = constant (d) none of the above

37. What is dimensional formula of gravitational field strength?
(a) M^0LT^{-2} (b) MLT^{-2}
(c) ML^2T^{-2} (d) $M^2T^2L^{-1}$

38. Which of the following is the dimensional formula for latent heat?
(a) ML^2T^{-2} (b) $M^0L^2T^{-2}$
(c) M^2LT^{-2} (d) M^0LT^{-2}

39. Given that g is acceleration due to gravity and R is the radius of the earth. Then $[g/R]^{1/2}$ possesses the dimensions of
(a) orbital speed (b) angular speed
(c) escape velocity (d) time period

40. Which of the following have the same dimensions as Planck's constant?
(a) momentum of force
(b) force/distance
(c) moment of momentum
(d) momentum/distance

41. Given that $\tan\theta = v^2/rg$ gives the angle of banking of the cyclist going round the curve. Here v is the speed of cyclist, r is the radius of the curve and g is acceleration due to gravity. Which of the following statements about this relation is true?
(a) it is both dimensionally as well as numerically correct
(b) it is neither dimensionally correct nor numerically correct
(c) it is dimensionally correct but not numerically
(d) it is numerically correct but not dimensionally

42. If L and R denote the inductance and resistance, then the dimensional formula for R/L is same as that for
(a) frequency (b) time period
(c) $(\text{frequency})^2$ (d) $(\text{time period})^2$

43. If C and R denote the capacitance and resistance then the dimensional formula for CR is same as that for
(a) frequency (b) time period
(c) $(\text{frequency})^2$ (d) $(\text{time period})^2$

44. If C and L denote the capacitance and inductance, then the dimensional formula for CL is same as that for
(a) frequency (b) time period
(c) $(\text{frequency})^2$ (d) $(\text{time period})^2$

45. Given that T stands for time period and l stands for length of simple pendulum. If g is the acceleration due to gravity, then which of the following statements about the relation $T^2 = l/g$ is correct?
(a) it is correct both dimensionally as well as numerically
(b) it is neither dimensionally correct nor numerically
(c) it is dimensionally correct but not numerically
(d) it is numerically correct but not dimensionally

46. If energy E, velocity V and time T are taken as the fundamental units, the dimensional formula for surface tension is

(a) $EV^{-2}T^{-2}$ (b) $E^{-2}VT^{-2}$
(c) $E^{-2}V^{-2}T$ (d) $E^{-2}V^{-2}T^{-2}$

47. A thermal physical quantity is measured in calorie per gram. Its dimensional formula will be

(a) ML^0T^{-2} (b) $M^2L^2T^0$
(c) M^2LT^{-2} (d) $M^0L^2T^{-2}$

48. The frequency of vibration of a string is given by

$$v = \frac{p}{2l}\left[\frac{F}{m}\right]^{\frac{1}{2}}$$

Here p is the number of segments in which the string is divided, F is the tension in the string and l is its length. The dimensional formula for m is

(a) $M^0L^0T^0$ (b) $ML^{-1}T^0$
(c) ML^0T^{-1} (d) M^0LT^{-1}

49. Given that C denotes capacitance of a capacitor and V is the potential difference across its plates. Then the dimensions of CV^2 are same as that of

(a) force (b) torque
(c) momentum (d) power

50. The dimensions of $[\mu_0\varepsilon_0]^{-1/2}$ are the same as that of

(a) time period (b) wavelength
(c) frequency (d) velocity

ANSWERS

1	2	3	4	5	6	7	8	9	10
(c)	(b)	(a)	(a)	(c)	(d)	(b)	(c)	(c)	(c)
11	12	13	14	15	16	17	18	19	20
(b)	(a)	(d)	(d)	(a)	(d)	(b)	(d)	(a)	(b)
21	22	23	24	25	26	27	28	29	30
(b)	(c)	(d)	(b)	(d)	(c)	(d)	(b)	(b)	(b)
31	32	33	34	35	36	37	38	39	40
(c)	(a)	(d)	(b)	(a)	(c)	(a)	(b)	(b)	(c)
41	42	43	44	45	46	47	48	49	50
(a)	(a)	(b)	(d)	(c)	(a)	(d)	(b)	(b)	(d)

EXPLANATIONS

1. Here $[N] = M^0L^{-2}T^{-1}$;

$[N_1] = [N_2] = M^0L^{-3}T^0$

and $[Z_1] = [Z_2] = M^0LT^0$.

Hence $[D] = \frac{[N]}{[N_1]} \times [Z_1]$

$$= \frac{M^0L^{-2}T^{-1}}{M^0L^{-3}T^0} \times M^0LT^0$$

$$= M^0L^2T^{-1}.$$

2. Change in momentum = impulse.

3. Impulse = force × time. Hence rate of change of impulse is equal to force.

4. [Frequency] = $M^0L^0T^{-1}$. Same is true for angular frequency.

5. Electromotive force is the potential difference of a cell or battery in the open circuit.

6. Strain is dimensionless quantity. The angle is also a dimensionless quantity.

7. [Angular frequency] = $M^0L^0T^{-1}$.

8. $\left[\frac{\text{Force} \times \text{displacement}}{\text{time}}\right]$

$$= \frac{[MLT^{-2}][M^0LT^0]}{[M^0L^0T]} = ML^2T^{-3}.$$

9. $\left(p + \frac{a}{V^2}\right)(V - b) = RT.$

Hence $pV - pb + \frac{a}{V} - \frac{ab}{V^2} = RT$ ...(i)

Hence pV, pb, $\frac{a}{v}$ and ab/V^2 have the same dimensions as RT.

10. The dimensional formula for each of the term in $\left(p+\frac{a}{V^2}\right)$ is same. That is $[p]=\left[\frac{a}{V^2}\right]$.
Hence $[a]=[pV^2]$

11. The dimensional formula for each of the term in $(V-b)$ is same.
Since V is volume, therefore b also represents volume.

12. $(G)=[F][r^2]/[M_1][M_2]$
$= MLT^{-2}\times L^2/M\times M = M^{-1}L^3T^{-2}$

13. Dimensional formula of $(\text{velocity})^2 \div \text{radius}$
$= (M^0LT^{-1})^2/M^0LT^0$
$= M^0LT^{-2} = [\text{Acceleration}]$

14. $[\text{Work}] = ML^2T^{-2}$
and $[\text{stress}] = ML^{-1}T^2$

15. From equation

$$pV - pb + \frac{a}{V} - \frac{ab}{V^2} = RT, \text{ we find:}$$

$[pV] = [RT]$.
or $[RT] = [pV]$
$= (ML^{-1}T^{-2})(M^0L^3T^0)$
$= ML^2T^{-2}$
$= [\text{Energy}]$

16. From the equation

$$pV - pb + \frac{a}{V} - \frac{ab}{V^2} = RT, \text{ we find :}$$

$$\left[\frac{ab}{V^2}\right] = [RT]$$

or $$\left[\frac{ab}{RT}\right] = [V^2] = M^0L^6T^0$$

17. Here kx is dimensionless.
Hence $[k] = [1/x] = M^0L^{-1}T^0$

20. Thrust is the total force on the given area, where as pressure is force per unit area.

21. $[gR] = [M^0LT^{-2}][M^0LT^0] = M^0L^2T^{-2}$.

22. $[m/k]$ = [mass/(force/length)]
= [mass × length/force]
$= [ML^0T^0][M^0LT^0]/[MLT^{-2}]$
$= M^0L^0T^2$.

23. Here $(\omega t+\phi_0)$ is dimensionless.

24. Here $[r]=[y]$. So $[r/y]$ is dimensionless. Same is the case with kx.

25. $[\text{Planck's constant}] = ML^2T^{-1}$.

26. $[\text{Stress}] = ML^{-1}T^{-2}$ and $[\text{strain}] = M^0L^0T^0$.

27. Dimensions of Frequency, Velocity gradient and angular speed are same. But that of potential gradient are different.

28. [velocity gradient] = [velocity/distance]
$= M^0LT^{-1}/M^0LT^0 = M^0L^0T^{-1}$ = [frequency].

29. Dimensional equation equates the derived unit to its dimensional formula.

30. $$\left[\frac{v^2}{rg}\right] = \frac{M^0L^2T^{-2}}{[M^0LT^0]\,[M^0LT^{-2}]} = M^0L^0T^0.$$

31. Relative density = Density of substance/ Density of water at 4°C. Relative density being a ratio of same quantities, it is dimensionless.

32. $$\left[\frac{v^2}{r}\right] = \frac{[M^0LT^{-1}]^2}{M^0LT^0}$$
$= M^0LT^{-2}$ = (acceleration)

33. [Energy gradient] = [Energy/distance]
$= [ML^2T^{-2}]/M^0LT^0 = MLT^{-2}$. But the dimensional formula for the quantities listed at (a), (b) and (c) is $ML^{-1}T^{-2}$.

34. Here $[k]$ = force/length $= ML^0T^{-2}$.

Hence $$\left[\frac{M}{k}\right]^{\frac{1}{2}} = \left[\frac{ML^0T^0}{ML^0T^{-2}}\right]^{\frac{1}{2}} = M^0L^0T.$$

35. Here ωt is is an angle. It is dimensionless. Same is true for x/R, because $[x]=[R]=M^0LT^0$.

36. Here *nu* gives the magnitude of the physical quantity, which is always constant.

37. [Gravitational field strength]
= [gravitational force per unit mass]
= [gravitational acceleration]
$= M^0LT^{-2}$.

38. Latent heat = heat absorbed per unit mass
Hence [Latent heat] = [heat/mass]
= [energy/mass]
$= [ML^2T^{-2}/ML^0T^0]$
$= M^0L^2T^{-2}$.

39. $$\left[\frac{g}{R}\right]^{\frac{1}{2}} = \left[\frac{M^0LT^{-2}}{M^0LT^0}\right]^{\frac{1}{2}}$$
$= M^0L^0T^{-1}$ = [angular speed]

40. [Planck's constant] = [Moment of momentum]
= [Momentum × distance] $= ML^2T^{-1}$.

41. Here [tan θ] = [v^2/rg] = $M^0L^0T^0$. Also, in the actual expression for the angle of banking of a road, there is no numerical factor involved. Therefore, the relation is both numerically and dimensionally correct.

42. For RL circuit $I = I_0e^{-Rt/L}$.
Here [Rt/L] is dimensionless.
Hence [R/L] = [$1/t$] = [frequency]

43. For RC circuit $q = q_0e^{-t/RC}$. Here [t/RC] is dimensionless number. Hence [t] = [RC] = [time period]

44. Time period of CL oscillations is given by $2\pi\sqrt{LC}$. Hence [CL]^2 = [time period]^2.

45. The correct relation for time period of simple pendulum is $T = 2\pi(l/g)^{1/2}$. So, the given relation is numerically incorrect as the factor 2π is missing.

46. [E] = ML^2T^{-2}, [V] = M^0LT^{-1}. [T] = M^0L^0T.

$$[\text{Surface tension}] = \frac{\text{Force}}{\text{Length}}$$

$$= \frac{MLT^{-2}}{M^0LT^0} = \frac{ML^2T^{-2}}{M^0L^2T^0} = \frac{E}{M^0L^2T^0}$$

$$= \frac{E\,T^{-2}}{M^0L^2T^{-2}} = \frac{E\,T^{-2}}{V^2} = EV^{-2}T^{-2}.$$

47. Calorie per gram = [heat/gram] = [Energy/mass] = (ML^2T^{-2}/ML^0T^0) = $M^0L^2T^{-2}$.

48. Here m represents mass per unit length of the string.

49. Energy stored in a capacitor = ½CV^2.
Hence [CV^2] = [Energy] = [torque].

50. $[\mu_0\varepsilon_0]^{-1/2}$ = [velocity of light in vacuum].
Also note that [ε_0] = $M^{-1}L^{-3}T^4I^2$ and [μ_0] = MLT^2I^{-2}.
Hence $[\mu_0\varepsilon_0]^{-1/2} = [L^{-2}T^4]^{-1/2}$ = M^0LT^{-1} = [velocity].

UNIT-2

KINEMATICS

DESCRIPTION OF MOTION IN ONE DIMENSION

MOTION

Motion is the change in position of the object with respect to time. It is of two types–

(i) Absolute motion (ii) Relative motion

Absolute Motion : Absolute motion is the motion with respect to a body which is at absolute rest. This type of motion is impossible.

Relative Motion : Relative motion is the motion with respect to a body which is at relative rest. For example, a person sitting in a moving train is at relative rest with respect to the train but it is in relative motion with respect to a person on the platform.

On the basis of change in position (x, y, z coordinates) of the object with respect to the surrounding. Motion can be divided into three parts.

(i) **Motion in One Dimension :** If only one of the three coordinates specifying the position of the object, change with respect to time, then the motion is called one dimensional motion. In this type of motion, the path followed by the body is a straight line, e.g., the motion of a man on a level road, motion of train on horizontal rails, motion under gravity etc.

(ii) **Motion in Two Dimensions :** If any two of the three coordinates specifying the position of the object change with respect to time, then the motion is called two dimensional motion. In this type of motion the body moves in a plane, e.g., circular motion and projectile motion.

(iii) **Motion in Three Dimensions :** If all the three coordinates of the position of the body change with respect to time, then the motion is called three dimensional motion. Examples of this type of motion are the motion of a bird, aeroplane, or a kite in sky.

VARIOUS TERMS REGARDING MOTION

(i) **Displacement :** Displacement is the change in position of the body in a certain direction. It is a vector quantity. Magnitude of displacement is the shortest distance between the initial and final positions and is the vector drawn from initial to final position is called displacement.

(ii) **Distance :** Distance is the total actual path covered by the body between initial and final states. It is a scalar quantity. Displacement may be positive, negative or zero but distance is always positive.

(iii) **Velocity :** Rate of change of displacement with respect to time is called velocity.

$$\text{Velocity} \quad \vec{v} = \frac{\text{displacement}}{\text{time}} = \frac{\vec{dx}}{dt}$$

$$\text{or} \quad \vec{v} = \frac{\vec{x}_2 - \vec{x}_1}{t_2 - t_1} \text{ m/sec,}$$

where $\vec{x}_2$ and $\vec{x}_1$ are the positions of the particle at instants t_1 and t_2.

It is a vector quantity, Velocity may be positive or negative.

(iv) **Uniform Velocity :** The velocity of an object is said to be uniform if it covers equal displacement in equal intervals of time. There is not acceleration if the body moves with uniform velocity.

(v) **Variable Velocity :** An object is said to have variable velocity if it covers unequal displacement in equal interval of time. Acceleration necessarily present in the motion. In this case either direction of velocity or magnitude or both change w.r.t. time, e.g., speed is constant in uniform circular motion but velocity is variable.

(vi) **Average Velocity :**

$$\text{Average velocity} = \frac{\text{Total displacement}}{\text{Total time}}$$

Average velocity is zero if the body returns to starting point in the given time interval.

Note : If the body covers first half distance with velocity V_1 and next half with velocity V_2 then

average velocity $= \dfrac{2V_1V_2}{V_1+V_2}$.

If a body travels with uniform velocity V_1 for time t_1 and with uniform velocity V_2 for time t_2, then

average velocity $= \dfrac{V_1t_1+V_2t_2}{t_1+t_2}$

(vii) Speed : Speed is the scalar form of velocity. It is defined as the distance travelled in one second. If the body covers a distance d in time t, then

speed $v = \dfrac{d}{t}$ m/sec.

(viii) Variable Speed : If the body covers unequal distance in equal interval of time, then it is said to be moving with a variable speed. Acceleration is always present if the speed of the body is variable.

Uniform Speed : The speed of the body is uniform if it covers equal distance in equal interval of time. Acceleration may or may not be there in the motion if the body is moving with uniform speed, e.g., a body moving in uniform circular motion has uniform speed but variable velocity, therefore, the acceleration is present in the circular motion.

(ix) Average Speed :

Average speed $= \dfrac{\text{Total distance}}{\text{Total time}}$

Note : If the body covers first half distance with speed u and next half with speed v then the average speed is $2\,uv/(u+v)$. If the body covers first one-third distance at speed V_1, next one-third at speed V_2 and last one-third at speed V_3, then average speed

$$V = \frac{3V_1V_2V_3}{V_1V_2+V_1V_3+V_2V_3}$$

(x) Acceleration : Rate of change of velocity with respect of time is known as acceleration. It is a vector quantity. If $\Delta\vec{V}$ is the change in velocity in time Δt, then

$$\vec{a} = \frac{\Delta\vec{V}}{\Delta t} \quad \text{or} \quad a = \frac{d^2x}{dt^2}.$$

Negative acceleration is known as retardation, which indicates that the velocity of the object is decreasing with respect to time.

(xi) Uniform Acceleration : If the velocity of the body changes in equal amount during same time interval; then the acceleration of the body is said to be uniform acceleration. Acceleration is uniform when neither its direction nor magnitude change with respect to time.

(xii) Variable Acceleration : If the velocity of body changes in different amounts during same time interval, then the acceleration of the body is known as variable acceleration. Acceleration is variable if either its direction or magnitude or both change with respect to time. For example the acceleration in uniform circular motion.

UNIFORM MOTION AND UNIFORM VELOCITY

A body is said to be moving with uniform velocity if it covers equal displacement in equal interval of time. There is no acceleration in this type of motion and its v–t graph is a straight line parallel to time axis.

The area bounded between v–t curve and time axis in a particular time interval gives the displacement of the body during that time interval.

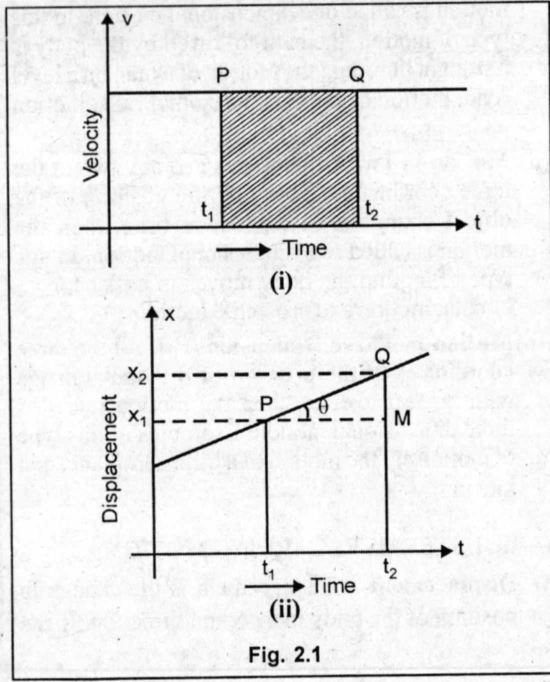

Fig. 2.1

In Fig. (i) the displacement of the body between time interval t_1 to t_2 = area $PQ\ t_1t_2$. The time-displacement graph of a body moving with uniform velocity is shown in Fig. From the graph, displacement $(x_2 - x_1)$ in time interval $(t_2 - t_1)$ can be found. This gives the velocity 'v' in this interval as

$$v = \frac{x_2 - x_1}{t_2 - t_1} \text{ or } v = \frac{QM}{PM}$$

$$= \tan\theta = \text{slope of } x - t \text{ graph.}$$

Thus, the slope of $x - t$ graph gives the velocity. Equation of motion of uniform motion is

$$x(t) = (x_0) + vt \qquad \text{...(i)}$$

where $x(t)$ is the displacement at any instant t and (x_0) is the displacement at $t = 0$. At a later instant t'.

$$x' = (x_0) + vt'$$

$$\therefore \quad x' - x = \{(x_0) + vt'\} - \{(x_0) + vt\} \qquad \text{...(ii)}$$

$$x' - x = v(t' - t)$$

or

$$x' = x + v(t' - t) \qquad \text{...(iii)}$$

If we denote $x - x_0 = s$ = distance travelled by the body in t sec, then

$$s = vt \qquad \text{...(iv)}$$

Equation (i), (ii), (iii) and (iv) can be used to analyse the kinematics of an object moving with uniform speed.

VARIABLE OR NON-UNIFORM MOTION

The velocity of the body is variable in this type of motion and the body covers unequal displacement in equal interval of time. If the direction or magnitude (or both) of velocity change with respect to time, then the motion is said to be variable or non-uniform.

Velocity-Time Graph in Variable or Non-Uniform Motion

(i) In the variable motion or non-uniform motion v–t graph is a straight line inclined at some angle with the time axis.

(ii) Any two points A and B are taken on the curve and two perpendiculars are drawn from it on velocity axis as well as on time axis. Now the acceleration can be calculated as follows

$$a = \frac{v_2 - v_1}{t_2 - t_1} = \frac{BC}{AC} = \tan\theta = \text{slope of } v - t \text{ graph.}$$

(iii) This graph is important because its study gives us to distance as well as displacement covered by the body in a given time interval.

Distance travelled by the body in a given time interval = Area of v–t graph (during that interval) added without considering sign.

Displacement = Area of v–t graph (during that interval) added with sign, e.g., in the figure given below

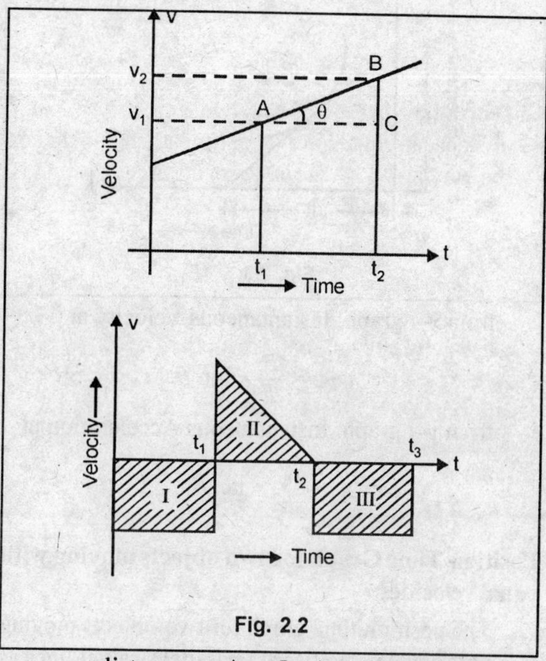

Fig. 2.2

$$\text{distance} = \text{Area I} + \text{Area II} + \text{Area III}$$

$$\text{Displacement} = \text{Area II} - \text{Area III} - \text{Area I}$$

(iv) We can plot time-displacement and time-acceleration graph with the help of above curve.

INSTANTANEOUS VELOCITY AND INSTANTANEOUS ACCELERATION

If the displacement and velocity graphs are curves instead of straight line then the velocity and acceleration at any instant can be calculated by drawing a tangent at that point and finding its slope. These values of velocities and acceleration are called instantaneous velocity and instantaneous acceleration respectively.

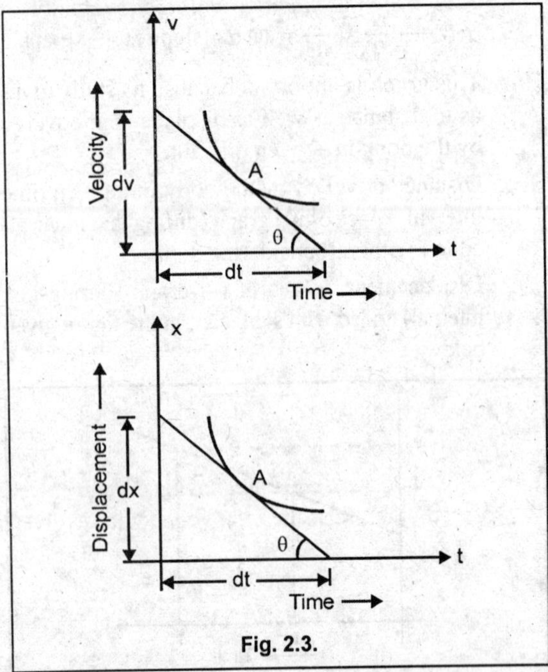

Fig. 2.3.

from x–t graph, Instantaneous Velocity at

$$A = \frac{dx}{dt} = \tan\theta$$

from v–t graph, Instantaneous Acceleration at

$$A = \frac{dV}{dt} = \tan\theta$$

Position-Time Graph for two objects moving with equal velocities

The position time graph for two objects moving with equal velocities are parallel straight lines as shown in figure. The objects P and Q are moving with equal velocities from position x_0 and x_0' at $t = 0$.

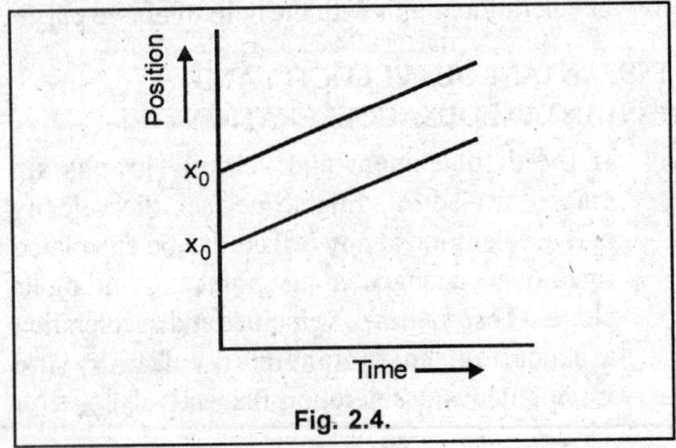

Fig. 2.4.

Position-Time Graph for two bodies moving with different velocities

The position time graph of two objects P and Q moving with different velocities (i.e., with some relative velocity) are straight lines of different slopes inclined to the time axis. The two lines must intersect each other. The position and time coordinates of the point of intersection indicates the place and time of their meeting.

From the graphs it can be concluded that

(i) The sign of their relative displacement $x_Q - x_P$ reverses after the point of meeting, i.e., if $x_Q > x_P$ before meeting then $x_Q < x_P$ after meeting.

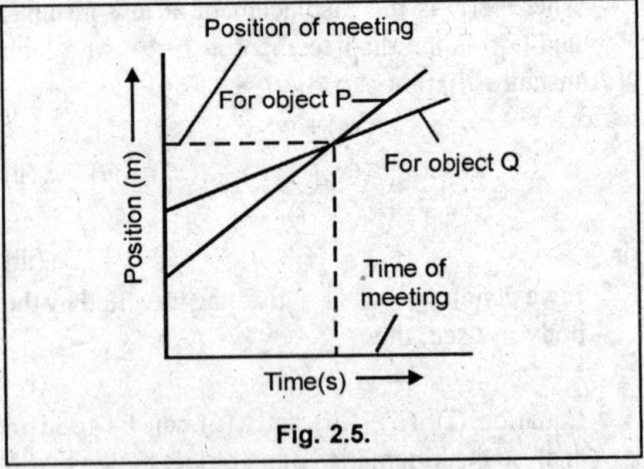

Fig. 2.5.

(ii) If the objects are moving in opposite directions then the magnitude of their relative velocity is $(v_P + v_Q)$. Therefore, their relative velocity is more than the velocity of either object, i.e., the relative velocity is greater than v_P as well as v_Q. Thus the two objects appear to move very fast.

ACCELERATION-TIME GRAPH

In acceleration-time graph aceleration of the body is plotted on Y-axis and time on X-axis. It has following important characteristics of this graph are as follows

(i) If the graph is straight line parallel to time axis, then the acceleration is constant.

(ii) If the graph is a straight line inclined with time axis but with positive slope, then the acceleration is uniformly increasing.

(iii) If the graph is a straight line inclined with time axis but with negative slope, then the

acceleration of the body is continuously decreasing.

(iv) The area under a–t graph and time axis gives the change in velocity of the body during that time interval.

(v) v–t graph can be plotted by a–t graph.

EQUATIONS OF MOTION

The equations of motion are as follows :

(i) $v = u + at$

(ii) $s = ut + (1/2)\,at^2$

(iii) $v^2 = u^2 + 2as$

where u = initial velocity, v = final velocity after t seconds, a = acceleration, s = distance travelled in t seconds.

Note : The distance travelled in nth second is given by

$$S_n = u + (2n-1)\,a/2$$

MOTION UNDER GRAVITY

(a) Downward Motion (↓)

(i) $v = u + gt$

(ii) $h = ut + \frac{1}{2}gt^2$

(iii) $v^2 = u^2 + 2gh$

(b) Upward Motion (↑)

(i) $v = u - gt$

(ii) $h = ut - \frac{1}{2}gt^2$

(iii) $v^2 = u^2 - 2gh$

RELATIVE VELOCITY

If the distance between the two bodies is changing either in magnitude or direction or both then each is said to have a relative velocity with respect to other.

The relative velocity of first body with respect to the second body is obtained by the vector addition of the negative velocity (velocity in opposite direction) of second body to the velocity of first body.

PARTICULARS CASES

(a) If the two bodies A and B are moving with velocities u and v in the same direction, then

Relative velocity of A with respect to $B = u - v$

Relative velocity of B with respect to $A = v - u$

(b) If the two bodies A and B are moving in opposite directions with velocities u and v then, relative velocity is given by

Relative velocity of A w.r.t. $B = u + v$

Relative velocity of B w.r.t. $A = -(u + v)$

(c) If the above two bodies are moving at right angles to each other, then the relative velocity is given by $V_{\text{rel}} = \sqrt{(u^2 + v^2)}$.

(d) If the above two bodies are moving, making an angle θ with each other, then the relative velocity is given by $V_{\text{rel}} = \sqrt{(u^2 + v^2 + 2uv\cos\theta)}$.

(e) If rain drops are falling vertically with a velocity v and a person is walking horizontally with a velocity u, then he should hold an umbrella at an angle θ with vertical given by $\tan\theta = u/v$, to prevent himself from being wet.

(f) If a boat moving with a velocity v in still water crosses a river which is flowing with a velocity u, then :

(i) To reach the opposite bank in minimum time, the boat must move at right angles to the current.

(ii) To go straight across to the opposite bank, the boat must move at an angle $\theta = \sin^{-1}\left(\frac{u}{v}\right)$ with the vertical or $\left[90^\circ + \sin^{-1}\frac{u}{v}\right]$ with the direction of current.

MOTION IN TWO AND THREE DIMENSIONS

SCALAR AND VECTOR QUANTITIES

The physical quantities are of two types: Scalars, Vectors.

(a) **Scalar Quantities:** There are many physical quantities which are completely described by their magnitude only (i.e. by a numerical value with

appropriate unit) and are added according to the ordinary rules of algebra.

(b) **Vector Quantities:**

(i) There are certain physical quantities whose complete description not only requires their magnitude (i.e., a numerical value with appropriate unit) but also their direction in space, e.g. velocity of a train.

(ii) Thus, the physical quantities which have magnitude and direction and which can be added according to the triangle rule, are called Vector quantities. Other examples of Vector quantities are displacement, acceleration, force, momentum, electric field, etc.

(c) **Types of Vectors**

(i) Like Vectors : Two vectors are said to be like vectors if they have same direction but different magnitude.

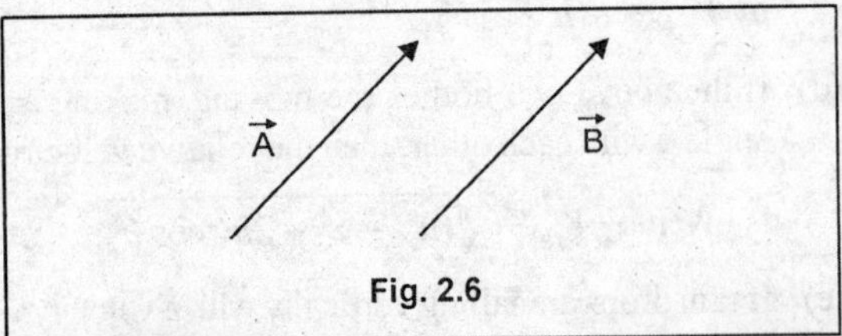

Fig. 2.6

(ii) Equal Vectors: Two vectors are equal, if they have the same magnitude and same or parallel directions.

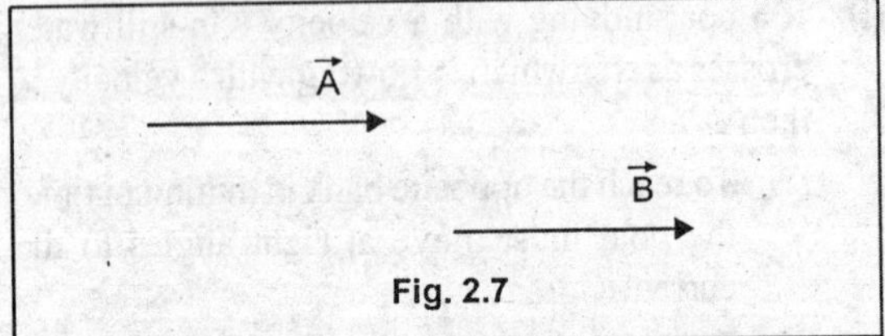

Fig. 2.7

(iii) Unlike Vectors: The vectors having opposite direction and different magnitude, are called unlike vectors.

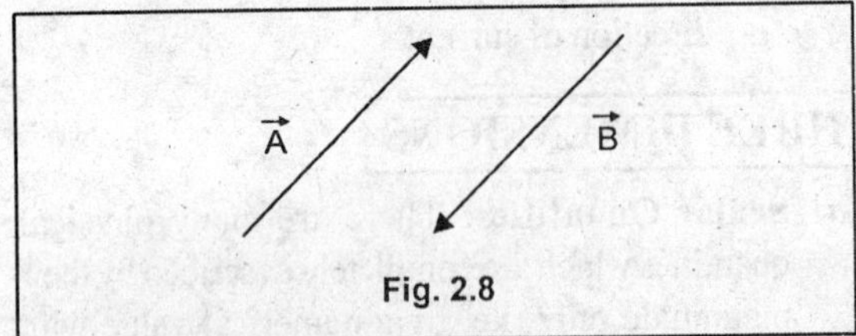

Fig. 2.8

(iv) Opposite Vectors: The vectors having same magnitude but opposite direction, are called opposite vectors.

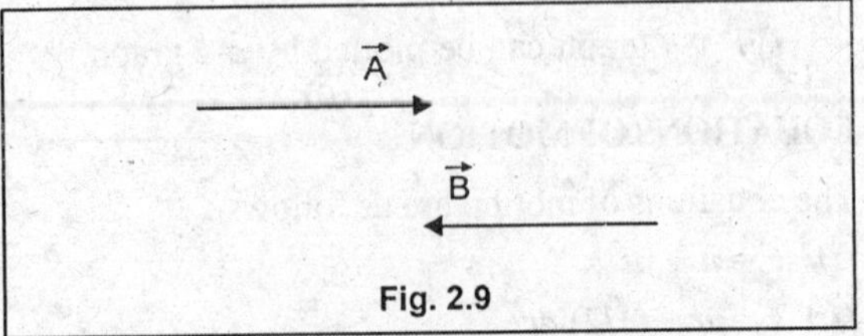

Fig. 2.9

(v) Unit Vectors: A vector divided by its magnitude is called a unit vector along the direction of the vector. Obviously, the unit vector has unit magnitude and direction is the same as that of the given vector.

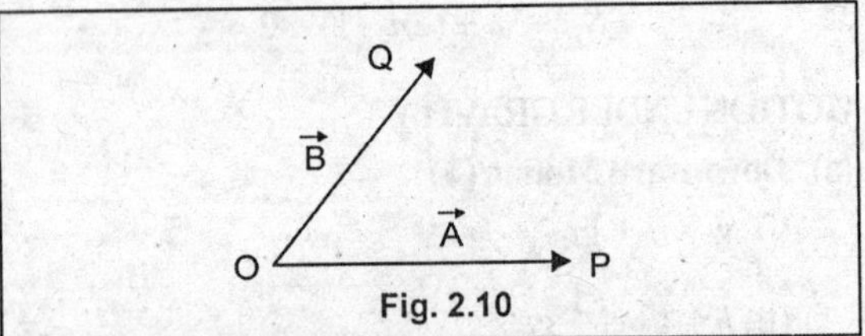

Fig. 2.10

A unit vector in the direction of some vector $\vec{A}$ is written as $\hat{A}$ and is read as 'A cap' or 'A hat'. Therefore, by definition.

$$\hat{A} = \frac{\vec{A}}{A} \quad \text{or} \quad \vec{A} = \hat{A}A$$

(d) **Null Vector:** It is defined as a vector having zero magnitude. It has a direction which is indeterminate as its magnitude is zero.

VECTOR ADDITION

(i) **Triangle law of vector addition:** Suppose two vectors $\vec{A}$ and $\vec{B}$ represent both in magnitude and direction the sides $\overrightarrow{PQ}$ and $\overrightarrow{QR}$ of the triangle PQR taken in same order. Then according to triangle law of vector addition, the resultant $\vec{R}$ is represented by the closing side PR taken in the opposite order.

(a) Magnitude of the resultant $\vec{R}$: Draw a perpendicular RS from the point R, on the side

PQ which meets the line PQ at point S when produced forward.

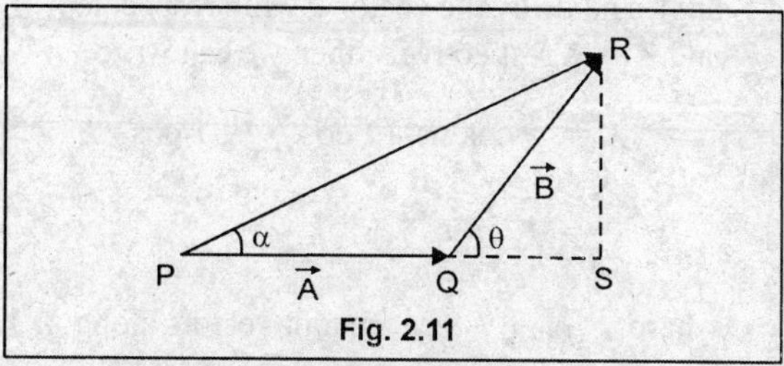

Fig. 2.11

Then, from the Δ PSR, we get

$$PR^2 = PS^2 + SR^2$$
$$= (PQ + QS)^2 + (SR)^2$$
$$= (PQ)^2 + (QS)^2 + 2PQ.QS + (SR)^2$$

But

$$(QS)^2 + (SR)^2 = (QR)^2$$

$$\therefore \quad PR^2 = PQ^2 + QR^2 + 2PQ.QS \quad ...(i)$$

From right angled triangle QRS, we get

$$\cos\theta = \frac{QS}{QR}$$

or $\quad QS = QR\cos\theta$

Therefore, equation (i) becomes

$$PR^2 = PQ^2 + QR^2 + 2\,PQ.QR\cos\theta$$

Now, $\quad PR = R, PQ = A, QR = B$

$$\therefore \quad R^2 = A^2 + B^2 + 2\,AB\cos\theta$$

$$\Rightarrow \quad R = \sqrt{A^2 + B^2 + 2AB\cos\theta} \quad ...(ii)$$

(b) Direction of the resultant $\vec{R}$: Suppose the resultant $\vec{R}$ makes an angle α with the direction of $\vec{A}$. Then from right angled triangle PRS, we get

$$\tan\alpha = \frac{RS}{PS} = \frac{RS}{PQ + QS} \quad ...(iii)$$

Now, $\quad PQ = A,$

$QS = B\cos\theta$

and $\quad RS = B\sin\theta$

$$\therefore \quad \tan\alpha = \frac{B\sin\theta}{A + B\cos\theta} \quad ...(iv)$$

(ii) Parallelogram law of Vector Addition: Suppose two vectors $\vec{A}$ and $\vec{B}$ inclined to each other at an angle θ be represented in magnitude and direction both by the concurrent sides $\overrightarrow{PQ}$ and $\overrightarrow{PT}$ of the parallelogram $PQRT$ (Fig. 3.7). Then according to parallelogram law, resultant of $\vec{A}$ and $\vec{B}$ is represented both in magnitude and direction by the diagonal $\overrightarrow{PR}$ of the parallelogram.

(a) Magnitude of the resultant $\vec{R}$: Drop a perpendicular from the point R on the line PQ which meets the line PQ at some point S (Fig. 2.12).

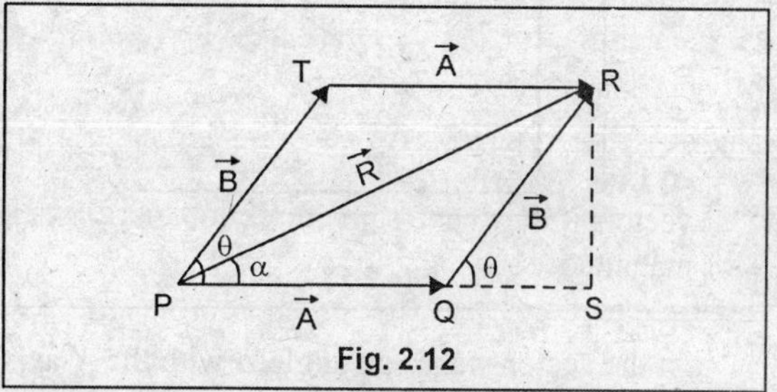

Fig. 2.12

From right handed triangle PSR, we get

$$PR^2 = PS^2 + SR^2$$
$$= (PQ + QS)^2 + SR^2$$
$$= PQ^2 + QS^2 + 2PQ.QS + SR^2$$

$$\because \quad QS^2 + SR^2 = QR^2$$

$$\therefore \quad PR^2 = PQ^2 + QR^2 + 2PQ.QS$$

Now $\quad PR = R, PQ = A$ and $QR = B$

Further, $\quad QS = B\cos\theta$

$$\therefore \quad R^2 = A^2 + B^2 + 2\,AB\cos\theta$$

$$\Rightarrow \quad R = \sqrt{A^2 + B^2 + 2AB\cos\theta} \quad ...(i)$$

(b) Direction of the resultant $\vec{R}$: Suppose the resultant vector $\vec{R}$ makes an angle α with vector $\vec{A}$. Then from right angled triangle PRS, we get

$$\tan\alpha = \frac{RS}{PS}$$

$$= \frac{RS}{PQ + QS} = \frac{B\sin\theta}{A + B\cos\theta}.$$

RESOLUTION OF VECTORS

(i) The process of splitting up a vector into two or more vectors is called resolution of a vector. The

vectors into which a given vector is split are called component vectors. The resolution of a vector into two mutually perpendicular vectors is called the rectangular resolution of vector in a plane or two dimensions.

(ii) Figure 2.13 shows a vector $\overrightarrow{OR} = \vec{r}$ in the *X-Y* plane drawn from the origin *O*.

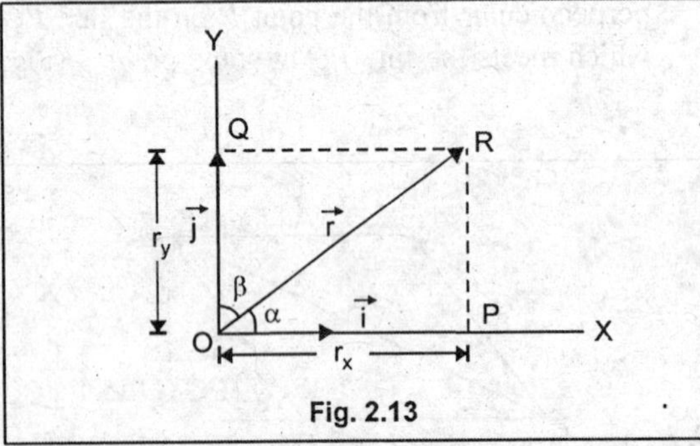

Fig. 2.13

Let the vector makes an angle α with the *X*-axis and β with the *Y*-axis. This vector is to be resolved into two component vectors along two mutually perpendicular unit vectors $\hat{i}$ and $\hat{j}$ respectively, where $\hat{i}$ and $\hat{j}$ are the unit vectors along *X*-axis and *Y*-axis respectively as shown in figure 3.8.

From point *R*, draw perpendicular *RP* and *RQ* on *X* and *Y*-axis respectively. The length *OP* is the projection of $\overrightarrow{OR}$ on *Y*-axis. According to parallelogram law of vector addition

$$\vec{r} = \overrightarrow{OR} = \overrightarrow{OP} + \overrightarrow{OQ}$$

Thus we have resolved the vector $\vec{r}$ into two parts, one along *OX* and the other along *OY*, the magnitude of the part along *OX* is $OP = r_x = r\cos\alpha$ and the magnitude of the part along *OY* is $OQ = r_y = r\cos\beta$, i.e., in terms of unit vector $\hat{i}$ and $\hat{j}$ we can write

$$\overrightarrow{OP} = \vec{r}\cos\alpha\,\hat{i} = r_x\hat{i}$$

and $$\overrightarrow{OQ} = \vec{r}\sin\alpha\,\hat{j} = r_y\hat{j}$$

Thus, $$\vec{r} = r\cos\alpha\,\hat{i} + r\cos\beta\,\hat{j}$$

$$= r_x\hat{i} + r_y\hat{j}$$

(iii) If the vector $\vec{r}$ is not in the *X-Y* plane, it may have non zero projections along *X*, *Y* and *Z* axes and we can resolve it into three components i.e. along the *X*, *Y* and *Z* axes. If α, β and γ be the angles made by the vector $\vec{r}$ with respect to *X*, *Y* and *Z* axes respectively, then we can write

$$\vec{r} = r\cos\alpha\,\hat{i} + r\cos\beta\,\hat{j} + r\cos\gamma\,\hat{k}$$

$$= r_x\hat{i} + r_y\hat{j} + r_z\hat{k}$$

where $\hat{i}$, $\hat{j}$ and $\hat{k}$ are the unit vectors along *X*, *Y* and *Z* axes respectively, the magnitude ($r\cos\alpha$) is called the component of $\vec{r}$ along *X*-axis, ($r\cos\beta$) is called the component along Y-axis and ($r\cos\gamma$) is called the component along Z-axis. Above equation also shows that **any vector in three-dimensions can be expressed as a linear combination of the three unit vectors $\hat{i}$, $\hat{j}$ and $\hat{k}$.**

SCALAR PRODUCT OF TWO VECTORS

(i) The scalar product of two vectors is defined as a scalar quantity having magnitude equal to the product of the magnitudes of two vectors and the cosine of the smaller angle between them.

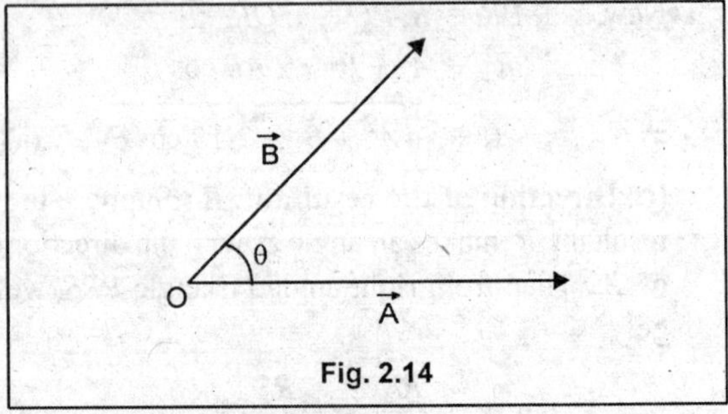

Fig. 2.14

Mathematically, if θ is the angle between vectors $\vec{A}$ and $\vec{B}$ fig. 2.14, then

$$\vec{A}\cdot\vec{B} = AB\cos\theta$$

(ii) Above equation can also be written as

$$\vec{A}\cdot\vec{B} = A\,(B\cos\theta) = B\,(A\cos\theta)$$

where $B\cos\theta$ is the magnitude of component of $\vec{B}$ along the direction of vector $\vec{A}$ and $A\cos\theta$ is the magnitude of component of $\vec{A}$ along the direction of vector $\vec{B}$ (Fig. 2.15).

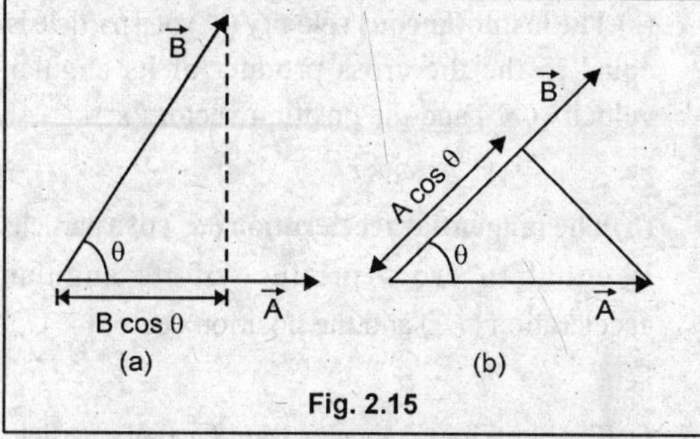

Fig. 2.15

Therefore, **the dot product of two vectors can also be interpreted as the product of the magnitude of one vector and the magnitude of the component of other vector along the direction of first vector.**

(iii) Dot product of two vectors can be positive or zero or negative depending upon θ which is less than 90° or equal to 90° or $90° < \theta < 180°$.

(iv) **Dot product of two vectors is always commutative**

i.e. $\vec{A}.\vec{B} = \vec{B}.\vec{A}$, $\vec{A}.\vec{B} = AB\cos\theta$

(θ is the angle between $\vec{A}$ and $\vec{B}$ measured in *ACQ* direction)

and $\vec{B}.\vec{A} = BA\cos(-\theta) = AB\cos\theta$

Thus $\vec{A}.\vec{B} = \vec{B}.\vec{A}$

(v) The dot product of a vector with itself gives square of its magnitude i.e.

$$\vec{A}.\vec{A} = AA\cos 0° = A^2$$

(vi) The dot product of two mutually perpendicular vectors is zero i.e. if two vectors $\vec{A}$ and $\vec{B}$ are perpendicular then

$$\vec{A}.\vec{B} = AB\cos 90° = 0$$

(vii) The dot product obeys the distributive law i.e.

$$\vec{A}.(\vec{B}+\vec{C}) = \vec{A}.\vec{B}+\vec{A}.\vec{C}$$

(viii) Two vectors are collinear, if their dot product is numerically equal to the product of their magnitudes

i.e. when $\theta = 0°$ or $180°$, $|\vec{A}.\vec{B}| = AB$

(ix) In case of unit vectors $\hat{i}, \hat{j}$ and $\hat{k}$, we have following two properties:

(a) $\hat{i}.\hat{i} = \hat{j}.\hat{j} = \hat{k}.\hat{k} = 1$ (as $\theta = 0°$)

(b) $\hat{i}.\hat{j} = \hat{j}.\hat{k} = \hat{k}.\hat{i} = 0$ (as $\theta = 90°$)

(x) **Dot product of two vectors in terms of their rectangular components in three dimensions:**

$$\vec{A}.\vec{B} = (A_x\hat{i}+A_y\hat{j}+A_z\hat{k}).(B_x\hat{i}+B_y\hat{j}+B_z\hat{k})$$
$$= A_xB_x + A_yB_y + A_zB_z$$

(xi) **Examples of some physical quantities which can be expressed as scalar product of two vectors:**

(a) Work (W) is defined as the scalar product of force ($\vec{F}$) and the displacement ($\vec{s}$)

i.e. $W = \vec{F}\cdot\vec{s}$

(b) Power (P) is defined as the scalar product of force ($\vec{F}$) and the velocity ($\vec{v}$)

i.e. $P = \vec{F}\cdot\vec{v}$

(c) Magnetic flux (ϕ) linked with a surface is defined as the dot product of magnetic induction ($\vec{B}$) and area vector (A)

i.e. $\phi = \vec{B}\cdot\vec{A}$

VECTOR PRODUCT OF TWO VECTORS

(i) The vector product of two vectors is defined as a vector having magnitude equal to the product of the magnitudes of two vectors with the sine of angle between them and direction ⊥ to the plane containing the two vectors in accordance with right handed screw rule or right hand thumb rule.

(ii) Mathematically, if θ is the angle between vectors $\vec{A}$ and $\vec{B}$, then

$$\vec{A}\times\vec{B} = AB\sin\theta\,\hat{n} \quad \text{...(i)}$$

The direction of vector $\vec{A}\times\vec{B}$ is the same as that of unit vector $\hat{n}$.

(iii) The cross product of the two vectors does not obey commutative law. As discussed above

$$\vec{A}\times\vec{B} = -(\vec{B}\times\vec{A})$$

i.e. $\vec{A}\times\vec{B} \neq (\vec{B}\times\vec{A})$

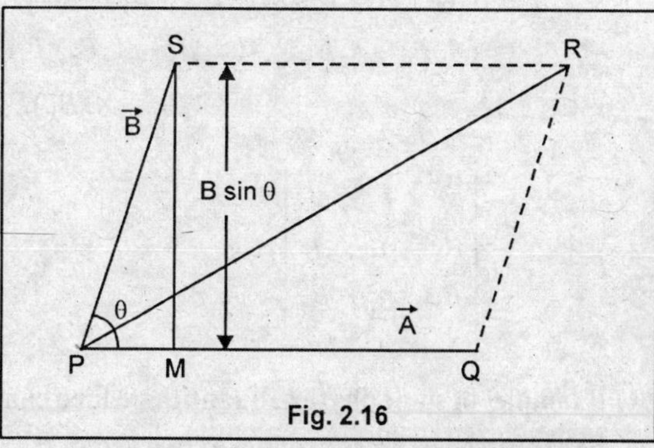

Fig. 2.16

(iv) The cross product follows the distributive law

i.e. $\vec{A}\times(\vec{B}+\vec{C}) = \vec{A}\times\vec{B}+\vec{A}\times\vec{C}$

(v) The cross product of a vector with itself is a null vector

i.e. $\vec{A}\times\vec{A} = (A)(A)\sin 0^\circ\,\hat{n}=0$.

(vi) The cross product of two vectors represents the area of the parallelogram formed by them.

Fig. 3.11 shows a parallelogram *PQRS* whose adjacent sides $\overrightarrow{PQ}$ and $\overrightarrow{PS}$ are represented by vectors $\vec{A}$ and $\vec{B}$ respectively.

Now, area of parallelogram $= QP\times SM = AB\sin\theta$.

Because, the magnitude of vector $\vec{A}\times\vec{B}$ is $AB\sin\theta$, hence cross product of two vectors represents the area of parallelogram formed by it.

(vii) In case of unit vectors $\hat{i},\hat{j},\hat{k}$, we obtain following two important properties:

(a) $\hat{i}\times\hat{i}=\hat{j}\times\hat{j}=\hat{k}\times\hat{k}=(1)(1)\sin 0^\circ\,(\hat{n})=0$

(b) $\hat{i}\times\hat{j}=(1)(1)\sin 90^\circ\,(\hat{k})=\hat{k}$

where, $\hat{k}$ is a unit vector $\perp$ to the plane of $\hat{i}$ and $\hat{j}$ in a direction in which a right hand screw will advance, when rotated from $\hat{i}$ to $\hat{j}$.

Also $\quad -\hat{j}\times\hat{i} = -(1)(1)\sin 90^\circ\,(-\hat{k})=\hat{k}$

Similarly, $\hat{j}\times\hat{k} = -\hat{k}\times\hat{j}=\hat{i}$

and $\quad \hat{k}\times\hat{i} = -\hat{i}\times\hat{k}=\hat{j}$

(viii) **Cross product of two vectors in terms of their rectangular components:**

$$\vec{A}\times\vec{B} = (A_x\hat{i}+A_y\hat{j}+A_z\hat{k})\times(B_x\hat{i}+B_y\hat{j}+B_z\hat{k})$$
$$= (A_yB_z-A_zB_y)\hat{i}+(A_zB_x-A_xB_z)\hat{j}+(A_xB_y-A_yB_x)\hat{k}$$

$$= \begin{vmatrix}\hat{i} & \hat{j} & \hat{k}\\ A_x & A_y & A_z\\ B_x & B_y & B_z\end{vmatrix}$$

(ix) **Examples of some physical quantities which can be expressed as cross product of two vectors:**

(a) The instantaneous velocity ($\vec{v}$) of a particle is equal to the the cross product of its angular velocity ($\vec{\omega}$) and the position vector ($\vec{r}$)

i.e. $\quad \vec{v} = \vec{\omega}\times\vec{r}$

(b) The tangential acceleration ($\vec{a}_t$) of a particle is equal to cross product of its angular acceleration ($\vec{\alpha}$) and the position vector ($\vec{r}$)

i.e. $\quad \vec{a}_t = \vec{\alpha}\times\vec{r}$

(c) The centripetal acceleration ($\vec{a}_c$) of a particle is equal to the cross product of its angular velocity (ω) and the linear velocity ($\vec{v}$)

i.e. $\quad \vec{a}_c = \vec{\omega}\times\vec{v}$

(d) The force $\vec{F}$ on a charge q moving inside magnetic field is equal to charge times the cross product of its velocity ($\vec{v}$) and magnetic induction ($\vec{B}$)

i.e. $\quad \vec{F} = q(\vec{v}\times\vec{B})$

(e) The torque of a force ($\vec{F}$) is equal to the cross product of the position vector ($\vec{r}$) and the force ($\vec{F}$) applied

i.e. $\quad \vec{\tau} = \vec{r}\times\vec{F}$

(f) The angular momentum ($\vec{L}$) is equal to cross product of position vector ($\vec{r}$) and linear momentum ($\vec{p}$) of the particle

i.e. $\quad \vec{L} = \vec{r}\times\vec{p}$.

PROJECTILE MOTION

Projectile fired at an Angle with Horizontal

(i) An object thrown into space and under the action of earth's gravity is called a projectile. When an object is thrown upward in a direction different from the vertical then its is acted upon by acceleration due to gravity acting vertically downwards and moves along a curved path in a vertical plane. This motion is called the projectile motion and its path is called trajectory. e.g. the motion of a bomb dropped from an aeroplane, the motion of a cricket ball or football after being hit.

(ii) The projectile motion can be supposed to be made of two simple motions i.e. motion in horizontal direction and motion in vertical direction.

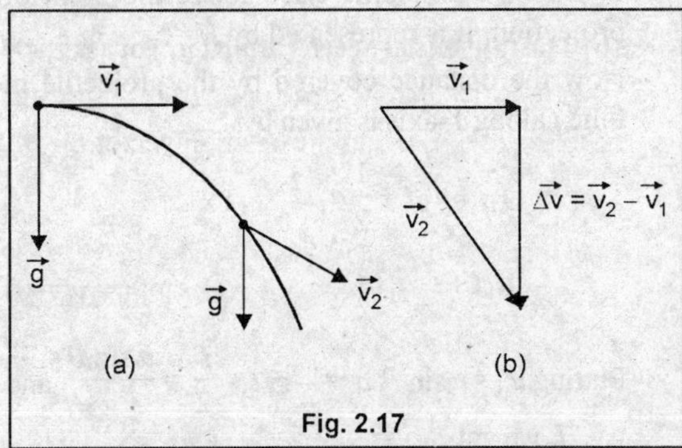

Fig. 2.17

These two motions are completely independent from each other. Consider a ball thrown in horizontal direction with an initial velocity $\vec{v}_1$. The ball moves on a curved path under the acceleration due to gravity $\vec{g}$ and after some time its velocity becomes $\vec{v}_2$ whose magnitude and direction are different from those of $\vec{v}_1$ (Fig. 2.17a). The change in velocity, $\Delta\vec{v}$, is obtained by subtracting the vector $\vec{v}_1$, from the velocity vector $\vec{v}_2$ (Fig. 2.17b). We find that **the direction of Δv is the same as that of the acceleration $\vec{g}$.** Hence, if a ball is dropped downwards from the roof of a building and simultaneously another ball is thrown in a horizontal direction, then both the balls will reach the ground at the same time but at different places.

(iii) Consider a projectile fired with velocity u at an angle θ with the horizontal from the point O on the ground. Take the point O as the origin, horizontal line OX, as positive direction of the X-axis and the vertical line OY in upward direction as the positive direction of Y-axis (Fig. 3.13). Let $t = 0$ is the instant, when projectile is fired from the point O. Hence initial coordinates of the projectile are:

$$x_0 = 0, \; y_0 = 0$$

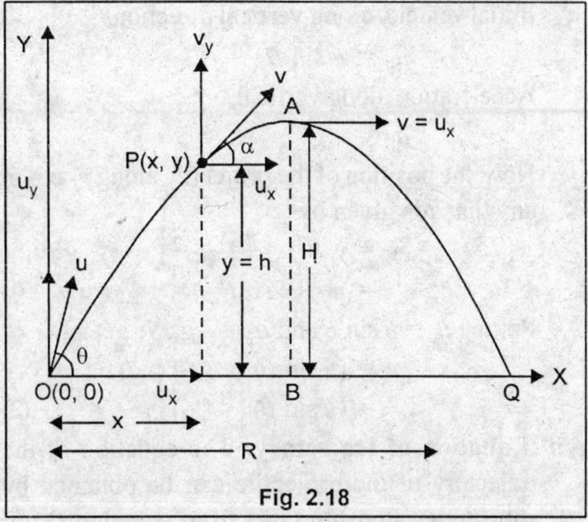

Fig. 2.18

(iv) Resolving u in horizontal and vertical components, we get

$$u_x = u \cos \theta$$

and $$u_y = u \sin \theta.$$

As the projectile moves, it covers distances along horizontal due to the horizontal component $u \cos \theta$ of the velocity of projection and along vertical due to the vertical component $u \sin \theta$. Let the projectile reaches point P at any instant t so that its positions along X and Y-axes are given by x and y respectively.

(v) **Motion along horizontal direction:** If friction due to air is neglected, then horizontal component of the velocity i.e. $u \cos \theta$ will remain constant. Thus initial velocity along horizontal direction, $u_x = u \cos \theta$, acceleration along horizontal, $a_x = 0$. Now, the position of the particle along X-axis at any time t is given by:

$$x = x_0 + u_x t + \tfrac{1}{2} a_x t^2$$

or $$x = u_x t + \tfrac{1}{2} a_x t^2 \qquad (\because x_0 = 0)$$

Putting $u_x = u \cos \theta$ and $a_x = 0$, we get

$$x = (u \cos \theta)\, t + \tfrac{1}{2} \times 0 \times t^2$$
$$= (u \cos \theta)\, t$$

or $$t = \frac{x}{u \cos \theta} \qquad \text{...(1)}$$

(vi) **Motion along vertical direction:** The velocity of projectile along vertical direction goes on decreasing due to gravity.

Initial velocity along vertical direction,

$$u_y = u \sin \theta$$

Acceleration along vertical,

$$a_y = -g$$

Now, the position of the projectile along y-axis at any time t is given by

$$y = y_0 + u_y t + \tfrac{1}{2} a_y t^2$$

$$= u_y t + \tfrac{1}{2} a_y t^2 \qquad (\because y_0 = 0)$$

Putting $u_y = u \sin \theta$ and $a_y = -g$, we get

$$y = (u \sin \theta)\, t + (\tfrac{1}{2})(-g)\, t^2$$

$$= (u \sin \theta)\, t - (\tfrac{1}{2})\, g t^2 \qquad \ldots(2)$$

(vii) **Equation of trajectory:** The equation of the trajectory of the projectile can be obtained by substituting the value of t from equation (1) in equation (2). Therefore, we get

$$y = (u \sin \theta) \times \frac{x}{u \cos \theta} - \frac{1}{2} g \times \left(\frac{x}{u \cos \theta} \right)^2$$

$$\text{or } y = x \tan \theta - \frac{1}{2} \frac{g}{u^2 \cos^2 \theta} x^2 \qquad \ldots(3)$$

This equation is quadratic in x and linear in y. Therefore, it represents a parabola i.e. **a projectile fired at some angle with the horizontal moves along a parabolic path.**

(viii) **Time of flight:** It is the time taken by the projectile to return to ground or the time for which the projectile remains in air above the horizontal plane from the point of projection.

It is denoted by T. Since motion from O to A and A to Q are perfectly symmetrical, the time of ascent (for journey from O to A) and time of descent (for journey from A to Q) will be each equal to $T/2$. Further, on reaching the highest point A, the vertical component of the velocity of the projectile must become zero i.e. $v_y = 0$.

Now, velocity of the projectile at any time t along Y-axis is given by

$$v_y = u_y + a_y t$$

Putting $u_y = u \sin \theta$, $a_y = -g$, $t = \dfrac{T}{2}$ and $v_y = 0$, we get

$$0 = u \sin \theta + (-g) \frac{T}{2}$$

$$\text{or} \qquad \boldsymbol{T = \frac{2u \sin \theta}{g}} \qquad \ldots(4)$$

(ix) **Maximum height attained:** It is the greatest height to which a projectile rises above the point of projection. It is represented by H.

Now the distance covered by the projectile in time t along Y-axis is given by

$$y = y_0 + u_y t + \frac{1}{2} a_y t^2$$

$$= u_y t + \frac{1}{2} a_y t^2 \qquad (\because y_0 = 0)$$

Putting $u_y = u \sin \theta$, $a_y = -g$, $t = \dfrac{T}{2} = \dfrac{u \sin \theta}{g}$ and $y = H$, we get

$$H = (u \sin \theta) \times \frac{u \sin \theta}{g} + \frac{1}{2}(-g) \left(\frac{u \sin \theta}{g} \right)^2$$

$$\text{or, } \boldsymbol{H = \frac{u^2 \sin^2 \theta}{2g}} \qquad \ldots(5)$$

(x) **Horizontal Range:** It is the distance covered by the projectile along the horizontal direction between the point of projection to the point on the ground where the projectile returns again. It is represented by R. Clearly, range R is the horizontal distance covered by the projectile with uniform velocity $u \cos \theta$ in time equal to the time of flight. Hence

$$R = u_x \times T$$

$$= u \cos \theta \times \frac{2u \sin \theta}{g}$$

$$= \frac{u^2 (2 \sin \theta \cos \theta)}{g}$$

As $2 \sin \theta \cos \theta = \sin 2\theta$, hence we have

$$\boldsymbol{R = \frac{u^2 \sin 2\theta}{g}} \qquad \ldots(6)$$

UNIFORM CIRCULAR MOTION

Angular Velocity and its Relation with Linear Velocity

(i) If an object moves on a circular path with a constant speed, then its motion is called uniform circular motion in a plane. The magnitude of

acceleration in such a motion remains constant but the direction changes continuously.

(ii) Consider a particle P moving on a circular path around the point O with a constant speed v. The position of the particle at any instant is represented by an angle θ between a radial line OP and a reference line OP_0 (Fig. 2.19). Although the magnitude (v) of the velocity $\vec{v}$ of the particle is constant, but its direction is changing from moment to moment. Figure shows the velocity vectors of the particle at different positions. In every position, the velocity vector $\vec{v}$ will be perpendicular to radius vector $\vec{r}$.

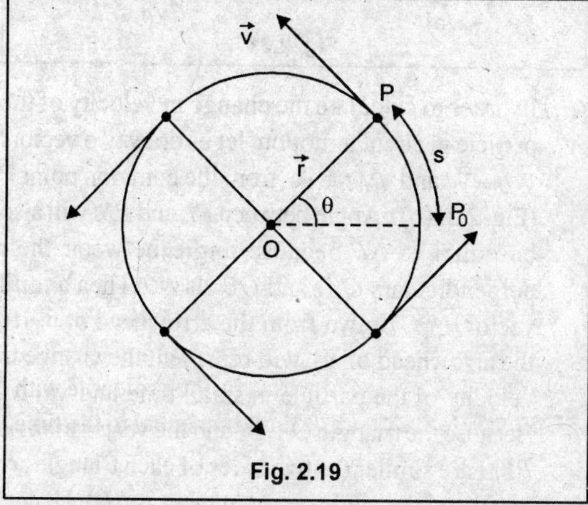

Fig. 2.19

(iii) **Angular Displacement:** Suppose a particle is initially (at $t = 0$) at point P_0 and reached the point A at any instant t_1 and point B at a later instant t_2, such that $\angle AOP_0 = \theta_1$ and $\angle BOP_0 = \theta_2$ (Fig. 2.20). Let the particle covers a distance Δs along the circular path in the time interval $t_2 - t_1$ ($= \Delta t$). It rotates through an angle $(\theta_2 - \theta_1)$ ($= \Delta\theta$) during this interval. This angle of rotation is called angular displacement of the particle. If radius of circular path be r, then the angular displacement is

$$\Delta\theta = \frac{\Delta s}{r} \qquad \ldots(1)$$

The unit of angular displacement is **radian**.

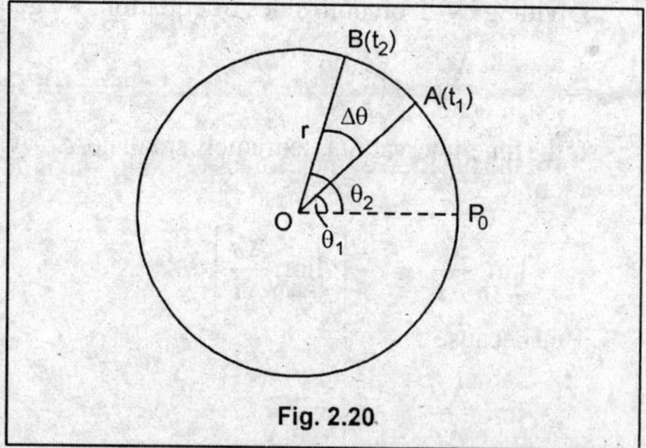

Fig. 2.20

(iv) **Angular Velocity:** The time rate of change of angular displacement of a particle is known as its angular velocity. It is denoted by ω and is measured in **radians per second**.

Because $\Delta\theta$ is the angular displacement of the particle in a small time-interval Δt, hence average angular velocity of the particle in this time-interval is

$$\omega = \frac{\Delta\theta}{\Delta t}$$

If time interval Δt is extremely small i.e. $\Delta t \to 0$, then the average angular velocity is equal to the instantaneous angular velocity, given by

$$\omega = \lim_{\Delta t \to 0} \frac{\Delta\theta}{\Delta t} = \frac{d\theta}{dt}$$

The particle undergoes an angular displacement of 2π radian (or 360°) in one complete revolution. Hence, if the time taken by particle to complete one revolution is represented by T (i.e. time period), then the average angular velocity of the particle is given by

$$\omega = \frac{2\pi}{T} \qquad \ldots(2)$$

If n represents the frequency of revolution or the particle completes n revolutions in 1 second, then

$$\omega = 2\pi n \qquad \ldots(3)$$

(v) **Relation between angular velocity and linear velocity:** According to equation (1), the angular displacement of the particle in time-interval Δt is

$$\Delta\theta = \frac{\Delta s}{r}$$

Dividing by Δt on both sides of equation, we get

$$\frac{\Delta\theta}{\Delta t} = \frac{1}{r}\frac{\Delta s}{\Delta t}$$

If the time-interval Δt is extremely small i.e. $\Delta t \to 0$ then,

$$\lim_{\Delta t\to 0}\frac{\Delta\theta}{\Delta t} = \frac{1}{r}\left[\lim_{\Delta t\to 0}\frac{\Delta s}{\Delta t}\right]$$

But because

$$\lim_{\Delta t\to 0}\frac{\Delta\theta}{\Delta t} = \omega$$

= instantaneous angular velocity

and $\lim_{\Delta t\to 0}\frac{\Delta s}{\Delta t} = v$

= instantaneous linear velocity

hence, $\omega = \frac{v}{r}$

or $v = r\omega$ ...(4)

Above equations show that for a given angular velocity (ω), the linear velocity (v) of the particle is directly proportional to the distance (r) of the particle from the centre i.e. **higher is the distance of the particle from the centre, higher will be its linear velocity.**

CENTRIPETAL ACCELERATION

(i) Although the speed of a particle performing uniform circular motion remains constant but its velocity changes continuously due to continuous change in its direction (as velocity is a vector quantity). This implies that there occurs an acceleration in uniform circular motion. Because the direction of this acceleration is always found towards the centre of the circle, hence it is called **centripetal acceleration.**

(ii) Consider a particle moving on a circular path of radius r and centre O, with a uniform speed v (Fig. 2.21). Direction of motion of the particle (or the direction of velocity) at every point of its path, will be along the tangent drawn at that point. Let $\vec{v}_1$ and $\vec{v}_2$ are the linear velocities of the particle at point A_1 and B_2 in a small time-interval Δt. Because the speed of the particle remains constant, hence $|\vec{v}_1| = |\vec{v}_2| = v$. But their directions will differ by angle $\Delta\theta$. So the change in velocity of the particle in moving from point A_1 to B_2 is equal to $\vec{v}_1 - \vec{v}_2 = \Delta\vec{v}$.

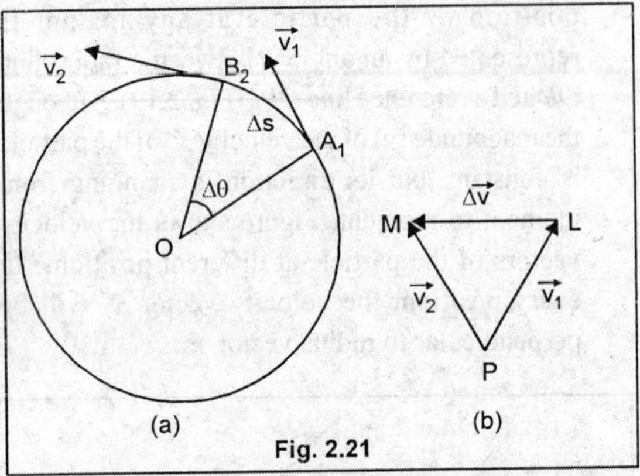

Fig. 2.21

(iii) In order to calculate the change in velocity of the particle in circular motion, let us draw two vectors $\overrightarrow{PL} = \vec{v}_1$ and $\overrightarrow{PM} = \vec{v}_2$ from the common point P (Fig. 2.21(b)). Angle between PL and PM will also be equal to $\Delta\theta$ because angle between their perpendiculars OA_1 and OB_2 is $\Delta\theta$. Then a third vector $\overrightarrow{LM}$ drawn from the arrowhead of $\vec{v}_1$ to the arrowhead of $\vec{v}_2$ will represent the change in velocity of the particle in small time interval Δt. Because the triangle OA_1B_2 and the vector triangle PLM are similar (as two sides of each triangle are equal and the angle between them is $\Delta\theta$). Hence,

$$\frac{A_1B_2}{OA_1} = \frac{LM}{PL}$$

or $$\frac{\Delta s}{r} = \frac{\Delta v}{v}$$

$$\therefore \quad \Delta v = \frac{v}{r}\Delta s$$

Dividing by Δt on both sides of equation, we get

$$\frac{\Delta v}{\Delta t} = \frac{v}{r}\frac{\Delta s}{\Delta t}$$

If Δt is extremely small i.e. $\Delta t \to 0$, then we have

$$\lim_{\Delta t\to 0}\frac{\Delta v}{\Delta t} = \frac{v}{r}\left(\lim_{\Delta t\to 0}\frac{\Delta s}{\Delta t}\right)$$

But because

$$\lim_{\Delta t \to 0} \frac{\Delta v}{\Delta t} = a = \text{instantaneous acceleration}$$

and $$\lim_{\Delta t \to 0} \frac{\Delta s}{\Delta t} = v = \text{instantaneous velocity}$$

Hence, $$a = \frac{v}{r}(v) = \frac{v^2}{r} \qquad \ldots(5)$$

From equation (4), we know that $v = r\omega$, hence

$$a = \frac{(r\omega)^2}{r} = \omega^2 r \qquad \ldots(6)$$

(iv) Above equation gives the magnitude of the acceleration $\vec{a}$ of the particle. The direction of acceleration vector $\vec{a}$ at any time will always be perpendicular to the velocity vector $\vec{v}$ of the particle at that time.

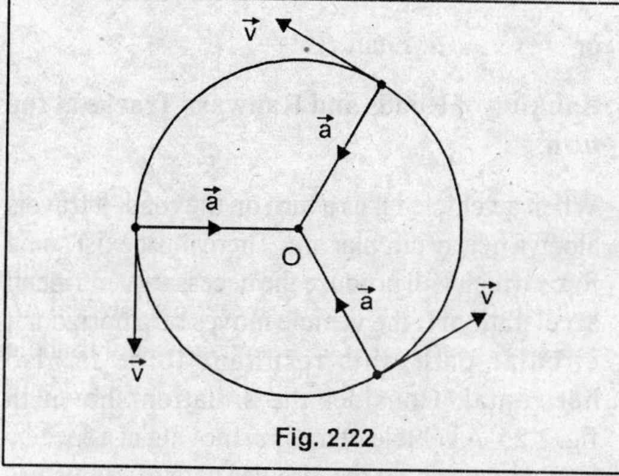

Fig. 2.22

It is due to the reason that when Δt is decreased, $\Delta\theta$ also decreases and like wise $\Delta\vec{v}$ becomes more and more perpendicular to $\vec{v}$ (Fig. 3.16b) and in the limiting case, when Δt approaches zero, $\Delta\vec{v}$ (which ultimately determines the acceleration vector) becomes perpendicular to the velocity vector.

Because velocity vector at any point is tangential to the circular path at that point, the acceleration vector acts along radius of the circle at that point and is directed towards centre *O* of the circle (Fig. 2.22). This is the reason that it is called centripetal acceleration. Its magnitude (v^2/r or $r\omega^2$) remains constant but its direction changes continuously and remains perpendicular to the direction of the velocity of the particle.

CENTRIPETAL FORCE

(i) We have already studied that if an object moves with a uniform speed v on a circular path of radius r, then it always experiences a centripetal acceleration whose magnitude remains constant ($= v^2/r$) but whose direction continuously changes and remains always directed towards the centre of the circle. According to Newton's second law of motion, an acceleration is always generated due to a force whose direction is the same as that of the acceleration.

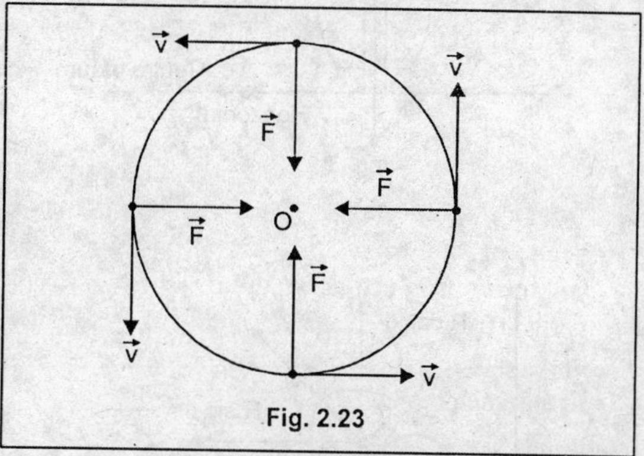

Fig. 2.23

Thus it is obvious that **an object moving on a circular path with uniform speed is always acted upon by a force, directed towards the centre of the circle (Fig. 2.23). This force is known as centripetal force.** If this force is absent, the circular motion will not be possible.

(ii) Centripetal force is not a new kind of force. Any of the forces found in nature such as gravitational force, frictional force, magnetic force, elastic force, electric force etc. may act as a centripetal force.

TWO SPECIAL EXAMPLES INVOLVING CENTRIPETAL FORCE

(A) A cyclist leans inward while taking a turn on the road:

(i) Fig. 2.24 (a) shows a cyclist taking a turn towards

his left hand on a circular path of radius *r*. Let m be the mass of the cyclist and the bicycle, and *v* the speed of the bicycle. Suppose the cyclist bends away from the vertical by an angle θ in order to generate a force necessary for circular motion. If *R* represents the reaction of the ground then *R* may be resolved into two components- horizontal and vertical (Fig. 2.24(b)).

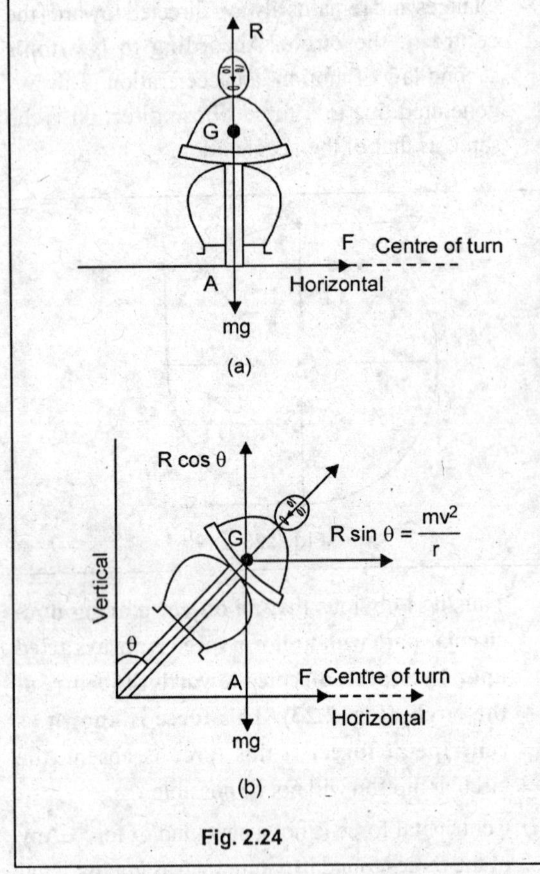

Fig. 2.24

(ii) The vertical component $R \cos \theta$ balances the weight mg of the cyclist and the horizontal component $R \sin \theta$ provides the necessary centripetal force for circular motion i.e.

$$R \sin \theta = \frac{mv^2}{r} \quad ...(1)$$

and $R \cos \theta = mg \quad ...(2)$

Dividing eqn. (1) by eqn. (2), we get

$$\tan \theta = \frac{v^2}{rg} \quad ...(3)$$

For less bending of cyclist, it is necessary that (a) speed *v* should be smaller and (b) radius *r* of the circular path should be greater.

(iii) Since the centripetal force mv^2/r is provided by the frictional force between the tyres and the road, hence the value of mv^2/r should be less than the limiting frictional force μR or $\mu m g$ otherwise the bicycle would overturn i.e. for no overturning of cyclist

$$\mu mg \geq \frac{mv^2}{r}$$

or $$\mu \geq \frac{v^2}{rg}$$

or $$\mu \geq \tan \theta .$$

(B) Banking of Roads and Railways Tracks at the turn:

(i) When a vehicle takes a turn on the road, it travels along a nearly circular arc. There must exist some force which will produce the necessary centripetal acceleration. If the vehicle moves on a horizontal circular path, this resultant force is also horizontal. Consider the situation shown in fig. 2.25. A vehicle of mass *m* moving at a speed *v* is taking a turn on the circular path of radius *r*.

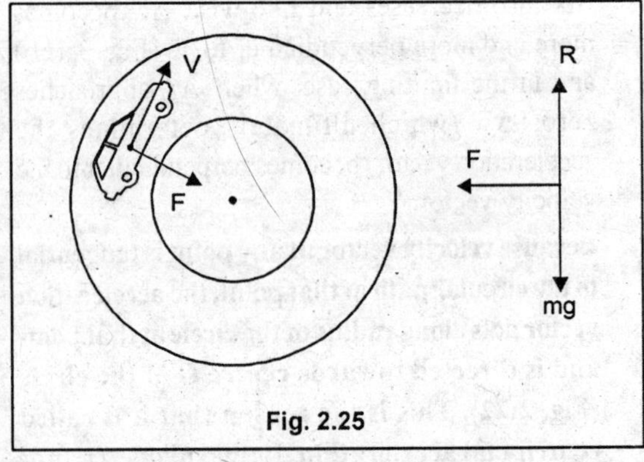

Fig. 2.25

The external forces acting on the vehicle are:

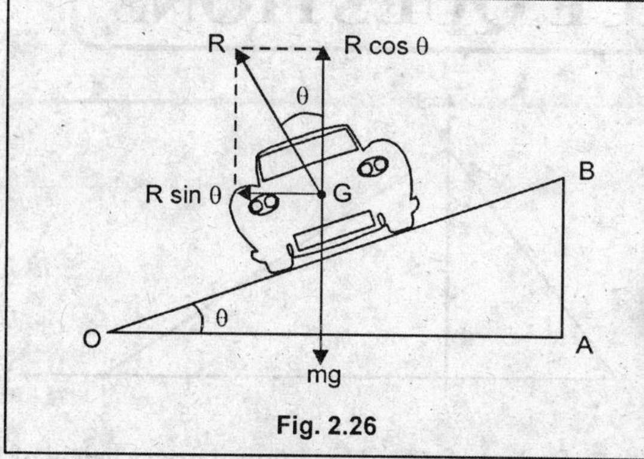

Fig. 2.26

(a) Weight (= mg) acting vertically downwards
(b) Normal reactional force (= R) acting vertically upward
(c) Frictional force (= F) acting towards the centre of horizontal circular path. (This is the static frictional force and is self adjustable)

(ii) The tyres get a tendency of skid outward and the frictional force which opposes this skidding acts towards the centre. Thus, for a safe turn, we must have

$$\frac{v^2}{r} = \frac{F}{m}$$

or $$F = \frac{mv^2}{r}$$

However, there is a limit to the magnitude of the frictional force. If μ is the coefficient of static friction between the tyres and the road, the magnitude of frictional force F cannot exceed μmg, so that

$$F \leq \mu mg$$

Thus for a safe turn:

$$\frac{mv^2}{r} \leq \mu mg, \qquad \mu \geq \frac{v^2}{rg} \qquad ...(1)$$

(iii) Friction is not always reliable at circular turns if high speeds and sharp turns are involved. In order to avoid the dependence on friction, the roads are banked at the turn (or given as slope) so that the outer part of the road is somewhat raised up as compared to the inner part (Fig. 2.26). The surface of the road makes an angle θ with the horizontal throughout the turn. The reactional force R now makes an angle θ with the vertical. At the correct speed, the horizontal component of R is sufficient to produce the force towards the centre. Further, the vertical component $R\cos\theta$ balances the weight of the vehicle. Hence

$$R\sin\theta = \frac{mv^2}{r}$$

and $R\cos\theta = mg$

These equations give

$$\tan\theta = \frac{v^2}{rg} \qquad ...(2)$$

(iv) Above equation shows that angle θ depends on the speed of the vehicle as well as on the radius of the turn. Thus the slope θ is proper for a particular speed of the car turning on a given circular path.

(v) If a vehicle is moving at a speed higher than the desired speed, it tends to slip outward at the turn, but then the frictional force acts inward and provides the additional centripetal force.

MULTIPLE CHOICE QUESTIONS

1. Two bodies A and B start from rest and from the same point with a uniform acceleration of 2 m/s^2. If B starts one second later, then the two bodies are separated, at the end of the next second, by
   (a) 1 m (b) 2 m
   (c) 3 m (d) 4 m.

2. A man is walking on a road with a velocity 3 km/h. Suddenly rain starts falling. The velocity of rain is 10 km/h in vertically downward direction. The relative velocity of rain is
   (a) $-\sqrt{13}$ km/h (b) $\sqrt{109}$ km/h
   (c) $\sqrt{7}$ km/h (d) 13 km/h.

3. A car is moving on a road and rain is falling vertically. Select the correct answer :
   (a) The rain will strike the behind screen only
   (b) The rain will strike the front screen only
   (c) The rain will strike both the screens
   (d) The rain will not strike any of the screens.

4. An insect crawls a distance of 4 m along north in 10 seconds and then a distance of 3m along east in 5 seconds. The average velocity of the insect is :
   (a) 7/15 m/sec (b) 1/5 m/sec
   (c) 5/15 m/sec (d) 12/15 m/sec.

5. A body projected vertically upwards with a velocity u returns to the starting point in 4 seconds. If $g = 10$ m/s^2, the value of u is
   (a) 20 ms^{-1} (b) 15 ms^{-1}
   (c) 10 ms^{-1} (d) 5 ms^{-1}.

6. A body A starts from rest with an acceleration a_1. After two seconds, another body B starts from rest with an acceleration a_2. If they travel equal distances in the 5th second after the start of A, then the ratio of $a_1 : a_2$ is equal to
   (a) 5:9 (b) 9:5
   (c) 5:7 (d) 7:5.

7. Refer Figure, find the ratio of speed in first two seconds to the speed in the next 4 seconds
   (a) 1:2 (b) 2:1
   (c) $\sqrt{2}:1$ (d) 3:1.

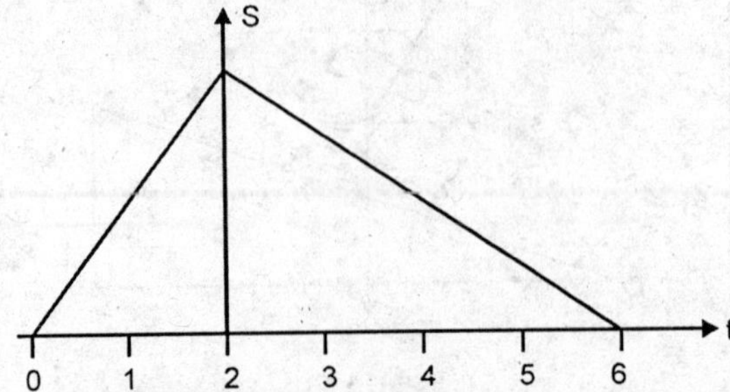

8. Body A of mass M is dropped from a height of 1 m and body B of mass 3 M is dropped from a height of 9 m. Ratio of time taken by the bodies 1 and 2 to reach the ground is ($g = 10$ m/s^2).
   (a) 1:1 (b) 1:3
   (c) 3:1 (d) 9:1.

9. A car moving with a speed of 25 m/s takes a U-turn in 5 seconds, without changing its speed. The average acceleration during these 5 sec is
   (a) 10 ms^{-2} (b) 5 ms^{-2}
   (c) 2.5 ms^{-2} (d) 7.5 ms^{-2}.

10. A car leaves station X for station Y every 10 minutes. The distance between X and Y is 60 km. The car travels at a speed of 60 km/h. A man drives a car from Y station towards X station at speed 60 km h^{-1}. If he starts at the moment when one of the cars leaves station X, how many cars would be meet on route ?
   (a) 10 (b) 11
   (c) 20 (d) 21.

11. A balloon starts rising from the ground with an acceleration of 1.25 m/s^2. After 8 s, stone is released from the balloon. The stone will
   (a) cover a distance of 30 m
   (b) have a displacement 50 m
   (c) reach the ground in 4 s
   (d) begin to move down after being released.

12. A stone is dropped from the top of a tower and travels 24.5 m in last second of its journey. The height of the tower is
   (a) 44.1 m (b) 49 m
   (c) 78.4 m (d) 72 m.

13. A body is released from the top of a tower of height h metres. It takes T seconds to reach the ground. The ball at the time $\frac{T}{2}$ second is

(a) at $\frac{h}{2}$ metres from the ground

(b) at $\frac{h}{3}$ metres from the ground

(c) at $\frac{3h}{4}$ metres from the ground

(d) depends upon the mass and volume of the ball.

14. Tripling the speed of a motor car multiplies the distance needed for stopping it by

(a) 3 (b) 6
(c) 9 (d) some other number.

15. A stone is dropped into a well in which the level of water is h metre below the top of the well. If v is velocity of sound, the time T after which the splash is heard is given by

(a) $T = 2h/v$ (b) $T = \sqrt{\frac{2h}{g}} + \frac{h}{v}$

(c) $T = \sqrt{\frac{2h}{g}} + \frac{h}{g}$ (d) $T = \sqrt{\frac{h}{2g}} + \frac{2h}{v}$

16. A ball thrown up is caught by the thrower 6s after start. The height to which the ball has risen is (take $g = 10\ ms^{-2}$)

(a) 10 m (b) 30 m
(c) 45 m (d) 90 m.

17. A particle of mass 2 kg moving with a constant acceleration covers a distance of 10 m in the third second and 16 m in the 4th second. The initial velocity of the particle is

(a) –5 m/s (b) 6 m/s
(c) 10 m/s (d) 8 m/s.

18. A point initially at rest moves along the X-axis. Its acceleration a varies with time as $a = 4t$. If it starts from the origin, the distance covered by it in 3 second is

(a) 12 m (b) 18 m
(c) 24 m (d) 36 m.

19. The velocity time graph of a body is shown in the figure. If the slope of the line is m, then the distance travelled by the body in time T is

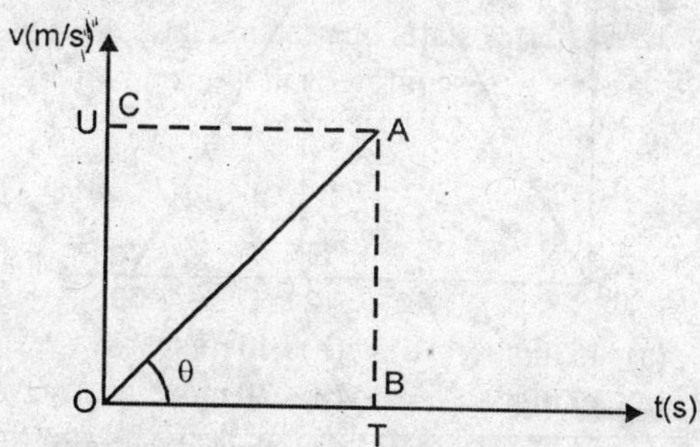

(a) $mU^2/2T$ (b) $U^2/2T$
(c) $2mU^2$ (d) $U^2/2m$.

20. A body released from the top of a tower falls through half the height of the tower in 3 seconds. It will reach the ground after nearly

(a) 3.5 sec (b) 4.24 sec
(c) 4.71 sec (d) 6 sec.

21. A body dropped from top of a tower fall through 40 m during the last two seconds of its fall. The height of tower is ($g = 10\ m/s^2$)

(a) 60 m (b) 45 m
(c) 80 m (d) 50 m.

22. The displacement of a body is given to be proportional to the cube of time elapsed. The magnitude of the acceleration of the body is

(a) increasing with time

(b) decreasing with time

(c) constant but not zero

(d) zero.

23. An automobile moving due west at a velocity of 72 km/h is brought to rest in 2 seconds by the application of brakes. How much distance does the automobile cover in these 2 seconds ?

(a) 25 m (b) 20 m
(c) 15 m (d) 10 m.

24. Figure shows the time acceleration graph for a particle in rectilinear motion. The average acceleration in first twenty seconds is

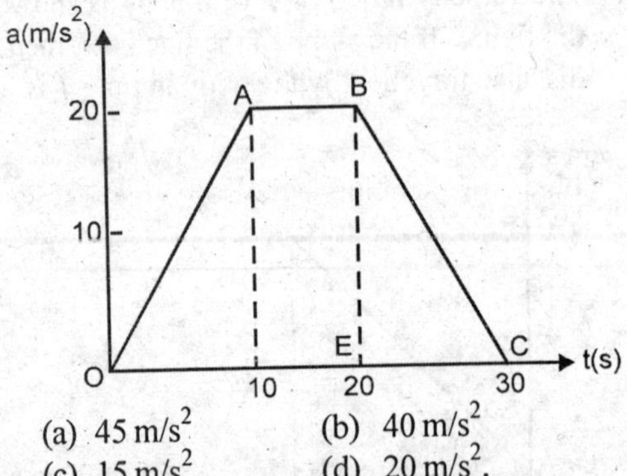

(a) 45 m/s^2 (b) 40 m/s^2
(c) 15 m/s^2 (d) 20 m/s^2.

25. A body starts from rest, what is the ratio of the distance travelled by the body during the 4th and 3rd second ?

(a) $\frac{7}{5}$ (b) $\frac{5}{7}$
(c) $\frac{7}{3}$ (d) $\frac{3}{7}$.

26. A projectile is thrown into space so as to have the maximum possible horizontal range equal to 400 m. Taking the point of projection as the origin, the co-ordinate of the point where the velocity of the projectile is minimum are
(a) (400, 100) (b) (200, 100)
(c) (400, 200) (d) (200, 200)

27. Which of the following is the largest, when the height attained by the projectile is the greatest?
(a) range
(b) time of flight
(c) angle of projectile with the vertical
(d) none of the above

28. Which of the following remains constant for a projectile fired from the earth?
(a) kinetic energy
(b) momentum
(c) horizontal component of velocity
(d) vertical component of velocity

29. A particle moves in a plane with uniform acceleration having direction different than that the instantaneous velocity. What is the maximum height?
(a) 2 R (b) R
(c) $R/2$ (d) $R/4$

30. In case of a projectile, what is the angle between the instantaneous velocity and acceleration at the highest point?
(a) zero (b) 45°
(c) 90° (d) 180°

31. A person sitting in the rear end of the compartment throws a ball towards the front end. The ball follows a parabolic path. The train is moving with uniform velocity of 20 ms^{-1}. A person standing outside on the ground also observes the ball. How will the maximum heights (y_m) attained and the ranges (R) seen by the thrower and the outside observer compare with each other?
(a) same y_m different R
(b) same y_m and R
(c) different y_m same R
(d) different y_m and R

32. Two bullets are fired horizontally with different velocities from the same height. Which will reach the ground first?
(a) slower one
(b) faster one
(c) both will reach simultaneously
(d) it cannot be predicted

33. The range of a projectile when fired at 75° with the horizontal is 0.5 km. What will be its range when fired at 45°?
(a) 0.5 km (b) 1.0 km
(c) 1.5 km (d) 2.0 km

34. The instantaneous height y of a projectile and the distance x covered by it are as follows
$$x = 8\,t, y = 5\,t - 2\,t^2$$
What is the acceleration due to gravity if distances are measured in metres and time in second?
(a) 2 ms^{-2} (b) 4 ms^{-2}
(c) 8 ms^{-2} (d) 10 ms^{-2}

35. The instantaneous height y and the horizontal distance x covered by a particle are as follows
$$y = bt^2, x = ct^2$$
What is the speed of the particle one second after the firing?
(a) $2\,(b + c)$ (b) $2(b - c)$
(c) $2\,(b^2 + c^2)^{1/2}$ (d) $2\,(b^2 - c^2)^{1/2}$

36. The range of a projectile is maximum. If the range is R, what is the maximum height?
(a) $2R$ (b) R
(c) $R/2$ (d) $R/4$

37. A ball is thrown horizontally from the top of a tower. What happens to the horizontal component of its velocity?
(a) increases
(b) decreases
(c) remains unchanged
(d) first decreases and then increases

38. A projectile is fired with a velocity of 10 ms^{-1} at an angle of 60° with the horizontal. Its velocity at the highest point is
(a) zero (b) 5 ms^{-1}
(c) 8.66 ms^{-1} (d) 10 ms^{-1}

39. A projectile can have the same range R for two angles of projection. If t_1 and t_2 be the times of flight in the two cases then what is the product of the two times of flight?
(a) $t_1 t_2 \propto R^2$ (b) $t_1 t_2 \propto R$
(c) $t_1 t_2 \propto \frac{1}{R}$ (d) $t_1 t_2 \propto \frac{1}{R^2}$

40. A ball is projected upwards from the top of tower with a velocity 50 ms^{-1} making angle 30° with the horizontal. The height of the tower is 70 m. After how many seconds from the instant of throwing will the ball reach the ground?
(a) 2 s (b) 5 s
(c) 7 s (d) 9 s

41. The distance travelled by a body dropped from the top of a tower is proportional to
(a) mass of the body
(b) weight of the body
(c) height of tower
(d) square of time

42. A heavy and a lighter body are dropped from the top of a tower. Which will reach the ground first?
(a) lighter one
(b) heavier one
(c) both will reach simultaneously
(d) cannot be predicted

43. A ball is thrown horizontally and another is just dropped from the top of tower. Which will reach the ground first?
(a) first ball
(b) second ball
(c) both will reach simultaneously
(d) depends upon the masses of the balls

44. A ball is projected from the top of a tower at an angle 60° with the vertical. What happens to the vertical component of its velocity?
(a) increases continuously
(b) decreases continuously
(c) remains unchanged
(d) first decreases and then increases

45. A ball is thrown at an angle θ with the horizontal. Its horizontal range is equal to its maximum height. This is possible when $\tan \theta =$ ......
(a) 0.5 (b) 1
(c) 2 (d) 4

46. Two projectiles are fired at different angles with the same magnitude of velocity such that they have the same range. At what angles they might have been projected?
(a) 10° and 50° (b) 25° and 65°
(c) 35° and 75° (d) none of the above

47. Four projectiles are fired with the same velocities at angles 25°, 40°, 55°, and 70° with the horizontal. The range of projectile will be largest for the one projected at angle
(a) 25° (b) 40°
(c) 55° (d) 70°

48. A bullet is fired horizontally with a velocity of 200 ms^{-1}. If acceleration due to gravity is 10 ms^{-2}, in the first second it will fall through a height of
(a) 5 m (b) 10 m
(c) 20 m (d) 200 m

49. A projectile is thrown at an angle of 40° with the horizontal and its range is R_1. Another projectile is thrown at an angle 40° with the vertical and its range is R_2. What is the relation between R_1 and R_2?
(a) $R_1 = R_2$ (b) $R_1 = 2R_2$
(c) $R_2 = 2R_1$ (d) $R_1 = 4R_2/5$

50. A ball thrown by one player reaches the other in 2 seconds. The maximum height attained by the ball above the point of projection will be about
(a) 2.5 m (b) 5 m
(c) 7.5 m (d) 10 m

ANSWERS

1	2	3	4	5	6	7	8	9	10
(c)	(b)	(b)	(c)	(a)	(a)	(b)	(b)	(a)	(b)
11	**12**	**13**	**14**	**15**	**16**	**17**	**18**	**19**	**20**
(c)	(a)	(c)	(c)	(b)	(c)	(a)	(b)	(d)	(b)
21	**22**	**23**	**24**	**25**	**26**	**27**	**28**	**29**	**30**
(b)	(a)	(b)	(c)	(a)	(b)	(b)	(c)	(b)	(c)
31	**32**	**33**	**34**	**35**	**36**	**37**	**38**	**39**	**40**
(a)	(c)	(b)	(b)	(c)	(d)	(c)	(b)	(b)	(c)
41	**42**	**43**	**44**	**45**	**46**	**47**	**48**	**49**	**50**
(d)	(c)	(c)	(d)	(d)	(b)	(b)	(a)	(a)	(b)

EXPLANATIONS

1. Body A will travel for 2 seconds and body B for 1 second. Separation between them $= S_1 - S_2$

$= \frac{1}{2}\times 2\times 2^2 - \frac{1}{2}\times 2\times 1^2 = 4 - 1 = 3\,\text{m}$

2. Rel. vel. of rain w.r.t. man

$= \sqrt{3^2 + 10^2} = \sqrt{109}$ km/h

3. The relative vel. of rain w.r.t. car is inclined to the vertical in the backward direction. Therefore, it will strike the front screen.

4. Average velocity

$= \frac{\text{net displacement}}{\text{total time}} = \frac{\sqrt{4^2+3^2}}{10+5} = \frac{5}{15}$ m/s

5. Here time of ascent = time of descent $= \frac{4}{2} = 2s$.

Taking vertical upward motion of body we have

$v = u, a = -10\text{ m/s}^2, v = 0, t = 2\text{s}$

As $v = u + at$ or $0 = u + (-10)\times 2$

or $u = 20$ m/s.

6. Distance travelled by A in 5th second,

$D_A = 0 + \frac{a_1}{2}(2\times 5 - 1) = \frac{9}{2}a_1$

Distance travelled by B in 3rd second,

$D_B = 0 + \frac{a_2}{2}(2\times 3 - 1) = \frac{5}{2}a_2$

As per question, $D_A = D_B$

so $\frac{9}{2}a_1 = \frac{5}{2}a_2$ or $\frac{a_1}{a_2} = \frac{5}{9}$

7. Speed in two seconds, $v = \frac{s}{2}$.

Speed in time interval 2 to 6 sec is

$v' = \frac{s}{6-2} = \frac{s}{4}\quad \therefore \frac{v}{v'} = \frac{s/2}{s/4} = 2.$

8. Time of fall, $t = \sqrt{2h/g}$ or $t \propto \sqrt{h}$

$\therefore \frac{t_1}{t_2} = \sqrt{\frac{h_1}{h_2}} = \sqrt{\frac{1}{9}} = \frac{1}{3}$

9. Average acc.

$= \frac{\text{change in vel.}}{\text{time taken}} = \frac{25-(-25)}{5} = 10\text{ ms}^{-2}$

10. Speed of every car is 60 km/h.

Distance between two stations = 60 km.

Time taken by car Y to reach the other station

$= \frac{60}{60} = 1h = 60$ min.

No. of cars leaving the station X in 60 min.

$= \frac{60}{10} = 6$. When car 1st reaches the station Y, the car sixth just starts its journey. The car Y will encounter the number of cars coming from X in route $= 6 + 5 = 11$.

11. Taking vertical upward motion of balloon for 8 sec.

$v = u + at = 0 + 1.25\times 8 = 10$ m/s.

$s = \frac{1}{2}at^2 = \frac{1}{2}\times 1.25\times 8^2 = 40$ m

Taking vertical downward motion of stone released from balloon, we have

$u = -10$ m/s, $a = 10\text{ m/s}^2$, $s = 40$ m; $t = ?$

as $s = ut + \frac{1}{2}at^2$

so, $40 = -10 \times t + \frac{1}{2} \times 10 \times t^2$

or $5t^2 - 10t - 40 = 0$

On solving, $t = 4$ s.

12. Here $D_t = 24.5$ m; $a = 9.8$ m/s^2, $u = 0$, $t = ?$, $s = ?$

As $D_t = u + \frac{a}{2}(2t - 1)$

$\therefore$ $24.5 = 0 + \frac{9.8}{2}(2t - 1)$

or $2t = \frac{49.0}{9.8} + 1 = 5 + 1 = 6$ or $t = 3$s.

$s = ut + \frac{1}{2}at^2 = 0 + \frac{1}{2} \times 9.8 \times 3^2 = 44.1$ m.

13. $s = ut + \frac{1}{2}at^2$

$h = 0 + \frac{1}{2}at^2$

$x = 0 + \frac{1}{2}a\left(\frac{T}{2}\right)^2 = \left(\frac{1}{2}aT^2\right) \times \frac{1}{4}$

$= \frac{h}{4}$ from top

i.e., $\frac{3h}{4}$ metre from the ground.

14. As $F \times s = \frac{1}{2}mv^2$

$\therefore$ $s \propto v^2$

When v is trippled, s becomes 9 times.

15. Stone falls with acceleration g while sound comes with constant velocity v. So

$$T = t_1 + t_2 = \sqrt{\frac{2h}{g}} + \frac{h}{v}$$

16. Time of ascent = time of descent = $\frac{6}{2} = 3$s.

From $v = u + at$

$0 = u - 10 \times 3,$

$u = 30$ ms^{-1}

From, $v^2 - u^2 = 2as.$

$0 - (30)^2 = 2 \times (-10)s$; $s = 45$ m.

17. From $D_n = u + \frac{a}{2}(2n - 1)$

$10 = u + \frac{a}{2}(2 \times 3 - 1)$ ...(i)

$16 = u + \frac{a}{2}(2 \times 4 - 1)$ ...(ii)

Subtract (i) from (ii), $6 = \frac{7a - 5a}{2} = a$

From (i), $10 = u + \frac{5}{2} \times 6,$

$\therefore$ $u = -5$ m/s

18. As acceleration is changing with time, we calculate distance travelled in each second separately.

Vel. at the end of 1st sec = $0 + 4 \times 1 = 4$ m/s

Vel. at the end of 2nd sec = 8 m/s

Vel. at the end of 3rd sec = 12 m/s

As distance = av. vel. × time

$\therefore$ Total distance = $s_1 + s_2 + s_3$

$= \frac{0+4}{2} + \frac{4+8}{2} + \frac{8+12}{2} = 2 + 6 + 10 = 18$ m.

19. Slope = $m = \tan\theta = \frac{AB}{OB} = \frac{U}{OB}$

or $OB = \frac{U}{m}$

Distance travelled = area of ΔOAB

$= \frac{OB \times AB}{2} = \frac{U}{m} \times \frac{U}{2} = \frac{U^2}{2m}$

20. From, $s = ut + \frac{1}{2}at^2$

$\frac{h}{2} = 0 + \frac{1}{2}a \times 3^2$ ...(i)

$h = 0 + \frac{1}{2}at^2$ ...(ii)

Divide (ii) by (i),

$2 = \frac{t^2}{9}$; $t = 3\sqrt{2} = 4.24$ s.

21. Let the body fall through the height of tower in t seconds. From, $D_n = u + \frac{a}{2}(2n - 1)$ we have, total distance travelled in last 2 seconds of fall is

$D = D_t + D_{(t-1)}$

$= \left[0 + \frac{g}{2}(2t - 1)\right] + \left[0 + \frac{g}{2}2(t - 1) - 1\right]$

$= \frac{g}{2}(2t - 1) + \frac{g}{2}(2t - 3) = \frac{g}{2}(4t - 4)$

$= \frac{10}{2} \times 4(t - 1)$

or $40 = 20(t - 1)$ or $t = 2 + 1 = 3$s.

Distance traveled in t seconds is

$s = ut + \frac{1}{2}at^2 = 0 + \frac{1}{2} \times 10 \times 3^2 = 45$ m.

22. Given, $s = kt^3$; $\therefore$ velocity, $v = \frac{ds}{dt} = 3kt^2$ and acceleration,

$$a = \frac{dv}{dt} = 6kt \text{ i.e., } a \propto t.$$

23. $u = 72 \text{ km/h} = 20 \text{ m/s}$

From, $v = u + at$

$0 = 20 - a \times 2$, or $a = 10 \text{ ms}^{-2}$

From, $v^2 - u^2 = 2as$

$0 - (20)^2 = 2(-10)\,s$ or $s = 20$ m.

24. Average acceleration $= \frac{\Delta v}{\Delta t}$

$= \frac{\text{Area of acceleration time graph}}{\text{Time}}$

$= \frac{\text{Area } OABE}{OE} = \frac{300}{20} = 15 \text{ m/s}^2$

25. $$\frac{D_4}{D_3} = \frac{0 + \frac{a}{2}(2\times 4 - 1)}{0 + \frac{a}{2}(2\times 3 - 1)} = \frac{7}{5}.$$

26. When the horizontal range is maximum, the maximum height attained is $R/4$. Velocity of projectile is minimum at the highest point.

27. y_m is maximum, when θ with the horizontal is 90°. In such a case time of flight is also maximum.

29. Only in case of parabolic motion the direction and magnitude of the acceleration remains same. In uniform circular motion direction changes.

30. At the highest point, the velocity is directed horizontally. The acceleration is vertically downwards.

31. The motion of the train will affect only the horizontal component of the velocity of the ball. Since, vertical component is same for both observers, the y_m will be same, but R will be different.

32. Time taken to reach the ground depends on the height from which the projectile is fired horizontally. That is same in both cases.

33. $R_1 = u^2 \sin 2\theta/g = u^2 \sin 150°/g$

$= u^2 \sin 30°/g = u^2/2g.$

$R_2 = u^2 \sin 90°/g = u^2/g.$

Therefore $R_2 = 2R_1$.

34. Acceleration due to gravity is $d^2y/dt^2 = 4 \text{ ms}^{-2}$.

35. $v_x = 2ct$ and $v_y = 2bt$.

Speed after one second will be

$$[(2b)^2 + (2c)^2]^{\frac{1}{2}} = 2(b^2 + c^2)^{\frac{1}{2}}.$$

36. Range is maximum for $\theta = 45°$.

In such a case $y_m = R/4$.

38. Horizontal component of velocity remains unchanged throughout the motion. At the highest point, the vertical component of velocity is zero.

39. Range is same for angles of projection θ and $(90 - \theta)$

$$t_1 = \frac{2u \sin\theta}{g},$$

$$t_2 = \frac{2u\sin(90-\theta)}{g} = \frac{2u\cos\theta}{g}$$

Hence $t_1 t_2 = 4\frac{u^2 \sin\theta\cos\theta}{g^2}$

$$= \frac{2}{g}\left[\frac{u^2 \sin 2\theta}{g}\right] = \frac{2}{g}R, \text{ where } R \text{ is range.}$$

40. Vertically upward component of velocity of projection is $(50 \sin 30°)\text{ ms}^{-1} = 25 \text{ ms}^{-1}$. If t is the time taken to reach the ground then using

$$x = v_0 t + \frac{1}{2}gt^2,$$

We find $70 = -25\times t + \frac{1}{2}\times 10 \times t^2$.

Which gives $t = -2$ s and 7 s.

Here -2 s is not valid.

41. $y = v_0 t + \frac{1}{2}gt^2$. Hence $v_0 = 0$.

45. Here maximum height = range.

That is $u^2 \sin^2\theta/2g = u^2 \sin 2\theta/g$.

That is $\sin^2\theta/\sin 2\theta = 2$.

46. Range is same for θ and $90 - \theta$.

47. $R = u^2 \sin 2\theta/g$. And in this case the $\sin 2\theta$ is the largest for $\theta = 40°$ as compared to that for $\theta = 25°, 55°, 70°$.

48. Horizontal velocity has no effect on the distance of vertical fall.

49. R is same for θ and $90 - \theta$.

50. $T = 2u\sin\theta/g = 2$.

Hence $u \sin\theta = g$, $y_m = u^2 \sin^2\theta/2g$

$= g^2/2g = g/2 \sim 5$ m.

UNIT-3

Laws of Motion

NEWTON'S FIRST LAW OF MOTION

(i) According to this law, **every body continues in its state of rest or of uniform motion in a straight line, unless it is compelled by some external force to change the state,** i.e.,

(a) if a body is at rest, then so as to set it in motion, a force has to be applied on it.

(b) if a body is moving with a constant speed along a straight line, then in order to decrease or increase its speed, a force has to be applied in the direction of motion or opposite to the direction of motion.

(c) if a body is moving with a constant speed along a straight line, then in order to change its direction of motion, a force has to be applied normal to the direction of motion.

(ii) Newton's first law of motion can be divided into two parts. The first part is concerned with a basic property of matter, called **Inertia.** It is that property of the body by virtue of which the body is unable to change its state by itself in the absence of external forces, *e.g.*, if a chair is at rest then it will remain at rest unless a force is applied on it. It can be set into motion only by applying a force on it. **The inherent property of the bodies that they do not change their state unless acted upon by an external force, is called inertia.**

(iii) The second part of the first law of motion gives a definition for force. It is a push or pull which either changes or tends to change the state of rest or uniform motion of a body.

MASS AND MOMENTUM

(i) The physical quantity which is a measure of the inertia of a body is called its inertial mass. The mass of a body can also be described as that which is able to interact with other body in accordance with the Newton's law of gravitation. In this situation the mass of the body is called as gravitational mass.

(ii) Mass is a scalar quantity and is measured in Kilograms.

(iii) In Newtonian Mechanics which we are presently discussing the mass of a body does not depend on its velocity.

(iv) **Momentum:**

(a) It is defined as the total quantity of motion contained in a body and is measured as the product of the mass of body and its velocity.

(b) Since the momentum is the product of a scalar (mass) and a vector (velocity), hence it is a vector quantity represented by $\vec{p}$. It is directed along the velocity.

(c) The momentum of a body of mass m moving with velocity $\vec{v}$ is given by

$$\vec{p} = m\vec{v}$$

(d) If a ball of mass m_1 and a car of mass m_2 $(m_2 > m_1)$ are moving with same velocity v and p_1 and p_2 are the momentum of ball and car respectively, then

$$\frac{p_1}{p_2} = \frac{m_1 v}{m_2 v}$$

or $$\frac{p_1}{p_2} = \frac{m_1}{m_2}$$

As $m_2 > m_1$, hence it implies that $p_2 > p_1$, i.e., if a ball and a car are moving with same velocity, the momentum of car will be greater than that of the ball. Similarly, if two objects of same masses are thrown with different velocities, the one moving with greater velocity will have greater momentum.

(e) If two objects of masses m_1 and m_2 moving with velocities v_1 and v_2 have equal momentum, then

$$m_1 v_1 = m_2 v_2$$

or $$\frac{v_1}{v_2} = \frac{m_2}{m_1}$$

In case, $m_2 > m_1$, then $v_2 < v_1$, i.e., **if two objects of different masses have same momentum, the lighter body possesses greater velocity.**

(f) The dimensional formula of momentum is $[MLT^{-1}]$ and its units are kg ms^{-1} is SI system.

NEWTON'S SECOND LAW OF MOTION

(i) According to this law, the time rate of change of momentum of a body is directly proportional to the external force applied on it and the change in momentum takes place in the direction of force.

(ii) If $\vec{p}$ be the momentum of a body and $\vec{F}$ be the external force acting on it, then according to Newton's second law of motion

$$\vec{F} \propto \frac{d\vec{p}}{dt}$$

or $$F = K\frac{d\vec{p}}{dt}$$

Here, K is a constant of proportionality. Its value depends on the unit adopted for measuring the force. Both in SI and cgs system, the unit of force is selected in such a manner so that $K = 1$. Hence above equation becomes:

$$\vec{F} = \frac{d\vec{p}}{dt} \qquad ...(1)$$

i.e., force is equal to the time rate of change of momentum and it leads to the quantitative measurement of the force.

(iii) A body of mass m moving with a velocity $\vec{v}$ has got a momentum $\vec{p} = m\vec{v}$. Hence

$$\vec{F} = \frac{d}{dt}(m\vec{v})$$

$$= m\frac{d\vec{v}}{dt} = m\vec{a} \qquad ...(2)$$

where $\vec{a} = (d\vec{v}/dt)$, is the acceleration produced in the motion of the body.

(iv) If the applied force produces acceleration $\vec{a}$ such that a_x, a_y and a_z are the magnitudes of the components of acceleration along X–axis, Y–axis and Z–axis respectively, then

$$\vec{F} = m(\hat{i}\ a_x + \hat{j}\ a_y + \hat{k}\ a_z) \qquad ...(3)$$

If F_x, F_y and F_z are the components of force along X–axis, Y–axis and Z–axis respectively, then

$$\vec{F} = \hat{i}F_x + \hat{j}F_y + \hat{k}F_z \qquad ...(4)$$

From equations (3) and (4), we get

$$F_x = ma_x,\ F_y = ma_y \text{ and } F_z = ma_z \qquad ...(5)$$

NEWTON'S THIRD LAW OF MOTION

(i) According to this law to every action, there is equal and opposite reaction.

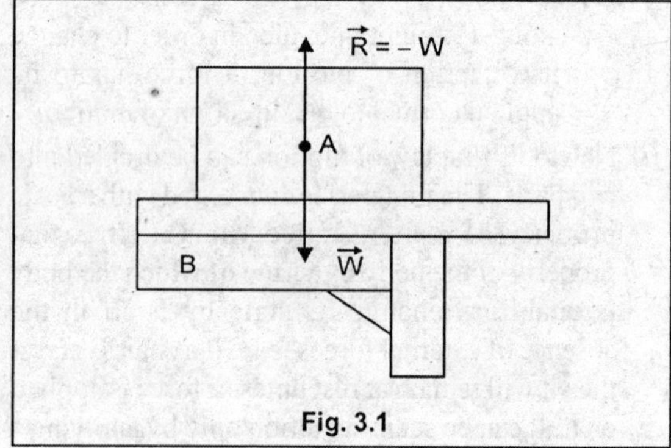

Fig. 3.1

(ii) Consider a body A of weight $\vec{W}$ resting on another body B (Fig. 3.1). The body exerts force equal to its weight $\vec{W}$ on the body B and according to Newton's third law of motion, body B gives an equal and opposite reaction $\vec{R}$ to the body A, i.e.,

$$\vec{W} = -\vec{R}$$

(iii) In general, if a body A exerts force $\vec{F}_{AB}$ (which may be gravitational, electrical or magnetic etc.) on a body B, then the body B will exert a force $\vec{F}_{BA}$ on body A, such that

$$\vec{F}_{AB} = -\vec{F}_{BA}$$

(iv) Further, as the action and reaction do not act on the same body, they never cancel each other.

(v) According to this law it is impossible to have a single force out of mutual interaction between two bodies.

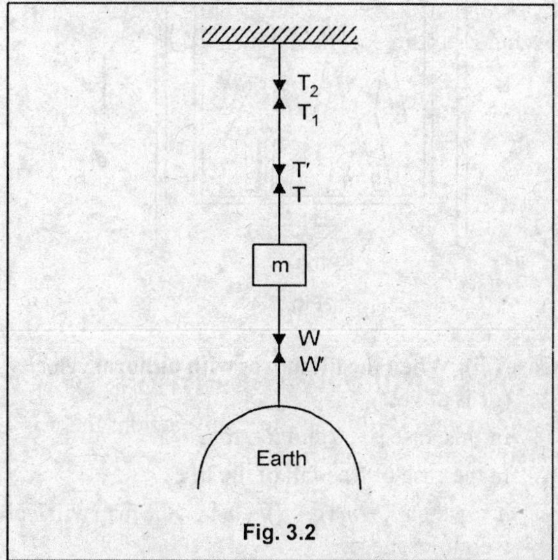

Fig. 3.2

Suppose a mass m is tied to a string and string hangs vertically from a rigid support. In this example, we find that

(a) The earth pulls mass m with a force W'. W and W' form an action-reaction pair acting on different bodies.

(b) The string pulls the mass m with a force T (= Tension in the string). The mass pulls the string with an equal and opposite force T'. Thus T and T' form another action- reaction pair.

(c) Next the rigid support pulls the string with a force T_2 and the string pulls the support with a force T_1. T_1 and T_2 form another action-reaction pair.

(vi) It should be noted here that force W' acting on the earth is so small compared to the huge mass of earth that the earth is not at all affected.

(vii) Further the forces acting on m are its weight W and tension T due to the string. Thus

$$\vec{T}+\vec{W} = m\vec{a}$$

Since m is at rest,

$$\vec{a} = 0$$

$$\therefore \quad \vec{T} = -\vec{W}$$

Although T and $\vec{W}$ are equal and opposite but they do not form action-reaction pair because they act on the same body.

FRAMES OF REFERENCE - INERTIAL FORCE

(i) A frame in which an observer is situated and makes his observations is known as his frame of reference. He fixes a point O as the origin of some coordinate system in this frame. We can describe all the physical quantities like position, velocity, acceleration etc. of an object in terms of this coordinate system. Normally, the earth is taken as a frame of reference because earth can be supposed to be at rest for all considerations.

(ii) Suppose we consider a stationary train on a track laid on the earth. If an observer is sitting in the train, he may choose for himself the train as a frame of reference with origin O'. Let the train now moves with a uniform velocity v with respect to earth. The observer at O finds that the frame with origin O' is moving with a velocity v relative to him. It is also possible for him to conclude that the frame O' is at rest and he is moving with a velocity $-v$ relative to O' though he remains stationary in the frame with origin O.

Both these conclusions are equivalent to each other. There is no way to check the truth of either of the two observations. In other words, a frame at rest is equivalent to any other frame which is moving with a constant velocity relative to it. Such frames are called **Inertial frames of reference.**

(iii) All the fundamental laws of physics are similar in all the reference frames which move with uniform velocity with respect to one another. In such frames Newton's laws of motion are valid.

(iv) As soon as a frame of reference starts accelerating, it become **noninertial** and Newton's laws of motion no more remain valid.

MOTION OF A MAN IN A LIFT

We consider the following cases:

Case (i): When the lift is accelerated upwards:

Suppose R be the upward thrust of the floor on the man (normal Reaction) and mg is the weight of the man acting downwards.

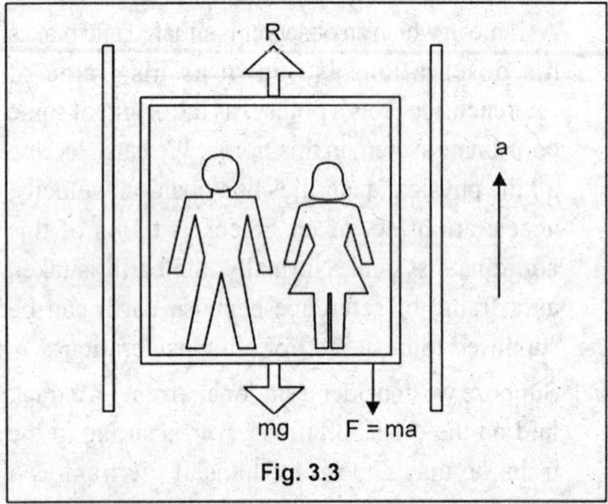

Fig. 3.3

Hence,

unbalanced force = mass × acceleration

or $R - mg = ma$

or $R = mg + ma = m(g + a)$

Thus, if the man is standing on weighing machine, it will show a larger weight than mg.

We can also analyse this problem in a different way, from the point of view of an accelerating frame, which is the lift. Because the acceleration a is directed upwards, the inertial force to be applied on the man is ma in the downward direction. As he is relatively at rest on the floor, the reaction R is balanced by $(mg + ma)$

Case (ii): When the lift is accelerated downward:

In this case, inertial force $F = ma$, is to be applied vertically upward (Fig. 3.4). Now

$$R + F = mg$$

or $R + ma = mg$

or $R = m(g - a)$

Now the weighing machine will show a weight smaller than mg.

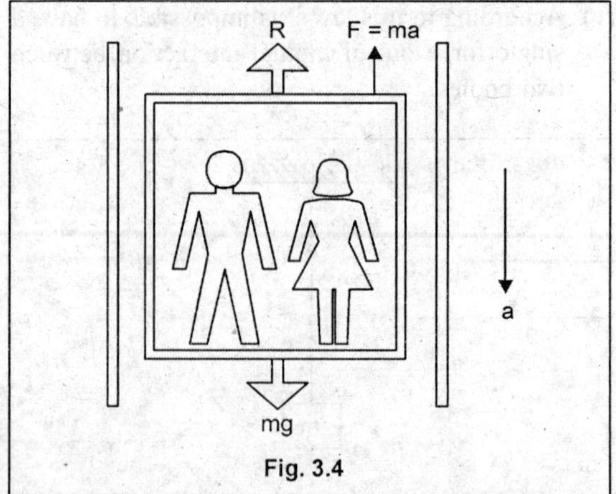

Fig. 3.4

Case (iii): When the lift moves with uniform velocity (or is at rest)

In this case $a = 0$ and $R =$ mg.

In the case of free fall of the lift,

$a = g$, then $R = m(g - g) = 0$, i.e., the man will feel weightlessness.

FRICTION

INTRODUCTION

(i) The property by virtue of which an opposing force is generated between two rough surfaces in contact which opposes the sliding of one surface over the other, is known as friction. The force which always acts in the direction opposite to that in which one surface has a tendency to slide over other surface or move is called as force of friction.

(ii) The frictional force between the two surfaces before the relative motion actually starts is known as static friction. The frictional force between two surfaces when the surfaces in contact are in relative motion is known as kinetic friction.

KINETIC FRICTION

(i) When two bodies in contact move with respect to each other, rubbing the surfaces in contact, the friction between them is called Kinetic friction. The directions of the frictional forces are such that the relative motion is opposed by the friction.

(ii) Let a body *A* placed in contact with *B* is moved with respect to it as shown in fig. 4.20. The force of friction (F) acting on *A* due to *B* will be opposite to the velocity of A with respect to *B*. In figure, this force is shown towards left. The force of friction (F) on *B* due to *A* is opposite to the velocity of *Bs* with respect to *A*. In fig. 3.5 this force is shown towards right.

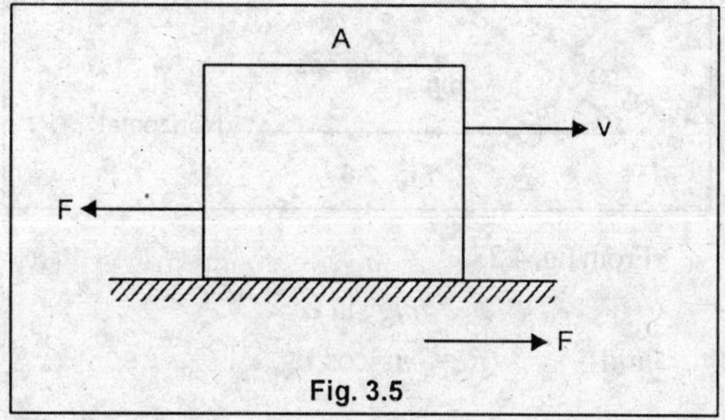

Fig. 3.5

(iii) **Direction of kinetic friction:** The kinetic friction on body *A* slipping against another body *B* is opposite to the velocity of *A* with respect to *B*. It should be noted here that the velocity coming into picture is with respect to the body applying the force of friction.

(iv) The magnitude of the kinetic friction is proportional to the normal force acting between the bodies.

i.e. $F_k = \mu_k N$ ...(1)

where *N* is the normal force. The proportionality constant μ_k is called the coefficient of Kinetic Friction. Its value depends upon the nature of two surfaces in contact. If the surfaces are smooth μ_k will be small; if the surfaces are rough μ_k will be large. It also depends upon the materials of two bodies in contact.

(v) According to equation (1) the coefficient of Kinetic friction does not depend on the speed of the sliding bodies. Once the bodies slip on each other, the frictional force if $\mu_k N$, whatever be the speed. This is nearly true for relative speeds not too large (say for speed < 10 m/s).

(vi) we also find from equation (1) that as long as the normal force *N* is same, the frictional force is independent of the area of the surface in contact.

STATIC FRICTION

(i) Frictional forces can also act between two bodies which are in contact but are not sliding with respect to each other. The friction in such cases is called static friction. For example, suppose many persons are trying to push a heavy box on the floor to take it out of a room.

(ii) **Magnitude of Static Frictional force:** The maximum static friction that a body can exert on other body in contact with it, is called limiting friction. This maximum or limiting friction is proportional to normal contact force between two bodies. We can write

$$f_{max} = \mu_s N$$

The constant of proportionality μ_s is called the coefficient of static friction. Its value again depends on the material and roughness of two surfaces in contact. In general, μ_s **is slightly greater than** μ_k.

ANGLE OF FRICTION

(i) Suppose a body of mass *m* is lying in rest position on a rough table as shown in figure 3.6. Its weight *mg* is acting downward and normal reaction *R* is acting in opposite direction. Suppose we pull the body by some horizontal force *P* and *F* is the frictional force preventing the motion of the body.

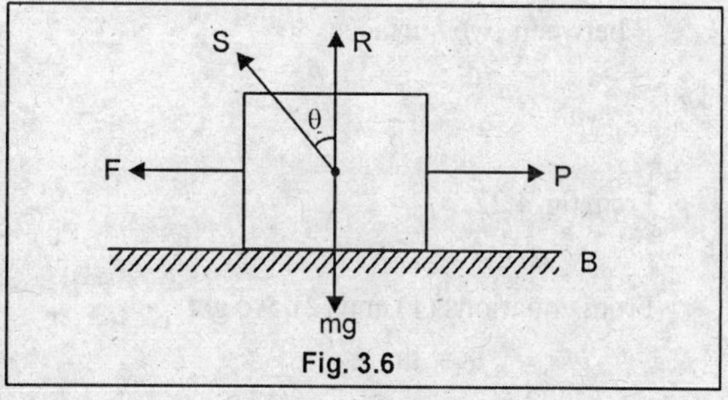

Fig. 3.6

Suppose *S* represents the resultant of *R* and *F* which makes an angle θ with *R*. Resolving *S* along *R* and *F*, we get

$$S \cos \theta = R$$

and $S \sin \theta = F$

i.e. $\tan \theta = F/R$

For equilibrium,

$$R = W = mg$$

and $F = P$

(ii) If we go on increasing the pulling force, the force of friction also goes on increasing till a stage is reached when the body is just at the point of motion. This stage is called as limiting equilibrium. The force of friction in this stage is called as Limiting Friction as is maximum.

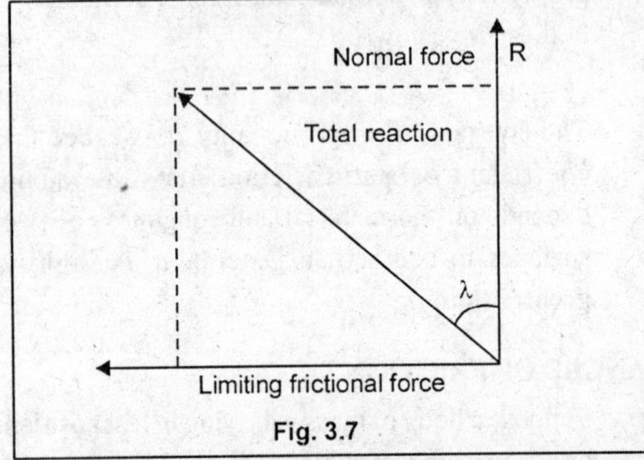

Fig. 3.7

The angle which the resultant of this maximum force and the normal reaction makes with the normal is called angle of friction. This is normally represented by λ.

(iii) The coefficient of friction μ is defined as the ratio of limiting frictional force F to the normal reaction R between two surfaces.

i.e. $$\mu = \frac{F}{R}$$

From fig. 4.22,

$$\tan \lambda = F/R$$

From equations (1) and (2), we get

$$\mu = \tan \lambda$$

ANGLE OF REPOSE (α)

Angle of repose is relevant to the motion of a body on a rough inclined plane. If a body placed on such an inclined plane, is just on the point of sliding down because of its own weight, then the angle of inclination of the plane with the horizontal (Fig. 3.8) is called the angle of repose (α) for the two surfaces in contact.

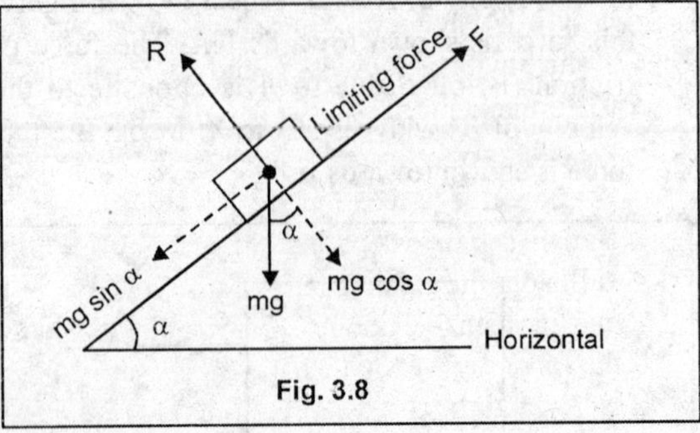

Fig. 3.8

From fig. 4.23,

$$F = mg \sin \alpha$$

and $$R = mg \cos \alpha$$

$$\therefore \quad \frac{F}{R} = \tan \alpha = \mu \quad \ldots(1)$$

Again $$\mu = \tan \lambda \quad \ldots(2)$$

Hence $$\alpha = \lambda$$

Angle of Repose = Angle of limiting friction

LAWS OF FRICTION

(i) The force of friction at the point of contact of two bodies is in the direction opposite to that in which the point of contacts starts moving.

(ii) When the body is just on the point of moving, the force of friction is limiting. The ratio of limiting friction to normal reaction bears a constant ratio and is denoted by μ. The limiting friction is μR.

(iii) The limiting friction is independent of areas in contact provided the normal reaction is unaltered.

(iv) When the body starts moving, the above law of limiting friction still holds good and is independent of the velocity.

LINEAR MOMENTUM AND ITS CONSERVATION PRINCIPLE

(i) The linear momentum of a particle of mass m moving with velocity v is defined as $\vec{p} = m\vec{v}$. **If no external force acts upon a system of two or**

more bodies, then the total momentum of the system remains constant. This is known as the principle of conservation of momentum.

(ii) Suppose two smooth bodies of masses m_1 and m_2 are moving in the same direction on a smooth surface with velocities $\vec{v}_1$ and $\vec{v}_2$ respectively. Their momenta are $\vec{p}_1 = m_1\vec{v}_1$ and $\vec{p}_2 = m_2\vec{v}_2$ respectively.

Suppose, the bodies collide in head-on direction and are separated again from each other. During collision, the bodies exerts force on each other due to which their momenta are changed. Suppose the force exerted on the first body by the second is $\vec{F}_{12}$ and the force exerted on the second body by the first is $\vec{F}_{21}$. Suppose, due to these forces the change in momentum of the first body is $\Delta\vec{p}_1$ and that of the second body is $\Delta\vec{p}_2$. The total change in momentum of the two bodies is $\Delta\vec{p}_1 + \Delta\vec{p}_2$.

During collision, both the bodies are in contact each other. Hence, at this instant, they are parts of one combined body. No external force is acting on this combined body. [Force $\vec{F}_{12}$ and $\vec{F}_{21}$ are being exerted by the two parts of a combined body on each other. Hence these are internal forces of the combined body, but not the external forces]. Hence according to Newton's second law, there will be no change in the momentum of the combined body, i.e.

$$\Delta\vec{p}_1 + \Delta\vec{p}_2 = 0$$

$$\text{or } \Delta(\vec{p}_1 + \vec{p}_2) = 0$$

Here $\Delta(\vec{p}_1 + \vec{p}_2)$ represents the change in the combined momentum of the bodies. It is evident from the above equation that there is no change in the combined momentum of the bodies (although there are individual changes in $\vec{p}_1$ and $\vec{p}_2$). In other words, the momentum of the system of two bodies remains constant, that is,

$$\vec{p}_1 + \vec{p}_2 = \text{Constant}$$

$$\text{or } m_1\vec{v}_1 + m_2\vec{v}_2 = \text{Constant}$$

(iii) If, after collision, the velocities of the bodies becomes $\vec{v}_1'$ and $\vec{v}_2'$, that is, their momenta become $m_1\vec{v}_1'$ and $m_2\vec{v}_2'$ respectively, then

$$m_1\vec{v}_1 + m_2\vec{v}_2 = m_1\vec{v}_1' + m_2\vec{v}_2'$$

$$\text{or } -m_1(\vec{v}_1' - \vec{v}_1) = m_2(\vec{v}_2' - \vec{v}_2)$$

This equation shows that **whatever is the change in momentum of the one body, the same change occurs in the momentum of the second body in the opposite direction.**

APPLICATIONS OF THE PRINCIPLE OF CONSERVATION OF LINEAR MOMENTUM

(i) **When a bullet is fired from a gun, the gun recalls or gives a kick in backward direction.**

Suppose M be the mass of gun and m the mass of bullet. Initially, both the gun and bullet are at rest. Suppose, the bullet moves with a velocity $\vec{v}$, when gun is fired and the gun moves with velocity $\vec{V}$.

According to the principle of conservation of linear momentum.

Total momentum of the gun and bullet before firing = total momentum of the gun and bullet after firing

i.e. $$0 = M\vec{V} + m\vec{v}$$

or $$\vec{V} = -(m/M)\vec{v}$$

(a) The negative sign shows that $\vec{V}$ and $\vec{v}$ are in opposite direction. i.e. if bullet moves forward, the gun will move in backward direction. The backward motion of the gun is called recoil of the gun.

(b) When bullet is fired from a gun, the bullet also exerts a reactionary-force on the gun which is pushed back and acquires an equal momentum in the backward direction. It is due to this reason that gunner feels a push in the backward direction.

(c) Since the mass of the gun (M) is much greater than the mass of the bullet (m), the velocity of recede of the gun is much less than the velocity of proceed of the bullet.

(d) If a bullet be fired by a light gun and another similar bullet by a heavy gun that the light gun will recede with a larger velocity and is likely to hurt the shoulder of the gunner more severely.

(ii) When a man jumps from a boat to the shore, the boat slightly moves away from the shore

Initially, the total momentum of the boat and the man is zero. When a man jumps from the boat, total momentum can be zero, only if the boat moves in a direction opposite to the direction of jumping of man.

(iii) Rocket Launching

As the fuel in rocket undergoes combustion, the gases so produced leave the body of the rocket with large velocity and give upthrust to the rocket. If we assume that the fuel is burnt at a constant rate, then the rate of change of momentum of the rocket will be constant. As more and more fuel gets burnt, the mass of the rocket goes on decreasing and it leads to increase of the velocity of rocket more and more rapidly.

ROCKET PROPULSION

(i) As discussed above, Rocket Propulsion is based on the law of conservation of momentum. This application is of special significance because rocket is a system, in which mass varies with time.

(ii) Suppose total mass of a rocket and its fuel is M_0 at $t = 0$. Let the gas is ejected at a constant rate $r = -(dM/dt)$ and at a constant velocity u with respect to the rocket.

The total mass of rocket and its remaining fuel, after time t is given by

$$M = M_0 - rt$$

If the velocity of the rocket at time t is v, the linear momentum of the system is

$$P = Mv = (M_0 - rt)v \qquad \ldots(1)$$

Consider a small time interval Δt. A mass $\Delta M = r\Delta t$ of the gas is ejected in this time and the velocity of the gas with respect to ground is

$\vec{v}_{\text{gas w.r.t. ground}}$

$= \vec{v}_{\text{gas w.r.t. rocket}} + \vec{v}_{\text{rocket w.r.t. ground}}$

$= -u + v$

in the forward direction.

The linear momentum of the system at $t + \Delta t$ is

$$= (M - \Delta M)(v + \Delta v) + \Delta M(v - u) \qquad \ldots(2)$$

Assuming no external force on the rocket-fuel system, from (1) and (2),

$(M - \Delta M)(v + \Delta v) + \Delta M(v - u) = Mv$

or $(M - \Delta M)(\Delta v) = (\Delta M)u$

or $\Delta v = \dfrac{(\Delta M)u}{M - \Delta M}$

or $\dfrac{\Delta v}{\Delta t} = \dfrac{\Delta M}{\Delta t} \cdot \dfrac{u}{M - \Delta M} = \dfrac{ru}{M - r\Delta t}$

Taking the limit as $\Delta t \to 0$

$$\frac{dv}{dt} = \frac{ru}{M} = \frac{ru}{M_0 - rt} \qquad \ldots(3)$$

This gives the acceleration of the rocket.

(iii) **Thrust on the Rocket**

$$F = M(dv/dt)$$
$$= ru$$
$$= -u(dM/dt)$$

Ignoring negative sign, we get

$$\boldsymbol{F = u(dM/dt)} \qquad \ldots(4)$$

i.e. **thrust on the rocket at any instant is equal to the product of the exhaust speed of the burnt gases and the rate of combustion of fuel at that instant.**

(iv) From eq. (3), we have

$$\frac{dv}{dt} = -\left(\frac{dM}{dt}\right)\frac{u}{M}$$

or $\quad dv = -u.\dfrac{dM}{M}$

When $\quad M = M_0, v = v_0 \qquad$ (at $t = 0$)

and when $M = M_1, v = v \qquad$ (at $t = t$)

Integrating above equation on both sides, we get

$$\int_{v_0}^{v} dv = -\int_{M_0}^{M} u.(dM/M)$$

or $\quad |v|_{v_0}^{v} = -u|\log_e M|_{M_0}^{M}$

or $\quad v - v_0 = -u[\log_e M - \log_e M_0]$

$\quad = u[\log_e M_0 - \log_e M]$

or $\quad v = v_0 + u\log_e(M_0/M) \qquad \ldots(5)$

This equation gives the velocity of rocket at any time t, when mass of the rocket is M.

If the initial velocity of the rocket is zero, then above equation becomes

$$v = u \log_e (M_0 / M) \quad \ldots(6)$$

(v) In above derivation, we have neglected the effect of gravity of the earth. If we take this also into consideration, then eq. (6) takes the form

$$v = u \log_e (M_0 / M) - gt \quad \ldots(7)$$

MULTIPLE CHOICE QUESTIONS

1. The velocity time graph of a lift moving downwards is a straight line inclined to the time axis at 45°. If mass of the lift is M kg, what is the effective weight (in newton) of the lift? Take $g = 10\ ms^{-2}$.
   (a) $10M$
   (b) $9M$
   (c) M
   (d) none of the above

2. A monkey of mass 20 kg is holding a vertical rope. The rope can break when a mass of 25 kg is suspended from it. What is the maximum acceleration with which the monkey can climb up along the rope?
   (a) $2.5\ ms^{-2}$
   (b) $5\ ms^{-2}$
   (c) $7\ ms^{-2}$
   (d) $10\ ms^{-2}$

3. A mass when dropped vertically from the top of a smooth inclined plane reached the ground with a velocity of $50\ ms^{-1}$. If it is allowed to move along the inclined plane, what will be the horizontal component of the velocity on reaching the ground? Angle of inclination of the plane is 30°.
   (a) $50\ ms^{-1}$
   (b) $25\sqrt{3}\ ms^{-1}$
   (c) $10\ ms^{-1}$
   (d) zero

4. In which of the following cases the net force is not zero?
   (a) a kite skilfully held stationary in the sky.
   (b) a ball freely falling from a height.
   (c) an aeroplane rising upwards at an angle of 45° with the horizontal with a constant speed.
   (d) a cork floating on the surface of water.

5. Two masses of 10 kg and 5 kg are suspended from a rigid support as shown in figure. The system is pulled down with a force of 150 N attached to the lower mass. The string attached to the support breaks and the system accelerates downwards.

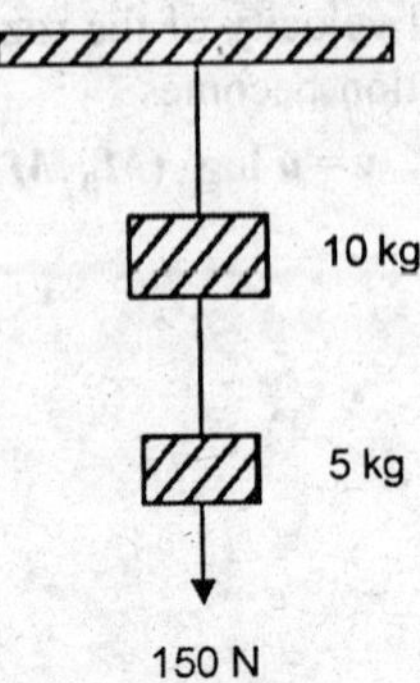

If the downward force continues to act, what is the acceleration of system?
   (a) $20\ ms^{-2}$
   (b) $10\ ms^{-2}$
   (c) $5\ ms^{-2}$
   (d) zero

6. Two masses M_1 and M_2 are attached to the ends of a string which passes over a pulley attached to the top of an inclined plane. The angle of inclination of the plane in θ. Take $g = 10\ ms^{-2}$

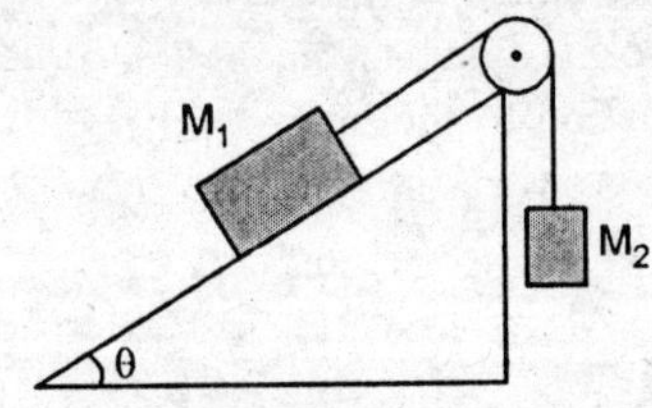

Given that $M_2 = 2M_1$ and M_2 moves vertically downwards with acceleration a. If the position of the masses are reversed the acceleration of M_2 down the inclined plane will be
   (a) $2a$ (b) a
   (c) $a/2$ (d) none of the above

7. Two masses M_1 and M_2 are attached to the ends of string which passes over the pulley attached to the top of a double inclined plane. The angles of inclination of the inclined planes are α and β. See figure and answer the following questions. Take $g = 10\ ms^{-2}$.

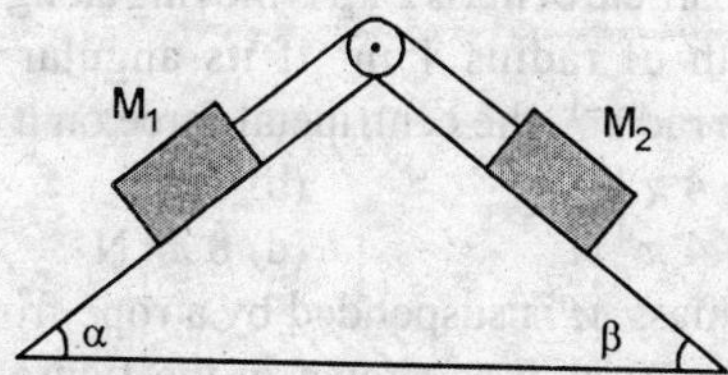

If $M_1 = M_2$ and $\alpha = \beta$, what is the acceleration of the system?

(a) zero (b) 2.5 ms^{-2}
(c) 5 ms^{-2} (d) 10 ms^{-2}

8. A sparrow flying in the air sits on a stretched telegraph wire. If weight of the sparrow is W, which of the following is true about the additional tension T produced in the wire
(a) $T=0$ (b) $T=W$
(c) $T<W$ (d) $T>W$

9. Which of the following statements is true for the jet plane flying horizontally at very high speed?
(a) gravity does not act on it.
(c) upward thrust of the air balances gravity.
(c) thrust due to the gas ejected balances gravity.
(d) the flow of air around the plane causes lift that balances the gravity.

10. A book is lying on an inclined plane having inclination to the horizontal θ °. What is the angle between the weight of the book and the reaction of the plane on the book?
(a) 0° (b) θ°
(c) 180° – θ° (d) 180°

11. A block is allowed to slide down an inclined plane of inclination θ. If, the inclined plane is lying on the floor of a lift which is falling down with a retardation a, what will be the acceleration of the block with which it will slide down?
(a) $(g+a) \sin \theta$ (b) $(g-a) \sin \theta$
(c) $g \sin \theta + a$ (d) $g \sin \theta - a$

12. A rope of mass M is held vertically by fixing its upper end to a rigid support. What will be the tension in the rope at a distance x from the rigid support? Given that the length of the rope is L, and acceleration due to gravity is g
(a) Mg (b) $\frac{L-x}{L} \times Mg$
(c) $\frac{L}{L-x} \times Mg$ (d) $\frac{x}{L} \times Mg$

13. Three masses M_1, M_2 and M_3 are attached with strings passing over a fixed and frictionless pulley as shown in the figure.

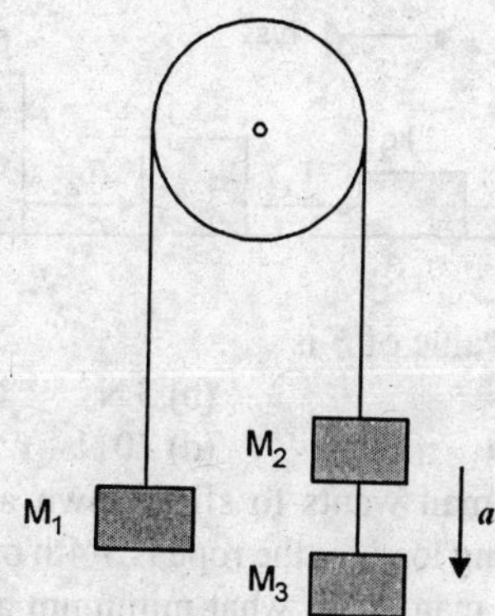

What is the acceleration of M_1?

(a) $\frac{M_3+M_2-M_1}{M_3+M_2+M_1}$ (b) $\frac{M_3-M_2+M_1}{M_3+M_2+M_1}$
(c) $\frac{M_3-M_2-M_1}{M_3+M_2+M_1}$ (d) $(M_2+M_3-M_1)g$

14. A body is at rest on the surface of the earth. Which of the following statements is correct?
(a) no force is acting on the body
(b) only weight of the body acts on it
(c) net downward force is equal to the net upward force
(d) none of the above

15. Two blocks of mass 4 kg and 6 kg are placed in contact with each other on a frictionless horizontal surface. See figure. The acceleration of the lighter mass will be

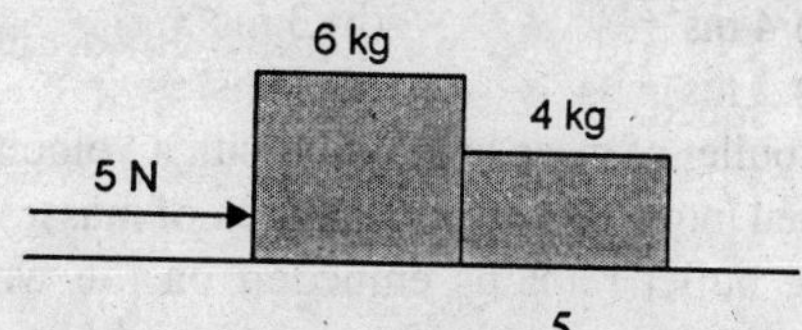

(a) 0.5 ms^{-2} (b) $\frac{5}{4}$ ms^{-2}
(c) $\frac{5}{6}$ ms^{-2} (d) none of the above

16. Three blocks masses 2 kg, 3 kg and 5 kg are connected to each other with light strings and

are then placed on a smooth frictionless surface. See figure below. Let the system be pulled with a force F from the side of lighter mass so that it moves with an acceleration of 1 ms^{-2}. T_1 and T_2 denote the tensions in the other strings.

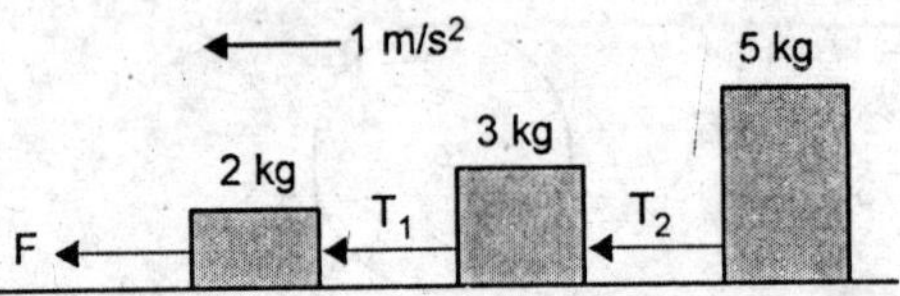

Then value of F is

(a) 2 N (b) 3 N

(c) 5 N (d) 10 N

17. A fireman wants to slide down a rope. The breaking load for the rope is 3/4th of the weight of the man. With what minimum acceleration should the fireman slide down? Acceleration due to gravity is g.

(a) $\frac{1}{4}g$ (b) $\frac{1}{2}g$

(c) $\frac{3}{4}g$ (d) zero

18. Two masses of 10 kg and 20 kg respectively are connected by a massless spring as shown in the figure. A pull of 100 N acts on the mass of 20 kg.

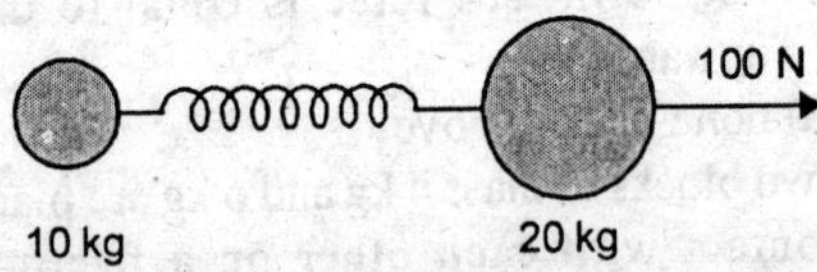

If the instantaneous acceleration of 10 kg mass be 2 ms^{-2}, the acceleration of 20 kg mass is

(a) 4 ms^{-2} (b) 3 ms^{-2}

(c) 2 ms^{-2} (d) 1 ms^{-2}

19. A bullet of mass m moving with a velocity v is fired into a large wooden block of masses M. If the bullet remains embeded on the wooden block, the velocity of the system will be

(a) $\frac{M}{M+m}v$ (b) $\frac{m}{M+m}v$

(c) $\frac{M}{M-m}v$ (d) $\frac{m}{M-m}v$

20. A particle of mass 2 kg is moving along a circular path of radius 1 m. If its angular speed is 2 π rad s^{-1}, the centripetal force on it is

(a) 4π N (b) 8π N

(c) $4\pi^4$ N (d) $8\pi^2$ N

21. A mass M is suspended by a rope from a rigid support at P as shown in the figure. Another rope is tied at the end Q, and it is pulled horizontally with a force F. If the rope PQ makes angle θ with the vertical then the tension in the string PQ is

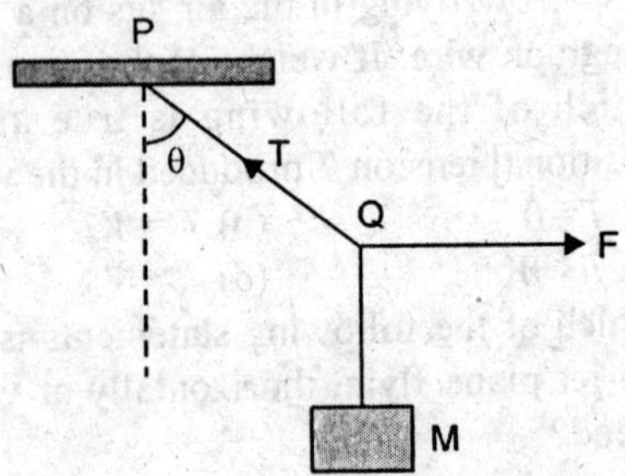

(a) $F \sin\theta$ (b) $F/\sin\theta$

(c) $F \cos\theta$ (d) $F/\cos\theta$

22. A block is suspended from a spring balance B, as shown in figure and it reads M_1. A beaker partially filled with water is placed on another spring balance B_2 as shown in figure (b) which reads M_2. If, we immerse the M_1 in the water in the beaker as shown in figure (c). What will be reading of balance B_1.

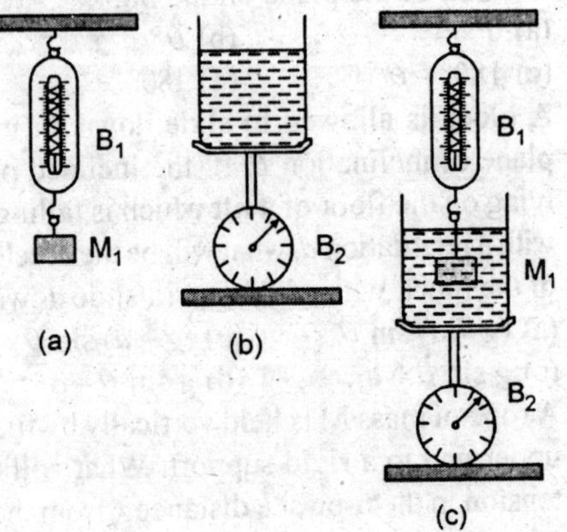

(a) M_1 (b) $\frac{M_1+M_2}{2}$

(c) Less than M_1 (d) More than M_1

23. A block moves down a smooth inclined plane of inclination θ. Its velocity on reaching the bottom is v. If it slides down a rough inclined plane of same inclination its velocity on reaching the bottom is v/n, where n is a number greater than 0. The coefficient of friction μ is given by

(a) $\mu = \tan\theta\left[1-\frac{1}{n^2}\right]$

(b) $\mu = \cot\theta\left[1-\frac{1}{n^2}\right]$

(c) $\mu = \tan\theta\left[1-\frac{1}{n^2}\right]^{\frac{1}{2}}$

(d) $\mu = \cot\theta\left[1-\frac{1}{n^2}\right]^{\frac{1}{2}}$

24. A heavy block of mass M is slowly placed on a conveyer belt moving with a speed v. The coefficient of friction between the block and the belt is μ. Through what distance will the block slide on the belt?

(a) $\frac{v}{\mu g}$ (b) $\frac{v^2}{\mu g}$

(c) $\frac{v}{2\mu g}$ (d) $\frac{v^2}{2\mu g}$

25. Two blocks of mass M_1 and M_2 are connected with a string passing over a pulley as shown in the figure. The block M_1 lies on a horizontal surface. The coefficient of friction between the block M and horizontal surface is μ. The system accelerates. What additional mass m should be placed on the block M_1 so that the system does not accelerate?

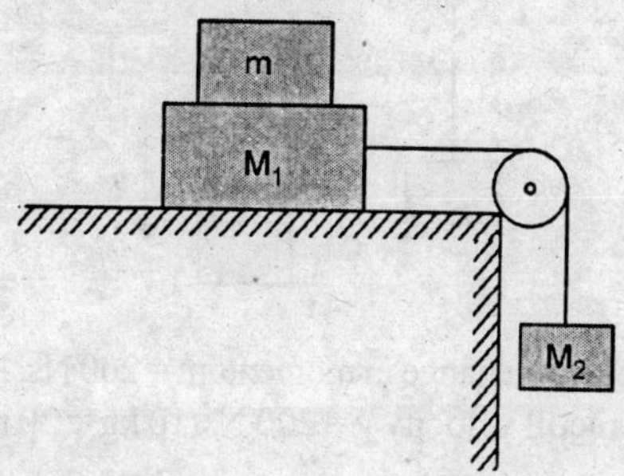

(a) $\frac{M_2+M_1}{\mu}$ (b) $\frac{M_2}{\mu}-M_1$

(c) $M_2-\frac{M_1}{\mu}$ (d) $(M_2-M_1)\mu$

26. The angle between frictional force and the instantaneous velocity of the body moving over a rough surface is

(a) zero

(b) $\pi/2$

(c) π

(d) equal to the angle of friction

27. A body is placed on an inclined plane and has to be pushed down. The angle made by the normal reaction with the vertical will be

(a) equal to the angle of repose

(b) equal to the angle of friction

(c) less than the angle of repose

(d) more than the angle of friction

28. Brakes of very small contact area are not used although friction is independent of area, because friction

(a) resists motion

(b) causes wear and tear

(c) depends upon nature of the materials

(d) operating in this case is sliding friction

29. Why a horse need to pull harder during the first few steps in pulling the cart?

(a) limiting friction is greater than dynamic friction.

(b) sliding friction is greater than rolling friction.

(c) no frictional force acts after the cart comes in motion.

(d) air friction is greater during first law steps of motion.

30. A body is sliding down an inclined plane having angle of friction θ. If the coefficient of friction is μ, then the acceleration of the body down the inclined plane is

(a) $g(\sin\theta+\mu\cos\theta)$

(b) $g(\sin\theta-\mu\cos\theta)$

(c) $g(\cos\theta+\mu\sin\theta)$

(d) $g(\cos\theta-\mu\sin\theta)$

ANSWERS

1	2	3	4	5	6	7	8	9	10
(b)	(a)	(b)	(b)	(a)	(d)	(a)	(d)	(d)	(c)
11	**12**	**13**	**14**	**15**	**16**	**17**	**18**	**19**	**20**
(a)	(b)	(a)	(c)	(a)	(d)	(a)	(a)	(b)	(d)
21	**22**	**23**	**24**	**25**	**26**	**27**	**28**	**29**	**30**
(b)	(c)	(a)	(d)	(b)	(c)	(c)	(b)	(a)	(b)

EXPLANATIONS

1. The slope of the graph is tan 45° = 1. Hence, the lift is falling with acceleration $a = 1\ \text{ms}^{-2}$. Taking $g = 10\ \text{ms}^{-2}$, effective weight of the lift is $M(g-a) = M(10-1)$ newton $= 9\ M$ newton.
2. Let the monkey climb up with acceleration a. Then tension caused in the rope will be $T = M(g+a)$ where M is the mass of the monkey. Maximum value of T is $25 \times g$.
   Hence $25 \times g = 20\,(g + a)$.
   Taking $g = 10\ \text{ms}^{-2}$, it gives $a = 2.5\ \text{ms}^{-2}$.
3. Let l be the length of the inclined plane and h be its height. Using $\upsilon^2 - \upsilon_0^2 = 2ax$, we find $h = 125$ m. And $l = h/\sin\theta = 250$ m. Acceleration down the inclined plane $= g\sin\theta$. So, velocity at the bottom will be $50\ \text{ms}^{-1}$ directed along the plane. Hence, its horizontal component will be $(50\cos 30°)\ \text{ms}^{-1} = 25\sqrt{3}\ \text{ms}^{-1}$
4. When the body falls freely, it is accelerated downwards. Hence, a force acts on it.
5. Total force on the system will be weight of the system + 150 N = 300 N.
   Hence acceleration of the system when force continues to act will be $300\ \text{N}/15\ \text{kg} = 20\ \text{ms}^{-2}$. $= a$ (say).
   Tension in the string will be $10 \times a = T + 10 \times g$. Which gives $T = 100$ N.
   When the force stops acting, the system falls freely.
8. Let the angle subtended by the wire at the point where the sparrow sits be 2θ. Then $2T\cos\theta = w$. Since θ is very near to 90°, as the wire will sag by a small amount. Hence $T >> w$.
10. See figure. Angle between action and reaction is 180°. And that between reaction and weight is $180° - \theta°$.

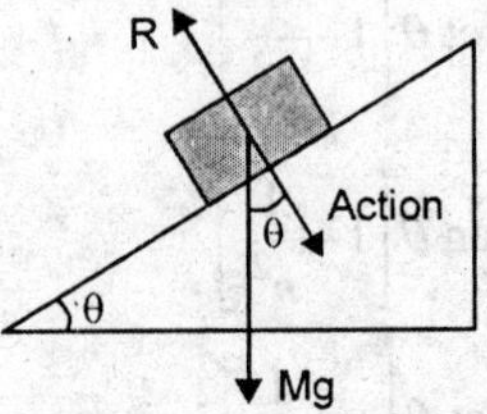

11. The effective value of the downward acceleration is $[g - (-a)]\sin\theta = (g+a)\sin\theta$.
12. The tension at a distance x from the support will be the weight of the rest of the rope having length $(L - x)$. Which comes out to be $(L - x)\,Mg/L$.
13. See figure. For the motion of M_1, M_2 and M_3, we have

$$T - M_1 g = M_1 a$$
$$\Rightarrow T_1 + M_2 g - T = M_2 a$$
$$\Rightarrow M_3 g - T_1 = M_3 a$$

Solving these equations find a and T_1.

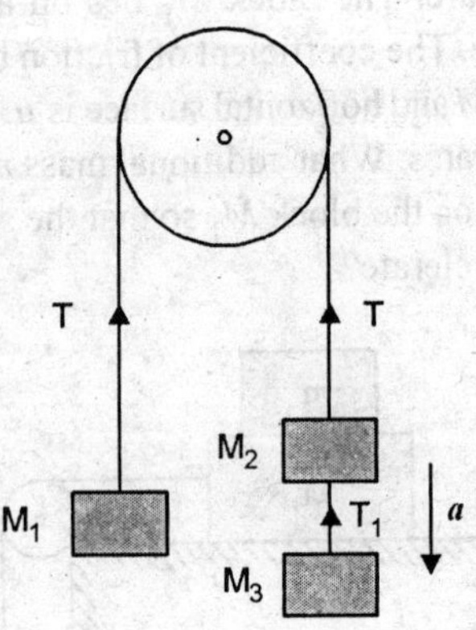

14. Impulse = change in momentum = 200 Ns. Hence the recoil velocity $v = 200\ \text{Ns}/10\ \text{kg} = 20\ \text{ms}^{-1}$.

15. The net force on the body is zero. Weight of the body is balanced by the reaction of the ground.

16. Here $F = (2+3+5)$ kg × 1 ms^{-2} = 10 N.

17. Let the acceleration of the fireman be a. Then $Mg - R = Ma$.

But maximum value of $R = \frac{3}{4}Mg$.

Hence $Mg - \frac{3}{4}Mg = Ma$.

That is $a = g/4$.

18. Force acting on 10 kg mass = 10 × 2N = 20 N. The mass of 10 kg will pull the mass of 20 kg backwards with a force of 20 N. Hence net force on the mass of 20 kg = 100 N – 20 N = 80 N. Acceleration 80 N / 20 kg = 4 ms^{-2}.

19. Here $mv = (M+m)V$.

20. $F_c = MR\omega^2 = 2 \times 1 \times (2\pi)^2$ N

21. See figure. In the triangle PLQ,

$\vec{QP} = \vec{T}, \vec{PL} = M\vec{g}$ and $\vec{LQ} = \vec{F}$.

The point Q is in equilibrium under the action of $\vec{T}, \vec{M}g$ and $\vec{F}$.

Here $T = PQ = LQ/\sin\theta = F/\sin\theta$.

Also $T = PQ = LP/\cos\theta = Mg/\cos\theta$.

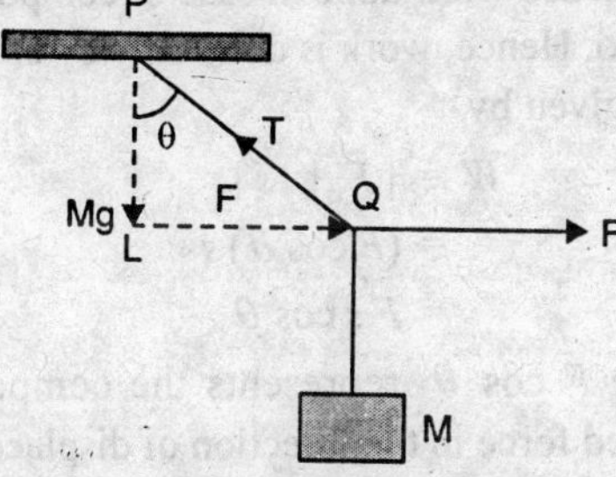

That is $F = T\sin\theta$ and $Mg = T\cos\theta$.

Therefore $[(Mg)^2 + (F)^2]^{1/2} = T$.

22. The reading in B_1 will decrease due to the up thrust caused by the buoyancy.

The component of the acceleration due to gravity along the plane will add up to the acceleration of the cabin.

23. Acceleration down the smooth inclined plane will be $g\sin\theta$. That on the rough inclined plane will be $(g\sin\theta - \mu g\cos\theta)$. If l be the length of the inclined plane, then

$l = \frac{1}{2}g\sin\theta(t)^2$

And $l = \frac{1}{2}g(\sin\theta - \mu\cos\theta)(nt)^2$

On solving we find $\mu = \tan\theta(1 - \frac{1}{n^2})$

We are using $v^2 - v_0^2 = 2ax$.

$v^2 = 2g\sin\theta \times 1$

$(v/n)^2 = 2g(\sin\theta - \mu\cos\theta) \times 1$.

On solving we again find the same value of μ.

24. The block will be acted by the force friction = μMg. It will be causing acceleration $a = \mu g$. The block slides on the belt till its velocity becomes v. Using $v^2 - v_0^2 = 2ax$ we find $x = v^2/2\mu g$.

25. The motion will stop when the force of friction is equal to the weight of M_2. That is, when $M_2 g = \mu(M_1 + m)g$.

26. Frictional force is always directed opposite to the direction of motion.

27. The body need not be pushed down, when the angle of inclination is equal to the angle of repose. In such a case it will automatically move down.

28. Although friction is independent of the area of the contact of rough surfaces, yet brakes of smaller size undergo wear and tear very fast.

30. Net downward force = $Mg\sin\theta - \mu Mg\cos\theta$

UNIT-4

WORK, ENERGY AND POWER

WORK

(i) **Whenever a force acting on a body is able to actually move it through some distance in the direction of force, then work is said to be done by the force.**

(ii) When a coolie moves on platform with load on his head, he exerts force along the vertical direction. But because no distance is covered along the vertical direction, hence work done by the coolie is zero.

WORK DONE BY A CONSTANT FORCE

(i) The work done by a force is measured by the product of the applied force and the displacement of the body in the direction of the applied force.

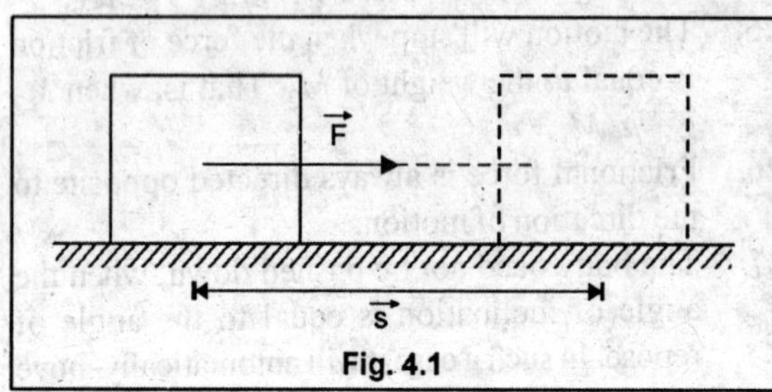

Fig. 4.1

If a force $\vec{F}$ acts on a body and produces a displacement $\vec{s}$ in the body in the direction of the force, then work done by the force is given by

$$W = Fs \quad \ldots(1)$$

where F and s are the magnitudes of the force vector and the displacement vector in the direction of the applied force respectively.

(ii) If force $\vec{F}$ does not act along the direction of displacement $\vec{s}$ (Fig. 4.2), then work is calculated by resolving the force $\vec{F}$ into two mutually perpendicular components:

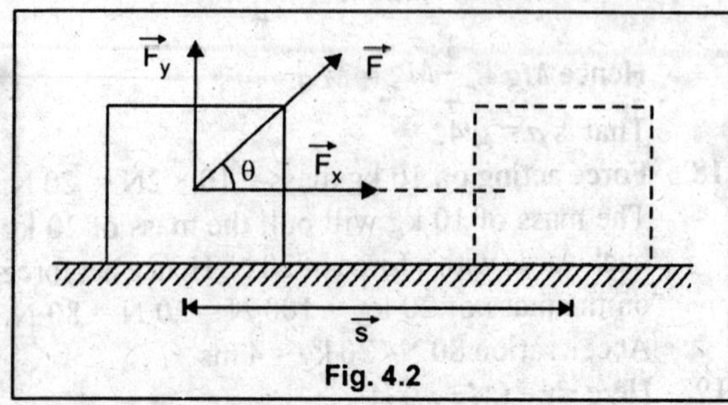

Fig. 4.2

(a) $\vec{F}_x$ along the direction of displacement $\vec{s}$ (having magnitude $F \cos \theta$)

(b) $\vec{F}_y$ along perpendicular to the displacement $\vec{s}$ (having magnitude $F \sin \theta$)

where θ is the angle between the directions of force vector $\vec{F}$ and displacement vector $\vec{s}$.

Since the body does not move in the direction of $\vec{F}_y$, hence work done in case of component $\vec{F}_y$ is zero. Hence, work is done only by component $\vec{F}_x$, given by

$$W = |\vec{F}_x|\,|\vec{s}| = (F \cos \theta)\, s = F s \cos \theta \quad \ldots(2)$$

Since $F \cos \theta$ represents the component of applied force in the direction of displacement of the body, hence in general we can write

Work = component of force in the direction of displacement × displacement

If we put $\theta = 0$ in eqn. (2), we have

$$W = F s \cos 0° = F s$$

which is same as given by eqn. (1), valid in the case when $\vec{F}$ and $\vec{s}$ were in same direction. Thus eqn. (2) is valid for all the situations. Since $\vec{F}$ and $\vec{s}$ are vectors, hence equation (2) can also be written as

$$W = \vec{F} \cdot \vec{s} \quad \ldots(3)$$

Hence, **work done by a force may be represented as the dot product of the force applied and the displacement caused by the force.** Because work done is the dot product of the vectors, it is a scalar quantity.

(iii) Also, if $\vec{F}$ and $\vec{s}$ are perpendicular to each other, then

$$W = \vec{F} \cdot \vec{s}$$
$$= Fs \cos 90° = 0$$

Thus if the displacement of the body is perpendicular to the force, no work is done, e.g. when a satellite revolves around the earth, the direction of force applied by the earth is always perpendicular to the direction of motion of the satellite. Hence work done on the satellite by the centripetal force is zero.

NATURE FOR WORK DONE

(i) Work done is given by

$$W = \vec{F} \cdot \vec{s}$$

According to this equation three possible situations arise regarding the sign or nature of work, which are given below:

(a) $W > 0$, if angle between $\vec{F}$ and $\vec{s}$ is **acute** or $\vec{F}$ and $\vec{s}$ are in the same direction.

(b) $W = 0$, if either $\vec{F}$ or $\vec{s}$ or both $\vec{F}$ and $\vec{s}$ are zero or $\vec{F}$ and $\vec{s}$ are perpendicular to each other.

(c) $W < 0$, if angle between $\vec{F}$ and $\vec{s}$ is **obtuse** or $\vec{F}$ and $\vec{s}$ are in opposite direction.

(ii) **Some illustrations of positive work done**

(a) When an object falls freely under gravitational force, the work done by gravitational force is **positive.**

(b) When a gas filled in a cylinder fitted with a movable piston is allowed to expand, the work done by the gas is **positive.**

(iii) **Some illustrations of Zero work done:**

(a) When a body is moved along a circular path of a string, the work done by the tension in the string is zero.

(b) When a person does not move from his position but he may be holding any amount of heavy load, the work done is zero.

(iv) **Some illustrations of negative work done:**

(a) When a body is made to slide over a rough surface, the work done by the frictional force is negative (as angle between $\vec{F}$ and $\vec{s}$ is 180°).

(b) When a gas filled in a cylinder fitted with a piston is compressed by applying some external force, then work done by external force is **negative.**

WORK DONE BY A VARIABLE FORCE

(i) There are many such examples in which a body may be moving under the effect of a variable force, e.g. when a body is moved away from the centre of earth, the magnitude of force continuously decreases but the direction always remains same. It is also possible that a body may move under the effect of a force, whose both magnitude and direction may be changing

(ii) Here we shall calculate the work done in moving a body from point A to B under the action of a variable force. Suppose at any instant, the body is at the point P and the force acting on it is $\vec{F}$.

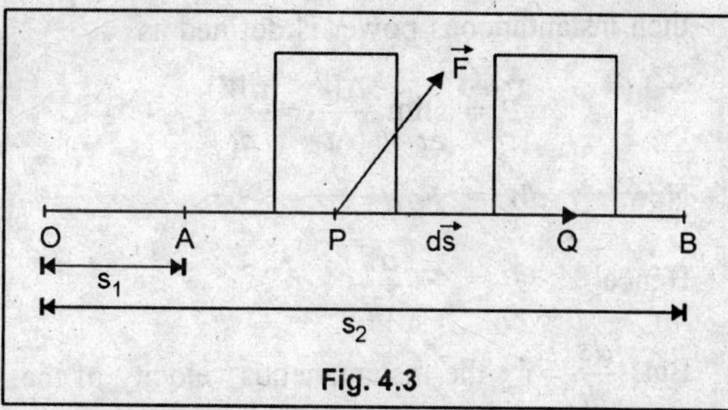

Fig. 4.3

Let the body travels from point P to point Q through a distance $d\vec{s}$ which is infinitesimally small. Although the force is variable between points P and Q but due to displacement PQ being very small, it may be taken as constant over this small displacement. Hence, small amount of the work done by the force $\vec{F}$ between points P and Q is given by

$$dW = \vec{F} \cdot d\vec{s}$$

(iii) Hence total work done in moving the body from point A to B is given by

$$W = \int dW = \int_A^B \vec{F} \cdot d\vec{s}$$

If s_1 and s_2 are the magnitude of initial and final displacements of the body at *A* and *B* with respect to the reference point *O*, then

$$W = \int_{s_1}^{s_2} \vec{F} \cdot d\vec{s}$$

In the case *F* and *ds* are along the same direction, then

$$W = \int_{s_1}^{s_2} F \cdot ds$$

POWER

(i) **The time rate of doing work is called power.** If *W* is the amount of work done in time, *t*, then average power, is

$$P_{av} = W/t \quad ...(1)$$

(ii) Since power is the ratio of two scalars, the average power is a scalar.

(iii) The power of an agent during a time interval may not be constant. The instantaneous power is defined as the limiting value of the average power of an agent in a small time interval, when the time interval approaches zero. Hence, if ΔW is the small amount of work done in a small time interval Δt, then instantaneous power is defined as

$$P = \lim_{\Delta t \to 0} \frac{\Delta W}{\Delta t} = \frac{dW}{dt}$$

Now, $dW = \vec{F} \cdot d\vec{s}$

Hence $P = \vec{F} \cdot \frac{d\vec{s}}{dt}$

But, $\frac{d\vec{s}}{dt} = \vec{v}$, the instantaneous velocity of the particle.

Hence $P = \vec{F} \cdot \vec{v} \quad ...(2)$

Thus, **instantaneous power of an agent is measured as the dot product of instantaneous velocity and the force acting on it at that instant.**

If θ is the angle between $\vec{F}$ and $\vec{v}$, then $P = Fv \cos \theta$

In case, $\theta = 0°$, $P = Fv$.

ENERGY

(i) **The energy of a body is defined as its capacity for doing work.** Since the energy of a body represents the total amount of work done, hence

(a) it is a scalar quantity just like work

(b) its dimensions are the same as that of work i.e. $[ML^2T^{-2}]$

(c) it is measured in the same units as the work i.e. **joule** and **erg**

(ii) Energy and Power are different from each other. Energy of a body implies the total amount of work that the body can do and it has nothing to do with the time taken to perform the work. On the other hand, **the power of the body depends on the time in which the work is done.**

(iii) Energy can exists in different forms such as mechanical energy, heat energy, sound energy, electrical energy, light energy etc. Here, we are concerned with the mechanical energy only which is of two types i.e. **Kinetic and Potential Energy.**

KINETIC ENERGY

(i) **The energy possessed by a body by virtue of its motion is called kinetic energy.**

(ii) Some examples of kinetic energy:

(a) The kinetic energy of running water is used to run the water mills.

(b) A bullet fired from a rifle can penetrate into a target because of its kinetic energy.

(iii) **Calculation of Kinetic Energy:** The kinetic energy of a body of mass *m* moving with velocity *v* can be calculated in any of the following two ways:

(a) either by calculating the amount of work done by the moving body against the external force, before it comes to rest.

(b) or by calculating the amount of work required to set the body into motion with the velocity *v* from its state of rest.

Let us calculate here kinetic energy of a body by the second method. Suppose a constant force $\vec{F}$ is applied on the body at rest till it starts moving with velocity $\vec{v}$ along the direction of force. Suppose $\vec{s}$ be the displacement of body during this time. Then work done by the force

$$W = \vec{F} \cdot \vec{s} = Fs \text{ (as } \theta = 0°) \quad ...(1)$$

If *a* is the acceleration produced in the motion of body, then according to Newton's second law of motion,

$$\vec{F} = m\vec{a}$$

Since all the vectors $\vec{s}, \vec{v}$ and $\vec{a}$ are along the direction of $\vec{F}$, the arrow heads may be dropped and we may use simply their magnitudes. Therefore, equation (1) takes the form

$$W = m\,as \quad ...(2)$$

Using the relation $v^2 - u^2 = 2\,as$, we have

$$v^2 = 2\,as$$

or $$a = v^2/2s \quad ...(3)$$

From equations (1) and (3), we have

$$W = m.(v^2/2s)\,s = ½\,mv^2$$

Since this work done on the body of mass m will set the body moving with velocity v from its state of rest, it is equal to kinetic energy of the body.

Hence,

Kinetic energy = ½ mv^2 ...(4)

WORK-ENERGY THEOREM

(i) If a body is initially at rest and a force $\vec{F}$ is applied on the body to move it through a distance $d\vec{s}$ along its own direction, then, work done

$$dW = \vec{F}\cdot d\vec{s} = F\,ds$$

According to Newton's second law of motion

$$F = ma$$

where a is the acceleration produced in the direction of froce on applying the force. Hence

$$dW = ma\,ds$$

$$= m.(dv/dt).ds \qquad [\because a = (dv/dt)]$$

or $$dW = m\,(ds/dt)\,dv$$

$$= mv\,dv \qquad [\because (ds/dt) = v]$$

Therefore, work done on the body in order to increase its velocity from zero to v is given by

$$W = \int_0^v mvdv = m\int_0^v vdv$$

$$= m\left[\frac{v^2}{2}\right]_0^v = \frac{1}{2}mv^2$$

This work is equal to kinetic energy of the body of mass m, when moving with velocity v.

If the force applied increases the velocity from v_1 to v_2, then

$$W = \int_{v_1}^{v_2} mvdv = m\int_{v_1}^{v_2} vdv$$

$$= m\left[\frac{v^2}{2}\right]_{v_1}^{v_2} = \frac{1}{2}mv_2^2 - \frac{1}{2}mv_1^2$$

Thus work done by a force acting on a body is equal to change in kinetic energy of the body. This is called as Work-Energy Theorem.

POTENTIAL ENERGY

Potential energy is the energy which a body has by virtue of its position in a conservative field and is represented by U. The potential energy of a body at any position say $\vec{s}$ in a conservative field is equal to the work done by the body in moving it from its present position $\vec{s}$ to some standard position say $\vec{s}_0$. The standard position is arbitrary and generally called the zero position because at this position the potential energy of the body is zero or the body has lost the capacity of doing work. The potential energy of a body will therefore be given by

$$U = \int_s^{s_0} \vec{F}\cdot d\vec{s} = -\int_{s_0}^{s} \vec{F}\cdot d\vec{s} \quad ...(1)$$

Hence potential energy of a body at position $\vec{s}$ in a conservative field is defined as the work done by an external agency against the action of a conservative force F, in order to bring it from some standard position $\vec{s}_0$ to the position s.

CONSERVATION OF ENERGY

(i) If a particle is displaced from position $\vec{s}_1$ to a position $\vec{s}_2$ under the influence of a conservative force $\vec{F}$, then according to work-energy theorem

$$\int_{s_1}^{s_2} \vec{F}\cdot d\vec{s} = T_2 - T_1 \quad ...(1)$$

But according to the definition of potential energy

$$\int_{s_1}^{s_2} \vec{F}\cdot d\vec{s} = U_1 - U_2 \quad ...(2)$$

Hence, from equations (1) and (2), we have

$$T_2 - T_1 = U_1 - U_2$$

or $$T_1 + U_1 = T_2 + U_2$$

Thus **for conservative forces the sum of kinetic and potential energies at any point remains constant throughout the motion. It does not depend upon time. This is known as law of conservation of mechanical energy.**

(ii) From above law, it also follows that

$$\Delta(T+U) = \Delta E = 0$$

i.e. $\Delta T + \Delta U = 0$

or $$\Delta T = -\Delta U \quad ...(3)$$

i.e. if the kinetic energy of a body increases its potential energy decreases by the same amount and vice-versa.

(iii) In addition to the above some non-conservative forces like friction is also acting on the particle, the total mechanical energy is no more constant. It changes by the amount of work done by the frictional force i.e.

$$\Delta(T+U) = \Delta E = W_f$$

where W_f is the work done against friction. The lost energy is transformed into heat and the heat energy produced is exactly equal to mechanical energy dissipated. We can therefore write

$$\Delta E + Q = 0$$

where Q is amount of heat produced. This shows that **energy may be transformed from one from to another but it cannot be created or destroyed i.e. the total energy always remains constant. This is known as the law of conservation of energy.**

COLLISION

(i) Collision between two particles is defined as the mutual interaction of the particles for a small interval of time due to which both the energy and momentum of the interacting particles change.

(ii) Examples of collision are collision between two vehicles on a road, collision between two billiard balls, collisions between two gas atoms at room temperature.

(iii) It is not necessary for two bodies undergoing collision to have physical contact with each other. In case of Rutherford's α-particle scattering experiment, α-particles were scattered due to electrostatic interaction between α-particle and the nucleus separated by some distance.

Thus a collision will take place if either of the two bodies come in physical contact with each other or even when path of one body is affected by the force exerted due to the other.

(iv) Collision between two bodies are broadly categorised into two types:

(A) Elastic Collision: The collision, in which both the momentum and kinetic energy of the system remain conserved, are called elastic collision. For example the collision between atomic and subatomic particles, the collision between two glass balls etc. Characteristics of elastic collision are as follows:

(a) The momentum is conserved

(b) Total energy is conserved

(c) Kinetic energy is conserved

(d) Forces involved in the interaction are of conservative nature

(e) Mechanical energy is not transformed into any other form of energy.

(B) Inelastic Collisions: The collisions in which only the momentum of the system is conserved but kinetic energy is not conserved are called inelastic collisions. Most of the collision in our day to day life are inelastic collisions. For example mud thrown on the wall is an example of perfectly inelastic collision. There is a complete loss of kinetic energy, as the mud remains sticking to the wall. Characteristics of inelastic collisions are as follows:

(a) momentum is conserved

(b) total energy is conserved

(c) kinetic energy is not conserved

(d) some or all of the forces involved are non-conservative in nature

(e) a part of whole of the mechanical energy may be transformed into other forms of energy.

(v) Thus in both types of collision,

(a) **momentum is conserved**

(b) **total energy is conserved**

(c) **it is the kinetic energy which may or may not be conserved.**

ELASTIC COLLISION IN ONE DIMENSION

(i) Consider two perfectly elastic bodies *A* and *B* of masses m_1 and m_2 moving along the same straight line with velocities v_1 and v_2 respectively (Fig. 4.4). We assume $v_1 > v_2$ so that the two bodies may collide. Let v'_1 and v'_2 be the final velocities of the bodies after the collision. The two bodies suffer head on collision and continue moving along the same straight line in the same direction. The two bodies will separate after collision only if $v'_2 > v'_1$.

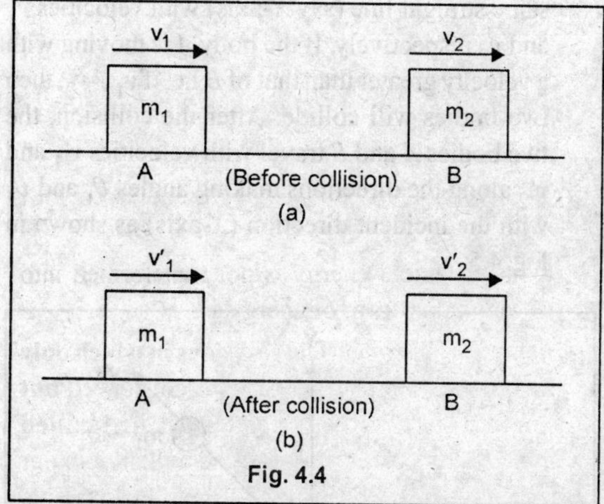

Fig. 4.4

(ii) Because the total linear momentum of the system remains constant, hence we have

$$m_1v_1 + m_2v_2 = m_1v'_1 + m_2v'_2 \quad \text{...(1)}$$

or $\quad m_1v_1 - m_1v'_1 = m_2v'_2 - m_2v_2$

or $\quad m_1(v_1 - v'_1) = m_2(v'_2 - v_1) \quad \text{...(2)}$

Since kinetic energy is also conserved in an elastic collision, we have

$$\frac{1}{2}m_1v_1^2 + \frac{1}{2}m_2v_2^2 = \frac{1}{2}m_1v_1'^2 + \frac{1}{2}m_2v_2'^2$$

or, $\quad m_1v_1^2 - m_1v_1'^2 = m_2v_2'^2 - m_2v_2^2$

or, $\quad m_1(v_1^2 - v_1'^2) = m_2(v_2'^2 - v_2^2) \quad \text{...(3)}$

Dividing equation (3) by equation (2), we obtain

$$v_1 + v'_1 = v'_2 + v_2$$

or $\quad v_1 - v_2 = v'_2 - v'_1 \quad \text{...(4)}$

Above equation shows that **in one dimensional elastic collision, the relative velocity of approach ($v_1 - v_2$) before collision is equal to the relative velocity of separation ($v'_2 - v'_1$) after collision.**

(iii) **Calculation of velocities after collision**

Let us first find the velocity of body *A* after collision. From equation (4), we get

$$v'_2 = v_1 - v_2 + v'_1$$

Substituting for v'_2 in equation (1), we get

$$m_1v_1 + m_2v_2 = m_1v'_1 + m_2(v_1 - v_2 + v'_1)$$

or $\quad m_1v_1 + m_2v_2 = m_1v'_1 + m_2v_1 - m_2v_2 + m_2v'_1$

or $\quad v'_1(m_1 + m_2) = (m_1 - m_2)v_1 + 2m_2v_2$

$$\therefore \quad v'_1 = \frac{(m_1 - m_2)v_1 + 2m_2v_2}{m_1 + m_2} \quad \text{...(5)}$$

Again from equation (4), we get

$$v'_1 = v'_2 - v_1 + v_2$$

Substituting for v'_1 in equation (1), we get

$$m_1v_1 + m_2v_2 = m_1(v'_2 - v_1 + v_2) + m_2v'_2$$

or $\quad m_1v_1 + m_2v_2 = m_1v'_2 - m_1v_1 + m_1v_2 + m_2v'_2$

or $\quad (m_2 - m_1)v_2 + 2m_1v_1 = (m_1 + m_2)v'_2$

$$\therefore \quad v'_2 = \frac{(m_2 - m_1)v_2 + 2m_1v_1}{m_1 + m_2} \quad \text{...(6)}$$

It is worth noting here that value of v'_2 can be directly written from expression for v'_1 by replacing m_1 by m_2, v_1 by v_2 and vice versa.

(iv) **Special cases:**

(a) When the two bodies are of equal masses: Suppose that

$$m_1 = m_2 = m \text{ (say)}$$

From equation (5), we get

$$v'_1 = \frac{(m - m)v_1 + 2mv_2}{m + m} = v_2$$

Also from equation (6), we get

$$v'_2 = \frac{(m - m)v_2 + 2mv_1}{m + m} = v_1$$

Thus, **if two bodies of equal masses undergo elastic collision in one dimension, then after the**

collision, the bodies will exchange their velocities.

(b) When target body i.e. body B is at rest: In this case, the body B is at rest i.e. $v_2 = 0$. Hence from equations (5) and (6), we obtain

$$v'_1 = \frac{(m_1 - m_2)v_1}{(m_1 + m_2)} \quad ...(7)$$

$$v'_2 = \frac{2m_1v_1}{(m_1 + m_2)} \quad ...(8)$$

When target body B is at rest, following interesting subcases may be possible:

(I) When the two bodies are of equal masses: Putting $m_1 = m_2 = m$ in equations (7) and (8), we have

$$v'_1 = 0 \text{ and } v'_2 = v_1 \quad ...(9)$$

Thus, **when body *A* collides against body *B* of equal mass at rest, the body *A* comes to rest and the body *B* moves on with the velocity of the body *A*.** This is sometimes observed, when a boy makes his glass ball hit a stationary glass ball, his own glass ball comes to rest, while the stationary ball starts moving with the same velocity. It can be easily shown in this case, that **the transfer of energy is hundred percent.**

(II) When the mass of body B is negligible as compared to that of A: When $m_2 << m_1$, then in equations (7) and (8), m_2 can be neglected in comparision to m_1 i.e. $m_1 - m_2 \approx m_1$ and $m_1 + m_2 \approx m_1$. Hence, we have

$$v'_1 = (m_1/m_1)\, v_1 = v_1 \quad ...(10)$$

and $$v'_2 = (2m_1/m_1)\, v_1 = 2v_1 \quad ...(11)$$

Thus, **when a heavy body *A* collides against a light body *B* at rest, the body *A* should keep on moving with same velocity and the body *B* will come in motion with velocity double that of *A*.** Thus, in principle, if a moving truck (heavy body) collides against a stationary drum, then the truck would keep on moving with the same velocity, while the drum would come in motion with a velocity double the velocity of the truck.

(III) When the mass of body *B* is very large as compared to that of *A*. When $m_2 >> m_1$, then in equations (7) and (8), m_1 can be neglected in comparison to m_2 i.e. $m_1 - m_2 \approx - m_2$ and $m_1 + m_2 \approx m_2$. Hence, we get

$$v'_1 = -(m_2/m_2)\, v_1 = -v_1$$

$$v'_2 = (2m_1/m_2)\, v_1 = 0 \qquad (\because m_2 >> m_1)$$

Thus, **when a light body *A* collides against a heavy body *B* at rest, the body *A* should start moving with same velocity just in opposite direction while the body *B* should practically remain at rest.** This result is in accordance to our observation that when a rubber ball hits a stationary wall, the wall remain at rest, while the ball bounces back with the same speed.

ELASTIC COLLISION IN TWO DIMENSIONS

(i) Let us consider two perfectly elastic bodies A and B of masses m_1 and m_2 moving along the same straight line (say X-axis) with velocities v_1 and v_2 respectively. If the body A is moving with a velocity greater than that of B i.e. if $v_1 > v_2$, then two bodies will collide. After the collision, the two bodies A and B travel with velocities v'_1 and v'_2 along the directions making angles θ_1 and θ_2 with the incident direction (X-axis) as shown in Fig. 4.5.

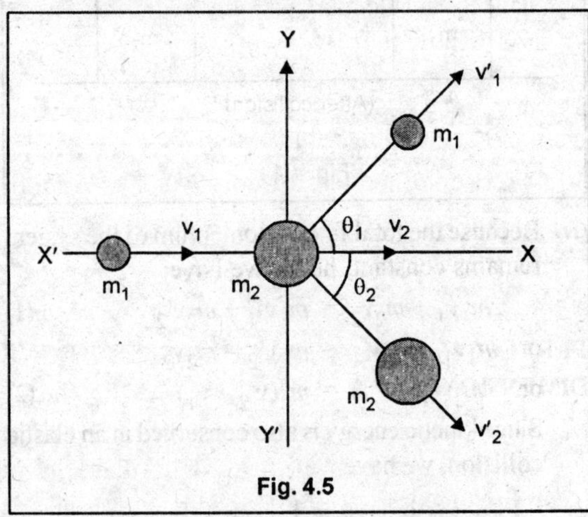

Fig. 4.5

(ii) Because, the collision is perfectly elastic, the kinetic energy must be conserved. Therefore,

$$\frac{1}{2}m_1v_1^2 + \frac{1}{2}m_2v_2^2 = \frac{1}{2}m_1v_1'^2 + \frac{1}{2}m_2v_2'^2 \quad ...(1)$$

Momentum is a vector quantity. As the two bodies move along different directions before and after the collision, the momentum of the two bodies must be separately conserved along *X*-axis and *Y*-axis. The component of momentum of body *A* after collision along *X*-axis = $m_1 v'_1 \cos\theta_1$

The component of momentum of body B after the collision along *X*-axis = $m_2 v'_2 \cos\theta_2$

Applying law of conservation of momentum along *X*-axis, we get,

$$m_1 v_1 + m_2 v_2 = m_1 v'_1 \cos\theta_1 + m_2 v'_2 \cos\theta_2 \quad ..(2)$$

The component of momentum of body *A* after collision along *Y*-axis = $m_1 v'_1 \sin\theta_1$ (along *OY*)

The component of momentum of body *B* after collision along *Y*-axis

$$= m_2 v'_2 \sin\theta_2 \quad \text{(along } OY'\text{)}$$
$$= -m_2 v'_2 \sin\theta_2 \quad \text{(along } OY\text{)}$$

Before collision, the component of momentum of body *A* or of body *B* along *Y*-axis is zero.

Therefore, applying law of conservation of momentum along *Y*-axis, we get

$$0+0 = m_1 v'_1 \sin\theta_1 + (-m_2 v'_2 \sin\theta_2)$$

or $\quad m_1 v'_1 \sin\theta_1 = m_2 v'_2 \sin\theta_2 \quad \ldots(3)$

(iii) In the study of collision between two bodies, we have to find the four quantities i.e. v'_1, v'_2, θ_1 and θ_2. Since there are only three equations connecting them, the values of all the four quantities cannot be found. In practice, the value of one variable, say final velocity of *A* or *B* or the direction of motion of *A* or *B* after collision is measured experimentally. Then the values of remaining three quantities are determined from equation (1), (2) and (3).

PERFECTLY INELASTIC COLLISION IN ONE DIMENSION

(i) **Final Velocity:** When perfectly inelastic bodies moving along the same line collide, they stick to each other. Let m_1 and m_2 be the masses and v_1 and v_2 be their velocities before the collision and V be the common velocities of the bodies after the collision. According to law of conservation of linear momentum

$$m_1 v_1 + m_2 v_2 = m_1 V + m_2 V$$

$$\therefore \quad V = \frac{m_1 v_1 + m_2 v_2}{m_1 + m_2}$$

(ii) **Loss of Kinetic Energy:** The kinetic energy before the collision

$$= \frac{1}{2} m_1 v_1^2 + \frac{1}{2} m_2 v_2^2$$

Kinetic Energy after the collision

$$= \frac{1}{2}(m_1 + m_2) V^2$$

Loss of Kinetic Energy due to the collision

$$= \frac{1}{2} m_1 v_1^2 + \frac{1}{2} m_2 v_2^2 - \frac{1}{2}(m_1 + m_2) V^2$$

$$= \frac{1}{2}\left[m_1 v_1^2 + m_2 v_2^2 - \frac{(m_1 v_1 + m_2 v_2)^2}{(m_1 + m_2)} \right]$$

$$= \frac{1}{2}\left[\frac{m_1 m_2 (v_1^2 + v_2^2 - 2 v_1 v_2)}{(m_1 + m_2)} \right]$$

$$= \frac{m_1 m_2 (v_1 - v_2)^2}{2(m_1 + m_2)}.$$

Obviously loss in kinetic energy is positive.

COEFFICIENT OF RESTITUTION

(i) We have seen that for a perfectly elastic collision velocity of separation = velocity of approach and for a perfectly inelastic collision velocity of separation = 0

(ii) Generally, the bodies are neither perfectly elastic nor perfectly inelastic. In that case, we can write velocity of separation = *e* (velocity of approach) where $0 < e < 1$. The constant *e* depends upon the material of the colliding bodies. This constant is known as coefficient of restitution. If $e = 1$, the collision is perfectly elastic and if $e = 0$, the collision is perfectly inelastic.

MULTIPLE CHOICE QUESTIONS

1. When a body is moving in a circular orbit, work done will be
(a) positive (b) negative
(c) zero (d) None of these

2. When a body moves with a constant speed along a circle
(a) no acceleration is produced in the body
(b) its velocity remains constant
(c) no work is done on it
(d) no force acts on the body

3. What is **F**. **ds**?
(a) Torque (b) Impulse
(c) Momentum (d) Work

4. A man lifts 20 kg mass upto 2m. The work done by him is
(a) 2 joule (b) zero
(c) none of these (d) 200 joule

5. A body, constrained to move in the y-direction is subjected to a force given by ($\vec{F} = 2\hat{i} + 15\hat{j} + 6\hat{k}$) N. What is the work done by this force in moving the body a distance to 10 m along the y-axis?
(a) 190 J (b) 160 J
(c) 150 J (d) 20 J

6. A 60 kg weight is dragged on a horizontal surface by a rope. If coefficient of friction is μ = 0.5, the angle of rope with surface is 60° and g = 9.8 m/sec^2, then work done is
(a) 294 joule (b) 15 joule
(c) 588 joule (d) 197 joule

7. A horizontal force of 5 N is required to maintain a velocity of 2 m/s for a block of 10 kg mass sliding over a rough surface. The work done by this force in one minute is
(a) 600 J (b) 60 J
(c) 6 J (d) 6000 J

8. A point of application of a force F = 3i – 2j + 2k Newtons is displaced by x = 3i -2j + k meters. Then the work done by the force is
(a) 5 J (b) 7 J
(c) 9 J (d) 11 J
(e) zero

9. A body is acted upon by a force $\vec{F} = -12\hat{i} + 5\hat{j}$. Work done by the force in moving the body from the origin to a point, coordinates of which are (5, 4) is
(a) 153 (b) 80
(c) 73 (d) 7

10. A force $\vec{F} = (5\hat{i} + 3\hat{j})$ N is applied over a particle which displaces it from its origin to the point $\vec{r} = (2\hat{i} - 1\hat{j})$ metres. The work done on the particle is
(a) – 7 joules (b) + 13 joules
(c) + 7 joules (d) + 11 joules

11. Work done by a frictional force is
(a) negative (b) positive
(c) zero (d) none of these

12. A chain of mass m and length L is placed on a table with one-fourth of it hanging freely from the edge of the table. The amount of work required to pull the chain on to the table is nmg L where n is equal to
(a) 1/32 (b) 1/16
(c) 1/8 (d) 1/4

13. A particle moves from the position $\vec{r}_1 = 3\hat{i} + 3\hat{j} - 2\hat{k}$ to the position $\vec{r}_2 = 13\hat{i} + 8\hat{j} + 8\hat{k}$ under the action of a force $2\hat{i} + \hat{j} + 4\hat{k}$. If the force and displacement are measured in SI units, the work done is (in J)
(a) 115 (b) 85
(c) 75 (d) none of these

14. A uniform chain of mass M and length L is lying on a smooth table with half of its length hanging vertically down the edge of the table. The work done in pulling the hanging part of the chain over the table is
(a) MgL / 2 (b) MgL / 4
(c) MgL / 8 (d) MgL / 16

15. A body moves a distance of 10 m along a straight line under the action of a 5 N force. If the work done is 25 J, then angle between the force and direction of motion of the body is
(a) 30° (b) 45°
(c) 60° (d) 75°

16. A body of mass 3 kg is under a force which causes a displacement in it, given by $s = t^2/3$ (in m). Find the work done by the force in 2 seconds
(a) 2 J (b) 3.8 J
(c) 5.2 J (d) 2.6 J

17. A force $\vec{F} = 5\hat{i} + 6\hat{j} - 4\hat{k}$ acting on a body, produces a displacement $\vec{S} = 6\hat{i} + 5\hat{k}$. Work done by the force is
(a) 10 units (b) 18 units
(c) 11 units (d) 15 units

18. The work done in pulling up a block of wood weighing 2 kN for a length of 10 m on a smooth plane inclined at an angle of 15° with the horizontal is
(a) 4.36 kJ (b) 5.17 kJ
(c) 8.91 kJ (d) 9.82 kJ

19. "A boy carrying a box on his head is walking on a level road from one place to another on a straight road is doing no work". This statement is
(a) correct (b) incorrect
(c) partly correct (d) insufficient data

20. The forces $F_1 = 3\hat{i} + 4\hat{j} - 3\hat{k}$ N and $F_2 = 2\hat{i} + \hat{j} + 4\hat{k}$ N act simultaneously on a body to displace it from the position of $3\hat{i} + 2\hat{j} - \hat{k}$ m to the position of $5\hat{i} + \hat{j} - 2\hat{k}$ m. The increase in the energy of the body is
(a) 16 J (b) 10 J
(c) – 8 J (d) 0

21. A string of mass m is stretched by a length ℓ. What is the work done where g is the acceleration due to gravity?
(a) 1/2 mgℓ (b) mgℓ
(c) 1/4 mgℓ (d) 4 mgℓ

22. A mass is hanging on a wire, due to which its length increases by *l*, then work done is
(a) 1/2 mgl (b) mgl
(c) zero (d) 2 mgl

23. A body of mass m is moving in a circle of radius r with a constant speed v. The force on the body is mv^2/r and is directed towards centre. Then the work done by this force in moving the body over half the circumference of the circle is
(a) 0 (b) $mv^2/r \times \pi r$
(c) mv^2rt (d) $\pi r^2 \times mv$

24. If a particle is rotating in a circle, which of the following is true?
(a) No work is done
(b) Particle has no acceleration
(c) Velocity of particle is constant
(d) No force is acting on the particle

25. A car weighing 500 kg working against a resistance of 500 N, accelerates from rest to 20 ms^{-1} in 100 m. ($g = 10\ ms^{-2}$). The work done by the engine of car is
(a) 1.0×15^5 J (b) 1.5×15^5 J
(c) 1.05×15^5 J (d) None of these

26. A force of $(3\hat{i} + 4\hat{j})$ N acts on a body and displaces it by, $(3\hat{i} + 4\hat{j})$ metres. The work done by the force is
(a) 10 J (b) 12 J
(c) 16 J (d) 25 J

27. Calculate the work done when a force $\vec{F} = 2\hat{i} + 3\hat{j} - 5\hat{k}$ units acts on a body producing a displacement $\vec{s} = 2\hat{i} + 4\hat{j} + 3\hat{k}$ units
(a) 30 units (b) 45 units
(c) 1 units (d) zero unit
(e) 15 units

28. A mass m is lowered with the help of a cord by distance d at a constant acceleration g/4. The work done by the cord will be
(a) mgd (b) mgd/4
(c) mgd/8 (d) 3/4 mgd

29. A force $\vec{F} = 4\hat{i} + 5\hat{j}$ newton displaces a particle through a distance $S = (3\vec{i} - \vec{j})$ metre, then find the work done
(a) – 7 joule (b) + 7 joule
(c) + 12 joule (d) – 12 joule

30. A mass M is lowered with the help of a string by a distance x at a constant acceleration g/2. The work done by the string will be
(a) Mgx (b) ½ Mgx
(c) ½ Mgx^2 (d) Mgx^2

31. A body moves a distance of 10 m under the action of force F = 10 N. If the work done is 25 J, the angle which the force makes with the direction of motion is
(a) 0° (b) 30°
(c) 60° (d) none of these

32. A uniform chain of length l and mass M lying on a smooth table and one-third of its length is hanging vertically down over the edge of the table. If g is the acceleration due to gravity, the work required to pull the hanging part on to the table is
(a) Mgl (b) Mgl/9
(c) Mgl/3 (d) Mgl/18

33. A force $\vec{F} = 6\hat{i} + 2\hat{j} - 3\hat{k}$ acts on a particle and produces a displacement of $\vec{S} = 2\hat{i} - 3\hat{j} - x\hat{k}$. If the work done is zero, the value of x is
(a) – 2 (b) 1/2
(c) 2 (d) 3

34. A lorry and a car, moving with the same kinetic energy, are brought to rest by applying the same retarding force, then
(a) lorry will come to rest in a shorter distance
(b) both will come to rest in the same distance
(c) car will come to rest in a shorter distance
(d) none of these

35. A force $\vec{F} = 6\hat{i} + 5\hat{j}$ newton acts and displaces the body through $\hat{S} = 3\hat{i} - 2\hat{k}$ meter. Then the work done will be
(a) 8 J (b) 28 J
(c) 18 J (d) 10 J

36. A force $\vec{F} = (5\hat{i} + 4\hat{j})$ N acts on a body and produces a displacement $\vec{S} = 6\hat{i} - 5\hat{j} + 3\hat{k}$ m. The work done will be
(a) 10 J (b) 20 J
(c) 30 J (d) 40 J

37. A body of mass 5 kg is placed at the origin, and can move only on the x-axis. A force of 10 N is acting on it in a direction making an angle of 60° with the x-axis and displaces it along the x-axis by 4 metres. The work done by the force is
(a) 2.5 J (b) 7.25 J
(c) 40 J (d) 20 J

38. A ball of mass M moves with velocity v and strikes with a wall having infinite mass and return with same velocity. Work done by the ball on the wall is
(a) zero (b) Mv J
(c) $\frac{M}{v}$ J (d) $\frac{v}{M}$ J

39. The work done by the centripetal force F when the body completes one rotation around the circle of radius R is
(a) 2πRF (b) 2 RF
(c) RF (d) Zero

40. A position dependent force $F = 7 - 2x + 3x^2$ newton acts on a small body of mass 2 kg and displaces it from x = 0 to x = 5m. The work done in joule is
(a) 70 (b) 270
(c) 35 (d) 135

41. A force acts on a 3 gm particle in such a way that the position of the particle as a function of time is given by $x = 3t - 4t^2 + t^3$, where x is in metres and t is in seconds. The work done during the first 4 second is
(a) 490 mJ (b) 450 mJ
(c) 912 mJ (d) 530 mJ

42. A 10 kg mass moves along x-axis. Its acceleration as a function of its position is shown in the figure. What is the net work done on the mass by the force as the mass moves from x = 0 to x = 8 cm?
(a) 8×10^{-2} joules (b) 16×10^{-2} joules
(c) 4×10^{-4} joules (d) 1.6×10^{-3} joules

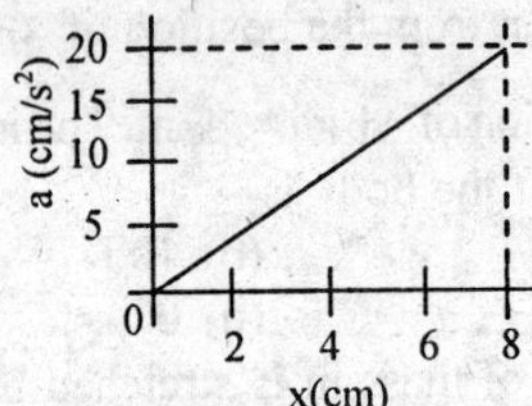

43. A force of $(3x^2 + 2x)$ N acts on system displacing it from x = 1 m to x = 3m. What is the work done?
(a) 20 J (b) 29 J
(c) 34 J (d) 42 J

44. Work done by a centripetal force F in taking round a particle along a circle of radius r through one-quarter of the circumference is
(a) Fr/4 (b) Fr/2
(c) Fr (d) zero

45. Natural length of a spring is 60 cm, and its spring constant is 4000 N/m. A mass of 20 kg is hung from it. The extension produced in the spring is, (Take g = 9.8 m/s^2)
(a) 4.9 cm (b) 0.49 cm
(c) 9.4 cm (d) 0.94 cm

46. When a body moves with constant speed in a circular path then
(a) it has constant acceleration
(b) it has constant velocity
(c) no work done
(d) none is correct

47. When a body moves in a circular path, no work is done by the force since,
(a) force and displacement are perpendicular to each other
(b) the force is always away from the centre
(c) there is no displacement
(d) there is no net force

48. Which of the following is non-conservative force?
(a) Viscous force (b) Gravitational force
(c) Electrostatic force (d) Interatomic force

49. Which statement is wrong? If a body is rotating around a circle with constant speed
(a) its velocity is accelerating
(b) force is conserved
(c) Kirchhoff's law obeys conservation of charge
(d) when electron falls on lower orbit from higher orbit, energy is released

50. KWh is a unit of
(a) power (b) quantity of charge
(c) energy (d) current

ANSWERS

1	2	3	4	5	6	7	8	9	10
(c)	(c)	(d)	(c)	(c)	(b)	(a)	(b)	(c)	(c)
11	**12**	**13**	**14**	**15**	**16**	**17**	**18**	**19**	**20**
(a)	(a)	(d)	(d)	(c)	(d)	(a)	(b)	(b)	(c)
21	**22**	**23**	**24**	**25**	**26**	**27**	**28**	**29**	**30**
(a)	(a)	(a)	(a)	(b)	(d)	(c)	(d)	(b)	(b)
31	**32**	**33**	**34**	**35**	**36**	**37**	**38**	**39**	**40**
(d)	(d)	(c)	(c)	(c)	(a)	(d)	(a)	(d)	(d)
41	**42**	**43**	**44**	**45**	**46**	**47**	**48**	**49**	**50**
(c)	(a)	(c)	(c)	(a)	(c)	(a)	(a)	(b)	(c)

HINTS / SOLUTIONS

1. Work done $W = \vec{F}.\vec{S}$. In this case, F and S are ⊥ to each other. This however, will not be zero if it is the case of non-uniform circular motion.

10. $W = \vec{F}.\vec{d} = (5\hat{i}+3\hat{j})\ (2\hat{i}-1\hat{j})$

$= 10-3 = +7$ Joule

15. The work done $W = \vec{F}.\vec{d}$

$W = Fd\cos\theta$

$\Rightarrow 25 = 5\times 10\times\cos\theta$

$\Rightarrow \cos\theta = 1/2$

$\Rightarrow \theta = 60°.$

16. Work done $= \int F.ds = \int m\left(\frac{d^2s}{dt^2}\right)ds$

Now, $s = \frac{t^2}{3}$

$\therefore \frac{ds}{dt} = \frac{2t}{3}$ and $\frac{d^2s}{dt^2} = \frac{2}{3}$

$$\therefore W = \int_{t=0}^{t=2} 3\times\frac{2}{3}\left(\frac{2t}{3}\right)dt$$

$$\text{or} \quad = \frac{4}{3}\left(\frac{t^2}{2}\right)_0^2 = \frac{4}{3}\times\frac{4}{2} = \frac{8}{3} = 2.6\,J.$$

19. Generally it is a said that he does no work, but this is wrong because while he does no work against his weight (i.e. gravitational force, mg) but he definitely does work against frictional froce (μ mg). Students must understand it clearly. If he is walking towards, say, north, he, in fact, is pushing earth towards south which means frictional force is acting on him towards north.

20. As

$$W = (\vec{F}_1 + \vec{F}_2)(\vec{r}_1 - \vec{r}_2) = (5\vec{i} + 5\vec{j} + \vec{k})(2\vec{i} - \vec{j} + 3\vec{k})$$

$= 10 - 5 + 3 = 8$ J.

∴ Energy increased in the body is $= -8$ J.

21. Work done = 1/2 × stress × strain
$= 1/2 \times mg \times \ell$

26. Force (F) = $(3\hat{i} + 4\hat{j})$N and displacement (d) $= (3\hat{i} + 4\hat{j})$metres

∴ Work done (W) $= \vec{F}.\vec{d} = (3\hat{i} + 4\hat{j}).(3\hat{i} + 4\hat{j})$
$= [(3 \times 3) + 16] = 9 + 16 = 25$ J.

29. Work done = F.d
$= (4\hat{i} + 5\hat{j})(3\hat{i} - \hat{j}) = 12 - 5 = 7$ joule

30. $W = F \cdot x = \frac{Mg}{2} x = \frac{Mgx}{2}$.

31. $Fs \cos\theta = W \Rightarrow \cos\theta = 25/100 = 1/4$.

32. Work done = Change in P.E.

$$= \frac{M}{3} g . \frac{\ell}{6} = \frac{Mg\ell}{18}.$$

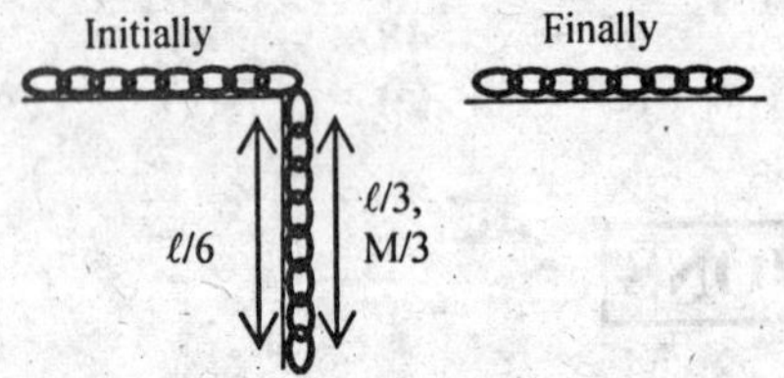

33. $\vec{F} = 6\hat{i} + 2\hat{j} - 3\hat{k}$ .... (i)

$\vec{S} = 2\hat{i} - 3\hat{j} + x\hat{k}$ .... (ii)

$W = \vec{F}.\vec{S} =$ zero

$\Rightarrow 12 - 6 - 3x = 0$.
$\therefore 6 = 3x$ or $x = 2$.

34. Both lorry and car have same K.E. that means velocity of car is more but when same retarding force acts on both, retardation caused in case of car is more.

35. $W = F.S = (6\hat{i} + 5\hat{j}).(3\hat{i} - 2\hat{k}) = 18$

36. Work done, $W = \vec{F}.\vec{S}$
$= (5\hat{i} + 4\hat{j}).(6\hat{i} - 5\hat{j} + 3\hat{k})$
$= 30 - 20 = 10$ J

37.

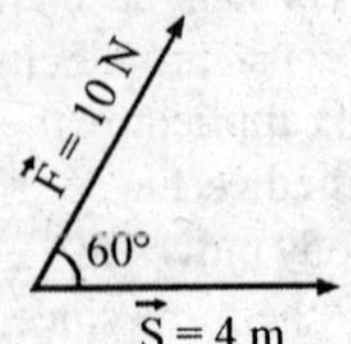

$W = Fd \cos\theta$
$= 10 \times 4 \cos 60° = 20$ J.

38. Work done = F.S.
Here S = 0 ∴ Work done = 0

39. Work = force × displacement
for circular round, displacement = 0
∴ W = 0.

41. $x = 3t - 4t^2 + t^3$

$$\therefore \frac{dx}{dt} = 3 - 8t + 3t^2 \quad \therefore \frac{d^2x}{dt^2} = -8 + 6t$$

∴ Force, F = mass × acceleration.
$= 3 \times 10^{-3}(-8 + 6t)$ N
∴ Work $= [3 \times 10^{-3}(-8 + 6t)] \times [3 - 8t + 3t^2]$
$= [3 \times 10^{-3}(-8 + 6 \times 4)] \times [3 - 8 \times 4 + 3 \times 4^2]$
$= 912 \times 10^{-3}$ J $= 912$ mJ.

42. $\int \vec{F} . \vec{ds}$ is the work done. It is equal to the area under the F – s graph. Instead of F, the graph is for accleration **a** versus displacement **s**. However, F = ma. So, the work done will be area under the graph multiplied by mass m.

∴ Work done = Area of triangle × mass

$$= \frac{1}{2}(8 \times 10^{-2} \times 20 \times 10^{-2}) \times 10 = 8 \times 10^{-2} \text{ J}.$$

43. $W = \int_1^3 F dx = \int_1^3 (3x^2 + 2x) dx = \left[\frac{3x^3}{3} + \frac{2x^2}{2}\right]_1^3$

$= 27 + 9 - 1 - 1 = 34$ J.

44. Displacement is one quarter of the circumference = r
∴ W = Fr

45. Length of the spring $= \ell = 60$ cm
spring constant of the spring $= k = 4000$ N/m

Load mass attached to the spring = 20 kg

Total load attached to the spring = 20 × 9.8 = 196 N

Let the extension produced = Δx

Now, force applied by the spring = Downward force applied on the spring by the weight

$$K\Delta x = mg, \Delta x = \frac{mg}{K} = \frac{20 \times 9.8}{4000}$$

$\Delta x = 0.049\ m, \Delta x = 4.9$ cm

50. The Kilo Watt hour is the energy consumed when 1000 Watts power is utilised for one hour.

UNIT-5

MOTION OF SYSTEM OF PARTICLES AND RIGID BODY

RIGID BODY

A body in which there is no displacement of the particles, even if a very large force is applied on it is called a rigid body.

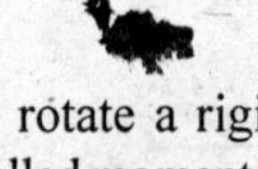

TORQUE (τ)

The tendency of a force to rotate a rigid body about the axis of rotation is called moment of force or torque due to the force. It is measured as the product of magnitude of force and the perpendicular distance of the line of action of the force from the axis of rotation.

Thus, Torque τ = force × perpendicular distance of force from axis of rotation.

Units of torque are N-m (not joule) and dimensional formula is $[ML^2T^{-2}]$.

Expression for torque in cartesian co-ordinate system

In order to calculate torque let us first calculate the work done in rotating a body in a plane. Let us consider a particle of mass m situated in $X-Y$ plane. The particle is moving in a circular path of radius r with respect to O. Let P and Q represent the positions of the particle at instants t and $(t + \Delta t)$ respectively. The position vectors of P and Q are $\vec{r}$ and $\vec{r} + \Delta\vec{r}$ with respect to the origin O. A force $\vec{F}$ is applied on the particle which causes its motion from P and Q. Let the angle $\angle POQ = \Delta\theta$, then $\vec{PQ} = \Delta\vec{r}$ is the displacement of the particle in time Δt.

The small work done by this force

$$\Delta W = \vec{F}.\Delta\vec{r} \quad \text{...(i)}$$

Let, F_x and F_y be the components of force along X and Y axes and Δx and Δy be the components of $\Delta\vec{r}$ along X and Y axes respectively then

$$\Delta W = \vec{F}.\Delta\vec{r} = (\hat{i}F_x + \hat{j}F_y).(\hat{i}\Delta x + \hat{j}\Delta y)$$

or $\quad \Delta W = Fx\,\Delta x + Fy\Delta y \quad$ ...(ii)

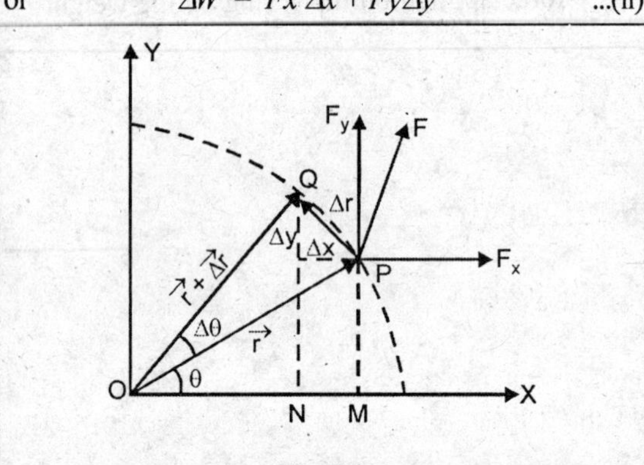

Fig. 5.1

Now, let the coordinates of P and Q be (x, y) and $(x + \Delta x)$ and $(y + \Delta y)$, then from right angled triangle OMP, we have

$OM = OP\cos\theta \quad$ and $\quad PM = OP\sin\theta$

or $\quad x = r\cos\theta$ and $y = r\sin\theta$.

Similarly from right angled triangle ONQ we have

$x + \Delta x = r\cos(\theta + \Delta\theta)$ and $y + \Delta y = r\sin(\theta + \Delta\theta)$

Now $\quad x + \Delta x = r[\cos\theta\cos\Delta\theta - \sin\theta\sin\Delta\theta]$

For small angles $\cos\Delta\theta = 1$, $\sin\Delta\theta = \Delta\theta$

$\therefore \quad x + \Delta x = r[\cos\theta - \Delta\theta\sin\theta] = x - y\Delta\theta$

or $\quad \Delta x = -y\Delta\theta$

Similarly $y + \Delta y = r[\sin\theta\cos\Delta\theta + \cos\theta\sin\Delta\theta]$

or $\quad y + \Delta y = r[\sin\theta + \Delta\theta.\cos\theta]$

or $\quad y + \Delta y = y + x\Delta\theta$

or $\quad \Delta y = x\Delta\theta$

Substituting the values of Δx and Δy in equation (ii), we get

$$\Delta W = Fx(-y\Delta\theta) + Fy(x\Delta\theta)$$

$$\Delta W = \Delta\theta[xFy - yFx]$$

Here, in this expression we define

$xf_y - yf_x = \tau$ as the magnitude of a physical quantity which when multiplied by angular displacement gives the work done in rotational motion just as force when multiplied by linear displacement gives work in translational motion. The quantity $xF_y - yF_x$ is called the torque of force about an axis passing through origin O and perpendicular to $X-Y$ plane.

Hence $\quad \Delta W = \tau\Delta\theta$

and $\quad \tau = xF_y - yF_x$

The above expression gives only the magnitude of the torque and not the direction.

DIRECTION OF TORQUE

The torque due to a force acts in a direction in which a right handed screw placed perpendicular to the $X-Y$ plane (plane of rotation) advance, when rotated in the direction of rotational motion. Thus if the motion is in $X-Y$ plane, then the torque will be along z-axis.

POWER OF TORQUE

The small work done by a torque τ acting on the body, in small angular displacement $\Delta\theta$ in time Δt is given by

$$\Delta W = \tau\Delta\theta \qquad ...(i)$$

Dividing equation (i) by Δt, wer get

$$\frac{\Delta W}{\Delta t} = \frac{\tau\Delta\theta}{\Delta t}$$

Now $\frac{\Delta W}{\Delta t} = P$, the average power during time interval Δt and $\frac{\Delta\theta}{\Delta t} = \omega$, the average angular speed of the particle during time interval Δt.

Thus, $\quad P = \tau\omega$

Expression for torque in polar coordinate system

Suppose that force vector $\vec{F}$ makes an angle ϕ with the position vector $\vec{r}$ of the particle and an angle α with x-axis. Let θ be the angle which the position vector $\vec{r}$ makes with x-axis, then

$$\phi = \alpha - \theta \qquad ...(i)$$

Now, $\quad F_x = F\cos\alpha$

and $\quad F_y = F\sin\alpha$

If the coordinates of P are (x, y) then,

$$x = r\cos\theta \quad \text{and} \quad y = r\sin\theta$$

Now, $\quad \tau = xF_y - yF_x$

$\therefore \quad \tau = r\cos\theta F_y - r\sin\theta F_x$

or $\quad \tau = r\cos\theta(F\sin\alpha) - r\sin\theta(F\cos\alpha)$

or $\quad \tau = rF[\sin\alpha\cos\theta - \cos\alpha\sin\theta]$

$\quad \tau = rF\sin(\alpha - \theta) = rF\sin\phi$

[From equation (i)]

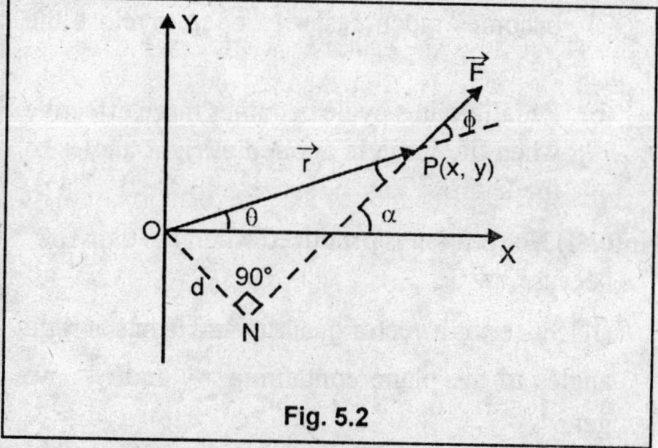

Fig. 5.2

Let ON be perpendicular on NP, then the perpendicular distance of F from O is $ON = d$, and from right angled triangle ONP,

$$ON = OP\sin\phi$$

or $\quad d = r\sin\phi$

Hence, $\quad \tau = Fd \qquad ...(iii)$

equation (iii) represents the expression for torque to a force.

Let F_r and F_θ be the radial and transverse components of force along $\vec{r}$ and θ respectively, then

$$F_r = F\cos\phi, F_\theta = F\sin\phi$$

Hence equation (ii) becomes

$$\tau = rF_\theta \qquad ...(iv)$$

i.e. torque = transverse component of the force × distance from axis of rotation.

Thus radial component of force does not contribute to the torque, only the transverse component contributes to the torque.

Now from equation (iii) it follows that the torque due to a force is maximum when

(i) **r is maximum :** For this reason :

(a) The door handles are provided at the edge of the door not at the hinges.

(b) To open a tightly fitted nut we use a wrench with a long arm.

(c) The handle of the water pump is made long to lift up water easily.

(ii) $\sin\theta$ is maximum i.e. $\theta = 90°$: For this reason.

(a) When the force is applied on the door in a direction at right angles to the plank, it becomes much easier to open or close the door.

(b) Pedalling in a cycle becomes more effective when the force is applied at right angles to the shaft.

Note. (I) No rotation is produced when $\theta = 0$ or $180°$ because $\tau = 0$.

(II) Since τ is a vector quantity and it acts at right angles to the plane containing $\vec{r}$ and $\vec{F}$, we get,

$$\vec{\tau} = \vec{\tau}$$

(III) Since, $\vec{r} = x\hat{i} + y\hat{j} + z\hat{k}$

and $\vec{F} = \vec{F}$

we have, $\vec{\tau} = c.(x\hat{i} + y\hat{j} + z\hat{k}) \times (F_x\hat{i} + F_y\hat{j} + F_z\hat{k})$

or $c \times (x\hat{i} + y\hat{j} + z\hat{k}) + (F_x\hat{i} + F_y\hat{j} + F_z\hat{k})$

$$= \hat{i}[yF_z - zF_y] - \hat{j}[xF_z - zF_x] + \hat{k}[xF_y - yF_x] \quad \text{...(v)}$$

but $\hat{i}[yF_z - zF_y] - \hat{j}[xF_z - zF_x] + \hat{k}[xF_y - yF_x]$

$$= \tau_x\hat{i} + \tau_y\hat{j} + \tau_z\hat{k} \quad \text{...(vi)}$$

Comparing (v) and (vi), we get

$\tau_x = yF_z - zF_y;\ \tau_y = zF_x - xF_z;\ \tau_z = xF_y - yF_x$

ANGULAR MOMENTUM

Angular momentum of a body is defined as the product moment of linear momentum about the axis of rotation of the product of linear momentum of the body and the perpendicular distance of its line of action from the axis of rotation.

Units of angular momentum are kg m^2 sec^{-1}. Its dimensional formula is $[ML^2T^{-1}]$.

EXPRESSION FOR ANGULAR MOMENTUM IN CARTESIAN COORDINATES

For a particle moving in $X - Y$ plane

$$\tau_2 = xF_y - yF_x$$

But $$F_x = \frac{dp_x}{dt} = \frac{d}{dt}(mv_x) = \frac{mdv_x}{dt}$$

Similarly $$F_y = \frac{dv_y}{dt}$$

$$\therefore \quad \tau_z = xm\frac{dv_y}{dt} - ym\frac{dv_x}{dt}$$

or $$\tau_z = m\left[x\frac{dv_y}{dt} - y\frac{dv_x}{dt}\right]$$

Now, $$\frac{d}{dt}(xv_y - yu_x) = x\frac{dv_y}{dt} + v_xv_y - y\frac{dv_x}{dt} - v_xv_y$$

or $$\frac{d}{dt}(xv_y - yv_x) = x\frac{dv_y}{dt} - y\frac{dv_x}{dt}$$

$$\therefore \tau_z = m\frac{d}{dt}[xv_y - yv_x] = \frac{d}{dt}[xmv_y - ymv_x]$$

or $$\tau_z = \frac{d}{dt}[xp_y - yp_x] \quad \text{...(i)}$$

Now, according to Newton's II law for rotatory motion

$$\tau = \frac{dL}{dt} \quad \text{...(ii)}$$

$\therefore$ Comparing (i) and (ii), we get

$L_z = xp_y - yp_x;\ L_y = zp_x - xp_z;\ L_x = yp_z - zp_y$

LAW OF CONSERVATION OF ANGULAR MOMENTUM

If the sum of external torques acting on the system is zero, then the total angular momentum of the system remaining constant. This is the law of conservation of angular momentum. For a system of N particles, the total external torque is due to the sum of external torques acting due to the external forces, since the internal forces do not contribute to the torque. Thus,

$$\vec{\tau}(\text{tot}) = \frac{d\vec{L}(\text{tot})}{dt}$$

If the sum of external torques acting on the system is zero, then

$$0 = \frac{d\vec{L}(\text{tot})}{dt}$$

$$\vec{L}(\text{tot}) = \text{constant vector.}$$

or $\vec{L}_1 + \vec{L}_2 + ... \vec{L}_N$ = constant vector.

Since the angular momentum can also be written as

$$L = I\omega \quad \therefore \; I\omega = \text{constant}$$

i.e., if I increases, ω decreases and vice-versa.

APPLICATIONS OF LAW OF CONSERVATION OF ANGULAR MOMENTUM

The phenomenon which obey the law of conservation of angular momentum are as follows :

(i) The angular velocity of a planet in its orbit round the sun increases when it gets nearer to sun, as M. I. of the planet about sun decreases and w increases.

(ii) An ice-skater or a ballet-dancer can increase her angular velocity by folding her arms or by folding her body, as this decreases moment of inertia and increases angular velocity.

(iii) The speed of the inner layers of the whirlwind about its axis in a tornado is very high because of small moments of inertia of inner layers.

(iv) A diver jumping from spring board some times exhibits sommer-saults in air before touching the water surface, because the diver curls his body to decrease moment of inertia and increase angular velocity. As he is about to reach the water surface he again outstretches his limbs. This again increases moment of inertia and the diver enters the water surface with a gentle speed.

(v) A helicopter is provided with two fans to conserve angular momentum.

(vi) The speed of rotation of a person standing on a rotating stool with his arms outstreched suddenly increases when he folds his hands, because moment of inertia decreases and velocity increases.

MOMENT OF INERTIA OF A PARTICLE

The moment of inertia of a particle about an axis is defined as the product of the mass of the particle and square of the perpendicular distance of the particle from axis of rotation.

$$\therefore \quad I = m \times r^2$$

Units of moment of inertia are gm. cm^2 in C.G.S. system and kg. m^2 in S.I. system. The dimensional formula of the moment of inertia is [ML^{2}T^0].

MOMENT OF INERTIA OF A RIGID BODY

Moment of inertia of a rigid body about any axis of rotation is defined as the sum of products of masses of the particles and the square of their respective distances from axis of rotation.

Let $m_1, m_2, m_3, ...$ be the masses of the particles and $r_1, r_2, r_3 ...$ be their respective distances from axis of rotation, then moment of inertia

$$I = m_1r_1^2 + m_2r_2^2 + m_3r_3^2 + ... m_nr_n^2$$

or $$I = \sum_{i=1}^{n} m_i r_i^2$$

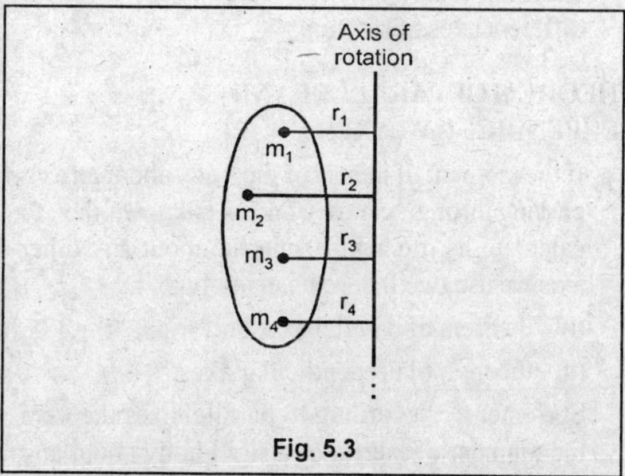

Fig. 5.3

if x_i and y_i are the coordinates of the ith particle, then

$$I = \sum_{i=1}^{n} m_i(x_i^2 + y_i^2)$$

RADIUS OF GYRATION

Radius of gyration is defined as the distance from axis of rotation at which if total mass of the body were supposed to be concentrated, the moment of inertia would be the same as with the actual distribution of mass of body in small particles.

Let K be the radius of gyration and M be the total mass of the body then moment of inertia

$$I = MK^2$$

Now $$I = m_1r_1^2 + m_2r_2^2 + \dots m_nr_n^2$$

If all the particle have equal mass m, then

$$I = m[r_1^2 + r_2^2 + \dots r_n^2]$$

$$\therefore \quad MK^2 = m[r_1^2 + r_2^2 + \dots r_n^2]$$

$$MK^2 = m \times n\left[\frac{r_1^2 + r_2^2 + \dots r_n^2}{n}\right]$$

But $m \times n = M$ = total mass of the body

$$\therefore \quad K^2 = \frac{r_1^2 + r_2^2 + r_3^2 + \dots r_n^2}{n}$$

or $$K = \sqrt{\left(\frac{r_1^2 + r_2^2 + r_3^2 + \dots r_n^2}{n}\right)}$$

Thus K = root mean square of the distance of the particles from axis of rotation.

Note. Radius of gyration of a rigid body is not a constant quantity but its value is different for different axes of rotation.

THEOREM OF PARALLEL AND PERPENDICULAR AXES

If the moment of inertia of the body about an axis passing through centre of mass is known then to calculate its moment of inertia about any other axis we use two theorems, namely

(i) theorem of parallel axes and

(ii) theorem of perpendicular axes.

Statement. According to parallel axes theorem the moment of inertia of a rigid body about any axis is equal to its moment of inertia about a parallel axis passing through centre of gravity plus the product of the mass of the body and the perpendicular distance between the two parallel axes.

Thus $$I = I_g + Ma^2$$

where I_g = M.I. of the body about an axis passing through centre of gravity,

Let M = Mass of the body

and a = perpendicular distance between the two parallel axes.

Proof. Consider a rigid body of mass M. Let AB be an axis passing through centre of gravity. Let CD be another axis parallel to AB and lying at a perpendicular distance a from the given axis AB. Let m be the mass of the particle at a distance r from the axis AB. Then, moment of inertia of the particle about CD is

$$dI = m\,(r + a)^2$$

and M.I. of the body about CD is

$$I = \Sigma m(r + a)^2$$

$$I = \Sigma mr^2 + \Sigma ma^2 + \Sigma 2mar$$

$$I = I_g + a^2\,\Sigma m + 0$$

[$\Sigma 2mar = 0$, because centre of mass is that point at which the total mass of the body is supposed to be concentrated]

$\therefore$ Now, $a^2\Sigma m = Ma^2$

$$\therefore \quad I = I_g + Ma^2$$

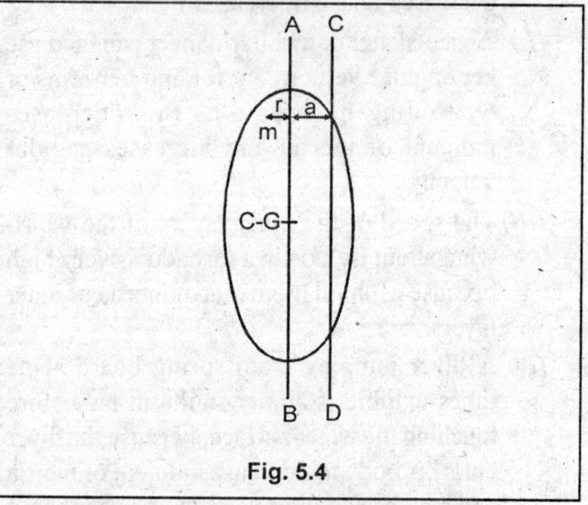

Fig. 5.4

THEOREM OF PERPENDICULAR AXES

Statement. According to perpendicular axes theorem the moment of inertia of a plane lamina about an axis is equal to the sum of its moments of inertia about any two mutually perpendicular axes in its plane and intersecting each other at the point where the perpendicular axis pass through it.

Thus $I_z = I_x + I_y$

Proof. Let us consider a laminar body. Let *OX* and *OY* be two mutually perpendicular axes lying in the plane of the body and *OZ* is the third axis perpendicular to the plane of the body and passing through the point of intersection of these axes. Let a particle of mass m be placed at point *P*(*x*, *y*).

The moment of inertia of mass *m* about *OZ* is

$$dI = mr^2 = m(x^2 + y^2)$$

∴ Moment of inertia of the body about *OZ* axis is

$$I = \Sigma m(x^2 + y^2) = \Sigma mx^2 + \Sigma my^2$$

or $$I = I_y + I_x [\because mx^2 = I_y ; \Sigma my^2 = I_x]$$

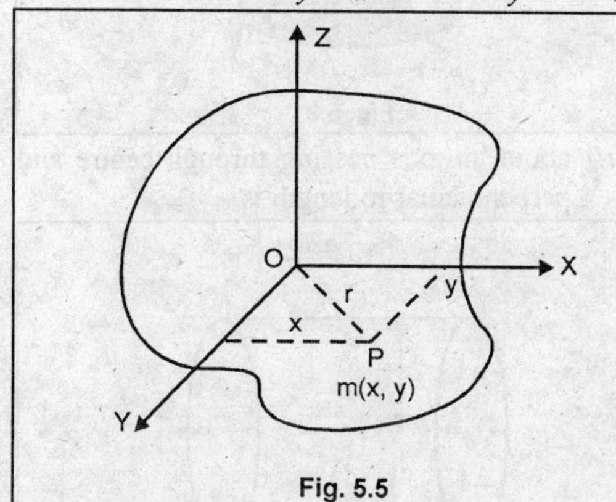

Fig. 5.5

CENTRE OF MASS

The centre of mass of the body is defined as a representative point which describes the translatory motion of a body and acts as if the total mass of the body is concentrated at this point and all the external forces are acting at this point.

If $\vec{r}_1, \vec{r}_2, \vec{r}_3 ..., \vec{r}_n$ are position vectors of masses $m_1, m_2, m_3, ..., m_n$ respectively, then the position of centre of mass of the system is given by

$$\vec{r}_{cm} = \frac{m_1 \vec{r}_1 + m_2 \vec{r}_2 + ... m_n \vec{r}_n}{m_1 + m_2 + ... + m_n} \quad ...(i)$$

If (x_{cm}, y_{cm}, z_{cm}) are coordinates of centre of mass of a system of particles of masses $m_1, m_2, ..., m_n$ at position $(x_1, y_1, z_1), (x_2, y_2, z_2), ..., (x_n, y_n, z_n)$ respectively, then

$$x_{cm} = \frac{m_1x_1 + m_2x_2 + ... + m_nx_n}{m_1 + m_2 + ... + m_n}$$

$$y_{cm} = \frac{m_1y_1 + m_2y_2 + ... + m_ny_n}{m_1 + m_2 + ... + m_n} \quad ...(ii)$$

$$z_{cm} = \frac{m_1z_1 + m_2z_2 + ... + m_nz_n}{m_1 + m_2 + ... + m_n}$$

For a continuous body, we suppose that the body is formed of a large number of infinitesimal mass elements. If *dm* is mass of such an element at position (*x*, *y*, *z*) relative to arbitrary origin, then the centres of mass of the body is given by

$$x_{cm} = \frac{\int x\, dm}{\int dm} = \frac{\int x\, dm}{M}$$

$$y_{cm} = \frac{\int y\, dm}{\int dm} = \frac{\int y\, dm}{M} \quad ...(iii)$$

$$z_{cm} = \frac{\int z\, dm}{\int dm} = \frac{\int z\, dm}{M}$$

where $M = \Sigma m = \int dm$ is the total mass of the body.

The velocity of centre of mass of a system of particles is given by

$$\vec{v}_{cm} = \frac{m_1 \vec{v}_1 + m_2 \vec{v}_2 + ... + m_n \vec{v}_n}{m_1 + m_2 + ... + m_n}$$

If external force acting on the system of particles is zero, then, linear momentum of the system

$$\vec{P} = \vec{p}_1 + \vec{p}_2 + ... + \vec{p}_n$$

$$= m_1 \vec{v}_1 + m_2 \vec{v}_2 + ... + m_n \vec{v}_n$$

= constant, so that

$$\vec{v}_{cm} = \text{constant.}$$

Thus in the absence of external forces, the velocity of centre of mass remains constant.

MOMENT OF INERTIA OF SOME REGULAR BODIES

1. **Circular Ring.** Moment of inertia of a circular ring

(i) about an axis passing through centre and perpendicular to plane of ring is $I = MR^2$

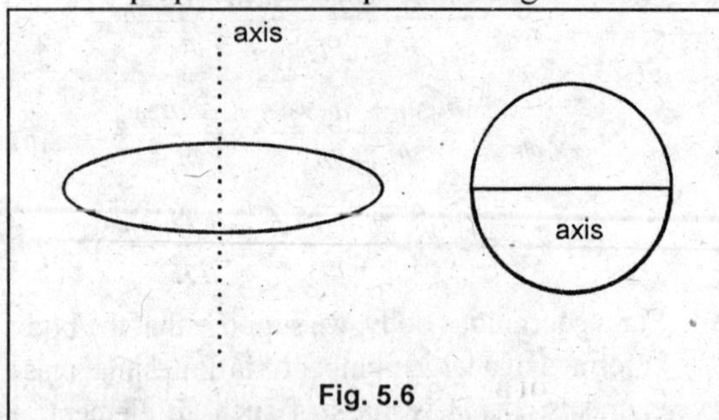

Fig. 5.6

(ii) about a diameter is $I = \frac{MR^2}{2}$

2. Thin Hollow Cylinder.

Moment of inertia of a thin hollow cylinder

(a) about its geometrical axis is $I = MR^2$

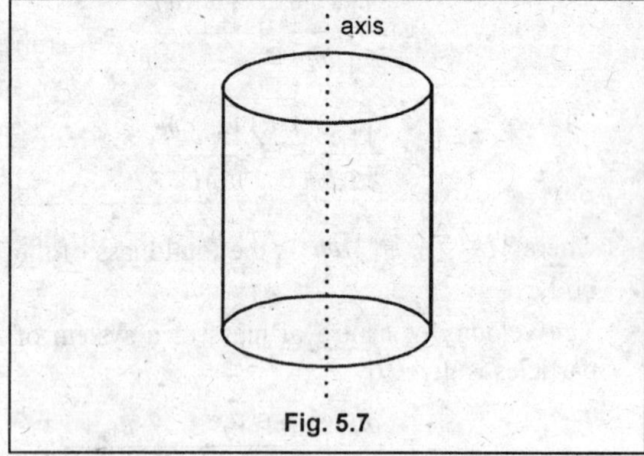

Fig. 5.7

3. Disc :

Moment of inertia of a disc

(i) about an axis passing through centre and perpendicular to plane of disc is $I = \frac{MR^2}{2}$

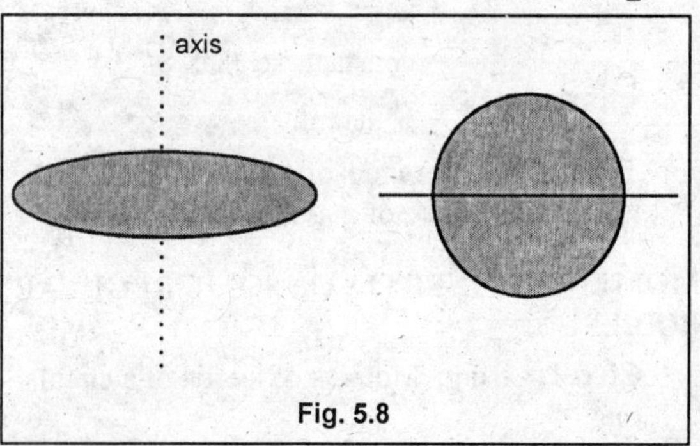

Fig. 5.8

(ii) about a diameter is $I = \frac{MR^2}{4}$.

4. A Solid Cylinder. Moment of inertia of a solid cylinder

(i) about its geometrical axis is $I = \frac{MR^2}{2}$

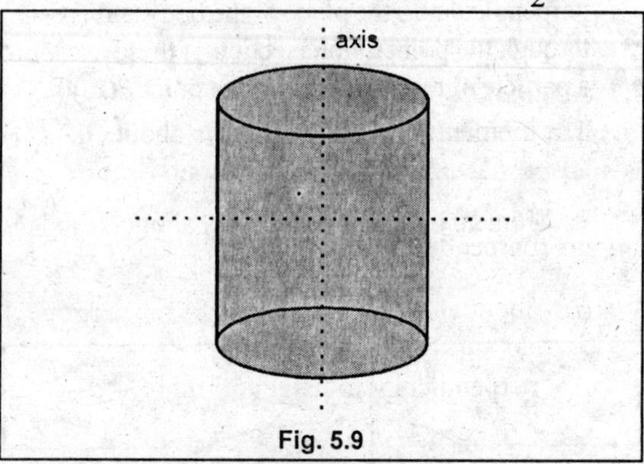

Fig. 5.9

(ii) about an axis passing through centre and perpendicular to length is

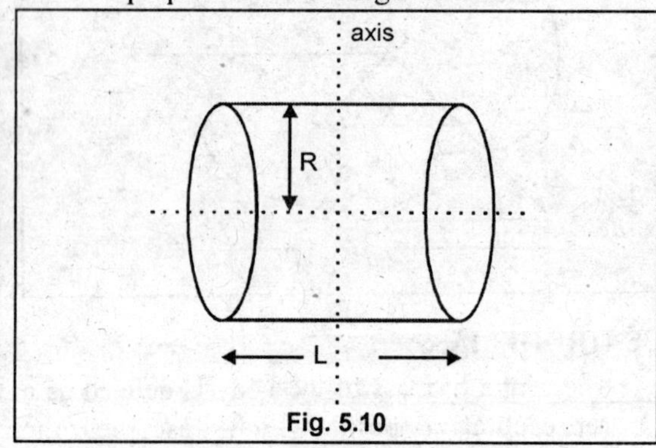

Fig. 5.10

$$I = M\left(\frac{R^2}{4} + \frac{L^2}{12}\right)$$

5. A Thin Spherical Shell. Moment of inertia of a thin spherical shell

(i) about a diameter is $I = \frac{2}{3}MR^2$

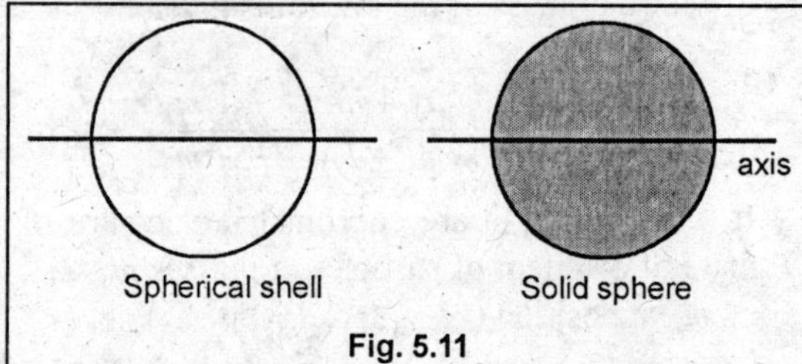

Fig. 5.11

(ii) about a tangent is $I = \frac{5}{3}MR^2$

6. **Solid Sphere.** Moment of inertia of a solid sphere

(i) about a diameter is

$$I = \frac{2}{5}MR^2$$

(ii) about a tangent is $I = \frac{7}{3}MR^2$

7. **A Thin Uniform Rod.** Moment of inertia of a thin uniform rod

(i) about an axis passing through centre and perpendicular to length of rod is $I = \frac{ML^2}{12}$

(ii) about an axis passing through an edge and perpendicular to length of rod is $I = \frac{ML^2}{3}$

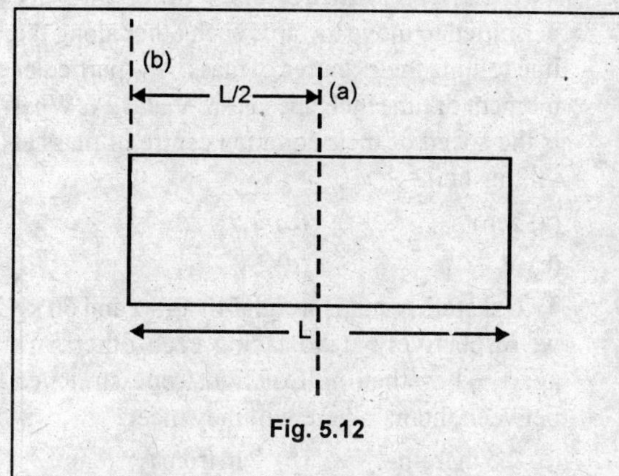

Fig. 5.12

8. **A cuboid ($l \times b \times h$).** Moment of inertia of a cuboid

(i) about an axis passing through centre and parallel to height h is

$$I = \frac{M(l^2 + b^2)}{12}$$

9. A Diatomic molecule whose atoms are of masses m_1 and m_2 at separation r.

Moment of inertia of diatomic molecule about an axis passing through centre of mass and perpendicular to bond length is

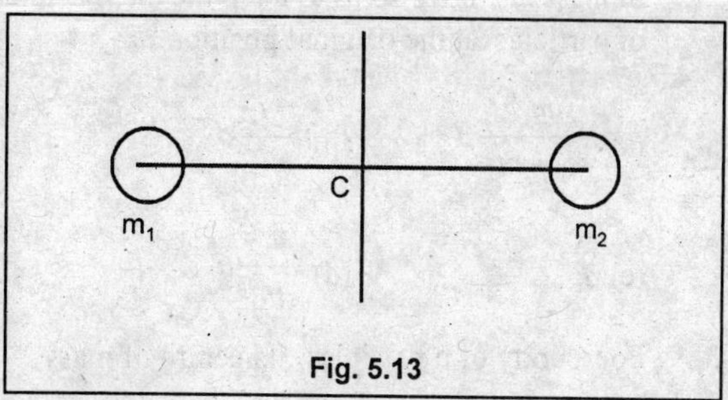

Fig. 5.13

Rotational Inertia. Conservation of Angular Momentum

$$I = \frac{m_1 m_2}{m_1 + m_2} r^2 = \mu r^2$$

where $\mu = \frac{m_1 m_2}{m_1 + m_2}$ is called the reduced mass.

MULTIPLE CHOICE QUESTIONS

1. In carbon monoxide molecule the carbon and oxygen atoms are separated by a distance of 1.2×10^{-10} m. The distance of centre of mass from the carbon atom is

(a) 0.56×10^{-10}m (b) 0.48×10^{-10}m

(c) 0.69×10^{-10}m (d) 0.75×10^{-10}m

2. Consider a system of two particles having masses m_1 and m_2. If the particle of mass m_1 is pushed towards the mass centre of particles through a distance d, by what distance would the particle of mass m_2 move so as to keep the mass centre of particles at the original position ?

(a) $\frac{m_1}{m_1+m_2}d$ (b) $\frac{m_1}{m_2}d$

(c) d (d) $\frac{m_2}{m_1}d$

3. For a body of n particles, its centre of mass

(a) is same as its C.G.

(b) is vector sum of moments of masses of particles divided by sum of masses

(c) is vector sum of moments of weights of masses divided by sum of masses

(d) is vector sum of torques divided by sum of masses

4. If the linear density of a rod of length 3 m varies as $\lambda = 2 + x$, then the position of the centre of gravity of the rod is

(a) 7/3 m (b) 12/7 m

(c) 10/7 m (d) 9/7 m

5. If position vector of mass 1 kg and 3 kg are $\hat{i}+\hat{j}+\hat{k}$ and $-\hat{i}-\hat{j}-\hat{k}$ respectively, then find position vector of centre of mass.

(a) $-\frac{1}{4}\left(\hat{i}+\hat{j}+\hat{k}\right)$ (b) $-\frac{3}{4}\left(\hat{i}-\hat{j}+\hat{k}\right)$

(c) $-\frac{1}{2}\left(\hat{i}+\hat{j}-\hat{k}\right)$ (d) $0\hat{i}+0\hat{j}+0\hat{k}$

6. Two identical balls each of radius 10 cm are placed touching each other. The distance of their centre of mass from the point of contact is

(a) zero (b) 5 cm

(c) 10 cm (d) 15 cm

7. A piece of mass at rest splits into 2 parts of mass M and m and velocity of the small fragments of mass m is ν, then the velocity of big fragment may be given as

(a) $V = \frac{M}{(M-m)\nu}$ (b) $V = \frac{(M-m)\nu}{M}$

(c) $V = \frac{m}{M}\nu$ (d) $V = \frac{M}{m}\nu$

8. Two particles attract each other and are permitted to move towards each other along the line joining their centres of mass. At a particular moment of time their speeds are V and 2V. What is the speed of their common centre of mass at this instant?

(a) zero (b) 1.5 V

(c) V (d) 3V

9. Two skaters A and B weighs 40 kg wt and 60 kg wt respectively stand facing each other 5 m apart. They then pull of light rope stretched between them. Where will they meet?

(a) 2.5 m from A (b) 2 m from A

(c) 3 m from A (d) 1.5 m from A

10. Two blocks of masses 10 kg and 4 kg are connected by a spring of negligible mass and placed on a frictionless horizontal surface. An impulse gives a velocity of 14 m/s to the heavier block in the direction of the lighter block. The velocity of the center of mass is

(a) 30 m/s (b) 20 m/s

(c) 10 m/s (d) 5 m/s

11. A solid sphere of radius R is placed on smooth horizontal surface. A horizontal force F is applied at height h from the lowest point. For the maximum acceleration of centre of mass, which is correct?

(a) h = R
(b) h = 2R
(c) h = 0
(d) No relation between h and R

12. If a force acts on a body at a point away from the centre of mass, then
(a) linear acceleration changes
(b) angular acceleration changes
(c) both change
(d) none changes

13. A wheel is rotating at 900 r.p.m. about its axis. When the power is cut off it comes to rest in 1 minute. The angular retardation in radians/s^2 is
(a) $\pi/2$ (b) $\pi/4$
(c) $\pi/6$ (d) $\pi/8$

14. A car is moving at a speed of 72 km/hr. The diameter of its wheels is 0.5 m. If the wheels are stopped in 20 rotations after applying brakes, then angular retardation produced by the brakes is
(a) – 45.5 rad/s^2 (b) – 29.5 rad/s^2
(c) – 33.5 rad/s^2 (d) – 25.5 rad/s^2

15. A car is initially at rest on a circular track that has a radius of 40 m. The car then starts to move counter clockwise around the track, accelerating at constant angular acceleration of 1.0 rad/sec^2. The time it takes for the car to move half of the wave around the track is
(a) $\sqrt{6.28}$ sec (b) $\sqrt{2.24}$ sec
(c) $\sqrt{3.14}$ sec (d) $\sqrt{4\pi}$ sec

16. In a bicycle the radius of rear wheel is twice the radius of front wheel. If r_F and r_r are the radius, v_F and v_r are the speeds of top most points of wheel, then
(a) $v_r = 2v_F$ (b) $v_F = 2v_r$
(c) $v_F = v_r$ (d) $v_F > v_r$

17. O is the centre of an equilateral triangle ABC. F_1, F_2 and F_3 are three forces acting along the sides AB, BC and AC as shown here. What should be the magnitude of F_3, so that the total torque about O is zero?
(a) $(F_1 + F_2)$ (b) $2(F_1 + F_2)$
(c) $(F_1 + F_2)/2$ (d) $(F_1 - F_2)$

18. The torque acting on a body is the rotational analogue of
(a) mass of the body
(b) linear kinetic energy of the body
(c) linear velocity of the body
(d) force in linear motion
(e) linear acceleration

19. If torque is zero then
(a) angular momentum is conserved
(b) linear momentum is converved
(c) energy is conserved
(d) angular momentum is not conserved

20. A particle is moving in the XY plane with constant velocity along a line parallel to the X-axis. Its angular momentum about the Z-axis
(a) is zero
(b) remains constant
(c) goes in increasing
(d) goes on decreasing

21. A particle of mass m is rotating in a circular path of radius r. If its angular momentum is L, the centripetal force acting on it is
(a) $\dfrac{L}{mr^2}$ (b) $\dfrac{L^2}{mr^2}$
(c) $\dfrac{L^2}{m^2r^2}$ (d) $\dfrac{L^2}{mr^3}$

22. A particle undergoes uniform circular motion. About which point on the plane of the circle, will the angular momentum of the particle remain conserved?
(a) Centre of the circle
(b) On the circumference of the circle
(c) Inside the circle
(d) Outside the circle

23. Angular momentum of a body is defined as the product of
(a) mass and angular velocity
(b) centripetal force and radius
(c) linear velocity and angular velocity
(d) moment of inertia and angular velocity
(e) mass and acceleration due to gravity

24. A child swinging on a swing in sitting position, stands up, then the time period of the swing will
(a) increase
(b) decrease
(c) remain same
(d) increase if the child is long and decrease if the child is short

25. A simple pendulum oscillates in a vertical plane. When it passes through the mean position, the tension in the string is 3 times the weight of the pendulum bob. What is the maximum displacement of the pendulum of the string with respect to the vertical?
(a) 30° (b) 45°
(c) 60° (d) 90°

26. The moment of inertia of the body (initially at rest) about a given axis is 1.2 kg m^2. In order to produce rotational kinetic energy of 1500 J, an angular acceleration of 25 rad/sec^2 must be applied about that axis for a period of
(a) 1 sec (b) 2 sec
(c) 8 sec (d) 10 sec

27. The time period of a compound pendulum is expressed by
(a) $2\pi\sqrt{\frac{l^2+K^2}{lg}}$ (b) $2\pi\sqrt{\frac{l^2+K^2}{g}}$
(c) $2\pi\sqrt{\frac{l^2+K}{g}}$ (d) $2\pi\sqrt{\frac{l+K^2}{lg}}$

28. The angular velocity of a body changes from ω_1 to ω_2 without applying any torque, but due to change in its moment of inertia. The ratio of radii of gyration in both the cases is
(a) $\omega_1 : \omega_2$
(b) $\omega_2 : \omega_1$
(c) $\sqrt{\omega_1} : \sqrt{\omega_2}$
(d) $\sqrt{\omega_2} : \sqrt{\omega_1}$

29. A closed tube, partly, filled with a liquid and set horizontal, is rotated about a vertical axis passing through its center. In the process, the moment of inertia of the system about its axis would
(a) decrease always
(b) increase always
(c) remain constant
(d) increase if tube is less than half filled otherwise decrease

30. A ring of radius 0.5m and mass 10 kg is rotating about its diameter with angular velocity of 20 rad/s. Its kinetic energy is
(a) 10 J (b) 100 J
(c) 500 J (d) 1000 J

31. A solid sphere, a hollow sphere and a disc have same mass and radius roll down the same inclined plane from rest. Which one will reach on the ground at least time?
(a) solid sphere
(b) hollow sphere
(c) disc
(d) all will reach in same time

32. A body of mass M slides down an inclined plane and reaches the bottom with velocity v. If a disc of same mass rolls down the same inclined plane, what will be its velocity on reaching the bottom?
(a) v (b) v/√2
(c) √(2/3) v (d) v/2

33. A disc is rolling (without slipping) on a horizontal surface. C is its centre and Q and P are two points equidistant from C. Let V_P, V_Q and V_C be the magnitude of velocities of points P, Q and C respectively, then

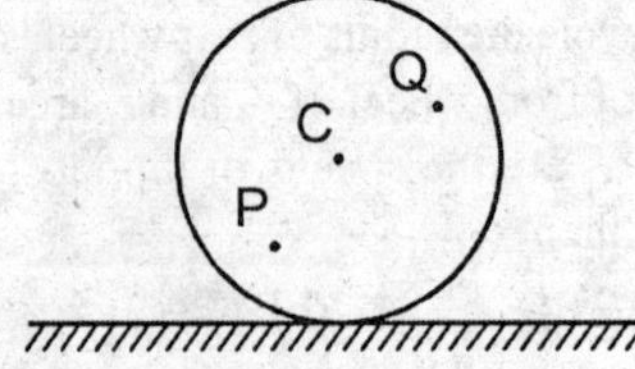

(a) $V_Q > V_C > V_P$
(b) $V_Q < V_C < V_P$
(c) $V_Q = V_P$, $V_c = \frac{1}{2} V_P$
(d) $V_Q < V_C > V_P$

ANSWERS

1	2	3	4	5	6	7	8	9	10
(c)	(b)	(b)	(b)	(b)	(a)	(c)	(b)	(c)	(c)
11	**12**	**13**	**14**	**15**	**16**	**17**	**18**	**19**	**20**
(d)	(c)	(a)	(d)	(a)	(c)	(a)	(d)	(a)	(b)
21	**22**	**23**	**24**	**25**	**26**	**27**	**28**	**29**	**30**
(d)	(a)	(d)	(b)	(d)	(b)	(a)	(d)	(b)	(d)
31	**32**	**33**							
(a)	(b)	(a)							

HINTS / SOLUTIONS

1. Let the centre of mass of the system be at O distant r from carbon atom.

Hence,

$$m_1 r = m_2 (R - r)$$

or $\quad 12\,r = 16 \times (1.2 \times 10^{-10} - r)$

$$28r = 16 \times 1.2 \times 10^{-10}$$

$$r = \frac{16 \times 1.2 \times 10^{-10}}{28}$$

$$= 0.69 \times 10^{-10}\,\text{m}.$$

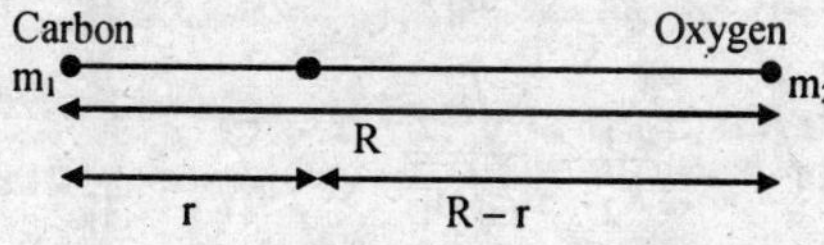

3. $$\text{CM} = \frac{\sum_{1}^{n} m_i \vec{r}_i}{\sum_{1}^{n} m_i}$$

4. Mass of an element dx of the rod dm = (2 + x) dx

∴ x coordinate of centre of gravity

$$x_{cm} = \frac{\int_0^L x\,dm}{\int_0^L dm} = \frac{\int_0^L x(2+x)dx}{\int_0^L (2+x)dx}$$

$$= \frac{\int_0^3 2x\,dx + \int_0^3 x^2 dx}{\int_0^3 2\,dx + \int_0^3 x\,dx} = \frac{\left[x^2\right]_0^2 + \left[\frac{x^3}{3}\right]_0^3}{\left[2x\right]_0^3 + \left[\frac{x^2}{2}\right]_0^3} = \frac{12}{7}\,\text{m}$$

7. This is from law of conservation of momentum.

10. V_e is independent of spring force.

11. Since there is no friction at the contact surface (smooth horizontal surface) there will be no rolling. Hence, the acceleration of the centre of mass of the sphere will be independent of the position of the applied force F. Therefore, there is no relation between h and R.

13. $\omega_i = \frac{900}{60} \times 2\pi = 30\pi$ rad/sec,

$\omega_f = 0$, t = 60 sec, $\alpha = ?$

$\omega_f = \omega i + \alpha t$

$$\therefore \alpha = \frac{\omega_f - \omega_i}{t} = \frac{0 - 30\pi}{60} = -\frac{\pi}{2}\,\text{rad/s}^2$$

14. Speed of the car = 72 km/hr

$$= \frac{72 \times 5}{18} = 20\,\text{m/s}$$

Diameter of each wheel = $\frac{0.5}{2}$ m

Number of rotations = 20

The angular speed

$$\omega = \frac{v}{r} = \frac{20}{0.25} = 80 \text{ rad / sec.}$$

Angular displacement

$\theta = 2\pi \times 20 = 40\,\pi$ rad

The angular retardation

$$\omega^2 = \omega_0^2 + 2\alpha\theta$$

$$0 = (80)^2 + 2\alpha(40\pi)$$

or $\alpha = -\frac{(80)^2}{80\pi} = -25.5 \text{ rad / s}^2.$

15. $\theta = \omega_0 t + ½\,\alpha t^2$ or $\theta = 0 + ½\,\alpha t^2$.

$$\therefore\ t = \sqrt{\frac{2\theta}{\alpha}} = \sqrt{\frac{2\pi}{1}} = \sqrt{2 \times 3.14} = \sqrt{6.28} \text{ sec.}$$

16. Let the velocity of c.m. of cycle is v, then $v_F = 2v$ and $v_r = 2v$ $\therefore v_F = v_r$

17. From triangle law, $\vec{F}_3 = \vec{F}_1 + \vec{F}_2$.

21. $L = mvr$

$\Rightarrow v = L/mr$

Centripetal force, $F = \frac{m}{r} \cdot \frac{L^2}{m^2 r^2} = \frac{L^2}{mr^3}$.

22. $\vec{L} = \vec{r} \times \vec{p}$ Where $\vec{L}$ is angular momentum, r is position vector and $\vec{p}$ linear momentum.

$\therefore$ for $\vec{L}$ to be constant, the following 3 values should remain unchanged 1. $|\vec{r}|$ 2. $|\vec{p}|$ 3. direction of $\vec{r} \times \vec{p}$, which is $\perp$ to the plane containing. This happens only when it is calculated about the centre of the circle.

25. $T = 3\,mg$;

$T - 3\,mg = mv^2/\ell$

$= 2mgv = \sqrt{2g\ell}½\,mv^2$

$= mg\ell\,(1 - \cos\theta)$

$\Rightarrow \quad \theta = 90°.$

26. Moment of inertia

$I = 1.2 \text{ kg m}^2$

Rotational kinetic energy = 1500 J

Angular acceleration, $\omega = 25$ rad/sec^2

From the relation of rotational kinetic energy

$$K = \frac{1}{2} I\omega^2$$

We have $\omega^2 = \frac{2K}{I} = \frac{2 \times 1500}{1.2} = 2500$

or $\omega = \sqrt{2500} = 50$ rad / sec.

27. Time period of a compound pendulum is

$$T = 2\pi\sqrt{\frac{l + k^2/l}{g}} = 2\pi\sqrt{\frac{l^2 + k^2}{lg}}$$

Note: Compound pendulum is any object of any shape or size which is hung (free to rotate) at any of its points and given a small swing. K is the radius of gyration about the hing and l is the distance between the point of suspension and the CG of the body.

28. Initial angular velocity $= \omega_1$

Final angular velocity $= \omega_2$

According to law of conservation of angular momentum

$$I_1\omega_1 = I_2\omega_2$$

$$\Rightarrow (Mk_1^2)\omega_1 = (Mk_2^2)\omega_2$$

$$\therefore \frac{k_1^2}{k_2^2} = \frac{\omega_2}{\omega_1}$$

or $\frac{k_1}{k_2} = \frac{\sqrt{\omega_2}}{\sqrt{\omega_1}}$

$$\therefore k_1 : k_2 = \sqrt{\omega_2} : \sqrt{\omega_1}$$

30. For a ring $I = MR^2$, I about the diameter $= MR^2 + MR^2 = 2MR^2$,

$K = \frac{1}{2} I\omega^2$

$= \frac{1}{2} \times 2MR^2\,\omega^2$

$= 10 \times 0.5 \times 0.5 \times 20 \times 20 = 1000$ J

31. On inclined plane

$$f = \frac{g \sin\theta}{1 + \frac{K^2}{R^2}} \text{ i.e. } f \propto \frac{R^2}{R^2 + K^2}$$

lower is the value of the radius of gyration, greater is the acceleration. Therefore, least time is taken to roll down.

$$\left.\begin{array}{l} \text{K for solid sphere} = \sqrt{\frac{2}{5}}\,R \\ \text{K for hollow sphere} = \sqrt{\frac{2}{3}}\,R \\ \text{K for disc} = \frac{R}{\sqrt{2}} \end{array}\right\} \text{about its diameter}$$

32. $v^2 = (2g \sin\theta) \times \ell$.

Acceleration down the inclined plane will be

$$a = \frac{M}{\left[M + \frac{I_{cm}}{R^2}\right]} g \sin\theta = \frac{2}{3} g \sin\theta.$$

Hence, when the disc rolls down, the velocity at the bottom is given by

$$v^2 = \left(2 \times \frac{2}{3} g \sin\theta\right) \times \ell.$$

This gives $v = \frac{V}{\sqrt{2}}$.

33. O is the instantaneous centre of rotation. All the points of the disc are having circular motion about O with the same angular velocity.

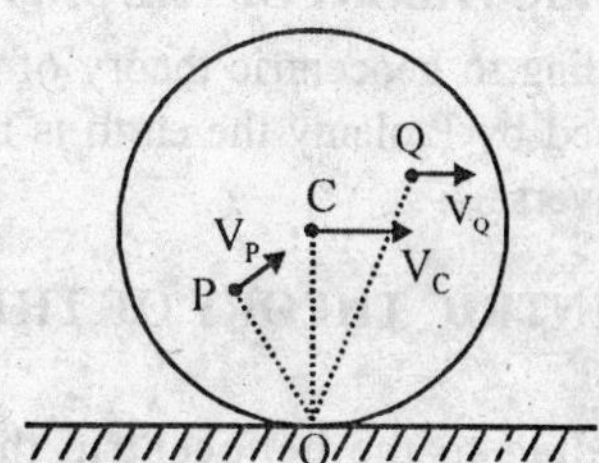

$\therefore$ $V_Q = \omega \times OQ$ $\quad V_C = \omega \times OC$

$V_p = \omega \times OP$

As $OQ > OC > OP$,

$\therefore$ $V_Q > V_C > V_P$

$\therefore$ Option (a) is correct.

UNIT-6

GRAVITATION

GEOCENTRIC THEORY OF THE UNIVERSE

According to geocentric theory of the universe proposed by Ptolemy the earth is the centre of the universe.

HELIOCENTRIC THEORY OF THE UNIVERSE

According to the heliocentric theory of the universe proposed by Copernicus the sun is the centre of the universe.

Kepler's laws of planetary motion

(i) Every planet revolves round the sun in an elliptical orbit with sun at one of the foci.

(ii) The line joining the sun to the planet (radius vector) sweeps out equal area in equal interval of time, i.e., the areal velocity is constant

i.e., $dA/dt = \text{constant}$

The consequence of this theory is that the linear velocity is different at different places. It is maximum at a place where the distance between the planet and the sun is minimum. The orbital velocity is minimum when the distance between the planet and the sun is maximum.

The other consequence of this law is that the angular momentum remains constant in planetary motion.

(iii) The square of time period of revolution is directly proportional to the cube of average distance between the planet and the sun $T^2 \propto R^3$ or the square of time period of revolution is proportional to the cube of semi-major axis of ellipse $T^2 \propto a^3$.

NEWTONS'S UNIVERSAL LAW OF GRAVITATION

On the basis of Kepler's laws of planetary motion, Newton stated his famous law of gravitation. According to Newton's universal law of gravitation stated on the basic of Kepler's laws of planetary motion every two objects in the universe attract each other. The force of attraction is directly proportional to the product of masses and inversely proportional to the square of distance between the two masses, i.e., if two masses, m_1 and m_2 are separated from each other by a distance r then

$$F \propto \frac{m_1 m_2}{r^2} \quad \text{or} \quad F = G.\frac{m_1 m_2}{r^2}$$

where G = universal gravitational constant

$G = 6.67 \times 10^{-11}$ Newton m^{-2} kg^{-2}

$G = 6.67 \times 10^{-8}$ dyne cm^{-2} gm^{-2}

Gravitational field

Gravitational field is the space surrounding the material body in which its attraction (gravitational) can be experienced.

Intensity of gravitational field

Intensity of gravitational field is defined as the force experienced by unit mass placed at any point in the gravitational field. Its units are Newton/kg and the dimensional formula is [LT^{-2}]. it is a vector quantity.

$\therefore E = F/m$

The intensity of gravitational field at a distance r from the point mass m is, $E = Gm/r^2$.

Intensity of gravitational field at a distance 'r' from the centre of earth is, $E = (GM_e)/r^2$ where M_e is the mass of earth. On the surface of earth $r = R_e$

$$\therefore \quad E = GM_e/R_e^2 = g$$

GRAVITATIONAL POTENTIAL

Gravitational potential at a point is defined as the work done in moving unit mass from infinity to that point against the field. If W work is done in moving a mass m then V = W/m.

It units are joule/kg. It is a scalar quantity. Its proper sign is negative.

The gravitational potential at a distance r from the centre of earth is, $V = -GM_e/r$ if $r > R_e$

Similarly the gravitational potential on the surface of earth is, $V = -GM_e/R_e$ where M_e is the mass of earth and R_e is the radius of earth.

Gravitational potential at a point distance r from a point mass 'm' $= -\frac{G_m}{r}$.

Note. The intensity of gravitational field at a point inside the hollow spherical shell is zero while the potential is constant.

Gravitational potential energy

The gravitational potential energy of a body at a point is defined as the amount of work done in bringing the body from infinity to that point against the field.

Let us calculate the gravitational potential energy of a mass m placed on the surface of earth. For this we assume that earth is a uniform sphere of radius R_e and mass M_e. Suppose the body of mass m is placed at Q, at a distance x from the centre of earth. The force acting on this mass, when it is at P is

$$F = \frac{GM_e m}{x^2}$$

The small work done in moving this mass through a small distance $PQ = dx$ is

$$dW = F.dx = \frac{GM_e m}{x^2}.dx$$

Thus the total work done in moving the mass 'm' from infinity to a point A, distance r from the centre of earth is

$$W = \int_{\infty}^{r} \frac{GMm}{x^2}\, dx$$

$$\therefore\ W = -\left[\frac{GMm}{x}\right]_{\infty}^{r} = -GMm\left[\frac{1}{r} - \frac{1}{\infty}\right]$$

$$\text{or}\ \ W = -\frac{GMm}{r}$$

Thus, the potential energy of mass m at a height r from the centre of earth is $U = -\frac{GM_e m}{r}$ and on the surface of earth it is $U = -\frac{GM_e m}{R_e}$.

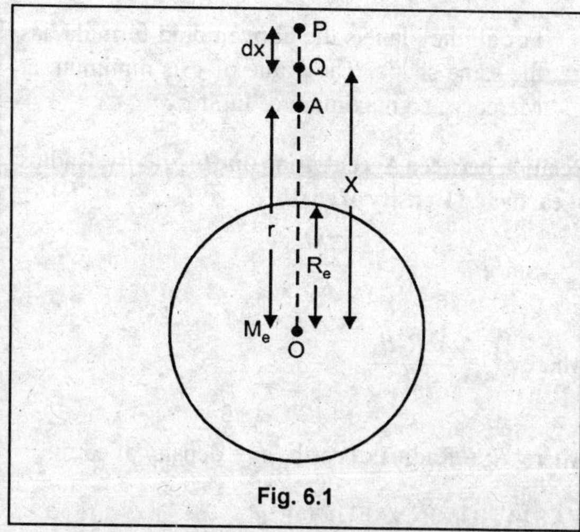

Fig. 6.1

The gravitational potential $V = \frac{U}{m}$

$\therefore$ The gravitational potential at a point distant 'r' from the centre of earth is

$$V = -\frac{GM_e}{r}$$

and on the surface of earth is

$$V = -\frac{GM_e}{R_e}$$

ACCELERATION DUE TO GRAVITY 'g'

Acceleration due to gravity is the acceleration produced in a body due to the force of gravity. Its value in S.I. system is 9.8 m/sec^2 and in F.P.S. system is 32 ft/sec^2.

Relation between g, G and M_e

Consider a body of mass m placed on the surface of earth of mass M_e. According to Newton's law gravitation, the gravitational force acting on the body is

$$F = \frac{GM_e m}{R_e^2}$$

But $F = mg_e \quad \therefore\ mg_e = \frac{GM_e m}{R_e^2}$

or $$g_e = \frac{GM_e}{R_e^2} \quad \text{or} \quad GM_e = g_e R_e^2$$

For all the planets the above noted formula has the same shape. The value of g is minimum at Mercury and maximum at Jupiter.

Relation between Acceleration due to gravity, Radius of earth and Density of earth

Since $g_e = \frac{GM_e}{R_e^2}$

where $M_e = \frac{4\pi R_e^3 d_e}{3}$

$\therefore \quad g_e = (4\pi R_e G d_e)/3$

where R_e = Radius of earth, d_e = density of earth.

VARIATION IN VALUE OF 'g'

It can be studied under three categories :

A. Variation of 'g' on the surface of earth. It is due to the following two reasons :

(a) Due to shape of earth. The earth is elliptical in shape. It is flatter at the poles and bulged out at the equator. Now, we know that $g \propto 1/R^2$, therefore the value of g at the equator is minimum and the value of g at the poles is maximum (Radius at poles is < Radius at equator).

(b) Due to rotation of earth. Since earth rotates about its axis hence every object placed on the surface of earth also rotates about the same axis. A centripetal force is required for circular motion. A component of true weight of the body provides this force and the other component is responsible for the observed value of g.

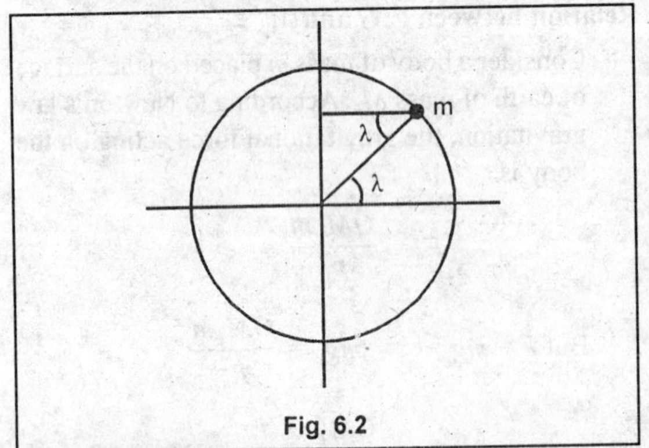

Fig. 6.2

If the observed value of g at the lattitude λ is represented by g_λ, then

$$g_\lambda = g_e - R_e\omega^2 \cos^2 \lambda$$

where ω is the angular velocity of rotation of the earth.

At equator $\lambda = 0°$; $\cos \lambda = 1$

$$\therefore \quad g_\lambda = g_e - R_e\omega^2.$$

At poles $\lambda = 90°$; $\cos \lambda = 0$

$$\therefore \quad g_\lambda = g_e.$$

Thus it is obvious that

(i) If the rate of rotation of earth increases then the value of g will decrease at all places except at the poles.

(ii) Maximum effect of rotation takes place at the equator, if the earth stops rotating then the value of g will increase by a factor $R_e\omega^2$ at equator.

(iii) If the earth starts rotating with an angular speed 17 times at the present speed of rotation then the objects will fly off the equator. (i.e. g will be zero at the equator).

(iv) If the observed value of g becomes zero at equator, then the length of day will be 1.4 hr.

B. Variation of 'g' above the surface of earth

The value of 'g' decreases as we go above the surface of the earth.

(i) Consider a body of mass m at a height 'h' above the surface of earth. Thus, the gravitational force on the body is

$$F = \frac{GM_e m}{(R_e + h)^2}$$

If g' is the value of gravity at a height 'h' above the surface of earth, then

$$mg' = \frac{GM_e m}{(R_e + h)^2}$$

$$\Rightarrow \quad g' = \frac{GM_e}{(R_e + h)^2} = \frac{g_e R_e^2}{(R_e + h)^2}$$

or

$$g' = \frac{g_e}{(1 + h/R_e)^2} = g_e\left[1 + \frac{h}{R_e}\right]^{-2}$$

where R_e is the radius of earth and M_e is the mass of earth, if $h \ll R_e$, then expanding binomially and neglecting higher powers of h/R_e, we get

$$g' = g_e\left(1 - \frac{2h}{R_e}\right)$$

∴ the decrease in the value of g on going up a height 'h' above the surface of earth,

$$\Delta g_e = \frac{2g_e h}{R_e}.$$

C. Variation of 'g' below the surface of earth

The value of 'g' decreases as we go below the surface of earth the effective mass of earth attracting the body decreases. Consider a body of mass m situated at a depth x from the surface of earth. Then the distance of the body from the centre of earth is $(R_e - x)$. Hence, there will be gravitational attraction between the mass m and a spherical region of radius $(R_e - x)$ of earth. If d_e is the density of earth, then the gravitational force on the body is

$$F = \frac{G\frac{4\pi(R_e - x)^3}{3} d_e . m}{(R_e - x)^2}$$

But, $F = mg'$

$$\therefore \quad mg' = \frac{4\pi G d_e (R_e - x)m}{3}$$

or $$g' = \frac{4\pi G d_e R_e}{3}\left(1 - \frac{x}{R_e}\right)$$

But $\frac{4\pi G d_e R_e}{3} = g_e$

hence, the value of 'g' at a depth x from the surface of earth is $g' = g\{1 - (x/R)\}$.

At the centre of earth $x = R$ hence $g = 0$.

The decrease in the value of 'g' at a depth 'x' below the surface of earth is $\Delta g = (gx/R)$.

PLANETS AND SATELLITE

Planets. Planets are the heavenly bodies revolving round the sun. They are nine in number, e.g. Mercury, earth, venus, jupiter, mars, saturn, uranus, neptune and pluto.

Satellites. Satellites are the heavenly bodies revolving Round the planets. They are of two types

(i) Natural satellites such as moon.

(ii) Artificial satellites launched by man such as Rohini, Aryabhatt etc.

ORBITAL VELOCITY

The velocity is given to a satellite in order to keep it in its orbit is known as orbital velocity (V_0). The necessary centripetal force required for circular motion is provided by the gravitational attraction between earth of mass M_e and satellite of mass m.

$$\therefore \quad \frac{GM_e m}{(R_e + h)^2} = \frac{mV_0^2}{R_e + h}$$

The orbital velocity of a mass m at a height 'h' above the surface of earth is

$$V_0 = \sqrt{\left[\frac{GM_e}{(R_e + h)}\right]}$$

where M_e = Mass of earth and R_e = Radius of earth

Also $$V_0 = R_e\sqrt{\left[\frac{g_e}{(R_e + h)}\right]}$$

If the satellite is very near to the surface of earth, then $h = 0$.

Hence $$V_0 = \sqrt{\left(\frac{GM_e}{R_e}\right)} = \sqrt{(g_e R_e)}$$

Time period of satellite

Let T be the time period of a satellite at a height 'h', then $T = \frac{\text{Circumference of the orbit}}{\text{Orbital velocity}}$

$$T = \frac{2\pi(R_e + h)}{V_0}$$

or $$T = 2\pi\sqrt{\left[\frac{(R_e + h)^3}{GM_e}\right]} = 2\pi\sqrt{\left[\frac{(R_e + h)^3}{g_e R_e^2}\right]}$$

Note.

(i) If the satellite is very near to the surface of earth ($h << R_e$), then

$$T = 2\pi\sqrt{\left(\frac{R_e}{g_e}\right)} = 84.6 \text{ min.}$$

Hence the minimum time period of the satellite is 84.6 min.

(ii) The angular velocity of satellite,

$$\omega = \sqrt{\left[\frac{GM_e}{(R_e + h)^3}\right]} = \sqrt{\left[\frac{g_e R_e^2}{(R_e + h)^3}\right]}$$

If the satellite is very near to the surface of earth then

$$\omega = \sqrt{g/R_e} = 0.001237 \text{ rad/sec.}$$

and $T^2 \propto (R_e + h)^3$,

i.e. Kepler's III law is true for circular motion also.

Total energy of satellite

Kinetic energy of the satellite,

$$K = \frac{1}{2}mv_0^2 \text{ or } K = \frac{GM_e m}{2R},$$

where m is the mass of satellite and R is the height of satellite from the centre of earth.

Potential energy of the sattellite, $U = -GM_e m/R$.

Negative sign indicates that the satellite is bound to the surface of earth. Hence the total energy of the satellite is

$$E = \text{K.E.} + \text{Potential energy}$$

$$E = (GM_e m/2R) - (GM_e m/R)$$

or $$E = -GM_e m/2R$$

or $$E = -\text{K.E.} \quad \text{or} \quad E = \frac{1}{2}\text{P.E.}$$

Total energy needed to put the satellite in its orbit at a height h

Let the satellite of mass m be launched at a height h above the surface of earth of radius R_e and mass M_e, then total energy required to place the satellite in an orbit of radius $(R_e + h)$ is

E = gain in K.E. + gain in P.E.

or $$E = \frac{1}{2}mv_0^2 + \left[-\frac{GM_e m}{(R_e + h)} - \left(-\frac{GM_e m}{R_e}\right)\right]$$

or $$E = \frac{1}{2}\frac{mGM_e}{(R_e + h)} - \frac{GM_e m}{(R_e + h)} + \frac{GM_e m}{R_e}$$

or $$E = \frac{-GM_e m}{2(R_e + h)} + \frac{GM_e m}{R_e}$$

or $$E = GM_e m\left[\frac{1}{R_e} - \frac{1}{2(R_e + h)}\right]$$

or $$E = g_e R_e^2 m\left[\frac{1}{R_e} - \frac{1}{2(R_e + h)}\right] = mg_e\left[R_e - \frac{R_e^2}{2(R_e + h)}\right]$$

Binding Energy of Satelite

The energy given to a satellite to escape away the satellite from the gravitational field of the planet is called binding energy. Binding energy of the satellite is

$$E = +(GM_e m/2R),$$

where R is the distance of satellite from the centre of earth.

ESCAPE VELOCITY

The minimum velocity required to the body to enable it to escape away from the gravitational field of earth is called escape velocity.

Let the mass of the planet be M and its radius R, then the escape velocity from its surface will be

$$V_e = \sqrt{(2GM/R)} = \sqrt{(8\pi R^2 dG/3)}$$

or $$V_e = \sqrt{(2gR)}.$$

Escape velocity from the surface of earth is 11.2 km/sec.

Relation between velocity of projection and shape of orbit

When a body is projected with a velocity v from any height in a horizontal direction, then

(i) If $v < v_0$, the body will finally fall to earth

(ii) If $v = v_0$, the body will rotate in circular path

(iii) If $v_0 < v < v_e$, the body will revolve in elliptical orbit.

(iv) If $v = v_e$, the body will leave the gravitational field of earth and escape away following a parabolical path

(v) If $v > v_e$, the body will escape, following a hyperbolical path.

Geostationary satellites or parking satellite

An artificial satellite revolving around the earth in an equatorial plane with a time period of 24 hrs in the same sense as that of earth, will appear stationary to the observer on earth. Such a satellite is known as Geostationary satellite or Parking satellite.

Weight of the object in artificial satellite or synchronous satellite

Since weight of a person is equal to the reaction on the foot of the man. In an artificial satellite the reaction the foot of the man is zero, hence the person does not experience any weight. This state is known as the state of weightlessness.

Let m be the mass of the person in the artificial satellite moving in a circular orbit of radius r around earth, then the centripetal force

$$\frac{GMm}{r^2} = \frac{mv^2}{2} \quad \text{...(i)}$$

Now, the forces acting on the foot of the person are

(i) gravitational force of earth (towards the centre of earth)

(ii) centrifugal force (away from the centre of earth)

(iii) the reaction (N) on the man away from centre.

$$N + \frac{mv^2}{r} = \frac{GMm}{r^2}$$

From equation (i) $N + \frac{GMm}{r^2} = \frac{GMm}{r^2}$

$$N = 0$$

Hence, the body will enjoy weightlessness.

It does not depend on the distance of the satellite from the earth.

Relation between escape velocity and orbital velocity

$$v_e = \sqrt{2}v_0$$

Relation between K.E. of escape and kinetic energy of orbital motion

Kinetic energy of escape = 2 × kinetic energy of orbital motion

There is no atmosphere on moon

On the surface of moon the value of acceleration due to gravity is very small and the radius of moon is also much smaller than that of earth hence the value of escape velocity on the surface of moon is much smaller than that on the surface of earth. It is only 2.5 km/sec. The root mean square velocity of all gases is more than this value therefore they escape away from the gravitational field of moon. Hence there is no atmosphere on moon.

The root mean square velocity of hydrogen is more than that of the escape velocity on earth hence hydrogen is not found in earth's atmosphere.

GRAVITATIONAL AND INERTIAL MASSES

The mass defined on the property of inertia is known as inertial mass and the mass defined on the property of gravity is known as gravitational mass.

Properties of Inertial Mass

1. It is equal to the ratio of magnitude of external force applied on the body to the acceleration produced in it by that force

$$m = F/a$$

2. It is proportional to the quantity of matter present in the body.
3. It is independent of shape, size and state of the body.
4. It is not affected by the presence of other bodies near it.
5. When various masses are put together, the inertial masses add according to scalar laws irrespective of the material of the bodies involved.
6. It increases with increase in velocity according to the relation $m = \frac{m_0}{\sqrt{(1 - v^2/c^2)}}$, where m_0 = rest mass of the body.

MULTIPLE CHOICE QUESTIONS

1. The acceleration due to gravity at a height 1/20th of the radius of the earth above the earth surface is 9 ms^{-2}. Its value at a point at an equal distance below the surface of the earth in ms^{-2} is about
(a) 8.5 (b) 9.5
(c) 9.8 (d) 11.5

2. Mars has about 1/10th as much mass as the earth and half as great a diameter. The acceleration of falling body on Mars in ms^{-2} is about (acceleration due to gravity on earth = 9.8 ms^{-2})
(a) 1.96 (b) 3.92
(c) 4.9 (d) 9.8

3. Sun is about 330 times heavier and 100 times bigger in radius than earth. The ratio of mean density of the sun to that of earth is
(a) 3.3×10^{-6} (b) 3.3×10^{-4}
(c) 3.3×10^{-2} (d) 1.3

4. What will happen to the weight of the body at the south pole, if the earth stops rotating about its polar axis ?
(a) no change (b) increases
(c) decreases but does not become zero
(d) reduces to zero

5. The radii of two planets are respectively R_1 and R_2 and their densities are respectively ρ_1 and ρ_2. The ratio of the accelerations due to gravity (g_1/g_2) at their surface is
(a) $\dfrac{R_1\rho_2}{R_2\rho_1}$ (b) $\dfrac{R_1\rho_1}{R_2\rho_2}$
(c) $\dfrac{\rho_1 R_2^2}{\rho_2 R_1^2}$ (d) $\dfrac{R_1 R_2}{\rho_2 \rho_2}$

6. If one moves from the surface of earth to moon, what will be the effect on its weight ?
(a) weight of a person decreases continuously with height from the surface of earth
(b) weight of a person increases with height from the surface of earth
(c) weight of a person first decreases with height and then increases with height from the surface of earth
(d) weight of a person first increases with height and then decreases with height from the surface of earth

7. If the earth of radius R, while rotating with angular velocity ω becomes stand still, what will be the effect on the weight of a body of mass m at a latitude of 45° ?
(a) remains unchanged
(b) decreases by $R\omega^2$
(c) increaes by $R\omega^2$
(d) increases by $R\omega^2/2$

8. One goes from the centre of the earth to a distance two third the radius of the earth, where will the acceleration due to gravity be the greatest ?
(a) at the centre of the earth
(b) at a depth half the radius of the earth
(c) at a depth one third the radius of the earth
(d) at a depth two third the radius of the earth

9. Two spherical planets A and B have same mass but densities in the ratio 8 : 1. For these planets, the acceleration due to gravity at the surface of A to its value at the surface of B is
(a) 1 : 4 (b) 1 : 2
(c) 4 : 1 (d) 8 : 1

10. If both the masses and radius of the earth, each decrease by 50%, the acceleration due to gravity would
(a) remain same (b) decrease by 50%
(c) decrease by 100%
(d) increase by 100%

11. Which of the following cannot be used for measuring time in a spaceship orbiting around the earth ?
(a) atomic clock (b) quartz watch
(c) electric clock (d) pendulum clock

12. A pendulum is taken to a place where the acceleration due to gravity is 1/6th that of earth's

surface. How would its length be changed to keep its time period same ?

(a) 1/12th (b) 1/6th
(c) 1/3rd (d) none of the above

13. The maximum vertical distance through which a full dressed astronaut can jump on the earth is 0.5 m. Estimate the maximum vertical distance through which he can jump on the moon, which has a mean density 2/3rd that of the earth and radius one quarter that of the earth.

(a) 1.5 m (b) 3 m
(c) 6 m (d) 7.5 m

14. If R is the radius of the earth and g is acceleration due to gravity on the earth's surface, the mean density of earth is

(a) $\frac{4\pi G}{3gR}$ (b) $\frac{3\pi G}{4gG}$
(c) $\frac{3g}{4\pi RG}$ (d) $\frac{\pi Rg}{12G}$

15. A clock S is based on oscillation of a spring and a clock P is based on pendulum motion. Both clocks run at the same rate on earth. On a planet having the same density as earth but twice the radius,

(a) S will run faster than P
(b) P will run faster than S
(c) both will run at the same rate as on the earth
(d) both will run at the same rate which will be different from that on the earth

16. At a distance 320 km above the surface of earth, the value of acceleration due to gravity will be lower than its value on the surface of the earth by nearly (radius of earth = 6400 km)

(a) 2% (b) 6%
(c) 10% (d) 14%

17. Units of gravitational intensity are

(a) ms^{-2} (b) Nkg^{-1}
(c) $kg\ ms^{-1}$ (d) $kg\ ms^{-2}$

18. Gravitational intensity at a place is given by

(a) G (b) g
(c) mg (d) none of the above.

19. Two planets of radii R_1 and R_2 are made from the same material. The ratio of the acceleration due to gravity g_1/g_2 at the surface of two planets is

(a) R_1/R_2 (b) R_2/R_1
(c) $(R_1/R_2)^2$ (d) $(R_2/R_1)^2$

20. In problem 13, the ratio of the time duration of his jump on the moon to that of his jump on earth is

(a) 1 : 6 (b) 6 : 1
(c) $\sqrt{6}:1$ (d) $1:\sqrt{6}$

21. At a point P, which is at a height of R metres from the surface of the earth, the gravitational potential will be (M = mass of the earth, R = radius of the earth)

(a) $GM/2R$ (b) $-GM/2R$
(c) $-GM/R$ (d) GM/R

22. Gravitational potential on the surface of earth is (M = mass of earth, R = radius of earth)

(a) $-GM/2R$ (b) $-gR$
(c) gR (d) GM/R

23. If earth were a hollow sphere, what would be gravitational field intensity at any point inside the earth ?

(a) 9.8 ms^{-2} (b) > 9.8 ms^{-2}
(c) < 9.8 ms^{-2} (d) zero

24. Intensity of gravitational field of earth is maximum at

(a) poles (b) equator
(c) centre of earth (d) same every where

25. The gravitational intensity at any point due to earth inside the earth is

(a) same as at surface
(b) increased as we go down
(c) same as at the centre of earth
(d) decreased as we go down.

26. If g is the acceleration due to gravity on the earth's surface, the gain in potential energy of the earth at a height equal to three times the radius R of the earth will be

(a) mgR (b) $\frac{1}{2}mgR$
(c) $\frac{1}{3}mgR$ (d) $\frac{3}{4}mgR$

27. Weight of a body is defined as the product of its mass and acceleration due to gravity i.e. $W = mg$. If weight of a body is 600 N and g is taken as 10 ms^{-2}, then the mass of the body will be

(a) 6 kg (b) 60 kg
(c) 600 kg (d) none of these

28. A mass m is placed at a point B in the gravitational field of mass M. When the mass m is brought from B to near point A, its gravitational potential energy will

(a) remain unchanged
(b) increase
(c) decrease
(d) become zero

29. There are two bodies of masses 100,000 kg and 1000 kg separated by a distance of 1 m. At what distance from the smaller body, the intensity of gravitational field will be zero ?

(a) $\frac{1}{9}$m (b) $\frac{1}{10}$m
(c) $\frac{1}{11}$m (d) $\frac{10}{11}$m.

30. At what distance in metre from the centre of the earth, the intensity of gravitational field will be zero ? Take mass of earth and moon as 5.98×10^{24} kg and 7.35×10^{22} kg respectively and the distance between moon and earth is 3.85×10^8 m.

(a) zero (b) 3.85×10^6
(c) 8×10^8 (d) 3.46×10^7

31. Two bodies of masses 100 kg and 1000 kg are separated by a distance of 1 m. What is the intensity of gravitational field at the mid point of the line joining them ?
$(G = 6.6 \times 10^{-11}$ Nm^2 kg$^{-2})$

(a) 2.4×10^{-9} N/kg (b) 2.4×10^{-8} N/kg
(c) 2.4×10^{-7} N/kg (d) 2.4×10^{-6} N/kg

32. A body of mass m rises to a height $h = R/5$ from the surface of earth, where R is the radius of earth. If g is the acceleration due to gravity at the surface of earth, the increase in potential energy is

(a) (4/5) mgh (b) (5/6) mgh
(c) (6/7) mgh (d) mgh

33. The gravitational potential difference between the surface of a planet and a point 20 m above it is 14 J kg^{-1}. The work done in moving a 2.0 kg mass by 8.0 m on a slope of 60° from the horizontal is equal to

(a) 7 J (b) 9.6 J
(c) 16 J (d) 32 J

34. In a gravitational field, if a body is bound, then total energy has

(a) positive value (b) negative value
(c) zero value (d) KE < PE

35. The gravitational potential difference between the surface of a planet and a point 100 m above its surface is 10 J kg^{-1}. If the gravitational field over this range is uniform, then the work done to raise the body of 5 kg from the surface to a height 40 m is

(a) 10 J (b) 20 J
(c) 40 J (d) 80 J

36. In the question no. 29, what will be the intensity of the gravitational field at the mid point of the line joining the bodies

(a) 2.6×10^{-5} N/kg (b) 2.6×10^{-7} N/kg
(c) 2.6×10^{-8} N/kg (d) 2.6×10^{-9} N/kg

37. The gravitational field in a region is given by $\vec{I} = (4\hat{i} + \hat{j})$ N/kg. Work done by this field is zero when a particle is moved along the line

(a) $x + y = 6$ (b) $x + 4y = 6$
(c) $y + 4x = 6$ (d) $x - y = 6$

38. A person brings a mass of 2 kg from P to Q. The increase in K.E. of the mass in 4J and the work done by the person on the mass is –10 J. The gravitational potential difference between Q and P is

(a) –3 J/kg (b) –7 J/kg
(c) 7 J/kg (d) 4 J/kg

39. The gravitational field due to a mass distribution is $I = \frac{C}{x^2}$ in x direction. Here C is constant. Taking the gravitational potential to be zero at infinity, potential at x is

(a) $\frac{2C}{x}$ (b) $\frac{C}{x}$
(c) $\frac{2C}{x^2}$ (d) $\frac{C}{2x^2}$

40. A uniform ring of mass M and radius R is placed directly above a uniform sphere of mass 8 M and of same radius R. The centre of the ring is at a distance of $d = \sqrt{3}R$ from the centre of the sphere. The gravitational attraction between the sphere and the ring is

(a) $\frac{GM^2}{R^2}$ (b) $\frac{3GM^2}{2R^2}$

(c) $\frac{2GM^2}{2R^2}$ (d) $\frac{\sqrt{3}GM^2}{R^2}$

41. The workdone in slowly lifting a body from earth's surface to a height R (radius of earth) is equal to twice the workdone in lifting the same body from earth's surface to a height h. Here h is equal to

(a) $\frac{R}{6}$ (b) $\frac{R}{4}$

(c) $\frac{R}{3}$ (d) $\frac{R}{2}$

42. At what height from the surface of the earth, the total energy of the satellite is equal to its potential energy at a height of $2R$ from the surface of earth (R = radius of earth)

(a) $\frac{R}{4}$ (b) $\frac{R}{2}$

(c) $2R$ (d) $4R$

43. A solid sphere is of density ρ and radius R. The gravitational field at a distance r from the centre of the sphere, where $r < R$, is

(a) $\frac{\rho\pi GR^3}{r}$ (b) $\frac{4\pi G\rho r^2}{3}$

(c) $\frac{4\pi G\rho R^3}{3r^2}$ (d) $\frac{4\pi G\rho r}{3}$

44. The self gravitational potential energy of a spherical shell of mass M and radius R is

(a) $-\frac{GM^2}{R}$ (b) $-\frac{GM^2}{2R}$

(c) $-\frac{GM^2}{4R}$ (d) $-\frac{3}{5}\frac{GM^2}{R}$

45. The period of a satellite in a circular orbit around a planet is independent of
(a) the mass of the planet
(b) the radius of the planet
(c) the mass of the satellite
(d) all the three parameters (a), (b) and (c)

46. What is the binding energy of earth-sun system neglecting the effect of other planets and satellites ? Mass of earth $M_e = 6 \times 10^{24}$ kg, mass of the sun $M_s = 2 \times 10^{30}$ kg. Distance between earth and sun,
$R = 1.5 \times 10^{11}$ m; $G = 6.6 \times 10^{-11}$ Nm^2 kg^{-2}.
(a) 8.8×10^{10} J (b) 8.8×10^{31}
(c) 5.2×10^{33} J (d) 2.6×10^{33} J

47. The distance between the earth and the moon is 3.85×10^8 m. At what distance from the earth's centre, the intensity of gravitational field will be zero ? The masses of earth and moon are 5.98×10^{24} kg and 7.35×10^{22} kg respectively.
(a) 3.46×10^8 m (b) 0.39×10^8 m
(c) 1.82×10^8 m (d) none of the above

48. The gravitational field due to a mass distribution is $E = K/x^3$ in the x-direction (K is a constant). Taking the gravitational potential to be zero at infinity, its value at a distance $x/\sqrt{2}$ is
(a) K/x (b) $K/2x$
(c) K/x^2 (d) $K/2x^2$

49. For a body to escape from earth, angle at which is should be fired is
(a) 45° (b) >45°
(c) <45° and (d) any angle

50. The plane of the elliptical orbit of a satellite revolving around earth passes through
(a) centre of earth (b) north pole
(c) south pole (d) none of the above

ANSWERS

1	2	3	4	5	6	7	8	9	10
(b)	(b)	(b)	(a)	(b)	(c)	(d)	(c)	(c)	(d)
11	**12**	**13**	**14**	**15**	**16**	**17**	**18**	**19**	**20**
(d)	(b)	(b)	(c)	(b)	(c)	(a, b)	(b)	(a)	(b)
21	**22**	**23**	**24**	**25**	**26**	**27**	**28**	**29**	**30**
(b)	(b)	(d)	(a)	(d)	(d)	(b)	(c)	(c)	(d)

31	32	33	34	35	36	37	38	39	40
(c)	(b)	(b)	(b)	(b)	(a)	(c)	(b)	(b)	(d)
41	**42**	**43**	**44**	**45**	**46**	**47**	**48**	**49**	**50**
(c)	(b)	(d)	(b)	(c)	(d)	(a)	(c)	(d)	(a)

HINTS / SOLUTIONS

1. Given $g_h = 9 = \frac{gR^2}{(R + R/20)^2} = \frac{20 \times 20}{21 \times 21} g$

or $g = \frac{9 \times 21 \times 21}{20 \times 20}$

Now, $g_d = g\left(1 - \frac{d}{R}\right)$

$= \frac{9 \times 21 \times 21}{20 \times 20}\left[1 - \frac{(R/20)}{R}\right]$

$= 9.5 \text{ ms}^{-2}$.

2. $g_m = GM_m/R_m^2$ and $g_e = GM_e/R_e^2$

$\therefore \frac{g_m}{g_e} = \frac{M_m}{M_e} \times \left(\frac{R_e}{R_m}\right)^2$

$= \frac{1}{10} \times (2)^2 = \frac{4}{10} = 0.4$

or $g_m = 0.4\, g_e$

$= 0.4 \times 9.8 = 3.92 \text{ ms}^{-2}$

3. As mass, $M = \frac{4}{3}\pi R^3 \rho$

or $\rho = \frac{3M}{4\pi R^3}$

$\therefore \frac{\rho_s}{\rho_e} = \frac{M_s}{M_e} \times \frac{R_e^3}{R_s^3} = 330 \times \left(\frac{1}{100}\right)^3$

$= 3.3 \times 10^{-4}$

4. As weight of body on pole = mg and g does not change at pole due to rotation of earth, so there is no change in the weight of body.

5. $g = \frac{GM}{R^2} = \frac{G}{R^2}\frac{4}{3}\pi R^3 \rho = \frac{4}{3}\pi GR\rho$

So, $\frac{g_1}{g_2} = \frac{R_1\rho_1}{R_2\rho_2}$.

6. The gravitational attraction on a body due to earth decreases with height and increases due to moon. At a certain height, it becomes zero and with further increase in height, the gravitational attraction of moon becomes more than that of earth.

7. $g' = g - R\omega^2 \cos^2\lambda$; When $\lambda = 45°$

then $g' = g - R\omega^2 (1/\sqrt{2})^2 = g - R\omega^2/2$.

When earth stops rotating, $w = 0$, so $g' = g$.

$\therefore \quad g - (g - gR\omega^2/2) = R\omega^2/2$.

8. The acceleration due to gravity at a depth d inside the earth is

$g' = g\left(1 - \frac{d}{R}\right) = g\left(\frac{R-d}{R}\right) = g\frac{r}{R}$

Where, $R - d = y$ = distance of a place from the centre of earth. Therefore $g' \propto r$.

9. Mass of two planets is same, so

$\frac{4}{3}\pi R_1^3 \rho_1 = \frac{4}{3}\pi R_2^3 \rho_2$

or $\frac{R_1}{R_2} = \left(\frac{\rho_2}{\rho_1}\right)^{1/3} = \left(\frac{1}{8}\right)^{1/3} = \frac{1}{2}$

$\frac{g_1}{g_2} = \frac{GM/R_1^2}{GM/R_2^2} = \left(\frac{R_2}{R_1}\right)^2 = (2)^2 = 4$

10. Here, $g = GM/R^2$ and

$g' = \frac{G(M/2)}{(R/2)^2} = \frac{2GM}{R^2} = 2g$

$\therefore$ % increase in $g = \left(\frac{g'-g}{g}\right) \times 100$

$= \left(\frac{2g-g}{g}\right) \times 100 = 100\%$.

11. In a spaceship orbiting around the earth, $g = 0$. Therefore a pendulum clock cannot be used for measuring time.

12. $T = 2\pi\sqrt{\frac{l}{g}}$; for constant value of T, l/g is constant. If g becomes $g/6$ then l should be $l/6$ for the same value of T.

13. On moon, $g_m = \frac{4}{3}\pi G(R/4)(2\rho/3)$

$$= \frac{1}{6}\left(\frac{4}{3}\pi GR\rho\right) = \frac{1}{6}g$$

Work done in jumping

$$= m \times g \times 0.5 = m \times (g/6)\, h_1$$

so $h_1 = 0.5 \times 6 = 3.0$ m

14. $g = \frac{GM}{R^2} = \frac{G}{R^2} \times \frac{4}{3}\pi R^3 \rho = \frac{4}{3}\pi GR\rho$

or $\rho = \frac{3g}{4\pi RG}$

15. $g = \frac{GM}{R^2} = \frac{G \times \frac{4}{3}\pi R^3 \rho}{R^2} = \frac{4}{3}\pi G\rho R$

i.e. $g \propto R$.

For pendulum clock, g will increase on the planet, so time period will decrease. But for spring clock, it will not change. Hence P will run faster than S.

16. $\frac{g'}{g} = 1 - \frac{2h}{R} = 1 - \frac{2 \times 320}{6400}$

$$= 1 - \frac{1}{10} = \frac{9}{10}$$

$\therefore$ % decrease in $g = \left(\frac{g - g'}{g}\right) \times 100$

$$= \frac{1}{10} \times 100 = 10\%$$

17. Intensity of gravitational field is equal to acceleration due to gravity at a point, which is maximum at poles.

18. Gravitational intensity at a point is equal to acceleration due to gravity at that point.

19. $g = \frac{GM}{R^2} = \frac{G}{R^2} \times \frac{4}{3}\pi R^3 \rho = \frac{4}{3}\pi G\rho R$

i.e., $g \propto R \quad \therefore \quad \frac{g_1}{g_2} = \frac{R_1}{R_2}$.

20. On earth, using relation $s = ut + \frac{1}{2}at^2$

we have, $\frac{1}{2} = 0 + \frac{1}{2}gt^2$ or $t = \frac{1}{\sqrt{g}}$.

On moon; $3.0 = 0 + \frac{1}{2}g_1 t_1^2 = \frac{1}{2} \times \frac{g}{6} t_1^2$

or $t_1 = \frac{6}{\sqrt{g}}$

$\therefore \frac{t_1}{t} = \frac{6/\sqrt{g}}{1/\sqrt{g}} = 6.$

21. Gravitational potential at a point

$$= \frac{-GM}{(2R)} = \frac{-GM}{2R}.$$

22. Gravitational potential at a point on the surface of earth,

$$V = \frac{-GM}{R} = \frac{-gR^2}{R} = -gR$$

23. Gravitational intensity at a point inside the hollow sphere is zero.

25. Gravitational intensity at a point inside the solid sphere is directly proportional to the distance of point from the centre of sphere *i.e.*, $I \propto r$.

26. Gravitational potential energy at any point at distance x from centre of earth is $E = -GMm/x$; At the surface of earth $x = R$, so,

$$E_1 = \frac{-GMm}{R} = -mgR$$

At height $3R$, from surface of earth, $x = 4R$

So, $E_2 = \frac{-GMm}{4R} = -mgR/4.$

Increase in potential energy

$$= \frac{-mgR}{4} + mgR = \frac{3}{4}mgR.$$

27. Weight $= 60 \times 10\,\text{N} = mg = m \times 10;$

so $m = 60\,\text{kg}.$

28. Gravitational potential energy of a body in the gravitational field, $E = \frac{-GMm}{r}$. When r decreases –ve value of E increases *i.e.* E decreases.

29. Let x be the distance of point from the smaller body where gravitational intensity is zero.

$$\therefore \frac{Gm_1}{(1-x)^2} = \frac{Gm_2}{x^2}$$

or $\frac{x}{1-x} = \sqrt{\frac{m_2}{m_1}} = \sqrt{\frac{1000}{100000}} = \frac{1}{10}$

or $10x = 1 - x$ or $x = (1/11)$ m.

30. Let x be the distance of point from the centre of earth where gravitational intensity is zero. Therefore,

$$\frac{GM_e}{x^2} = \frac{GM_m}{(3.85\times10^8 - x)^2}$$

or $$\frac{x}{3.85 \times 10^8 - x} = \sqrt{\frac{M_e}{M_m}}$$

$$= \sqrt{\frac{5.98\times10^{24}}{7.35\times10^{22}}} = 9$$

or $$\frac{x}{9} + x = 3.85\times10^8$$

or $$x = 9\times3.85\times10^8/10$$

$$= 3.46\times10^7 \text{ m.}$$

31. Resultant gravitational intensity at a mid point on the line joining the two mass bodies is

$$I = \frac{Gm_2}{(r/2)^2} - \frac{Gm_1}{(r/2)^2} = \frac{4G}{r^2}(m_2 - m_1)$$

$$= \frac{4\times6.6\times10^{-11}}{1^2}(1000-100)$$

$$= 2.4\times10^{-7} \text{ N/kg.}$$

32. Gravitational force on a body at a distance x from the centre of earth $F = \frac{GMm}{x^2}$. Work done,

$$W = \int_R^{R+h} F\,dx = \int_R^{R+h} \frac{GMm}{x^2}dx$$

$$= GMm\left[-\frac{1}{x}\right]_R^{R+h}$$

$$= mgR^2\left[\frac{1}{R} - \frac{1}{R+h}\right]$$

This work done appears as increase in potential energy ΔE_p. So

$$\Delta E_p = mgR^2\left[\frac{1}{R} - \frac{1}{R+h}\right]$$

$$= mg(5h)^2\left[\frac{1}{5h} - \frac{1}{6h}\right] = \frac{5}{6}mgh.$$

33. Gravitational intensity,

$$I = \frac{dV}{dx} = \frac{14}{20} = 0.7 \text{ N kg}^{-1}$$

Acceleration due to gravity,

$$g = I = 0.7 \text{ N kg}^{-1}$$

Work done under this field in displacing a body on a slope of 60° through a distances

$$= m(g\sin 60^\circ)\,s$$

$$= 2\times(0.7\times\sqrt{3}/2)\times8 = 9.6 \text{ J}$$

34. For a bound body, total energy of the body is negative. It is due to the fact that the energy is required to free the body from the gravitational attraction.

35. Acceleration due to gravity, g = electric intensity = rate of change of potential

$$= \frac{10}{100} = \frac{1}{10}$$

The work done in moving upwards a body of 5 kg through 40 m will be = mgh

$$= 5\times(1/10)\times40 = 20 \text{ J.}$$

36. Gravitational intensity at the middle point is

$$E = \frac{Gm_1}{(r/2)^2} - \frac{Gm_2}{(r/2)^2} = \frac{4G}{r^2}(m_1 - m_2)$$

$$= \frac{4\times6.6\times10^{-11}}{1^2}(100000-1000)$$

$$= 2.64\times10^{-11}\times99000$$

$$= 2.6\times10^{-5} \text{ N/kg.}$$

37. Work done by the gravitational field is zero, when displacement is perpendicular to gravitational field. Here, gravitational field, $\vec{I} = 4\hat{i} + \hat{j}$. If θ_1 is the angle which $\vec{I}$ makes with positive x-axis, then

$$\tan\theta_1 = \frac{1}{4} \text{ or } \theta_1 = \tan^{-1}\left(\frac{1}{4}\right) = 14°6'$$

If θ_2 is the angle which the line $y + 4x = 6$ makes with positive x-axis, then

$$\theta_2 = \tan^{-1}(-4) = 75°\,56'$$

So $\theta_1 + \theta_2 = 90°$.

i.e. the line $y + 4x = 6$ is perpendicular to $\vec{I}$.

38. $W_{P\to Q}$ = (P.E. at Q – P.E. at P) + (K.E. at Q – K.E. at P)

or $W_{P\to Q} = m(V_Q - V_P) + (K_Q - K_P)$

or $-10 = 2(V_Q - V_P) + 4$

or $V_Q - V_P = -7$ J/kg.

39. $V = \int_{\infty}^{x} I\, dx = -\int_{\infty}^{x} \frac{C}{x^2}\, dx = \frac{C}{x}.$

40. Refer Figure, Gravitational intensity due to the ring at a distance $d = \sqrt{3}\, R$ on its axis is

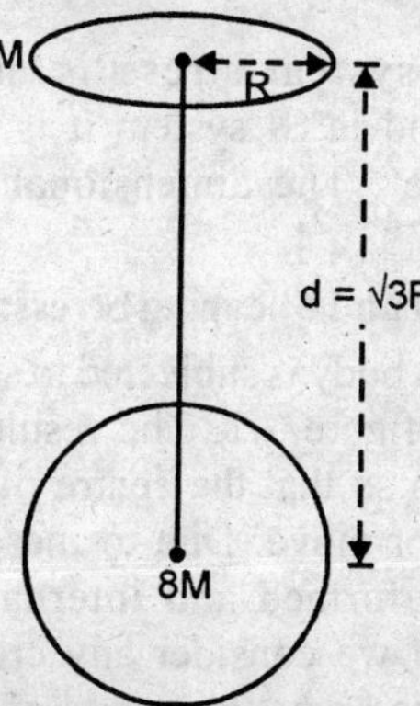

$$I = \frac{GMd}{(d^2 + R^2)^{3/2}} = \frac{GM \times \sqrt{3}R}{(3R^2 + R^2)^{3/2}} = \frac{\sqrt{3}\, GM}{8R^2}$$

Force on sphere

$$(8M)\, I = (8M) \times \frac{\sqrt{3}\, GM}{8R^2} = \frac{\sqrt{3}\, GM^2}{R^2}.$$

41. Work done = increase in gravitational pot. energy

$$W_1 = -\frac{GMm}{(R+R)} + \frac{GMm}{R} = \frac{GMm}{2R} = \frac{mgR}{2}$$

Work done in lifting the body to height h is

$$W_2 = -\frac{GMm}{(R+h)} + \frac{GMm}{R} = \frac{GMmh}{R(R+h)} = \frac{mg\, Rh}{(R+h)}$$

As $W_1 = 2W_2$, so $\frac{mgR}{2} = \frac{2mg\, Rh}{(R+h)}$

or $h = \frac{R}{3}$

42. Total energy of a satellite at a height h

$$= \frac{GMm}{2(R+h)}$$

Potential energy at a height 2R from surface of Earth $= -\frac{GMm}{2R+R} = -\frac{GMm}{3R}$

As per question, $-\frac{GMm}{2(R+h)} = -\frac{GMm}{3R}.$

or $h = \frac{R}{2}.$

43. When $r < R$, Gravitational field intensity,

$$I = \frac{GM}{R^3}\, r = \frac{Gr}{R^3}\left(\frac{4}{3}\pi R^3 \rho\right) = \frac{4\pi G\rho r}{3}$$

44. When mass of the shell is m, its potential is

$$= -\frac{Gm}{R}$$

Work done in increasing the elementary mass dm is

$$dW = -\frac{Gm}{R}\, dm$$

Total work done = self potential energy

$$= \int_0^M -\frac{Gm}{R}\, dm = -\frac{GM^2}{2R}.$$

45. The period of a satellite in a circular orbit is independent of mass of the satellite.

46. Binding energy of the system $= \frac{GM_e\, M_s}{2r}$

$$= \frac{6.6 \times 10^{-11} \times 6 \times 10^{24} \times 2 \times 10^{30}}{2 \times 1.5 \times 10^{11}}$$

$= 2.6 \times 10^{33}$ J.

47. $\frac{GM_e}{x^2} = \frac{GM_m}{(r-x)^2}$

or $\frac{r-x}{x} = \sqrt{\frac{M_m}{M_e}}$

$$= \sqrt{\frac{7.35 \times 10^{22}}{5.98 \times 10^{24}}} = 0.11$$

or $r = 0.11x + x = 1.11x$

or $x = r/1.11 = 3.85 \times 10^8/1.11$

$= 3.47 \times 10^8\ \text{m} \simeq 3.46 \times 10^8\ \text{m}$

48. $dV = -Edx$

or $V = -\int_{\infty}^{x/\sqrt{2}} E\, dx = -\int_{\infty}^{x/\sqrt{2}} Kx^{-3}\, dx = K/x^2$

49. The body can be fired at any angle because the energy is sufficient to take the body out of the gravitational field of earth.

UNIT-7

PROPERTIES OF BULK MATTER

ELASTIC AND PLASTIC BEHAVIOUR OF SOLIDS

(i) The property of the materials by virtue of which the bodies are restored to their natural shape and size (or oppose the deformations produced in them) after the removal of external force is called elasticity.

(ii) If a body completely regains its original form after removal of external forces, it is called a Perfectly Elastic Body. In fact, the concept of a **perfectly elastic body** is an idealisation and no materials behave as perfectly elastic. **A quartz fibre is the nearest approach to a perfectly elastic body.**

(iii) A body that does not even partially regain its original shape and size on the removal of deforming force (however small the magnitude of deforming force may be) and remains in the deformed state, is called a **Perfectly Inelastic or Plastic Body**. Generally, when the deforming forces are removed, the body partially regains the original form. Such bodies are called **Partially Elastic**. Wet soil, paraffin wax etc. are the example of nearly plastic bodies.

STRESS

(i) The restoring force developed per unit area in the body when subjected to deforming force, is called be stress, i.e.,

$$\text{Stress} = \frac{\text{Restoring Force}}{\text{Area}}$$

(ii) Since the restoring forces are equal and opposite to the external deforming forces (so long as deforming force is within elastic limit or no permanent deformation is produced), therefore, the stress may be measured as the external force acting per unit area, i.e.,

$$\text{Stress} = \frac{\text{External Force applied}}{\text{Area}} = \frac{F}{A}$$

(iii) In the cgs system stress is measured in dynes/cm^2 and in SI system it is measured in newton/metre^2. The dimensional formula for stress is $[ML^{-1}T^{-2}]$.

(iv) **Longitudinal and Shearing Stress:**

(a) Suppose a body is subjected to several forces as shown in figure 7.1. The resultant of these forces is zero so that the centre of mass of the body does not move. Due to these forces, the body gets deformed and internal forces are developed. If we consider any cross-sectional area ΔA of the body, then parts of the body on the two sides of area ΔA exert forces $\vec{F}, -\vec{F}$ on each other. These internal forces $\vec{F}, -\vec{F}$ appear because of deformation.

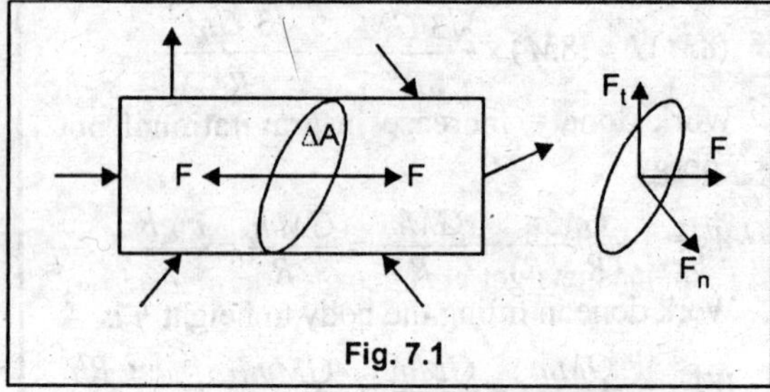

Fig. 7.1

(b) The force $\vec{F}$ may be resolved in two components F_t and F_n tangential and normal to area ΔA respectively. **Longitudinal or normal stress** over the area ΔA is defined as

$$S_n = \frac{F_n}{\Delta A} \quad \text{...(1)}$$

and the **tangential stress or shearing stress** over the area ΔA is defined as

$$S_t = \frac{F_t}{\Delta A} \quad \text{...(2)}$$

(c) The longitudinal stress is of two types. If the two parts of the body on the two sides of ΔA pull each other, then the longitudinal stress is called as **Tensile stress**. This is the case when a rod or a wire is stretched by equal and opposite forces. If the rod is pushed at the two ends with equal and opposite forces, it will be under compression. Here the two parts of the body on the two sides of any cross-section ΔA push each other. The longitudinal stress is then called **compressive stress.**

(v) **Volume stress:** When a body is subjected to forces acting everywhere on the surface in such a way that the force at every point is normal to the surface and the magnitude of force on any small surface area is proportional to the area, then the force per unit area is called **Volume Stress.** This is the case when a small solid body is immersed in a fluid. If the pressure at the location of the solid is P, the force on any area ΔA is $P\Delta A$ directed perpendicularly to the area. Therefore, volume stress over an area ΔA is defined as

$$S_v = \frac{F}{\Delta A} \quad \text{...(3)}$$

which is the same as the pressure.

STRAIN

(i) If a body is subjected to deforming force its dimensions get changed and the body is said to be deformed or strained. **The ratio of change in dimension of the body to the original dimensions is called strain.** Since a body can have three types of deformations, i.e., in length, in volume or in shape, likewise there are three types of strains namely **longitudinal strain, volume strain and shear strain.**

(ii) **Longitudinal strain:** Suppose the length of a rod increases from its natural value L to $L + \Delta L$, when pulled by equal and opposite forces along the length. The fractional change $\Delta L/L$ is called the longitudinal strain, i.e.,

$$\text{longitudinal strain} = \frac{\text{change in length}}{\text{original length}} = \frac{\Delta L}{L}$$

If the length increases from its natural length, the longitudinal strain is called **tensile strain.** If the length decreases from its natural length, the longitudinal strain is called **compressive strain.**

(iii) **Volume strain:** If a body is subjected to a volume stress, there occurs a change in its volume. The fractional change in volume is known as volume strain. If V is the volume of unstressed body and $V + \Delta V$ is the volume when subjected to volume stress, then volume strain is defined as

$$\text{Volume strain} = \frac{\Delta V}{V}$$

(iv) **Shearing strain:** If a body is acted upon by an external force tangential to a surface of the body, the opposite surface being kept fixed, it suffers a change in shape; its volume remaining unchanged. In such a case, the body is said to be sheared. **The ratio of the displacement of a layer in the direction of the tangential force and the distance of that layer from the fixed surface is called the shearing strain.**

HOOKE'S LAW AND MODULII OF ELASTICITY

(i) Hooke's law states that if the deformation is small, strain produced in a body is directly proportional to the corresponding stress, i.e.,

$$\text{stress} \propto \text{strain or } \frac{\text{stress}}{\text{strain}} = \text{constant}$$

This constant of proportionality is called **modulus of elasticity or the coefficient of elasticity of the material.** Its value depends upon the nature of material and the manner in which the body is deformed called as Young's Modulus, Shear Modulus and Bulk Modulus.

(ii) **Young's Modulus:** If a rod is stretched by equal and opposite forces F each, a tensile stress F/A is produced in the rod where A is the area of cross-section. The length of the rod increases from its natural value L to $L + \Delta L$, i.e., tensile strain is $\Delta L/L$.

According to Hooke's Law, for small deformations

$$Y = \frac{\text{Tensile stress}}{\text{Tensile strain}} \quad \text{...(1)}$$

which is a constant for the given material, known as Young's Modulus for the material. In the situation described above, the Young's modulus is

$$Y = \frac{F/A}{\Delta L/L} = \frac{FL}{A \Delta L} \quad ...(2)$$

If the rod is compressed, compressive stress and compressive strain appear. Their ratio Y is same as that for the tensile case.

(iii) **Shear Modulus or Modulus of Rigidity:** Within Elastic limit, the ratio of tangential stress to shear strain is called the Shear Modulus or the modulus of rigidity of the material of the body. It is denoted by η.

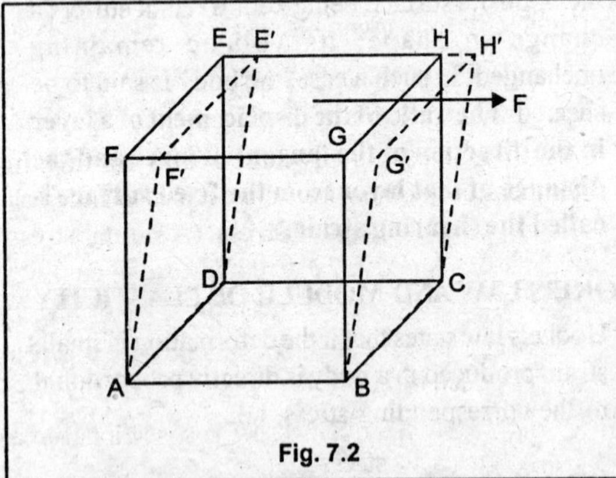

Fig. 7.2

Consider a rectangular block, whose lower surface ABCD is rigidly fixed and upper surface EFGH is subjected to tangential force F (Fig. 7.2). Let A be the area of each face and AF = L be the perpendicular distance between them. When the tangential force F is applied at the upper surface EFGH, then all the layers parallel to EFGH are displaced in the direction of force. The displacement of a layer is proportional to its distance from the fixed surface. The rectangular block thus takes the form of a parallelopiped ABCDE′F′G′H′. Let the upper layer is displaced through a distance FF′ = l. Suppose $\angle FAF' = \theta$. Here θ is the angle through which the line AF, initially perpendicular to the fixed surface, is turned and is called the angle of shear or shearing strain.

In practice, for solids, θ is very small so that in $\Delta AFF'$

$$\theta \approx \tan\theta = \frac{FF'}{AF} = \frac{l}{L}$$

If A be the area of the upper face EFGH, then shearing stress = F/A

∴ Modulus of rigidity of the material of block.

$$\eta = \frac{F/A}{\theta} = \frac{F}{A\theta}$$

The unit of η is newton/metre^2 and its dimensional formula is $[ML^{-1}T^{-2}]$.

(iv) **Bulk Modulus:** On applying uniform pressure all over the surface of a body, the volume of the body changes, but its shape remains unchanged. Such a strain may appear in all the three states of matter; solid, liquid and gas. When strain is small, the ratio of the volume stress to the volume strain is called the bulk modulus of the material of the body. It is denoted by B.

If P be the volume stress (same as pressure) and ΔV be the decrease in volume, then Bulk Modulus is defined as

$$B = -\frac{P}{\Delta V/V} = -\frac{PV}{\Delta V}.$$

The unit of B is also newton/metre^2 and dimensional formula is $[ML^{-1}T^{-2}]$.

ELASTIC POTENTIAL ENERGY IN A STRETCHED WIRE

(i) Potential energy corresponding to the molecular forces is minimum when a body is in its normal shape. Let us consider this potential energy to be zero. When the body is deformed, internal forces are developed in a direction opposite to the deforming forces. Hence in the process of deforming a body work has to be done against these internal forces. Thus, the potential energy of the body is increased. This is called the **elastic potential energy**. Here we shall find out an expression for the increase in elastic potential energy when a wire is stretched from its natural length.

(ii) Consider a wire having initial length L and cross sectional area A is fixed rigidly at one end and a stretching force is applied at the other end. This force is so adjusted that the wire is only slowly stretched so that at any moment during stretching the external force is equal to the tension in the wire.

(iii) Suppose at any moment during extension the tension in the wire is F while extension is x. Hence longitudinal stress $= F/A$ and longitudinal strain $= x/L$

If Y be the Young's Modulus of the material of wire, then

$$Y = \frac{F/A}{x/L}$$

or
$$F = \frac{YA}{L}x \quad \text{...(1)}$$

The work done by the external force in a further extension dx is

$$dW = F\,dx = (YA/L)\,x\,dx$$

The total work done by the external force in an extension 0 to l is

$$W = \int_0^l \frac{AY}{L} x\,dx = \frac{AY}{2L} l^2$$

This work is stored in the wire as its elastic potential energy.

Thus, the elastic potential energy of the stretched wire is

$$U = \frac{AY}{2L} l^2 \quad \text{...(2)}$$

This may be written as

$$U = \frac{1}{2}\left[AY\left(\frac{l}{L}\right)\right] l$$

= ½ × Max. stretching force × extension...(3)

Equation (2) may also expressed as

$$U = \frac{1}{2}\left[Y\left(\frac{l}{L}\right)\left(\frac{l}{L}\right)(AL)\right]$$

= ½ × Stress × Strain × Volume

= ½ Y (strain)^2 Volume ...(4)

TENSION IN A STRETCHED WIRE

Consider a wire of length L and area of cross section A is clamped rigidly between two supports. When it is allowed to cool, it contracts in length and exerts a pulling force on each support. Let Y be the Young's Modulus and α the coefficient of linear expansion of the material of wire. If l be the decrease in length of the wire corresponding to a temperature fall Δt, then

$$\alpha = \frac{\text{decrease in length}}{\text{initial length} \times \text{temperature fall}}$$

$$= \frac{l}{L\Delta t}$$

or $\quad l = L\,\alpha\,\Delta t$

$\therefore$ Longitudinal strain $= (l/L) = \alpha\,\Delta t$

Hence, corresponding stress

= Young's Modulus × Strain

$= Y\alpha\Delta t$

As this stress is produced due to fall in temperature of the wire, hence it is also called as **Longitudinal Thermal Stress.** (A similar stress will be developed in the wire if instead of cooling, the wire is allowed to be heated).

Hence, the tension developed in the wire is given as

Tension F = Stress × Cross sectional area

$= Y\alpha\,\Delta t\,A$

$= \boldsymbol{YA\alpha\,\Delta t}$

SURFACE TENSION

(i) The free surface of every liquid has always a tendency to contract to a minimum possible surface area and thus behaves like a stretched membrane having a tension in all directions parallel to the surface. This tension in the surface of a liquid is called the surface tension. Thus, surface tension is that characteristic property of a liquid by virtue of which, its free surface possess a tendency to contact so as to acquire a minimum possible surface area.

(ii) **Surface tension definition:** Imagine a line AB drawn on the free surface of a liquid in any direction (Fig. 7.3). In order to have the minimum surface area, the surface on either side of this line exerts a pulling force on the surface on the other side. This force lies in the plane of the surface and is perpendicular to the line AB. The magnitude of this force per unit length of line AB is taken as a measure of the surface tension of

the liquid. Thus if F is the total force acting on either side of the line AB of length l, then the surface tension is given by $T = F/l$

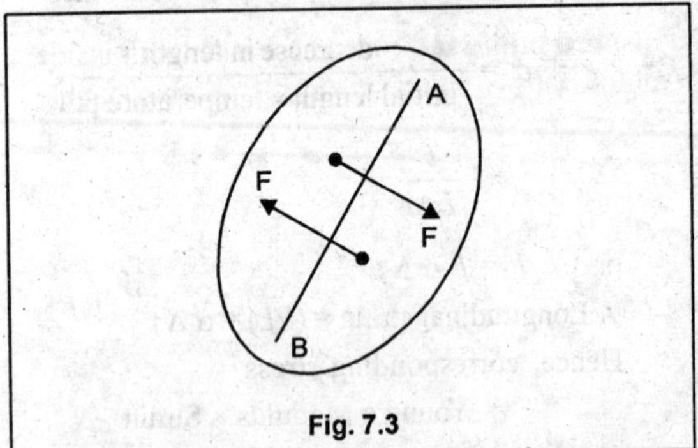

Fig. 7.3

If $l = 1$, then $T = F$. **Hence the surface tension of a liquid can be measured as the force per unit length on an imaginary line drawn on the liquid surface, acting perpendicular to it on either side and tangentially to the liquid surface.**

(iii) The unit of surface tension is dyne/cm in cgs system and Newton/metre in SI system. The dimensional formula for surface tension is $[ML^0T^{-2}]$.

(iv) The value of the surface tension of a liquid decreases with rise in temperature and becomes zero at the critical temperature.

SURFACE ENERGY

The molecules in the surface have some additional energy due to their position. This additional energy per unit area of the surface is called surface energy. It may also be defined as the work done in increasing the area of the surface film by unity.

RELATION BETWEEN SURFACE TENSION AND SURFACE ENERGY

(i) Consider a liquid film formed between a rectangular wire frame $ABCD$ and a straight wire PQ which can slide on the rectangular wire frame without friction (Fig. 7.4). Due to surface tension, the film will have a tendency to contract and in this process, the straight wire PQ will be pulled inward. However, the wire PQ can be held in position under a force F equal and opposite to the force acting on wire PQ all along its length due to surface tension in soap film.

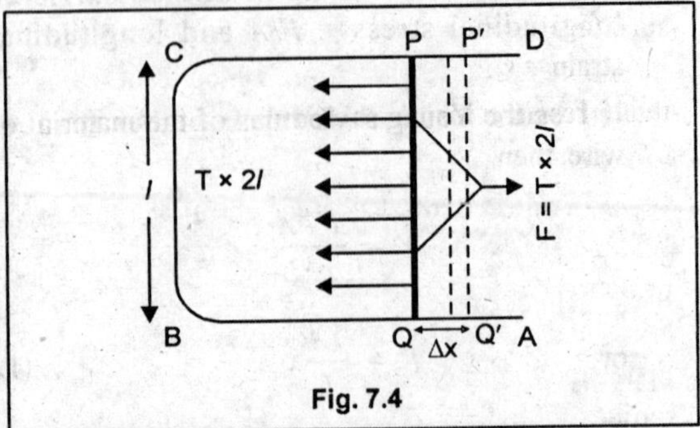

Fig. 7.4

Let T be the force due to surface tension per unit length, then

$$L = T \times 2l$$

where l is the length of wire PQ. The length is taken twice due to the fact that the film has got two free surfaces.

(ii) Suppose the straight wire PQ is moved through a small distance Δx so as to take new position $P'Q'$. In this process, area of the film has been increased by $2l \times \Delta x$ on both sides and work done by the force F is given by

$$W = F \times \Delta x = (T \times 2l) \times \Delta x$$

But $2\,l \times \Delta x$ is the total increase in area of both the surfaces of the film. Let it be ΔA. Then

$$W = T \times \Delta A$$

or

$$T = W/\Delta A$$

(iii) In above equation, if $\Delta A = 1$, then $T = W$. **Thus the work done in increasing the surface area by unity will be equal to the surface tension *T*. Hence surface tension of a liquid film by unity at constant temperature.**

EXCESS PRESSURE INSIDE A LIQUID DROP AND A BUBBLE

(i) A liquid surface possesses a tendency to have minimum surface area due to property of surface tension. Small liquid drops and bubbles are found to have spherical shape.

However, a big drop of liquid is not spherical in shape. It is because of negligible effect of gravity in case of a small drop. Since small drops and bubbles are spherical in shape, hence it implies that for a given volume, a sphere must be possessing minimum surface area. Because the surface area of a drop does not reduce to zero inspite of the surface tension, hence it indicates that **pressure inside the drop is higher than outside.**

(ii) **Inside a liquid drop:** Consider a drop of liquid of surface tension T and radius R. Suppose the pressures inside and outside the drop of liquid are p_i and p_o respectively. Then, excess pressure inside the liquid drop $= p_i - p_o$ (Fig. 7.5). Let the radius of the drop is increased from R to $R + \delta R$ under the pressure difference $(p_i - p_o)$.

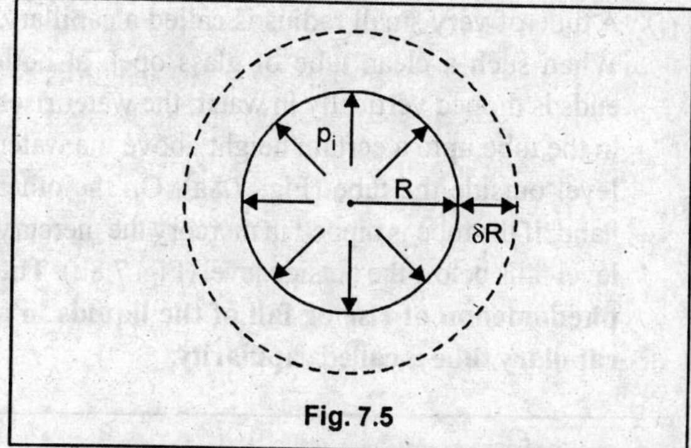

Fig. 7.5

The outward force acting on the drop = pressure difference × surface area

$$F = (p_i - p_o) \times 4\pi R^2$$

Hence small amount of work done in increasing the radius of drop by δR is

$$dW = F(\delta R)$$

$$= (p_i - p_o) \times 4\pi R^2 \times \delta R \quad ...(1)$$

This work is done by the excess of pressure against the force of surface tension and is stored inside it in the form of its potential energy.

Therefore, increase in potential energy of the drop.

dU = surface tension × increase in surface area

or $dU = T \times \{4\pi(R + \delta R)^2 - 4\pi R^2\}$

$$= T \times \{4\pi R^2 + 8\pi R\delta R + 4\pi(\delta R)^2 - 4\pi R^2\}$$

Since δR is small, hence the term containing $(\delta R)^2$ can be neglected

$$\therefore \quad dU = 8\pi TR\delta R \quad ...(2)$$

Thus, from equations (1) and (2), we have

$$dW = dU$$

$$4\pi R^2 (p_i - p_o)\,\delta R = 8\pi TR\delta R$$

$$(p_i - p_o) = 2T/R \quad ...(3)$$

(iii) **Inside a liquid bubble:** There is air both inside and outside a liquid bubble. If a liquid bubble increases in size from radius R to $R + \delta R$, then area of its inner surface as well as outer surface will increase.

∴ Increase in potential energy of the liquid bubble

$$dU = 2 \times T\{4\pi(R + \delta R)^2 - 4\pi R^2\}$$

$$= 16\pi TR\delta R \quad ...(4)$$

As obtained above, small amount of work done in increasing the radius of bubble from R to $R + \delta R$ is given by

$$dW = 4\pi R^2 (p_i - p_o)\,\delta R \quad ...(5)$$

Hence again equation (4) and (5), we get

$$4\pi R^2 (p_i - p_o)\,\delta R = 16\pi TR\delta R$$

$$\therefore \quad (p_i - p_o) = 4T/R \quad ...(6)$$

(iv) **Inside an air bubble :** An air bubble has one surface. In a liquid drop, air is outside the drop and liquid is inside it. In air bubble, liquid is outside the spherical core of air. Thus, just like a liquid drop, an air bubble also has only one free surface.

Hence in case of air bubble also, excess of pressure inside an air bubble

$$p_i - p_o = 2T/R \quad ...(7)$$

ANGLE OF CONTACT

(i) Whenever a liquid comes in contact with a solid surface, the shape of the liquid surface near the

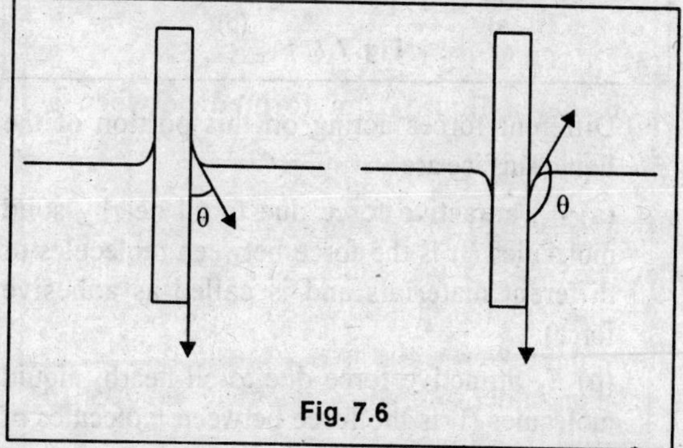

Fig. 7.6

contact gets in general curved. When a glass plate is dipped in water, the surface near the plate becomes concave as if water is pulled up by the plate but if the glass plate is dipped in mercury, the surface near the plate becomes convex as if mercury is depressed near the plate (Fig. 7.6).

(ii) The angle of contact is the angle between the tangent planes at the solid surface and the liquid surface at the point of contact. In this tangent plane to the solid surface is to be drawn towards the liquid and the tangent plane to the liquid is to be drawn away from the solid. Figure 8.6 demonstrates the construction of angle of contact. **For the liquids that rise along the solid surface, the angle of contact is less than 90°. For the liquids that are depressed along the solid surface, the angle of contact is greater than 90°** e.g. θ is equal to 0° for water-glass pair and 140° for mercury-glass pair.

(iii) Let us now analyse why a liquid surface gets in general curved near the contact with a solid surface. A liquid surface in equilibrium cannot bear any stress parallel to the surface. Hence the resultant force of any small portion of the surface must be perpendicular to the surface there. Consider a small portion of the liquid surface near its contact with the solid surface (Fig. 7.7).

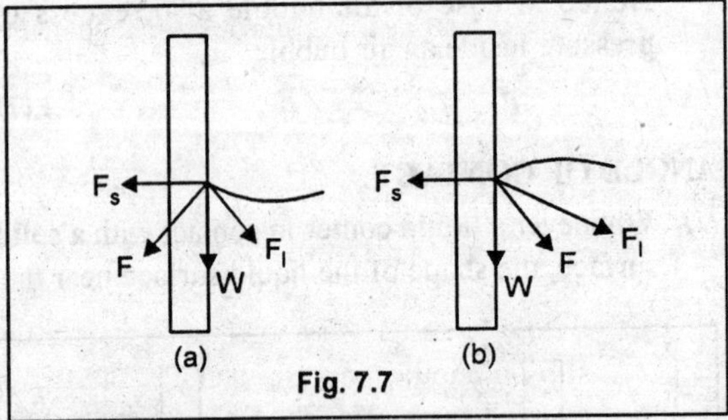

Fig. 7.7

(iv) Different forces acting on this portion of the liquid surface are:

(a) F_s, attractive force due to all nearby solid molecules (It is the force between molecules of different materials and is called as adhesive force).

(b) F_l, attractive force due to all nearby liquid molecules (It is the force between molecules of same material and is called as cohesive force).

(c) W, the weight of the portion of liquid surface considered.

(v) The direction of the resultant of F_s, F_l and W decides the shape of the surface near the contact. The liquid surface acquires such a shape that the surface is perpendicular to this resultant. **If the resultant passes through the solid (Fig. 7.7a) the surface is concave upward and the liquid rises along the solid. If the resultant passes through (Fig. 7.7b) the liquid, the surface is convex upward and the liquid is depressed along the solid.**

CAPILLARITY

(i) A tube of very small radius is called a capillary. When such a clean tube of glass open at both ends is dipped vertically in water, the water rises in the tube upto a certain height above the water level outside the tube (Fig. 7.8a). On the other hand, if the tube is dipped in mercury the mercury level falls below the outside level (Fig. 7.8b). **The phenomenon of rise or fall of the liquids in a capillary tube is called capillarity.**

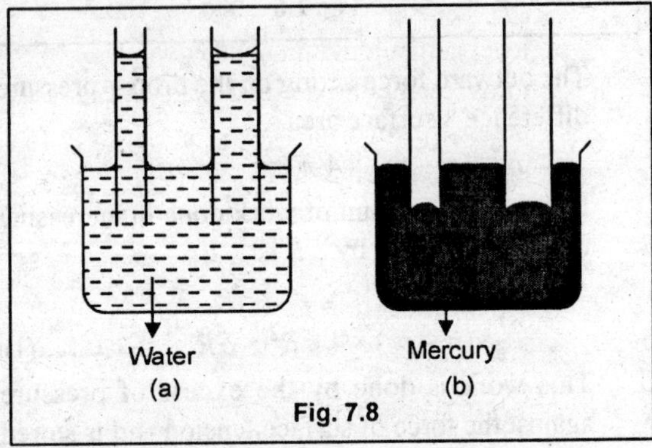

Fig. 7.8

The liquids which wet glass (for which the angle of contact is acute) rise up in the capillary tube while those which do not wet glass (for which the angle of contact is obtuse) are depressed down in the capillary.

(ii) The extent to which a liquid rises or falls in a tube depends upon the diameter of the tube. The narrower the tube, the higher is the rise or fall of the liquid in the tube.

(iii) **Explanation of capillary rise:**

(a) The phenomenon of capillarity arises due to surface tension of liquids. When a glass capillary tube is dipped in water, the water meniscus inside the tube is concave. The pressure just below the meniscus is less than pressure just above it by $2T/R$, where T is the surface tension of water and R is the radius of curvature of the meniscus. The pressure on the surface of water is atmospheric pressure P. The pressure just below the plane surface of water outside the tube is also P but that just below the meniscus inside the tube is $P-(2T/R)$ (Fig. 7.9(a)).

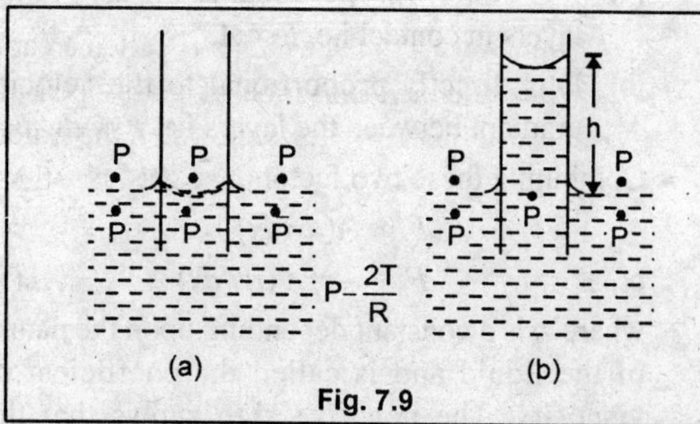

Fig. 7.9

(b) Since pressure at all points lying at the same level in the liquid must be equal. Hence, in order to overcome the deficiency of pressure ($=2T/R$) below the meniscus, water rises in the capillary upto such a height h (Fig. 7.9(b)) that the pressure due to water-column of height h becomes equal to $2T/R$, i.e.,

$$hdg = 2T/R \qquad ...(1)$$

where d is the density of water and g is the acceleration due to gravity.

(c) Let r be the radius of the capillary tube and θ be the angle of contact of water-glass, then the radius of curvature R of the meniscus is given by $R = r/\cos\theta$ (Fig. 7.10).

Hence from equation (1)

$$hdg = \frac{2T}{r/\cos\theta} = \frac{2T\cos\theta}{r};$$

$$\Rightarrow \qquad \boldsymbol{h = \frac{2T\cos\theta}{rdg}} \qquad ...(2)$$

Above equation shows that as r decreases, h increases, i.e., **narrower the tube, greater is the height to which liquid rises in the tube.**

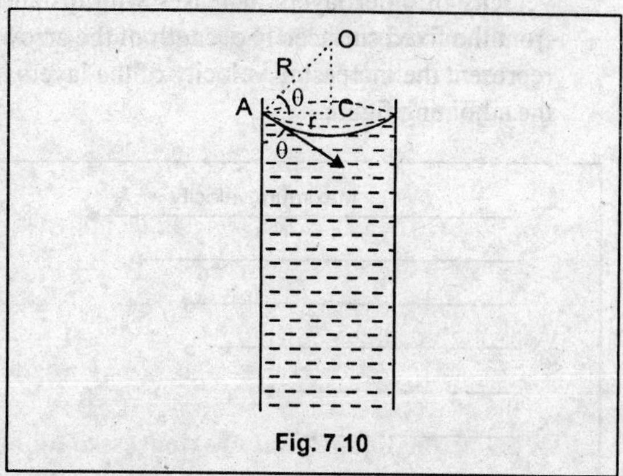

Fig. 7.10

(iv) For the liquid having concave meniscus (such liquids wet the walls of the tube), the angle of contact θ is acute and $\cos\theta$ is positive. Therefore, equation (2) gives a positive value for the height of the liquid and we say that such a liquid will show rise, when a tube is dipped in it. The liquid having convex meniscus (such liquids do not wet the walls of the tube), for which θ is obtuse, $\cos\theta$ will be negative and equation (2) gives a negative value for h i.e. such liquids should get depressed in the tube. This is what we really observe when a glass tube is immersed in mercury or molten lead.

VISCOSITY

(i) When a solid body slides over another solid body, a frictional force acts between them which opposes the relative motion of the bodies. Similarly, when a layer of a liquid slips or tends to slip on another layer in contact, the two layers exerted tangential forces on each other. The directions are such that the relative motion between the layers is opposed. **This property of a liquid to oppose relative motion between its layers is called viscosity.** The force between the layers opposing relative motion between them are known as viscous forces. The viscosity may be thought of an internal friction of a liquid in motion.

(ii) Suppose a liquid is flowing on a fixed horizontal surface *AB* (Fig. 7.11). The liquid layer which is in contact with the fixed surface is at rest, while the velocity of other layers increases with distance from the fixed surface. The length of the arrows represent the increasing velocity of the layers in the adjoining figure.

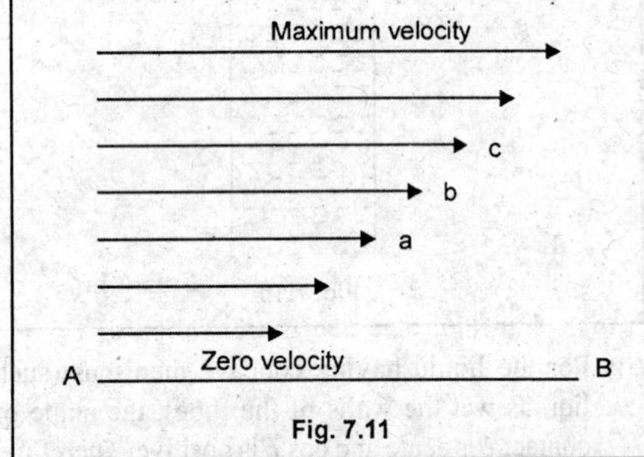

Fig. 7.11

Thus there exists a relative motion between the different layers of the liquid. Consider three successive parallel layers, *a*, *b* and *c* whose velocities are in the increasing order. The layer *a* tends to retard the layer *b*, while *b* tends to retard *c*. Thus each layer tends to decrease the velocity of the layer above it. Similarly, each layer tends to increase the velocity of layer below it. This means that in between any two layers of the liquid, internal tangential forces act which try to destroy the relative motion between the layers. These forces are called viscous forces. If the flow of liquid is to be maintained, an external force must be applied to overcome the backward viscous force. In the absence of the external force, the viscous force would soon bring the liquid to rest.

(iii) Suppose a liquid is flowing over a horizontal solid surface in the form of parallel layers. Consider two layers *P* and *Q* at a distance x and $(x + dx)$ from the solid surface moving with the velocities v and $(v + dv)$ respectively (Fig. 7.12). Then dv/dx denotes the rate of change of velocity with distance in the direction of increasing distance and is called as velocity gradient. Now, due to viscosity a force *F* acts in opposite direction to destroy the relative motion between the layers.

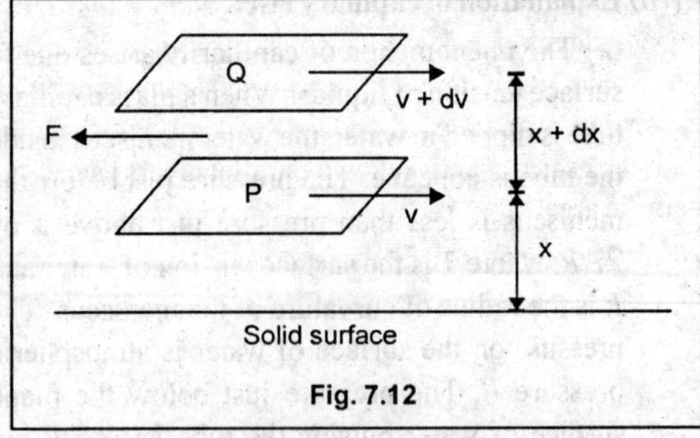

Fig. 7.12

(iv) According to Newton, the viscous force *F* depends upon the following factors:

(a) It is directly proportional to the area of the layers in contact i.e. $F \propto A$.

(b) It is directly proportional to the velocity gradient between the layers i.e. $F \propto dv/dx$.

Combining these two factors, we get

$$F \propto A(dv/dx)$$

or,
$$F = -\eta A\,(dv/dx) \qquad \ldots(1)$$

where η is a constant depending upon the nature of the liquid and is called the coefficient of viscosity. The negative sign shows that the viscous force is directed in a direction opposite to the direction of the motion of the liquid.

If $A = 1$ and $dv/dx = 1$, then numerically $\eta = F$.

Hence, **coefficient of viscosity of a liquid is defined as the tangential viscous force, which maintains a unit velocity gradient between two parallel layers, each of unit area.**

(v) **Dimension of η :** We know that

$$F = \eta A\,(dv/dx)$$

$$\therefore \qquad \eta = \frac{F}{A} \times \frac{dx}{dv}$$

$$= \frac{[MLT^{-2}][L]}{[L^2][LT^{-1}]} = [ML^{-1}T^{-1}]$$

(vi) **(a)** In CGS system, the unit of η is dynes s/cm^2 or g/cm/sec and is called **poise**. The coefficient of viscosity of a liquid is said to be one poise if a tangential force of 1 dyne maintains a velocity gradient of 1 gm/sec/cm between two parallel layers each 1 cm^2 in area.

(b) In SI system, the unit of η is Nsm^{-2} and is called **deca poise.** The coefficient of viscosity of a liquid is said to be 1 deca poise if a tangential force of 1 newton maintains a velocity gradient of 1 $kgs^{-1}m^{-1}$ between two parallel layers each 1 m^2 in area.

$$\textbf{1 deca poise} = \textbf{1 N s m}^{-2} = (10^5 \text{ dynes}) \text{ s} \times (100 \text{ cm})^{-2} = \textbf{10 poise.}$$

BERNOULLI'S THEOREM

It states that total energy of an ideal bluid having steady, irrotational flow is constant. Ideal fluid is one which is incompressible and non-viscous. Thus, the quantity

$$p + \rho gh + \frac{1}{2}\rho v^2 = \text{constant}$$

along any streamline. Here
p = fluid pressure
ρ = mass density of fluid
g = acceleration due to gravity
h = vertical height
v = fluid velocity.
This can also be written as below.

$$\frac{p}{gh} + h + \frac{1}{2}\frac{v^2}{g} = \text{constant}$$

In this form, we call

$\frac{p}{gh}$ as pressure head,

h as gravitational head,

$\frac{1}{2}\frac{v^2}{g}$ as velocity head.

STOKES' LAW AND TERMINAL VELOCITY

(i) A spherical body falling through a viscous medium (e.g., rain drop falling through air), generates a relative motion between different layers of the fluid. The layer which is in contact with the body moves with the velocity of body itself and the layer next to it, has lesser velocity, the next still lesser and so on, while the layer at a considerable distance from the body remains at rest. As a result of this relative motion, a backward dragging force is produced in upward direction which opposes the motion of the body. The backward dragging force increases with increase in velocity of the moving body and finally if the body is small, the backward dragging force immediately balances the driving force and the body starts falling with a constant velocity known as the **terminal velocity** of the body.

(ii) Stokes proved that the backward dragging force acting on a small sphere of radius r, moving with uniform velocity v through a medium of viscosity η is

$$F = -6\pi\eta rv \quad ...(1)$$

This equation is known as **Stokes' Formula.**

Minus sign indicates that the direction of F is opposite to the direction of v.

(iii) In order to derive this law, Stokes made the following assumptions:

(a) The medium is perfectly homogeneous (liquid or gas) and is of infinite extension.

(b) The body falling through the medium is perfectly rigid, smooth and spherical in shape.

(c) The flow of fluid is steady and streamlined.

(d) There is no slip between the body and medium.

(iv) **Terminal velocity:** Suppose a small spherical body of radius r falls through a large column of a viscous fluid of density α and coefficient of viscosity η. Let ρ be the density of the material of body. As the body falls, the following three forces act on the body:

(a) **Weight of the body acting vertically downwards** which is given by

$$W = (4/3)\pi r^3 \rho g$$

(b) **Upthrust or Buoyant force B acting vertically upwards** which is equal to the weight of the fluid displaced i.e.

$$B = (4/3)\pi r^3 \sigma g$$

(c) **Viscous force F acting vertically upward** (in a direction opposite to the motion of the body). The viscous force goes on increasing as the velocity of the falling body increases. A stage comes, when the weight of the body becomes just equal to the sum of the upthrust and viscous force. In that stage, the body falls with constant maximum velocity, called the **terminal velocity**. If v_T is the terminal velocity attained, then according to Stokes' law, the viscous force is given by

$$F = 6\pi\eta r v_T$$

Hence, total force acting on the body in upward direction is

$$B + F = (4/3)\,\pi r^3 \sigma g + 6\,\pi\eta r v_T$$

In equilibrium

$$W = B + F$$

or, $\quad (4/3)\pi r^3 \rho g = (4/3)\,\pi r^3 \sigma g + 6\,\pi\eta r v_T$

or, $(4/3)\pi r^3(\rho - \sigma) g = 6\,\pi\eta r v_T$

$\Rightarrow \quad v_T = (2/9)\,[r^2\,(\rho - \sigma)\,g/\eta]$ ...(5)

In case, density of medium is very low (e.g. body falling through air), then density of medium (*s*) may be neglected as compared to the density of material (*r*) of the spherical body. Then equation (5) becomes

$$v_T = \frac{2r^2 \rho g}{9\eta} \quad \text{...(6)}$$

FLOW OF LIQUID THROUGH A UNIFORM CAPILLARY TUBE

(i) Poisseuille derived the formula for the flow of a liquid through a horizontal tube of uniform bore under a constant pressure difference p between its ends. Consider a horizontal tube of length l and radius r. The velocity of the flowing liquid is maximum along the axis and zero at the walls of the tube. Let the tube is divided into a large number of coaxial cylindrical shells. Suppose in steady state, the velocity of the cylindrical liquid layer at a distance x from the axis of the tube is v. Hence at every point at this liquid layer, the velocity gradient perpendicular to direction of flow is $(-\,dv/dx)$.

(ii) Let us consider the force acting on a liquid cylinder of radius x. As the liquid outside this cylinder is flowing with a smaller velocity, hence it exerts a backward viscous force on the cylinder. By Newton's Law, viscous force

$$F = \eta\,(2\pi x l)\left(-\frac{dv}{dx}\right)$$

Due to pressure difference, the force tending to accelerate this liquid cylinder $= p\pi x^2$

Since there is no acceleration of liquid,

$$\therefore \quad p\pi x^2 = -\eta\,(2\pi x l)\frac{dv}{dx}$$

or, $$\frac{dv}{dx} = -\frac{px}{2\eta l}$$

Integrating, we get

$$v = -\frac{p}{2\eta l}\left(\frac{x^2}{2}\right) + c$$

When $x = r$, $v = 0$,

$$\therefore \quad c = \frac{p}{2\eta l} r^2;$$

$$\Rightarrow \quad v = \frac{p}{2\eta l}(r^2 - x^2)$$

(iii) Now suppose a thin cylindrical shell of radii x and $x + dx$. The volume of liquid flowing per sec, through it is given by

$$dV = \text{area of shell} \times \text{velocity}$$

$$= (2\pi x\,dx)\frac{p}{4\eta l}(r^2 - x^2)$$

$\therefore$ Volume of liquid flowing per second through a tube of radius r is given by

$$V = \frac{\pi p}{2\eta l}\int_0^r (r^2 - x^2)\,x\,dx$$

$$= \frac{\pi p^4}{8\eta l}.$$

MULTIPLE CHOICE QUESTIONS

1. An ice cube contains a large air bubble. The cube is floating on the surface of water contained in a trough. What will happen to the water level, when the cube melts?
   (a) it will remain unchanged
   (b) it will fall
   (c) it will rise
   (d) first it will fall and then rise
2. A steel ball is floating in a trough of mercury. If we fill the empty part of the trough with water, what will happen to the steel ball?
   (a) it will continue in its position
   (b) it will move up
   (c) it will move down
   (d) it will execute vertical oscillations
3. A wooden block is floating in a trough of water. If the trough falls freely, then upward thrust on the wooden block will be
   (a) same as before
   (b) more than earlier
   (c) zero
   (d) equal to the weight of the block in air
4. If there were no gravity, which of the following will not be there for a fluid?
   (a) viscosity
   (b) surface tension
   (c) pressure
   (d) Archimede's upward thrust
5. A person is carrying a bucket in one hand and a fish in the other. If he puts fish in the bucket, how will the load carried by the person change?
   (a) no change
   (b) it will be more
   (c) it will be less
   (d) it will depend on the mass of the fish
6. The density of ice is 0.9 g cm^{-3}. What percentage by volume of the block of ice floats outside the water?
   (a) 10% (b) 45%
   (c) 75% (d) 90%
7. A boat carrying steel balls is floating on the surface of water in a tank. If the balls are thrown into the tank one by one, how will it affect the level of water?
   (a) it will remain unchanged
   (b) it will rise
   (c) it will fall
   (d) first it will rise and then fall
8. An ice cube contains a glass ball. The cube is floating on the surface of water contained in a trough. What will happen to the water level, when the cube melts?
   (a) it will be unchanged
   (b) it will fall
   (c) it will rise
   (d) first it will fall and then rise
9. A bird is sitting in a wire cage, which is hanging from a spring balance. How will the reading change when the bird flies inside the cage?
   (a) it will remain unchanged
   (b) it will be less than earlier
   (c) it will be more than earlier
   (d) it cannot be predicted
10. What makes a ship made of steel float, whereas a steel needle sinks in water?
    (a) viscosity
    (b) surface tension
    (c) power of its engine
    (d) none of the above
11. For a floating body to be in stable equilibrium, where should its centre of buoyancy be located?
    (a) above the centre of gravity
    (b) below the centre of gravity
    (c) at the centre of gravity
    (d) it may be anywhere
12. A boat floating in a tank is carrying passengers. If the passengers drink water, how will it affect the water level of the tank?
    (a) it will go down
    (b) it will rise

(c) it will remain unchanged
(d) it will depend on atmospheric pressure

13. A body is just floating on the surface of a liquid. The density of the body is same as that of the liquid. The body is slightly pushed down. What will happen to the body?
(a) it will slowly come back to its earlier position
(b) it will remain submerged, where it is left
(c) it will sink
(d) it will come out violently

14. An inflated balloon is floating on the surface of water. What will happen if it is pushed down so as to submerge it some distance below the surface?
(a) it will slowly come back to its earlier position.
(b) it will remain submerged
(c) it will sink to the bottom
(d) it will violently come out

15. Which will be easier to lift?
(a) 10 kg of iron
(b) 10 kg of loosely packed feathers
(c) 10 kg of water
(d) there will be no difference in either case

16. A bird is resting on the floor of an air tight box suspended from a spring balance. If the bird starts flying how will the reading of spring balance change?
(a) it will remain unchanged
(b) it will be less than earlier
(c) it will be more than earlier
(d) it cannot be predicted

17. A body floats in water with one fourth of its volume above the surface of water. If placed in oil it floats with one third of its volume above the surface of oil. The density of oil is
(a) $\frac{2}{3}$ (b) $\frac{3}{4}$
(c) $\frac{4}{9}$ (d) $\frac{9}{8}$

18. An iceberg is floating in sea water. The density of ice is 0.92 g cm^{-3} and that of sea water is 1.03 g cm^{-3}. What percentage of the iceberg will be below the surface of water?
(a) 3% (b) 11%
(c) 89% (d) 92%

19. A wooden block of volume 1000 cm^3 is suspended from a spring balance. It weighs 12 N in air. It is suspended in water such that half of the block is below the surface of water. The reading of the spring balance is
(a) 10 N (b) 9 N
(c) 8 N (d) 7 N

20. A vessel contains oil (density 0.8 g cm^{-3}) over mercury (density 13.6 g cm^{-3}). A homogeneous sphere floats with half of its volume immersed in mercury and the other half in oil. The density of material of the sphere in g cm^{-3} is
(a) 7.2 (b) 12.8
(c) 14.4 (d) none of the above

21. A ball weighing 20 N is suspended from a spring balance B_1. A beaker containing water is placed on the pan of another spring balance B_2, which reads 50 N. If the ball is now immersed in the water contained in the beaker, which of the statements about the balance B_1 and B_2 is correct?
(a) balance B_1 reads more than 20 N
(b) balance B_2 reads less than 50 N
(c) balance B_1 reads less than 20 N and balance B_2 reads more than 50 N
(d) balance B_1 reads more than 20 N and balance B_2 reads less than 50 N

22. A wooden raft of mass 30 kg is floating on the surface of water. Density of raft is 600 kg m^{-3}. How much mass can be placed on the raft to make it just sink?
(a) 20 kg (b) 30 kg
(c) 40 kg (d) 50 kg

23. A body when placed in water, floats in it completely immersed. The volume of the body is 100 cm^3. It is placed in jar. The mass of the jar and water is 400 g. After placing the body in it, the total mass will be
(a) 250 g (b) 400 g
(c) 450 g (d) 500 g

24. The block of solid-I floats in water with one fourth of its volume outside and solid-II floats in water with one fourth of its volume inside.
$$\frac{\text{Density of solid - I}}{\text{Density of solid - II}} =$$

(a) $\frac{1}{4}$ (b) $\frac{3}{4}$
(c) 3 (d) none of the above

25. A disc of area A is placed at the bottom of a water tank. The thrust due to water column on it is F. If another disc of area $2A$ is placed at the bottom of same water tank, the thrust on it will be
(a) $F/2$ (b) F
(c) $2F$ (d) $4F$

26. A disc of area A is placed at the bottom of a water tank. The pressure of water column on it is p. If another disc of area $2A$ is placed at the bottom, of the same water tank, the pressure on it will be
(a) $p/2$ (b) p
(c) $2p$ (d) $4p$

27. A rectangular block is 5 cm × 5 cm × 10 cm. The block is floating in water with 5 cm side vertical. If it floats with 10 cm side vertical, what change will occur in the level of water?
(a) no change
(b) it will rise
(c) it will fall
(d) it may rise or fall depending on the density of block

28. A wooden cube floats just inside the water when a mass of 300 g is placed on it. If the mass is removed, the cube floats with 3 cm above the water surface. The length of the side of cube is
(a) 10 cm (b) 15 cm
(c) 20 cm (d) 30 cm

29. If we blow air through a hole at the top of a closed tube containing liquid, the pressure increases
(a) in all directions
(b) only in downward direction
(c) only on the sides
(d) neither downwards nor on the sides

30. Why the dam of water reservoir is thick at the bottom?
(a) quantity of water increases with depth
(b) density of water increases with depth
(c) pressure of water increases with depth
(d) because of some reason other than those mentioned above

31. A trough full of water is placed on a spring balance. If we put our hand in water without touching the trough, how will the reading of the balance change?
(a) it will remain unchanged
(b) it will decrease
(c) it will increase
(d) it is not possible to predict

32. A metallic block of density 5 g cm^{-3} and having dimensions 5 cm × 5 cm × 5 cm is weighed in water. Its apparent weight will be
(a) 5 × 5 × 5 × 5 gf
(b) 4 × 4 × 4 × 4 gf
(c) 5 × 4 × 4 × 4 gf
(d) 4 × 5 × 5 × 5 gf

33. Which of the following is not the unit for pressure?
(a) Nm^{-2} (b) pascal
(c) atmosphere (d) poiseuille

34. One atmospheric pressure is approximately equivalent to
(a) 1.01×10^4 Nm^{-2} (b) 1.01×10^5 Nm^{-2}
(c) 1.01×10^6 Nm^{-2} (d) none of the above

35. What is the barometric height of a liquid of density 3.4 g cm^{-3} at a place where that for mercury barometer is 70 cm?
(a) 70 cm (b) 140 cm
(c) 280 cm (d) none of the above

36. Sudden fall of pressure at a place indicates
(a) storm (b) rain
(c) fair weather (d) cold wave

37. Why the aeroplanes are made to run on the runway before take off?
(a) it decreases friction
(b) it decreases viscous drag of the air
(c) it decreases atmospheric pressure
(d) it provides required lift to the aeroplane

38. What is meant by the statement "pressure of gas is 13.6 cm of Hg"?
(a) density of mercury is 13.6 g cm^{-3}
(b) pressure is equivalent to that of 13.6 cm mercury column
(c) at sea level mercury barometer reads 13.6 cm
(d) pressure is equal to 13.6 atmosphere

39. Which of the following is equivalent to Pa?
(a) dyn /cm^2 (b) bar
(c) atm (d) none of the above

40. One of the unit earlier used for expressing pressure was called bar. 1 bar is equivalent to
(a) 10^4 Pa (b) 10^5 Pa
(c) 10^6 Pa (d) 10^7 Pa

41. Hydraulic brakes work on the basis of
(a) Pascal's law
(b) Bernoulli's principle
(c) Poiseuille's law
(d) Archimede's principle

42. Why is it easier to swim in sea water?
(a) atmospheric pressure is highest at the sea level
(b) sea water contains salt
(c) density of sea water is higher than the ordinary water
(d) because of some reason other than those mentioned above

43. A jet plane flies in air because
(a) upthrust of air balances the weight
(b) weight of the air displaced is equal to the weight of the aeroplane
(c) gravity does not act on the aeroplane
(d) of some reason other than those mentioned above

44. Density of ice is ρ and that of water is σ. What will be the decrease in volume when a mass M of ice melts?
(a) $\dfrac{M}{\sigma-\rho}$ (b) $\dfrac{\sigma-\rho}{M}$
(c) $M\left[\dfrac{1}{\rho}-\dfrac{1}{\sigma}\right]$ (d) $\dfrac{1}{M}\left[\dfrac{1}{\rho}-\dfrac{1}{\sigma}\right]$

45. Area of cross-section of the press-plunger of a Bramah press is 2 cm^2 and that of pump plunger is 0.02 cm^2. If we apply a downward force of 10 N on the pump plunger, the load that can be lifted is given by
(a) 10 N (b) 100 N
(c) 1000 N (d) 10000 N

46. The unit of thrust is
(a) Nm^{-1} (b) Nm^{-2}
(c) Nm^{-2} s (d) N

47. The pressure p and thrust G are related with area A as
(a) $p = GA$ (b) $G = pA$
(c) $p = \sqrt{G}A$ (d) $G = \sqrt{p}A$

48. Which of the following works on Pascal's law?
(a) aneroid barometer
(b) hydraulic lift
(c) venturimeter
(d) sprayer

49. Eight drops of water, each of radius 2 mm are falling through air at a terminal velocity of 8 cm s^{-1}. If they collapse to form a single drop, the terminal velocity of the combined drop will be
(a) 8 cm s^{-1} (b) 16 cm s^{-1}
(c) 24 cm s^{-1} (d) 32 cm s^{-1}

50. Water flows through a horizontal pipe of radius 1 cm at a speed of 8 cm s^{-1}. What will be the speed of flow of water under similar conditions, if the radius of the pipe is doubled?
(a) 8 cm s^{-1} (b) 4 cm s^{-1}
(c) 2 cm s^{-1} (d) 1 cm s^{-1}

ANSWERS

1	2	3	4	5	6	7	8	9	10
(a)	(b)	(c)	(d)	(a)	(a)	(c)	(b)	(b)	(d)
11	**12**	**13**	**14**	**15**	**16**	**17**	**18**	**19**	**20**
(c)	(c)	(c)	(d)	(b)	(a)	(d)	(c)	(d)	(a)
21	**22**	**23**	**24**	**25**	**26**	**27**	**28**	**29**	**30**
(c)	(a)	(d)	(c)	(c)	(b)	(a)	(a)	(a)	(c)
31	**32**	**33**	**34**	**35**	**36**	**37**	**38**	**39**	**40**
(c)	(d)	(d)	(b)	(c)	(a)	(d)	(b)	(d)	(b)
41	**42**	**43**	**44**	**45**	**46**	**47**	**48**	**49**	**50**
(a)	(c)	(d)	(c)	(c)	(d)	(b)	(b)	(d)	(c)

HINTS / SOLUTIONS

1. The weight of the water displaced = weight of ice cube + weight of air. Since, the weight of the air is negligible, so the volume of the water produced due to the melting of ice will be same as the volume of the water displaced.
2. The water will lie above the mercury. The steel ball will continue to float above the mercury and will be covered by water. The upthrust due to the water displaced will make the ball move up.
3. During free fall, weight is zero. And so is upthrust.
4. Archimede's upthrust is equal to the weight of the liquid displaced. In the absence of gravity, the weight is zero.
5. The load carried = weight of bucket + weight of the fish.
6. Let the mass of ice be M. Then mass of water displaced will also be M. Volume of water displaced will be $V_1 = M/1$. Volume of ice $V_2 = M/0.9$. Hence % age of the volume outside

$$= \frac{\frac{M}{0.9} - \frac{M}{1}}{\frac{M}{0.9}} \times 100 = (1-0.9)\times 100 = 10\%.$$

7. As explained above, when the steel balls are put in the tank, the volume of the water displaced is equal to the volume of the steel balls. This is less than the volume of the water having weight equal to that of steel balls. Hence, the water level will fall.
8. The weight of the water displaced = weight of ice + weight of glass ball. When the ice melts, the glass ball will be immersed in water. The water displaced due to the immersion of glass ball will be equal to its volume. Which will be less than the volume of the water having weight equal to the weight of ball. Hence, the water level will fall.
9. The air pushed down by the wings of the bird will go out of the wires.
10. The ship is given special shape so that the weight of the water displaced is more than the weight of the ship.
11. If centre of buoyancy is at the centre of gravity, the torque due to the weight and upthrust is zero.
12. There will be increase in the load. This will displace more water. But water displaced will be equal to the water drunk by the passengers. So, the water level will not change.
13. The weight of the body is equal to the upthrust. It will sink due to the downward push.
14. It will come up due to the large upthrust and negligible weight of the balloon.
15. The weight decreases due to upthrust. And the upthrust is equal to the weight of air displaced, which is more in case of losely packed feathers.
16. The system is closed. So, the downward push by the bird and lift so obtained will be internal forces. Hence, there will be no change in the reading of the spring balance.
17. $(V \times \frac{3}{4}) \times 1 \times g = (V \times \frac{2}{3})\rho \times g.$
18. Mass of ice berg
= Mass of water displaced = M (say)

Volume of iceberg, $V_1 = \frac{M}{0.92}$.

Volume of water displaced, $V_2 = \frac{M}{1.03}$.

Percentage of iceberg below the water surface

$$= \frac{V_1 - V_2}{V_1} \times 100 = 89.3\%.$$

19. Volume of water displaced = 500 cm^3. Its mass is 0.5 kg and weight is 5 N. Hence loss of weight is also 5 N.
20. Let ρ be the density of the sphere and V be its volume.

Then $V\rho g = \left[\frac{V}{2} \times 13.6 + \frac{V}{2} \times 0.8\right] g$.

21. The reading of B_1 decreases due to upthrust and there is equal increase in the reading of B_2 due to reaction.

22. The volume of raft $V = M/\rho$
$= (30/600)\ m^3 = 0.05\ m^3$.
The maximum water it can displace
$= V \times 1000\ kg = 50\ kg$.
So, we can place 50 kg – 30 kg
= 20 kg mass on the raft.

23. Since the body floats completely immersed, therefore density of the body = density of water. Hence mass of the body is (100 × 1) g.
So, total mass = 400 g + 100 g = 500g.

24. For solid-I,
$\left(V \times \frac{3}{4}\right) \times 1 \times g = V\rho_1 g$. That is $\rho_1 = \frac{3}{4}$
For solid-II,
$\left(V \times \frac{1}{4}\right) \times 1 \times g = V\rho_2 g$. That is $\rho_2 = \frac{1}{4}$.

25. Pressure is independent of area.
And thrust = pressure × area.

26. Pressure is independent of area.
And thrust = pressure × area.

27. Water displaced = mass of the block, which does not change in the two situations.

28. Let the side of the cube be L. Then volume of water displaced due to mass. The water displaced is 300 g and its volume is 300 cm^3.
Hence $3 \times L \times L = 300$ that is $L = 10$ cm.

29. In liquids, pressure is same in all directions.

30. Pressure at the bottom is maximum. To with stand it, the bottom is made thick.

31. The downward reaction equal to the thrust on the hand will be added up to the weight of trough.

32. Loss of weight = weight of (5 × 5 × 5) cm^3 of water = 5 × 5 × 5 gf. Hence apparent weight
= (5 × 5 × 5 × 5 – 5 × 5 × 5) gf.
= (4 × 5 × 5 × 5) gf.

33. Poiseuille is the unit of viscosity.

34. $P = h\rho g$
$= 0.76 \times (13.6 \times 1000) \times 9.8$
$= 1.01 \times 10^5\ Nm^{-2}$

35. $h_1 \rho_1 g_1 = h_2 \rho_2 g_2$.
Hence $h_2 = h_1 \rho_1/\rho_2$
$= 70 \times 13.6/3.4 = 280$ cm.

36. Fall in pressure means air will rush to that place from the place where pressure is more.

37. The shape of the wings is such that the air running around them causes loss of pressure on the upper side. This, in accordance with Bernoulli's theorem causes lift.

39. $Pa = 1\ Nm^{-2}$.

43. The flow of air around the wings provides the lift.

44. Decrease in volume
= Volume of ice – Volume of water of same mass.

45. Pressure is same on both sides.
Hence $F_1/A_1 = F_2/A_2$.
$\therefore F_2 = F_1 A_2/A_1 = 10 \times 2/0.02 = 1000$ N

49. Terminal velocity is directly proportional to the square of the radius of the drop. Let the radius of each small drop be r and that of single drop formed by the combination of 8 drops be R.
Then $\frac{4}{3}\pi R^3 = 8 \times \frac{4}{3}\pi r^3$.

50. $A_1 v_1 = A_1 v_2$. When radius is doubled, the area becomes four times. Hence, velocity becomes one fourth.

UNIT-8

THERMODYNAMICS

INTRODUCTION

(i) The branch of science that deals with the relation between heat and mechanical energy is called thermodynamics. It is mainly concerned with the transformation of heat into mechanical work and vice versa. It is our daily experience that mechanical work can be converted into heat. For example, heat is generated when we rub our hands or two pieces of metal together. Heat can also be converted into mechanical work, as in the steam engine.

DEFINITION OF SOME TERMS USED IN THERMODYNAMICS

(i) Thermodynamic system: A collection of extremely large number of particles having a certain value of pressure, volume and temperature is called a thermodynamic system. For example, a large collection of gas molecules is a thermodynamic system. A thermodynamic system can be in solid, liquid or gaseous state. A system wholly enclosed in an adiabatic boundary, so that there is no transfer of heat to the surroundings is called as isolated system. A system wholly enclosed in a diathermic boundary, so that there is an exchange of heat with surroundings but no exchange of matter, is called a closed system.

(ii) Thermodynamic variables: The thermodynamic state of a system can be described in terms of the various properties of the system, such as its composition, volume, pressure, temperature etc. These are called the thermodynamic variables of the system. In the case of gases, the variables are volume, pressure, temperature etc. In the case of liquids, these variables can be density, surface tension, temperature, etc. and in the case of solids they could be elasticity, area, volume, temperature, etc. There are also some other thermodynamic variables such as internal energy (U), entropy (S) etc. All the thermodynamic variables can be expressed in terms of P, V and T.

(iii) Equation of State: A relation between pressure, volume and temperature for a system is called its equation of state. The state of a thermodynamic system is completely defined in terms of its pressure, volume and temperature.

For example, for 1 mole of an ideal gas, the equation of state is

$$PV = RT$$

In simple systems, such as gases, any two variables out of the three variables P, V, T determine the state of the system. The third variable can be known by using the equation of state.

(iv) Thermal equilibrium: The two systems are said to be in thermal equilibrium with each other, if they have same temperature. Thus, the temperature is a property which determines, whether the two systems will be in thermal equilibrium or not. In other words, temperature is such a thermodynamic property that all the systems having the same temperature must be in thermal equilibrium.

(v) Thermodynamic process: A thermodynamic process takes place, if the thermodynamic variables of the system change with time. Thermodynamic process are of following types:

(a) **Isothermal process:** A thermodynamic process that takes place at constant temperature is called isothermal process.

(b) **Adiabatic process:** A thermodynamic process in which system is not allowed to exchange heat with surroundings is called adiabatic process.

(c) **Isochoric process:** A thermodynamic process that takes place at constant volume is called isochoric process.

(d) **Isobaric process:** A thermodynamic process that takes place at constant pressure is called isobaric process.

(e) **Cyclic process:** A thermodynamic process in which state of the system remains unchanged is called cyclic process.

(vi) **Sign convention for a thermodynamic process:** The following sign conventions are generally used for the study of thermodynamical process:

(a) Work done by a system is taken as positive, while work done on a system is taken as negative.

(b) Heat absorbed by a system is taken as positive, while the heat lost by the system is taken as negative.

(c) The increase in internal energy of a system is taken as positive while the decrease in internal energy is taken as negative.

PV-DIAGRAM OR INDICATOR DIAGRAM

(i) The state of a thermodynamic can be completely described if only two thermodynamic variables are known to us because the third variable is automatically fixed by the equation of state of the system. A graphical representation of the state of the system with the help of two thermodynamic variables is called indicator diagram of the system. In case the two thermodynamic variables are *P* and *V*, the diagram is called *P-V* diagram.

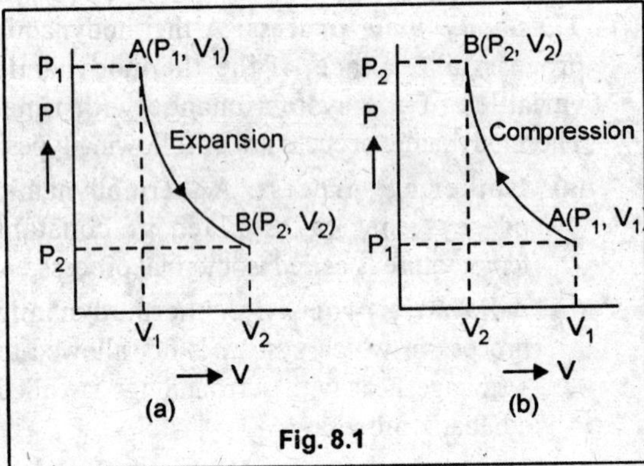

Fig. 8.1

(ii) Adjoining fig. 8.1 (a) shows a *P-V* diagram, when the system undergoes expansion from the state *A* (P_1, V_1) to state *B* (P_2, V_2). On the other hand, fig. 8.1 (b) represents the *P-V* diagram for the system undergoing compression.

WORK DONE BY A THERMODYNAMIC SYSTEM DURING EXPANSION

(i) Suppose a cylinder fitted with a frictionless and weightless piston contains a gas and some weights are placed on the piston.

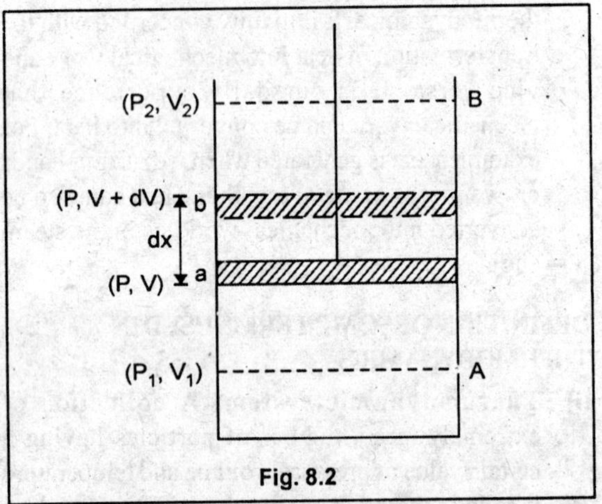

Fig. 8.2

If we remove the weights from the piston, the gas will expand doing work against the piston. On the other hand, if we place additional weights on the piston, the gas will be compressed and work will be done on the gas.

(ii) Suppose the gas is allowed to expand from the initial state *A*, corresponding to pressure P_1 and volume V_1 to the final state *B* corresponding to pressure P_2 and volume V_2. We shall calculate work done by the gas first by analytical method and then by indicator diagram method.

(iii) **Analytical method:** Suppose at any instant during expansion, the pressure and volume of the gas are *P* and *V* respectively (Fig. 8.2). Let the piston moves through infinitesimally small distance *dx* against the constant pressure *P*, so that volume becomes $V + dV$. Then small work done,

$$dW = \text{Force on piston} \times \text{small distance moved}$$

Let *A* be the area of cross-section of the piston, then force on the piston will be *PA*. Therefore,

$$dW = PA\,dx$$

Now,

$Adx = dV$ = small increase in volume

$\therefore\ dW = PdV$

The total work done W during the expansion of the gas from initial state $A(P_1, V_1)$ to the final state $B(P_2, V_2)$ can be calculated by integrating equation (1) between V_1 to V_2. Therefore, total work done is given by

$$W = \int_{V_1}^{V_2} PdV \qquad ...(2)$$

If, during expansion, pressure of the gas remains constant, then equation (1) simplifies to:

$$W = P\int_{V_1}^{V_2} dV = P(V_2 - V_1) \qquad ...(3)$$

During expansion, work is done by the gas and hence it is positive. In case of compression, work is done on the gas and is negative.

(iv) **Indicator diagram method:** Suppose the point A and B on the indicator diagram (Fig. 8.3) represent the initial state (P_1, V_1) and the final state (P_2, V_2) respectively. Suppose a be any point on the indicator diagram and P and V be the values of pressure and volume corresponding to it.

Let the volume increases from V to $V + dV$ corresponding to the point b on the indicator diagram such that pressure remains constant.

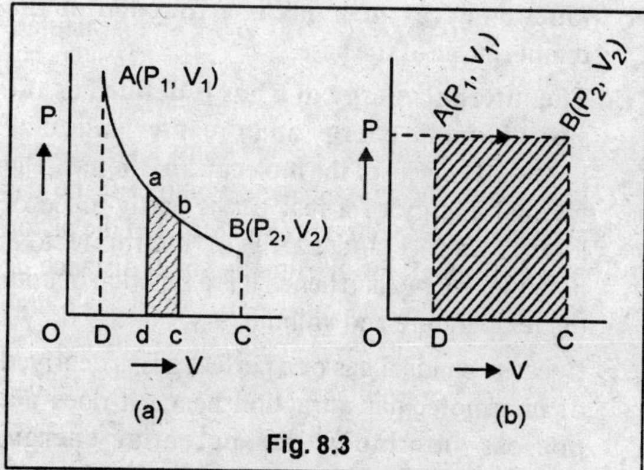

Fig. 8.3

Then, $ad = bc = P$

and $cd = dV$

Now, small work done in changing from state a to state b,

$$dW = PdV$$
$$= ad \times cd$$
$$= \text{area of the shaded strip } abcd$$

Thus the total work done during the expansion by the gas from the initial state A (P_1, V_1) to final state B (P_2, V_2) can be obtained by adding the areas of all such strips formed between AD and BC under the PV-diagram. Obviously, the total work done will be

$$W = \text{area } ABCD \qquad ...(4)$$

(v) Thus, **work done by a system is numerically equal to area under the *PV*-diagram. During expansion, the work is done by the system and the area *ABCD* under *PV*-diagram is traced in clockwise direction.**

(vi) Thus, **if area under *PV*-diagram is traced in clockwise direction, then work done will be positive and will be negative during compression), if the area is traced in anticlockwise direction.**

(vii) It follows from equations (2) and (4) that total work done during change from state (P_1, V_1) to state (P_2, V_2) is given by

$$\boldsymbol{W = \int_{V_1}^{V_2} PdV}$$
$$= \textbf{area under } \boldsymbol{PV}\textbf{-diagram}$$

(viii) If pressure remains constant during expansion of the gas from initial state to final state, then indicators diagram will be a straight line AB parallel to volume axis as shown in figure. Here also, total work done

$$W = P(V_2 - V_1)$$
$$= \text{area of the rectangle } ABCD$$

or $\qquad = \text{area under } PV\text{-diagram.}$

WORK DONE DURING A CYCLIC PROCESS

(i) When a system after passing through various intermediate states returns back to its original state, then it is called a **cyclic process.**

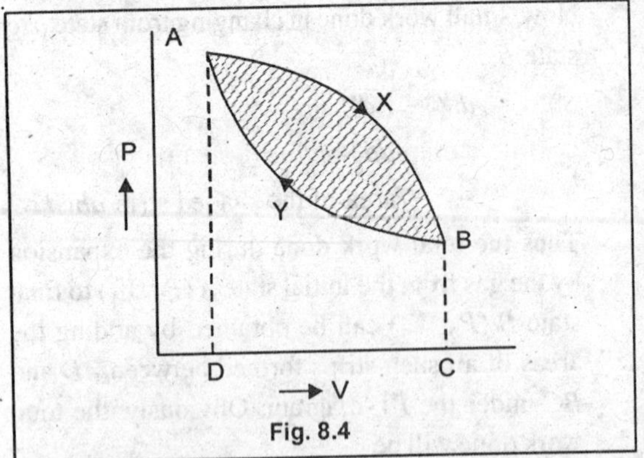

Fig. 8.4

(ii) Suppose a gas enclosed in a cylinder is expanded from initial state *A* to final state *B* along path *AXB* (Fig. 8.4). If W_1 be the work done by the system during expansion, then

$$W_1 = +\text{area } AXBCDA$$

(iii) Now the gas is compressed from state *B* to state *A* along the path *BYA* so as to return the system to the initial state. If W_2 be the work done on the system during compression, then

$$W_2 = -\text{area } BYADCB$$

According to sign convention, work done on the system is taken as negative.

(iv) Therefore, net amount of work done along the cyclic path *AXBYA*,

$$W = W_1 + W_2$$
$$= +\text{area } AXBCDA - \text{area } BYADCB$$
$$= \text{area } AXBYA$$

Thus, net amount of work done along the cyclic path is numerically equal to the area of the cyclic path. For the cyclic path shown in fig. 8.4, as the area comes out to be positive, net work will be done by the system. It should also be noted here that the cyclic path has been traced in clockwise direction and the expansion curve *AXB* lies above the compression curve *BYA*.

(v) If one draws a cyclic path in anti-clockwise direction, the expansion curve will be below the compression curve. In this case, although net work done will again be equal to area of the closed cyclic path but it will now be negative. It implies that net work will now be done on the system.

INTERNAL ENERGY

(i) As discussed in the chapter on kinetic theory of gases, the molecules of an ideal gas are in a state of ceaseless random motion and do not attract each other. The concept of zero attraction is not realized in actual practice. Experiments show that the molecules of a gas actually exert mutual force of attraction on one another. Whenever two bodies are present at a finite distance apart, they possess potential energy. Therefore, the molecules of a real gas possess intermolecular potential energy. If the volume of the gas increases, work will be performed by the gas against the intermolecular attraction and hence the potential energy of the gas will increase. Therefore, **intermolecular potential energy of a real gas is function of its volume.**

(ii) Because the molecules of a gas are always in a state of random motion, hence according to kinetic theory of gases, the average kinetic energy of the gas molecule is given by

$$E_{av} = \frac{3}{2}kT$$

where k is Boltzman's constant. As the temperature increases, the average kinetic energy of the molecule will also increase. Therefore, **kinetic energy of a gas is a function of the temperature of the gas.**

(iii) **The internal energy of a gas is defined as the sum of kinetic energy and the intermolecular potential energy of the molecules of the gas.** The internal energy of a real gas is partly made of kinetic energy and partly of intermolecular potential energy and hence it is a function of both the temperature and volume.

(iv) Because an ideal gas or a perfect gas is deprived of intermolecular attraction hence it does not possess intermolecular potential energy. Therefore, **internal energy of an ideal gas is wholly kinetic in nature and is a function of temperature only.**

FIRST LAW OF THERMODYNAMICS

(i) Suppose, in a thermodynamic process, an amount of heat ΔQ is given to the gas and an amount of work ΔW is done by it i.e. the total energy of the gas must increase by an amount $(\Delta Q - \Delta W)$. As a result of this

(a) either the entire gas together with its cylinder may start moving or

(b) the internal energy of the gas molecules may increase.

If the energy does not appear in form (a) then this net energy $(\Delta Q - \Delta W)$ must be responsible for the increase in internal energy of the gas molecules. Hence, ΔU represents the change in internal energy of the gas, then we have

$$\Delta U = \Delta Q - \Delta W$$

or

$$\Delta Q = \Delta U + \Delta W \qquad \text{...(5)}$$

(ii) Equation (5) is called as the **first law of thermodynamics**. In an ideal monoatomic gas, the internal energy of the gas is simply translational kinetic energy of all its molecules. In general, the internal energy may be due to vibrational kinetic energy, rotational kinetic energy and potential energy corresponding to intermolecular forces.

(iii) Equation (5), is, in fact, the law of conservation of energy. According to the law of conservation of energy, the energy can neither be created nor it can be destroyed but can change itself from one form to another.

(iv) Equation (5) may be analyzed from a different angle also. This equation shows that if we take a system from an initial state i to a final state f by several different processes, $\Delta Q - \Delta W$ should be same in all the processes. This is due to the reason that $\Delta Q - \Delta W = \Delta U - (U_f - U_i)$ depends only on the initial and final states. This implies that both ΔQ and ΔW may be different in different processes, but $\Delta Q - \Delta W$ is the same for all the processes taking away the system from initial state to final state. Thus, we do not write $\Delta Q = Q_f - Q_i$ or $\Delta W = W_f - W_i$ but we do write $\Delta U = U_f - U_i$. Thus first law of thermodynamics leads to a basic conclusion that **there exists an internal energy function U that has a fixed value in a given state.**

(v) While applying first law of thermodynamics following points regarding the sign of ΔQ, ΔW and ΔU must be taken care of:

(a) work done by the system is taken positive, while work done on the system is taken as negative.

(b) heat gained (added) by a system is taken as positive while heat lost (extracted) by the system is taken as negative.

(c) the increase in internal energy of system is taken as positive while the decrease in internal energy is taken as negative.

ISOTHERMAL PROCESS

(i) **The process in which the pressure and volume of the system change but temperature remains constant is called an isothermal process.**

(ii) An isothermal process may be achieved

(a) if the gas is enclosed in a vessel whose walls are made of a highly conducting material and

(b) the gas is compressed or allowed to expand very slowly.

(iii) When the gas expands, cooling will take place. But because the gas expands very slowly; hence before the temperature of the gas falls, heat is conducted into the cylinder through the conducting walls from the surroundings i.e. temperature of the gas remains almost constant. On the other hand, when the gas is compressed slowly, the heat produces escapes to the surroundings through the conducting walls before it could increase the temperature of the gas i.e. temperature of the gas again remains almost constant.

(iv) The internal energy remains constant in isothermal process in case of an ideal gas because internal energy of an ideal gas depends on temperature only.

(v) Since $dU = 0$ in this process, hence in accordance to first law of thermodynamics, the amount of heat supplied is equal to the work done by the gas.

(vi) As the change in temperature is zero, hence the molar heat capacity in such process is

$$C_{\text{isothermal}} = \frac{\Delta Q}{n\Delta T} = \text{infinity}$$

(vii) For one mole of an ideal gas, $PV = RT$.

As temperature remains constant in an isothermal process, hence PV = constant.

Above equation (called as Boyle's law) represents the equation of an isothermal process for an ideal gas.

(viii) **First law of thermodynamics applied to isothermal process:**

Internal energy of an ideal gas depends on temperature only. Because temperature remains constant in an isothermal process, hence there is no change in internal energy in this process i.e., $dU = 0$. Therefore, according to first law of thermodynamics,

$$dQ = dU + dW$$

or $$\mathbf{dQ = dW}$$

(a) In the process of isothermal expansion, as work is done by the system, hence dW is positive. Consequently dQ will also be positive. Therefore, **if a gas is to expand isothermally, then an amount of heat equivalent to work done by the gas will have to be supplied to it from the external source.**

(b) In the process of isothermal compression, as work is done on the system, hence dW is negative. Consequently dQ will also be negative. Therefore, **if a gas is to compress isothermally, then an amount of heat equivalent to work done on the gas will have to be removed from it.**

(c) When a gas undergoes isothermal expansion or compression, there is no change in the internal energy of the gas.

WORK DONE DURING ISOTHERMAL PROCESS

(i) Consider one mole of a perfect gas contained in a cylinder having conducting walls and fitted with a frictionless, movable piston. When the piston moves through infinitesimally small distance dx, the small work done

$$dW = PA\,dx = PdV$$

where A is the area of cross-section of the piston.

(ii) Therefore, when the system goes from initial state $A(P_i, V_i)$ to the final state $B(P_f, V_f)$, total work done,

$$W = \int_{V_i}^{V_f} PdV$$

Now, for one mole of ideal gas,

$$PV = RT$$

or $$P = \frac{RT}{V}$$

$$\therefore \quad W_T = \int_{V_i}^{V_f} \frac{RT}{V} dV$$

$$= RT \int_{V_i}^{V_f} \frac{dV}{V}$$

$$= RT\,[\log_e V]_{V_i}^{V_f}$$

or $$W_T = RT \log_e \frac{V_f}{V_i}$$

$$\mathbf{W_T = 2.303\,RT \log_e \frac{V_f}{V_i}} \quad \text{...(1)}$$

ADIABATIC PROCESS

(i) The process in which pressure, volume and temperature of the system change but there is no exchange of heat between the system and the surroundings is called an adiabatic process.

(ii) An adiabatic process may be achieved

(a) if the gas is enclosed in a vessel whose walls are made of a highly insulating material and,

(b) the gas is compressed or allowed to expand very quickly.

(iii) When the gas expands, cooling will take place. Because the process takes place very quickly and the walls are made of insulating material, hence no heat can enter the system from surroundings. On the other hand, when the gas is compressed quickly, heat cannot escape to surroundings through the insulating walls and temperature of gas gets increased.

(iv) Internal energy of the system always changes in case of an adiabatic process taking place in an ideal gas.

(v) Since $\Delta Q = 0$, hence work done by the gas in an adiabatic process equals to decrease in its internal energy or work done on the gas during compression is equal to increase in its internal energy.

(vi) Since $\Delta Q = 0$ in this process, hence the molar heat capacity in such a process is

$$C_{\text{adiabatic}} = \Delta Q/n\Delta T = \text{zero}$$

(vii) Adiabatic process takes place according to Poisson's law

$$PV^{\gamma} = \text{constant}$$

RELATION BETWEEN *P*, *V* AND *T* IN AN ADIABATIC PROCESS

(i) **Relation between *P* and *V*:** Let us consider an adiabatic process taking place in an ideal gas. Suppose during a short part of the process, the pressure, volume and temperature change from P, V, T to $P + dP$, $V + dV$ and $T + dT$ respectively and the internal energy changes from U to $U + dU$. Because no heat is supplied in this process, hence according to first law of thermodynamics

$$0 = dU + PdV \quad \text{...(1)}$$

We know that,

$$C_v = \frac{1}{n}\frac{dU}{dT}$$

or $$dU = n\,C_v\,dT$$

Thus, from (1),

$$n\,C_v dT + PdV = 0 \quad \text{...(2)}$$

Since the gas is ideal, hence

$$PV = nRT$$

or $$PdV + VdP = nRdT$$

or $$dT = \frac{PdV + VdP}{nR}$$

Substituting this equation for dT in (2),

$$C_v\left[\frac{PdV + VdP}{R}\right] + PdV = 0$$

or $$(C_v + R)\,PdV + C_v VdP = 0$$

or $$C_p PdV + C_v VdP = 0$$

or $$\frac{C_p}{C_v}\frac{dV}{V} + \frac{dP}{P} = 0$$

or $$\gamma\frac{dV}{V} + \frac{dP}{P} = 0$$

where $\gamma = C_p/C_v$

or $$\gamma\frac{dV}{V} = -\frac{dP}{P}$$

If the initial pressure and volume be P_i and V_i respectively and the final pressure and volume be P_f and V_f respectively, then

$$\int_{V_i}^{V_f} \gamma\frac{dV}{V} = -\int_{P_i}^{P_f}\frac{dP}{P}$$

or $$\gamma \log\frac{V_f}{V_i} = -\log\frac{P_f}{P_i}$$

or $$\log\left[\frac{V_f}{V_i}\right]^{\gamma} = \log\left[\frac{P_i}{P_f}\right]$$

or $$\frac{V_f^{\gamma}}{V_i^{\gamma}} = \frac{P_i}{P_f}$$

or $$P_i V_i^{\gamma} = P_f V_f^{\gamma}$$

or $$\mathbf{PV^{\gamma} = constant} \quad \text{...(3)}$$

(ii) **Relation between *P* and *T*:** We know that,

$$PV = nRT$$

$$\therefore \quad V = nRT/P$$

Putting above equation in (3), we have

$$P\,(nRT/P)^{\gamma} = \text{constant}$$

or $$\mathbf{P^{(1-\gamma)}\,T^{\gamma} = constant} \quad \text{...(4)}$$

(iii) **Relation between *V* and *T*:** Again from the equation

$$PV = nRT$$

$$P = nRT/V$$

Putting again in equation (3),

$$(nRT/V)\, V^{\gamma} = \text{constant}$$

or $$TV^{\gamma-1} = \text{constant} \qquad \ldots(5)$$

FIRST LAW OF THERMODYNAMICS APPLIED TO ADIABATIC PROCESS

Since in adiabatic process, no heat enters or leaves the system, hence $dQ = 0$. Thus, for adiabatic process, the first law of thermodynamics takes the form

$$dU + dW = 0$$

or $$dW = -dU$$

(a) In the process of adiabatic expansion, as work is done by the system, hence dW is positive and likewise dU will be negative. Therefore, **if a gas expands adiabatically, its internal energy is decreased by an amount equal to work done by the system i.e. gas will cool down.**

(b) In the process of adiabatic compression, as work is done on the system, hence dW is negative and likewise dU will be positive. Therefore, **if a gas is compressed adiabatically, its internal energy is increased by an amount equal to work done on the system i.e. gas will be heated.**

WORK DONE DURING ADIABATIC PROCESS

(i) Let us consider one mole of a perfect gas enclosed in a cylinder having insulating walls and fitted with a frictionless, movable piston. When the piston moves through infinitesimally small distance dx, the small work done

$$dW = PAdx = PdV$$

where A is the area of cross section of the piston.

(ii) When the system goes from initial state $A(P_i, V_i)$ to the final state $B(P_f, V_f)$, total work done

$$W_s = \int_{V_i}^{V_f} PdV$$

Now for an adiabatic change, Poisson's law tells us that

$$PV^{\gamma} = K = \text{a constant}$$

or $$P = KV^{-\gamma}$$

Hence work done in an adiabatic process

$$W_s = \int_{V_i}^{V_f} KV^{-\gamma} dV$$

$$= K\int_{V_i}^{V_f} V^{-\gamma} dV$$

$$= K\left[\frac{V^{1-\gamma}}{1-\gamma}\right]_{V_i}^{V_f}$$

$$= \frac{K}{1-\gamma}[V_f^{1-\gamma} - V_i^{1-\gamma}]$$

$$= \frac{1}{1-\gamma}[KV_f^{1-\gamma} - KV_i^{1-\gamma}]$$

Now, $$K = P_i V_i^{\gamma} = P_f V_f^{\gamma}$$

$$\therefore \quad W_s = \frac{1}{\gamma-1}[P_i V_i^{\gamma} V_i^{1-\gamma} - P_f V_f^{\gamma} V_f^{1-\gamma}]$$

$$= \frac{1}{\gamma-1}[P_i V_i - P_f V_f] \qquad \ldots(1)$$

(iii) If temperature of the system in initial and final states are T_i and T_f respectively, then

$$P_i V_i = RT_i \quad \text{and} \quad P_f V_f = RT_f$$

$$\therefore \quad \boldsymbol{W_s = \frac{1}{\gamma-1}[RT_i - RT_f]}$$

$$\boldsymbol{= \frac{R}{\gamma-1}[T_i - T_f]} \qquad \ldots(2)$$

Above equation gives the work done for one mole of a perfect gas during adiabatic process.

HEAT ENGINE, HEAT PUMP AND SECOND LAW OF THERMODYNAMICS

(i) Three conditions must be fulfilled to utilize heat for useful work:

(a) A device called engine with a working substance is essential.

(b) The engine must work in a reversible cyclic process.

(c) The engine must operate between two temperatures. It will absorb heat from a hot body (called source), convert a part of it into

useful work and reject the rest to a cold body (called sink) (Fig. 8.5).

(ii) **Efficiency of heat engine:** Suppose an engine takes an amount of heat Q_1 from high-temperature bodies, converts a part W of it into work and rejects an amount of heat Q_2 to low temperature bodies or sink. Hence, the heat absorbed by the engine is $(Q_1 - Q_2)$. From the first law, no part of this heat is used up in increasing the internal energy since change in internal energy (dU) is zero as the system returns to the initial state after the completion of the cycle. Thus $(Q_1 - Q_2)$ represents the amount of heat converted into useful work i.e. $W = (Q_1 - Q_2)$.

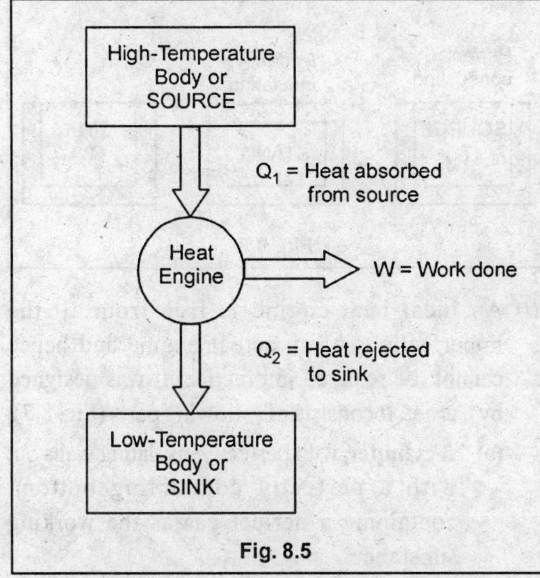

Fig. 8.5

The efficiency of the engine is defined as

$$\eta = \frac{\text{Work done by the engine}}{\text{Heat absorbed}}$$

$$= \frac{Q_1 - Q_2}{Q_1} = 1 - \frac{Q_2}{Q_1}$$

or $$\eta = \frac{W}{Q_1} = 1 - \frac{Q_2}{Q_1}.$$

(iii) Heat pump or Refrigerator:

(a) We have seen above that in a heat engine, the working substance extracts some heat Q_1 from the source at a higher temperature, converts a part of it into work W and rejects the rest Q_2 to the sink at lower temperature. One can also proceed in the reverse way where the working substance takes heat Q_2 from a sink at a lower temperature. Then an amount W of work is done on it by the surrounding and a higher amount of heat $Q_1 = Q_2 + W$ is rejected to the source at a higher temperature (Fig. 8.6).

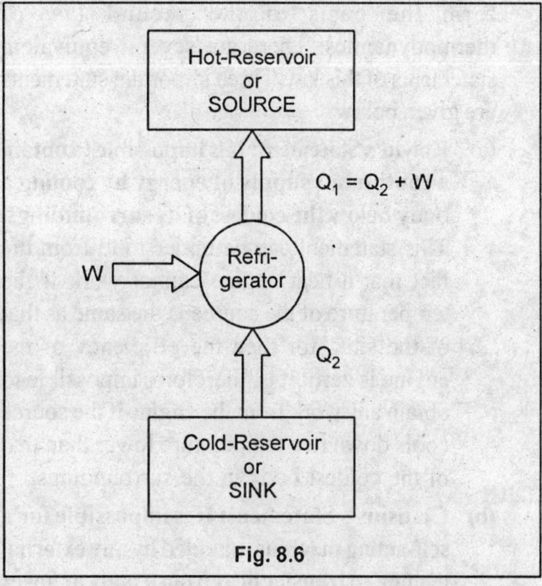

Fig. 8.6

(b) Such a device which, by doing work on it, is made to extract heat from a colder body is called a refrigerator and the working substance is called refrigerant.

(c) First the gas is allowed to expand adiabatically. Then it is allowed to expand isothermally in contact with the sink, the heat Q_2 being extracted from the sink in the process. The gas is then adiabatically compressed until it heats up to a temperature equal to the that of source. Finally the gas is compressed isothermally till the initial state is reached with the cylinder in contact with the source. The heat Q_1 generated in the process is transferred to the source. Clearly,

$Q_1 = Q_2 + W$, where W is the work done on the gas in the cycle.

(iv) We have seen that in a heat engine, the useful work done $(Q_1 - Q_2)$ is less than the heat Q_1. If Q_2 were zero, the efficiency of the engine would be = 1 or 100%. This as never been realized. Similarly if, in a refrigerator, the heat given out at the higher temperature were equal to heat absorbed at the lower temperature, the efficiency of the refrigerator would be 100%. Such a perfect refrigerator is never realized. These impossibilities form the basis of the second law of thermodynamics. There are several equivalent statements of this law. Three important statements are given below:

(a) **Kelvin's Statement: It is impossible to obtain a continuous supply of energy by cooling a body below the coldest of its surroundings.** This statement can be understood from the fact that a heat engine cannot work if the temperature of the source is the same as that of the sink, for then the efficiency of the engine is zero. It is, therefore, impossible to obtain any work from the engine if the source cools down to a temperature lower than that of the coldest body in the surroundings.

(b) **Clausius's Statement: It is impossible for a self-acting machine, unaided by any external agency, to transfer heat from a body at lower temperature to a body at a higher temperature.**

(c) **Planck's Statement: It is impossible to construct an engine which, operating in a cycle, will produce an effect other than extracting heat from a reservoir and performing an equivalent amount of work.** This statement implies that the working substance, working in a cycle, cannot convert all the heat in extracts into work, it has to reject some heat to the sink.

CARNOT'S IDEAL HEAT ENGINE

(i) A device which converts heat into mechanical work continuously, is known as heat engine. The substance used, which on absorbing heat performs external work is called the working substance. The working substance repeatedly undergoes a cycle of operation. The efficiency of engines was found to vary between 5% and 55%, which means that at most only 55% of the total heat energy supplied is converted into work.

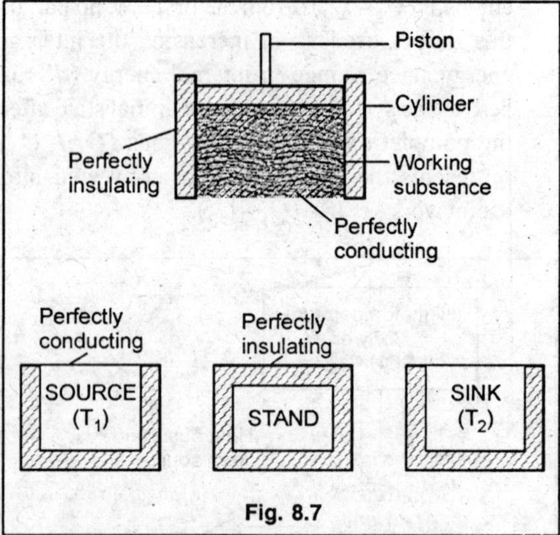

Fig. 8.7

(ii) An ideal heat engine is free from all the imperfections of an actual engine and hence cannot be realized in practice. It was designed by Carnot. It consists of following parts (Fig. 8.7).

(a) **A cylinder,** with perfectly insulating walls but with a perfectly conducting bottom, containing a perfect gas as the working substance.

(b) **A hot body or source,** of infinitely large thermal capacity, maintained at a constant high temperature $T_1 K$.

(c) **A cold body or sink,** at a constant lower temperature $T_2 K$.

(d) **A perfectly insulating stand** for the cylinder.

(iii) Carnot's engine has to be operated in a special way in order to obtain continuous work from it. This special way is called the Carnot's cycle. The gas in the cylinder is taken around the following reversible cycle of four operations as shown in figure and explained as below:

(a) **Operation I: Isothermal expansion:** the cylinder containing the working substance (1 mole of an ideal gas) is placed in contact with the heat source so that the working substance acquires the constant temperature T_1 of the source.

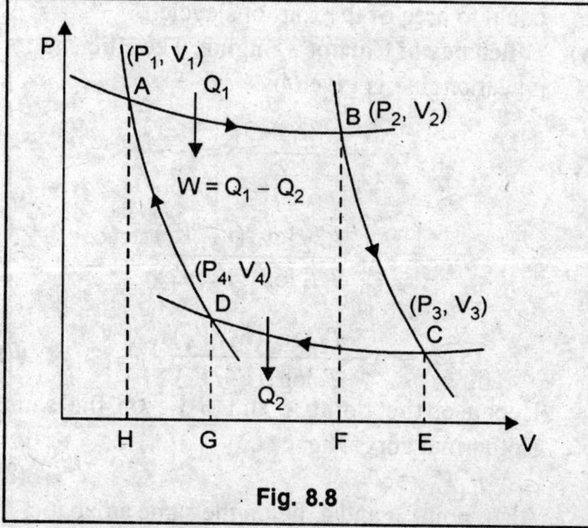

Fig. 8.8

Now the gas is allowed to expand very slowly. As the gas expands, it draws heat from the source through perfectly conducting base and the piston slowly moves upwards. These conditions ensure a constant temperature T_1 of the gas and the gas thus expands isothermally from initial state $A\ (P_1, V_1)$ to the state $B\ (P_2, V_2)$ along the isothermal curve AB at temperature T_1 (Fig. 8.8). Let Q_1 be the quantity of heat absorbed by the gas from the source and W_1 be the work done by the gas. As the process is isothermal in nature, hence work done by the gas is given by:

$$Q_1 = W_1$$

$$= \int_{V_1}^{V_2} PdV$$

$$= RT_1 \log_e \frac{V_2}{V_1}$$

$$= \text{Area } ABFH \qquad \ldots(1)$$

(b) **Operation II: Adiabatic expansion:** The cylinder is now removed from the source and is placed in contact with the insulating stand. The working substance is completely thermally isolated from the surroundings. Therefore, as the gas is allowed to expand further, the expansion will be adiabatic in nature. Let W_2 be the work done by the gas during adiabatic expansion along BC between the states represented by points B (P_2, V_2) and C (P_3, V_3) till the temperature of the working substance becomes T_2 i.e., equal to that of the sink. As the process is now adiabatic in nature, hence work done by the gas is given by:

$$W_2 = \int_{V_2}^{V_3} PdV$$

$$= \frac{R(T_1 - T_2)}{\gamma - 1}$$

$$= \text{Area } BCEF \qquad \ldots(2)$$

(c) **Operation III: Isothermal compression:** The cylinder is now removed from the stand and placed on the sink at a temperature $T_2 K$. The working substance is now compressed slowly so that as the heat is developed, it easily flows to the sink through the conducting base of the cylinder. Thus the temperature of the working substance will remain constant at T_2. The isothermal compression is carried out along curve CD between the state $C\ (P_3, V_3)$ and state $D\ (P_4, V_4)$. Let Q_2 be the amount of heat rejected by the working substance to the sink and W_3 be the work done on it. As the process is again isothermal in nature, hence

$$Q_2 = W_3$$

$$= -\int_{V_3}^{V_4} PdV$$

$$= \int_{V_4}^{V_3} PdV$$

$$= RT_2 \log_e \frac{V_3}{V_4}$$

$$= \text{Area } CEDG \qquad \ldots(3)$$

(negative sign indicates the volume decreases in isothermal compression.)

(d) Operation IV: Adiabatic compression: The cylinder is removed from the sink and placed again on the insulated stand. The working substance is further compressed along adiabatic curve DA so that it returns to the initial state. The temperature of the working substance becomes equal to that of source (T_1). Let W_4 the work done on the working substance between the state D (P_4, V_4) and the state (P_1, V_1). Then,

$$W_4 = \int_{V_4}^{V_1} (P)(-dV)$$

$$= -\int_{V_4}^{V_1} PdV$$

$$= \int_{V_1}^{V_4} PdV$$

$$= \frac{R(T_1 - T_2)}{\gamma - 1}$$

$$= \text{Area } ADGH \qquad \ldots(4)$$

(iv) Net work done by the working substance in one complete cycle: In operations I and II, work is done by the working substance and hence W_1 and W_2 are positive. On the other hand, in operations III and IV, work is done on the working substance and hence W_3 and W_4 are negative.

∴ Net work done by the working substance in one complete cycle.

$$W = W_1 + W_2 + (-W_3) + (-W_4)$$

From equations (2) and (4), we find that $W_2 = W_4$

$$\therefore \quad W = W_1 - W_3$$

Again, from equations (1) and (3), we have

$$W_1 = Q_1 \text{ and } W_3 = Q_2$$

$$\therefore \quad W = W_1 - W_3 = Q_1 - Q_2 \qquad \ldots(5)$$

Thus, **in Carnot's heat engine, during each cycle, the mechanical work obtained is equal to the net amount of heat absorbed by the working substance.**

Further,

$$W = \text{Area } ABFG + \text{Area } BCEF - \text{Area } CEDG - \text{Area } ADGH$$

$$W = \text{Area } ABCD \qquad \ldots(6)$$

i.e. in Carnot's heat engine, during each cycle, the mechanical work obtained is numerically equal to area of the Carnot's cycle.

(v) Efficiency of Carnot's Engine: The efficiency of a heat engine is given by

$$\eta = \frac{W}{Q_1} = \frac{Q_1 - Q_2}{Q_1} = 1 - \frac{Q_2}{Q_1}$$

$$= 1 - \frac{RT_2 \log_e(V_3/V_4)}{RT_1 \log_e(V_2/V_1)}$$

$$= 1 - \frac{T_2 \log_e(V_3/V_4)}{T_1 \log_e(V_2/V_1)} \qquad \ldots(7)$$

Because, the point A and B lie on the same isothermal curve, hence

$$P_1V_1 = P_2V_2 \qquad \ldots(8)$$

Also, point B and C lie on the same adiabatic,

$$\therefore \; P_2V_2^{\gamma} = P_3V_3^{\gamma} \qquad \ldots(9)$$

Further the points C and D lie on the same isothermal,

$$\therefore \; P_3V_3 = P_4V_4 \qquad \ldots(10)$$

Finally, the points D and A lie on the same adiabatic,

$$P_4V_4^{\gamma} = P_1V_1^{\gamma} \qquad \ldots(11)$$

Multiplying equations (8), (9), (10) and (11), we get

$$P_1V_1P_2V_2^{\gamma}\, P_3V_3P_4V_4^{\gamma} = P_2V_2P_3V_3^{\gamma}\, P_4V_4P_1V_1^{\gamma}$$

or $$V_2^{\gamma-1}\, V_4^{\gamma-1} = V_3^{\gamma-1}\, V_1^{\gamma-1}$$

or $$V_2V_4 = V_3V_1$$

or $$\frac{V_3}{V_4} = \frac{V_2}{V_1}$$

Putting above equation in equation (7), we get

$$\eta = 1 - \frac{T_2}{T_1} \qquad \ldots(12)$$

MULTIPLE CHOICE QUESTIONS

1. The density of water at 20°C is 998 kg m^{-3} and that at 40°C is 992 kg m^{-3}. The coefficient of cubical expansion of water is
(a) 0.2×10^{-4}/°C (b) 0.4×10^{-4}/°C
(c) 0.6×10^{-4}/°C (d) none of the above

2. An iron ball is heated. The percentage increase will be the largest in
(a) diameter (b) surface area
(c) volume (d) density

3. A glass flask of volume 1000 cm^3 is completely filled with mercury at 0°C. The coefficient of cubical expansion of mercury is 182×10^{-6}/°C and that of glass is 30×10^{-6}/°C. If the flask is now placed in boiling water at 100°C, how much mercury will over flow?
(a) 30 cm^3 (b) 18.2 cm^3
(c) 15.2 cm^3 (d) 3 cm^2

4. Two rods of length L_1 and L_2 are made of materials having coefficients of linear expansions as α_1 and α_2 respectively. If $L_1 - L_2$ is independent of temperature, then which of the following relations is correct?
(a) $L_1\alpha_1 = L_2\alpha_2$ (b) $L_1\alpha_2 = L_2\alpha_1$
(c) $L_1L_2 = \alpha_1\alpha_2$ (d) none of the above

5. The area under the indicator diagram gives
(a) heat gained or lost by the system
(b) work done on the system or by the system
(c) average kinetic energy of the particles of the system
(d) none of the above

6. A process in which the heat content of the system remains constant is called
(a) isobaric (b) isochoric
(c) isothermal (d) none of the above

7. A process in which the volume remains constant is called
(a) isobaric (b) isochoric
(c) isothermal (d) none of the above

8. Which of the following is not the property of both heat and work.
(a) transient phenomenon
(b) boundary phenomenon
(c) path function
(d) exact differential

9. What is the value of pV/T for one mole of ideal gas?
(a) 8.4 cal mol^{-1} K^{-1} (b) 4.2 cal mol^{-1} K^{-1}
(c) 2 cal mol^{-1} K^{-1} (d) none of the above

10. An ideal gas expands freely in a perfectly rigid and insulated cylinder. Which of the following parameters connected with it varies?
(a) temperature alone
(b) internal energy alone
(c) both temperature and internal energy
(d) neither temperature nor internal energy

11. When heat is added to a system, which of the following is not possible?
(a) internal energy of the system increases
(b) work is done by the system
(c) neither internal energy increases nor work is done by the system
(d) internal energy increases and also work is done by the system

12. In which process the indicator diagram is straight line parallel to volume axis?
(a) isobaric (b) isothermal
(c) adiabatic (d) irreversible

13. The first law of thermodynamics is based on the law of conservation of
(a) energy (b) mass
(c) momentum (d) none of the above

14. Thermodynamics is concerned with
(a) measurement of heat
(b) transfer of heat
(c) change of state
(d) none of the above

15. Isothermal is a graph between (P is pressure, V is volume, T is absolute temperature)
(a) P and T (b) P and V
(c) V and T (d) PV and T

16. Which of the following cannot determine the state of a thermodynamic system?
(a) pressure and volume
(b) volume and temperature
(c) temperature and pressure
(d) any one of the thermodynamic variables

17. Which of the following is the best container for gas during isothermal process?
(a) glass vessel (b) copper vessel
(c) wood vessel (d) thermos flask

18. Isothermal is a process represented by the equation
(a) pV = a constant (b) p/V = a constant
(c) p/T = a constant (d) pV^{γ} = constant

19. The first law of thermodynamics forbids interconversion of
(a) heat and work
(b) internal energy and work
(c) potential energy and kinetic energy
(d) none of the above

20. System A is in thermal equilibrium with B and B is separately in thermal equilibrium with C. Then A and C are in thermal equilibrium. From which law of thermodynamics it follows?
(a) zeroth (b) first
(c) second (d) third

21. In which of the following process all the three thermodynamic variables, that is pressure, volume and temperature can change?
(a) isobaric (b) isothermal
(c) isochoric (d) adiabatic

22. For the same rise in temperature of one mole of gas at constant volume the heat required for triatomic gas is k times that required for monoatomic gas. What is the value of k?
(a) 0.5 (b) 1
(c) 1.5 (d) 2

23. A sample of perfect gas is compressed isothermally to half its volume. If it is compressed adiabatically to the same volume, the final pressure of the gas will be
(a) more
(b) less
(c) same
(d) more or less depending on the initial temperature of the gas

24. Study of T-S curves will come under .... law of thermodynamics.
(a) zeroth (b) 1st
(c) 2nd (d) 3rd

25. Why does air of the atmosphere becomes cold at higher altitudes? Choose the best answer.
(a) decrease in density
(b) variation in pressure
(c) expansion of the air
(d) height above the surface of the earth

26. The first law of thermodynamics forbids flow of heat
(a) from low temperature to higher temperature
(b) from lower pressure to higher pressure
(c) from bodies with more heat content to the one with less heat content
(d) none of the above cases

27. In which of the process, the internal energy of the system remains constant?
(a) adiabatic (b) isochoric
(c) isobaric (d) isothermal

28. In which of the following processes the system always returns to the original thermodynamic state?
(a) adiabatic (b) isobaric
(c) cyclic (d) reversible

29. Which of the following states of matter have two specific heats?
(a) solid (b) gas
(c) liquid (d) fluid

30. The internal energy of a real gas is independent of
(a) pressure (b) temperature
(c) volume (d) none of the above

31. The internal energy of a perfect gas is
(a) wholly kinetic
(b) wholly potential
(c) sum of potential and kinetic energy of the molecules
(d) difference of kinetic and potential energies of the molecules

32. The internal energy of a perfect gas is independent of
(a) pressure (b) temperature
(c) volume (d) none of the above

33. A sink, that is a system where heat is rejected is essential for the conversion of heat into work. From which law the above inference follows?
(a) zeroth (b) first
(c) second (d) third

34. Which of the following laws of thermodynamics leads to the inference that it is difficult to convert whole of heat into work?
(a) zeroth (b) first
(c) second (d) third

35. A heat engine is a device to
(a) convert work into heat
(b) convert heat into work
(c) increase the efficiency
(d) transfer heat from lower to higher temperature

36. Thermodynamic system returns to its original state, which of the following is not possible?
(a) the work done is zero
(b) the work done is positive
(c) the work done is negative
(d) the work done is independent of the path followed

37. If the temperature of the sink is absolute zero, the efficiency of the heat engine should be
(a) zero (b) 50%
(c) 100% (d) none of the above

38. For maximum efficiency of an engine with a given source of heat, the temperature of the sink should be
(a) equal to that of the source
(b) slightly less than that of the source
(c) 0°C
(d) 0 K

39. When the temperature difference between the source and the sink increases, the efficiency of the heat engine
(a) increases
(b) decreases
(c) is not affected
(d) may increase or decrease depending upon the nature of the working substance

40. What is the name of the device used to transfer heat from a subsystem at lower temperature to the surroundings at higher temperature?
(a) heat engine
(b) refrigerator
(c) Carnot's engine
(d) no such device exists

41. The temperature of the source of a Carnot heat engine is 0°C and that of sink is –39°C. The efficiency of the heat engine is
(a) zero (b) 14.3%
(c) 39% (d) none of the above

42. Two steam engines X and Y have their source at 1000 K and 1100 K and their sinks are at 500 K and 400 K respectively. In η_x and η_y be their efficiencies then which of the following statements about their efficiencies is true?
(a) $\eta_x > \eta_y$
(b) $\eta_x < \eta_y$
(c) $\eta_x = \eta_y$
(d) the data is not sufficient to make the above prediction

43. The efficiency of the Carnot heat engine
(a) is independent of the temperature of the source and the sink
(b) is independent of the working substance
(c) can be 100%
(d) is not affected by the thermal capacity of the source or the sink

44. Which of the following conditions of the Carnot ideal heat engine can be realised in practice?
(a) infinite thermal capacity of the source
(b) infinite thermal capacity of the sink
(c) perfectly non conducting stand
(d) none of the above

45. For 100% efficiency of a Carnot engine the temperature of the source should be
(a) –273°C (b) 0°C
(c) 273°C (d) none of the above

46. A Carnot engine has an efficiency 50% when its sink is at a temperature of 27°C. The temperature of the source is
(a) 273°C (b) 300°C
(c) 327°C (d) 373°C

47. In a Carnot heat engine the temperature of the working substance at the end of the cycle is
(a) equal to that at the beginning
(b) more than that at the beginning
(c) less than that at the beginning
(d) determined by the amount of heat rejected at the sink

48. For an engine operating between the temperature t_1°C and t_2°C, the efficiency will be

(a) $\frac{t_2}{t_1}$ (b) $\frac{t_2+273}{t_1+273}$

(c) $\frac{t_1-t_2}{t_1}$ (d) $\frac{t_1-t_2}{t_1+273}$

49. The efficiency of the heat engine working between the freezing point and boiling point of water is very near to

(a) 50% (b) 25%

(c) 12.5% (d) 6.25%

50. A Carnot engine whose source is at 400 K, takes 200 cal of heat and rejects 150 cal to the sink. What is the temperature of the sink?

(a) 800 K (b) 400 K

(c) 300 K (d) none of the above

ANSWERS

1	2	3	4	5	6	7	8	9	10
(d)	(c)	(c)	(a)	(b)	(d)	(b)	(b)	(c)	(c)
11	12	13	14	15	16	17	18	19	20
(c)	(a)	(a)	(b)	(b)	(d)	(b)	(a)	(d)	(a)
21	22	23	24	25	26	27	28	29	30
(d)	(d)	(a)	(d)	(c)	(d)	(d)	(c)	(b)	(a)
31	32	33	34	35	36	37	38	39	40
(a)	(b)	(c)	(c)	(b)	(d)	(c)	(d)	(a)	(b)
41	42	43	44	45	46	47	48	49	50
(b)	(b)	(b)	(d)	(d)	(c)	(a)	(d)	(b)	(c)

HINTS / SOLUTIONS

1. $\rho_0 = \rho(1+\gamma T)$.
2. Volume coefficient is largest. Density decreases instead of increasing, when temperature increases.
3. Volume of mercury overflowed = change in volume of mercury – change in volume of flask.
4. Here $\Delta L_1 = \Delta L_2$.
   That is $L_1(1+\alpha_1 T) = L_2(1+\alpha_2 T)$.
   Which gives $L_1 - L_2 = (L_2\alpha_2 - L_1\alpha_1)\, T$.
   Since $L_1 - L_2$ is independent of temperature.
   Therefore: $L_2\alpha_2 - L_1\alpha_1 = 0$.
6. It is called adiabatic.
8. Work is exact differential but heat is not an exact differential.
9. $pV = RT$. Hence $pV/T = R = 2$ cal mol^{-1} V^{-1}.
10. It is adiabatic expansion . As the temperature falls, so does the internal energy.
11. $\Delta Q = \Delta W + \Delta U$. Hence when heat is added either ΔW or ΔU or both are non zero.
12. In isobaric process, the pressure remains constant.
16. At least two variables out of p, V and T are required to represent the state of a thermodynamic system.
17. For isothermal process, heat generated should go out immediately. But in the adiabatic process, it should not go out at all.
22. C_v for monoatomic gas is (3/2), R and that for triatomic gas is $3R$. $Q_2/Q_1 = 3R\,(3/2)\,R = 2$.
23. For isothermal compression $P_2 = \frac{P_1 V_1}{V_2}$. For adiabatic compression $P_2 = P_1\left(\frac{V_1}{V_2}\right)^{\gamma}$. Since $\gamma > 1$, hence P_2 will be more as compared to that in case of isothermal compression.
24. For isothermal process, heat generated should go out immediately. But in the adiabatic process,

it should not go out at all.

26. First law of thermodynamics is concerned with the conservation of energy and not with the flow of heat.

29. Gases have C_p and C_v.

30. The internal energy of a real gas consists of KE and PE, which depend on temperature and volume.

31. There is no inter molecular force for perfect gas. So, intermolecular potential energy does not exist.

32. The internal energy of perfect gas consists of only translational KE, therefore it depends on temperature alone.

36. Work done is equal to the area enclosed by the $P-V$ diagram.

37. $\eta = \frac{T_1 - T_2}{T_1}$. Hence $\eta \propto (T_1 - T_2)$

When $T_2 = OK, \eta = 1 = 100\%$

38. $\eta = \frac{T_1 - T_2}{T_1}$. Hence $\eta \propto (T_1 - T_2)$

When $T_2 = OK, \eta = 1 = 100\%$

39. $\eta = \frac{T_1 - T_2}{T_1}$. Hence $\eta \propto (T_1 - T_2)$

When $T_2 = OK, \eta = 1 = 100\%$

41. $\eta = \frac{273 - 234}{273} = \frac{39}{273} = \frac{1}{7} = 0.143 = 14.3\%$

42. $\eta_x = \frac{1000 - 500}{1000} = \frac{1}{2}$,

$$\eta_y = \frac{1100 - 400}{1100} = \frac{7}{11}.$$

Hence $\eta_x < \eta_y$.

45. The temperature of the source should be infinite.

46. $\eta = \frac{T_1 - T_2}{T_1} = 1 - \frac{T_2}{T_1}$. Hence

$$T_1 = \frac{T_2}{1-\eta} = \frac{300K}{\frac{1}{2}} = 600K = 327°C$$

48. In the expression $\eta = \frac{T_1 - T_2}{T_1}$, the T_1 and T_2 are in kelvin.

49. $\eta = \frac{373 - 273}{373} = 0.268 = 26.8\%$

50. $\eta = \frac{Q_1 - Q_2}{Q_1} = \frac{200 - 150}{200} = \frac{1}{4}$.

$\eta = \frac{1}{4} = 1 - \frac{T_2}{T_1}$. This gives

$$T_2 = \frac{3}{4} T_1 = \frac{3}{4} \times 400\ K = 300\ K$$

UNIT-9

OSCILLATIONS & WAVES

OSCILLATIONS

PERIODIC MOTION

The motion which repeats itself in position and phase after regular intervals of time is known as periodic motion e.g., motion of sun around earth, motion of simple pendulum, motion of arms of a clock etc.

OSCILLATORY OR VIBRATORY MOTION

The movement of a body on either side of a point in definite time interval, is known as oscillatory or vibratory motion. Time taken by the body to complete one oscillation is known as time-period e.g., motion of a mass suspended from a spring, motion of simple pendulum etc.

Each oscillatory motion is periodic but each periodic motion is not oscillatory.

The time after which the body retraces its path is called the time-period and the number of vibration made in one second is called frequency.

Frequency $= 1/T$ [T = time period]

Displacement and Amplitude

Displacement is a physical quantity which varies uniformly with time in an oscillatory motion. The maximum value of displacement is called amplitude.

Function representing Simple Harmonic Motion

Let $y = a\cos\frac{2\pi t}{T} + b\sin\frac{2\pi t}{T}$,

Substituting $a = A\sin\theta$, $b = A\cos\theta$, we have

$$y = A\sin\theta\cos\frac{2\pi t}{T} + A\cos\theta\sin\frac{2\pi t}{T}$$

or $$y = A\sin\left(\frac{2\pi t}{T} + \theta\right) \quad \text{...(i)}$$

Equation (i) represents simple harmonic motion of amplitude A and angular frequency $2\pi/T$. The initial phase or epoch is θ, where $\tan\theta = a/b$, and amplitude $A = \sqrt{(a^2 + b^2)}$.

Simple Harmonic Motion and its Characteristics

A motion in which the acceleration of the body is proportional to its displacement from the mean position and is always directed towards the mean position is known as the simple harmonic motion. Important characteristics of simple harmonic motion are as follows :

(i) Motion is on both sides of mean position. The maximum displacement on one side of mean position is called amplitude.

(ii) The body repeats its motion in a definite interval of time.

(iii) Acceleration is always proportional to the displacement and is directed opposite to it.

Acceleration $\propto -y$

(iv) The motion of foot of perpendicular dropped from the particle moving in a circle on the horizontal and vertical diameters is called S.H.M.

Equation of simple harmonic motion

The equation of S.H.M. is $y = A\sin\omega t$. The values of t and corresponding displacements are given in the following table.

t	*Displacement 'y'*	t	*Displacement 'y*
0	0	$5T/8$	$-A/\sqrt{2}$
$T/8$	$+A/\sqrt{2}$	$3T/4$	$-A$
$T/4$	$+A$	$7T/8$	$-A/\sqrt{2}$
$3T/8$	$+A/\sqrt{2}$	T	0
$T/2$	0		

The graphical representation of the above data is shown in the figure below :

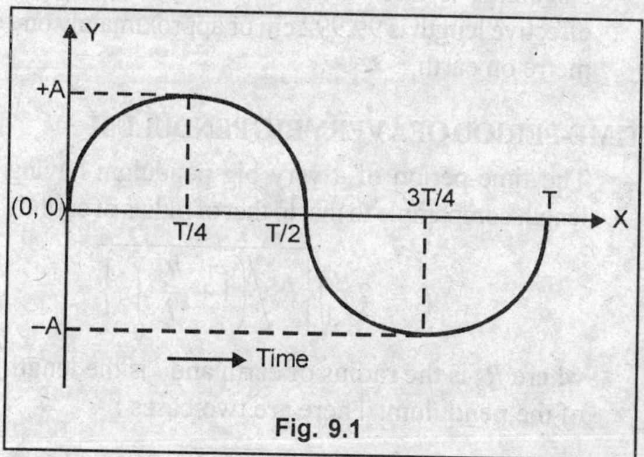

Fig. 9.1

PHASE

The property of wave motion which tells us the position and direction of motion of the particle at any instant is called phase. It is measured either by the angle which the particle makes with the mean position or by fraction of time period or by fraction of wavelength.

If the equation of S.H.M. is $y = A\sin(\omega t + \theta)$, then $(\omega t + \theta)$ is called the phase of the particle at any instant 't' and θ is the initial phase or epoch of the particle.

Two particles executing S.H.M. if they are in same phase of vibration cross their mean position in same direction and are in opposite phase if they cross the mean position in opposite directions. The phase difference between two particles in same phase is 2π while the phase difference between the two particles in opposite phase is π.

Velocity of a particle executing S.H.M.

We know $y = A\sin\omega t$

$dy/dt = A\omega\cos\omega t$ or $v = \omega\sqrt{(A^2 - y^2)}$

At $y = 0$ (i.e. at mean position) velocity is maximum and $v_{max} = A\omega$.

At $y = A$ (i.e., at extreme position) velocity is minimum and $v_{min} = 0$.

Kinetic energy of a particle executing S.H.M.

Kinetic energy, $K = (1/2)mv^2 = (1/2)m\omega^2(A^2 - y^2)$.

The kinetic energy is maximum at $y = 0$ i.e. at mean position and $K_{max} = (1/2)m\omega^2A^2$, similarly the kinetic energy is minimum at $y = A$, i.e. at extreme position and $K_{min} = 0$.

Acceleration of a particle executing S.H.M.

$$\text{Acceleration} = \frac{d^2y}{dt^2} = -\omega^2 A\sin\omega t.$$

$\therefore$ Acceleration $= -\omega^2 y$

The negative sign indicate that the acceleration is directed towards the mean position.

Acceleration is maximum at extreme position (i.e., at $y = A$) and the maximum acceleration is given by

Maximum acceleration $= \omega^2 A$

Acceleration is minimum at $y = 0$, i.e. at mean position and the minimum acceleration is zero.

Note. The acceleration is maximum at a place where the velocity is minimum and vice versa.

Potential energy of a particle executing S.H.M.

Potential Energy, U = Average force × displacement

or $U = \left(\frac{0 + F}{2}\right)y$ or $U = \frac{m\omega^2 y^2}{2}$

Maximum potential energy is at $y = \pm A$ and is given by $U_{max} = (1/2)m\omega^2A^2$.

Minimum potential energy is at $y = 0$ and is given by $U_{min} = 0$.

Total energy of a particle executing S.H.M.

Total energy, E = K.E. + P.E.

or $E = (1/2)m\omega^2(A^2 - y^2) + (1/2)m\omega^2y^2$

or $E = (1/2)m\omega^2A^2$

or $E = 2\pi^2 mA^2n^2$,

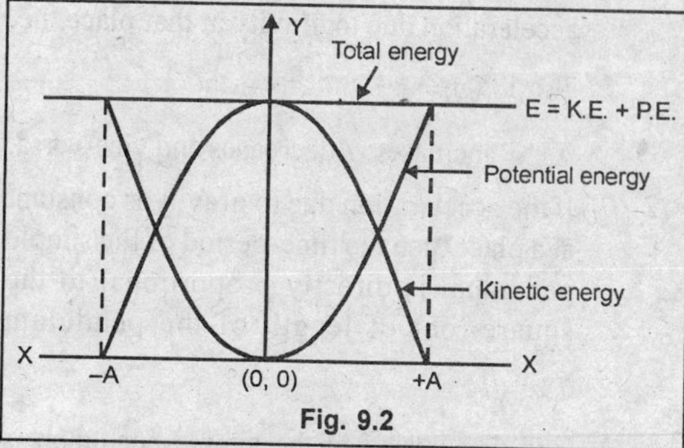

Fig. 9.2

where n is the frequency of vibrations. It is obvious that the total energy of a particle executing

S.H.M. remains constant during the motion, it changes from potential to kinetic and vice-versa. The curves representing K.E., P.E. and total energy are shown in figure.

SIMPLE PENDULUM

An ideal simple pendulum consists of a heavy point mass suspended from a rigid support by means of an elastic inextensible string.

Ideal simple pendulum is not a practical possibility hence a heavy metal sphere is suspended by a light thread from a rigid support.

The metal sphere is called bob and the point from where the pendulum is suspended is called centre of suspension. The distance between the centre of suspension and centre of gravity of the bob is known as the effective length of the pendulum.

The time-period of the simple pendulum is $T = 2\pi\sqrt{(l/g)}$.

It is obvious that :

(i) The time-period of the simple pendulum is independent of amplitude, if the amplitude is small, while if the amplitude is large then the time-period is given by

$$T = 2\pi\sqrt{\left(\frac{l}{g}\right)\left[1+\frac{1}{2^2}\sin^2\frac{\theta_m}{2}+\frac{1}{2^2}\cdot\frac{3^2}{4^2}\sin^4\frac{\theta_m}{2}+\ldots\right]}$$

Thus the period increases with increasing amplitude.

(ii) If the length is constant, then the time-period is inversely proportional to square-root of acceleration due to gravity at that place, i.e. $T \propto 1/\sqrt{g}$.

As 'g' increases, T decreases and vice-versa.

(iii) If the acceleration due to gravity is constant at a place then the time-period of the simple pendulum is directly proportional to the square-root of length of the pendulum $T \propto \sqrt{l}$.

(iv) The time-period of the simple pendulum is independent of the mass and material of the bob.

SECONDS PENDULUM

The simple pendulum, having a time-period of 2 seconds is known as seconds pendulum. Its effective length is 99.992 cm or approximately one metre on earth.

TIME-PERIOD OF A VERY BIG PENDULUM

The time-period of a very big pendulum having length comparable to that to that of radius of earth is

$$T = 2\pi\sqrt{\left\{R_e\Big/\left(1+\frac{R_e}{l}\right)g\right\}}$$

where R_e is the radius of earth and l is the length of the pendulum. There are two cases :

(a) If $l = R_e$ then $T = 2\pi\sqrt{(R_e/2g)} = 84.6/\sqrt{2}$ min.

(b) If $l = \infty$ then $T = 2\pi\sqrt{(R_e/g)} = 84.6$ min.

CONICAL PENDULUM

Conical pendulum consists of a bob suspended by a metal wire fixed at one end and rotating in a horizontal circle at the other end.

It is shown in the adjoining figure.

The tension 'T' in the wire can be resolved into two components

(i) $T\cos\theta$, vertical component

(ii) $T\sin\theta$, horizontal component

$\therefore \quad T\cos\theta = mg$

and $T\sin\theta = mr\omega^2$ in equilibrium position.

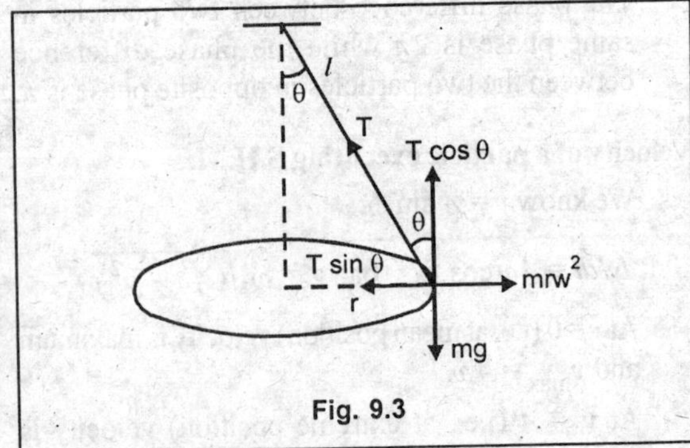

Fig. 9.3

COMPOUND PENDULUM

Compound pendulum is A rigid body capable of rotating in a vertical plane about a horizontal axis passing through any point in the body is called compound pendulum. Its time-period is given by

$$T = 2\pi\sqrt{(I/mgd)},$$

where I is the Moment of Inertia of the body about the centre of suspension, m is the mass of body and 'd' is the distance of centre of gravity from the centre of suspension

TORSIONAL PENDULUM

A rigid executing angular simple harmonic motion in a horizontal plane about a vertical axis passing through centre of body is called torsional pendulum.

In angular simple harmonic motion the restoring torque is proportional the angular displacement i.e. $I(d^2\theta/dt^2) = -C\theta$

where C is restoring couple per unit twist.

$\therefore \quad d^2\theta/dt^2 = -C/I.\ \theta$

Comparing this equation with Acc. $= -\omega^2\theta$,

we get $\quad \omega = 2\pi\sqrt{(I/mgd)},$

$\therefore \quad T = 2\pi/\omega = 2\pi\sqrt{(I/C)}$

Where I is the Moment of Inertia of the moving system about the axis of rotation.

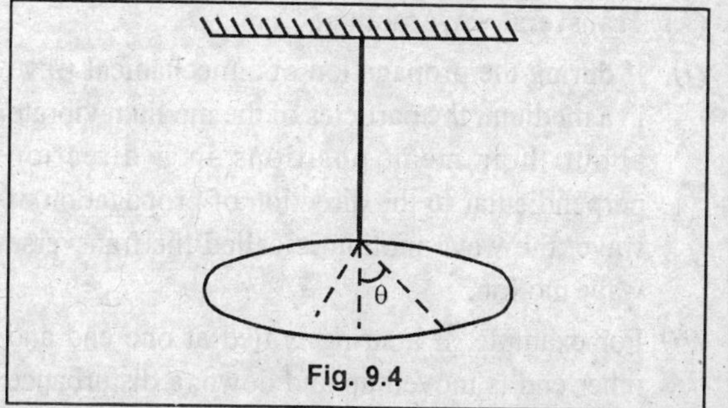

Fig. 9.4

SIMPLE HARMONIC OSCILLATIONS OF SPRINGS

Springs have a property that when they are stretched or compressed then a restoring force is immediately developed in them while try to bring them back to their initial state. If the expression produced in the spring is 'x', then

$$F = Kx$$

Where K is a constant known as spring constant or force constant or stiffness constant. K is numerically equal to $K = F/x = mg/x$.

Its units are Newton/metre. The time period of a spring loaded by mass 'm' is

$$T = 2\pi/\omega = 2\pi\sqrt{(I/C)}$$

SPRINGS IN SERIES

When two springs connected in series are made to oscillate, then their time-period is given by

$$T = 2\pi\sqrt{[m(K_1 + K_2)/K_1K_2]}$$

The equivalent spring constant, K in this case is given by $1/K_1 = 1/K_1 + 1/K_2 + 1/K_3 + ... + 1/K_n$ for n springs.

SPRINGS IN PARALLEL

When two springs connected in parallel are made to oscillate then their time-period is given by

$$T = 2\pi\sqrt{[m(K_1 + K_2)]}$$

and the equivalent spring constant is

$K = K_1 + K_2 + K_3 + ...\ K_n$ for n springs.

Note. If the spring of spring constant K is cut into n equal parts, then the spring constant of each part will become Kn, on the other hand if the spring is stretched such that its length becomes n times the previous length, then the spring constant of the spring becomes K/n.

WAVES

WAVE MOTION

(i) To understand the concept of wave motion and its important characteristics, we consider here an example of a stone dropped in still water of a pond. When the stone strikes the calm water surface at some place, a disturbance is created at that place. The disturbance or water ripples spread out on the water surface around the point, where the stone falls. The water ripples move away in the form of crests and troughs. If small pieces of paper are now thrown on the surface of water, it is found that they do not travel with the wave from the place where the stone strikes, but only execute

motion in upward and downward directions. Which shows that whereas the waves are formed due to a repeated periodic motion of the water molecules but the water molecules do not move themselves alongwith the waves.

(ii) The mechanism of wave propagation on the water surface can be explained on the basis of two properties of medium, viz. Elasticity and Inertia. When the stone strikes the water surface at some place, it creates a cavity at that place. Due to property of elasticity, water opposes the change in its level and starts filling in the cavity from all directions. Because the water coming from all directions is in motion, it, due to property of inertia of motion, continues to come into the cavity even after it is completely filled. As a result of this level of water at that place becomes higher than the surrounding level. Water again opposes it due to property of elasticity and falls down. Thus the water particles at that place move up and down. These particles transfer their motion to the surrounding molecules and come back to their original positions. The neighbouring particles, in turn, transfer their motion to their next molecules and this process goes on.

(iii) Above example thus shows that the water particles do not leave their positions permanently, they simply execute periodic motion about their mean positions while the disturbance produced by the stone moves outward continuously. In other words, the energy initially given by the stone to the water particles is continuously transmitted through water.

PROGRESSIVE WAVE

(i) Wave motion will die out soon due to frictional force present in the medium. However, if we generate the wave in a medium continuously, the particles of the medium oscillate continuously. In this situation, the disturbance produced in the medium is called a progressive wave.

(ii) An important characteristic of progressive wave can be demonstrated by doing a simple experiment. Take some pieces of corks, place them at different points on the surface of water and produce waves by dipping stick in water. It is observed that one by one all the corks begin to oscillate up and down about their mean positions. The cork nearest the stick starts oscillating earliest and the farthest one in the last. Hence, if we observe all the corks simultaneously at any instant, they will be found in different states of their oscillations. Some one will be in its mean position, the other one above its mean position and some other one below its mean position. Some corks will be moving upwards while some other downwards i.e. different corks will be in different phases of their oscillation.

(iii) Thus, **when a progressive wave propagates in a medium, then, at any instant, all the particles of the medium oscillate in the same way but the phase of oscillation changes from particle to particle.**

TWO TYPES OF WAVE MOTION OR MECHANICAL WAVES

The wave motion is classified into two catogories namely transverse and longitudinal wave motion, depending upon the direction of oscillation of the particle during the propagation of progressive mechanical waves in a medium.

(A) Transverse wave motion:

(i) If during the propagation of a mechanical wave in a medium, the particles of the medium vibrate about their mean positions in a direction perpendicular to the direction of propagation of wave, the wave motion is called the transverse wave motion.

(ii) For example, if a string is tied at one end and other end is moved up and down, a disturbance in the form of a pulse travels along the length of the string i.e. particles of the string vibrate along a direction perpendicular to the direction along which the disturbance travels. Hence the waves in the string are transverse. The stretched string of sitar, violin, sonometer etc. execute transverse vibrations.

(iii) All electromagnetic waves are transverse in character.

(iv) A transverse wave travels in the form of **Crests** and **Troughs** (Fig. 9.5). A crest is a portion of the medium, which is highly raised above the normal positions of rest of the particles of the medium while a trough is a portion of the medium, which is highly depressed below the normal positions of rest of the particles of the medium.

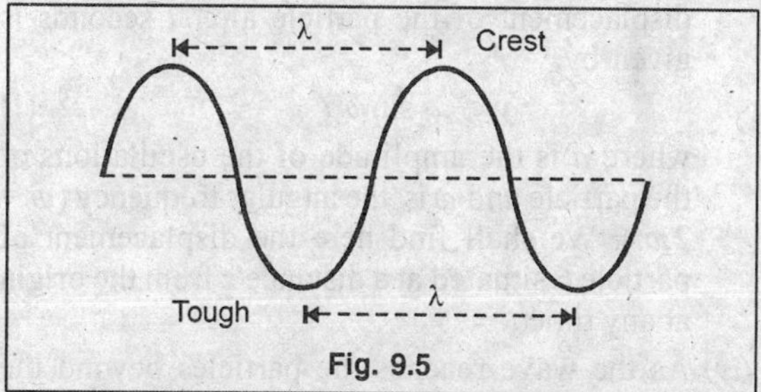

Fig. 9.5

(v) The distance travelled by the disturbance in the time, the particle of the medium completes one vibration, is called the wavelength. It is found that, it is equal to the distance between two successive crests or troughs and is denoted by λ as shown in fig. 9.5.

(vi) For the propagation of transverse waves, medium must also necessarily have the property of rigidity. As gases have no rigidity, hence transverse waves cannot be produced in gases. In liquids, transverse waves cannot be formed in the interior. They can be formed only one surface of liquids because there is some rigidity on the surface because of surface tension. In case of solids, transverse waves can always be produced because there is sufficient rigidity in solids.

(vii) The velocity of transverse wave motion is given by

$$v = \frac{\text{distance travelled}}{\text{time taken}}$$

Since, wavelength (λ) is the distance travelled by the wave in time T, in which the particle of the medium completes one vibration, we get

$$v = \frac{\lambda}{\mathrm{T}} = \left(\frac{1}{T}\right)\lambda = n\lambda$$

where $n = 1/T$, is the frequency of the vibrating particle or the frequency of the wave motion i.e. the number of waves produced per second in the medium.

(B) Longitudinal wave motion

(i) If during the propagation of a mechanical wave in a medium, the particles of the medium oscillate parallel to the direction of propagation of the wave, the wave motion is called the longitudinal wave motion.

(ii) For example, when one end of a long spring is tied to a hook in a wall and the other end is moved forward and backward, then every turn of the spring oscillates parallel to the length of the spring and longitudinal waves propagate through the spring.

(iii) If the whole spring is observed simultaneously at any instant, then we find that at some places the turns of the spring are seen to be closer and at some other places they are seen to be farther than in the normal state of the spring. The places where the turns are closer are said to be in the state of compression while the places where the turns are farther are said to be in the state of rarefaction.

(iv) The states of compression and rarefaction continue to move forward along the length of spring. The distance travelled by the disturbance in the time, the particle of the medium completes one vibration is called wavelength. In case of a longitudinal wave it is found that it is equal to the distance between two successive compressions or rarefactions.

(v) The velocity of longitudinal waves is also given by

$$v = n\lambda$$

(vi) Longitudinal waves can be produced in all types of material medium (solid, liquid and gas). The waves produced in the air are always longitudinal. The wave produced in the interior of liquids are longitudinal, although transverse waves are possible only on the surface of liquids.

(vii) During the propagation of longitudinal waves in a medium, the density and pressure of the medium are higher at the places of compression than in

the normal state of the medium; but lower at the places of rarefaction than in the normal state.

IMPORTANT CHARACTERISTICS OF WAVE MOTION

Important characteristics of a transverse or longitudinal wave motion are as follows:

(i) Wave motion is a kind of disturbance travelling in a material medium with certain fixed velocity.

(ii) In a wave motion, there is no transfer of the particles of the medium from one part to another part of the medium. The particles of the medium execute vibratory motion about their mean positions.

(iii) The disturbance (or wave motion) from one particle reaches the next neighbouring particle a little later and as the disturbance reaches, it also starts executing vibratory motion about its mean position.

(iv) The velocity of every oscillating particle of the medium is different at its different positions in one oscillation but the velocity of wave motion is always constant i.e. **particle velocity varies with respect to time, while the wave velocity is independent of time.**

(v) For the propagation of wave motion, the medium must have the properties of elasticity and inertia.

(vi) During the propagation of wave motion, energy is propagated from one part of the medium to another, without any actual transfer of the particles of material medium.

(vii) The net displacement of an oscillating particle is zero over one complete oscillation.

EQUATION OF A PLANE PROGRESSIVE WAVE

(i) If during the propagation of a progressive wave, the particles of the medium perform simple harmonic motion about their mean positions then the wave is known as a simple harmonic progressive wave.

(ii) Suppose a plane simple harmonic wave travels from the origin O along the positive direction of X-axis from left to right. Fig. 9.6(a) shows the equilibrium positions of particles 1, 2, 3, ... When the wave propagates, these particles oscillate about their equilibrium positions. Fig. 9.6(b) shows the instantaneous positions of these particles at any instant during the propagation of wave. The curve joining these positions represents the wave.

(iii) If time is counted from the instant when the particle 1 at the origin just passes through mean position in positive direction, then the displacement of the particle after t seconds is given by

$$y = a \sin \omega t \qquad ...(1)$$

where a is the amplitude of the oscillations of the particle and ω is the angular frequency ($\omega = 2\pi n$). We shall find here the displacement of particle 6 situated at a distance x from the origin at any time t.

(iv) As the wave reaches the particles beyond the particle 1, the particles starts vibrating about their mean positions. If the speed of the wave be v, then it will reach particle 6, distance x from the particle 1, in x/v sec. Therefore, the particle 6 will start vibrating x/v sec after the particle 1. This implies that the displacement of the particle 6 at a time t will be the same as that of the particle 1 at a time x/v sec earlier i.e. at the time $[t-(x/v)]$. The displacement of particle 1 at time $[t-(x/v)]$ can be obtained by putting $[t-(x/v)]$ in place of t in equation (1). Hence the displacement of the particle 6, distance x from the origin, at time t is given by

$$y = a \sin \omega [t-(x/v)] \qquad ...(2)$$

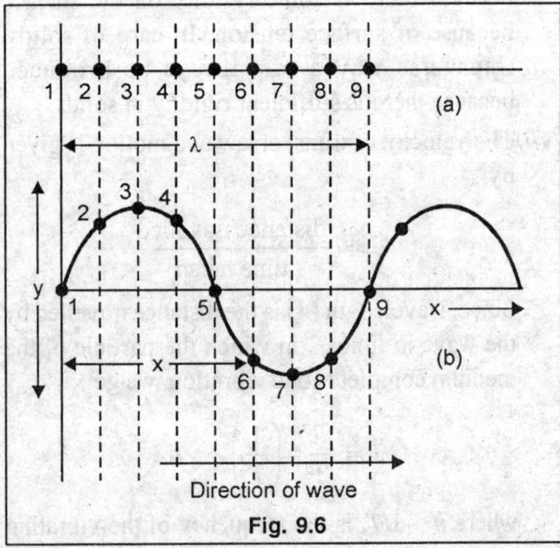

Fig. 9.6

(v) But $\omega = 2\pi n$, hence we can also write equation (2) as

$$y = a \sin 2\pi n [t - (x/v)] \quad ...(3)$$

Now, $n = v/\lambda$, where λ is the wavelength. Therefore,

$$y = a \sin (2\pi v/\lambda) [t - (x/v)]$$

or

$$y = a \sin (2\pi/\lambda) (vt - x) \quad ...(4)$$

Again, $v = n\lambda = \lambda/T$

where T is the time period.

Therefore,

$$y = a \sin (2\pi/\lambda) [\{(\lambda/T)t\} - x],$$

$$\boldsymbol{y = a \sin 2\pi [(t/T) - (x/\lambda)]} \quad ...(5)$$

This is the equation of a plane progressive simple harmonic wave travelling along positive X-axis.

REFLECTION OF SOUND WAVES

(i) Since sound propagates in the form of waves, it shows both the phenomenon of reflection and refraction. When sound wave travelling in a medium strikes the surface separating the two media, a part of incident wave is reflected back into initial medium obeying ordinary laws of reflection while the rest is partly absorbed and partly refracted or transmitted into second medium.

(ii) The particles at the boundary are unable to vibrate when a sound wave gets reflected from a rigid boundary. Thus, a reflected wave is generated which interferes with the oncoming wave to produce zero displacement at the rigid boundary. At these points of zero displacement, the pressure variation is maximum. This implies that **the phase of wave is reversed but the nature of sound wave does not change i.e. on reflection the compression is reflected back as compression and rarefaction as rarefaction.** If the incident wave is represented by the equation: $y = a \sin (\omega t - kx)$, then the equation of reflected wave takes the form $y = a' \sin (\omega t + kx + \pi) = -a' \sin (\omega t + kx)$ where a' is the amplitude of reflected wave.

(iii) A sound wave is also reflected if it encounters a rare medium or free boundary or low pressure region. A practical example is when a sound wave travels in a narrow open tube. When the wave reaches an open end, it gets reflected. The force on the particles there due to the outside air is quite small and hence, the particles vibrate with the increasing amplitude. As a result, the pressure there remains at the average value. This implies that **there is no change in the phase of wave but the nature of sound wave is changed i.e. on reflection the compression is reflected back as rarefaction and vice-versa.** If the incident wave is:

$$y = a \sin (\omega t - kx),$$

then the equation of reflected wave takes the form

$$y = a' \sin (\omega t + kx)$$

where a' is the amplitude of reflected wave.

REFRACTION OF SOUND

When sound wave passes from one homogeneous medium to another homogeneous medium, it deviates from its path. This is called as phenomenon of refraction. If i and r are the angles of incidence and refraction, then according to Snell's law

$$\frac{\sin i}{\sin r} = \frac{v_1}{v_2} = \text{constant}$$

where v_1 and v_2 are the velocities of sound in first and second medium respectively.

PRINCIPLE OF SUPERPOSITION

(i) When two or more progressive waves travel in a medium simultaneously, each wave travels independently, as if the other waves were not present at all. Such a process by which the different waves travelling through a medium simultaneously overlap one another without losing their individual nature and shape is called superposition of waves.

(ii) For example, consider two wave pulses P and Q of equal displacements of same sign (both upwards) and travelling along the length of a string with equal speeds but in opposite direction (Fig. 9.7(a)).

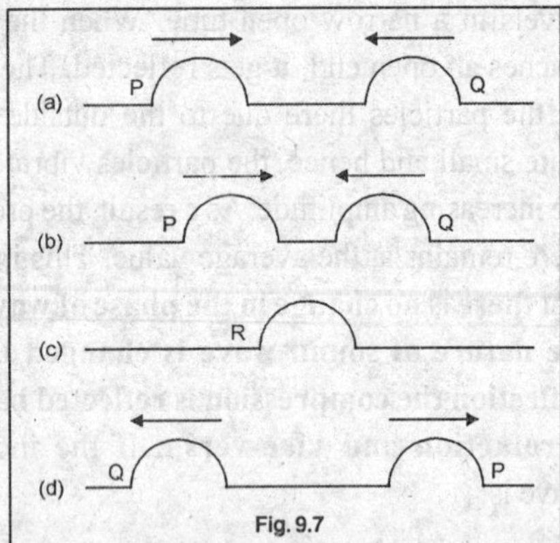

Fig. 9.7

Fig. 9.7(b) shows two wave pulses at a later instant. Fig. 9.7(c) shows the effect at a time t, when the two wave pulses superpose upto each other. It is observed that at such an instant i.e. at time t, a wave pulse R having displacement equal to twice that of the either wave pulse (equal to sum of the displacements of two wave pulses) is produced. After some more time, the wave pulse P and Q move along the string as shown in Fig. 10.3(d). The two wave pulses P and Q travel retaining their shapes after they superpose on each other at time t.

(iii) On the other hand, if the two wave pulses P and Q of equal displacements but of opposite sign move with equal speeds in opposite directions along the length of string as shown in Fig. 9.8 (a), then the two pulses get near each other after small time as shown in Fig. 9.8 (b), superpose on each other producing a resultant wave pulse R of zero displacement as shown in Fig. 9.8 (c) and after crossing each other, continue to move, retaining their shapes as shown in Fig. 9.8 (d).

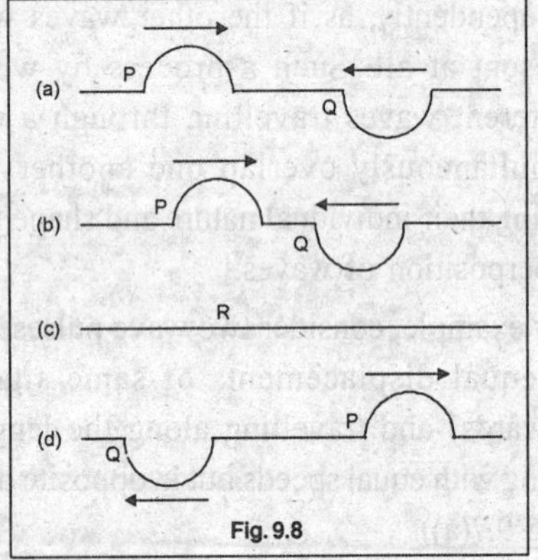

Fig. 9.8

(iv) The above observations show that the resultant wave is obtained by adding the displacements of the two wave pulses according to law of vector addition. This is known as principle of superposition of waves and can be summarized as follows:

When two or more waves travel in a medium simultaneously in such a way that each wave represents its separate motion individually, then the resultant displacement of particle of the medium at any time is equal to the vector sum of the individual displacements.

(v) In general, if $\vec{y}_1, \vec{y}_2, \ldots\ldots, \vec{y}_n$ are the displacements at a point, where the n waves superpose on each other, then the resultant displacement at that point is given by

$$\vec{y} = \vec{y}_1 + \vec{y}_2 + \ldots\ldots + \vec{y}_n$$

For two wave pulses of equal displacements in same direction i.e. $|\vec{y}_1| = |\vec{y}_2| = A$ (say), the magnitude of resultant displacement on superposition will be

$$|\vec{y}| = A + A = 2A$$

For two wave pulses of equal but opposite displacements say A and $-A$, the magnitude of the resultant displacement on superposition will be

$$|\vec{y}| = A + (-A) = 0$$

(vi) The superposition of two waves give rise to following three important effects :

(a) When two waves of same frequency or wavelength moving with same speeds in the same direction in a medium superpose on each other, they give rise to an effect called interference of waves.

(b) When two waves of slightly different frequency moving with the same speed in the same direction in a medium superpose on each other, they given rise to beats.

(c) When two waves of same frequency moving with same speed in opposite direction in a medium superpose on each other, they give rise to the stationary waves.

BEATS IN SOUND WAVES

(i) When two harmonic waves of nearly equal frequency travelling in a medium along the same direction superpose upon each other, the intensity of the resultant sound at a point in the medium rises and falls regularly with time. This rise and fall in the intensity of sound is called the phenomenon of beats. One rise and one fall form one beat. The number of times the intensity of sound rises and falls in one second is called beat frequency and it is found to be equal to the difference in frequencies of the two superposing harmonic waves.

(ii) The human ear cannot hear the beats, if the beats formed are more than ten per second. In other words, so that the human ear can detect the beats, the difference in the frequencies of the two harmonic waves should not be more than ten. It is because of the persistence of hearing.

(iii) **Qualitative explanation for the formation of beats:** The phenomenon of beats is a special example of the interference of sound waves with respect to time at a fixed point. When two sound sources are sounded simultaneously, two waves start travelling in the medium in the same direction. If these two waves meet at a point in the same phase then the intensity of sound at that point is maximum but if they meet in opposite phase then the intensity of sound is minimum. If the frequencies of the two waves are identical, then the phase difference between two waves approaching at any point remains constant. Hence the intensity of sound at that point remains constant. But if there is a slight difference in the frequencies of the waves, then the phase difference at any point varies regularly with respect to time i.e. at that point the waves go on meeting alternately in the same phase and in the opposite phases i.e. **the resultant intensity of sound at that point rises and falls alternately.**

(iv) **Graphical explanation for the formation of beats:** Consider that two harmonic waves of nearly equal frequencies are travelling in the medium in same direction. Suppose the frequencies of two waves are $v_1 = 50$ Hz and $v_2 = 40$ Hz respectively and their amplitudes are equal. In 1/5 second, the two waves will cover the same distance. But in this distance, the number of waves due to first and second waves will be respectively 10 and 8 as shown in fig. 9.9(a) and fig. 9.9(b).

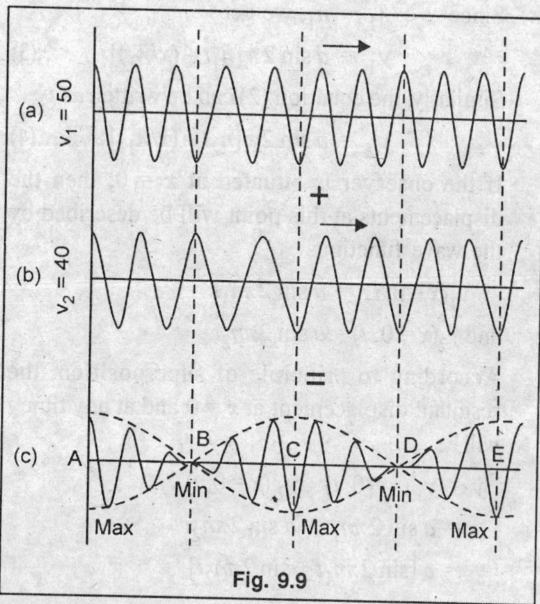

Fig. 9.9

When the two waves superpose on each other, the resultant displacement at each point can be determined by using the principle of superposition i.e. by adding the displacements due to two waves according to vector algebra at each point. The resultant wave form will be as shown in fig. 9.9 (c). The amplitude and hence the intensity becomes maximum, minimum, maximum, minimum and maximum at the points *A*, *B*, *C*, *D* and *E* respectively. Thus we see that two beats are formed, one between *A* and *C* and second between *C* and *E*. Because these two beats are formed in 1/5 second, the number of beats formed per second will be 10 i.e. equal to difference of frequencies of the two harmonic waves.

(v) **Quantitative explanation for the formation of beats:** Consider that two harmonic waves of equal amplitudes and frequencies n_1 and n_2 are travelling in a medium in the same direction with equal speeds v. Let the wave functions of the two waves be

$$y_1 = a\sin(2\pi/\lambda_1)(vt-x) \quad ...(1)$$

and $$y_2 = a\sin(2\pi/\lambda_2)(vt-x) \quad ...(2)$$

The equation (1) can be written as

$$y_1 = a\sin 2\pi[(v/\lambda_1)t-(x/\lambda_1)]$$

Since $v/\lambda_1 = n_1$, we get

$$y_1 = a\sin 2\pi[n_1 t-(x/\lambda_1)] \quad ...(3)$$

Similarly, the equation (2) can be written as

$$y_2 = a\sin 2\pi[n_2 t-(x/\lambda_1)] \quad ...(4)$$

If the observer is situated at $x = 0$, then the displacements at this point will be described by the wave functions

$$y_1(x=0,t) = a\sin 2\pi n_1 t$$

and $y_2(x=0,t) = a\sin 2\pi n_2 t$.

According to principle of superposition, the resultant displacement at $x = 0$ and at any time t will be

$$y = y_1(x=0,t)+y_2(x=0,t)$$
$$= a\sin 2\pi n_1 t + a\sin 2\pi n_2 t$$
$$= a[\sin 2\pi n_1 t+\sin 2\pi n_2 t]$$
$$= 2a\sin 2\pi\left(\frac{n_1+n_2}{2}\right)t\cos 2\pi\left(\frac{n_1-n_2}{2}\right)t$$
$$= \left[2a\cos 2\pi\left(\frac{n_1-n_2}{2}\right)t\right]\sin 2\pi\left(\frac{n_1+n_2}{2}\right)t \quad ...(5)$$

Above equation represents a harmonic wave of frequency $[(n_1+n_2)/2]$ and of amplitude

$$A = 2a\cos 2\pi\left(\frac{n_1-n_2}{2}\right)t \quad ...(6)$$

which varies with time.

(a) The resultant amplitude will be maximum if

$$\cos 2\pi\left(\frac{n_1-n_2}{2}\right)t = \pm 1$$

or, $$\pi(n_1-n_2)t = n\pi$$

or, $$t = n/(n_1-n_2),$$

where $n = 0, 1, 2, 3, ...$

i.e. $t = 0$,

$$\frac{1}{(n_1-n_2)}, \frac{2}{(n_1-n_2)}, \frac{3}{(n_1-n_2)}, ...$$

Thus, at $x = 0$, the resultant amplitude and hence the intensity of sound will again become maximum after a fixed interval of time equal to $[1/(n_1-n_2)]$.

Therefore, frequency of maximum intensity

$$= \frac{1}{1/(n_1-n_2)} = (n_1-n_2)$$

(b) The resultant amplitude will be minimum, if

$$\cos 2\pi\left(\frac{n_1-n_2}{2}\right)t = 0$$

or, $$\pi(n_1-n_2)t = (2n+1)\pi/2,$$

where $$n = 0, 1, 2...$$

or $$t = \frac{1}{2(n_1-n_2)}, \frac{2}{2(n_1-n_2)}, \frac{3}{2(n_1-n_2)}, ...$$

Thus, at $x = 0$, the intensity of sound will again become minimum after a fixed interval of time equal to

$$\frac{2}{2(n_1-n_2)} \text{ or } \frac{1}{2(n_1-n_2)}$$

Therefore, **frequency of minimum intensity**

$$= \frac{1}{1/(n_1-n_2)} = (n_1-n_2)$$

Thus, frequency of maximum intensity and minimum intensity of the sound on superposition of two waves are equal. The one maximum in the intensity will be followed by a minimum, then by a maximum in intensity and so on. As one beat is formed, when intensity of sound again becomes maximum after once becoming minimum, the number of beats per second or beat frequency will be $= (n_1-n_2)$.

LONGITUDINAL STATIONARY WAVES AND VIBRATIONS OF AIR COLUMNS

(i) Some musical instruments, in which sound is produced through vibrations of air columns are flute, whistle, clarinet etc. When air is blown at the mouth of a bottle, sound is produced due to vibrations of air column inside the bottle. Here we shall study the vibrations of air-columns in the cylindrical tubes of uniform diameter. Such sound-producing tubes are called organ pipes. The tube which is closed at one end and open at the other is called a closed organ pipe; and the tube which is open at both ends is called an open organ pipe.

(ii) **Vibrations of air column in closed organ pipe:**

(a) A longitudinal wave travels in the air of the pipe from the open end towards the closed end when a vibrating source is brought near the open end of a closed pipe. The closed end, behaving like a rigid boundary, reflects this wave and sends it back towards the open end (The closed end of the pipe reflects the longitudinal wave like a rigid boundary, that is, it reflects the state of compression in the form of a compression and the state of rarefaction in the form of a rarefaction).

The open end acting like a free boundary reflects it and sends again towards the close end (The open end of the pipe reflects the longitudinal wave like a free boundary, that is, it reflects the state of compression in the form of a rarefaction and the state of rarefaction in the form of a compression). Thus two longitudinal waves travel in the air-column in opposite directions which superpose and produce stationary longitudinal waves. At the closed end of the pipe the particles of air have no freedom to vibrate, hence there is always a node at the closed end. On the other hand, at the open end of the pipe the air particles have the greatest freedom to vibrate, hence there is always an antinode at the open end.

(b) If the air is blown lightly at the open end of the closed organ pipe, then the air-column would vibrate, as shown in Fig. 9.10 (a), with an antinode (A) at the open end and a node (*N*) at the closed end. In this situation, air column is said to vibrate in fundamental mode because there are no other nodes or antinodes in between the two ends of pipe. This is simplest possible tone produced in a closed organ pipe and may also be called as tone of minimum possible frequency or the first harmonic. If l be the length of the pipe and λ_1 the fundamental wavelength, then

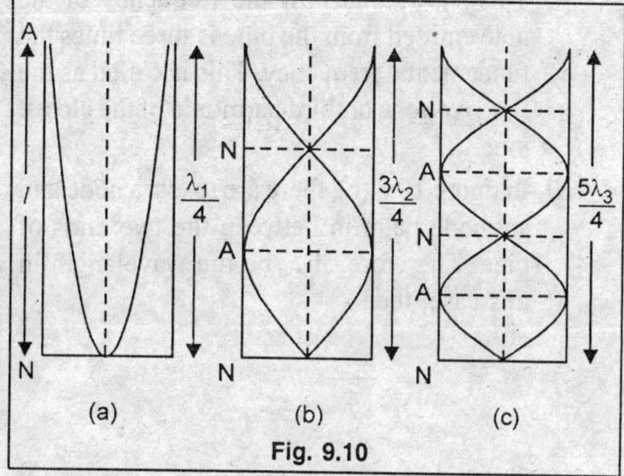

Fig. 9.10

$$l = \lambda_1/4$$

or $$\lambda_1 = 4l \qquad \text{...(1)}$$

because the distance between an antinode and the nearest node is $\lambda/4$.

If n_1 be the fundamental frequency of the pipe and v the velocity of sound in air, then

$$n_1 = \frac{v}{\lambda_1} = \frac{v}{4l} \qquad \text{...(2)}$$

(c) Tones of frequencies higher than the fundamental tone can be produced if, air is blown forcefully at the open end of the pipe. These are called overtones. In this case, additional nodes and antinodes are formed between the two ends of pipe as shown in Fig. 9.10 (b) and Fig. 9.10 (c). In the Fig. 9.10(b), there is one extra node and antinode pair formed between the two ends of pipe.

Hence in this case wavelength will differ from that of previous case. Let the new wavelength be λ_2. It follows from Fig. 10.6 (b), that

$$l = \frac{3\lambda_2}{4}$$

$$\lambda_2 = \frac{4l}{3} \quad ...(3)$$

Thus, if n_2 be the corresponding frequency of the tone produced in the pipe, then

$$n_2 = \frac{v}{\lambda_2} = 3\frac{v}{4l} = 3\ n_1 \quad ...(4)$$

This shows that now the frequency of the note emitted from the pipe is three times the fundamental frequency. This is called as the first overtone or third harmonic of the closed pipe.

(d) In figure 10.6 (c), there are to extra node and antinode pairs in between the two ends of pipe. Therefore, if l_3 be the wavelength in this case, then

$$l = \frac{5\lambda_3}{4}$$

or $$\lambda_3 = \frac{4l}{5} \quad ...(5)$$

If n_3 be the corresponding frequency, then

$$n_3 = \frac{v}{\lambda_3} = \frac{5v}{4l} = 5n_1 \quad ...(6)$$

i.e. in this case, the frequency of the note emitted is five times the fundamental frequency. This is called as the second overtone or fifth harmonic of the closed pipe.

(e) It follows from above discussion that the frequencies of the fundamental tone and overtones of a closed organ pipe have the following ratios with each other:

$n_1 : n_2 : n_3 : ... = 1 : 3 : 5 : ...$

In other words, **only odd harmonics are produced in a closed organ pipe.**

(iii) Vibrations of air column in open organ pipe:

(a) A longitudinal wave travels from this end towards the other end when a vibrating source is brought near the one end of an open pipe. The other end, acting like a free boundary, reflects this wave and sends towards the first end. Thus two longitudinal waves travel in the air-column in opposite directions which superpose and form stationary waves. Because the pipe is open at both ends, there is an antinode at each end.

(b) If air is blown lightly at one end of the pipe, then the air column would vibrate, as shown in fig. 9.11 (a) with antinode (*A*) at each end and a node (*N*) in the middle. In this situation, air column of open organ pipe is said to vibrate in fundamental mode because there is no extra node and antinode in between the two ends of the pipe. This is again the simplest possible tone or tone of minimum possible frequency produced by an open pipe. It may be also called as first harmonic of the open pipe. If l is the length of the pipe and λ_1 is the fundamental wavelength, then

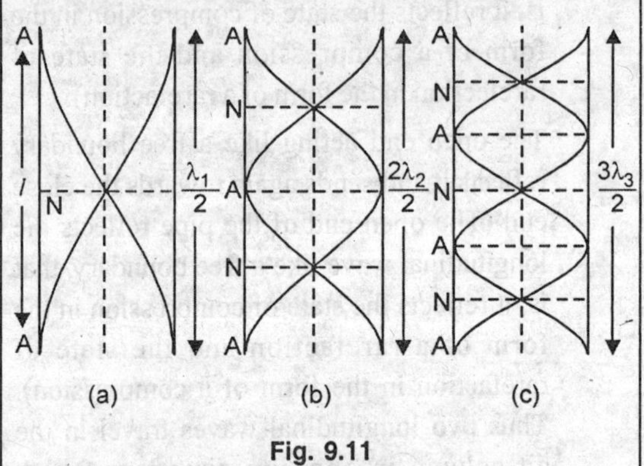

Fig. 9.11

$$l = \lambda_1/2$$

or $$\lambda_1 = 2l \quad ...(7)$$

If n_1 be the corresponding fundamental frequency of the pipe and v the velocity of sound in air, then again

$$n_1 = \frac{v}{\lambda_1} = \frac{v}{2l} \quad ...(8)$$

(c) If air is blown forcefully at the end of the pipe, then overtones are produced. In this case, additional nodes and antinodes are formed in between the two ends of the pipe as shown in fig. 9.11(b) and fig. 9.11(c). In fig. 9.11(b), there is one extra node and antinode pair in between the two ends of the pipe. Therefore, if λ_2 be the wavelength in this case, then

$$l = \frac{2\lambda_2}{2}$$

or $$\lambda_2 = \frac{2l}{2} \qquad \text{...(9)}$$

If n_2 be the corresponding frequency of the note emitted by the pipe, then

$$n_2 = \frac{v}{\lambda_2} = \frac{2v}{2l} = 2n_1 \qquad \text{...(10)}$$

i.e. the frequency of this note is twice the frequency of the fundamental note. This is called as the first overtone or the second harmonic of the open pipe.

(d) In fig. 10.7 (c), there are two extra node and antinode pairs in between the two ends of the pipe. Therefore, if λ_3 be the wavelength of this case, then

$$l = \frac{3\lambda_3}{2}$$

or $$\lambda_3 = \frac{2l}{3} \qquad \text{...(11)}$$

If n_3 be the corresponding frequency of the note emitted by the pipe, then

$$n_3 = \frac{v}{\lambda_3} = \frac{3v}{2l} = 3n_1 \qquad \text{...(12)}$$

i.e. in this case the frequency of the note emitted is three times the fundamental frequency. This called as the second overtone or third harmonic of the pipe.

(e) It follows from above discussion that the frequencies of the fundamental tone and overtones of an open organ pipe have the following ratios with each other:

$$n_1 : n_2 : n_3 :... = 1:2:3:...$$

In other words, **both the even and odd harmonic are produced in an open pipe.**

STATIONARY WAVES IN A STRING FIXED AT BOTH ENDS

(i) There are also some such musical instruments like sitar, violine, etc., in which musical sounds are produced by the vibrations of the stretched strings. Here we shall study the different modes of vibrations of a string which is rigidly fixed at both the ends.

(ii) When a string or a wire clamped to rigid supports at its ends in plucked in the middle and released, the transverse progressive waves travel towards each end of the string or wire. The speed of these waves is given by

$$v = \sqrt{\frac{T}{m}} \qquad \text{...(1)}$$

where T is the tension in the string or wire and m is the mass per unit length of the string or wire. The waves travelling towards the rigid ends of the string are reflected from these ends and due to superposition of the incident and the reflected waves, transverse stationary waves are set up in the wire.

(iii) Since the ends of the string are fixed, there is a node N at each end and an antinode A in the middle. We know that the distance between two consecutive nodes is $\lambda/2$, where λ is wavelength. Hence if l be the length of the string between the clamped ends, then

$$l = \lambda/2$$

or $$\lambda = 2l$$

If n be the frequency of vibration of the wire, then

$$n = \frac{v}{\lambda} = \frac{v}{2l}$$

Putting the value of v from (1), we get

$$n = \frac{1}{2l}\sqrt{\frac{T}{m}} \qquad \text{...(2)}$$

This is the frequency of the note emitted by the vibrating string. It is clear from equation (2) that the frequency of the sound emitted from a vibrating stretched string can be changed in two ways; by changing the length of the string or by changing the tension in the string.

(iv) **Fundamental tone:** When a stretched string (or wire) is plucked in the middle and released, the string usually vibrates in one segment only. Nodes (*N*) are formed at the two ends of the string while one antinode (*A*) in the middle.

In this situation, the note emitted by the string is called the fundamental tone. If l be the length of the string, and λ_1 be the wavelength in this case, then

$$l = \frac{\lambda_1}{2}$$

or $$\lambda_1 = 2l$$

If n_1 represents the fundamental or minimum frequency of the vibrating string and v the speed of the transverse waves in the wire, then

$$n_1 = \frac{v}{\lambda_1} = \frac{v}{2l} = \frac{1}{2l}\sqrt{\frac{T}{m}} \quad ...(3)$$

(v) **First overtone:** The same length of the string can also be made to vibrate in more than one segment.

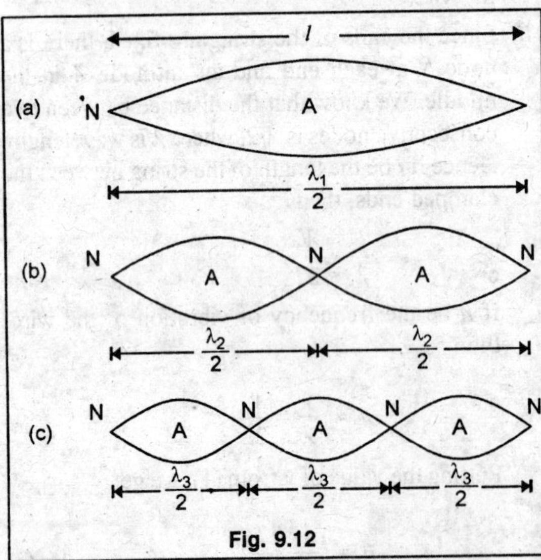

Fig. 9.12

If we touch the middle-point of the string by a feather and pluck it at one fourth of its length from one end, then the string vibrates in two segments. In this case, in addition to nodes at the ends of the string, there will be a node (*N*) at the middle point also, and in between these three nodes there will be two antinodes (*A*). Therefore, if λ_2 be the wavelength in this case, then

$$l = \frac{\lambda_2}{2} + \frac{\lambda_2}{2} = \frac{2\lambda_2}{2}$$

or $$\lambda_2 = \frac{2l}{2}$$

If the frequency of the wire be now n_2, then

$$n_2 = \frac{v}{\lambda_2} = \frac{2v}{2l}$$

$$= \frac{2}{2l}\sqrt{\frac{T}{m}} = 2n_1 \quad ...(4)$$

i.e. in this case the frequency of the tone produced by the vibrating string is two times the frequency of fundamental tone. This tone is called the first overtone or second harmonic.

(vi) **Second overtone:** If the string is made to vibrate in three segments and the wavelength in this case be λ_3, then

$$l = \frac{\lambda_3}{2} + \frac{\lambda_3}{2} + \frac{\lambda_3}{2} = \frac{3\lambda_3}{2}$$

or, $$\lambda_3 = \frac{2l}{3}$$

If the frequency of the vibrating string in this mode be n_3, then

$$n_3 = \frac{v}{\lambda_3} = \frac{3v}{2l}$$

$$= \frac{3}{2l}\sqrt{\frac{T}{m}} = 3n_1 \quad ...(5)$$

i.e. in this case the frequency of the emitted tone is three times the frequency of the fundamental tone. This tone is called second overtone or third harmonic.

(vii) Similarly, if the string is made to vibrate in four, five ... segments then still higher overtones can be produced. If the string vibrates in p segments, then its frequency is given by

$$n_p = \frac{P}{2l}\sqrt{\frac{T}{m}} = pn_1 \quad \text{...(6)}$$

(viii) From the above calculation we find that the frequencies of the fundamental tone and the overtones of a stretched string have the following ratios with each other:

$n_1 : n_2 : n_3 : ... = 1 : 2 : 3 : ...$

In other words, **both even and odd harmonics are produced in a stretched string.**

DOPPLER'S EFFECT IN SOUND

(i) If an observer is situated at a fixed distance from a sound-source, the frequency of sound heard by him is the same as produced by the source. But if the sound-source, or the observer, or both, are in state of motion; then the frequency of the sound appears to be changed to the observer. **This phenomenon of the apparent change in the frequency of the source due to a relative motion between the source and the observer is called as Doppler's effect.**

(ii) It is observed that the frequency of the sound appears to be increased, when the source of the sound and the observer are approaching each other but appears to be decreased, when the two move away from each other. For example, to an observer standing on a railway platform, the sound of the whistle of an engine appears shrill or of high frequency, when the engine is approaching him. But as soon as the engine crosses him and starts receding, the sound of the whistle appears suddenly grave or of low frequency.

(iii) It should be noted here that frequency of the sound always appears to increase, when source of sound moves towards a stationary observer or an observer moves toward a stationary source of sound or both move towards each other. On the other hand, the frequency of sound is found to decreases, when source of sound moves away from the stationary observer or the observer moves away from the stationary source of sound or both move away from each other.

(iv) Doppler's effect can be studied in the following cases:

Part (A): When sound-source is in motion and observer is at rest: Suppose S and O be the positions of the sound-source and the observer respectively. Let n be the actual frequency of the source and v the velocity of sound. These n waves will be emitted from the source in one second which will travel with velocity v. If the source is stationary then these n waves will spread in the distance SO, where $SO = v$ (Fig. 9.13(a)). To the observer O, the wavelength of the waves will be $\lambda = v/n$.

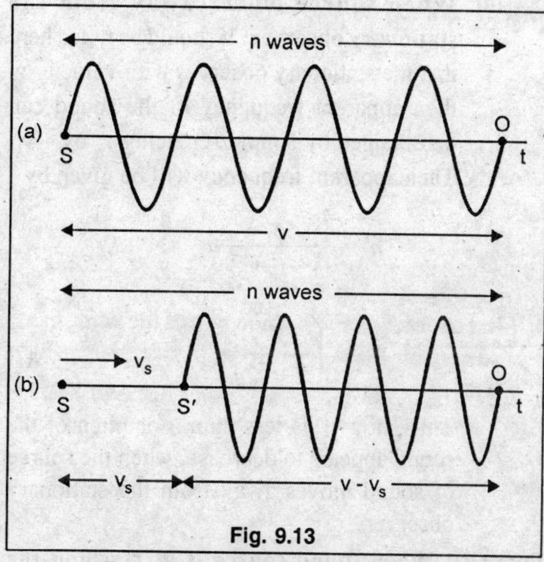

Fig. 9.13

(a) When source moves towards stationary observer: If the source S is in motion with velocity v_s towards the stationary observer, then after 1 sec, the source will reach the point S', such that $SS' = v_s$. Then the n waves emitted by the source in 1 sec will now spread in a distance $(v - v_s)$ only, because in 1 sec the source itself moves a distance v_s towards the observer (Fig. 9.13(b)). Therefore, to the observer, the apparent wavelength of the sound will be

$$\lambda' = \frac{v - v_s}{n}$$

If n' is the apparent frequency, then

$$n' = \frac{v}{\lambda'} = \frac{v}{(v - v_s)/n}$$

$$= \left(\frac{v}{v - v_s}\right) n \quad ...(1)$$

Thus we find that n' is greater than n i.e. pitch (or frequency) of the sound appears to increase, when the source of sound moves towards the stationary observer. It should be noted here that the velocity of the source of sound cannot be greater than the velocity of sound otherwise n' will become negative.

(b) **When source moves away from the stationary observer:** It should be noted here that the stationary observer with velocity v_s then apparent frequency of the sound can be obtained by simply replacing v_s by $-v_s$. Then apparent frequency will be given by

$$n' = \frac{v}{v - (-v_s)} n$$

$$= \left(\frac{v}{v + v_s}\right) n \quad ...(2)$$

Thus, now n' is less than n or pitch of the sound appears to decrease, when the source of sound moves away from the stationary observer.

Part (B): When sound source is at rest and the observer is in motion: In the adjoining fig. 9.14, S and O again represent the positions of source and observer respectively. The source S is emitting n number of waves per second, each having wavelength $\lambda = v/n$. If the n waves crossing the ear of the observer in 1 sec, the wave emitted right in the beginning will reach some point A, while that emitted in the last, will just reach at the point O where observer is situated. Thus, distance OA contains n waves which cross the ear of the observer in 1 sec (Fig. 9.14 (a)).

(a) **When observer moves towards the source:** Suppose the observer is moving towards the stationary source with velocity v_o. After 1 second it will reach the point O' such that $OO' = v_o$. Because of this motion, the number of waves crossing the ear of observer will be n waves contained in distance OA plus the number of waves contained in distance OO' i.e. v_o/λ. Therefore, apparent frequency of sound will be

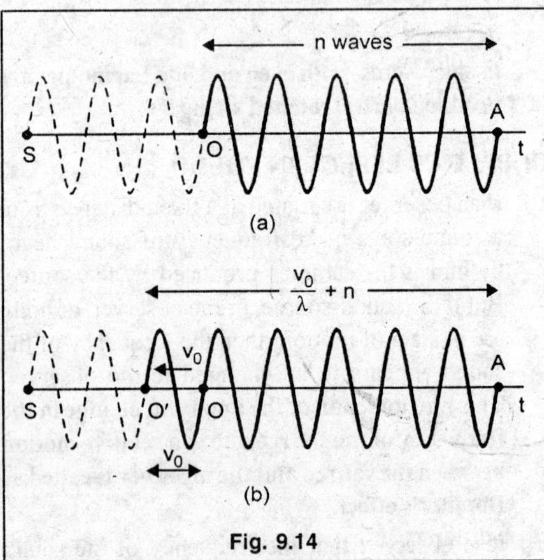

Fig. 9.14

$$n' = n + \frac{v_o}{\lambda} = n + \frac{v_o}{v/n}$$

$$= n + \frac{nv_o}{v} = \left(\frac{v + v_o}{v}\right) n \quad ...(3)$$

Thus, n' is greater than n i.e. pitch of the sound appears to increase, when the listener moves towards the stationary source.

(b) **When observer moves away from the source:** In this case, the number of waves crossing the ear of observer in one second will be less than n. However, the apparent frequency can be easily determined by simply replacing v_o by $-v_o$ in equation (3). Therefore, apparent frequency of the sound, when observer is moving away from the source is given by

$$n' = \left[\frac{v+(-v_o)}{v}\right]n$$

$$= \left(\frac{v-v_o}{v}\right)n \quad ...(4)$$

Now, n' is less than n i.e. frequency of sound appears to decrease, when the observer moves away from the source. It may be noted here again that velocity of the observer cannot be greater than the velocity of sound otherwise n' will become negative.

Part (C) : When source and Observer both are in motion : From the above discussion, it follows that

(i) When source is in motion and observer is stationary, Doppler effect is due to apparent change in the size of the wavelengths of waves and

(ii) When source is at rest and observer is in motion, Doppler effect is due to change in the number of waves crossing the ear of the observer.

We shall now use above conclusions to derive the expressions for apparent frequency of sound in different cases of both the source and observer in motion.

(a) When both the source and observer move towards each other: Suppose n' is the apparent frequency, when source alone is in motion with velocity v_s towards the observer (which is stationary). Then, from equation (1), we get:

$$n' = \left(\frac{v}{v-v_s}\right)n \quad ...(5)$$

where n is the actual frequency and v, the velocity of sound.

Now, suppose observer is also moving with velocity v_o towards the source, which appears to be emitting waves of frequency n'. Due to motion of the observer, the frequency will change from n' to n'', which according to equation (3) is given by

$$n'' = \left(\frac{v+v_o}{v}\right)n' \quad ...(6)$$

From equation (5) and (6), we get

$$n'' = \frac{v+v_o}{v} \times \frac{v}{v-v_s} n$$

$$= \left(\frac{v+v_o}{v-v_s}\right)n \quad ...(7)$$

Above equation shows that

(I) The apparent frequency will be greater than the actual frequency.

(II) The observer may not move with velocity greater than that of the velocity of sound otherwise n' will become negative which is not possible.

(b) When the source moves towards the observer and observer moves away from the source: In this case apparent frequency can be obtained by replacing v_o by $-v_o$ in equation (7). Thus, apparent frequency is given by

$$n'' = \frac{v+(-v_o)}{v-v_s} n$$

$$= \left(\frac{v-v_o}{v-v_s}\right)n \quad ...(8)$$

In such a case, n'' may be greater or less than n depending upon v_o is less than or greater than v_s or both greater than v.

Similarly, expressions for apparent frequency of the sound, when both the source and the observer move away from each other or when the source moves away from the observer but the observer moves towards the source can be obtained by changing signs of v_o or v_s or both in equation (7) and (8).

MULTIPLE CHOICE QUESTIONS

1. Displacement-time equation of a particle executing S.H.M. is, $x = 4 \sin \omega t + 3 \sin (\omega t + \pi/3)$. Here x is in centimeters and t in seconds. The amplitude of oscillation of the particle is approximately
(a) 5 cm (b) 6 cm
(c) 7 cm (d) 9 cm

2. The S.H.M. of a particle is given by the equation $y = 3 \sin \omega t + 4 \cos \omega t$. The amplitude is
(a) 7 (b) 12
(c) 1 (d) 5

3. Two mutually perpendicular simple harmonic vibrations have same amplitude, frequency and phase. When they superimpose, the resultant form of vibration will be
(a) a straight line (b) a parabola
(c) a circle (d) an ellipsoid.

4. The displacement y of a particle executing periodic motion is given by $y = 4 \cos^2 (t/2) \sin (1000\, t)$. This expression may be considered to be a result of the superposition of how many independent harmonic motions ?
(a) five (b) two
(c) three (d) four

5. A mass M is suspeneded from a spring of negligible mass. The spring is pulled a little and then released so that the mass executes simple harmonic oscillations with a time period T. If the mass is increased by m, then the time period becomes $\left(\frac{5}{4}T\right)$. The ratio of $\frac{m}{M}$ is
(a) 9/16 (b) 5/4
(c) 25/16 (d) 4/5

6. A spring has a force constant K and a mass m is suspended from it. The spring is cut in half and the same mass is suspended from one of the halves. If the frequency of oscillation in the first case is α, then frequency in the second case will be
(a) α (b) $\alpha/2$
(c) $\alpha\sqrt{2}$ (d) 2α.

7. A spring having a spring constant 'K' is loaded with a mass 'm'. The spring is cut into two equal parts and one of these is loaded again with the same mass. The new spring constant is
(a) K (b) $2K$
(c) $K/2$ (d) K^2

8. A mass m is suspended from the two coupled spring connected in series. The force constant for springs are K_1 and K_2. The time period of the suspended mass will be
(a) $T = 2\pi \sqrt{\frac{m}{K_1 - K_2}}$
(b) $T = 2\pi \sqrt{\frac{m K_1 K_2}{K_1 - K_2}}$
(c) $T = 2\pi \sqrt{\frac{m}{K_1 + K_2}}$
(d) $T = 2\pi \sqrt{\frac{m(K_1 + K_2)}{K_1 K_2}}$

9. In the Figure, S_1 and S_2 are identical springs. The oscillation frequency of the mass m is f. If one spring is removed, the frequency will become

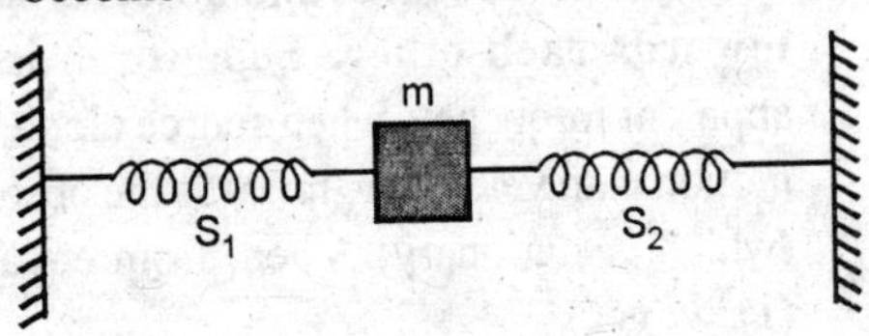

(a) f (b) $f \times 2$
(c) $f \times \sqrt{2}$ (d) $f / \sqrt{2}$

10. A mass m suspended from a massless spring stretches it by a distance. If pulled slightly more and let go, it will oscillate with a time period T where
(a) $T = 2\pi \sqrt{g / y}$ (b) $T = 2\pi \sqrt{my / g}$
(c) $T = 2\pi \sqrt{y / g}$ (d) $T = \sqrt{y / g}$

11. A spring of force constant K is cut into two pieces whose lengths are in the ratio 1 : 2. What is the force constant of the longer piece

(a) $\frac{K}{2}$ (b) $\frac{3K}{2}$

(c) $2K$ (d) $3K$

12. For a body of mass m attached to the spring, the spring factor is given by (ω, the angular frequency)

(a) m/ω^2 (b) $m\omega^2$

(c) $m^2\omega$ (d) $m^2\omega^2$

13. The vertical extension in a light spring by a weight of 1 kg suspended from the wire is 9.8 cm. The period of oscillation is

(a) 20π sec (b) 2π sec

(c) $2\pi/10$ sec (d) 200π sec

14. 1 kg weight is suspended to a weightless spring and it has time period T. If now 4 kg weight is suspended from the same spring, the new time period will be

(a) T (b) $T/2$

(c) $2T$ (d) $4T$

15. When a mass is attached to a spring, its length is increased by 20 cm. It is now further lowered and released. The time period is

(a) $2\pi/7$ sec (b) 7 sec

(c) 2π sec

(d) enough data not available

16. Two masses m_1 and m_2 are suspended together by a massless spring of constant K. When the masses are in equilibrium, m_1 is removed without disturbing the system. Then the angular frequency of oscillation of m_2 is

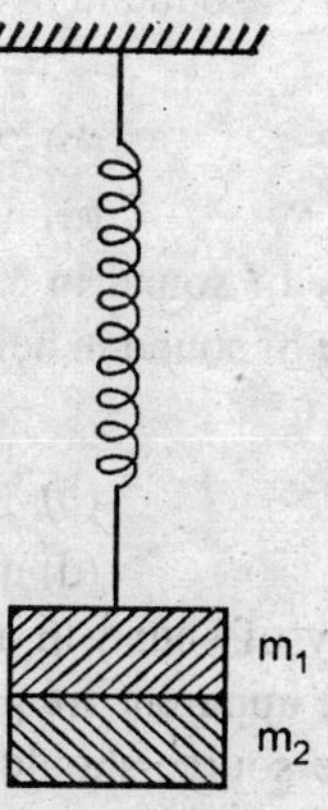

(a) $\sqrt{K/m_1}$

(b) $\sqrt{K/m_2}$

(c) $\sqrt{K/(m_1+m_2)}$

(d) $\sqrt{K/(m_1-m_2)}$

17. A simple spring has length l and force constant K. It is cut into two springs of lengths l_1 and l_2 such that $l_1 = nl_2$ (n = an integer). The force constant of the spring of length l_2 is

(a) $K(1+n)$

(b) $(K/n)(1+n)$

(c) K

(d) $K/(n+1)$

18. A simple spring has length l and force constant K. It is cut into two springs of lengths l_1 and l_2 such that $l_1 = nl_2$ (n = an integer). The force constant of spring of length l_1 is

(a) $K(1+n)$

(b) $(K/n)(1+n)$

(c) K

(d) $K/(n+1)$

19. A mass M, attached to a spring, oscillates with a period of 2 sec. If the mass is increased by 4 kg, the time period increases by one second. Assuming that Hooke's law is obeyed, the initial mass M was

(a) 3.2 kg (b) 1 kg

(c) 2 kg (d) 8 kg

20. A spring of force constant K is cut into three equal parts. The force constant of each part will be

(a) K (b) $3K$

(c) $K/3$ (d) $9K$

21. A spring has force constant k and a mass m is suspended from it. The spring is cut in two parts in the ratio 1 : 3, and the same mass is suspended from the smaller part. If the frequency of oscillation in the first case is n, then the frequency in the second case will be

(a) $2n$ (b) $3n$

(c) $\frac{n}{\sqrt{3}}$ (d) $\frac{\sqrt{3}}{2}n.$

22. A mass M is suspended from a spring of

negligible mass. The spring is pulled a little and then released so that the mass executes simple harmonic oscillation with a time period T. If the mass is increased by m, then the time period becomes $\left(\frac{5}{4}T\right)$ The ratio of $\frac{m}{M}$ is

(a) $\frac{9}{16}$ (b) $\frac{25}{16}$

(c) $\frac{4}{5}$ (d) $\frac{5}{4}$

23. A weightless spring which has a force constant k oscillates with frequency n when a mass m is suspended from it. The spring is cut into two equal halves and a mass 2 m is suspended from it. The frequency of oscillation will now become

(a) n (b) $2n$

(c) $\frac{n}{\sqrt{2}}$ (d) $n(2)^{1/2}$

24. The spring constant from the adjoining combination of spring is

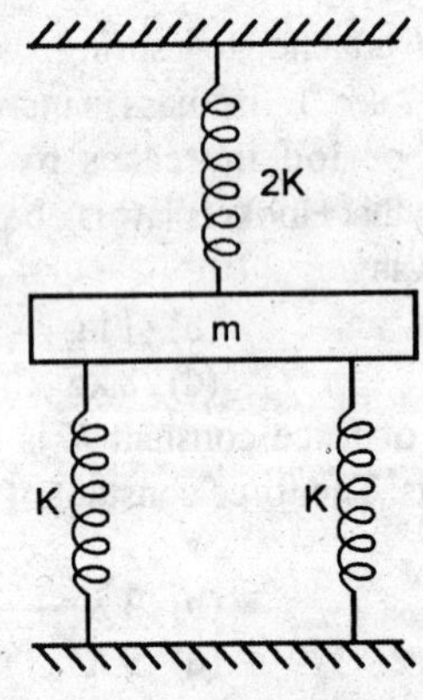

(a) K (b) $2K$

(c) $4K$ (d) $5K/2$

25. The period of oscillation of a mass 1.6 kg suspended from a spring is 2 seconds. If along with it another mass m kg is also suspended, the period of oscillation increases by one second. The mass m will be

(a) 1 kg (b) 2 kg

(c) 1.6 kg (d) 2.6 kg

26. Under similar conditions of temperature and pressure, in which of the following gases the velocity of sound will be the largest?

(a) H_2 (b) N_2

(c) O_2 (d) CO_2

27. The velocity of sound at 0°C is 332 ms^{-1}. At what temperature will it be 664 ms^{-1}?

(a) 1092°C (b) 819°C

(c) 546°C (d) 273°C

28. Velocity of sound in air at the given temperature

(a) decreases with increase in pressure

(b) may increase on decrease with pressure

(c) is independent of the variation in pressure

(d) varies directly as the square root of pressure

29. A person hears the sound of jet aeroplane after it has passed over his head. The angle of the jet plane with the horizontal when the sound appears to be coming vertically downwards is 60°. If the velocity of the sound is c, then the velocity of the jet plane should be

(a) 2 c (b) $\frac{c}{\sqrt{3}}$

(c) $\sqrt{3}\,c$ (d) c

30. A student sees a jet plane flying from east to west. When the jet is seen just above his head, the sound of jet appears to reach him making angle 60° with the horizontal from east. If the velocity of sound is c, then that of the jet plane is

(a) 2 c (b) $\frac{\sqrt{3}}{2}c$

(c) $\frac{2}{\sqrt{3}}c$ (d) $\frac{c}{2}$

31. The velocity of sound in oxygen at NTP is v. The velocity of sound in hydrogen at NTP will be

(a) 4 v (b) $2\sqrt{2}$

(c) 2 v (d) none of the above

32. The velocity of sound in oxygen at NTP is v. The velocity of sound in helium at NTP should be

(a) 4 v (b) $2\sqrt{2}$

(c) 2 v (d) none of the above

33. The velocity of sound in air is 330 ms^{-1}. To increase the apparent frequency of the sound by 50%, the source should move towards the

stationary observer with a velocity equal to
(a) 330 ms^{-1} (b) 220 ms^{-1}
(c) 165 ms^{-1} (d) 110 ms^{-1}

34. When both source and listener approach each other with a velocity equal to half the velocity of sound, the change in frequency of the sound as detected by the listener is
(a) zero (b) 25%
(c) 50% (d) none of the above

35. When both source and listener move in the same direction with a velocity equal to half the velocity of sound, the change in frequency of the sound as detected by the listener is
(a) zero (b) 25%
(c) 50% (d) none of the above

36. In which one of the following cases the jet aeroplane is flying at supersonic speed?
(a) its sound makes 30° with the vertical, when the jet is passing over the head of the listener
(b) its line of sight makes 30° with the vertical when sound appears to be coming vertically downwards
(c) its sound makes 60° with the vertical, when sound appears to be coming vertically downwards
(d) its line of sight makes 60° with the vertical, when sound appears to be coming vertically downwards

37. The wavelength of the sound produced by a source is 0.8 m. If the source moves towards the stationary listener at 32 ms^{-1}, what will be apparent wavelength of the sound? The velocity of sound is 320 ms^{-1}?
(a) 0.32 m (b) 0.40 m
(c) 0.72 m (d) 0.80 m

38. The difference between the apparent frequency of sound that is heard by the stationary listener, when the source approaches and then recedes with the same velocity is 5% of the natural frequency. Given that the velocity of sound is 320 ms^{-1}, the velocity of the source is
(a) 4 ms^{-1} (b) 8 ms^{-1}
(c) 12 ms^{-1} (d) 10 ms^{-1}

39. The pitch of the sound as detected by the observer is independent of
(a) original frequency
(b) the velocity of sound in the medium
(c) relative velocity of source and observer
(d) none of the above factors

40. The velocity of sound is 330 ms^{-1}. To hear a sound with 50% higher frequency, a listener should move towards the stationary source with a velocity equal to
(a) 330 ms^{-1} (b) 220 ms^{-1}
(c) 165 ms^{-1} (d) 110 ms^{-1}

41. Two factories are sounding their sirens at 800 Hz. A man goes from one factory to the other at a speed of 2 ms^{-1}. The velocity of sound is 320 ms^{-1}. The number of beats heard by the person in one second will be
(a) 2 (b) 4
(c) 8 (d) 10

42. A train is approaching the platform with a speed of 4 ms^{-1}. Another train is leaving the platform with the same speed. The velocity of sound is 320 ms^{-1}. If both the trains sound their whistles at frequency 280 hertz, the number of beats heard per second will be
(a) 6 (b) 7
(c) 8 (d) 10

43. A source of sound moves towards a stationary listener. The apparent pitch of the sound is found to be higher than its actual value. This happens because
(a) wavelength of sound waves decreases
(b) wavelength of sound waves increases
(c) the number of waves received by the listener increases
(d) the number of waves received by the listener decreases

44. Radio waves of wavelength λ are sent from a radar towards an aeroplane. If the aeroplane is moving towards the radar station, the wavelength of the radiowaves, received after reflection from the aeroplane will be
(a) λ
(b) more than λ
(c) less than λ
(d) more or less than λ, depending on the speed of aeroplane

45. In case of vibrating string, the frequency of the first overtone is equal to frequency of the
(a) fundamental note (b) first harmonic
(c) second harmonic (d) none of the above

46. A source of sound is moving towards a high wall with a speed of 20 ms^{-1}. The frequency of the sound produced by the source is 400 Hz. If the sound travels at 340 ms^{-1}, what will be the beat frequency heard by a man standing near the wall?
(a) zero (b) 2
(c) 5 (d) 10

47. The wavelength of light received from a galaxy is 10% greater than that received from identical source on the earth. The velocity of the galaxy relative to the earth is
(a) 3×10^8 ms^{-1} (b) 3×10^7 ms^{-1}
(c) 3×10^6 ms^{-1} (d) 3×10^5 ms^{-1}

48. A car sounding its horn at 480 Hz moves toward a high wall at a speed of 20 ms^{-1}. If the speed of sound is 340 ms^{-1}, the frequency of the reflected sound heard by the passenger sitting in the car will be nearest to
(a) 480 Hz (b) 510 Hz
(c) 540 Hz (d) 570 Hz

49. The sound of minimum frequency emitted by a vibrating string is not termed as
(a) first overtone
(b) first harmonic
(c) fundamental tone
(d) none of the above

50. If tension in the string is increased from 1 kN to 4 kN, other factors remaining unchanged, the frequency of the second harmonic will
(a) be halved
(b) remain unchanged
(c) be doubled
(d) become four times

ANSWERS

1	2	3	4	5	6	7	8	9	10
(b)	(d)	(a)	(c)	(a)	(c)	(b)	(d)	(d)	(c)
11	**12**	**13**	**14**	**15**	**16**	**17**	**18**	**19**	**20**
(b)	(b)	(c)	(c)	(a)	(b)	(a)	(b)	(a)	(b)
21	**22**	**23**	**24**	**25**	**26**	**27**	**28**	**29**	**30**
(a)	(a)	(a)	(c)	(b)	(a)	(b)	(c)	(b)	(d)
31	**32**	**33**	**34**	**35**	**36**	**37**	**38**	**39**	**40**
(a)	(b)	(d)	(d)	(a)	(d)	(c)	(b)	(d)	(c)
41	**42**	**43**	**44**	**45**	**46**	**47**	**48**	**49**	**50**
(d)	(b)	(a)	(c)	(c)	(a)	(b)	(c)	(a)	(c)

HINTS / SOLUTIONS

1. $x = 4 \sin \omega t + 3 \sin (\omega t + \pi/3)$

Comparing it with the equations

$x = r_1 \sin \omega t + r_2 \sin (\omega t + \phi)$

2. $y = 3 \sin \omega t + 4 \cos \omega t$

Let $3 = r \cos \theta$ and $4 = r \sin \theta$

then $y = r \cos \theta \sin \omega t + r \sin \theta \cos \omega t$

$= r \sin (\omega t + \theta)$

where $r = \sqrt{3^2 + 4^2} = 5.$

3. $x = a \sin \omega t$ and $y = a \sin \omega t$

So $x = y$. It will be a straight line equally inclined from X and Y-axis.

4. $y = 4 \cos^2\left(\frac{t}{2}\right) \sin (1000\, t)$

$$= 2 \cos \frac{t}{2} \left[\sin\left(1000t + \frac{t}{2}\right) - \sin\left(1000t - \frac{t}{2}\right)\right]$$

It is superposition of three independent harmonic motions.

5. $T = 2\pi\sqrt{\dfrac{M}{K}}$ and $T_1 = 2\pi\sqrt{\dfrac{M+m}{K}}$

or $\dfrac{T_1}{T} = \sqrt{\dfrac{M+m}{M}}$ or $\dfrac{5}{4} = \left(1+\dfrac{m}{M}\right)^{1/2}$

or $\dfrac{m}{M} = \dfrac{25}{16} - 1 = \dfrac{9}{16}$.

6. $v = \dfrac{1}{2\pi}\sqrt{\dfrac{K}{m}}$

and $v_1 = \dfrac{1}{2\pi}\sqrt{\dfrac{K_1}{m}} = \dfrac{1}{2\pi}\sqrt{\dfrac{2K}{m}} = \sqrt{2}\,v$.

7. If k is the spring constant of each splitted part of spring, then $K = \dfrac{k \times k}{k+k} = \dfrac{k}{2}$ or $k = 2K$.

8. The effective spring constant of two springs in series is; $K = \dfrac{k_1 k_2}{k_1 + k_2}$. There period,

$$T = 2\pi\sqrt{\frac{m}{K}} = 2\pi\sqrt{\frac{m(k_1+k_2)}{k_1 k_2}}$$

9. Here effective spring factor, $K = 2k$; Frequency of oscillation, $f = \dfrac{1}{2\pi}\sqrt{\dfrac{2k}{m}}$; when one spring is removed, then spring factor $= k$; New frequency of oscillation

$$f' = \frac{1}{2\pi}\sqrt{\frac{k}{m}} = \frac{f}{\sqrt{2}}.$$

10. Restoring force $= Ky = mg$ or $K = mg/y$

$$T = 2\pi\sqrt{\frac{m}{K}} = 2\pi\sqrt{\frac{m}{mg/y}} = 2\pi\sqrt{\frac{y}{g}}.$$

11 & 12. $T = 2\pi\sqrt{\dfrac{m}{k}}$ or $K = \dfrac{4\pi^2 m}{T^2} = \omega^2 m$.

Let k is the force constant of smaller piece of spring. Then the longer piece is a combination of two smaller pieces in series. Their effective force constant, $k_1 = k/2$. In a bigger spring the smaller pieces are connected in series, so

$$\frac{1}{K} = \frac{1}{k} + \frac{2}{k} = \frac{3}{k} \text{ or } k = 3K.$$

$\therefore \quad k_1 = 3K/2.$

13. $T = 2\pi\sqrt{\dfrac{l}{g}} = 2\pi\sqrt{\dfrac{9.8}{980}} = \dfrac{2\pi}{10}$ s.

14. $T' = 2\pi\sqrt{\dfrac{4}{K}} = 2 \times 2\pi\sqrt{\dfrac{1}{K}} = 2T$.

15. $T = 2\pi\sqrt{\dfrac{l}{g}} = 2\pi\sqrt{\dfrac{20}{980}} = \dfrac{2\pi}{7}s$

16. When both the masses are there, then angular frequency $\omega = \sqrt{K/(m_1+m_2)}$; is there, when m_1, is removed then

$$\omega' = \sqrt{K/m_2} \text{ and } T' = 2\pi\sqrt{\frac{m_2}{K}}$$

17 & 18. Let k be the force constant of spring of length l_2. Since $l_1 = nl_2$, where n is an integer, so the spring made of $(n+1)$ equal parts in length each of length l_2.

$$\therefore \quad \frac{1}{K} = \frac{(n+1)}{k} \text{ or } k = (n+1)K.$$

The spring of length $l_1 = (nl_2)$ will be equivalent to n springs connected in series where spring constant $k' = \dfrac{k}{n} = (n+1)\dfrac{K}{n}$.

19. $T = 2 = 2\pi\sqrt{\dfrac{M}{K}}$

and $2 + 1 = 2\pi\sqrt{\dfrac{M+4}{K}}$

or $3 = 2\pi\sqrt{\dfrac{M+4}{K}}$ so $\dfrac{4}{9} = \dfrac{M}{M+4}$

or $4M + 16 = 9M$ or $M = 16/5 = 3.2$ kg.

20. If k is the force constant of each part, then

$$\frac{1}{K} = \frac{3}{k} \text{ or } k = 3K.$$

21. Let k be the force constant of smaller piece of spring. Then the longer piece is a combination of three smaller pieces in series. Their effective force constant $k_1 = k/3$. In a bigger spring, the smaller pieces are connected in series, so

$$\frac{1}{K} = \frac{1}{k} + \frac{3}{k} = \frac{4}{k} \text{ or } k = 4K$$

$$n = \frac{1}{2\pi}\sqrt{\frac{K}{m}}$$

and $$n' = \frac{1}{2\pi}\sqrt{\frac{K'}{m}} = \frac{1}{2\pi}\sqrt{\frac{4K}{m}} = 2n.$$

22. $T = 2\pi\sqrt{\frac{M}{K}}$ and $\frac{5T}{4} = 2\pi\sqrt{\frac{M+m}{K}}$

or $$\left(\frac{5}{4}\right)^2 = \frac{M+m}{M}$$

or $$25M = 16M + 16m \text{ or } \frac{m}{M} = \frac{9}{16}.$$

23. $$n = \frac{1}{2\pi}\sqrt{\frac{k}{m}};\ n' = \frac{1}{2\pi}\sqrt{\frac{k'}{2m}}$$

$$= \frac{1}{2\pi}\sqrt{\frac{2k}{2m}} \qquad [\because k' = 2m]$$

$\therefore$ $n' = n.$

24. Here all the three springs are connected in parallel to mass m. Hence equivalent spring constant $k = K + K + 2K = 4K$.

25. $$2 = 2\pi\sqrt{\frac{1.6}{k}};(2+1) = 2\pi\sqrt{\frac{1.6+m}{k}}$$

$$\therefore \frac{3^2}{2^2} = \frac{1.6+m}{1.6}.$$ On solving, $m = 2$ kg.

26. Velocity of sound $\propto \left[\frac{1}{\text{density}}\right]^{\frac{1}{2}}$.

27. $$\frac{c_1}{c_2} = -\left[\frac{T_1}{T_2}\right]^{\frac{1}{2}}.$$

Here $c_1 = 332\ \text{ms}^{-1}$, $T_1 = 0°\text{C} = 273$ K,

$c_2 = 664\ \text{ms}^{-1}$. Hence $T_2 = 273 \times \left(\frac{c_2}{c_1}\right)^2$

$= 273 \times 4 = 1092$ K. $= 819°$C.

30. Distance covered by sound to reach the student = (distance covered by jet) × cos 60°.

Hence velocity of jet $= \frac{\text{Velocity of sound}}{2}$

31. Density of oxygen is 16 times that of hydrogen. Hence velocity of sound in hydrogen $= [16]^{1/2} v = 4v$.

32. $$\frac{c_1}{c_2} = \left[\frac{\rho_2}{\rho_1}\right]^{1/2}.$$

Density of helium = 8 × density of oxygen.

33. $v' = 1.5v$. Hence $\frac{c}{c - u_s}v = 1.5v$.

This gives $u_s = c/3$.

34. Here $u_L = u_s = c/2$. Positive sign is to be taken with u_s and –ve sign with u_L. That is $u_L = -c/2$ and $u_s = +c/2$. Therefore $v' = \frac{c + c/2}{c - c/2}v = 3v$.

Hence $\Delta v = 2v = 200\%$.

35. $$v' = \frac{c - u_L}{c - u_s}v$$

Where +ve sign is taken with u_L and u_s if they are in the same direction as c, otherwise –ve sign is taken. Here $u_L = c/2$ and $u_s = c/2$. Positive sign is to be taken with both. Hence $v' = v$. So, there is no change in frequency.

36. Distance covered by sound to reach the person = (distance covered by jet) × cot 60°. Hence velocity of jet = velocity of sound/$\sqrt{3}$.

37. $$v' = \frac{c}{c - u_s}v = \frac{320}{320 - 32}v = \frac{10}{9}v.$$

Hence $$\lambda' = \frac{c}{v'} = \frac{c}{v} \times \frac{v}{v'}$$

$$= \lambda\frac{v}{v'} = 0.8\ \text{m} \times \frac{9}{10} = 0.72\ \text{m}.$$

38. When source approaches $v'_a = \frac{c}{c - u_s}v$.

When source recedes $v'_r = \frac{c}{c + u_r}v$.

Also $(v'_a - v'_r) = \frac{2cu_s}{c^2 - u_s^2}v = \frac{5}{100}v$.

For 5% change in frequency $u_s < c$.

Hence u_s^2 may be neglected as compared to c^2.

Therefore we can write $\frac{2cu_s}{c^2} = \frac{1}{20}$.

40. $v' = 1.5\,v$. Hence $\dfrac{c+u_L}{c}v = 1.5\,v$.

This gives $u_L = c/2$.

41. $v'_a = \dfrac{c+u}{c}v$

$= \dfrac{320+2}{320}\times 800\text{ Hz} = \dfrac{322}{320}\times 800\text{ Hz}$.

$v'_r = \dfrac{c-u}{c}v$

$= \dfrac{320-2}{320}\times 800\text{ Hz} = \dfrac{318}{320}\times 800\text{ Hz}$

$v'_a - v'_r = \dfrac{322-318}{320}\times 800\text{ Hz}$

$= \dfrac{4\times 800}{320}\text{ Hz} = 10\text{ Hz}.$

42. $v'_a = \dfrac{c}{c-u}v = \dfrac{320}{320-4}\times 280 = \dfrac{320}{316}\times 280\text{ Hz}$

$v'_r = \dfrac{c}{c+u}v = \dfrac{320}{320+4}\times 280 = \dfrac{320}{324}\times 280\text{ Hz}$

$v'_a - v'_r = 320\times 280\left[\dfrac{1}{316}-\dfrac{1}{324}\right]\text{ Hz}$

$= \dfrac{320\times 280}{316\times 324}\times 8\text{ Hz} = 7\text{ Hz}.$

44. Here $v' = \dfrac{c}{c-2u}v$. When the aeroplane approaches with velocity u. Hence v' increases and so λ decreases.

46. Here the frequency of the direct waves received by the man near the wall = frequency of the reflected wave. Hence beat frequency is zero.

47. $\dfrac{\Delta\lambda}{\lambda} = \dfrac{v}{c}$. Here $\dfrac{\Delta\lambda}{\lambda} = 10\% = \dfrac{10}{100}$, and $c = 3\times 10^8\text{ ms}^{-1}$, hence $v = 3\times 10^8\text{ ms}^{-1}\times \dfrac{10}{100}$ $= 3\times 10^7\text{ ms}^{-1}$.

48. $v' = \dfrac{c+u}{c-u}v = \dfrac{360}{320}\times 480 = 540.$

49. First over tone is the second harmonic.

50. $v \propto \sqrt{F}$. When tension F increases from 1 kN to 4 kN the frequency is doubled.

UNIT-10

ELECTROSTATICS

INTRODUCTION : ELECTRIC CHARGE

The study of the phenomenon associated with stationary charges is called electrostatics.

1. Electric charge is a fundamental property like Length, Mass, and Time. Electric charges are of two types- Positive and Negative.
2. Every atom as a whole is electrically neutral, i.e. its total +ve charge is equal to total –ve charge. The charge are produced by transfer of atomic electrons. (The smallest unit of charge is either the –ve charge associated with electron or +ve charge with proton) from one body to other.
3. *(i)* A positive ion is an atom from which one or more electrons has been removed, i.e. **positive charge implies the deficiency of electrons.**

   (ii) A negative ion is an atom to which one more electrons has been added, i.e. **negative charge implies excess of electrons.**
4. **Units of Charges:**

   SI system – coulomb

   CGS system – Stat coulomb or esu of charge

   Electro Magnetic Unit – Absolute coulomb (ab coulomb) or emu of charge.
5. **Properties of charges:**

   (i) Like charges repel while opposite charges attract each other.

   (ii) Charge is conserved, i.e. charges are neither created nor destroyed.

   (iii) A charged body attracts a lighter neutral body.

   (iv) Charge is Quantized - Whatever charge exists in nature, it is always an Integer Multiple of Fundamental Charge (e), i.e. $Q = \pm ne$, where n is an integer.

   (v) Charge is relativistically invariant, i.e. charge is not affected by its motion.

COULOMB'S LAW

According to this law the electrostatic force F (either attractive or repulsive) between two stationary point charges q_1 and q_2 in free space (i.e. air or vacuum)

(i) is directly proportional to the product of the two charges.

(ii) is inversely proportional to square of the distance between the charges and

(iii) acts along the line joining the two charges.

Let r be the distance of charges q_2 from q_1 then

$$F \propto \frac{q_1 q_2}{r^2}$$

or $$F = C'\frac{q_1 q_2}{r^2} \qquad ...(1)$$

where C' represents constant of proportionality. Value of constant C depends on two factors.

(a) System of units.

(b) Medium in which charges are placed.

Electrostatic force in SI system between two points charges placed in free space, is

$$F = \frac{1}{4\pi\varepsilon_0}\frac{q_1 q_2}{r^2} \qquad ...(2)$$

When the medium between the two charges is not vacuum but replaced by some dielectric medium having dielectric constant K, then electrostatic force between two charges becomes

$$F' = \frac{1}{4\pi\varepsilon_0 K}\frac{q_1 q_2}{r^2}$$

$$= \frac{1}{4\pi\varepsilon}\frac{q_1 q_2}{r^2} \qquad ...(3)$$

where $\varepsilon = \varepsilon_0 K$ = permittivity of dielectric medium.

ELECTRIC FIELD

The region in which a charged particle placed at any point experiences a force, is called electric field. Electric field is measured in terms of electric field intensity $(\vec{E})$. The electric field intensity $\vec{E}$ at any point in an electric field is equal to force experienced by unit positive test charge q_0 placed at that point i.e.

$$\vec{E} = \frac{\vec{F}}{q_0}$$

ELECTRIC LINES OF FORCE

According to Faraday an electric field can be represented by means of electric lines of forces which help us to give both the magnitude and direction of electric field Intensity at any point in the following way –

(i) Electric lines of force is an imaginary line in the electric field, the tangent at any point of which gives the direction of electric field at that point.

(ii) The magnitude of Electric field intensity at any point is measured by the number of electric lines of force passing normally through unit area around that point.

IMPORTANT PROPERTIES OF LINES OF FORCE

(i) Electric lines of force diverge from a + ve charge and converge at a – ve charge.

(ii) Electric lines of forces never cross each other, otherwise there will be two direction of electric field at the point of intersection which is not possible.

(iii) Electric lines of force contract lengthwise but expand laterally.

CALCULATION OF ELECTRIC FIELD INTENSITY

In order to calculate the electric field intensity due to a point charge q, at some point P lying at a distance r we place a test charge q_0 at the point P.

According to coulomb's law, force on charge q_0 due to electric field produced by charge q, is

$$F = \frac{1}{4\pi\varepsilon}\frac{qq_0}{r^2};$$

$$\therefore \quad E = \frac{F}{q_0} = \frac{1}{4\pi\varepsilon}\frac{q}{r^2}$$

ELECTRIC POTENTIAL

The electric potential at any point in an electric field is defined as the works done on the system against the electric force in moving an unit positive test charge from infinity (i.e. from beyond the electric field) to that point. If W is the work done in bringing the charge q_0 from infinity to given point, then potential at that point:

$$V = \frac{W}{q_0} \qquad \ldots(7)$$

$$\text{Now,} \quad W = \int dw = \int_{\infty}^{R} \vec{F}.\vec{dr} = \int_{\infty}^{R} F\,dr \cos 180°$$

$$= \int_{\infty}^{R} q_0\,E dr = \int_{\infty}^{R} q_0 \frac{1}{4\pi\varepsilon_0}\frac{q}{r^2}\,dr$$

$$= \frac{q_0 q}{4\pi\varepsilon_0}\int_{\infty}^{R} -\frac{dr}{r^2} = \frac{qq_0}{4\pi\varepsilon_0}\frac{1}{R}$$

$$\therefore \quad V = \frac{W}{q_0} = \frac{1}{4\pi\varepsilon_0}\frac{q}{R}$$

ELECTRIC POTENTIAL DIFFERENCE

An electric potential difference always exists between two points in an electric field, if work is done against or by the electric force is moving a unit positive test charge from one point to other.

ELECTRIC POTENTIAL ENERGY

The electric potential energy of a group of point charge is defined as the work done on the system is assembling the group of charge from the situation when they were at infinite distances from each other i.e. their initial electrical potential energy = 0 or initially there is no interaction between them. Electric potential energy of any point charges q_1 and q_2 separated by a distance r_{12} is

$$U_{12} = \frac{1}{4\pi\varepsilon}\frac{q_1 q_2}{r_{12}} \quad ...(10)$$

ELECTRIC DIPOLE

Two equal, small and opposite charges separated by a very small distance $2l$ constitute an electric dipole.

(i) Charge $+q$ and $-q$ are called as +ve and –ve poles of electric dipole.

(ii) The line joining the two charges of dipole is called as dipole axis.

(iii) Every electric dipole has got associated with it a physical quantity, called as electric dipole moment.

(iv) Electric dipole moment is a vector quantity, represented by $\vec{p}$ having magnitude equal to $q\,2l$ and direction from $-q$ to $+q$

$$\vec{p} = q\,2\vec{l} \quad ...(11)$$

CALCULATION OF ELECTRIC FIELD AND POTENTIAL

(a) At some axial point:

The electric field at distance d from the centre O of dipole is

$$E = E_1 - E_2$$

$$= \frac{q}{4\pi\varepsilon}\left[\frac{1}{(d-l)^2} - \frac{1}{(d+l)^2}\right]$$

$$= \frac{1}{4\pi\varepsilon}\frac{2pd}{(d^2-l^2)^2}$$

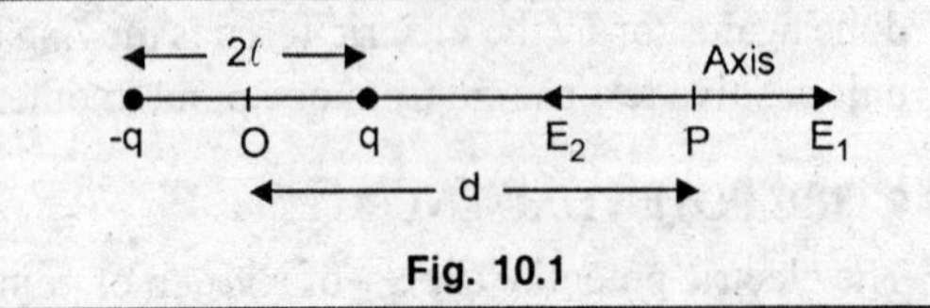

Fig. 10.1

For short dipole, $d >> l$.

Hence,

$$E_{\text{axial}} = \frac{1}{4\pi\varepsilon}\frac{2p}{d^3} \quad ...(12)$$

along the direction of $\vec{p}$

Electric potential at P,

$$V = \frac{q}{4\pi\varepsilon}\left[\frac{1}{d-l} - \frac{1}{d+l}\right]$$

$$= \frac{1}{4\pi\varepsilon}\frac{2ql}{(d^2-l^2)}$$

$$= \frac{1}{4\pi\varepsilon}\frac{p}{(d^2-l^2)}$$

For short dipole,

$$V = \frac{1}{4\pi\varepsilon}\frac{p}{d^2} \quad ...(13)$$

(b) At some bisectorial point:

$$\left|\vec{E}_1\right| = \left|\vec{E}_2\right| = \frac{1}{4\pi\varepsilon}\frac{q}{(d^2+l^2)}$$

$$E = E_1\cos\theta + E_2\cos\theta$$

$$= 2E_1\cos\theta$$

$$= 2\frac{1}{4\pi\varepsilon}\frac{q}{(d^2+l^2)} \times \frac{\ell}{\sqrt{(d^2+l^2)}}$$

$$= \frac{1}{4\pi\varepsilon}\frac{P}{(d^2+l^2)^{3/2}}$$

For short dipole, $d >> l$

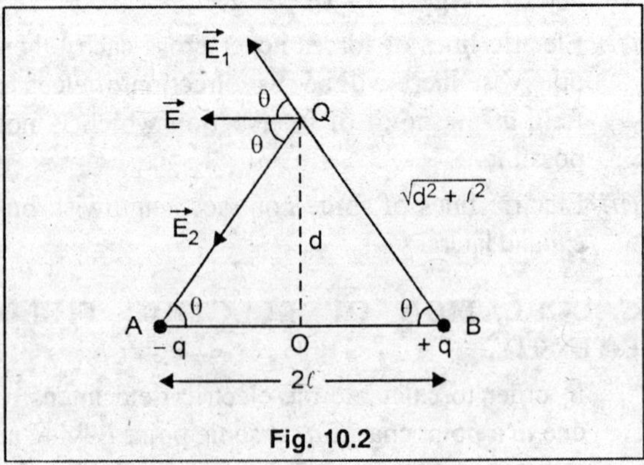

Fig. 10.2

Hence,

$$E_{\text{Bisector}} = \frac{1}{4\pi\varepsilon}\frac{P}{d^3} \quad ...(14)$$

opposite to direction of $\vec{p}$

Electric potential at Q,

$$V = \frac{1}{4\pi\varepsilon}\left[\frac{q}{BQ} - \frac{q}{AQ}\right]$$

But $AQ = BQ = \sqrt{(d^2 + l^2)}$

Hence $V = 0$ ...(15)

TORQUE ACTING ON AN ELECTRIC DIPOLE PLACED IN AN UNIFORM ELECTRIC FIELD

(i) An electric field whose magnitude as well as direction are same at every point is called uniform electric field. It is represented by electric lines of forces which are parallel, equidistant and pointing in same direction.

(ii) When an electric dipole, having dipole moment p ($= q.2l$) is placed in an uniform electric field E, with its axis making an angle θ with respect to the direction of electric field, then equal, parallel and opposite forces ($+q\vec{E}$ and $-q\vec{E}$) act on its two poles. As these forces also act along different lines of action, hence they form a force-couple. Due to this force-couple, dipole rotates and tries to align itself along the direction of electric field.

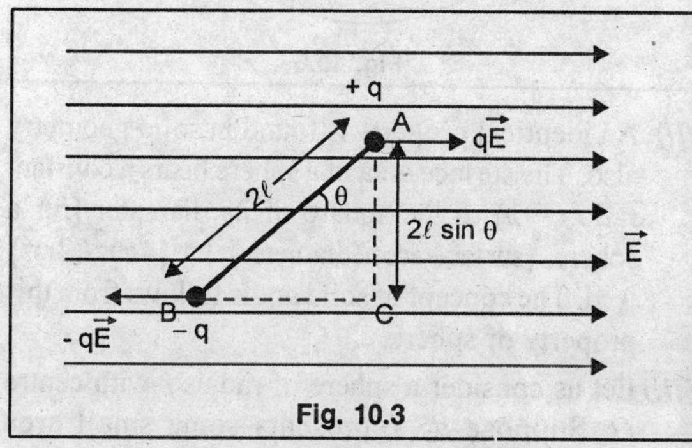

Fig. 10.3

(iii) Torque acting on electric dipole

$$\tau = \text{moment of force-couple}$$
$$= \text{force} \times \perp \text{distance}$$
$$= qE \times AC$$
$$= qE \times 2l \sin\theta$$
$$= (q.2l)\, E \sin\theta$$
$$= pE \sin\theta$$

Vector form:

$$\vec{\tau} = \vec{P} \times \vec{E}$$

WORK DONE IN ROTATING AN ELECTRIC DIPOLE IN AN UNIFORM ELECTRIC FIELD

Torque acting on an electric dipole when placed in an uniform electric field E, with its axis making an angle θ w.r.t. direction of $\vec{E}$, is

$$\tau = \text{pE} \sin\theta$$

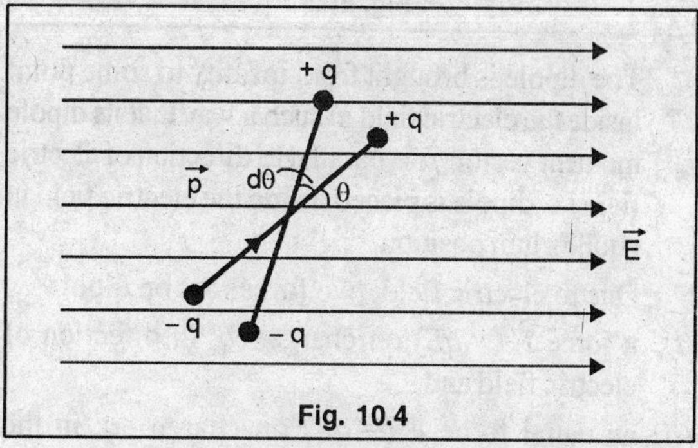

Fig. 10.4

Due to this torque, electric dipole has got a tendency to rotate in clockwise direction. If we want to rotate the electric dipole further through an angle $d\theta$, then work done on electric dipole (as it is being rotated against its natural tendency) is

$$dW = \tau.\, d\theta$$
$$= pE \sin\theta\, d\theta.$$

Hence total work done on electric dipole in rotating it through an angle θ from its equilibrium position (when electric dipole moment vector $\vec{p}$ is along the direction of electric field $\vec{E}$) is

$$W = \int dW$$
$$= \int_0^\theta pE \sin d\theta$$
$$= -[pE\cos\theta]_0^\theta$$
$$= pE(1 - \cos\theta)$$

ELECTRIC POTENTIAL ENERGY OF AN ELECTRIC DIPOLE IN AN ELECTRIC FIELD

The work done in bringing the dipole from infinity to some point inside the electric field is called the electric potential energy of electric dipole.

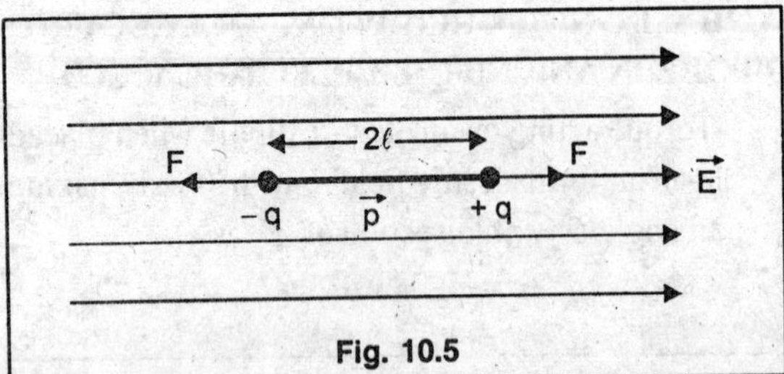

Fig. 10.5

The dipole is brought from infinity to some point inside the electric field in such a way that its dipole moment vector $\vec{p}$ is parallel to direction of electric field i.e. dipole is placed inside the electric field in equilibrium position.

Due to electric field, two forces act on dipole

(i) a force F (= qE) on charge $+q$, in direction of electric field and

(ii) an equal force F (= qE) on charge $-q$, in the opposite direction.

Hence for bringing the dipole in the field.

(i) Work is done by the system in case of charge $-q$ but

(ii) Work is done on the system in case of charge $+q$

As charge $-q$ covers distance $2l$ more than the charge q, therefore

$$W_{BY} > W_{ON}$$

i.e. Net work done in bringing the dipole from infinity to a point inside the electric field $= -qE.2l = -pE.$

This work is equal to the potential energy U_0 of the electric dipole when it is placed in electric field parallel to it.

i.e. $\quad U_0 = -pE$

In this position dipole is in stable equilibrium. Now if we rotate the dipole in the field through an angle θ, then work done on electric dipole is

$$W = pE(1 - \cos\theta).$$

Hence electric potential energy of dipole in θ position is

$$\begin{aligned} U_\theta &= U_0 + W \\ &= -pE + pE(1 - \cos\theta) \\ &= -pE\cos\theta \\ &= -\vec{p}.\vec{E}. \end{aligned}$$

GAUSS'S THEOREM

Solid angle:

(i) In plane geometry we study an important property that the circumference of a circle bears a constant ratio (= π) to its diameter. This property is used to define plane angle in terms of radian. The angle (in radian) subtended by an arc of length dl of a circle of radius r at its centre is given by

$$d\theta = \frac{dl}{r}$$

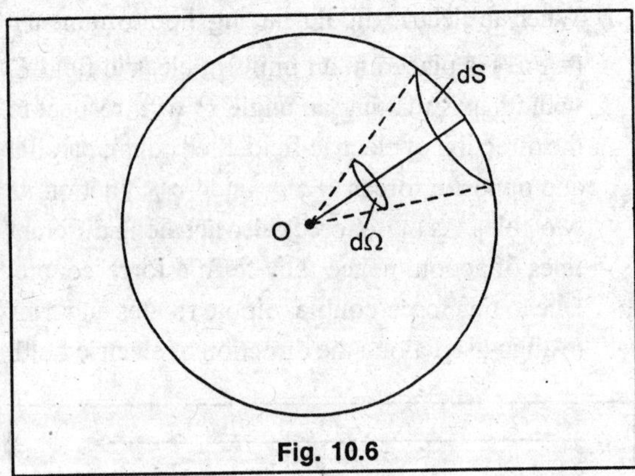

Fig. 10.6

(ii) An identical property is found in solid geometry also. The surface area of a sphere bears a constant ratio (= π) to the square of its diameter [for a sphere, {surface area/(diameter)^2} = {$4\pi r^2/(2r)^2$} = π]. The concept of solid angle follows from this property of sphere.

(iii) Let us consider a sphere of radius r with centre O. Suppose dS represents some small area element of the spherical surface. If all the points on the circumference of the area element are joined to the centre O, then solid angle $d\Omega$ subtended by the area element dS at the centre of the sphere is defined as

$$d\Omega = \frac{dS}{r^2} \qquad \text{...(1)}$$

(iv) The unit of solid angle is **steradian** and is a dimensionless quantity.

Electric Flux:

(i) Flux is the property of any vector field. The surface integral of a vector field over a given surface is also known as flux of the vector field through that surface. The word flux means flow of some kind and is adopted from hydrodynamics.

(ii) It can be easily seen that the volume, τ, of a liquid flowing per unit time out from a given cross-section S is just equal to the surface integral of the vector field defined by the velocity vector $\vec{v}$.

i.e. $$\tau = \int_S \vec{v}.d\vec{S} \qquad ...(2)$$

(iii) For vector fields other than the velocity vector field, there is nothing actually flowing i.e. for electric and magnetic fields, we cannot visualize anything actually flowing. However, the term flux is used for these vector fields also and is taken to mean the outward flow of the concerned vector field.

(iv) **The electric flux associated with electric field is a measure of total number of lines of forces passing normally through the surface held in the electric field.** It is represented by ϕ.

(v) Let us consider a small elementary area dS of a closed surface S. Suppose $\vec{E}$ be the electric field at the elementary area and θ be the angle between the electric field and vector area $d\vec{S}$. Then, electric flux through the area element $d\vec{S}$ is given by

$$d\phi = \vec{E}.d\vec{S} = (E\cos\theta)\, dS \qquad ...(3)$$

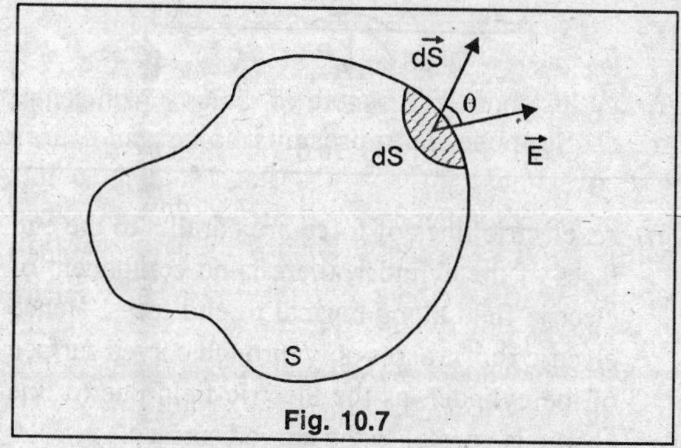

Fig. 10.7

(vi) Now, $E\cos\theta$ is the normal component of the electric field (i.e. component of the electric field along normal to the area element) and is represented by E_n. Hence we can also write equation (3) as

$$\begin{aligned} d\phi &= \vec{E}.d\vec{S} \\ &= (E\cos\theta)\, dS \\ &= E_n dS \qquad ...(4) \end{aligned}$$

(vii) Hence, electric flux through a small elementary area is equal to the product of the small area element and the normal component of the electric field. The electric flux through the whole surface S can be found by integrating above equation over the whole surface S i.e. total electric flux through the surface S is given by

$$\phi = \int_S \vec{E}.d\vec{S} = \int_S E_n\, dS \qquad ...(5)$$

i.e. **the electric flux linked with a surface in an electric field may be defined mathematically as the surface integral of the electric field over that surface.**

Gauss's theorem:

(i) **According to Gauss's theorem, total electric flux through a closed surface enclosing a charge is equal to $1/\varepsilon_0$ times the magnitude of the charge enclosed.** (ε_0 is the permittivity of free space). If ϕ is the total electric flux through a closed surface enclosing a charge q, then

$$\phi = \frac{q}{\varepsilon_0}$$

(ii) Suppose S represents any closed surface enclosing a charge q. Let $d\vec{S}$ be an elementary area located at a distance r from the charge q. If $\vec{E}$ is the electric field at the area element, then electric flux linked with the area element is given by

$$d\phi = \vec{E}.d\vec{S}$$

and the total electric flux through the closed surface S is expressed as

$$\phi = \int_S \vec{E}.d\vec{S}$$

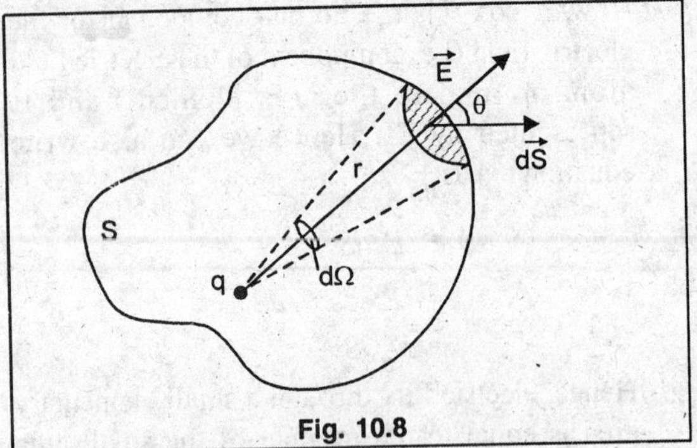

Fig. 10.8

Hence, Gauss's theorem may also be written as

$$\int_s \vec{E}.d\vec{S} = \frac{q}{\varepsilon_0} \quad ...(6)$$

(iii) **Proof:** If θ be the angle between the directions of $\vec{E}$ and $d\vec{S}$, then

$$\int_s \vec{E}.d\vec{S} = \int_s E\, dS \cos\theta$$

The magnitude of the electric field due to charge q at the area element is given by

$$E = \frac{1}{4\pi\varepsilon_0}\frac{q}{r^2}$$

Therefore,

$$\int_s \vec{E}.d\vec{S} = \int_s \frac{1}{4\pi\varepsilon_0}\frac{q}{r^2} dS \cos\theta$$

$$= \frac{q}{4\pi\varepsilon_0}\int_s \frac{dS\cos\theta}{r^2}$$

Using equation

$$\int_s \frac{dS\cos\theta}{r^2} = 4\pi$$

we get

$$\int_s \vec{E}.d\vec{S} = \frac{q}{4\pi\varepsilon_0} \times 4\pi = \frac{q}{\varepsilon_0}$$

Mathematically, Gauss's theorem can also be stated as follows:

If a charge is enclosed in a close surface, then surface integral of the electric field over a closed surface is equal to $1/\varepsilon_0$ times the charge enclosed.

(iv) Gauss's theorem is very helpful in calculating electric field in those cases where electric field is symmetrical around the source producing it. Electric field can be calculated very easily by the clever choice of a closed surface that encloses the source charge. Such a surface is called Gaussian surface. An imaginary closed surface enclosing a charge is called the Gaussian surface of that charge. This surface should pass through the point where electric field is to be calculated and must have a shape according to the symmetry of source.

APPLICATIONS OF GAUSS'S THEOREM

(A) Electric field due to a line charge

(i) Suppose a thin infinitely long straight line charge having a uniform charge density λ at all points on the line. It follows from the symmetry of the problem that electric field due to line charge at a distance r in any plane at right angles to the line charge is of same magnitude and is directed radially outward. Hence, to calculate electric field due to line charge at point P distant r from it, a cylinder of radius r and length l with the line charge as its axis may be treated as the Gaussian surface.

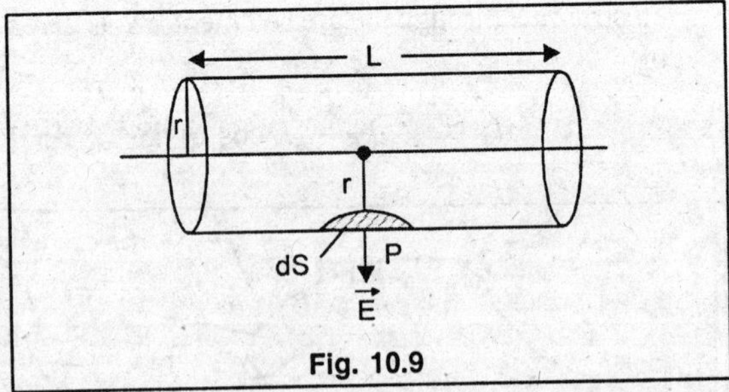

Fig. 10.9

(ii) As electric lines of force are parallel to the end faces of the cylinder, there is no component of electric field along normal to end faces. Hence electric flux crosses only through curved surface of the cylinder, as the electric field due to line charge is normal to the curved surface.

(iii) Let E be magnitude of electric field at point P, then electric flux through the Gaussian surface is given by

$$\phi = \int \vec{E}.d\vec{S} = \int E.dS$$

$$= E\int dS = E.2\pi rl$$

where $2\pi rl$ = area of the curved surface of a cylinder of radius r and length l.

(iv) Charge enclosed by the Gaussian surface, $q = \lambda l$. According to Gauss's theorem, we have

$$\phi = \frac{q}{\varepsilon_0}$$

or $$2\pi rlE = \frac{\lambda l}{\varepsilon_0}$$

$\therefore$ $$E = \frac{\lambda}{2\pi\varepsilon_0 r} \quad \text{...(1)}$$

(B) Electric field due to a uniformly charged cylinder

(i) Suppose a cylinder of radius a has a positive charge uniformly distributed all over its surface with surface charge density σ. Symmetry considerations, one again, point out that electric field is radial. The magnitude of electric field is constant at all the points which are at the same distance r from the axis of the cylinder. The proper Gaussian surface of the problem is a right cylinder coaxial with the given charged cylinder.

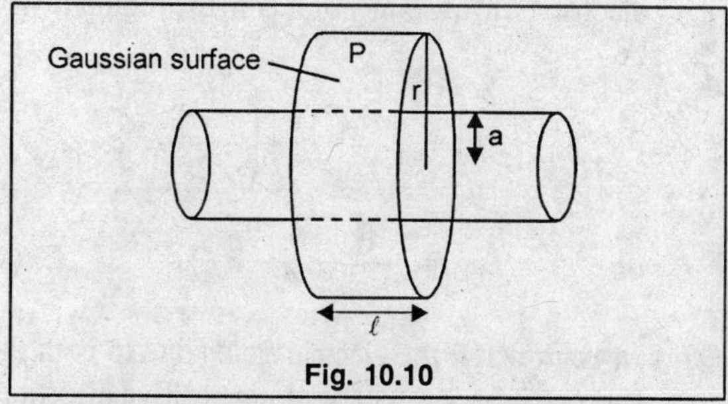

Fig. 10.10

(ii) In this problem also, the contribution to the surface integral will be only due to curved surface of the cylinder as $\vec{E}$ is normal to it. The ends will not contribute to the surface integral because $\vec{E}$ is parallel to them. Hence flux through the Gaussian surface is $E(2\pi rl)$. Because the charge enclosed by the Gaussian surface is $\sigma\,(2\pi al)$, hence according to Gauss's theorem

$$E(2\pi rl) = \frac{\sigma(2\pi al)}{\varepsilon_0}$$

or $$E = \frac{\sigma a}{\varepsilon_0 r} \quad \text{...(2)}$$

(iii) The charge per unit length of the charged cylinder is, obviously,

$$\sigma(2\pi a \times 1) = 2\pi a\sigma$$

If we represent this by λ, we get

$$\lambda = 2\pi a\sigma$$

or $$a\sigma = \frac{\lambda}{2\pi} \quad \text{...(3)}$$

From equation (2) and (3), we get

$$E = \frac{\lambda}{2\pi\varepsilon_0 r} \quad \text{...(4)}$$

This is the same as the formula for the field around a line of charge. Hence **electric field outside a charged cylinder is the same as though the charge were concentrated along axis.** The field inside the charged cylinder is zero because there is no charge inside the cylinder.

(C) Electric field due to an infinite plane sheet of charge

(i) Suppose a thin plane infinite sheet of charge, having a uniform surface charge density σ on both sides (In a thin sheet of charge, the same charge shows up on the two sides).

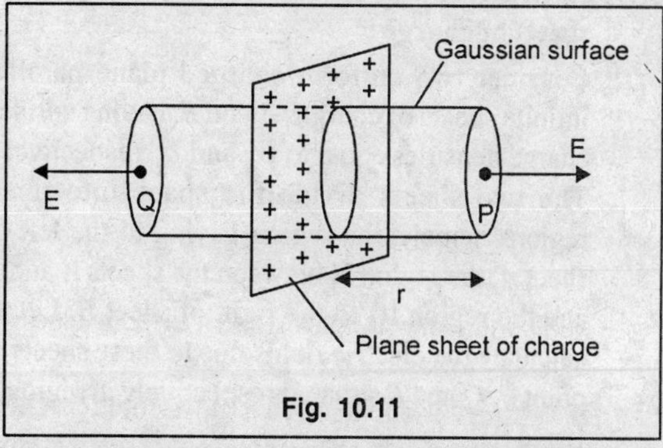

Fig. 10.11

Symmetry of the problem tells us that electric field must be perpendicular to the plane sheet of charge and directed outward. Further, electric fields at the points lying on opposite sides of sheet and equidistant from it, must be equal and opposite.

(ii) To find electric field due to the plane sheet of charge at any point P distant r from it, choose a cylinder of area of cross-section A through the point P as the Gaussian surface. Because electric lines of forces are parallel to the curved surface of the cylinder, the flux due to the electric field of the plane sheet of charge passes only through the two circular caps of the cylinder. If E is the magnitude of electric field at point P, then electric flux crossing through the Gaussian surface is given by

$$\phi = \int_S \vec{E}.d\vec{S}$$

$$= \int_{S_1} \vec{E}.d\vec{S} + \int_{S_2} \vec{E}.d\vec{S}$$

where S_1 and S_2 are the surface areas of the left and right circular ends of the cylinder.

If $S_1 = S_2 = A$, then

$$\phi = EA + EA = 2\,EA$$

(iii) As charge enclosed by the Gaussian surface, $q = \sigma A$, hence according to Gauss's theorem, we get

$$2EA = \frac{\sigma A}{\varepsilon_0}$$

or $$E = \frac{\sigma}{2\varepsilon_0} \qquad ...(5)$$

(D) Electric field due to two infinite plane parallel sheets of charge

(i) Consider two uniform charged plane parallel infinite sheets of charges A and B, having surface charge densities equal to σ_A and σ_B respectively. The two sheets divide the space into three regions namely, the region I lying to the left of sheet A, the region II between the sheets A and B and the region III to the right of sheet B. Let us calculate the electric fields due to these sheets at point P, Q and R situated respectively in region I, II and III.

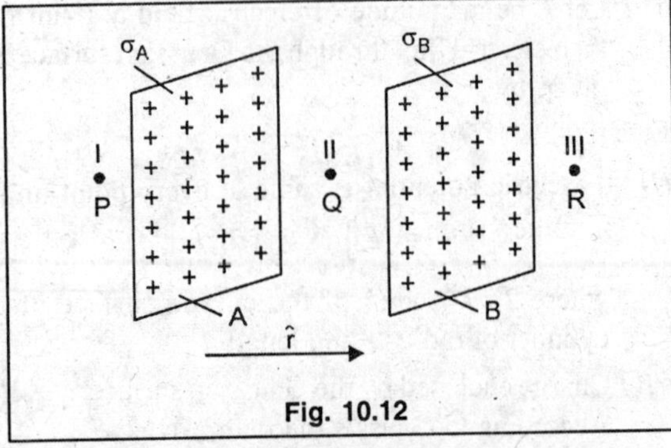

Fig. 10.12

(ii) In region I, electric fields due to both the sheets of charge will be from right to left (opposite to the direction; in which distances are measured as positive). Because, electric field due to a sheet of charge is given by equation (5), the electric field due to sheets A and B at some point P in the region I will be

$$\vec{E}_P = \left(-\frac{\sigma_A}{2\varepsilon_0}\hat{r}\right) + \left(-\frac{\sigma_B}{2\varepsilon_0}\hat{r}\right)$$

where $\hat{r}$ is an unit vector ⊥ to the sheets and directed towards R.H.S.

$$\therefore \quad \vec{E}_P = -\frac{1}{2\varepsilon_0}(\sigma_A + \sigma_B)\hat{r} \qquad ...(7)$$

(iii) **In region II,** electric field due to sheet of charge A will be from left to right (along positive direction) and that due to sheet of charge B will be from right to left (along negative direction). Hence, electric field at some point Q in the region II will be

$$\vec{E}_Q = \left(\frac{\sigma_A}{2\varepsilon_0}\hat{r}\right) + \left(-\frac{\sigma_B}{2\varepsilon_0}\hat{r}\right)$$

or $$\vec{E}_Q = \frac{1}{2\varepsilon_0}(\sigma_A - \sigma_B)\hat{r} \qquad ...(8)$$

(iv) **In region III,** the electric fields due to both the sheets of charges will be along positive direction. Therefore, electric field at some point R in the region III will be

$$\vec{E}_R = \left(\frac{\sigma_A}{2\varepsilon_0}\hat{r}\right) + \left(\frac{\sigma_B}{2\varepsilon_0}\hat{r}\right)$$

or, $$\vec{E}_A = \frac{1}{2\varepsilon_0}(\sigma_A + \sigma_B)\hat{r} \quad ...(9)$$

EQUIPOTENTIAL SURFACE

(i) If electric potential is same at every point of a surface, then such a surface is called as equipotential surface.

(ii) If a charge q is moved on such a surface from one point to other, then work done is equal to zero.

$$W = q\,\Delta V = 0$$

[$\because \Delta V = 0$ on E.P. surface]

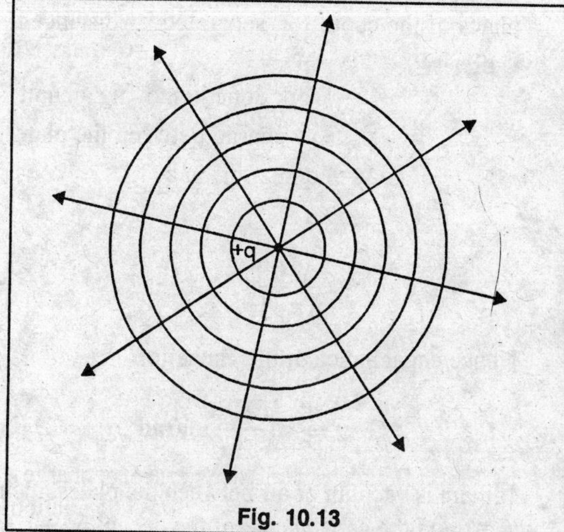

Fig. 10.13

(iii) Electric lines of forces are perpendicular to E.P. surface at its every point, otherwise there will be a component of electric field parallel to surface and work done in moving a charge on the surface will not be equal to zero.

(iv) Equipotential surfaces of a point charge will be infinite number of concentric spherical surfaces, all having their centres located at the point charge.

CAPACITANCE OF CONDUCTOR

The potential of a conductor gets raised when it is given a charge. The quantity of charge given to a conductor is found to be directly proportional to the potential raised by it. If q is the charge given to conductor and V is potential raised due to it, then

$$q \propto V$$

or $$q = CV$$

where C is a constant, known as capacitance of the conductor. From above equation, we get

$$C = q/V \quad ...(1)$$

If $V = 1$, then

$$C = q$$

Hence capacitance of a conductor is just equal to charge required to raise its potential by unity.

Unit of capacitance in SI system

$$= \frac{\text{Unit of charge}}{\text{Unit of potential}}$$

$$= \frac{\text{Coulomb}}{\text{Volt}}$$

$$= \text{Farad}$$

Dimensions of capacitance

$$[C] = \frac{[q]}{[V]} = \frac{[q]}{[W/q]}$$

$$= \frac{[q][q]}{[W]} = \frac{[A^2T^2]}{[ML^2T^{-2}]}$$

$$= [M^{-1}L^{-2}T^4A^2]$$

CAPACITOR

An arrangement which can store sufficient quantity of charge is called a capacitor.

If q is the charge given to a conductor and V is the potential raised due to it, then capacity of conductor is

$$C = \frac{q}{V}$$

Capacitance of a capacitor: If $+q$ and $-q$ are the charges on the two plates of a capacitor and V is the potential difference between them, then capacitance of the capacitor

$$C = \frac{q}{V}$$

If $V = 1$, then $C = q$ i.e. capacitance of a capacitor is defined as the charge required to be given to a plates of the capacitor, to produce unit potential difference between its plates.

CAPACITANCE OF A PARALLEL – PLATE CAPACITOR

Case I: When it is filled completely with a dielectric medium

A parallel plate capacitor consists of two long, plane, metallic plates which are placed parallel to each other at a small distance apart. Usually, some dielectric or insulating substance (instead of air) is filled between the plates.

Let A metre^2 be the area of each plate, and d be the distance between two plates. Let K be the dielectric constant of the insulating medium filled between the plates.

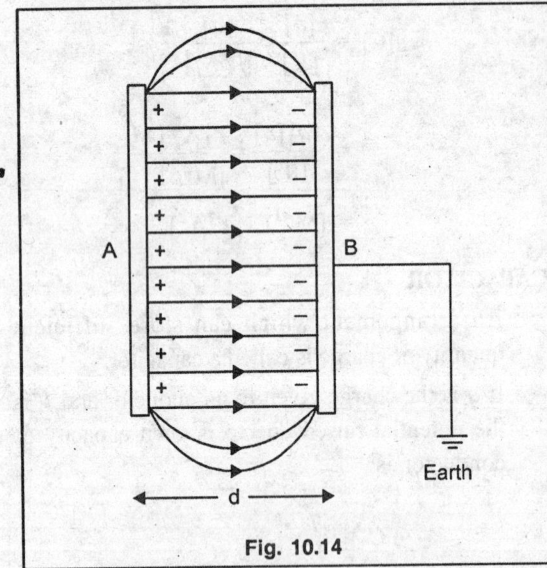

Fig. 10.14

When charge $+q$ coulomb is given to the plate A of the capacitor, charge $-q$ coulomb is induced on the front surface of other plate B and $+q$ coulomb on the back surface. Since the plate B is earthed, charge $+q$ coulomb on the back surface goes to earth. As a result of this, two plates will have equal and opposite charges and electric field produced between them will be uniform everywhere except near the edges. Moreover, the surface of each plate is an equipotential surface, hence electric field will also be perpendicular to the plates.

If σ represents the surface density of charge on each plate ($=q/A$), then intensity of electric field at any point between two oppositely charged plates is

$$E = \frac{\sigma}{K\varepsilon_0} = \frac{q}{K\varepsilon_0 A} \quad \text{...(1)}$$

Hence potential difference V between the two plates of the capacitor, separated by distance d, is given by

V = Work done in moving an unit +ve charge between the plates

= Force × distance

$= Ed$

$$= \frac{qd}{K\varepsilon_0 A}$$

Hence capacitance of the capacitor

$$C = \frac{q}{V} = \frac{K\varepsilon_0 A}{d} \text{ farad} \quad \text{...(2)}$$

If there is vacuum or air between the plates, then $K=1$ and the capacitance of the capacitor

$$C_0 = \frac{\varepsilon_0 A}{d} \text{ farad} \quad \text{...(3)}$$

Hence from equation (2) and (3),

$$\frac{C}{C_0} = K \quad \text{...(4)}$$

As K is always greater than one hence by filling a dielectric medium between the plates, capacitance of the capacitor is increased K times.

Case II: When capacitance is filled partially with a dielectric medium

Suppose a dielectric slab of thickness t and dielectric constant K is placed between the plates of capacitor. Now, the thickness of air space will be $(d-t)$.

Intensity of electric field in air space, is

$$E_0 = \frac{q}{\varepsilon_0 A}$$

and that in dielectric slab is

$$E = \frac{q}{K\varepsilon_0 A}$$

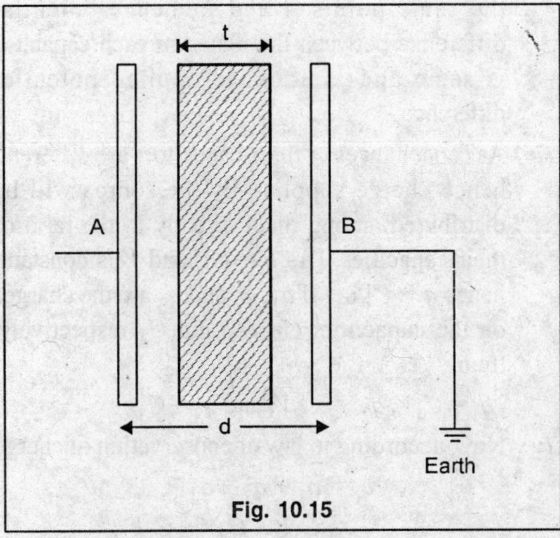

Fig. 10.15

Hence potential difference V between the plates of capacitor, is

$$V = W_{\text{air}} + W_{\text{Dielectric}}$$

$$= E_0 (d-t) + E.t$$

$$= \frac{q}{\varepsilon_0 A}(d-t) + \frac{q}{K\varepsilon_0 A}t$$

$$= \frac{q}{\varepsilon_0 A}\left[(d-t) + \frac{t}{K}\right]$$

$$= \frac{q}{\varepsilon_0 A}\left[d - t\left\{1 - \left(\frac{1}{k}\right)\right\}\right]$$

Hence capacitance of a capacitor filled partially with a dielectric, is given by

$$\boldsymbol{C_{pd} = \frac{q}{V} = \frac{\varepsilon_0 A}{d - t\ [1-(1/K)]}} \quad \ldots(1)$$

COMBINATIONS OF CAPACITORS

(I) Series Combination

(i) In this case, the first plate of first capacitor is connected to +ve terminal of battery, the second plate is connected to first plate of the second capacitor, the second plate of the second capacitor and so on, the second plate of the last capacitor is connected to earth.

(ii) When charge $+q$ is given to the first plate of the first capacitor C_1, charge $-q$ is induced on the inner surface of the second plate of C_1 and its free charge $+q$ flows to the first plate of second capacitor C_2. Thus the first plate of each capacitor has a charge $+q$ while the second plate has a charge $-q$. i.e. charge is same on each capacitor and is equal to charge supplied by the source.

(iii) As charge is same on each capacitor and capacities of different capacitors are different, hence potential difference applied between the points A and B is distributed among three capacitors reciprocally in the ratio of their capacities. [As $V = q/C$ and q is constant, hence $V \propto 1/C$] i.e. if V_1, V_2 and V_3 are the potential difference between the plates of capacitors C_1, C_2 and C_3 respectively, then

$$V_1 = \frac{q}{C_1}, V_2 = \frac{q}{C_2}, V_3 = \frac{q}{C_3} \quad \ldots(1)$$

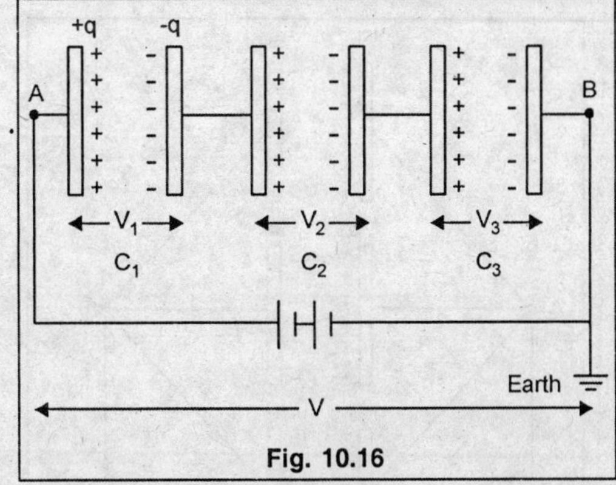

Fig. 10.16

(iv) If total potential difference between the points A and B is V, then according to law of conservation of energy,

$$V = V_1 + V_2 + V_3$$

$$= \frac{q}{C_1} + \frac{q}{C_2} + \frac{q}{C_3} \quad \ldots(2)$$

(v) If the combination of three capacitors is supposed to be replaced by a single capacitor having capacitance C, then it will be equivalent to the combination if on giving same charge q, the potential difference between its plates becomes V i.e. we can write

$$V = \frac{q}{C} \quad ...(3)$$

Hence from equation (2) and (3)

$$\frac{q}{C} = q\left[\frac{1}{C_1}+\frac{1}{C_2}+\frac{1}{C_3}\right]$$

or
$$\frac{1}{C} = \frac{1}{C_1}+\frac{1}{C_2}+\frac{1}{C_3} \quad ...(4)$$

(vi) **(a)** Equivalent capacitance is even less than the lowest capacitance of combination.

(b) Charge is same on each capacitor and is equal to charge supplied by source i.e.

$$CV = C_1V_1 = C_2V_2 = C_3V_3 \quad ...(5)$$

(II) Parallel Combination

(i) In this case, first plates of all the capacitors are connected to one point (say +ve terminal of source) while second plates to other point (say –ve terminal of source). Let three capacitors having capacities C_1, C_2 and C_3 are connected between points A and B. The point B is connected to earth.

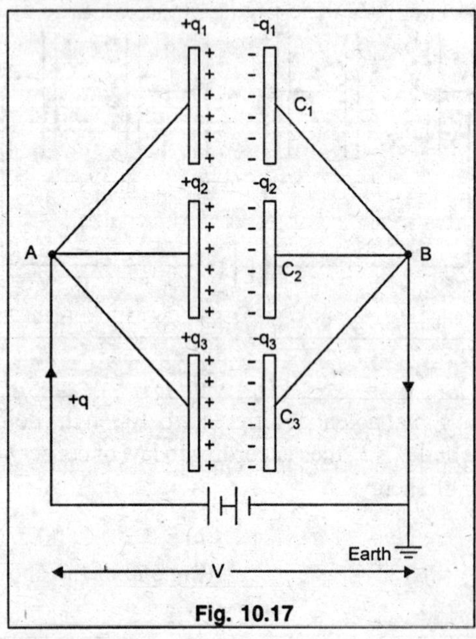

Fig. 10.17

(ii) Suppose charge $+q$ is given to the point A by means of a battery connected between points A and B. This charge is distributed on three capacitors according to their capacities. By induction, equal amounts of –ve charges area produced on inner surfaces of second plates of the capacitors and free +ve charges developed on outer surfaces go into earth.

(iii) As all the three capacitors are connected between the same points A and B, hence potential difference between the plates of each capacitor is same and is equal to applied potential difference V.

(iv) As capacitances of three capacitors are different, hence charge supplied by the source will be distributed among them directly in the ratio of their capacities. [As $q = CV$ and V is constant, hence $q \propto C$] i.e. If q_1, q_2 and q_3 are the charges on the capacitors C_1, C_2 and C_3 respectively, then

$$q_1 = C_1V, q_2 = C_2V, \text{ and } q_3 = C_3V$$

(v) Now, according to law of conservation of charge

$$\begin{aligned} q &= q_1 + q_2 + q_3 \\ &= C_1V + C_2V + C_3V \\ &= V(C_1 + C_2 + C_3) \quad ...(1) \end{aligned}$$

(vi) If the combination of three capacitors is supposed to be replaced by a single capacitor having capacity C, then it will be equivalent to the combination if on giving it a charge q the potential difference between its plates becomes V i.e.

$$q = CV \quad ...(2)$$

Hence from (1) and (2),

$$CV = V(C_1 + C_2 + C_3)$$

i.e.
$$C = C_1 + C_2 + C_3 \quad ...(3)$$

(vii) **(a)** Equivalent capacitance > highest capacitance of the combination.

(b) Potential difference is same across each capacitor and is equal to applied potential difference, i.e.

$$\frac{q}{C} = \frac{q_1}{C_1} = \frac{q_2}{C_2} = \frac{q_3}{C_3} \quad ...(4)$$

MULTIPLE CHOICE QUESTIONS

1. A cylindrical conductor is placed near another positively charged conductor. The net charge acquired by the cylindrical conductor will be
(a) positive only
(b) negative only
(c) zero
(d) either positive or negative depending upon the distance

2. Maximum value of electric intensity due to a charged sphere is at
(a) centre (b) surface
(c) infinity (d) none of the above

3. A one coulomb charge is placed on an insulated stand at the centre of a spherical conductor of radius 1 m. The sphere is given a charge of 1 C. The electrostatic force experienced by the charge at the centre will be
(a) zero (b) 1 N
(c) 9×10^9 N (d) none of the above

4. A positively charged rod is brought near an uncharged conductor. If the rod is then suddenly withdrawn the charge left on the conductor will be
(a) positive (b) zero
(c) negative (d) none of the above

5. The electrostatic potential energy of a charge of 5 C at a point in the electrostatic field is 50 J. The potential at that point is
(a) 0.1 V (b) 5 V
(c) 10 V (d) 250 V

6. The work done by an agency to carry a – 10 C charge from infinity to a point in electrostatic field is 50 J. The potential at that point is
(a) 0.2 V (b) 5 V
(c) – 5 V (d) – 500 V

7. Work done in carrying 2 C charge in a circular path of radius 3 m around a charge of 10 C is
(a) zero (b) 6.66 J
(c) 15 J (d) 60 J

8. For a material to behave as good conductor, which of the following conditions is a must?
(a) each atom should have large number of electrons
(b) each molecule should have large number of electrons
(c) total number of electrons in it should be zero
(d) none of the above conditions

9. $E = - dV/dr$. Here negative sign signified that
(a) E is opposite to V
(b) E is negative
(c) E increases when V decreases
(d) E is directed in the direction of decreasing V

10. Which of the following is not the property of equipotential surfaces?
(a) they do not cross each other
(b) they are concentric spheres for uniform electric field
(c) rate of change of potential with distance on them is zero
(d) they can be imaginary surfaces

11. The work done in displacing a charge of 2 C through 0.5 m on an equipotential surface is
(a) zero (b) 1 J
(c) 4 J (d) none of the above

12. What is the direction of the lines of force at any point on the equipotential surface?
(a) parallel to it (b) normal to it
(c) be inclined (d) none of the above

13. The potential of a spherical conductor of radius 3 m is 6 V. The potential at its centre is
(a) zero (b) 2 V
(c) 6 V (d) 18 V

14. A charged spherical conductor has potential of 6 V and its radius is 2 m. The electric intensity at its centre is
(a) zero (b) 3 NC^{-1}
(c) 12 NC^{-1} (d) none of the above

15. Electric intensity is equal to
(a) time rate of change of potential
(b) minimum rate of change of potential with distance
(c) maximum rate of change of potential with distance
(d) none of the abovc

16. A circle has been drawn round a point positive charge ($+q$) on its centre. The work done in taking a unit positive charge once round it is
(a) 1 J (b) $2\pi q$ J
(c) q J (d) zero

17. The force on a unit +ve charge when placed at any point in the electric field is called
(a) intensity (b) potential
(c) moment (d) none of the above

18. An electron moves with a velocity $\vec{v}$ in an electric field $\vec{E}$. If the angle between $\vec{v}$ and $\vec{E}$ is neither 0 nor π, the path followed by the electron is
(a) straight line (b) circle
(c) ellipse (d) parabola

19. Electric lines of force about a +ve point charge are
(a) circular and clockwise
(b) circular and anticlockwise
(c) radial outwards
(d) radial inwards

20. A charge is moved against electric repulsion in an electric field. Which of the following is correct?
(a) work is done by the electric field
(b) the potential energy of the charge decreases
(c) the strength of electric field decreases
(d) none of the above

21. What is the electric potential at the centre of a charged shell of radius 0.1 m if the potential at its surface is 10 V?
(a) 10V (b) 1V
(c) 0.1 V (d) zero

22. 10 C of charge is moved by 0.1 m on an equipotential surface. The work done in doing so is
(a) 10V (b) 1V
(c) 0.1 V (d) zero

23. What is the angle between maximum value of potential gradient and the equipotential surface?
(a) zero (b) $\pi/4$
(c) $\pi/2$ (d) π

24. Electric potential is
(a) scalar and dimensionless quantity
(b) vector and dimensionless quantity
(c) scalar and dimensional quantity
(d) vector and dimensional quantity

25. Two small spheres each carrying a charge q are placed 1 m apart. The electric force between them is F. If one sphere is taken around the other. The work done is
(a) F (b) $2\pi F$
(c) $F/2\pi$ (d) zero

26. Four charges each equal to q are placed at the corners of a square of side l. The electric potential at the centre of the square is
(a) $\frac{1}{4\pi\varepsilon_0}\frac{4q}{l}$ (b) $\frac{1}{4\pi\varepsilon_0}\frac{4q}{\sqrt{2}\,l}$
(c) $\frac{1}{\pi\varepsilon_0}\frac{\sqrt{2}\,q}{l}$ (d) $\frac{1}{\pi\varepsilon_0}\frac{2q}{l}$

27. Where is the electric potential due to a charged shell constant?
(a) outside it
(b) inside it
(c) both inside and outside it
(d) neither inside nor outside it

28. Where does the electric potential due to a charged conducting shell vary inversely as the distance from its centre?
(a) both inside and outside it
(b) only inside it
(c) only outside it
(d) neither inside nor outside it

29. A solid conducting sphere having a charge Q is surrounded by an uncharged concentric conducting spherical shell. The potential difference between the surface of solid sphere and the shell is V. The shell is now given a charge $-3Q$. The new potential difference between the same surfaces will be
(a) V (b) $2V$
(c) $4V$ (d) $-2V$

30. Electric potential V due to a dipole is related to the distance r of the observation point as

(a) $V \propto r$ (b) $V \propto r^{-1}$
(c) $V \propto r^2$ (d) $V \propto r^{-2}$

31. Two concentric spheres of radii R and r have similar charges with equal surface densities (σ). What is the electric potential at their common centre?

(a) $\frac{\sigma}{\varepsilon_0}$ (b) $\frac{\sigma}{\varepsilon_0}(R-r)$

(c) $\frac{\sigma}{\varepsilon_0}(R+r)$ (d) none of the above

32. Four charges 2 C, –3 C, –4 C and 5 C respectively are placed at the corners of a square. Which of the following statements is true for the point of intersection of the diagonals?

(a) electric field is zero but electric potential is non zero
(b) electric field is not zero but electric potential is zero
(c) both electric field and electric potential are zero
(d) neither electric field nor electric potential is zero

33. A charge of 5 C is placed at the centre of a spherical gaussian surface of radius 5 cm. The electric flux through the surface is

(a) 0.1 C (b) 0.5 C
(c) 1 C (d) 5 C

34. Gauss's law helps in

(a) determination of electric force between point charges
(b) situations where Coulomb's law fails
(c) determining electric potential due to symmetric charge distributions
(d) determining electric potential due to symmetric charge distributions

35. Electric flux in an electric field $\vec{E}$ through area $d\vec{S}$ is given by

(a) $\vec{E}\cdot d\vec{S}$ (b) $\varepsilon_0\vec{E}\cdot d\vec{S}$

(c) $\frac{\vec{E}\cdot d\vec{S}}{\varepsilon_0}$ (d) $\vec{E}\times d\vec{S}$

36. An electric dipole when placed in a uniform electric field will have minimum potential energy. The angle between dipole moment and electric field is

(a) zero (b) $\pi/2$
(c) π (d) $3\pi/2$

37. Two thin and infinite parallel plates have uniform densities of charge + σ and – σ. The electric field in the space outside the plates is

(a) $\frac{\sigma}{2\,\varepsilon_0}$ (b) $\frac{\sigma}{\varepsilon_0}$

(c) $\frac{2\,\sigma}{\varepsilon_0}$ (d) zero

38. Two thin and infinite parallel plates have uniform densities of charge + σ and – σ. What is the electric field in the space between them?

(a) $\frac{\sigma}{2\,\varepsilon_0}$ (b) $\frac{\sigma}{\varepsilon_0}$

(c) $\frac{2\,\sigma}{\varepsilon_0}$ (d) zero

39. Electric field due to an infinite sheet of charge having surface density σ is E. Electric field due to an infinite conducting sheet of same surface density of charge is

(a) $E/2$ (b) E
(c) $2\,E$ (d) $4\,E$

40. A cubical gaussian surfaces encloses 30 C of charge. The electric flux through each surface of the cube is

(a) 30 C (b) 15 C
(c) 10 C (d) 5 C

41. Charge on a spherical conductor resides

(a) at its surface
(b) at its centre
(c) throughout the body
(d) none of the above

42. For an irregularly shaped charged conductor, the potential is

(a) more at the flat parts
(b) more at the spherical parts
(c) more at the sharp edges
(d) same every where

43. Which of the following is discontinuous across the charged conducting surface?
(a) electric field
(b) electric potential
(c) both electric field and potential
(d) neither electric field nor electric potential

44. A gaussian surfaces encloses no charge. Which of the following is true for a point inside it?
(a) electric field must be zero
(b) electric potential must be zero
(c) both electric potential and intensity must be zero
(d) none of the above

45. If the radius of a soap bubble is doubled, its capacitance will be
(a) doubled (b) unchanged
(c) halved (d) increased by 50%

46. A soap bubble is charged to a potential of 16 V. Its radius is then doubled. The potential of the bubble now will be
(a) 16V (b) 8V
(c) 4V (d) 2V

47. Two positively charged conductors are put in contact. The final value of which of the following quantities of both the conductors will be less than the initial value of one of the conductors?
(a) capacitance (b) charge
(c) potential (d) none of the above

48. Which of the following is the correct relation between the units of capacitance, potential and charge?
(a) $q = CV$ (b) $q = C^{-1} V$
(c) $q = C^{-1} V^{-1}$ (d) $q = CV^{-1}$

49. A number of charged liquid drops coalesce. Which one of the following quantity does not change?
(a) charge
(b) capacitance
(c) potential
(d) electrostatic energy

50. The capacitance of a conductor in vacuum is 10 *F*. If it is put in a medium of relative permittivity 5, the capacitance will be
(a) unchanged (b) 2 *F*
(c) 50 *F* (d) $9 \times 10^9 \times 5 \times 10\,F$

ANSWERS

1	2	3	4	5	6	7	8	9	10
(c)	(b)	(a)	(b)	(c)	(c)	(a)	(d)	(d)	(b)
11	12	13	14	15	16	17	18	19	20
(a)	(b)	(c)	(a)	(c)	(d)	(a)	(d)	(c)	(d)
21	22	23	24	25	26	27	28	29	30
(a)	(d)	(c)	(c)	(d)	(c)	(b)	(c)	(a)	(d)
31	32	33	34	35	36	37	38	39	40
(c)	(b)	(d)	(c)	(b)	(a)	(d)	(b)	(c)	(d)
41	42	43	44	45	46	47	48	49	50
(a)	(d)	(a)	(d)	(a)	(b)	(c)	(d)	(a)	(c)

HINTS / SOLUTIONS

1. The +ve charges induced on one side will be equal to the –ve charge induced on the other side. So, the net charge will be zero.

3. Electric field inside the charged conductor is zero. So, the force on the charge inside it is also zero.

5. Potential = potential energy/test charge.

6. Potential = potential energy/test charge.

7. Electrostatic force is conservative. So, when the charge returns to the starting point, the work done is zero.

10. For uniform electric field the equipotential surfaces are plane and parallel to each other.

11. Work done in displacing a charge $= q \times \Delta V$. On the equipotential surface $\Delta V = 0$. Hence work done is also zero.

13. Electric potential inside a charged sphere is every where same as that in the surface.

14. Electric intensity inside a charged sphere is zero.

16. Electric field is conservative. So, the work done in carrying a charge on a closed path is zero.

18. Force on the electron e is $\vec{E}$. It is inclined to the instantaneous velocity. So, the acceleration is constant in magnitude and motion of electron will be parabola as is the case of projectile fired in the gravitational field.

21. Electric potential inside the charged shell is everywhere same as on the surface.

22. $W = q \times \Delta V$. Since $\Delta V = 0$, therefore $W = 0$.

23. Maximum value of potential gradient gives electric intensity.

25. Electric field is conservative. So, work done in taking a charge on the closed path is zero.

26. Electric potential due to each charge at the centre of the square is $\frac{1}{4\pi\varepsilon_0}\frac{\sqrt{2}q}{l}$.

Hence total potential is

$$4 \times \frac{1}{4\pi\varepsilon_0}\frac{\sqrt{2}q}{l} = \frac{1}{\pi\varepsilon_0}\frac{\sqrt{2}q}{l}$$

29. The difference of potential between the solid sphere and the hollow spherical shell depends only on their radii and the charge on the inner solid sphere.

$$V \propto \frac{Q}{R_1} - \frac{Q}{R_2}$$

When charge $-3Q$ is placed on outer sphere, the potential of inner sphere is $\frac{Q}{R_1} - \frac{3Q}{R_2}$.

That of outer sphere is $\frac{-Q}{R_2} - \frac{3Q}{R_2} = -\frac{4Q}{R_2}$

Difference is again $\frac{Q}{R_1} + \frac{Q}{R_2}$.

31. Let Q and q be the charges on the spheres. Then potential at the common centre is given by

$$U = \frac{1}{4\pi\varepsilon_0}\frac{Q}{R} + \frac{1}{4\pi\varepsilon_0}\frac{q}{r}$$

$$= \frac{1}{\varepsilon_0}\left[\frac{Q}{4\pi R^2} \times R + \frac{q}{4\pi r^2} \times r\right]$$

But $\frac{Q}{4\pi R^2} = \frac{q}{4\pi r^2} = \sigma$.

Hence $U = \frac{\sigma}{\varepsilon_0}[R + r]$

32. $V = \frac{1}{4\pi\varepsilon_0}\frac{1}{\sqrt{2}l}[2 - 3 - 4 + 5] = 0.$

However electric intensity will be

$$\vec{E} = \frac{1}{4\pi\varepsilon_0}\left[\frac{2}{2l^2}\hat{i} - \frac{3}{2l^2}\hat{j} - \frac{4}{2l^2}\hat{i} + \frac{5}{2l^2}\hat{j}\right]$$

Which is not zero. E will be

$$\frac{1}{4\pi\varepsilon_0}\frac{(2^2 + 2^2)^{1/2}}{2l^2} = \frac{1}{4\pi\varepsilon_0}\frac{2}{\sqrt{2}l^2}$$

33. Electric flux = charge enclosed.

36. $U_p = -\vec{p}_e\vec{E}$. So, U_p (minimum) $= -p_e E$. This happens when angle between p_e and $\vec{E}$ is 0°.

37. Electric intensity due to a sheet of charge having surface density $\sigma/2\,\varepsilon_0$ That due to $-\sigma$ is $-\sigma/2\varepsilon_0$. Total intensity

$\sigma/2\varepsilon_0 - (-\sigma/2\varepsilon_0) = \sigma/\varepsilon_0.$

And outside will be $-\sigma/2\varepsilon_0 + \sigma/2\varepsilon_0 = 0$.

38. Electric intensity due to a sheet of charge having surface density $\sigma/2\,\varepsilon_0$ That due to $-\sigma$ is $-\sigma/2\varepsilon_0$ Total intensity

$\sigma/2\varepsilon_0 - (-\sigma/2\varepsilon_0) = \sigma/\varepsilon_0.$

And outside will be $\sigma/2\varepsilon_0 + \sigma/2\varepsilon_0 = 0$.

39. Conducting sheet has two surfaces. So, electric field will be due to two surface densities of charge.

40. Total number of surface = 6. Total flux = 30 C. So, flux through each surface = 5 C.

45. When radius is doubled, the capacitance is also doubled. Since, the charge remains unchanged, therefore $V = q/C$ is halved.

46. When radius is doubled, the capacitance is also doubled. Since, the charge remains unchanged, therefore $V = q/C$ is halved.

47. Common potential will be in between two initial values. So, it will be less than the potential of one of the conductors.

49. When n drops coalesce radius of the single drop so formed becomes $n^{1/3}r$. So, the capacitances also becomes $n^{1/3}$ times. Potential is $nq/Cn^{1/3}$. Hence potential of the single drop is $n^{2/3}$ times. The potential energy, which is given by $\frac{1}{2}n^2q^2/Cn^{1/3}$ becomes $n^{5/3}$times.

50. Capacitance in a medium
= dielectric constant × capacitance in vacuum.

UNIT-11

CURRENT ELECTRICITY

ELECTRIC CURRENT

Electric current is the rate of flow of electric charge through any point of the circuit per unit time. It is denoted by I.

If a charge 'q' flows through the circuit for time 't', then current $I = q/t$.

If a charge 'dq' flows through the circuit for time 'dt' then $I = dq/dt$. Therefore $q = \int_0^t I\,dt$ Current is a *scalar* quantity.

Conventional direction of flow of current is opposite to the flow of electrons or from high potential to low potential.

Unit of electric current is **ampere.**

$$1 \text{ ampere} = \frac{1 \text{ coulomb}}{1 \text{ sec}}$$

$$= \text{flow of } 6.25 \times 10^{18} \text{ electrons/sec.}$$

CURRENT DENSITY

Current density is the current flowing normally through unit area of cross-section. It is a vector quantity and is represented by 'j'. If a current 'I' flows uniformly through area A, then the current density $j = I/A$.

Units of j are ampere m^{-2} and dimensions are $[AL^{-2}]$

If $\vec{A}$ is the vector area and $\vec{j}$ is the current density, then $I = \vec{j}.\vec{A}$ or $I = jA\cos\theta$, where θ is the angle between $\vec{j}$ and $\vec{A}$.

If the area is of irregular shape, then current,

$$I = \int \vec{j}.\vec{ds}$$

ATOMIC VIEW OF CONDUCTOR

(i) A large number of "free electrons" or "conduction electrons" are contained in every conductors.

(ii) The free electrons can move in between interatomic spaces.

(iii) The irregular velocity of free electrons is given by

$$v_{rms} = \sqrt{\left(\frac{3kT}{m}\right)} \approx 10^{+5} \text{ m/sec,}$$

where m = mass of electron, k = Boltzmann constant, T = absolute temperature.

(iv) The free electrons collide with each other. The collisions are elastic, i.e. there is no loss of energy during collisions.

(v) The distance travelled between two successive collisions is called **free path** and the average of all the free paths is called the mean **free path.**

(vi) Time taken between two successive collisions is called relaxation time. It is of the order of 10^{-14} sec.

(vii) The average flow of free electrons in the conductor which is not connected to the battery is zero, i.e. the number of free electrons crossing any section of the conductor from left to right is equal to the number of electrons crossing that section from right to left. Thus until the conductor is connected to the battery no current flows through it.

DRIFT SPEED OF FREE ELECTRONS

When the ends of the metallic conductor are connected to the battery a potential difference is established across the terminals of the wire. An electric field is developed across the ends of the wire. This field accelerates the electrons, but the speed of the electrons does not increase because they lose energy due to collisions with the positive ions. Thus, the electric field gives a constant velocity to the free electrons along the length of the wire. This velocity is called "drift velocity" (v_d) of electrons. The order of drift velocity is 10^{-4} m/sec.

Relation between electric current and drift velocity

The relation between current and drift velocity is $I = neAv_d$

As we know that the current density is given by $j = I/A$, hence $v_d = j/ne$.

This is the relation between current density and drift velocity.

ELECTRIC RESISTANCE

The opposition offered by the substance to the flow of charge is known as electrical resistance. If the potential difference between the ends of the conductor is V and the current in the conductor is I, then the electric resistance of the conductor will be given by $R = V/I$.

The resistance of the conductor

(i) $R \propto$ length of conductor

(ii) $R \propto \dfrac{1}{\text{area of cross-section}}$

The unit of resistance R in the MKS system is 'ohm'. Dimensions of electric resistance are $[ML^2T^{-3}A^{-2}]$. Besides the length and area of cross-section the resistance depends on material of conductor.

$$1 \text{ ohm} = \frac{1 \text{ volt}}{1 \text{ amp}} = \frac{10^8 \text{ e.m.u. of potential}}{10^{-1} \text{ e.m.u. of current}}$$

$$= 10^9 \text{ e.m.u. of resistance}$$

ELECTRICAL CONDUCTANCE

The reciprocal of the resistance is called the 'electric conductance' and its units the 'mho' or 'ohm^{-1}'. It is represented by G. Hence $G = 1/R$.

OHM'S LAW

According to Ohm's law, if physical state of a conductor (such as temperature), are unchanged then the ratio of the potential difference applied at its ends and the current flowing through it is constant.

Thus, if the potential difference applied at the ends of the conductor be V and the current flowing through it be I, then according to the ohm's law, we have $V/I = R =$ constant.

A graph drawn between the applied potential difference V and the current I flowing through the conductor is a straight line. This law is true for metallic conductors only.

OHMIC CIRCUITS

The circuits in which Ohm's law is followed are called ohmic circuits $V-I$ graph is a straight line passing through the origin. The reciprocal of slope of $V–I$ curve gives the resistance of the conductor.

UNOHMIC CIRCUITS

The circuits in which Ohm's law is not obeyed are called unohmic circuits. The $V–I$ graph is a curve, e.g. torch bulb, electrolyte, semiconductors, thermonic valves etc. as shown by curves (a), (b), (c).

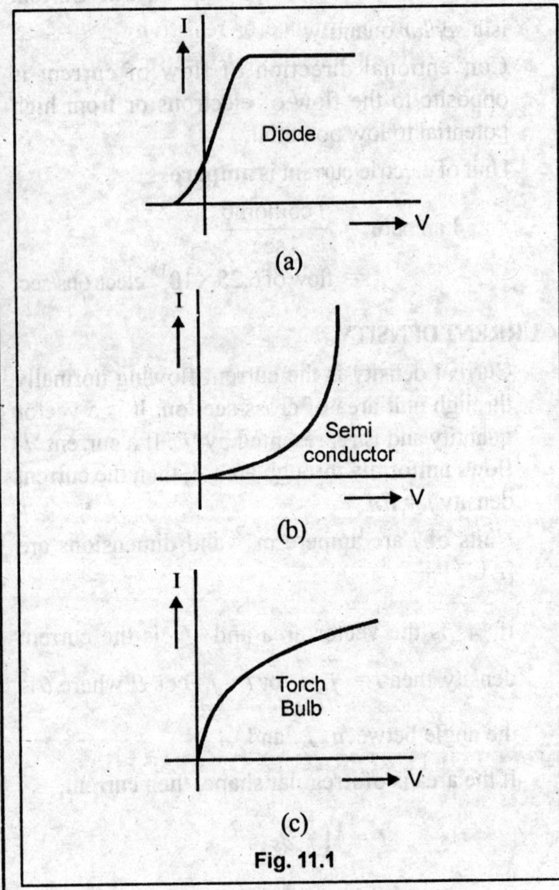

Fig. 11.1

Note. On proving ohms law, we have

$$i = neA\left(\frac{eV\tau}{ml}\right)$$

or $$V = \frac{ml}{ne^2\tau A}i \qquad ...(i)$$

or $V \propto i.$

This is Ohm's law.

Comparing equation (i) with $V = iR$, we get,

$$R = \frac{ml}{ne^2\tau A}i \qquad ...(ii)$$

Comparing equation (ii) with $R = \frac{\rho l}{A}$, we get

$$r = \frac{m}{ne^2\tau}$$

where r is known as the specific resistance of the material of wire and is constant for a particular material.

SPECIFIC RESISTANCE OR RESISTIVITY

The specific resistance or resistivity is defined as the ratio of intensity of electric field 'E' at any point in the conductor to the current density 'j' at that point. It is represented by 'ρ'. Therefore,

$$\rho = \frac{m}{ne^2\tau}$$

if l = 1m, A = 1 m^2 then, $R = r$.

Hence, the resistance of a wire of 1 metre length and 1 m^2 area of cross-section is called the specific resistance. Its units are ohm-metre and its dimensional formula is [ML^{3}T^{-3} A^{-2}].

It is also defined as the resistance of a cube of side 1 m of the given material.

SPECIFIC CONDUCTANCE OR CONDUCTIVITY

The reciprocal of specific resistance of a material is called specific conductance or conductivity. It is represented by σ. Thus

$$\sigma = 1/\rho \text{ but } \rho = E/j$$

$$\therefore \quad \sigma = j/E \text{ or } j = \sigma E$$

EFFECT OF TEMPERATURE ON RESISTIVITY

1. Resistivity of metals

Electric resistance of the metallic wire increases when its temperature is raised. Since the resistance of the wire is given by $R = ml/n\rho^2 A\tau$, where n is the number of free electrons per unit volume of the wire, m is the mass and e is the charge of the electrons. For a given wire, l, A, and n are constant; hence

$$R \propto 1/\tau.$$

As the temperature of the wire rises, the root-mean-square speed v_{rms} of its free electrons increases ($v_{rms} \propto \lambda/\tau$) and the relaxation time τ decreases. Hence, the resistance R of the wire increases, i.e. the resistivity of the material of the wire [$\rho = R(A/l)$] increases. The electric conductance of the wire decreases.

Let the resistance of the wire at 0 °C and t °C be R_0, R_t respectively, then the value of R_t is given by

$$R_t = R_0 (1 + \alpha t)$$

where α is a constant which is called the 'temperature coefficient of resistance' of the material of the wire. From eq. (i) we have

$$\alpha = \frac{R_t - R_0}{R_0 \times t} \text{ per °C}$$

If R_0 = 1 ohm., t = 1 °C then $\alpha = (R_t - R_0)$ = increase in resistance.

Hence if the resistance of a wire at 0 °C be 1 ohm, then on raising its temperature to 1 °C, the increase in its resistance will be equal to the temperature coefficient of resistance' of the material of that wire. For most of the metals the value of α is nearly 1/273 per °C. Hence by equation (i), we have

$$R_t = R_0\left(1 + \frac{t}{273}\right) = R_0\frac{(273 + t)}{273} = R_0\left(\frac{T}{273}\right)$$

where T is absolute temperature. Thus, $R_t \propto T$. Therefore the resistance of a pure metallic wire or the resistivity of metal is directly proportional to its absolute temperature.

2. Resistivity of Alloys

With rise in temperature the resistivity of alloys also increases. But this increase is much smaller compared to pure metals.

There are certain alloys such as manganin, constanton, nichrome, etc., whose resistivity is little affected by temperature, i.e., their temperature coefficient of resistance is negligible. Due to their high resistivity and negligible temperature coefficient of resistance.

these alloys are used to make wires for standard resistances, resistance boxes, etc.

3. Resistivity of Semi conductors

Substances whose electric conductance is large compared to insulators, but small compared to conductors are called 'semi-conductors'. Silicon, germaniumm selenium, carbon, etc. are semiconductors. The resistivity of semiconductors decreases with rise in temperature, i.e., their temperature coefficient of resistance is negative. The reason is that with rise in temperature the number of free electrons i.e. the value of n goes on increasing due to the breakage of covalent bonds. Therefore the resistance $R = \left(\frac{ml}{ne^2 \tau A}\right)$ goes on decreasing. Although in these substances also the relaxation time t decreases with rise in temperature, but the increase in the value of n is larger compared to the decrease in t. Hence, the net effect of rise in temperature is that the resistance decreases, i.e. the conductance increases.

4. Resistivity of Electrolytes

With rise in temperature the resistivity of electrolytes also decreases. The reason is that with rise in temperature the viscosity of electrolytes decreases so that ions get more freedom to move inside the electrolytes. Hence the resistivity (or resistance) of the electrolytes deccreases.

SUPERCONDUCTIVITY

An abnormal relation is seen between temperature and resistance in some substances. As the temperature is lowered, the resistance of the substances decreases slowly like pure metals, but at a certain minimum temperature, the resistance decreases rapidly and become zero. For example, the resistance of mercury become zero at 4 K. This phenomenon is called 'super-conductivity', and it occurs at low temperatures (from 10 K to 0.1 K).

Effect of Stretching a wire on its resistance

There are two cases :

(i) Following Length of the Wire is Changed. Let l_1 and l_2 be the initial and final lengths of the wire and r_1 and r_2 are the initial and final radii then, since the mass of the wire is constant

initial volume = final volume

$$\pi r_1^2 l_1 = \pi r_2^2 l_2 \quad \text{or} \quad \frac{l_1}{l_2} = \frac{r_2^2}{r_1^2}$$

Now $$R_1 = \frac{\rho l_1}{\pi r_1^2} \text{ and } R_2 = \frac{\rho l_2}{\pi r_2^2}$$

$$\therefore \quad \frac{R_1}{R_2} = \frac{l_1 r_2^2}{l_2 r_1^2} = \frac{l_1^2}{l_2^2} \qquad \therefore R \propto l^2$$

(ii) When Radius of the wire is changed. Let l_1 and l_2 be the initial and final lengths and r_1 and r_2 be the initial and final radii. Since the mass is constant,

$\therefore$ Initial volume = Final volume, i.e. $\pi r_1^2 l_1 = \pi r_2^2 l_2$

$$\Rightarrow \quad \frac{l_1}{l_2} = \frac{r_2^2}{r_1^2}$$

but $$R_1 = \frac{\rho l_1}{\pi r_1^2} \text{ and } R_2 = \frac{\rho l_2}{\pi r_2^2}$$

$$\therefore \quad \frac{R_1}{R_2} = \frac{l_1 r_2^2}{l_2 r_1^2} = \frac{r_2^4}{r_1^4} \quad \text{or } R \propto \frac{1}{r^4}$$

COMBINATIONS OF RESISTANCES

There are following two combinations of resistances :

(i) Resistance in Series

The combinations of three resistances in series is shown in the adjoining figure. Same current I flows through all the wires. V_1, V_2, V_3 are the potential differences along each wire and V the net potential difference. Same current I flows through different wires. Therefore

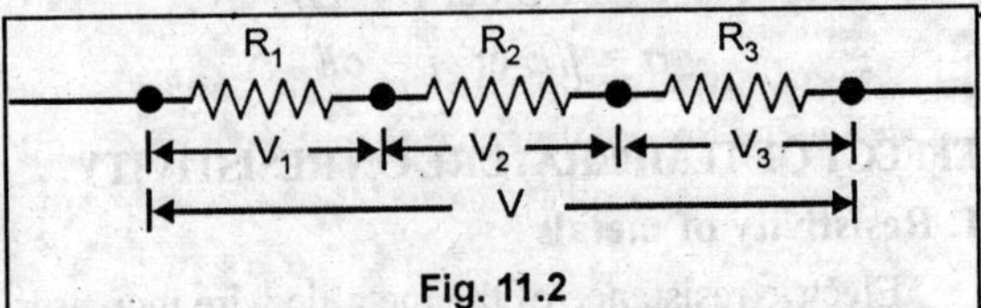

Fig. 11.2

$$V_1 = IR_1, V_2 = IR_2, V_3 = IR_3$$

$$\therefore \quad V = V_1 + V_2 + V_3$$

$$\text{or} \quad V = IR_1 + IR_2 + IR_3 \quad \text{but } V = IR$$

$$\therefore \quad IR = IR_1 + IR_2 + IR_3$$

or $\quad R = R_1 + R_2 + R_3$

(ii) Resistances in parallel

The combination of three resistances R_1, R_2, R_3 in parallel is shown in the adjoining figure

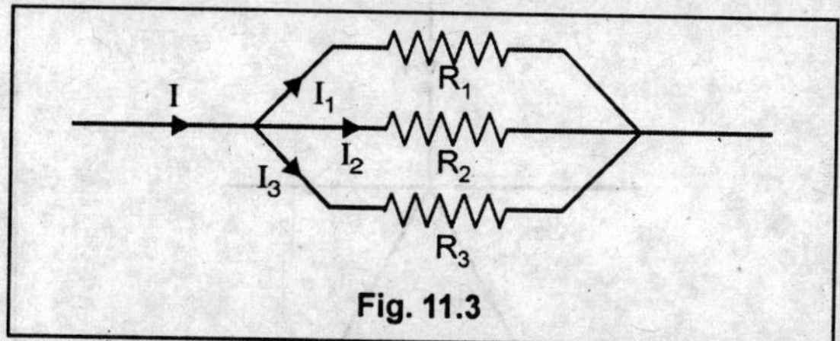

Fig. 11.3

If a battery of e.m.f. E is connected across the combination, then the potential difference across each resistance is E, i.e.

$$E = I_1R_1 = I_2R_2 = I_3R_3$$

or $\quad I_1 = E/R_1, I_2 = E/R_2, I_3 = E/R_3$

$\therefore$ total current $I = I_1 + I_2 + I_3$ but $I = E/R$,

Hence $\quad \frac{E}{R} = \frac{E}{R_1} + \frac{E}{R_2} + \frac{E}{R_3}$

or $\quad \frac{1}{R} = \frac{1}{R_1} + \frac{1}{R_2} + \frac{1}{R_3}$

As the value of equivalent resistance is less than the resistance of the smallest individual resistance and hence the resistance are connected in parallel, if the resistance in the circuit is to be reduced.

ELECTRIC CELL

A device which maintains the flow of charges continuously in a circuit is called the electric cell.

E.M.F. OF CELL

It is defined in two ways :

(i) **Qualitative Definition.** The potential difference across the terminals of the cell in an open circuit is called the e.m.f.

(ii) **Quantitative definition.** The energy given by the cell in the flow of unit charge in the whole circuit (including the cell) is called the 'electromotive force (e.m.f.) of the cell. The e.m.f. is a characteristic of the cell which depends upon the nature of the plates and the electrolyte used in the cell. It is not affected by the quantity of the electrolyte or the size of the plates or the distance between the plates.

Suppose during the flow of a charge of q coulomb in an electric circuit, the energy supplied (or the work done) by a cell is W joule then the E.M.F. of the cell is

$$E = (W/q) \text{ joule/coulomb or volt.}$$

POTENTIAL DIFFERENCE

Suppose during the flow of a charge of q coulomb in a part of an electrical circuit, W' joule work is done or W' joule energy is consumed, then the potential difference across that part will be $V = W'/q$ volt. It is measured by a voltmeter.

INTERNAL RESISTANCE OF A CELL

The resistance offered by the electrolyte to the flow of current in the cell is called internal resistance of the cell. Internal resistance (r) of the cell depends on following factors.

(i) **Distance between the electrodes.** The internal resistance of the cell increases with increase in the distance between the plates of the cell.

(ii) **Concentration of the electrolyte.** Internal resistance of the cell increases with increase in the concentration of the electrolyte.

(iii) **Area of electrodes.** Internal resistance of a cell decreases with increase in the area of the plates immersed in the solution.

(iv) **Polarisation in the cell.** Greater the polarisation, greater is the internal resistance.

POTENTIAL DIFFERENCE ACROSS THE TERMINALS OF THE CELL

Suppose the current i flows in the circuit for time t. If the charge flown in the circuit in time t be q, then the energy given by the cell is

$$W = Eq.$$

But $\quad q = it.$

$$\therefore \quad W = Eit$$

Outside the cell, the potential difference across the ends of the resistance R is V. Hence the external work done outside the cell is $W_{ext} = V.i.t.$

Let the internal resistance of the cell be r. Hence when the current i flows in the circuit, the potential drop in the electrolyte inside the cell will be $V' = ir$. Therefore, the work done inside the cell is

$$W_{int} = V.i.t = i^2rt. \qquad (\because V' = ir)$$

From the law of conservation of energy, we have

$$W = W_{ext} + W_{int},$$

$$\therefore \quad E_{it} = V_{it} + i^2rt$$

or $\quad E = V + ir$

or $\quad V = E - ir$

It is clear that (i) when the cell is giving current, i.e. when it is being discharged, then the potential difference V between its plates is less than its e.m.f E., (ii) larger the value of i, smaller will be the value of V. It means that larger is the current drawn from the cell, smaller will be the potential difference between its plates.

If in the above equation (i), $i = 0$, then $V = E$. i.e. when no current is being drawn from the cell, then the potential difference between the plates of the cell is equal to the e.m.f.

VALUE OF THE CURRENT IN THE CIRCUIT

Let the current in the circuit be i, then the potential difference across the ends of the resistance R will be

$$V = iR$$

Substituting the value of V in eq. (i), we get

$$iR = E - ir,$$

or $\quad E = iR + ir = i(R + r)$

i.e. $\quad i = E/(R + r) \quad$ ...(iii)

Here $(R + r)$ is the total (external + internal) resistance of the circuit.

KIRCHHOFF'S LAWS

Kirchhoff in 1842 gave two laws for determining the current and resistance in a complicated circuit. Which are as follows :

(i) In an electric circuit, the algebric sum of the currents meeting at any junction in the circuit is zero, i.e.

$$\Sigma i = 0$$

While applying this law, the current going towards the junction is taken as positive while that going away is taken as negative.

In the following figure

$$i_1 + i_3 - i_2 - i_4 - i_5 = 0$$

or $\quad i_1 + i_3 = i_2 + i_4 + i_5$

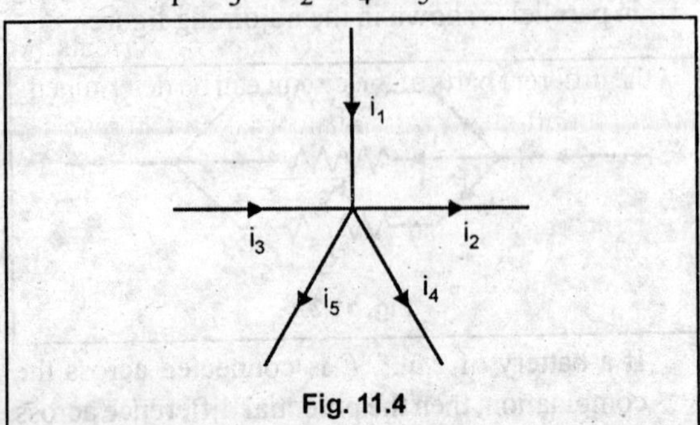

Fig. 11.4

Thus the sum of the currents flowing towards the junction is equal to the sum of the currents flowing away from the junction.

Therefore when a steady current flows in a circuit then there is neither any accumulation of charge at any point in the circuit nor any charge is removed from there. Thus, Kirchhoff's first law expresses the conservation of charge.

(ii) In any closed mesh of a circuit the sum of the products of the current and the resistance in each part of the mesh is equal to the algebraic sum of the e.m.f's in that mesh, i.e.

$$\Sigma iR = \Sigma E$$

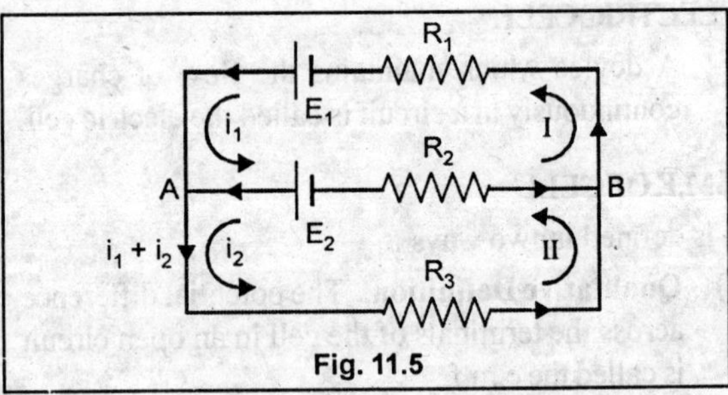

Fig. 11.5

While applying this law, when we traverse in the direction of current then the product of the current and the corresponding resistance is taken as positive, and the e.m.f. is taken as positive when we traverse from the negative to the positive electrode of the cell through the electrolyte. Applying Kirchoff's II law to mesh 1, we have (See Fig. 11.5)

$$i_1R_1 - i_2R_2 = E_1 - E_2$$

Similarly, for the mesh 2, we have

$$i_2R_2 + (i_1 + i_2)R_3 = E_2$$

From these equations the values of currents in the different parts of the circuit can be determined. Kirchhoff's II law is in accordance with energy conservation.

COMBINATIONS OF CELLS

As a cell is a source of electric current, a single cell cannot give a strong current, hence two or more cells are to be combined to get strong current. The combination of cells is called a 'battery'. Cells can be combined in three ways : (1) In series, (2) In parallel and (3) In mixed grouping.

1. In series.

In series combination, the negative pole of the first cell is connected to the positive pole of the second cell, the negative pole of the second to the positive pole of the third, the negative pole of the third to the positive pole of the fourth, and so on (Fig.)

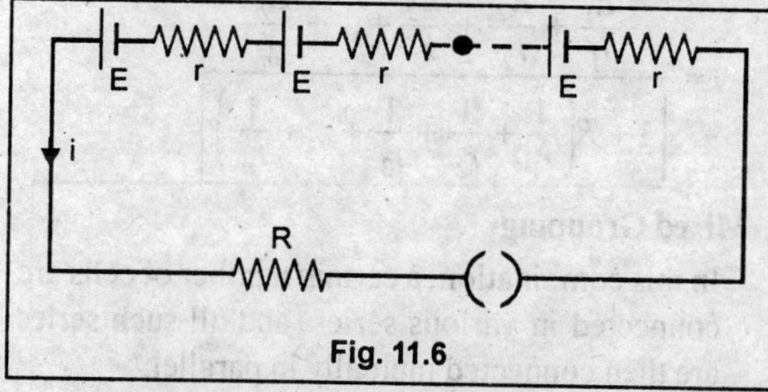

Fig. 11.6

Suppose, n cells each of e.m.f E and internal resistance r are connected in series. These cells are sending current in an external resistance R, then,

Total e.m.f. of the cell = nE.

Total internal resistance = nr.

$\therefore$ Total resistance of the circuit = $(nr + R)$.

Let i be the current in the circuit then $i = \dfrac{nE}{nr + R}$

Two cases arise here :

(i) If $nr << R$, then from equation (i), $i = \dfrac{nE}{R}$ (approx), i.e. if the internal resistance of the connected cells is much smaller then the external resistance, then the current given by these cells will be nearly n times, the current given by one cell. Hence, when the internal resistance of the connected cells is much smaller than the external resistance, then the cells should be connected in the series to obtain a strong current.

(ii) If $nr >> R$, then $i = \dfrac{nE}{nr} = \dfrac{E}{r}$ (approx), i.e. if the internal resistance of the connected cells is much greater than the external resistance, then nearly the same current is obtained by n cells as by a single cell. Hence, there is no advantage of connecting cells in series.

2. In Parallel

In parallel combination, the positive poles of all the cells are connected to one point, and the negative poles to another point (Fig.). Suppose n cells, each of e.m.f E and internal resistance r, are connected in parallel and this battery of n cells is connected to an external resistance R. Since the cells are connected in parallel, the e.m.f. of the battery will also be E. Let the equivalent internal resistance of the cell be R_1, then

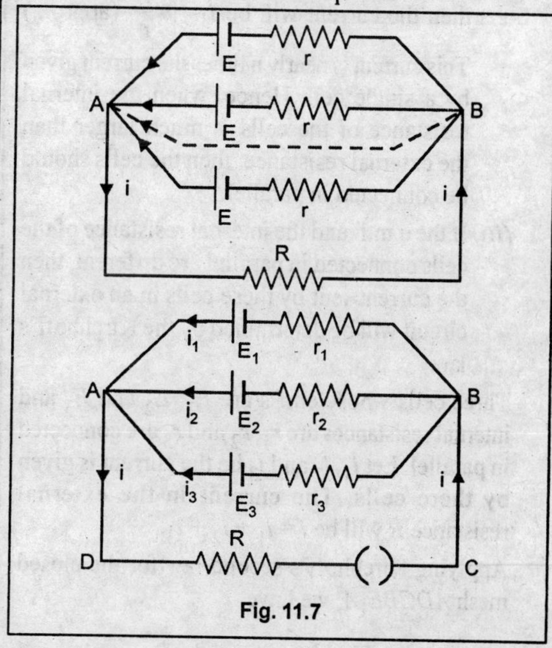

Fig. 11.7

$$\frac{1}{R_1} = \frac{1}{r} + \frac{1}{r} + ... \text{ upto } n \text{ terms} = \frac{n}{r}$$

or $$R_1 = \frac{r}{n}$$

$\therefore$ Total resistance of the circuit $= \left(\frac{r}{n} + R\right)$. If the current in the external circuit be i,

then $$i = \frac{E}{(r/n) + R} = \frac{nE}{r + nR}$$

Two cases arise here

(i) If $\frac{r}{n} << R$, i.e. if the internal resistance of the cells is much smaller than the external resistance then r can be neglected in comparison to nR. Then from equation (i),

$i = \frac{E}{R}$ (approx), i.e. the total current will be equal to the current given by a single cell. Hence connecting the cells of small internal resistance in parallel has no advantage.

(ii) If $\frac{r}{n} >> R$, i.e. if the internal resistance of the cells is larger than the external resistance, then the current will be $i = n\frac{E}{r}$ (approx.)

This current is nearly n times the current given by a single cell. Hence, when the internal resistance of the cells is much larger than the external resistance, then the cells should be connected in parallel.

(iii) If the e.m.f. and the internal resistance of the cells connected in parallel are different, then the current sent by these cells in an external circuit will be determined by the Kirchhoff's law.

Three cells whose emf's are E_1, E_2 and E_3 and internal resistances are r_1, r_2 and r_3 are connected in parallel. Let i_1, i_2 and i_3 be the current is given by there cells. The current in the external resistance R will be $i = i_1 + i_2 + i_3$.

Applying Kirchhoff's second law for the closed mesh $ADCBE_1A$, we have

$$iR + i_1 r_1 = E_1 \quad \text{or} \quad i_1 = \frac{E_1 - iR}{r_1}$$

Similarly, for the closed meshes $ADCBE_2A$ and $ADCBE_3A$, we have

$$i_2 = \frac{E_2 - iR}{r_2} \text{ and } i_3 = \frac{E_3 - iR}{r_3}$$

Substituting these values of i_1, i_2 and i_3 in the above equation, we get

$$i = \frac{E_1 - iR}{r_1} + \frac{E_2 - iR}{r_2} + \frac{E_3 - iR}{r_3}$$

$$= \frac{E_1}{r_1} + \frac{E_2}{r_2} + \frac{E_3}{r_3} - iR\left\{\frac{1}{r_1} + \frac{1}{r_2} + \frac{1}{r_3}\right\}$$

or $$i\left[1 + R\left(\frac{1}{r_1} + \frac{1}{r_2} + \frac{1}{r_3}\right)\right] = \frac{E_1}{r_1} + \frac{E_2}{r_2} + \frac{E_3}{r_3}$$

or $$i = \frac{\frac{E_1}{r_1} + \frac{E_2}{r_2} + \frac{E_3}{r_3}}{\left[1 + R\left(\frac{1}{r_1} + \frac{1}{r_2} + \frac{1}{r_3}\right)\right]}$$

For n cells to be in parallel, we have

$$i = \frac{\frac{E_1}{r_1} + \frac{E_2}{r_2} + \frac{E_3}{r_3} + ... + \frac{E_n}{r_n}}{\left[1 + R\left(\frac{1}{r_1} + \frac{1}{r_2} + \frac{1}{r_3} + ... + \frac{1}{r_n}\right)\right]}$$

3. Mixed Grouping

In this combination, a certain number of cells are connected in various series, and all such series are then connected mutually in parallel.

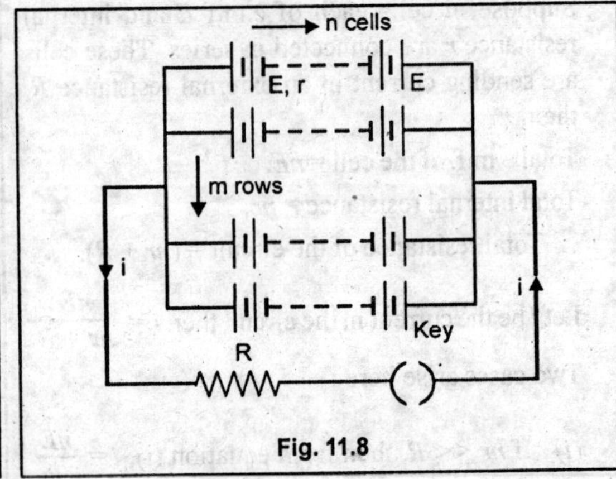

Fig. 11.8

Suppose n cells are connected in each series, and such m rows are connected in parallel (Fig.) Let E be the e.m.f. of each cell and r be the internal resistance. This battery of cells is sending current in an external resistance R.

The total e.m.f. of n cells connected in one series is nE. Since all the series are connected in parallel the e.m.f. of the battery as a whole will also be nE.

Similarly, the total internal resistance of cells in a series is nr. Such m rows are connected in parallel. Hence, if the internal resistance of the whole battery be R_1, then

$$\frac{1}{R_1} = \frac{1}{nr} + \frac{1}{nr} + \ldots \text{ upto } m \text{ terms} = \frac{m}{nr}$$

or $R_1 = \frac{nr}{m}$

$\therefore$ Total resistance of the circuit $= \{(nr/m) + R\}$.

Let the current in the external circuit be i, then

$$i = \frac{nE}{(nr/m) + R} = \frac{mnE}{nr + mR}$$

It is obvious from equation (i) that for the value of i to be maximum, the value of $(nr + mR)$ should be minimum. Now

$$nr + mR = \left\{\sqrt{(nr)} - \sqrt{(mR)}\right\}^2 + 2\sqrt{(mnRr)}.$$

Therefore, for $(nr + mR)$ to be minimum,

$$\left\{\sqrt{(nr)} - \sqrt{(mR)}\right\} = 0$$

or $\sqrt{(nr)} = \sqrt{(mR)}$ or $nr = mR$ or $R = nr/m$

But nr/m is the internal resistance of the whole battery. Hence in mixed grouping the current in the external circuit will be maximum when the internal resisance of the battery is equal to external resistance. Substituting $nr/m = R$ in equation (i), we can see that the maximum current in the external circuit will be $nE/2R$.

POTENTIOMETER

A device used to measure the potential difference between two points or to measure the e.m.f. of a cell is called potentiometer.

Construction. It consists of 10^{-12} metre long uniform wire of constantan or manganin, spread uniformly over a wooden board in the form of parallel pieces each of length one metre. All the pieces of the wire are connected in series by thick copper strips. Binding screws are attached at the ends A and B of the wire. A metre scale is fixed parallel to the length of the wires. The jockey J can slide along the length of the wire.

Principle. There are two circuits that should be connected accross the potentiometer wire for the measurement of potential difference or emf of a cell.

(i) Main Circuit. It consists of a battery B_1, whose positive terminal is connected to the end A and the negative terminal to the end B through a key (K) and a Rheostat (Rh). The function of main circuit is to maintain a steady current in the wire and hence a constant potential difference across the terminal of the wire. The current due to main circuit cell is represented by (⇒) in galvanometer.

(ii) Auxillary Circuit. The positive terminal of the cell E, whose emf is to be measured is connected to the terminal A of the wire and the negative terminal of the cell is connected to the jockey through a Galvanometer (G). The current due to the auxillary circuit cell is in the direction of (⇒).

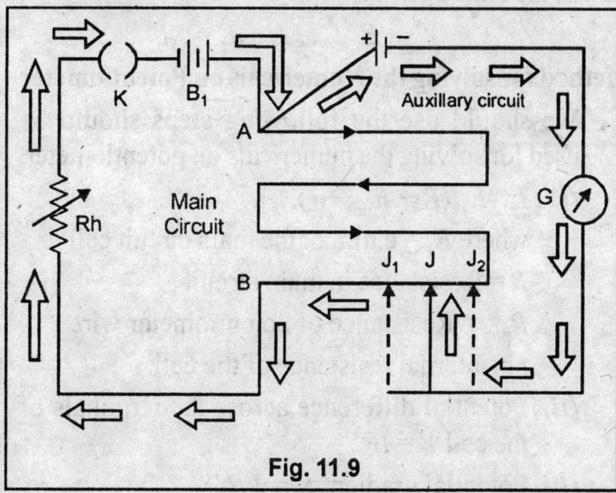

Fig. 11.9

It is obvious that the currents flowing in the Galvanometer due to main circuit auxillary circuit are in opposite directions. Now, suppose the jockey is made to touch a point J_1 on the wire such that the potential difference between A and J_1 is less than the emf of cell E, then the current due to the main circuit cell is less than the current due to auxillary circuit, hence the needle of the galvanometer will be deflected to one side.

If the jockey is touched to a point J_2 on the wire such that the potential difference between A and J_2 is higher than the emf of the cell E, then the current of main circuit will be more than the current from the auxillary circuit cell. In this case the needle of the galvanometer is deflected to opposite side.

It is obvious that in between J_1 and J_2 there will be a point 'J' such that when the Jockey is made to touh J, there will be no deflection in the galvanometer. The point J is called the 'null point'. The potential difference between A and J will be equal to the e.m.f. of the cell.

Let the current flowing in the wire be i and the resistance of unit length of the wire be r. Hence, if the length of the portion AJ of the wire be 'l' cm and the potential difference between the points A and J be V, then

$$V = \text{Current} \times \text{Resistance}$$

$$V = i \times lr = Kl$$

where $K = i\,r$ = Potential difference across unit length of potential gradient.

In the Null position

$$V = E \quad \therefore \quad E = Kl$$

Method for solving the Numericals on Potentiometer

We should use the following steps should be used for solving the numericals on potentiometer.

(i) $I = E_1/(R + R_{pot} + r)$,
where E_1 = e.m.f. of the main circuit cell
R = Resistance in main circuit
R_{pot} = Resistance of potentiometer wire
r = internal resistance of the cell.

(ii) Potential difference across the terminals of the cell $V = IR_{pot}$

(iii) Potential gradient $K = V/L$,
where L = total length of the potentiometer wire

(iv) E.m.f. of the cell $E = K_l$ where l = balancing length.

HEATING EFFECT OF ELECTRIC CURRENT

The amount of work done in moving a unit charge from one point to the other is called potential difference between two points. If a positive charge is moved from a point at a higher potential to a point at a lower potential, energy is liberated. In actual practice, flow of electrons takes place from lower to higher potential. The loss of energy by the electrons in moving from lower to higher potential appears in the form of heat. When a steady flow of current is maintained through a conductor, the energy liberated is converted into heat.

Suppose a conductor AB having a potential difference V.

Potential at $A = V_A$

Potential at $B = V_B$

$$V_A > V_B$$

$$V = V_A - V_B$$

Potential energy of a electron at A

$$= (-e\,V_A)$$

Potential energy of an electron at B

$$= (-e\,V_B)$$

Current flowing through the conductor

$$= I$$

Charge flow in time dt

$$q = I.dt$$

Number of electrons flowing from B to A in time dt

$$= \frac{q}{e} = \left(\frac{I\,dt}{e}\right)$$

Loss in potential energy of the electron

$$dW = \left(\frac{I\,dt}{e}\right)\left[(-eV_B) - (-eV_A)\right]$$

$$dW = \frac{I\,dt\,e}{e}(V_A - V_B)$$

$$dW = I\,dt\,V \quad \text{...(i)}$$

Power, $$P = \frac{dW}{dt} = \frac{V\,I\,dt}{dt}$$

$$P = VI \quad \text{...(ii)}$$

Units: V is measured in volts, I in amperes and P in watts.

$$V = IR$$

$$\therefore \quad P = I^2 R$$

If the current flows for a time t, the energy liberated,

$$W = Pt \text{ joules}$$

$$W = V.I\,t \text{ joules}$$

$$W = I^2 Rt \text{ joules}$$

Heat developed

$$H = \frac{W}{J}$$

$$J = 4.2 \text{ J/cal}$$

$$\therefore \quad H = \frac{W}{4.2} = \frac{VIt}{4.2} = \frac{I^2Rt}{4.2}$$

Units : H is in calories, V in volts, I in amperes, R in ohms and t in seconds.

MEASUREMENT OF ELECTRIC POWER

The electric power consumed by an electrical appliance is expressed in watts, by the product of potential difference at the terminals (expressed in volts) and the current (expressed in amperes). The unit of power in SI unit is called watt.

$$1 \text{ watt} = 1 \text{ joule/s}$$

The Board of Trade Unit (BOT) usually adopted for purpose of public supply is called kilowatt-hour. It is the power consumed by any appliance in one hour at the rate of one kilowatt.

Kilowatt-hours (kWh)

$$= \frac{\text{Volts} \times \text{Amperes} \times \text{Hours}}{1000}$$

$$= \frac{\text{Watts} \times \text{Amperes}}{1000}$$

The horse power, normally used by engineers and technologists as the unit of power, is equal to 746 watts.

Kilowatt-hour is the unit of electrical energy. Watt is the unit of power.

$$\text{Watts} = \text{Volts} \times \text{Amperes}$$

Watt-hour is also the unit of electrical energy

$$\text{Watt–hours} = \text{Volts} \times \text{Amperes} \times \text{Hours}$$

$$= \text{Watt} \times \text{Hours}$$

$$1 \text{ kWh} = 1000 \times 3600 \text{ joules}$$

$$= 3.6 \times 10^6 \text{ J.}$$

CHEMICAL EFFECTS OF ELECTRIC CURRENT

The phenomenon of the conduction of electricity through liquids was first studied by Faraday in about 1833. Pure liquids, with the exception of mercury, are, in general, bad conductors of electricity at ordinary temperatures, but the conductivity of a liquid increases if the solution contains a metallic salt or an acid. The molecules of a salt in solution are supposed to break up into two parts. One part possesses a positive electricity and the other possesses an equal and opposite quantity of negative electricity. This process of the breaking up of the molecules of a salt in solution is called *dissociation.* The two parts are called the *ions*. When an electric field is applied between two electrodes dipping in the solution, the +vely charged ions (cations) move towards the –ve electrode (cathode) and the –vely charged ions (anions) move towards the +ve electrode (anode). *The process of decompositions of a compound by the application of on electric field is called electrolysis.* The liquid containing the compound is called an electrolyte and the vessel containing the electrolyte is called a *voltmeter*. Anions carry –ve charge and move towards the anode. Cations carry +ve charge and move towards the cathode. For this reason anions are said to be electro-negative and cations are said to be electro-positive in character. In general, all metals and hydrogen are *electro-positive* and all non-metals are electro-negative.

DEFINITIONS

Chemical equivalent of a substance is equal to the ratio of the atomic weight to valency, e.g., the atomic weight of silver is 107.88 and valency of silver is one, hence the chemical equivalent of silver is 107.88. Similarly the atomic weights of oxygen, copper, zinc and sodium are 16, 63.5, 65.37 and 23 respectively and their valencies are 2, 2, 2 and 1. Hence the chemical equivalents of the above substances are 8, 31.75, 32.68 and 23 in the same order.

The gram – equivalent of a substance is equal to its chemical equivalent expressed in grams. In the same way a gram atom of a substance is equal to its atomic weight in grams and a gram-molecule is equal to its molecular weight in grams.

From Faraday's law of electrolysis, one coulomb of electricity liberates Z grams of the substance, where, Z is the electro-chemical equivalent of the substance. The quantity of electricity needed to liberate a substance equal to its chemical equivalent expressed in grams and is equal to $\frac{\text{chemical equivalent}}{Z}$ coulombs.

For silver, the electro-chemical equivalent is equal to 0.001118 and the chemical equivalent is 107.88. Hence, the quantity of electricity required to liberate 107.88 g of silver $= \frac{107.88}{0.001118} = 96{,}500$ coulombs (approximetly). The same quantity of electricity viz., 96,500 coulombs can librate 1.008g of hydrogen, 32.68 g of zinc, 31.75 g of copper, 23 g of sodium etc. The figures given being the corresponding chemical equivalents of the substances. The quantity of electricity i.e. 96,500 coulombs is called Faraday.

The number of atoms (N) present in 1 gram-atom of a substance is a constant and is equal to 6.0192×10^{23}. N is called the Avogadro's number. In the case of a singly ionised or a monovalent atom, the charge carried by an ion.

$$= \frac{\text{Faraday}}{N}$$

$$= \frac{96{,}500}{6.0192 \times 10^{23}}$$

$$= 1.603 \times 10^{-19} \text{ coulomb}$$

and this is equal to the charge on an electron. For divalent and trivalent ions, the charge carried by the ions will be two and three times the electronic charge respectively. If each ions (monovalent) carries a charge e, then N ions will carry a charge Ne and this quantity of charge is equal to Faraday.

$\therefore$ 1 Fraday = Avogadro's Number × Charge on the electron.

FARADAY'S LAWS OF ELECTROLYSIS

The two laws of electrolysis are stated as follows:

(i) The mass of ion liberated from an electrolyte at the respective electrodes is directly proportional to the quantity of electricity which passes through it,

$$W \propto Q$$

But, $Q = It$

where Q is the charge, I is current and t is the time. If I is expressed in amperes and t in seconds, then Q will be in coulombs.

$\therefore$ $W \propto It$ or $W = ZIt$

where Z is a constant called the electro-chemical equivalent of the substance. The units of Z will be g/coulombs, if W is expressed in grams.

$$\therefore \quad Z = \frac{W}{I \times t} g/C$$

The electro-chemical equivalent of a substance is defined as the mass of the ion in grams liberated at the electrode when when one coulomb of electricity is passed through the electrolyte.

(ii) If the same quantity of electricity passes through different electrolytes, the masses of the ions liberated at the respective electrodes are proportional to their chemical equivalents.

Let W be the mass of ion liberated, then,

$$W \propto \text{chemical equivalent}$$

or $$\frac{W}{\text{Chemical equivalent}} = \text{constant}$$

provided the same quantity of electricity passes through different electrolytes.

MULTIPLE CHOICE QUESTIONS

1. The length of a conductor is doubled and its radius is halved, its resistance is
(a) unchanged (b) doubled
(c) quadrupled (d) eight times its value

2. The length of a conductor is doubled and its radius is halved, its specific resistance is
(a) unchanged (b) halved
(c) doubled (d) quadrupled

3. The length and area of cross-section of a conductor are doubled its resistance is
(a) unchaged (b) halved
(c) doubled (d) quadrupled

4. The length of a conductor is doubled. Its conductance will be
(a) unchanged (b) halved
(c) doubled (d) quadrupled

5. The resistance of a wire is $R\Omega$. The wire is stretched to double its length keeping volume constant. Now the resistance of the wire will become
(a) $4R\Omega$ (b) $2R\Omega$
(c) $R/2\Omega$ (d) $R/4\Omega$

6. A resistance of 2Ω is to be made from a copper wire (specific resistance 1.7×10^{-8} Ωm) using a wire of length 50 cm. The radius of the wire is
(a) 0.0116 mm (b) 0.0367
(c) 0.116 mm (d) 0.367 mm

7. A wire 50 cm long and 1 mm^2 in cross-section carries a current of 4A when connected to a 2V battery. The resistivity of the wire is
(a) 2×10^{-7} Ωm (b) 5×10^{-7} Ωm
(c) 4×10^{-6} Ωm (d) 1×10^{-6} Ωm

8. A pot. diff. of 20 V is applied across a conductance of 8S. The current in the conductor is
(a) 2.5 A (b) 28A
(c) 160A (d) none of the above

9. A wire 1 m long has a resistance of 1Ω. If it is uniformly stretched, so that its length increases by 25%, then its resistance will increase by
(a) 25% (b) 50%
(c) 56.25% (d) 77.33%

10. If an increase in length of copper wire is 0.5% due to stretching, the percentage increase in its resistance will be
(a) 0.1% (b) 0.2%
(c) 1% (d) 2%

11. If n is the number density of free electrons in a metallic wire, then the resistance is proportional to
(a) n (b) n^2
(c) $1/n$ (d) $1/n^2$

12. There are two concentric spheres of radius (a) and (b) respectively. If the space between them is filled with medium of resistivity ρ, then the resistance of the intergap between the two spheres will be
(a) $\frac{\rho}{4\pi(b+a)}$ (b) $\frac{\rho}{4\pi}\left(\frac{1}{b}-\frac{1}{a}\right)$
(c) $\frac{\rho}{4\pi}\left(\frac{1}{a^2}-\frac{1}{b^2}\right)$ (d) $\frac{\rho}{4\pi}\left(\frac{1}{a}-\frac{1}{b}\right)$

13. Conductivity of a conductor depends upon
(a) length (b) area of cross-section
(c) volume (d) temperature

14. The practical unit of resistance is ohm, and it is equal to
(a) 10^{11} e.m.u. (b) 10^{10} e.m.u.
(c) 10^{9} e.m.u. (d) 10^{8} e.m.u.

15. Identify the set in which all the three materials are good conductors of electricity
(a) Cu, Ag and Au
(b) Cu, Si and diamond
(c) Cu, Hg and NaCl
(d) Cu, Ge and Hg

16. If a certain piece of copper is to be shaped into a conductor of minimum resistance, its length (L) and cross-sectional area A shall be respectively

(a) $L/3$ and $4A$ (b) $L/2$ and $2A$
(c) $2L$ and $A/2$ (d) L and A

17. A given piece of wire of length l cross-sectional area A, and resistance R is stretched uniformly to a wire of length $2l$. The new resistance is
(a) $R/2$ (b) R
(c) $2R$ (d) $4R$

18. A square aluminium rod is 1m long and 5 mm on edge. What must be the radius of another aluminium rod whose length is 1 m and which has the same resistance as the previous rod.
(a) 5mm (b) 4.2mm
(c) 2.8mm (d) 1.4mm

19. A nichrome wire 1 m long and 1 mm^2 in cross-section area draws 4 ampere at 2 volt. The resistivity of nichrome is
(a) $1 \times 10^{-7}\ \Omega$-m (b) $2 \times 10^{-7}\ \Omega$-m
(c) $4 \times 10^{-7}\ \Omega$-m (d) $5 \times 10^{-7}\ \Omega$-m

20. A steady current is set up in a metallic wire of non-uniform cross-section. How is the rate of flow of electrons (R) related to the area of cross-section (A) ?
(a) $R \propto A^{-1}$ (b) $R \propto A$
(c) $R \propto A^2$ (d) R is independent of A

21. Specific resistance of copper, constantan and silver are $1.78 \times 10^{-8}, 39.1 \times 10^{-8}$ and $10^{-8}\ \Omega$-m respectively. Which of these is the best conductor of heat and electricity ?
(a) copper (b) constantan
(c) silver (d) all of them

22. Two unequal resistances are connected in parallel across a cell. Which of the following statement is true ?
(a) current through smaller resistance is more
(b) current through larger resistance is more
(c) current is same through both the resistances
(d) nothing is definite, as it depends upon the e.m.f. of the cell and the circuit conditions

23. Two plates R and S are in the form of a square and have the same thickness. A side of S is twice the side of R. Compare their resistances. The direction of current is shown by an arrow head. Figure

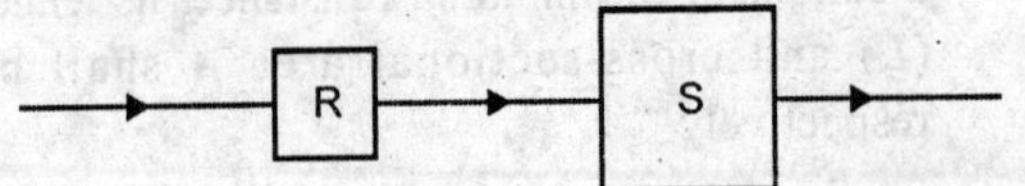

(a) the resistance of R is twice that of S
(b) both have the same resistance
(c) the resistance of S is four times that of R
(d) the resistance of R is half that of S

24. A given piece of wire of length l and radius r and resistance R is stretched uniformly to a wire of radius $r/2$. The new resistance is
(a) $16R$ (b) $4R$
(c) $R/4$ (d) $R/16$

25. Corresponding to the resistance $4.7 \times 10^6\ \Omega \pm 5\%$, which is order of colour coding on carbon resistors,
(a) yellow, violet, blue, gold
(b) yellow, violet, green, gold
(c) orange, blue, green gold
(d) orange, blue, blue gold

26. Which of the following is a characteristic temperature for the thermocouple?
(a) temperature of cold junction
(b) temperature of hot junction
(c) neutral temperature
(d) temperature of inversion

27. What is the nature of graph between temperature and thermo emf?
(a) hyperbola (b) straight line
(c) parabola (d) some other curve

28. The thermocouple can not act as
(a) refrigerator (b) a.c. generator
(c) parabola (d) voltmeter

29. Seebeck effect is inverse of
(a) Peltier effect (b) Joule's effect
(c) Thomson's effect (d) none of the above

30. What is the nature of graph between temperature and thermoelectric power?
(a) parabola (b) straight line
(c) hyperbola (d) none of the above

31. In the Seebeck series Bi occurs first followed by Cu and Fe among other. The Sb is the last in the series. If ξ_1 be the thermo emf at the given temperature difference for Bi – Sb thermocouple and ξ_2 be that for Cu – Fe thermocouple, which of the following is true?
(a) $\xi_1 = \xi_2$
(b) $\xi_1 < \xi_2$
(c) $\xi_1 > \xi_2$
(d) data is not sufficient to predict it

32. The thermo electric power at the neutral temperature is
(a) – ve
(b) zero
(c) + ve
(d) depends on the temperature of cold junction

33. What is thermoelectric power?
It is the rate of change of thermo emf with
(a) temperature
(b) time
(c) distance
(d) thermo electric current

34. What is the unit of electrochemical equivalent?
(a) kg A^{-1} (b) kg C^{-1}
(c) kg V^{-1} (d) none of the above

35. Which of the following is not the cause of low conductivity of electrolytes?
(a) low drift speed of ions
(b) high resistance by the solution to the motion of the ions
(c) low number density of charge carriers
(d) ionisation of the salt

36. As the temperature of hot junction increases, the thermo emf
(a) always increases
(b) always decreases
(c) may increase or decrease
(d) neither increases nor decreases

37. If the temperature of the hot junction of a thermocouple changes from 80°C to 100°C, the percentage change in thermoelectric power is
(a) 8 % (b) 10 %
(c) 20 % (d) 25 %

38. Same current passed through different electrolytes for given time liberates ions in proportion to their
(a) electrochemical equivalent
(b) chemical equivalent
(c) atomic masses
(d) atomic numbers

39. The amount of ions liberated by 96500 C of charge passed through the electrolyte is called
(a) electrochemical equivalent
(b) chemical equivalent
(c) gram equivalent
(d) none of the above

40. Mass of the ions liberated during electrolysis by 1 A current in one second is called
(a) equivalent weight
(b) chemical equivalent
(c) electrochemical equivalent
(d) none of the above

41. Voltameter cannot be used to measure
(a) current
(b) electrochemical equivalent
(c) potential difference
(d) charge

42. What determines the emf between the two metals placed in an electrolyte?
(a) relative position of metals in the electrochemical series
(b) distance between them
(c) strength of electrolyte
(d) nature of electrolyte

43. How much electric charge should pass through acidulated water to release 22.4 litre of hydrogen gas at NTP?
(a) 6.02×10^{23} C (b) 2×96500 C
(c) 22.4 C (d) 1 C

44. Electric current is passed through the following solutions. In which case hydrogen will be liberated at the cathode?
(a) sugar (b) sodium hydroxide
(c) sulphuric acid (d) copper sulphate

45. What carries current in an electrolyte?
(a) electrons only
(b) –ve ions only
(c) +ve ions only
(d) both +ve and –ve ions

46. Silver and zinc voltameter are connected in series and same current is passed through both of them for same time. If x kg of silver is liberated then the amount of zinc liberated will be very near to
(a) x (b) $x/5$
(c) $x/3$ (d) $x/2$

47. If 1 A of current is passed through $CuSO_4$ solution for 10 seconds, then the number of copper ions deposited at the cathode will be about
(a) 1.6×10^{19} (b) 3.1×10^{19}
(c) 4.8×10^{19} (d) 6.2×10^{19}

48. The degree of dissociation of the electrolyte does not depend on
(a) concentration
(b) dielectric constant of electrolyte
(c) volume
(d) temperature

49. The ratio of the number of hydrogen to that of oxygen atoms liberated in the electrolysis of acidulated water is
(a) 1 : 4 (b) 1 : 2
(c) 2 : 1 (d) 4 : 1

50. How much current should pass through acidulated water for 100 s to liberate 0.224 litre of hydrogen?
(a) 22.4 A (b) 19.3 A
(c) 9.65 A (d) 1 A

ANSWERS

1	2	3	4	5	6	7	8	9	10
(d)	(a)	(a)	(b)	(a)	(b)	(d)	(c)	(c)	(c)
11	12	13	14	15	16	17	18	19	20
(c)	(d)	(d)	(c)	(a)	(a)	(d)	(c)	(d)	(a)
21	22	23	24	25	26	27	28	29	30
(c)	(a)	(b)	(a)	(b)	(c)	(c)	(b)	(d)	(b)
31	32	33	34	35	36	37	38	39	40
(c)	(b)	(a)	(b)	(d)	(c)	(d)	(b)	(c)	(c)
41	42	43	44	45	46	47	48	49	50
(c)	(a)	(b)	(c)	(d)	(c)	(b)	(c)	(c)	(b)

HINTS / SOLUTIONS

1, 3. Use $R = \rho l/A$

4. Conductance $G = 1/R = A/\rho l$

i.e. $G \propto 1/l$

5. When wire is stretched to double its length, its resistance becomes four times.

6. $A = \pi r^2 = \rho l/R$ or $r = (\rho l/\pi R)^{1/2}$

7. $\rho = R\dfrac{A}{l} = \dfrac{V}{I}\dfrac{A}{l} = \dfrac{2}{4}\times\dfrac{10^{-6}}{0.5} = 10^{-6}\,\Omega\text{m}$

8. $R = 1/8\,\Omega$

and $I = V/R = 20\,(1/8) = 160\text{ A}$

9. New length, $l' = l + \dfrac{25}{100}l = \dfrac{125}{100}l$;

Let new area of cross-section $= A'$. Then

$$Ald = A'l'd \text{ or } A' = Al/l'$$

or $$A' = A \times l \Big/ \left(\frac{125}{100}\times l\right) = \frac{100}{125}A$$

$$R = \frac{\rho l}{A} \text{ and } R' = \frac{\rho l}{A'}$$

$$= \frac{\rho\left(\frac{125}{100}\right)l}{\left(\frac{100}{125}\right)A} = \frac{\rho l}{A}\left(\frac{125}{100}\right)^2$$

$$= 1.5625\,R$$

% increase in resistance

$$= \left(\frac{R' - R}{R}\right)\times 100$$

$$= \left(\frac{1.5625 - 1}{1}\right)\times 100 = 56.25\%$$

10. Approximate change in resistance $= 2 \times$ % change in length by stretching

11. $R = \dfrac{ml}{ne^2\tau A}$ i.e. $R \propto \dfrac{1}{n}$

12. Consider a concentric spherical shell of radius x and thickness dx as shown in Fig. Its resistance; dR is

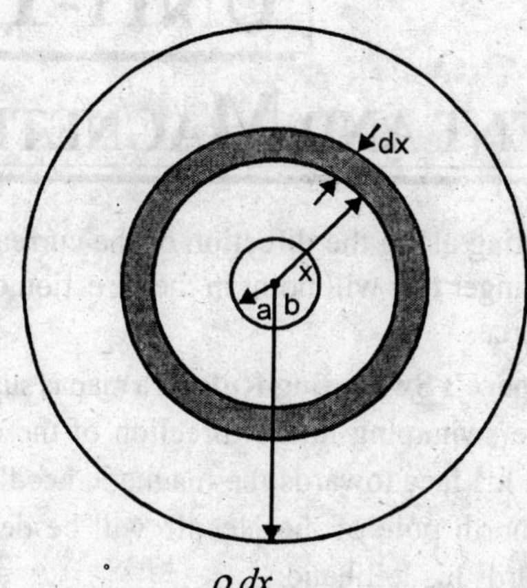

$$dR = \frac{\rho\, dx}{4\pi x^2}$$

$\therefore$ Total resistance,

$$R = \frac{\rho}{4\pi}\int_a^b \frac{dx}{x^2} = \frac{\rho}{4\pi}\left[\frac{1}{a} - \frac{1}{b}\right].$$

14. $$1 \text{ ohm} = \frac{1 \text{ volt}}{1 \text{ ampere}}$$

$$= \frac{10^8 \text{ e.m.u. of potential}}{(1/10) \text{ e.m.u. of current}}$$

$$= 10^9 \text{ e.m.u. of resistance.}$$

16. $R = \dfrac{\rho l}{A}$ or $R \propto \dfrac{l}{A}$

17. On stretching the wire, volume remains unchanged

$\therefore$ $A'l' = Al$

or $A' = Al/l' = Al/2l = A/2$

$\therefore$ $R' = \rho l'/A'$

$= \rho_2 l/(A/2) = 4\rho l/A = 4R$

18. Resistance of two wires of equal length and of same material will be same if their area of cross section is same. Therefore $A_1 = A_2$

or $b^2 = \pi r^2$

or $r = [b^2/\pi]^{1/2} = [(5)^2/(22/7)]^{1/2}$

$= 2.8$ mm.

19. $$\rho = \frac{RA}{l} = \frac{V}{I}\frac{A}{l} = \frac{2}{4}\times\frac{(10^{-6})}{1}$$

$$= 5\times 10^{-7}\ \Omega\text{m}.$$

20. Rate of flow of electrons will depend upon drift velocity and drift velocity is inversely proportional to area of cross-section, i.e. $v_d \propto 1/A$. Therefore

$$R \propto 1/A$$

21. The best conductor of electricity is one whose resistance is least. As $R = \rho l/A$. Therefore, for the given value of l and A, $R \propto \rho$.

22. When resistance are connected in parallel to a cell, the potential difference across each resistance is the same.

Current = Pot. diff./resistance.

23. Both plates have same thickness, thus area of cross-section facing current, $A_R/A_S = 1/2$. Also length of sides

$$l_R/l_S = 1/2$$

$$\text{Thus } \frac{R_R}{R_S} = \frac{l_R}{l_S}\times\frac{A_S}{A_R} = 1 \text{ or } R_R = R_S.$$

24. $R \propto 1/r^4$.

37. $dS/d\theta = \beta$ a constant.

Here $d\theta$ is 25%. Therefore dS should also be 25%.

46. Equivalent weight of silver and zinc respectively are 108 and 33. Same is the ratio of their chemical equivalents.

47. No. of copper ions

$$= \frac{\text{current} \times \text{time}}{\text{charge on electron} \times \text{valency}}$$

$$= \frac{1\times 10}{1.6\times 10^{-19}\times 2} = 3.125\times 10^{19}$$

UNIT-12

MAGNETIC EFFECTS OF CURRENT AND MAGNETISM

MAGNETIC EFFECT OF CURRENT

In 1820 it was discovered that an electric current is always accompained by a magnetic field. This is known as magnetic effect of current.

LINES OF FORCE DUE TO INFINITELY LONG STRAIGHT CURRENT CARRYING CONDUCTOR

Magnetic field is established around when a current is passed through it a straight conductor. It is important to note that :

(i) The lines of force around a straight conductor are in the form of concentric circle with their centre at the conductor.

(ii) If the conductor is vertical, then the lines of force are horizontal and vice-versa.

(iii) The direction of field at any point is at right angles to the line joining the conductor to that point.

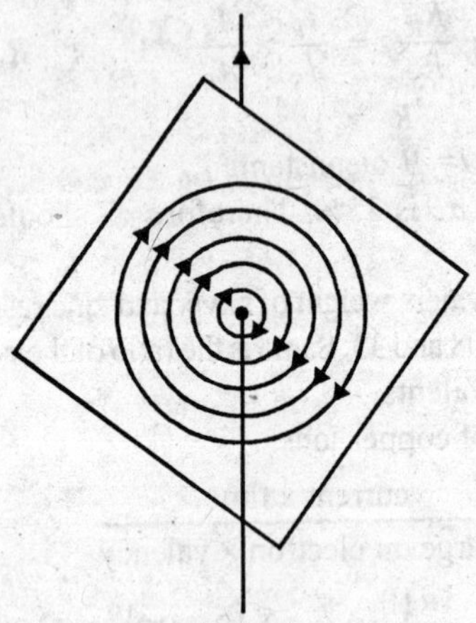

Fig. 12.1

RULES REGARDING THE DIRECTION OF FIELD

To determine the direction of magnetic field any of the following rules may be adopted.

(i) **Right Hand Palm Rule.** If the linear conductor is grasped in the palm of the right hand with thumb pointing along the direction of the current, then the finger tips will point in the direction of lines of force.

(ii) **Ampere's Swimming Rule.** If a man is supposed to be swimming in the direction of the current with his face towards the magnetic needle, then the north pole of the Needle will be deflected towards his left hand.

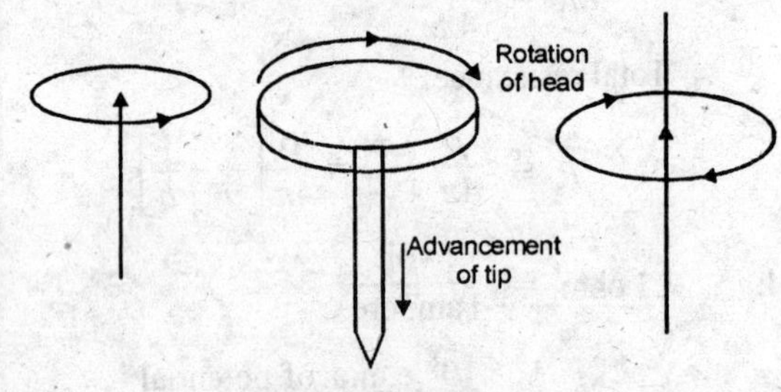

Fig. 12.2

(iii) **Maxwell's Cork Screw Rule.** If a right handed cork screw is rotated so that its tip moves in the direction of flow of current through the conductor, then the rotation of the head of the screw gives the direction of magnetic lines of force.

BIOT-SAVART LAW

In 1819 Biot and Savart on completely experimental observations, stated a formula for calculating the magnetic field at a point P due to current flowing in the conductor.

The magnetic field $\vec{dB}$ at the point P due to the small current element of length $\vec{dl}$ is

$$\vec{dB} = \frac{\mu_0}{4\pi} I . \frac{\vec{dl} \times \vec{r}}{r^3},$$

where μ_0 is a constant known as permeability of vacuum (or free space) and its value is

$$\mu_0 = 4\pi \times 10^{-7} \frac{\text{Wb}}{\text{amp} \times \text{metre}}$$

or $\mu_0 = 4\pi \times 10^{-7}$ Tm A^{-1}

Biot Savart law can also be written as

$$\vec{dB} = \frac{\mu_0}{4\pi} \cdot \frac{I\, \vec{dl} \times \vec{r}}{r^2} \quad \text{...(ii)}$$

where $\hat{r}$ is the unit vector directed from the element to the point P.

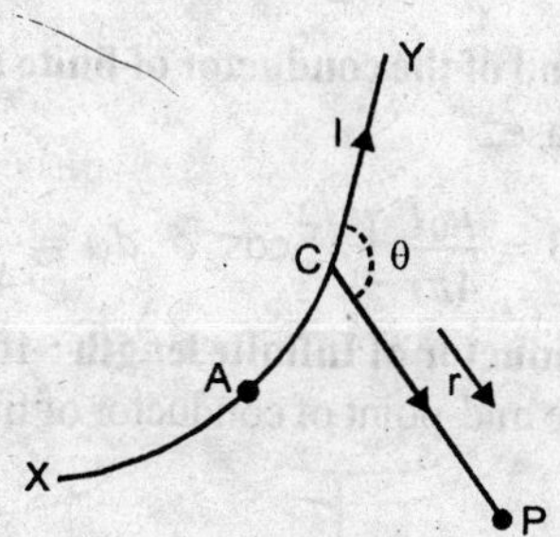

Fig. 12.3

The magnitude of the field is given by

$$dB = \frac{\mu_0}{4\pi} \cdot \frac{I\, dl \sin\theta}{r^2}$$

The direction of $\vec{dB}$ is the direction of the vector $\vec{dl} \times \vec{r}$. Therefore at the point P, the direction of $\vec{dB}$ is perpendicular to the plane of paper and is directed inwards.

From equation (iii) it follows that the field dB due to small current carrying conductor is

(i) directly proportional to the current, i.e. $dB \propto I$.

(ii) directly proportional to the length of the element, i.e. $dB \propto dl$

(iii) directly proportional to the sine of angle θ between the direction of the current and the radius vector of the point. If $\theta = 0$ or π, then dB = 0. Thus for all the points along the length of the element, the field is zero. the element and perpendicular to its length.

(iv) inversely proportional to the square of the distance r of the point P from the element, i.e. $dB \propto 1/r^2$

This is also called the inverse square law.

Note. The magnetic field due to the whole conductor XY is obtained by intergrating $\vec{dB}$ over the entire length of the conductor, so the magnetic field due to whole conductor is given by

$$\vec{B} = \vec{dB}$$

or
$$\vec{B} = \frac{\mu_0}{4\pi} \int \frac{I\, \vec{dl} + \vec{r}}{r^2}$$

COMPARISON BETWEEN COULOMB'S LAW AND BIOT-SAVART LAW

Coulomb's law in electrostatics and magnetic field due to a current carrying conductor have following similarities.

(i) Magnetic field is produced by a current element $I\, dl$, whereas the electric field is produced by an electric charge 'q'.

(ii) The magnitude of electric as well as magnetic field varies as the inverse of square of the distance of the conductor from the current element.

FIELD AT A POINT DUE TO LONG STRAIGHT CURRENT CARRYING CONDUCTOR

Suppose current I is flowing through a long current carrying conductor. Consider a small element CD of length dl on the conductor. The field at P due to the conductor is

$$|\vec{dB}| = \frac{\mu_0 I\, dl \sin\theta}{4\pi x^2},$$

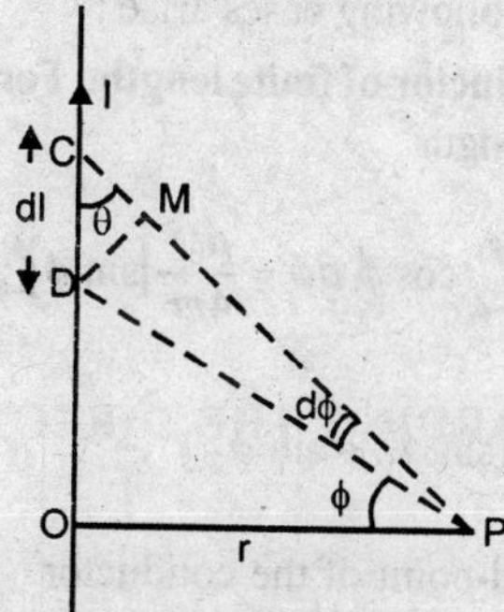

Fig. 12.4

where x is the distance of the point P from the current element CD and θ is the angle between

CD and the line joining it with the point P. The field is perpendicular to the plane containing P and the wire.

Since, the contribution at P of different current elements have the same direction, hence the total magnetic field is given by

$$B = \int \frac{\mu_0}{4\pi} \frac{Idl \sin \theta}{x^2} \quad ...(i)$$

From the figure, in ΔCDM,

$$\frac{DM}{CD} = \sin \theta \quad \therefore \quad \frac{DM}{\sin \theta} = dl$$

Hence from equation (i), we get

$$B = \frac{\mu_0 I}{4\pi} \int \frac{DM}{x^2} \quad ...(ii)$$

But, angle $= \frac{\text{arc}}{\text{radius}}$, hence, $d\phi = \frac{DM}{x}$

Hence, from equation (ii), we get

$$B = \frac{\mu_0 I}{4\pi} \int \frac{d\phi}{x}$$

But, in ΔOPD, $r/x = \cos \phi$

$\therefore \quad 1/x = (\cos \phi) / r$

Putting the value of $1/x$ in equation (iii), we get

$$B = \frac{\mu_0 I}{4\pi r} \int \cos \phi \, d\phi \quad ...(iii)$$

Equation (iii) gives the general equation for the field, but following cases arise :

(I) For a conductor of finite length. For a conductor of finite length

$$B = \frac{\mu_0 I}{4\pi r} \int_{-\phi_1}^{\phi_2} \cos \phi \, d\phi = \frac{\mu_0 I}{4\pi r} [\sin \phi]_{-\phi_1}^{\phi_2}$$

or $$B = \frac{\mu_0 I}{4\pi r} [\sin \phi_1 + \sin \phi_2]$$

At the mid-point of the conductor

$$\phi_1 = \phi_2 = \phi$$

$$\therefore \quad B = \frac{\mu_0 I}{2\pi r} [\sin \phi]$$

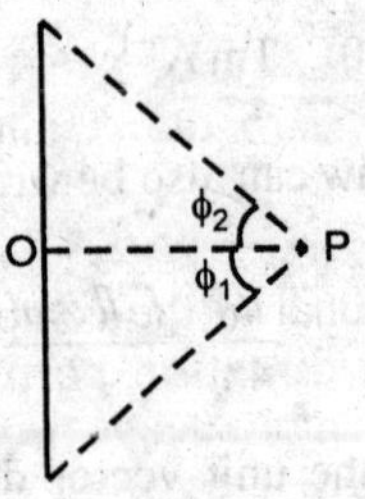

Fig. 12.5

(II) At one end of the conductor of finite length

In this case,

$$B = \frac{\mu_0 I}{4\pi r} \int_0^{\pi/2} \cos \phi \, d\phi = \frac{\mu_0 I}{4\pi r}$$

(III) For conductor of Infinite length : If the point P lies at the mid-point of conductor of finite length, then

$$B = \frac{\mu_0 I}{4\pi r} \int_{-\pi/2}^{\pi/2} \cos \phi \, d\phi = \frac{\mu_0 I}{2\pi r}$$

(IV) At one end of conductor of infinite length :

In this case $B = \frac{\mu_0 I}{4\pi r} \int_0^{\pi/2} \cos \phi d\phi = \frac{\mu_0 I}{4\pi r}$

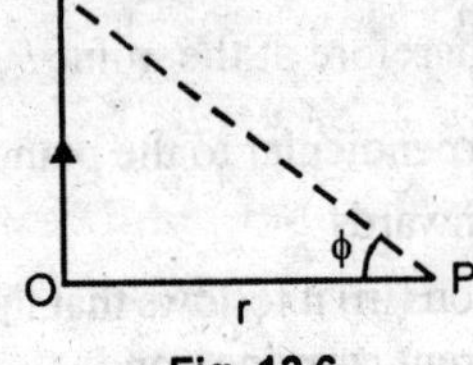

Fig. 12.6

FORCE ON A MOVING CHARGE IN A MAGNITUDE FIELD-LORENTZ FORCE

Let us consider a charge $+q$ moving in a uniform magnetic field of strength $\vec{B}$ directed along Y-axis. The charge $+q$ is moving in $X - Y$ plane making an angle θ with the direction of $\vec{B}$ as shown in the Fig. The charged particle experiences a force $\vec{F}$ along Z-axis i.e. perpendicular to the plane of $\vec{v}$ and $\vec{B}$ in outward direction, such that following rules are obeyed :

(i) The magnitude of force is directly proportional to the magnitude of charge, i.e. $F \propto q$

(ii) The magnitude of force is directly proportional to the component of velocity along a direction perpendicular to the direction of the magnetic field i.e.,

$$F \propto v \sin \theta$$

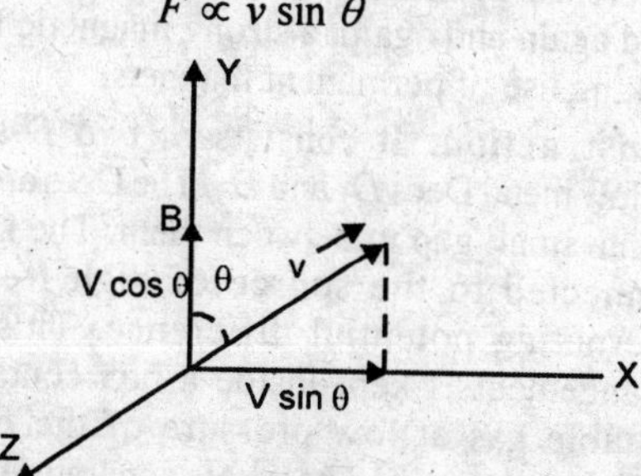

Fig. 12.7

Combining the two factors, we have

$$F \propto q v \sin \theta \quad \text{or } F = B q v \sin \theta$$

where the constant of proportionality $\vec{B}$ represents the strength of the magnetic field in which the charge is moving.

Vectorially the above expression can be written as

$$\vec{F} = q(\vec{v} \times \vec{B})$$

It is clear by the property of cross product that $\vec{v}$ is perpendicular to the plane containing $\vec{F}$ and $\vec{B}$.

AMPERE'S CIRCUITAL LAW

This law states that the line integral of magnetic flux density $(\vec{B})$ around any closed path or circuit is equal to μ_0 (permeability of free space) times the total current I enclosed by the closed circuit. Mathematically

$$\oint \vec{B}.\vec{dl} = \mu_0 I$$

APPLICATIONS OF AMPERE'S CIRCUITAL LAW

This law finds its application to many a problems in the electromagnetism. Some of them are as follows :

(i) Magnetic field due to a toroidal solenoid

A toroidal solenoid is an anchor ring around which a large number of turns of a copper wire are wrapped as shown in the figure. Consider a toroidal solenoid having n turns per unit length. O is the centre of toroid and a the radius of the circle.

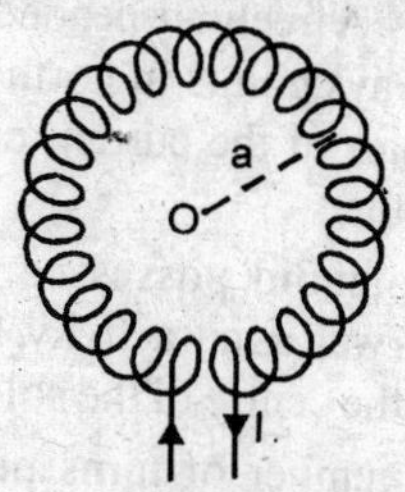

Fig. 12.8

Suppose, a current I is passed through the solenoid. The magnetic field produced will be same at all points on the circcumference of the circle and at any point, it will act along the tangent to the circle.

By Ampere's circuital law, $\oint \vec{B}.\vec{dl} = \mu_0$ (the current enclosed by a circle of radius a).

$$\therefore \quad \oint \vec{B}.\vec{dl} = \mu_0 (2\pi an . I),$$

where $2\pi na$ = total number of turns in the toroid and hence the total current through it = $2\pi naI$.

Since, $\vec{dl}$ and $\vec{dl}$ are parallel to each other,

$$\therefore \quad \oint \vec{B}\, dl \cos \theta = \mu_0 (2\pi anI)$$

$$\text{or} \quad B \oint dl = \mu_0 (2\pi anI)$$

$$\therefore \quad B(2\pi a) = (2\pi anI)\mu_0 \quad \text{or } B = \mu_0 nI$$

(ii) Magnetic field due to a straight long solenoid

A straight solenoid consists of a hollow tube over which a large number of turns of insulated copper wire are uniformly wound.

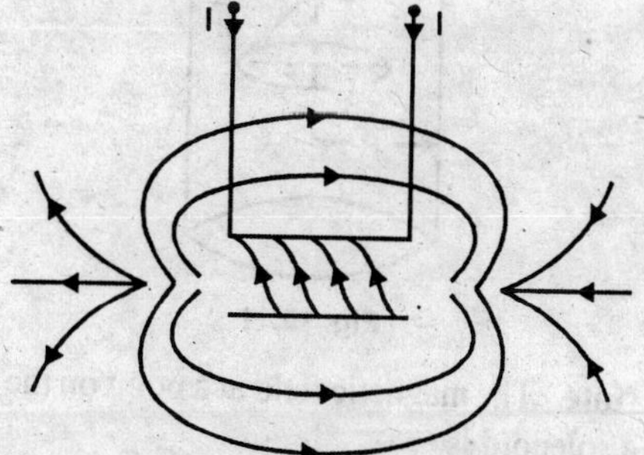

Fig. 12.9

When a current I is passed through the solenoid, each turn of the solenoid behaves as if a small bar magnet is placed along its axis and hence the solenoid also behave as a bar magnet placed along the axis. A freely suspended current carrying solenoid always points in north-south direction. Two like poles of the current carrying solenoid repel each other.

Thus the solenoid possesses the property of directivity as well as attractivity, like a bar magnet. The field at the centre of the solenoid is $B = \mu_0 nI$ where n = number of turns per unit length of solenoid. If N = total number of turns in the solenoid of length l, then, $n = N/l$.

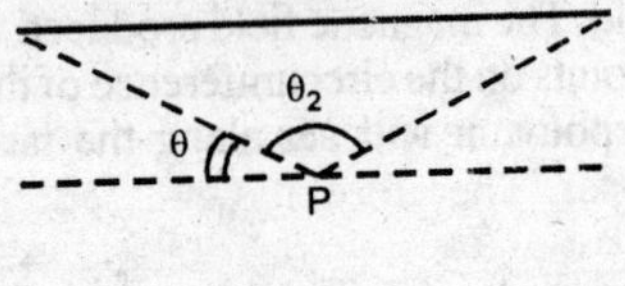

Fig. 12.10

The only dissimilarity between a solenoid and a bar magnet is that in the solenoid the field is maximum at the centre ($B = \mu_0 nI$) and minimum ($B = \mu_0 nI/2$) at the ends while in case of a bar magnet the field is maximum at the poles and zero at the centre.

If the solenoid has a core of magnetic material having relative permeability μ_r, then the field at its axis is given by $B = \mu_0 \mu_r nI$.

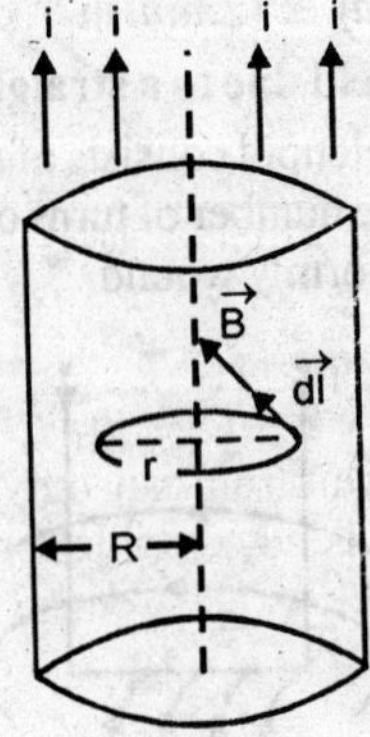

Fig. 12.11

Note. The magnetic field at a point on the axis of a solenoid is

$$B = \mu_0 ni\,[\cos\theta_1 - \cos\theta_2]$$

CYCLOTRON

It was designed by Lawerence and Livingstone in 1931. It is a device to acceleratre charged particles to high energies starting with a low initial energy.

Principle. It is based on the principle that the positive ions can be accelerated to high energies with a comparatively smaller alternating potential difference by making them to cross the electric field again and again, a strong magnetic field by making use of permanent magnets.

Construction. It consists of two *D*-shaped, hollow metal Dees D_1 and D_2. The Dees are placed with a small gap in between them. The Dees are connected to the source of high frequency alternating potential difference. This whole arrangement is kept inside a box containing a suitable gas at low pressure of the order of 10^{-3} mm. mercury. The whole apparatus is placed in between poles of a strong electromagnet *NS* as shown in figure. The magnetic field is perpendicular to the plane of the Dees.

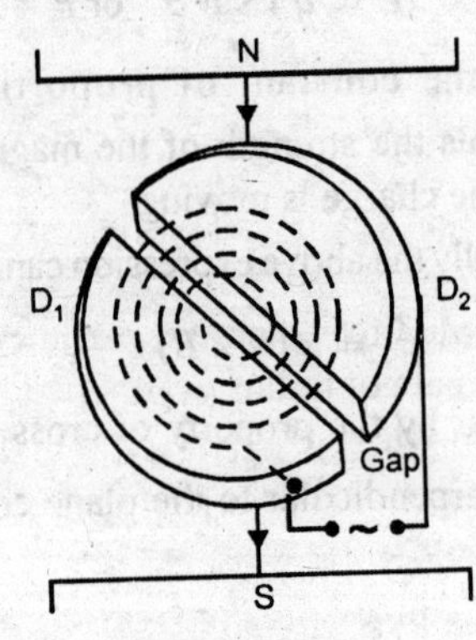

Fig. 12.12

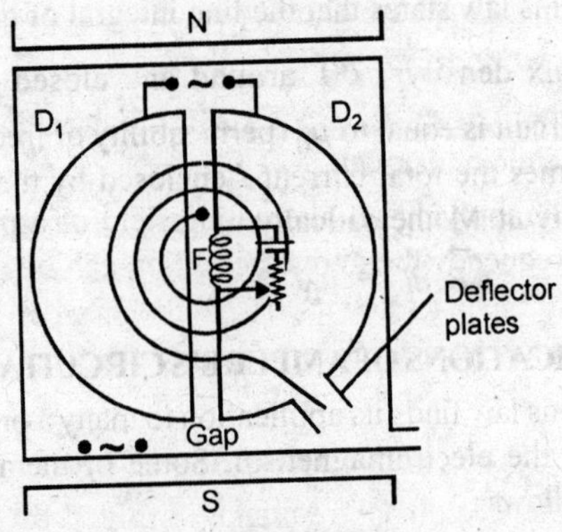

Fig. 12.13

A tungsten filament heated electrically is placed inside the gap between the Dees.

Theory. The filament emits an electron in the gap when it is heated. This electron collides with the atoms of the gas filled in the chamber and produces a positive ion (say an α-particle). This α-particle is accelerated towards that Dee which is negative at that time. The path of the α-particle inside the Dees is semicircular. When the charged particle again enters into the gap, the polarity of the Dees change and the other Dee becomes negative. The charged particle gets accelerated again and is attracted towards the other Dee. Its velocity increases and hence it moves in a circular path of greater radius. Thus, as the charged particles come again and again into the field they are accelerated more and more. They are finally taken out of the Dee's with the help of deflector plates.

Suppose a charged particle having a charge 'q' is accelerated in a magnetic field of induction B. It is attracted by the Dee which is negative at that time and starts moving towards it with a velocity v. The motion of charged particle at right angles to the magnetic field creates a Lorentz force on the particle due to which the particle bends into a circular path of radius $r = mv/Bq$.

The path of the particle inside the Dees is semicircular and the time which the particle spends inside the Dees is given by

$$t = \frac{\text{Length of semicircular path}}{\text{Velocity}} = \frac{\pi r}{v}.$$

Putting the value of r, we get $t = \pi m/Bq$

The above time is independent of velocity of the charged particle as well as the radius of the semicircular path.

By applying an alternating field of a particular frequency the above condition can be achieved for the positive ions. If T is the time period of the magnetic field then

$$t = T/2 = \pi m/Bq,$$

$$\therefore \quad T = 2\pi m/Bq$$

The cyclotron frequency is given by $\nu = 1/T = Bq/2\pi m$

This is known as magnetic resonance frequency.

Maximum energy of the positive Ions. Let the velocity acquired by the positive ion when it moves along the circular path of largest radius R be v_{max}, then, $v_{max} = BqR/m$.

The maximum energy acquired by the positive ion is

$$E = \frac{1}{2}mv_{max}^2 = \frac{B^2q^2R^2}{2m}.$$

Limitations of Cyclotron. As the charged particle is accelerated, its velocity increases and hence the mass increases, according to the formula,

$$m = \frac{m_0}{\sqrt{(1 - v^2/c^2)}}$$

Hence the time spent inside the Dees ($t \propto m$) also increases. Therefore, the charged particle takes more and more time inside the Dees. Since the electric field changes after a fixed interval, the charged particle lags behind the field, finally it becomes impossible to accelerate the charged particle as it becomes completely out of step of the applied A.C.

The above difficulty can be overcome in following two ways :

(i) As v increases, $\sqrt{(1 - v^2/c^2)}$ decreases.

Increase B such that $B\sqrt{(1 - v^2/c^2)}$ remains constant. Such a cyclotron is known as synchrotron.

(ii) As v increase, the frequency of the cyclotron decreases. The electric field is adjusted so that the frequency of the applied field is always equal to that of the charged particle. Such a cyclotron is called as frequency modulated cyclotron or synchro-cyclotron.

Note. A cyclotron can only accelerate heavy particles. It is not suitable for accelerating light particles such as electrons.

Betatron is used to acelerate electrons.

MAGNETISM

TORQUE ON A CURRENT LOOP IN A MAGNETIC FIELD

Consider a rectangular loop $PQRS$ suspended in

a uniform magnetic field of flux density $\vec{B}$. The loop carries a current I flowing in it. Let $PQ = RS = l$ and width $QR = SP = b$.

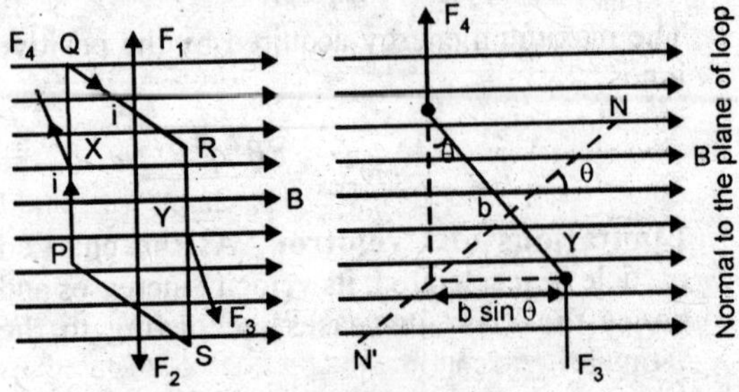

Fig. 12.14

As we know that a current-carrying conductor placed in magnetic field experiences a force. So, there is a force on each side of the current-loop in the direction determined by the Fleming's left hand rule. The vertical sides PQ and RS, each of length l, are always perpendicular to the magnetic field B. Hence, the forces on these are

$$F_4 = F_3 = ilB$$

The forces F_3 and F_4 are equal, parallel and opposite to each other, but their lines of action are different. Hence they form a deflecting couple. Due to this couple, the current-loop gets deflected from its position.

Let at any instant, the normal to the plane of loop makes an angle θ with the direction of the magnetic field B as shown in the Fig. Then at this instant, the moment of the deflecting couple is

τ = one force × perpendicular distance between the forces $= il_B \times b \sin \theta$.

But $\quad l \times b = A$ (area of the loop).

$\therefore \quad \tau = iAB \sin \theta.$

Since the forces F_1 and F_2 acting on the remaining two sides QR and SP of the loop are equal and opposite to each other but their line of action is the same. Hence they cancel each other. Thus the net force on the current-loop is zero only the couple $\tau = iAB \sin \theta$ acts on it. This couple deflects the loop to a position in which the axis of the loop is parallel to the magnetic field (i.e. the plane of the loop is perpendicular to the magnetic field B). In this position ($\theta = 0$), the moment of couple becomes zero.

If there are n turns in the coil, then the total torque acting on it is

$$\tau = B \sin A \sin \theta$$

This expression is valid for any shape of the coil.

Notes.

(i) If the plane of the coil is parallel to the magnetic flux density $\vec{B}$, then $\theta = 90°$.

(ii) If the plane of the coil is at right angles to the magnetic flux density $\vec{B}$, then $\theta = 0°$.

(iii) If the plane of the coil makes any other angle α with the field direction, then $\theta = (90° - \alpha)$.

MAGNETOSTATICS

COUPLE ON A BAR-MAGNET IN A MAGNETIC FIELD

A current-loop placed in a magnetic field experiences a couple which has a tendency to rotate the loop to make its axis parallel to the magnetic field. Similarly, a bar-magnet suspended in a magnetic field rotates to a position in which the axis of magnet is parallel to the magnetic field. In fact, a bar-magnet placed in a magnetic field is acted upon by a couple which has a tendency to keep the axis of magnet parallel to the magnetic field. In accordance with the atomic model of magnet, each atom of the magnet is equivalent to a small current-loop and all these current-loops are aligned in the same direction. In a magnetic field, the sum of couples on these small loops, is the couple acting on the magnet.

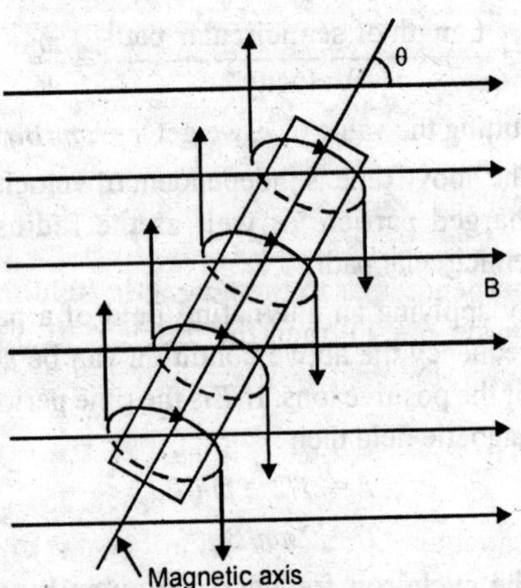

Fig. 12.15

Since we know that in a magnetic field B, the couple on a current-loop placed at an angle θ with the direction of the field is

$$\tau = (IA)B\sin\theta,$$

where A is the area of the current-loop. Let N be the total number of current-loops in the bar magnet, then the couple acting on the whole magnet is

$$\tau = (NIA)B\sin\theta. \quad ...(i)$$

The behaviour of a bar-magnet, or of a current-carrying coil in a magnetic field is similar to the behaviour of an electric dipole in an electric field. Hence, a bar-magnet, and a current-coil, etc. are also called 'magnetic dipoles'. The torque, τ acting on an electric dipole placed in an electric field E at an angle θ with the direction of the field is

$$\tau = pE\sin\theta, \quad ...(ii)$$

where p is the moment of the electric dipole. Comparing equation (i) and (ii), we find that the quantity (NIA) is equivalent to the moment p of the electric dipole. It is called the 'magnetic dipole moment' or the 'magnetic moment' M of the bar-magnet. Thus, $M = NIA$.

Hence, the torque acting on a bar-magnet is

$$\tau = MB\sin\theta \text{ or } \vec{\tau} = \vec{M} \times \vec{B}$$

MAGNETIC DIPOLE MOMENT

Suppose a magnetic dipole is placed at an angle θ with the direction of a uniform magnetic field B. The moment of the couple acting on the dipole is given by

$$\tau = MB\sin\theta$$

where M is the moment of the magnetic dipole. If the axis of the magnetic dipole be perpendicular to the magnetic field B($\theta = 90°$ or $\sin\theta = 1$), then the moment of the couple acting on it will be maximum. If it be τ_{max}, then

$$\tau_{max} = MB \quad \therefore \quad M = \tau_{max}/B$$

If $B = 1$, then $M = \tau_{max}$. Hence, the magnetic moment of a magnetic dipole is the moment of the couple which acts on the dipole when kept perpendicular to a uniform unit magnetic field.

Units and Dimensions : The unit of the magnetic moment,

$$M = \frac{\text{unit of } \tau_{max}}{\text{unit of } B}$$

$$= \frac{\text{newton - metre}}{\text{newton/(amp - metre)}} = \text{amp - metre}^2$$

The dimensions of magnetic moment M are $[L^2A]$.

Work done in rotating a magnetic dipole in a magnetic field

Consider a small magnetic dipole of dipole moment θ placed in a magnetic field of intensity $\vec{B}$. The torque acting on the dipole is

$$\tau = MB\sin\theta.$$

The small work done by this torque, in rotating the dipole through an angle θ is

$$dW = \tau d\theta = MB\sin\theta\, d\theta$$

Hence, the total work done in deflecting the dipole through an angle θ is

$$W = \int_0^\theta \tau\, d\theta = MB\int_0^\theta \sin\theta\, d\theta$$

$$\therefore \quad W = M_B[1 - \cos\theta]$$

Particular cases

(i) if $\theta = 0$, $\cos\theta = 1$, then $\quad W = M_B[1 - 1] = 0$

(ii) if $\theta = 90°$, $\cos\theta = 0$, then $\quad W = MB$

(iii) if $\theta = 180°$, $\cos\theta = -1$, then $\quad W = 2MB$

POTENTIAL ENERGY OF A MAGNETIC DIPOLE PLACED IN A MAGNETIC FIELD

Consider a magnetic dipole of dipole moment M placed in a uniform magnetic field of strength B such that rotation of the dipole makes an angle θ with the direction of the field. Then, magnitude of the torque acting on the dipole is $\tau = MB\sin\theta$.

This torque tends to align the magnetic dipole along the direction of field. If the dipole is rotated against the action of this torque, work has to be done. Suppose, the dipole is rotated through an infinitesimally small angle $d\theta$ under the action of a constant torque τ.

Then small amount of work done in rotating the dipole through an infinitesimally small angle $d\theta$, is

$$dW = \tau d\theta = MB\sin\theta\, d\theta$$

If the dipole is rotated from initial position $\theta = \theta_1$ to the final position $\theta = \theta_2$, then the total work done is given by

$$W = \int_{\theta_1}^{\theta_2} MB \sin\theta \, d\theta = MB \int_{\theta_1}^{\theta_2} \sin\theta \, d\theta$$

$$= MB\left[-\cos\theta\right]_{\theta_1}^{\theta_2} = -MB(\cos\theta_2 - \cos\theta_1)$$

The work done in rotating the dipole is stored as its potential energy (U). Thus,

$$U = -MB(\cos\theta_2 - \cos\theta_1) \quad ...(i)$$

Assume that the potential energy of the dipole will be zero, when $\theta = 90°$. Then potential energy of the dipole in any position can be obtained by setting $\theta_1 = 90°$ and $\theta_2 = \theta$ in equation (ii)

$U = -MB(\cos\theta - \cos 90°)$ or $U = -MB\cos\theta$

$U = -\vec{M}.\vec{B}$

Vectorially,

Particular Cases

(i) When $\theta = 0°$, $U = -MB\cos 0° = -MB$ (minimum)

(ii) When $\theta = 90°$, $U = -MB\cos 90° = 0$

(iii) When $\theta = 180°$, $U = -MB\cos 180° = MB$ (maximum)

Thus, dipole possesses minimum potential energy, when $\vec{M}$ and $\vec{B}$ are parallel and maximum potential energy when $\vec{M}$ and $\vec{B}$ are anti-parallel.

BAR MAGNET

MAGNETIC POLES

A magnet has two poles. When a magnet is brought near a heap of iron fillings the ends of the magnet show the maximum attraction. These ends where the magnetic attraction is maximum are called poles of the magnet.

A magnet suspended freely, always points in $N-S$ direction. The pole which points towards north is called **north pole (N)** and the pole that points towards the south is called **south pole (S)**. The SI unit of strength of a magnetic pole is ampere metre (A m).

EFFECTIVE LENGTH OF MAGNET

The distance between the poles of the magnet is called the effective length of the magnet.

MAGNETIC MOMENT

The product of pole strength (m) and effective length ($2l$) of the magnet is called the Magnetic Moment. Thus $M = m \times 2l = 2ml$.

Its units are Ampere-m^2 and it is a vector quantity. Its direction is along the axis of the magnet from north pole of the magnet to the south pole.

MAGNETIC FIELD

The region around a pole in which magnetic effect can be experienced is called magnetic field.

Properties of magnetic lines of force

The properties of magnetic lines of force are as follows

(1) Magnetic lines of force travel from north pole to south pole outside the magnet and from south to north pole inside the magnet.

(2) Magnetic lines of force are closed curves.

(3) Magnetic lines of force emerge out normally from the magnetised surface.

(4) The tangent drawn at any point of the magnetic lines of force represent the direction of magnetic field at that point.

(5) Two lines of force never intersect each other.

(6) Magnetic lines of force try to contract in length and repel each other laterally.

(7) The lines of force of uniform field are parallel to each other.

(8) The field is strong at places where the lines of force are crowded while it is weak at places where they are farther apart.

INTENSITY OF MAGNETIC FIELD

The number of lines of force crossing unit area of the surface, normally is called intensity of magnetic field.

OR

The force acting on unit pole placed in the magnetic field is called intensity of magnetic field.

i.e. $\quad H = (\mu_0/4\pi).(m/r^2)$

TANGENT LAW

Suppose we have two uniform magnetic fields at right angles to one another and if a magnet *NS* is placed in such a combination of fields, then it will be acted upon by two forces (*mF, mF*) equal, parallel and opposite tending to set it parallel to the direction of *F*; and two other forces (*mH, mH*) also equal, parallel and opposite, tending to set it parallel to the direction of *H*.

The magnet will be acted upon by two couples tending to rotate the magnet in opposite directions. It will set in a direction θ, such that the two couples balance each other.

Deflecting couple due to the force (*mF, mF*) $= mF \times NO$

$= mF.2l \cos\theta = (2ml)\, F \cos\theta = MF \cos\theta$

Restoring couple due to the forces (*mH, mH*) $= mH \times SO$

$= mH.2l \sin\theta = (2ml)\, H \sin\theta = MH \sin\theta$

∴ When the magnet is in the equilibrium position,

$$MF \cos\theta = MH \sin\theta$$

or
$$F = H\frac{\sin\theta}{\cos\theta} = H\tan\theta$$

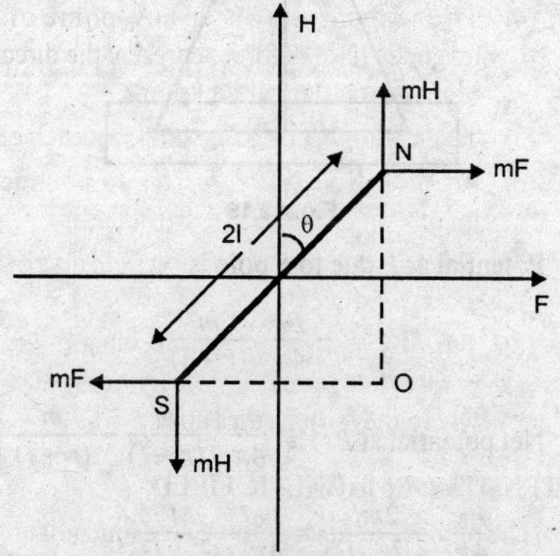

Fig. 12.16

Thus a magnet simultaneously acted upon by two uniform fields at right angles to each other will be deflected through an angle θ, such that the tangent of the angle of deflection gives the ratio of the two fields.

$$\tan\theta = F/H \quad \text{...(i)}$$

This is called Tangent Law.

FIELD DUE TO A SMALL BAR MAGNET (MAGNETIC DIPOLE)

(i) In End-on position

In End-on position the point lies on the axis of the magnet. Let *r* be the distance of the point *P* from the centre *O* of the magnet. Let $2l$ be the length of the magnet and *m* be its pole strength. Then $NP = (r - l)$, $SP = (r + l)$.

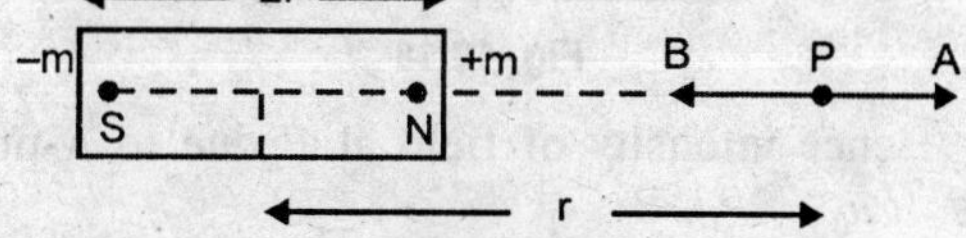

Fig. 12.17

The intensity due to the *N*-pole

$$\vec{PA} = \frac{\mu_0}{4\pi}\frac{m}{NP^2} = \frac{\mu_0}{4\pi}\cdot\frac{m}{(r-l)^2}$$

and, the intensity due to the *S*-pole,

$$\vec{PB} = \frac{\mu_0}{4\pi}\frac{m}{(SP^2)} = \frac{\mu_0}{4\pi}\cdot\frac{m}{(r+l)^2}$$

Thus, the resultant intensity is

$$B = \frac{\mu_0}{4\pi}\left[\frac{m}{(r-l)^2} - \frac{m}{(r+l)^2}\right] = \frac{\mu_0}{4\pi}\cdot\frac{4mlr}{(r^2-l^2)^2}.$$

$$B = \frac{\mu_0}{4\pi}\frac{2Mr}{(r^2-l^2)^2}$$

for a small magnet $r^2 >> l^2$, hence

$$B = \frac{\mu_0}{4\pi}\frac{2M}{r^3}$$

The direction of $\vec{B}$ is along the line joining the two poles from *S* pole to *N* pole.

(ii) Broad side-on position

In broad side-on the point lies on the magnetic equator of the magnet i.e. on the right bisector of the magnet.

Let us consider a magnet *NS* of pole strength *m* and length $2l$. *P* is the point on the right bisector of this magnet such that $OP = r$. Then,

$$SP = NP = (r^2 + l^2)^{1/2}$$

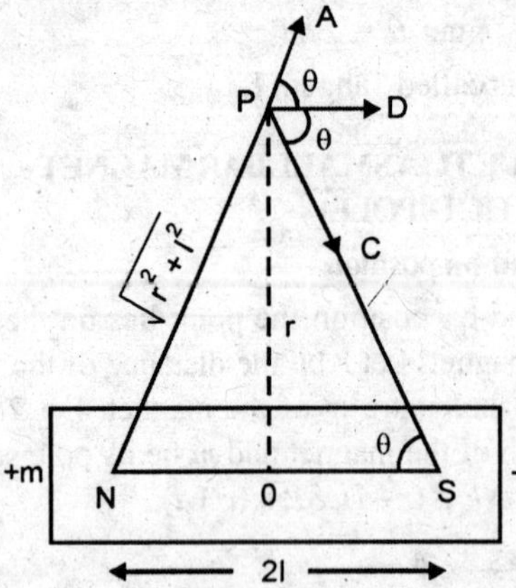

Fig. 12.18

Hence intensity of field at P due to N-pole $= \frac{\mu_0}{4\pi} \cdot \frac{m}{(r^2 + l^2)}$ along $\overrightarrow{PA}$. The intensity of field at P due to S-pole $= \frac{\mu_0}{4\pi} \cdot \frac{m}{(r^2 + l^2)}$ along $\overrightarrow{PC}$.

Each of these intensities can be resolved into two components : (i) along $\overrightarrow{PD}$ and (ii) perpendicular to $\overrightarrow{PD}$. The components perpendicular to $\overrightarrow{PD}$ being equal and opposite neutralise each other while the components parallel to $\overrightarrow{PD}$ add up.

Thus the resultant intensity at P is

$$B = \frac{\mu_0}{4\pi} \cdot \frac{m}{(r^2 + l^2)} \cos\theta + \frac{\mu_0}{4\pi} \frac{m}{(r^2 + l^2)} \cos\theta$$

or $$B = \frac{\mu_0}{4\pi}\left[\frac{2m}{(r^2 + l^2)} \cdot \frac{l}{(r^2 + l^2)^{1/2}}\right] = \frac{\mu_0}{4\pi} \cdot \frac{M}{(r^2 + l^2)^{3/2}}$$

For a small magnet $r^2 >> l^2$, hence $B = \frac{\mu_0}{4\pi} \cdot \frac{M}{r^3}$

The direction of $\vec{B}$ is parallel to the axis from N-pole to S-pole.

MAGNETIC POTENTIAL

The work done in carrying a unit N-pole from infinity to any point against the field is called the magnetic potential at that point.

OR

A quantity whose space rate of variation in any direction gives the intensity of the magnetic field is called magnetic potential. i.e. $B = -\frac{dV}{dx}$.

MAGNETIC POTENTIAL DUE TO A POINT POLE

Magnetic potential due to point pole, at a distance r from the pole of strength m is given by

$$V = \frac{\mu_0}{4\pi} \cdot \frac{m}{r} \frac{\text{joule}}{\text{weber}}.$$

POTENTIAL DUE TO A MAGNETIC DIPOLE

(i) At a point in end-side on position : Potential at P due to N pole of magnet of pole strength m and length $2l$ is $V_1 = \frac{\mu_0}{4\pi} \cdot \frac{m}{r - l}$.

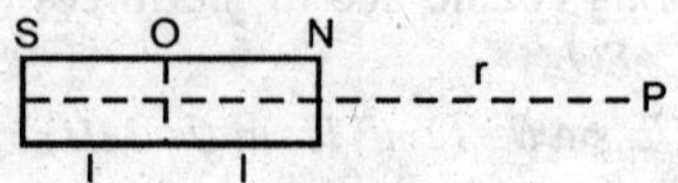

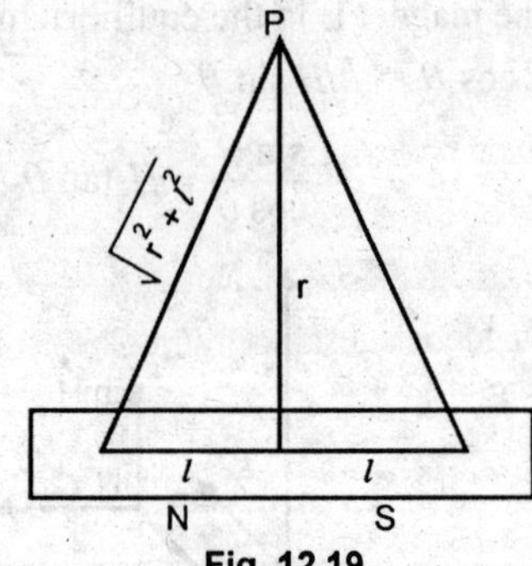

Fig. 12.19

Potential at P due to S pole is

$$V_2 = -\frac{\mu_0}{4\pi} \cdot \frac{m}{(r+1)}.$$

$\therefore$ Net potential at P, $V = \frac{\mu_0}{4\pi}\left[\frac{m}{(r-l)} - \frac{m}{(r+l)}\right]$

or $$V = \frac{\mu_0}{4\pi} \cdot \frac{2ml}{(r^2 - l^2)} = \frac{\mu_0}{4\pi} \frac{M}{(r^2 - l^2)}.$$

For a very short magnet, $l^2 << r^2$, hence

$$V = \frac{\mu_0}{4\pi} \cdot \frac{M}{r^2}.$$

(ii) At a point in the broadside-on position : Potential at P due to N pole

$$= \frac{\mu_0}{4\pi} \cdot \frac{m}{\sqrt{(r^2 + l^2)}}$$

Potential at P due to S pole $= \frac{\mu_0}{4\pi} \cdot \frac{m}{\sqrt{(r^2 + l^2)}}$.

$\therefore$ Net potential at P due to $NS = 0$.

Thus potential at any point lying on the magnetic equator of a magnet is zero in both CGS and MKS systems.

Note. The magnetic potential at a point lying on a line passing through the centre and making angle θ with axis is given by

$V = \frac{\mu_0}{4\pi} \cdot \frac{M \cos\theta}{(r^2 - l^2)}$ For small dipole $r^2 >> l^2$, hence

$$V = \frac{\mu_0}{4\pi} \cdot \frac{M \cos\theta}{r^2}.$$

CLASSIFICATION OF MAGNETIC SUBSTANCES

Curie and Faraday observed that almost all substances have certain magnetic properties. Placing many substances in magnetic fields he studied their behaviour. On the basis of magnetic behaviour of different materials, he divided them into three categories : (1) diamagnetic substances, (2) paramagnetic substances and (3) ferromagnetic substances.

1. Diamagnetic Substances

(i) When these substances are placed in a magnetic field they acquire feeble magnetism opposite to the direction of the magnetic field.

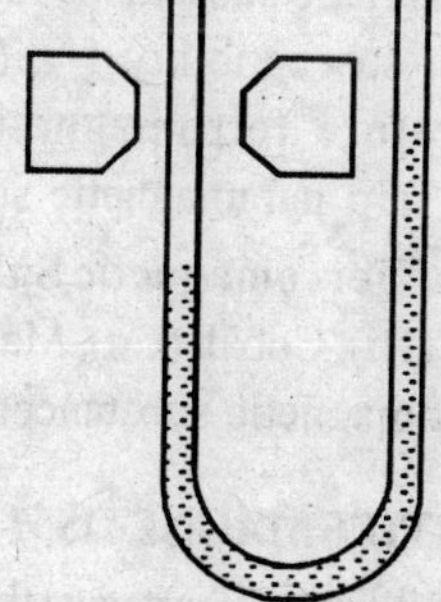

Fig. 12.20

(ii) When these substances are brought near the ends of a powerful magnet they are somewhat repelled. They are called 'diamagnetic' substances, and their magnetism is called the 'diamagnetism.'

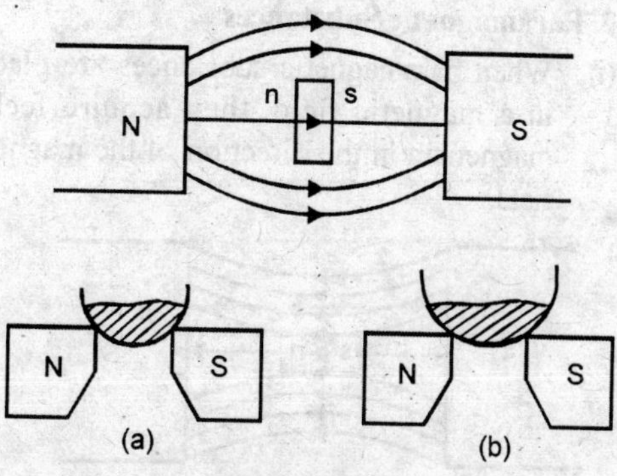

Fig. 12.21

(iii) If a diamagnetic solution is poured into a U-tube and one arm of this U-tube is placed between the poles of a strong magnet, the level of the solution in that arm is depressed (Fig. b).

(iv) When a rod of diamagnetic material is suspended freely between two magnetic poles, then its axis becomes perpendicular to the magnetic field (Fig. a). The poles produced on the two sides of the rod are similar to the nearer magnetic poles.

(v) In a non-uniform magnetic field, the diamagnetic substances are attracted towards the weaker parts of the field. If we take a diamagnetic liquid in a glass crucible, and put it over two nearby magnetic poles, then the liquid is depressed in the middle (Fig. a) where the field is strongest. Now, if the distance between the poles is increased, the liquid rises in the middle, because now the field is strongest near the poles.

(vi) Permeability of diamagnetic substances is less than 1 (i.e. $\mu < 1$).

(vii) Susceptibility of diamagnetic substances is small and negative.

(viii) Susceptibility of diamagnetic substances is independent of temperature.

Examples of Diamagnetic Substance : Bismuth (Bi), Zinc (Zn), Copper (Cu), Silver (Ag), Gold (Au), (Diamond) (C), Salt (NaCl), Water (H_2O), Mercury (Hg), Nitrogen (N_2), Hydrogen (H_2), etc. are diamagnetic substances.

2. Paramagnetic Substances

(i) When paramagnetic substances are placed in a magnetic field, they acquire feeble magnetism in the direction of the magnetic field.

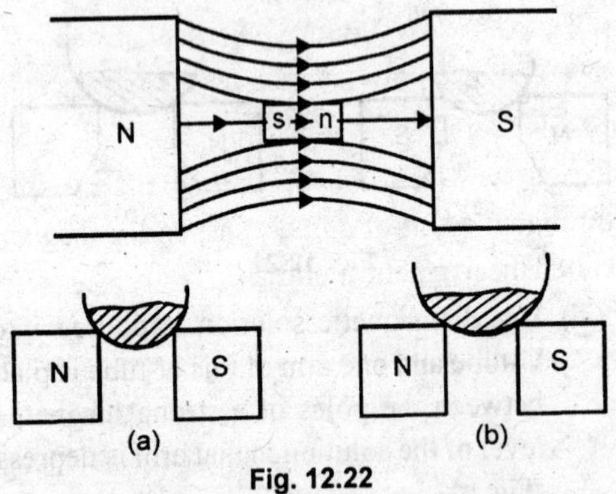

Fig. 12.22

(ii) When paramagnetic substances are brought closed to the ends of a powerful magnet, they are attracted towards the magnet.

(iii) When a rod of paramagnetic material is suspended freely between two magnetic poles, then its axis becomes parallel to the magnetic field (Fig. 17.10). The poles produced at the ends of the rod are opposite to the nearer magnetic poles.

(iv) If a paramagnetic solution is poured in a U-tube and one arm of the U-tube is placed between two strong poles, the level of the solution in that arm rises.

(v) In a non-uniform magnetic field, the paramagnetic substances tend to move from weaker to stronger parts of the magnetic field. If a paramagnetic liquid taken in a glass cruicible is put over two nearby magnetic poles, then the liquid rises in the middle (Fig. (a), (b)) where the field is strongest. Now, if the distance between the poles is increased, the liquid depresses in the middle and rises near the edges, because now the field is strongest near the poles.

(vi) Permeability of paramagnetic substances is slightly greater than 1 i.e. $\mu > 1$.

(vii) Susceptibility of paramagnetic substances is small and positive.

(viii) Paramagnetic substances follow Curie law, i.e. their susceptibility x is inversely proportional to the absolute temperature i.e. $\chi \propto (1/T)$. As the temperature increases, the susceptibility decreases and at a particular temperature known as Curie temperature, paramagnetic substance changes to diamagnetic substance. Curie temperature is different for different substances.

Examples of Paramagnetic substances Aluminium (Al), Sodium (Na), Platinum (Pt), Manganese (Mn), Copper Chloride ($CuCl_2$), Oxygen (O_2), etc. are paramagnetic substances.

3. Ferromagnetic Substances

(i) When ferromagnetic substances are placed in a magnetic field, they are strongly magnetised in the direction of the field.

(ii) Ferromagnetic substances are attracted fast towards a magnet when brought closer to either of its ends.

(iii) They pcssess all the properties of paramagnetic substances with much greater intensity.

(iv) Susceptibility of ferromagnetic substances is large and positive.

(v) Permeability of ferromagnetic substances is much greater than 1, ($\mu >> 1$).

(vi) Ferromagnetic substances follow Curie law i.e. their susceptibility $\chi \propto (1/T)$. At Curie temperature ferromagnetic substances change into paramagnetic substances.

Examples of Ferromagnetic Substances. Iron (Fe), Nickel (Ni), Cobalt (Co), Magnetic (Fe_3O_4), etc. are ferromagnetic substances.

CAUSE OF EARTH'S MAGNETISM

In 1600 Sir William Gilbert gave the idea that there is powerful magnet within the earth's crust.

However, the existence of such a magnet within earth is not possible due to following reasons

(i) The temperature in the interior of the earth is so high that it is not possible for any magnet to retain its magnetism.

(ii) If there were a magnet in the earth, then the position of earth's magnetic poles would have never changed.

(iii) There is no reason as to how the magnet within the earth has been magnetised.

Many theories put forward by different scientists regarding the magnetisation of earth are as follows

(i) In 1849 Grover put the view that the earth's magnetism is due to electric currents flowing near the outer surface of the earth. These currents are generated due to sun. Hot air, rising from the region near equator, goes towards northern and southern hemispheres and becomes electrified. These currents magnetise the ferromagnetic materials near the outer surface of the earth.

(ii) The temperature inside earth's crust is very high, therefore there are many conducting materials including iron and nickel in the molten state within the central core of the earth. Conventional currents are set up in this semi-fluid core due to earth's rotation about its axis. Because of this, the process of self-excited dynamo starts within earth. Therefore, electric current, and hence magnetism, is generated within earth. Most of the erarth's magnetism is supposed to be generated due to this reason.

(iii) The third view about earth's magnetism is that gases are present in ionised state in the atmosphere High-energy rays coming from sun collide with the atoms of gases in the upper layers of the atmosphere and ionise them. The radioactivity of the atmosphere and the cosmic rays also ionise the gases. A conducting layer of charged particles called ionosphere is formed. With the rotation of earth iono-sphere also rotates. Hence, strong electric currents flow due to earth's rotation. Earth's magnetic field is generated due to these currents.

ELEMENTS OF EARTH'S MAGNETISM

There are three elements of earth's magnetism (i) Angle of declination, (ii) Angle of dip, (iii) Horizontal component of earth's field.

Geographic Meridian : A vertical plane passing through the axis of rotation of the earth is called the geographical meridian.

Magnetic Meridian : A vertical plane passing through the axis of a freely suspended magnet is called the magnetic meridian.

ANGLE OF DECLINATION

The acute angle between the magnetic meridian and the geographical meridian is called the 'angle of declination' at any place.

ANGLE OF DIP

The angle between the axis of the freely suspended magnetic needle in the magnetic meridian and the horizontal direction is called the 'angle of dip'. The magnetic axis of a freely suspended needle represents the direction of the earth's magnetic field. Hence the angle of dip at a place is the angle between the direction of earth's magnetic field and the horizontal in the magnetic meridian at that place.

HORIZONTAL COMPONENT OF EARTH'S MAGNETIC FIELD

The earth's magnetic field B_e in the magnetic meridian may be resolved into a horizontal component H and vertical component V at any place.

In Fig., NS is a freely-suspended magnetic needle. The vertical plane $OPQR$ passing through the axis of the needle is the magnetic meridian. The plane $OLMR$ is the geographical meridian. The angle α between these two planes is the angle of declination. The angle between the axis OQ of the magnetic needle and the horizontal OP is the angle of dip θ.

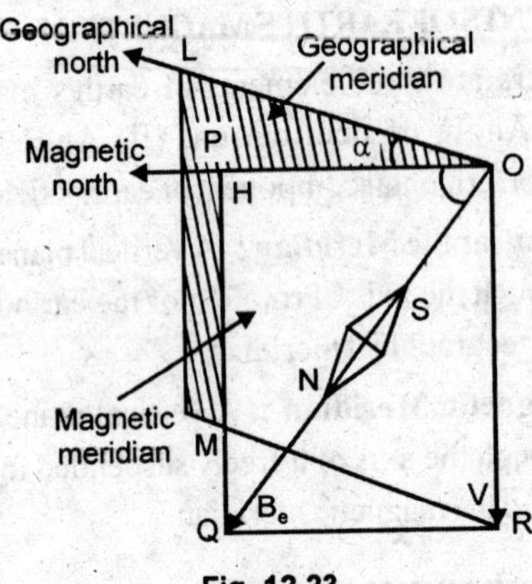

Fig. 12.23

The axis OQ of magnetic needle represents the direction of earth's magnetic field B_e. The field B_e may be resolved into horizontal and vertical components (H and V). From the figure, we have horizontal component of earth's magnetic field

$$H = B_e \cos \theta \quad \text{...(i)}$$

and vertical component of earth's magnetic field

$$V = B_e \sin \theta \quad \text{...(ii)}$$

Squaring and adding equation (i) and (ii), we get

$$H^2 + V^2 = B_e^2 \cos^2 \theta + B_e^2 \sin^2 \theta = B_e^2.$$

$$B_e = \sqrt{(H^2 + V^2)}$$

Dividing equation (ii) by equation (i), we have

$$\frac{V}{H} = \frac{B_e \sin \theta}{B_e \cos \theta} = \tan \theta.$$

We can decide the direction of B_e if α and θ at any place are known and if we know the values of H and θ, the magnitude of B_e can be determined. Thus α, θ and H give us full information about earth's magnetic field at any place. Hence these are called the "element of earth's magnetic field".

MULTIPLE CHOICE QUESTIONS

1. The wire loop $PQRS$ formed by joining two semicircular wires of radii R_1 and R_2 carries a current I as shown. The magnitude of magnetic induction at the centre O is

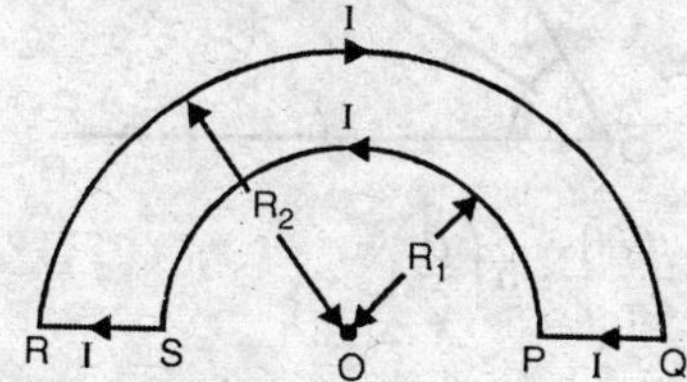

(a) $(\mu_0/4)\,I(R_1/R_2 - 1/R_1)$
(b) $(\mu_0/4)\,I(1/R_1 - 1/R_2)$
(c) $\mu_0 I(1/R_2 - 1/R_1)$
(d) $\mu_0 I(1/R_1)$

2. A straight conductor carrying a direct current i amp. is split into circular loop as shown in figure. Then the magnetic induction at the centre of the circular loop of radius r meter is

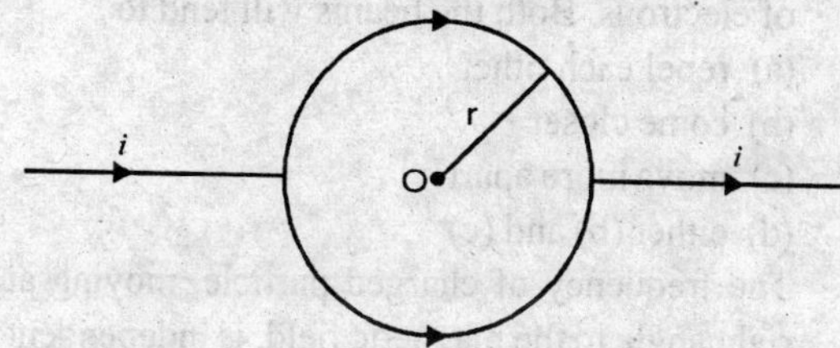

(a) 0 (b) ∞
(c) $\dfrac{\mu_0 i}{2\pi r}$ (d) $\dfrac{\mu_0 i}{2r}$

3. A current carrying coil is bent sharply so as to convert it into a double loop both carrying a current in the same direction. If B is the initial magnetic field at the centre and if the current in the two coils is opposite to each other, the final magnetic field will be

(a) zero (b) $2B$
(c) $4B$ (d) $8B$

4. A current carrying coil is bent sharply so as to convert it into a double loop both carrying a current in the same direction. If B is the initial magnetic field at the centre, then the final concentric magnetic field will be

(a) zero (b) $2B$
(c) $4B$ (d) $8B$

5. Equal current I flows in two segments of a circular loop in the direction shown in figure. Radius of the loop is r. The magnitude of magnetic field induction at the centre of the loop is

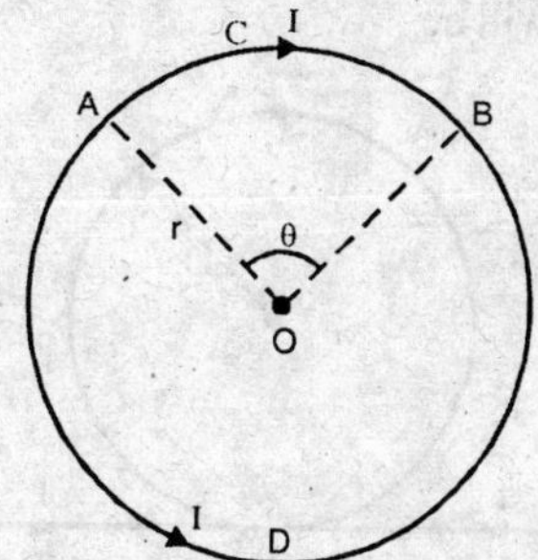

(a) zero (b) $\dfrac{\mu_0 I\theta}{4\pi r}$
(c) $\dfrac{\mu_0}{2\pi}\dfrac{I}{r}(\pi - \theta)$ (d) $\dfrac{\mu_0}{2\pi}\dfrac{I}{r}(2\pi - \theta)$

6. Magnetic field at the centre of a circular loop of area A is B. The magnetic moment of the loop will be

(a) $\dfrac{BA^2}{\mu_0 \pi}$ (b) $\dfrac{BA^{3/2}}{\mu_0 \pi}$
(c) $\dfrac{BA^{3/2}}{\mu_0 \pi^{1/2}}$ (d) $\dfrac{2BA^{3/2}}{\mu_0 \pi^{1/2}}$

7. Net magnetic field at the centre of the circle O due to a current through a loop as shown in figure is ($\theta < 180°$)

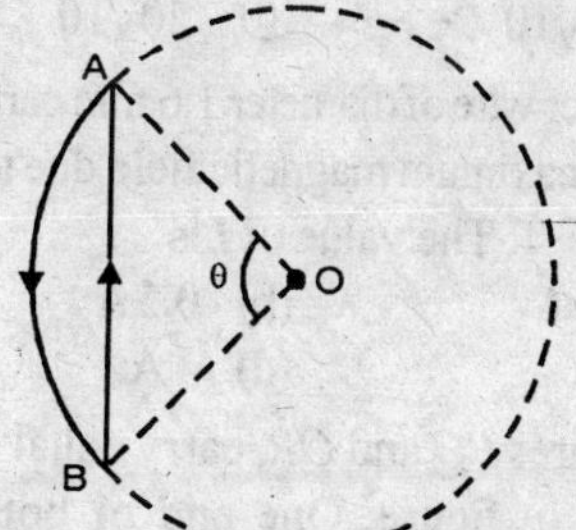

(a) zero
(b) perpendicular to paper inwards
(c) perpendicular to paper outwards
(d) perpendicular to the paper inwards if $\theta \leq 90°$ and perpendicular to paper outwards if $90° \leq \theta < 180°$.

8. An infinite long straight conductor is bent into the shape as shown in the figure. It carries a current of I ampere and the radius of the circular loop is r metre. Then magnetic induction at its centre will be

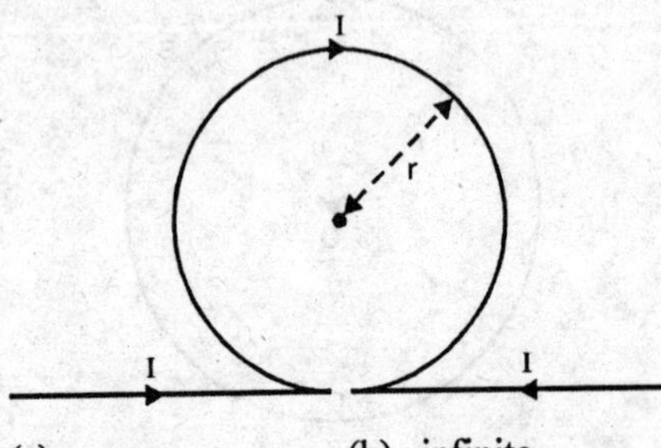

(a) zero (b) infinite

(c) $\frac{\mu_0}{4\pi}\frac{2I}{r}(\pi+1)$ (d) $\frac{\mu_0}{4\pi}\frac{2I}{r}(\pi-1)$

9. A positively charged particle moving with velocity $\vec{v}$ enters a region of space having a constant magnetic induction $\vec{B}$. The particle will experience the largest deflecting force when the angle between the vectors $\vec{v}$ and $\vec{B}$ is
(a) 45° (b) 90°
(c) 180° (d) 30°

10. Ratio of magnetic field induction at the centre of a current carrying coil of radius r and at a distance $3r$ on its axis is
(a) $\sqrt{10}$ (b) $2\sqrt{10}$
(c) $10\sqrt{10}$ (d) $20\sqrt{10}$

11. A copper wire of diameter 1.6 mm carries a current I. The maximum magnetic field due to this wire is 5×10^{-4} T. The value of I is
(a) 0.2 A (b) 0.5 A
(c) 2 A (d) 4 A

12. Two wires PQ and QR, carry equal currents I as shown in figure. One end of both the wires extends to infinity. $\angle PQR = \theta$. The magnitude of the magnetic field at O on the bisector angle of these two wires at a distance r from point Q is

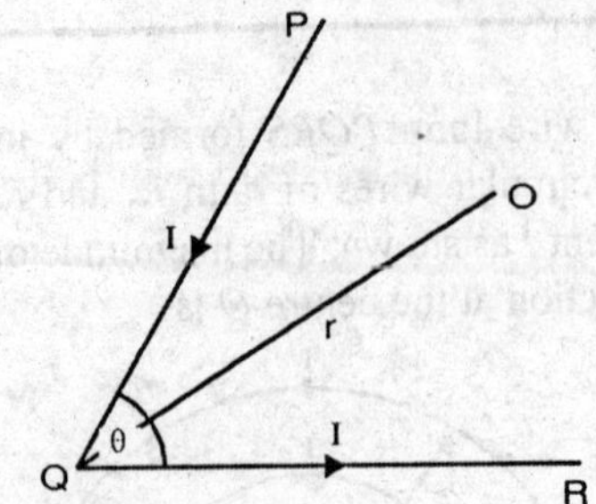

(a) $\frac{\mu_0}{4\pi}\frac{1}{r}\sin\left(\frac{\theta}{2}\right)$

(b) $\frac{\mu_0}{4\pi}\frac{1}{r}\cot\left(\frac{\theta}{2}\right)$

(c) $\frac{\mu_0}{4\pi}\frac{1}{r}\tan\frac{\theta}{2}$

(d) $\frac{\mu_0}{4\pi}\frac{I}{r}\frac{(1+\cos\theta/2)}{(\sin\theta/2)}$

13. A beam of protons is moving parallel to a beam of electrons. Both the beams will tend to
(a) repel each other
(b) come closer
(c) move more apart
(d) either (b) and (c)

14. The frequency of charged particle, moving at right angle to the magnetic field, is independent of
(a) the radius of circular trajectory
(b) the speed of particle
(c) both (a) and (b)
(d) the magnetic induction B

15. An electron (mass = 9×10^{-31} kg, charge = 1.6×10^{-19} C) moving with a velocity of 10^6 m/s enters a magnetic field. If it describes a circle of radius 0.1m, then strength of magnetic field must be
(a) $4.5 \times 10^{-5}\,T$ (b) $1.4 \times 10^{-5}\,T$
(c) $5.5 \times 10^{-5}\,T$ (d) $2.6 \times 10^{-5}\,T$

16. The mass of a proton is 1847 times that of electron. If an electron and a proton are injected in a uniform electric field at right angle to the direction of the field, with the same kinetic energy, then

(a) the proton trajectory will be less curved than that of electron
(b) both the trajectories will be straight
(c) both the trajectories will be equally curved
(d) the electron trajectory will be less curved than that of proton.

17. A uniform electric field and a uniform magnetic field are pointed in the same direction. If an electron is projected in the same direction, the electron
(a) velocity will increase in magnitude
(b) velocity will decrease in magnitude
(c) will turn to its left
(d) will turn to its right

18. A uniform magnetic field acts at right angle to the direction of motion of electron. As a result of this, the electron describes a circular path of radius 2 cm. If the speed of electron is doubled, the radius of circular path will becomes
(a) 4 cm (b) 2 cm
(c) 1 cm (d) 8 cm

19. An electron moving with kinetic energy 6×10^{-16} joules enters a field of magnetic induction 6×10^{-3} weber/m^2 at right angle to its motion. The radius of its path is
(a) 3.42 cm (b) 4.23 cm
(c) 5.17 cm (d) 7.7 cm

20. A charge moving with velocity v in x-direction is subjected to a field of magnetic induction in the negative x-direction. As a result, the charge will
(a) retard along x-axis
(b) move along a helical path around x-axis
(c) remain unaffected
(d) starts moving in a circular path

21. A deutron of kinetic energy 50 keV is describing a circular orbit of radius 0.5m, in a plane perpendicular to magnetic field $\vec{B}$. The kinetic energy of a proton that describes a circular orbit of radius 0.5 m in the same plane with the same magnetic field $\vec{B}$ is
(a) 200 keV (b) 50 keV
(c) 100 keV (d) 25 keV

22. A cathode ray beam is bent in a circle of radius 2 cm by a magnetic induction 4.5×10^{-3} weber/m^2. The velocity of electron is
(a) 3.43×10^7 m/s (b) 5.37×10^7 m/s
(c) 1.23×10^7 m/s (d) 1.58×10^7 m/s

23. Radius of curvature of a charged particle, in a uniform magnetic field, is directly proportional to
(a) momentum of particle
(b) intensity of the field
(c) charge on the particle
(d) energy of the particle

24. The work done by a magnetic field, on a moving charge is
(a) zero because $\vec{F}$ acts parallel to $\vec{v}$
(b) positive because $\vec{F}$ acts perpendicular to $\vec{v}$
(c) zero because $\vec{F}$ acts perpendicular to $\vec{v}$
(d) negative because $\vec{F}$ acts parallel to $\vec{v}$

25. A proton moving in a straight line enters a strong magnetic field along the field direction. How will its path and velocity change ?
(a) path is circular but speed constant
(b) path is same but velocity increases
(c) path is same and velocity remains constant
(d) path is same and motion is retarded

26. S.I. unit of magnetic permeability is
(a) A-m (b) Am^2
(c) H-m (d) H/m

27. Potential at any point on equatorial line of dipole is
(a) $\mu_0 M/4\pi d^2$ (b) $\mu_0 M/4\pi d^3$
(c) zero (d) none of these

28. The line joining a point to the centre of a short magnet makes angle θ with the axis. Potential at a point distant d from the centre of magnet, on this line is
(a) $\dfrac{\mu_0 M \sin\theta}{4\pi d^2}$ (b) $\dfrac{\mu_0 M \cos\theta}{4\pi d^2}$
(c) $\dfrac{\mu_0 M}{4\pi d^3}$ (d) none of these

29. Magnetic potential at a point distant d from a magnetic pole of strength m is

(a) $\frac{\mu_0}{4\pi}\frac{m}{d}$ (b) $\frac{\mu_0}{4\pi}\frac{m}{d^2}$

(c) $\frac{\mu_0}{4\pi}\frac{2m}{d}$ (d) none of these

30. Which of the following is not a magnetic substances ?

(a) brass (b) iron
(c) cobalt (d) nickel

31. A magnet of magnetic moment M is freely suspended in a constant uniform magnetic field of intensity H. If magnet is delfected by an angle θ from direction of H, the work done is

(a) $MH \cos\theta$ (b) $MH(1-\cos\theta)$
(c) $MH \sin\theta$ (d) $MH(1-\sin\theta)$

32. A bar magnet is released into a copper ring directly below it. The acceleration of the magnet will be

(a) equal to the acceleration due to gravity at that place
(b) less than the acceleration due to gravity at that place
(c) greater than the acceleration due to gravity at that place
(d) twice the acceleration due to gravity at that place

33. Force between two magnetic poles depends on

(a) pole strength only
(b) distance only
(c) medium only
(d) all the three above

34. What is the resultant magnetic moment of two magnets, each of magnetic moment M in the following figures :

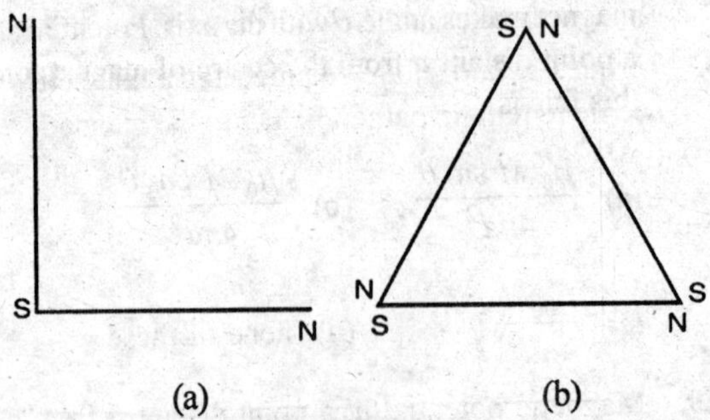

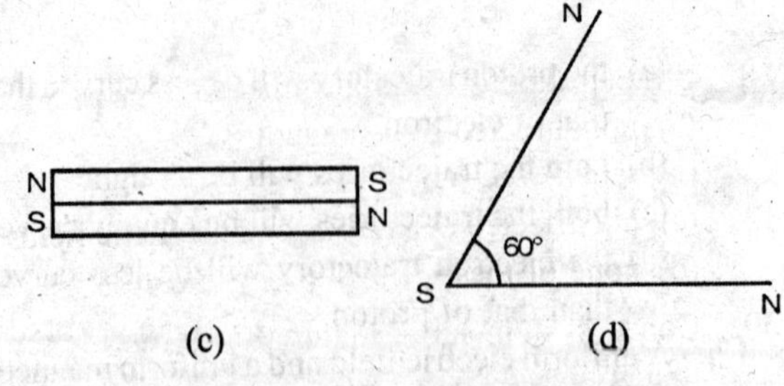

(a) $\sqrt{2}\,M$; zero $\sqrt{3}\,M$; zero
(b) $\sqrt{2}\,M$; zero ; zero; $\sqrt{3}\,M$
(c) $\sqrt{2}\,M$; $\sqrt{3}\,M$; zero ; zero;
(d) none of the above

35. A bar magnet is held at right angles to a uniform magnetic field. The couple acting on the magnet is to be halved by rotating it from this position. The angle of rotation is

(a) 60° (b) 45°
(c) 30° (d) 75°

36. Two magnets of equal magnetic moments M each are placed as shown in Figure. The resultant magnetic moment is

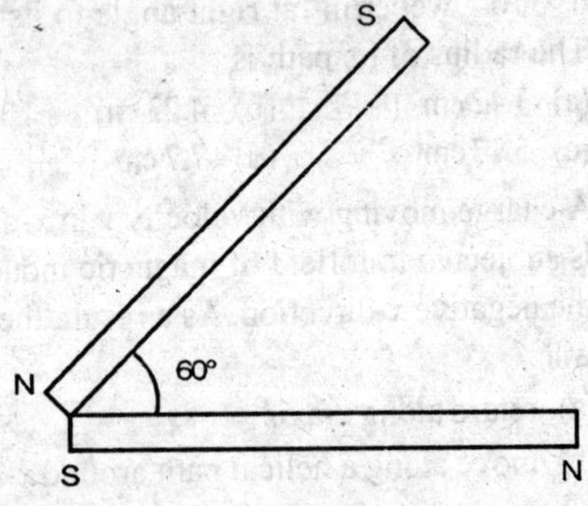

(a) M (b) $\sqrt{3}\,M$
(c) $\sqrt{2}\,M$ (d) $M/2$

37. Two small magnets, each of magnetic moment $10\,Am^2$ are placed in end of position 0.1 m apart from their centres. The force acting between them is

(a) 0.6 N (b) 0.6×10^7 N
(c) 0.6×10^{-7} N (d) none of the above

38. A non magnetic material is that which is
(a) not attracted by a magnet
(b) repelled by a magnet
(c) not affected even by strong magnetic fields
(d) none of these

39. Can a system have magnetic moment even though its net charge is zero ?
(a) Yes (b) No
(c) sometimes yes and sometimes no
(d) cannot say

40. The source of magnetic field is
(a) isolated magnetic pole
(b) static electric charge
(c) current loop
(d) none of the above

41. Two magnets have the same length and the same pole strength. But one of the magnets has a small hole at its centre. Then
(a) both have equal magnetic moment
(b) one with hole has smaller magnetic moment
(c) one with hole has larger magnetic moment
(d) one with hole loses magnetism through the hole

42. A thin magnet is cut into two equal parts by cutting it parallel to its length. If the original time period of vibration is 4 sec, the time period of each part in the same field will be
(a) 4s (b) 2s
(c) $4\sqrt{2}s$ (d) none of these

43. Two identical coils carrying same current have common centre but have their planes at right angles to each other. If the field due to each coil is B, the resultant field will be
(a) $\sqrt{2}B$ (b) $\frac{1}{\sqrt{2}}B$
(c) 2B (d) zero

44. A steel wire of length l has a magnetic moment M. It is bent into L shape from the middle. The new magnetic moment is
(a) M (b) $M/\sqrt{2}$
(c) $M/2$ (d) $2M$

45. The magnetic moment of a short magnet is 8 Am^2. The magnetic induction 20 cm away from its mid point on the axial line is
(a) 1×10^{-4}T (b) 2×10^{-4}T
(c) 4×10^{-4}T (d) 8×10^{-4}T

46. The moment of a magnet is 0.1 Am^2 and the force acting on each pole in a uniform magnetic field of 0.36 oersted is 1.44×10^{-4} N. The distance between the poles of magnet is
(a) 2.5 cm (b) 5.0 cm
(c) 1.25 cm (d) 1.17 cm

47. A magnet can be completely demagnetised by
(a) breaking the magnet into small pieces
(b) heating it slightly
(c) droppping into cold water
(d) applying a reverse field of appropriate strength

48. If the distance between two similar poles of equal strength is doubled, to get the same repulsive force, the pole strength of each pole should be
(a) increased by $\sqrt{2}$ times
(b) halved
(c) doubled
(d) increased by 4 times

49. Two short bar magnets with magnetic moments 400 *ab*-amp cm^2 and 800 *ab*-amp cm^2 are placed with their axis in the same straight line with similar poles facing each other and with their centres at 20 cm from each other. Then the force of repulsion is
(a) 12 dyne (b) 6 dyne
(c) 800 dyne (d) 150 dyne

50. Torques τ_1 and τ_2 are required for a magnetic needle to remain perpendicular to the magnetic fields B_1 and B_2 at two different places. The ratio B_1/B_2 is
(a) $\frac{\tau_2}{\tau_1}$ (b) $\frac{\tau_1}{\tau_2}$
(c) $\frac{\tau_1 + \tau_2}{\tau_1 - \tau_2}$ (d) $\frac{\tau_1 - \tau_2}{\tau_1 + \tau_2}$

ANSWERS

1	2	3	4	5	6	7	8	9	10
(b)	(a)	(a)	(c)	(c)	(d)	(b)	(d)	(b)	(c)
11	**12**	**13**	**14**	**15**	**16**	**17**	**18**	**19**	**20**
(c)	(d)	(d)	(c)	(c)	(c)	(b)	(a)	(a)	(c)
21	**22**	**23**	**24**	**25**	**26**	**27**	**28**	**29**	**30**
(c)	(d)	(a)	(c)	(c)	(d)	(c)	(b)	(a)	(a)
31	**32**	**33**	**34**	**35**	**36**	**37**	**38**	**39**	**40**
(b)	(b)	(d)	(b)	(a)	(a)	(a)	(c)	(a)	(a, c)
41	**42**	**43**	**44**	**45**	**46**	**47**	**48**	**49**	**50**
(b)	(a)	(a)	(b)	(b)	(a)	(d)	(c)	(a)	(b)

HINTS / SOLUTIONS

1. Magnetic field at O due to semicircular are PS of radius R_1 will be $B_1 = \frac{\mu_0 \pi I}{4\pi R_1}$. Its direction is perpendicular to coil directed outwards. Magnetic field at O due to semicircular arc PQ of radius R_2 will be,

$$B_2 = \frac{\mu_0 \pi I}{4\pi R_2}$$

Its direction is perpendicular to coil directed inwards. The resultant magnetic field at O,

$B = B_1 - B_2$ outwards.

or $$B = \frac{\mu_0}{4\pi} I\pi\left[\frac{1}{R_1} - \frac{1}{R_2}\right]$$

$$= \frac{\mu_0 I}{4}\left[\frac{1}{R_1} - \frac{1}{R_2}\right]$$

2. The magnetic field at the centre O due to current through upper side of semicircular current loop is equal and opposite to that due to lower side of semicircular current loop.

3. The magnetic field due to current through one coil is equal and opposite to that due to other, hence the resultant magnetic field is zero.

4. As $B = \frac{\mu_0}{4\pi}\frac{2\pi n i}{r}$; so $B \propto \frac{n}{r}$

Thus $$\frac{B_2}{B_1} = \frac{n_2}{n_1} \times \frac{r_1}{r_2} = \frac{2}{1} \times \frac{r}{r/2} = 4$$

or $B_2 = 4B_1$.

5. Magnetic field induction at O due to current through ACB is

$$B_1 = \frac{\mu_0}{4\pi}\frac{I\theta}{r}$$

It is acting perpendicular to the paper downwards. Magnetic field induction at O due to current through ADB is

$$B_2 = \frac{\mu_0}{4\pi}\frac{I}{r}(2\pi - \theta)$$

It is acting perpendicular to paper upards.

∴ Total magnetic field at O due to current loop is

$$B = B_2 - B_1 = \frac{\mu_0}{4\pi}\frac{I}{r}(2\pi - \theta) - \frac{\mu_0}{4\pi}\frac{I}{r}\theta$$

$$= \frac{\mu_0}{2\pi}\frac{I}{r}(\pi - \theta)$$

acting perpendicular to paper upwards.

6. $B = \frac{\mu_0}{4\pi}\frac{2\pi I}{r} = \frac{\mu_0 I}{2r}$ or $I = \frac{2Br}{\mu_0}$;

Also $A = \pi r^2$ or $r = \left(\frac{A}{\pi}\right)^{1/2}$

Magnetic moment, $M = IA = \frac{2Br}{\mu_0} A$

$$= \frac{2BA}{\mu_0} \times \left(\frac{A}{\pi}\right)^{1/2} = \frac{2BA^{3/2}}{\mu_0 \pi^{1/2}}$$

7. The current through loop is anticlockwise. Hence magnetic field at the points within the loop is perpendicular to paper outwards. As the magnetic lines of force form a closed path and tangent to line of force tells the direction of magnetic field at that point. Hence magnetic field at O is perpendicular to paper inwards.

8. The field induction at O due to straight part of conductor is $B_1 = \frac{\mu_0}{4\pi}\frac{2i}{r}$. The field induction at O due to circular coil is $B_2 = \frac{\mu_0}{4\pi}\frac{2\pi i}{r}$. Both fields will act in opposite direction, hence the total field induction at O will be

$$B = B_2 - B_1 = \frac{\mu_0}{4\pi}(\pi - 1)\frac{2i}{r}$$

$$= \frac{\mu_0}{4\pi}\frac{2i}{r}(\pi - 1)$$

10. The desired ratio

$$= \frac{\mu_0 I/2r}{\dfrac{\mu_0 I r^2}{2(r^2+9r^2)^{3/2}}} = (10)^{3/2} = 10\sqrt{10}$$

11. Maximum magnetic field due to wire carrying current is at surface and is given by

$$B = \frac{\mu_0}{4\pi}\frac{2I}{R} \text{ or } I = \frac{B.R}{2\times(\mu_0/4\pi)}$$

$$\therefore \quad I = \frac{5\times10^{-4}\times\left(\dfrac{1.6}{2}\times10^{-3}\right)}{2\times10^{-7}} = 2\text{ A.}$$

12. Perpendicular of O from PQ or QR, $a = r\sin\theta/2$

Magnetic field induction at O due to current through PQ and QR is

$$B = \frac{\mu_0}{4\pi}\frac{I}{a}[\sin(90-\theta/2) + \sin 90°]\times 2$$

$$= \frac{\mu_0}{2\pi}\frac{I}{r\sin\theta/2}(\cos\theta/2 + 1)$$

$$= \frac{\mu_0}{2\pi}\frac{I}{r}\frac{(1+\cos\theta/2)}{\sin\theta/2}$$

13. There will be an electrostatic force of attraction between beam of protons and beam of electrons and there will be magnetic attraction due to currents by virtue of motion of protons and electrons in the same direction and magnetic repulsion due to currents by virtue of motion of protons and electrons in the opposite direction.

14. $v = \frac{Bq}{2\pi m}$ which is independent of r and v.

15. $Bqv = \frac{mv^2}{r}$ or $B = \frac{mv}{rq} = \frac{(9\times10^{-31})\times10^6}{0.1\times(1.6\times10^{-19})}$
$= 5.5\times10^{-5}$ T.

16. Kinetic energy, $E_k = \frac{1}{2}mv^2$ or $mv^2 = 2E_k$.

Force on the charged particle in electric field $F = Eq$. Acceleration of the charged particle in the direction of electric field,

$$a = Eq/m$$

Taking the motion of charged particle at right angle to the initial direction of motion i.e., motion along the direction of electric field for the displacement y in the electric field.

$$u = 0, a = Eq/m, t = t, s = y.$$

As, $$s = ut + \frac{1}{2}at^2$$

$$\therefore \quad y = 0\times t + \frac{1}{2}\frac{Eq}{m}t^2 = \frac{1}{2}\frac{Eq}{m}t^2 \quad (1)$$

If x is the length of region of electric field, then $t = x/v$

From (1), $y = \frac{1}{2}\frac{Eq}{m}\times\frac{x^2}{v^2} = \frac{1}{2}\frac{Eq\,x^2}{2E_k}$

As y is independent of m, hence both the trajectories will be equally curved.

17. When electron is moving along the direction of electric and magnetic field, it experience no force due to magnetic field, but experience force due to electric field, which is $\vec{F} = e\vec{E}$. It acts opposite to the direction of electric field, hence velocity of electron will decrease.

18. $r = \frac{mv}{Bq}$ i.e. $r \propto v$ so $r_2/r_1 = v_2/v_1$
$= 2v_1/v_1 = 2$ or $r_2 = 2r_1 = 2\times2 = 4$ cm.

19. $E_k = \frac{1}{2}mv^2$ or $mv = \sqrt{2E_k m}$ and

$$r = \frac{mv}{Bq} = \frac{\sqrt{2E_k m}}{Bq}$$

20. Here angle between $\vec{v}$ and $\vec{B}$ is 180° and sin 180° = 0. $\therefore F = qvB \sin 180° = 0$.

21. $r = \frac{\sqrt{2mE}}{Bq} = \frac{\sqrt{2m_1 E_1}}{Bq}$ or

$$E_1 = \frac{mE}{m_1} = \frac{(2m_1)}{m_1} \times 50 \text{ keV} = 100 \text{ keV}$$

22. $v = \frac{Bqr}{m}$

$$= \frac{4.5 \times 10^{-3} \times 1.6 \times 10^{-19} \times 2 \times 10^{-2}}{9 \times 10^{-31}}$$

$= 1.6 \times 10^7$ m/s. $\approx 1.58 \times 10^7$ m/s

23. $r = \frac{mv}{Bq}$ *i.e.* $r \propto mv$

24. Force on moving charge while moving in magnetic field is ; $\vec{F} = q(\vec{v} \times \vec{B})$ where $\vec{F}$ is perpendicular to $\vec{v}$. Work done/sec = $\vec{F} \cdot \vec{v}$ = $Fv \cos 90° = 0$.

25. Force on proton moving along the direction of magnetic field, $F = qvB \sin 0° = 0$. Hence the path and velocity of proton remains unchanged.

26. $\mu_0 = \frac{B}{H} = \frac{\text{T}}{\text{Am}}$

$= TA^{-1} m^{-1} = Hm^{-1}$. [$\because TA^{-1}$ is henry (H)]

27. On equatorial line, $V = 0$

28. Mag. potential at any point due to a short magnet is

$$V = \frac{\mu_0}{4\pi} \frac{M \cos \theta}{d^2}.$$

29. Mag. potential $V = \frac{\mu_0}{4\pi} \frac{m}{d}$.

30. Brass is non magnetic.

31. $\theta_1 = 0°, \theta_2 = \theta$

$W = -MH(\cos \theta_2 - \cos \theta_1)$

$= -MH(\cos \theta - \cos 0°)$

$= MH(1 - \cos \theta)$

32. A bar magnet falling freely induces current in copper ring, that opposes the motion of the bar magnet. Therefore, acceleration of bar magnet is less than accleration due to gravity at that place.

33. Force between two magnetic poles depends on pole strength, distance and medium between the poles.

34. $M' = \sqrt{M^2 + M^2} = \sqrt{2}M$..

As magnetic moments are in a closed loop in Figure 16.22 (b)

$\therefore$ $M = 0$

In Figure 16.22 (c) $M' = M - M = 0$

In Figure 16.22 (d),

$$M' = \sqrt{M^2 + M^2 + 2MM \cos 60°} = \sqrt{3}M$$

35. $\tau_1 = MB \sin 90° = MB$

As $\tau_2 = \frac{1}{2}\tau_1$

$\therefore$ $MB \sin \theta = \frac{1}{2} MB \therefore \sin \theta = \frac{1}{2}, \theta = 30°$

Angle of rotation = 90° − 30° = 60°.

36. As magnetic moments are directed along *SN*, angle between $\vec{M}$ and $\vec{M}$ is $\theta = 120°$ (from Figure)

$\therefore$ Resultant magnetic moment

$$= \sqrt{M^2 + M^2 + 2MM \cos 120°}$$

$$= \sqrt{M^2 + M^2 + 2M^2(-1/2)} = M$$

37. Force between two magnetic dipoles is given by

$$F = \frac{\mu_0}{4\pi} \frac{6 M_1 M_2}{r^4}$$

$$= \frac{10^{-7} \times 6 \times 10 \times 10}{(0.1)^4} = 0.6 \text{ N}$$

38. A non magnetic material is that which is not at all affected even by strong magnetic fields.

39. Yes, for example, a neutron has some magnetic moment. Atoms of para and ferro magnetic materials are neutral and still they have some net magnetic moment.

40. Magnetic field is associated with an isolated magnetic pole and also with a current loop.

41. Hole reduces the effective length of the magnet and hence magnetic moment reduces.

42. Pole strength of each pole is halved, so is magnetic moment. As mass of each part is halved, moment of inertia I is halved.

As $T = 2\pi\sqrt{\dfrac{I}{MB}}$

$$\therefore \quad T' = \sqrt{\frac{(1/2)\,I}{(1/2)\,MB}} = T$$

Hence T remains the same *i.e.* 4 seconds.

43. As planes of two coils are at right angle to each other, so must be their fields.

$\therefore$ Resultant field $= \sqrt{B^2 + B^2} = B\sqrt{2}$..

44. Strength of each pole $= M/l$

Distance between the poles on bending the wire into L shape

$$= \sqrt{(l/2)^2 + (l/2)^2}$$

$$= \frac{l}{2}\sqrt{2} = \frac{l}{\sqrt{2}}$$

$$\therefore \quad M' = \frac{M}{l} \times \frac{l}{\sqrt{2}} = \frac{M}{\sqrt{2}}$$

45. $$B = \frac{\mu_0}{4\pi}\frac{2M}{d^3} = \frac{10^{-7} \times 2 \times 8}{(20 \times 10^{-2})^3} = 2 \times 10^{-4}\,T.$$

46. Here, $M = 0,1\,Am^2, B = 0.36$ oersted $= 0.36 \times 10^{-4}$ T

$F = 1.44 \times 10^{-4}$ N, $2l = ?$

As $F = mB$

$$\therefore \quad m = \frac{F}{B} = \frac{1.44 \times 10^{-4}}{0.36 \times 10^{-4}} = 4\text{A/m}$$

As $M = m \times 2l$

$$\therefore \quad 2l = \frac{M}{m} = \frac{0.1}{4}\text{ m} = 2.5\text{ cm}$$

47. For complete demagnetisation of a magnet, we must apply a reverse field of appropriate strength on the magnet.

48. $$F = \frac{\mu_0}{4\pi}\frac{mm}{r^2} = \text{constant}$$

When r is doubled, m.m should become 4 times or m should be doubled.

49. $$F = \frac{\mu_0}{4\pi}\frac{6M_1\,M_2}{r^4} = \frac{6M_1\,M_2}{r^4}$$

$$\left(\because \text{ in cgs system, } \frac{\mu_0}{4\pi} = 1\right)$$

$$= \frac{6 \times 800 \times 400}{20 \times 20 \times 20 \times 20} = 12 \text{ dyne}$$

50. As $\tau = MB\sin\theta$

$$\therefore \quad \tau_1 = MB_1 \sin 90° = MB_1$$

$$\tau_2 = MB_2 \sin 90° = MB_2$$

$$\therefore \quad \frac{MB_1}{MB_2} = \frac{\tau_1}{\tau_2} \text{ or } \frac{B_1}{B_2} = \frac{\tau_1}{\tau_2}.$$

UNIT-13

Electromagnetic Induction and Alternating Currents

ELECTROMAGNETIC INDUCTION

In 1831 Faraday discovered that if a magnet approaches a closed circuit, containing a galvanometer (Fig), an electric current is produced in the circuit. The direction of the current so induced in the circuit is reversed, when the magnet recedes from the coil. Also the direction of the current is opposite when a *S* pole approches the coil, to what it is when a *N*-pole approaches it. The more rapid the change, the greater is the deflection produced in the galvanometer. It is quite immaterial, whether the magnet approaches the coil or the coil approaches the magnet. The current so produced lasts only so long as the relative motion between the coil and the magnet lasts.

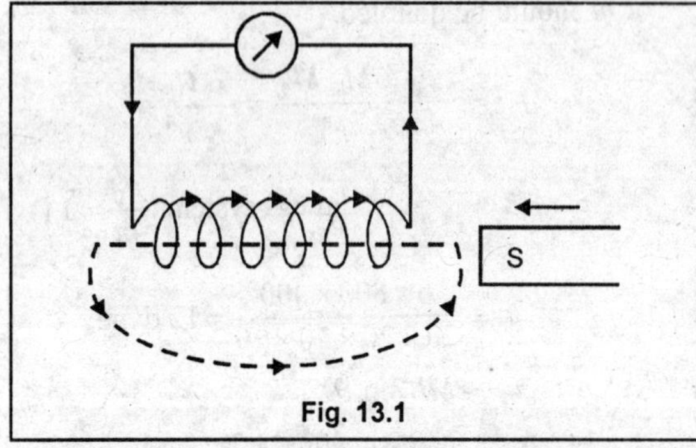

Fig. 13.1

The above observations can be summed up as follows :

"Whenever the magnetic lines of force linked with a closed circuit change an induced e.m.f. is always produced in the circuit and lasts only so long as the change lasts." The induced e.m.f. giving rise to such currents is called the induced electromotive force and the phenomenon is called **electromagnetic induction.**

FARADAY'S LAWS OF ELECTROMAGNETIC INDUCTION

(i) Whenever the number of lines of force i.*e.* magnetic flux linked with any closed circuit change, an induced current flows through the circuit which lasts only so long as the change lasts. An increase in the number of lines of force produces an inverse current, while a decrease of such lines produces a direct current.

(ii) The induced emf, *e* is equal to the negative rate of change of magnetic flux : If $\Delta\phi$ be the change in magnetic flux in a time interval Δt, then the induced emf in the circuit is

$$e = -\frac{\Delta\phi}{\Delta t}$$

In the limit $\Delta t \to 0$, $e = -\frac{d\phi}{dt}$

The negative sign indicated that the induced e.m.f. opposes the change in magnetic flux (Lenz's law). If the rate of change of magnetic flux be in weber/second, the induced emf *e* will be in volt. If the coil has *N* turns, then the emf will be induced in each turn and the emf of all the turns will be added up. If the turns of the coil are very close to each other, the magnetic flux passing through each turn will be same. So, the induced emf in the whole coil will be

$$e = -N\frac{\Delta\phi}{\Delta t} = -\frac{\Delta(N\phi)}{\Delta t}$$

$N\phi$ is called the number of 'flux linkages' in the coil.

INDUCED CURRENT AND INDUCED CHARGE

If the rate of change of magnetic flux in a coil of *N* turns is $\Delta\phi/\Delta t$, then the induced emf in the circuit is given by

$$e = -N(\Delta\phi/\Delta t).$$

Let the coil be closed and the total resistance of is circuit be *R*, then the induced current in the circuit will be

$$i = \frac{e}{R} = \frac{N}{R}\frac{\Delta\phi}{\Delta t}.$$

From this equation it is clear that the induced current in the circuit depends upon the resistance whereas the induced emf is independent of resistance. The charge flowing through the circuit in time-interval Δt will be given by

$$q = i \times \Delta t$$

$$= \frac{N}{R}\frac{\Delta\phi}{\Delta t} \times \Delta t = \frac{N}{R}\Delta\phi$$

$$= \frac{\text{number of turns} \times \text{change in magnetic flux}}{\text{resistance}}$$

From above equation it is clear that the induced charge does not depend upon the time-interval. The charge in the circuit will remain the same whether the change in magnetic flux be rapid or slow.

LENZ'S LAW

According to Lenz's Law the direction of the induced e.m.f. is always such as to oppose the change that cause it. This is in accordance with the principle of conservation of energy. Let the north pole of a magnet approach a coil (Fig.). Then the lines of force threading the coil will increase, which will induce an e.m.f. in the coil. The current in the coil should be anti-clockwise as seen from the side of the magnet, and so the face of the coil facing the north pole is also a north pole, and thus tending to repel the approaching magnet, due to which the current is induced.

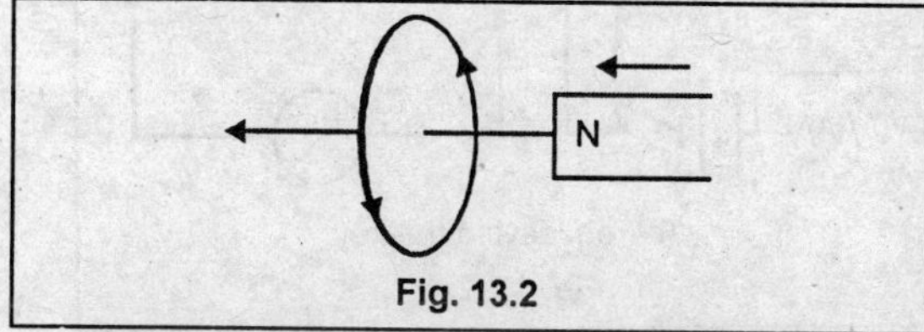

Fig. 13.2

Similarly, if the current in the circuit increases, the induced emf tries to decrease it while if the current in the circuit decreases, the induced emf tends to increase it.

DIRECTION OF INDUCED CURRENT FLEMING'S RIGHT-HAND RULE

If on stretch the right-hand thumb and two nearby fingers perpendicular to one another, the first finger points in the direction of magnetic field and the thumb in the direction of motion of the conductor, then the middle finger will point in the direction of the induced current (Fig.)

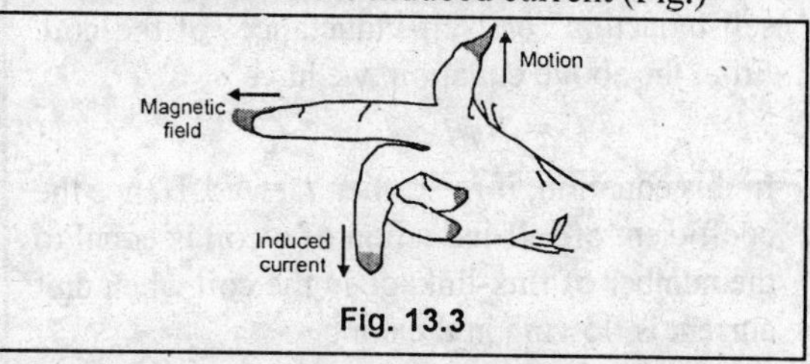

Fig. 13.3

TYPES OF ELECTROMAGNETIC INDUCTION

It is of two types

1. **Self Induction.** The current in the circuit increases or decreases whenever the key in the circuit is closed or opened. The variation of current causes a variation in magnetic flux linked with the circuit ($\because \phi \propto B \propto i$) hence, an induced emf is developed in the circuit. This emf is called self induced emf and the phenomenon is called self induction. Induced emf follows Lenz's Law. *i.e.* induced current always opposes the change in the main current. When the main current is increased (by the rheostat), the induced current flows opposite to the main current and opposes the increase in the main current (Fig. a). When the main current is decreased, then the induced current flows in the same direction as the main current and opposes the decrease in the main current (Fig. b).

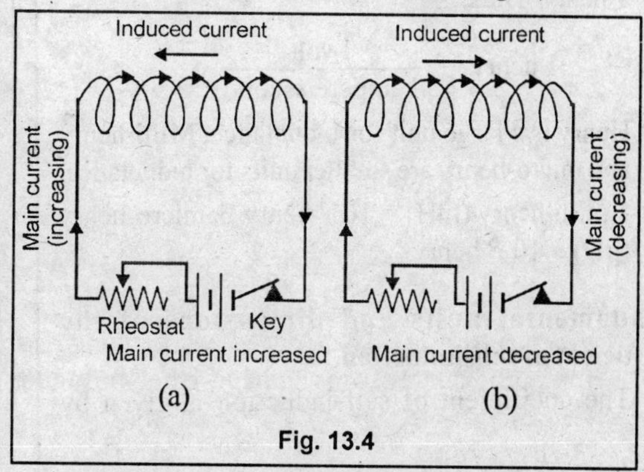

Fig. 13.4

Coefficient of self inductance. Def. (I). Consider a coil having N turns. Let the current flowing through the coil be i and the flux linked with each turn be ϕ, then the total flux linkage will be $N\phi$. Now,

$$N\phi \propto i \quad \text{or} \quad N\phi = Li$$

where L is a constant called the 'coefficient of self-induction' or 'self-inductance' of the coil. From the above equation, we have

$$L = N\phi/i$$

In this equation, if $i = 1$, then $L = N\phi$. Hence the coefficient of self-induction of a coil is equal to the number of flux-linkage in the coil when unit current is flowing in the coil.

Def. (II). From Faraday's law of electromagnetic induction

$$e = -\frac{\Delta}{\Delta t}(N\phi) = -\frac{\Delta(Li)}{\Delta t}$$

or $$e = -L\frac{\Delta i}{\Delta t}$$

If $$\frac{\Delta i}{\Delta t} = \frac{1 \text{ amp.}}{\text{sec.}}$$

then $e = L$ (numerically), hence the coefficient of self-induction of a coil is numerically equal to the emf induced in the coil due to unit rate of change of current in the coil.

Units of Coefficient of Self Induction. The unit of coefficient of self-induction is henry. If an emf of 1 volt is induced in a coil due to a change of current in it at the rate of 1 ampere/second, then the coefficient of self-induction of the coil is 1 henry. Thus

$$1 \text{ henry} = \frac{1 \text{ volt}}{1 \text{ ampere/second}}$$

Henry is a large unit for inductance. Milli-henry and micro-henry are smaller units for inductance. 1 milli-henry (mH) = 10^{-3} henry, 1 micro-henry (μH) = 10^{-6} henry.

Fundamental units and dimensions of the coefficient of self-induction

The coefficient of self-induction is given by

$$L = \frac{e}{\Delta i/\Delta t} = \frac{e\Delta t}{\Delta i}$$

$$\therefore \text{ unit of } L = \frac{\text{volt} \times \text{second}}{\text{ampere}} = \frac{(\text{joule/coulomb}) \times \text{sec.}}{\text{ampere}}$$

$$= \frac{\text{newton} \times \text{metre} \times \text{sec.}}{\text{coulomb} \times \text{ampere}}$$

$$= \frac{(\text{kg-metre-second}^{-2}) \times \text{metre} \times \text{sec.}}{(\text{ampere} \times \text{sec.}) \times \text{ampere}}$$

$$= \text{kg-metre}^2\text{-second}^{-2}\text{-ampere}^{-2}.$$

$\therefore$ Dimensions of $L = [ML^2T^{-2}A^{-2}]$.

MUTUAL INDUCTION

If two coils are placed near each other and the current flowing in one of them is changed then an emf is induced in the second coil. This phenomenon of electromagnetic induction is called 'mutual induction'. The first coil is known as the 'primary coil' and the second is known as the 'secondary coil'. The induced emf follows Lenz's Law.

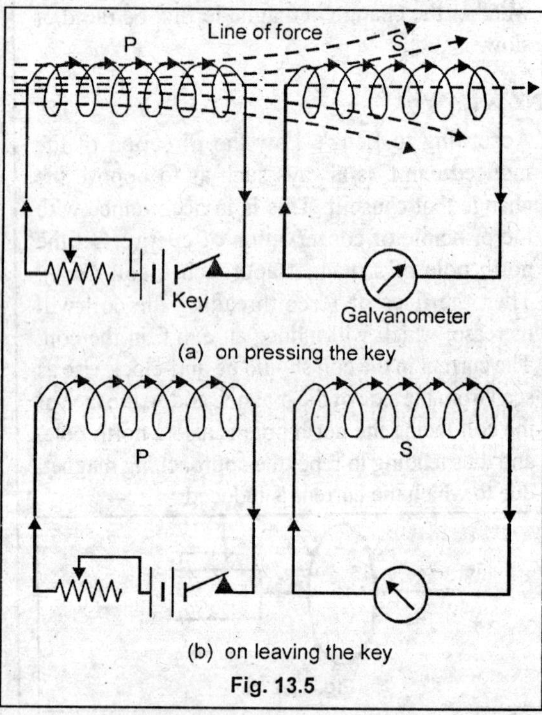

Fig. 13.5

COEFFICIENT OF MUTUAL INDUCTANCE

Def. (i) Let us consider two coils (Primary and secondary) placed very near to each other. Let N_1 and N_2 be the number of turns in the coils and i be the current flowing in the first coil.

Let due to this current, the magnetic flux linked with each turn of the secondary coil be ϕ_2. If N_2 be the number of turns in the secondary coil, then the number of flux-linkages in the coil will be

$N_2\phi_2$. This number is proportional to the current i_1 flowing in the primary coil,

i.e., $N_2\phi_2 \propto i_1$, or $N_2\phi_2 = Mi_1$,

where M is a constant called the 'coefficient of mutual induction' or 'mutual inductance' between the two coils. From the above equation, we have

$$M = \frac{N_2\phi_2}{i_1}$$

In this equation, if $i_1 = 1$, then $M = N_2\phi_2$. Hence the coefficient of mutual induction between two coils is equal to the number of magnetic flux-linkage in one coil when a unit current flows in the 'other'.

Def. (ii). From Faraday's Law $e = -\Delta\phi/\Delta t$

$$= -\Delta(N_2\phi_2)/\Delta t$$

But $N_2\phi_2 = Mi_1$,

$$\therefore \quad e_2 = -\frac{\Delta(Mi_i)}{\Delta t} = -M\frac{\Delta i_1}{\Delta t}$$

or
$$M = \frac{-e_2}{\Delta i_1 / \Delta t}$$

if $\Delta i_1/\Delta t = 1$, then $M = e_2$ (numerically). Hence, the coefficient of mutual induction between two coils is equal to the numerical value of the induced emf in one coil which is produced due to unit rate of changed of current in the other.

The unit of the coefficient of mutual induction is 'henry'.

TRANSFORMER

Transformer is a device used to obtain suitable A.C. voltage. It never works on D.C. There are of two types of transformer

(a) **Step-up Transformer.** It is used to convert low voltage high current to high voltage low current.

(b) **Step-down transformer.** It is used to convert high voltage low current to low voltage high current.

Principle. Transformer works on the principle of mutual induction i.*e.* when a magnetic flux linked with one coil changes, an induced e.m.f. is produced in the other coil.

Construction. It consists of two separate coils wound on a laminated iron core. The two coils are called primary coil P and secondary coil S. The a.c. input is applied across the primary coil and the transformed output is obtained across the secondary coil. The laminated iron core is prepared by joining together similar iron strips after coating them with varnish. Such a core helps to minimise energy losses due to production of eddy currents.

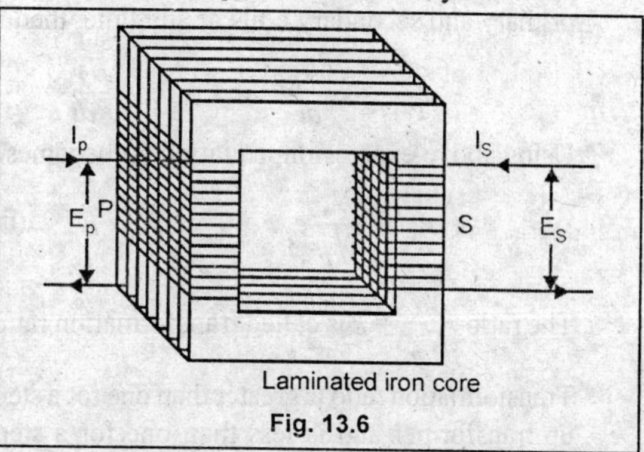

Fig. 13.6

Working. The number of turns in secondary coil (N_s) of a step-down transformer is less than that of primary coil (N_p), i.e., $N_s < N_p$. It converts a high voltage at low current into low voltage at high current.

Theory. The magnetic flux linked with the primary coil continuously change when an alternating source of e.m.f. is connected across it. The changing magnetic flux gets linked up with secondary coil through the laminated core, which in turn produces the alternating e.m.f. across the secondary coil. The soft iron core is capable of coupling practically whole of the magnetic flux generated in primary coil with the secondary coil. If the magnetic field lines remains confined to the soft iron core, then all the field lines across the primary coil link up with the each turn of secondary coil. Therefore, magnetic flux linked with the two coils is simply proportional to their number of turns. If N_p and N_s are number of turns in primary and secondary coils and ϕ_p and ϕ_s are magnetic flux linked with them, then

$$\frac{\phi_s}{\phi_p} = \frac{N_s}{N_p} \quad \text{or} \quad \phi_s = \frac{N_s}{N_p}.\phi_p \quad ...(i)$$

Differentiating with respect to time, we get

$$\frac{d\phi_s}{dt} = \frac{N_s}{N_p}.\frac{d\phi}{dt} \quad ...(ii)$$

According to Faraday's law, induced e.m.f. produced is given by

$$e = -\frac{d\phi}{dt}$$

Hence if e_p and e_s are induced e.m.f. produced in primary and secondary coils at any time, then

$$e_p = -\frac{d\phi_p}{dt} \text{ and } e_s = -\frac{d\phi_s}{dt}$$

Using above expression, equation (i) becomes

$$e_s = \frac{N_s}{N_p} e_p \quad ...(iii)$$

The ratio $\frac{N_s}{N_p} = k$ is called transformation ratio.

Transformation ratio is greater than one for a step-up transformer and is less than one for a step-down transformer.

If we assume that there are no energy losses, the **instantaneous output power = instantaneous input power.**

$$e_s i_s = e_p i_p$$

where, i_p and i_s are the values of current in primary and secondary coil respectively at the instant, when respective values of the voltage across them are e_p and e_s.

Hence $\frac{e_s}{e_p} = \frac{i_p}{i_s}$

Thus, a step-up transformer increases the voltage by decreasing the current and a step-down transformer decreases the voltage by increasing the current in accordance with a law of conservation of the energy. In other words, a **transformer simply transforms the voltages and currents, and it is not a generator of electricity.**

GENERATOR OR DYNAMO

A device by which we can convert mechanical energy to electrical energy is called Dynamo.

ALTERNATING CURRENT GENERATOR (A.C. DYNAMO)

Principle. Alternating current generator is based on the principle of the electromagnetic induction. When a coil is rotated about an axis perpendicular to the direction of uniform magnetic field, an induced e.m.f. is produced across it.

Construction. The A.C. generator consists of the following parts :

(1) **Armature.** The armature is a rectangular coil *ABCD* consisting of a large number of turns wound over a soft iron core. The soft iron core is used to increase the magnetic flux.

(2) **Field magnet.** Field magnet is a strong magnet having concave poles. The armature is rotated between the two poles of this magnet so that axis of the armature is perpendicular to magnetic field lines.

(3) **Slip ring.** The leads from the arms of the armature are connected to the two rings R_1 and R_2 separately. As the armature and hence the leads rotate, the rings R_1 and R_2 also rotate about the central axis.

(4) **Brushes.** Brushes (B_1, B_2) are used to pass on the current from armature to the external load *R*. As the rings rotate, the brushes remain in constant touch with the rings and always keep on pressing against them.

Working. The working of the a.c. generator is illustrated with the help of five different positions of the armature *ABCD* at time $t = 0, \frac{T}{4}, \frac{T}{2}, \frac{3T}{4}$ and *T* respectively as shown in Fig. below.

At $t = 0$, the armature *ABCD* is vertical with arm *AB* up and *CD* down. During the interval $t = 0$ to $t = \frac{T}{2}$, arm *AB* moves down and *CD* moves up.

The direction of current can be found with the help of Fleming's right hand rule. The current in the armature will flow in the direction *DCBA*.

During the interval $t = \frac{T}{2}$ to $t = T$, just the arm *AB* moves up and *CD* moves down. Hence during this interval, the current in the armature will flow in the direction *ABCD*.

The arms *AB* and *CD* of armature move momentarily parallel to the field. whenever, the armature is vertical, hence the rate of change of magnetic flux is zero. So, the induced e.m.f. $\left(e = -\frac{d\phi}{dt}\right)$ is also zero. Thus at time $t = 0$, $\frac{T}{2}$ and T, there is no induced e.m.f. in the coil.

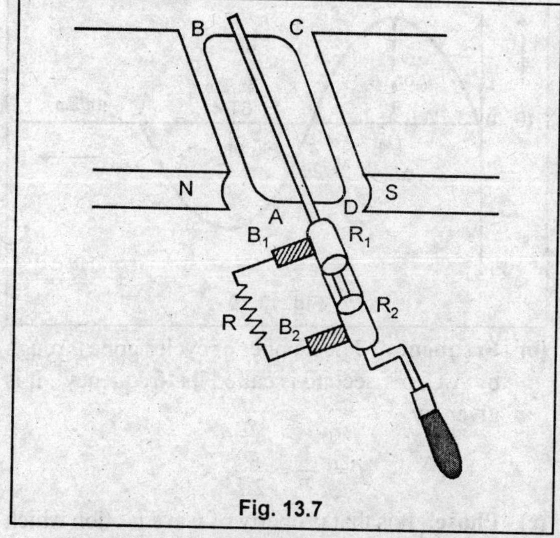

Fig. 13.7

In the horizontal position of armature, the arms cut the magnetic lines of force at once, so the rate of change of magnetic flux is fastest and maximum e.m.f. is induced in this position. Thus at time $t = \frac{T}{4}$ and $\frac{3T}{4}$, the induced e.m.f. produced is maximum.

Hence output e.m.f. across R during a complete rotation will vary sinusoidally.

Expression for instantaneous E.M.F produced in the armature of

A.C. Dynamo. Let us consider an armature of the a.c. generator having n turns and placed in uniform magnetic field B.

Suppose at any instant 't' the normal to the plane of coil makes an angle θ with the field direction. If ω is uniform angular velocity of the rotation of the coil, then $\theta = \omega t$.

In this position of the coil, the component of the field perpendicular to plane of coil is $B \cos \theta$ and hence magnetic flux linked with the coil at this instant is

$$\phi = nBA \cos \theta = nBA \cos \omega t \quad \text{...(i)}$$

where A is area of the coil. The induced e.m.f.

$$e = -\frac{d\phi}{dt} = -\frac{d}{dt}(nBA \cos \omega t) = -nBA\frac{d}{dt}(\cos \omega t)$$

$$= -nBA(-\sin \omega t)(\omega) = nBA\,\omega \sin \omega t$$

$$e = nBA\,\omega \sin \omega t \quad \text{...(ii)}$$

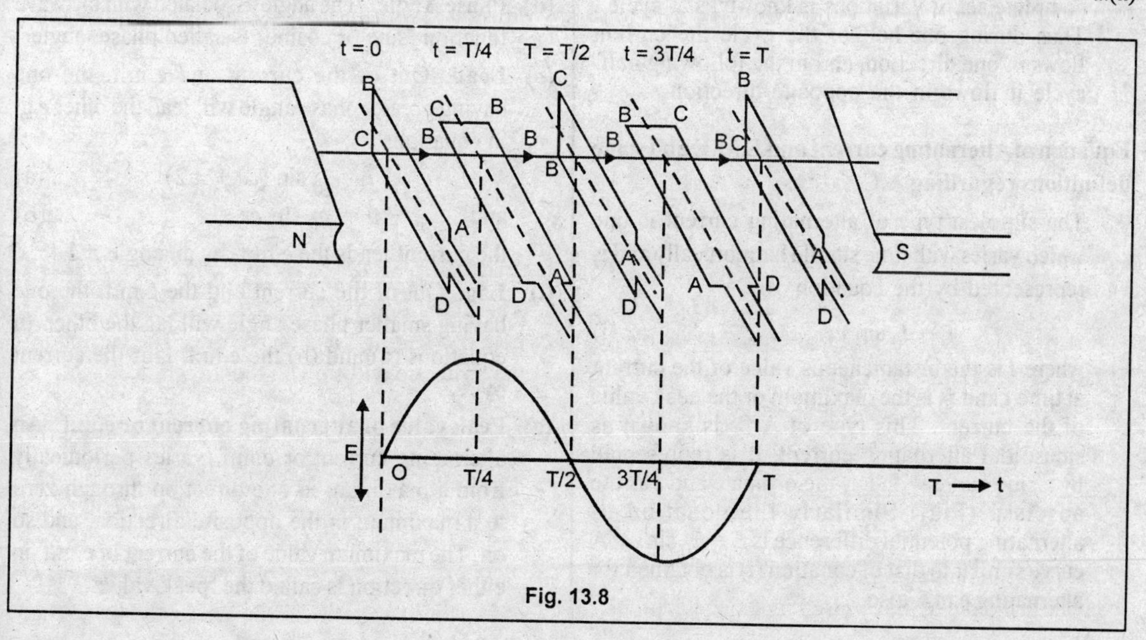

Fig. 13.8

The equation (ii) gives the instantaneous induced e.m.f. in the coil. Since $\omega_0 = nBA\,\omega$ is maximum value of the e.m.f. hence, we have

$$e = e_0 \sin \omega t.$$

It is clear from equation (ii) and (i) that the magnetic flux and induced e.m.f. have a phase difference of 90° and when flux is zero, induced e.m.f. is maximum.

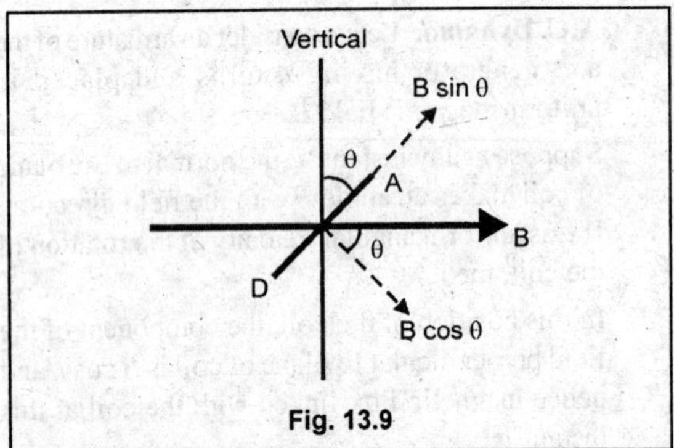

Fig. 13.9

ALTERNATING CURRENT (A.C.)

The current which periodically changes in magnitude and direction is called alternating current. It increases from zero to a maximum value, then decreases to zero and reverses in direction, increases to a maximum in this direction, and then decreases to zero. The complete set of variations is known as a 'cycle'. Thus during one-half of the cycle the current flows in one direction, and in the following half-cycle it flows in the opposite direction.

Equation of Alternating current and E.M.F. and some definitions regarding A.C.

The simplest type of alternating current is one which varies with time simple harmonically and is represented by the equation

$$i = i_0 \sin \omega t. \quad \text{... (i)}$$

where i is the instantaneous value of the current at time t and i_0 is the maximum or the peak value of the current. This type of A.C. is known as sinusoidal alternating current. It is represented by a sine curve with i as the ordinate and t as the abscissa (Fig.) Similarly the equation of alternating potential difference is $E = E_0 \sin \omega t$. A curve similar to that of equation (i) is obtained for alternating e.m.f. also.

(a) Time Period. The time by A.C. to go through one cycle of changes is called its 'period'. If in equation (i), we change t by $2\pi/\omega$, the same value of i is obtained. Hence the period T of A.C. is $2\pi\,\omega$.

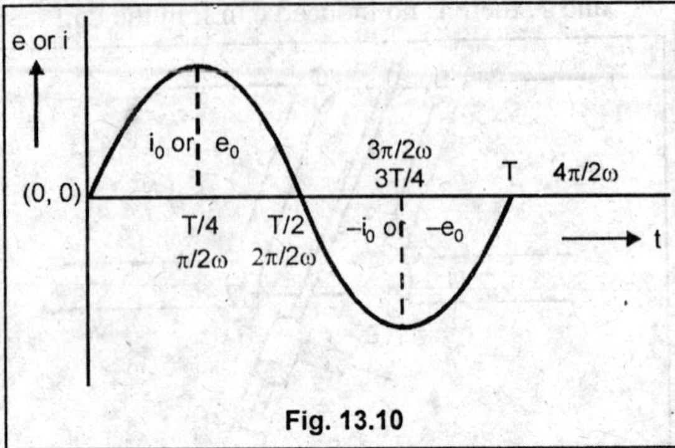

Fig. 13.10

(b) Frequency. The number of cycles gone through by A.C. per second is called its 'frequency'. It is given by

$$f = \frac{1}{T} = \frac{\omega}{2\pi}.$$

(c) Phase. It is that property of wave motion which tells us the position of the particle at any instant as well as its direction of motion. It is measured either by the angle which the particle makes with the mean position or by fraction of time period.

(d) Phase Angle. The angle associated with the wave function (sine or cosine) is called phase angle.

(e) Lead. Out of the current and e.m.f. the one having greater phase angle will lead the other *e.g.* in equations

$$i = i_0 \sin (\omega t + \pi/2) \quad \text{...(a)}$$

and

$$e = e_0 \sin \omega t \quad \text{...(b)}$$

the current leads the e.m.f. by an angle $\pi/2$.

(f) Lag. Out of the current and the e.m.f. the one having smaller phase angle will lag the other. In equations (a) and (b) the e.m.f. lags the current by $\pi/2$.

(g) Peak value of alternating current or e.m.f. An alternating current or e.m.f. varies periodically from a maximum in one direction through zero to a maximum in the opposite direction, and so on. The maximum value of the current or e.m.f. in either direction is called the 'peak value'.

MEAN VALUE OF ALTERNATING CURRENT

Let an alternating current be represented by

$$i = i_0 \sin \omega t$$

where i_0 is the peak value. Obviously the mean value of the current over a complete cycle is zero. It has no significance. Hence the 'mean value' of alternating current is defined as its average over half a cycle. For positive half cycle

$$i_{\text{mean}} = \frac{1}{T/2}\int_0^{T/2} i\, dt$$

Substituting $i = i_0 \sin \omega t$ and $T = (2\pi/\omega)$, we get

$$i_{\text{mean}} = \frac{\omega}{\pi}\int_0^{\pi/\omega} i_0 \sin \omega t\, dt = \frac{\omega}{\pi}\frac{i_0}{\omega}(-\cos \omega t)_0^{\pi/\omega}$$

$$= \frac{i_0}{\pi}[\cos \pi - \cos 0] = \frac{i_0}{\pi}[-1-1] = \frac{2}{\pi}i_0$$

Similarly the mean value of alternating e.m.f. is $2E_0/\pi$. For negative half cycle the mean value of alternating current is $-2i_0/\pi$ and the average value of e.m.f. for negative half cycle is $-2E_0/\pi$, so the average value of e.m.f. or current for complete cycle is zero.

Root-mean-square value of an alternating current

The square-root of the average of i^2 during a complete cycle, where i is the instantaneous value of the alternating current is called the root mean square (rms) value of the alternating current.

Now, the average value i^2 over a complete cycle is given by $\overline{i^2} = \frac{1}{t}\int_0^T i^2\, dt.$

Substituting $i = i_0 \sin \omega t$ and $T = 2\pi/\omega$, we get

$$\overline{i^2} = \frac{\omega}{2\pi}\int_0^{2\pi/\omega} i_0^2 \sin^2 \omega t\, dt$$

$$= \frac{\omega}{2\pi} i_0^2 \int_0^{2\pi/\omega} \frac{(1-\cos 2\omega t)}{2} dt$$

$$= \frac{\omega}{2\pi}\frac{i_0^2}{2}\left[t - \frac{\sin 2\omega t}{2\omega}\right]_0^{2\pi/\omega}$$

$$= \frac{\omega}{2\pi}\frac{i_0^2}{2}\left(\frac{2\pi}{\omega}\right) = \frac{i_0^2}{2}$$

Hence the root-mean-square value of the alternating current is given by

$$i_{\text{rms}} = \sqrt{(\overline{i^2})} = \frac{i_0}{\sqrt{2}} = 0.71\, i_0$$

Similarly, the root-mean-square value of the alternating voltage represented by

$E = E_0 \sin \omega t$ is given by

$$E_{\text{rms}} = \frac{E_0}{\sqrt{2}} = 0.71 E_0$$

If an alternating current given by $i = i_0 \sin \omega t$ passes through a resistance R, the instantaneous rate of heating is i^2R.

Hence the average rate of heating during a cycle,

$$= \frac{1}{T}\int_0^T i^2 R\, dt = \frac{R}{T}\int_0^T i^2\, dt = \frac{i_0^2 R}{2}$$

$$\left[\because \frac{1}{T}\int_0^T i^2\, dt = \frac{i_0^2}{2}\right]$$

$$= (i_{\text{rms}})^2 R \qquad \left[i_{rms} = \frac{i_0}{2}\right]$$

Which would be produced by a direct current of value i, if $i = i_{\text{rms}}$. Hence the rms value of an alternating current can also be defined as that direct current which produces the same rate of heating in a given resistance. Hence, the rms value of alternating current is also called as the 'effective' or the 'virtual' value of the current

$$i_{\text{virtual}} = \frac{i_0}{\sqrt{2}} = i_{rms}.$$

Similarly, the rms value of an alternating voltage can be defined as that direct voltage which produces the same rate of heating in a given resistance. The rms value of alternating voltage is also called as the 'effective' or the 'virtual' value of the voltage.

$$E_{\text{virtual}} = \frac{E_0}{\sqrt{2}} = E_{rms}.$$

IMPEDANCE

The ratio of the effective voltage to the effective current in any circuit is called the impedance Z of the circuit. It units are ohm.

PHASORS AND PHASOR DIAGRAMS

While studying A.C. circuits, we shall come across alternating voltages and currents having same frequency but differ in phase with each other. It is observed that the study of A.C. circuit becomes quite easy, if alternating currents and voltages are treated as vectors or more correctly as 'phasors'. While representing the alternating current and voltage vectors, the phase angle between the two quantities is also represented in the vector diagram.

A diagram representing alternating voltage and current as vector with the phase angle between them is called a phasor diagram.

CIRCUIT CONTAINING *L*, *C* AND *R*

Let us consider an alternating source of e.m.f. of r.m.s. value E_V connected to a series combination of an inductor of inductance L, a resistor of resistance R and a capacitor of capacitance C as shown in Fig. (a).

The equation of alternating e.m.f. is

$$E = E_0 \sin \omega t. \quad ...(i)$$

Let the r.m.s. value of current in the *LCR*-circuit be I_V and the r.m.s values of voltages across inductance L, capacitor C and resistance R be V_L, V_C and V_R respectively. The magnitude of r.m.s. value of current I_V is same in L, C, and R as they are in series. The r.m.s. value of alternating e.m.f. of the source i.e. E_V is equal to vector sum of V_L, V_C and V_R. Let us draw the phasor diagram for current and voltages.

Now, V_R and I_V are in phase. Therefore, both V_R and I_V are represented along OX. Fig. (b).

Also, V_L leads I_V by phase angle angle ($\pi/2$). Therefore, V_L is represented along O_Y.

Further, V_C lags I_V by phase angle ($\pi/2$). Therefore, V_C is represented along OY'.

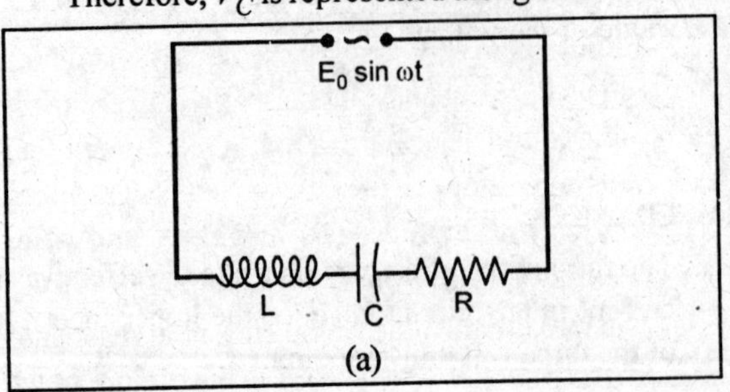

(a)

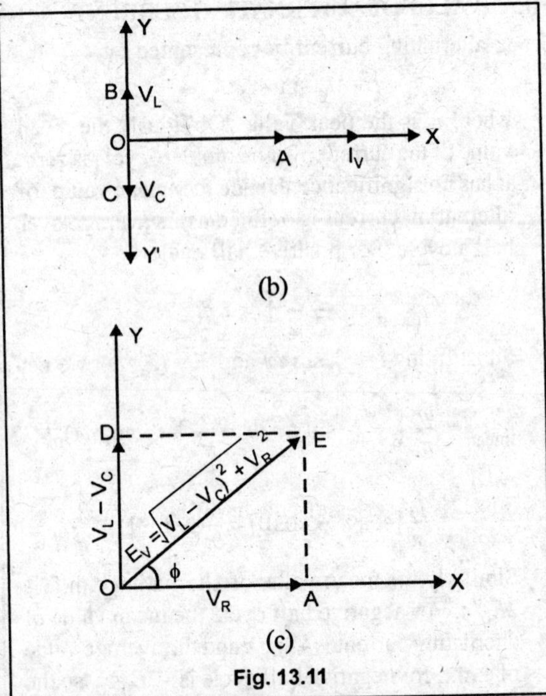

Fig. 13.11

Let OA, OB and OC represent the magnitude of V_R, V_L and V_C respectively. In case $V_L > V_C$ (as shown in Fig. (c)), then OD represents $V_L - V_C$, the resultant of V_L and V_C. Finally, OE, the resultant of OA and OD represents E_V. Thus, from phasor diagram, we have

$$OE = \sqrt{(OA^2 + AE^2)}$$

or $$E_V = \sqrt{\{(V_R^2 + (V_L - V_C)^2\}}$$

Now $$V_R = I_V R, V_L = I_V X_L \text{ and } V_C = I_V X_C$$

where $X_L = \omega L$ and $X_C = \dfrac{1}{\omega C}$.

Hence,

$$E_V = \sqrt{\{(I_V R)^2 + (I_V X_L - I_V X_C)^2\}}$$

$$= I_V \sqrt{\{R^2 + (X_L - X_C)^2\}}$$

or $$I_V = \frac{E_V}{\sqrt{\{R^2 + (X_L - X_C)^2\}}} \quad ...(ii)$$

Further, from phasor diagram, it follows that in *LCR*-series circuit, E_V leads I_V in case $V_L > V_C$ or $X_L > X_C$ by phase angle ϕ given by

$$\tan\phi = \frac{AE}{OA} = \frac{V_L - V_C}{V_R} = \frac{I_V X_L - I_V X_C}{I_V R}$$

or $$\tan\phi = \frac{X_L - X_C}{R} = \frac{\omega L - 1/\omega C}{R} \quad ...(iii)$$

If Z is the impedance of LCR-series circuit, then

$$I_V = \frac{E_V}{Z} \quad ...(iv)$$

From equations, (ii) and (iv), we have

$$Z = \sqrt{\{R^2 + (X_L - X_C)^2\}} = \sqrt{\left\{R^2 + \left(\omega L - \frac{1}{\omega C}\right)^2\right\}} \quad ...(v)$$

The phase relationship between current and e.m.f in L.C.R. series circuit in different cases are as follows :

(i) When $\omega L > \frac{1}{\omega C}$. From equation (iii) it follows that $\tan\phi$ is positive, *i.e.* ϕ is positive. Hence in such a case, e.m.f. leads the current.

(ii) When $\omega L < \frac{1}{\omega C}$. From equation (iii) it follows that $\tan\phi$ is negative *i.e.* ϕ is negative. Hence in such a case, e.m.f. lags behind the current.

(iii) When $\omega L = \frac{1}{\omega C}$. From equation (iii), it follows that $\tan\phi$ is zero, i.e. ϕ is zero. Hence, in such a case, current and e.m.f. are in phase with each other.

When $\omega L = \frac{1}{\omega C}$, the impedance of the circuit would be just equal to R (minimum). In other words, the LCR-series circuit will behave as a purely resistive circuit. Due to the minimum value of impedance, the current in LCR-series circuit will be maximum. This condition is known as resonance.

RESONANCE IN L-C-R (SERIES) CIRCUIT

In L-C-R series circuit resonance takes place when the impedance of the circuit is minimum or the current is maximum.

The value of angular frequency (ω_0) for which the current in series A.C. circuit acquires a maximum value and the impedance of the circuit reaches a minimum value is called the natural or resonant angular frequency.

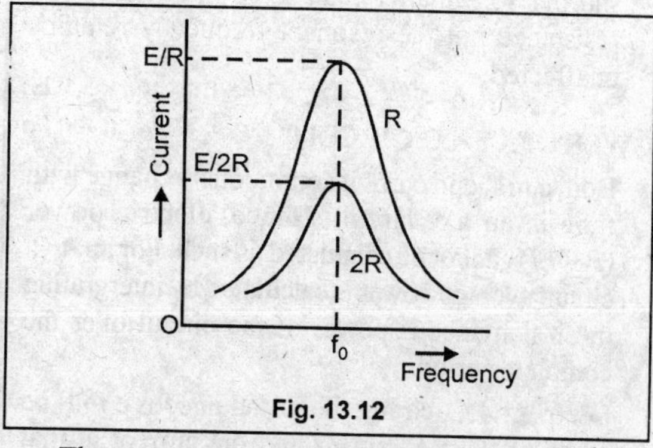

Fig. 13.12

Thus, at $\omega = \omega_0$, Z = minimum, but $Z \neq 0$, therefore it follows that Z will be minimum and I_V will be maximum, if

$$\omega_0 L - \frac{1}{\omega_0 C} = 0 \quad \text{or} \quad \omega_0 L = \frac{1}{\omega_0 C}$$

or $$\omega_0 = \frac{1}{\sqrt{(LC)}}, \text{ but } \omega_0 = 2\pi f_0$$

$$\therefore f_0 = \frac{1}{2\pi\sqrt{(LC)}}$$

where f_0 is the resonant frequency. Obviously at resonant frequency :

the maximum value of current, $(I_V)_{max} = \frac{E_V}{R}$.

Thus the resonant frequency depends on the product of L and C, and is independent of R.

If R, L and C remain fixed, and the frequency f of the applied e.m.f. is raised continuously from zero, the peak current varies as shown in Fig. At first the current is very small, increases to a maximum when the frequency increases to its resonance value f_0, and then falls again. **It is to be noted that before reesonance the current leads the applied e.m.f. at resonance it is in phase, and after resonance it lags behind the e.m.f.**

The maximum value of the current at resonance depends on the resistance R in the circuit, being smaller for larger R. In the Fig. two curves are plotted, one when the circuit resistance is R and the other when the circuit resistance is $2R$. The resonant current in the second case is half the value in the first case. Also, the resonance is sharper for smaller resistance than for larger resistance but the resonant frequency remains unaffected.

POWER OF AN A.C. CIRCUIT

Both e.m.f. and current continuously change with time in an a.c. circuit. Hence, electric power ($P = EI$) cannot be calculated as such. For an $A.C.$ circuit average power is calculated by intergrating the instantaneous power of the circuit over the complete period.

Let in an $A.C.$ circuit the instantaneous e.m.f. be given by $E = E_0 \sin \omega t$ and the current at that instant be given by $I = I_0 \sin (\omega t \pm \phi)$, where ϕ is the phase difference between current and e.m.f., I_0 and E_0 are the peak values of current and e.m.f. respectively and $\omega = 2\pi/T$, where T is the period of $A.C.$ The instantaneous power of $A.C.$ is given by

$$P_t = EI = E_0 \sin \omega t \,.\, I_0 \sin (\omega t \pm \phi)$$

or $$P_t = E_0 I_0 \sin \omega t\, [\sin \omega t \cos \phi \pm \cos \omega t \sin \phi]$$

or $$P_t = E_0 I_0 \{\sin^2 \omega t \cos \phi \pm \sin \omega t \cos \omega t \sin \phi]$$

or $$P_t = E_0 I_0 \left[\frac{(1-\cos 2\omega t)}{2}\cos\phi \pm \frac{\sin 2\omega t}{2}\sin\phi\right]$$

or $$P_t = \frac{E_0 I_0}{2}[\cos\phi - \cos 2\omega t \cos\phi \pm \sin 2\omega t \sin\phi]$$

or $$P_t = \frac{E_0 I_0}{2}[\cos \phi - \cos (2\omega t \mp \phi)]$$

Hence the average power in the circuit is

$$\overline{P} = \frac{1}{T}\int_0^T EI\, dt = \frac{E_0 I_0}{2T}\int_0^T \{\cos\phi - \cos(2\omega t \mp \phi)\, dt$$

$$= \frac{E_0 I_0}{2T}\left[t \cos \phi - \frac{\sin (2\omega t \mp \phi)}{2\omega}\right]_0^T$$

$$\therefore \overline{P} = \frac{E_0 I_0}{2}\cos \phi = \frac{E_0}{\sqrt{2}}\cdot\frac{I_0}{\sqrt{2}}\cos\phi$$

or $$\overline{P} = E_{rms} \,.\, I_{rms} \cos \phi.$$

In this expression $\cos \phi$ is known as the power factor. Value of $\cos \phi$ depends on the nature of the circuit. For L, C, and L-C circuits, the power factor is zero ($\because \phi = 90°$) for R circuit $\cos \phi = 1$ ($\because \phi = 0$) and for all other circuits $\cos \phi = R/Z$ where Z is the impedance of the circuit.

MULTIPLE CHOICE QUESTIONS

1. Tesla is a unit of
   (a) magnetic flux
   (b) electric flux
   (c) magnetic Induction
   (d) potential difference

2. A magnetic field generates a flux of 4×10^{-6} Wb in a long bar of steel of cross section 0.5×10^{-4} m^2, the flux density of the magnetic field in Wb/m^2
   (a) 8×10^{-6} (b) 2×10^{-6}
   (c) 8×10^{-2} (d) 2×10^{-8}

3. The unit of magnetic flux is
   (a) Debye (b) Henry
   (c) Weber (d) Rutherford

4. The magnetic flux linked with a vector area $\vec{A}$ in a uniform magnetic field $\vec{\mathbf{B}}$ is
   (a) $\vec{B} \times \vec{A}$ (b) AB
   (c) $\vec{A}.\vec{B}$ (d) $\frac{B}{A}$

5. The magnetic field in a coil of 100 turns and 40 cm^2 area is increased from 1 tesla to 6 tesla in 2 seconds. The magnetic field is perpendicular to the coil. The emf generated in it is
   (a) 10^4 V (b) 1.2 V
   (c) 1.0 V (d) 10^{-2} V

6. Faraday's law of electromagnetic induction states that the induced e.m.f. in a circuit is
   (a) proportional to density of lines of force
   (b) inversely proportional to the rate of change of lines of force
   (c) proportional to the total magnetic field produced
   (d) directly proportional to the rate of change of lines of force

7. Lenz's law states that the direction of the induced e.m.f. in a conductor is such as to
   (a) move the conductor parallel to itself
   (b) generate a magnetic field parallel to the conductor
   (c) align the conductor parallel to earth's magnetic field
   (d) develop forces opposing the cause of the induced e.m.f.

8. The induced e.m.f. in a circuit according to Faraday's law of electromagnetic induction is
   (a) inversely proportional to the total number of lines of force through the circuit
   (b) inversely proportional to the rate of change of lines of force through the circuit
   (c) directly proportional to the rate of change of lines of force through the circuit
   (d) directly proportional to the total number of lines of force through the circuit

9. Two identical coaxial circular coils carry a current i each, circling in the same direction. If the coils approach each other, you will observe that
   (a) the current in each remains the same
   (b) the current in one increases whereas in the other decreases
   (c) the current in each increases
   (d) the current in each decreases

10. Refer to the figure. Maximum deflection in the Galvanometer (G) occurs when

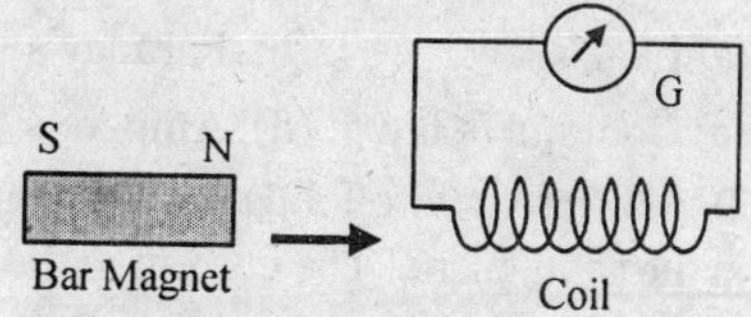

(a) the magnet is pushed to the coil

(b) the magnet is rotated in the coil

(c) the magnet is stationary at the centre of the coil

(d) the number of turns in the coil is reduced.

11. **Directions**: The question given below is followed by threc suggested completions or answers (i), (ii), and (iii). While answering follow the instructions below for encircling the correct response.

Answer

(a) if only (i) is correct

(b) if only (ii) is correct

(c) if only (i) and (ii) are correct

(d) if only (i) and (iii) are correct.

Lenz's law in e.m. induction follows naturally if one uses :

(i) Principle of conservation of energy.

(ii) Principle of conservation of momentum.

(iii) The principle that action and reaction are always equal and opposite.

(a) (b)

(c) (d)

12. A moving conductor coil in a magnetic field produces an induced emf. This is in accordance with

(a) Lenz's law (b) Faraday's law

(c) Coulomb's law (d) Ampere's law.

13. A metallic ring is hung on a wall. A magnet's north pole is brought near it. Induced current is

(a) zero

(b) infinity

(c) in anticlockwise direction

(d) in clockwise direction.

14. Which law applies to the phenomenon of electromagnetic induction?

(a) Lenz's law (b) Faraday's law

(c) Coulomb's law (d) Ampere's law

15. Two different wire loops are concentric and lie in the same plane. The current in the outer loop is clockwise and increasing with time. The induced current in the inner loop then is

(a) clockwise

(b) zero

(c) counterclockwise

(d) in a direction that depends on the ratio of the loop radii.

16. According to Faraday's Law of electromagnetic induction

(a) The direction of induced current is such that it opposes the cause producing it

(b) The magnitude of induced emf produced in a coil is directly proportional to the rate of change of magnetic flux

(c) The direction of induced emf is such that it opposes the cause producing it

(d) None of the above

17. The direction of induced emf during electromagnetic induction is given by

(a) Faraday's law (b) Lenz's law

(c) Maxwell's law (d) Ampere's law

18. The north pole of a long horizontal bar magnet is being brought closer to a vertical conducting plane along the perpendicular direction. The direction of the induced current in the conducting plane will be

(a) horizontal (b) vertical

(c) clockwise (d) anticlockwise

19. The north pole of long horizontal bar magnet is being bought closer to a vertical conducting plane along the perpendicular direction. The direction of the induced current in the conducting plane will be

(a) horizontal (b) vertical

(c) clocking (d) anticlockwise

20. The induced currents always produced expanding magnetic fields round their conductors in a direction that opposes the original magnetic field. This law is called.

(a) Ohm's law (b) Kirchhoff's law

(c) Lenz's law (d) Fleming's rule

21. The concept of rotating magnetic field, which is the basis of practically all alternating current machinery, was conceived by

(a) Tesla (b) Young

(c) Planck (d) Franck and Hertz

22. The frequency of the electric current supplied in houses in India is

(a) 40 Hz (b) 50 Hz
(c) 100 Hz (d) 150 Hz

23. The rms value of voltage in a circuit is 100 V. Then the peak voltage is (in volts)

(a) $100/\sqrt{2}$ (b) $100\sqrt{2}$
(c) $300/\sqrt{2}$ (d) $300\sqrt{2}$

24. A normal domestic electric supply is an alternating current whose average value is

(a) zero
(b) half the peak value
(c) the peak value multiplied by $\pi/2$
(d) the peak value divided by $\pi/2$

25. A generator produces a voltage that is given by E = 240 sin 120 t volt, where t is in seconds. The frequency and e.m.f. voltage respectively are

(a) 60 Hz and 240.
(b) 19 Hz and 120.
(c) 19 Hz and 170.
(d) 754 Hz and 170.

26. The peak value of I_o and E_o of the current and voltage respectively in alternating current are related to their effective values I_{eff} and E_{eff} by

(a) $I_{eff}/\sqrt{2}$ and $E_{eff}/\sqrt{2}$
(b) $I_{eff}/\sqrt{2}$ and $\sqrt{2}\,E_{eff}$
(c) $\sqrt{2}\,I_{eff}$ and $E_{eff}/\sqrt{2}$
(d) $\sqrt{2}\,I_{eff}$ and $\sqrt{2}\,E_{eff}$

27. The root mean square value of an alternating current of 50 hertz frequency is 10 ampere. The time taken by the alternating current in reaching from zero to maximum value and the peak value will be

(a) 2×10^{-2} sec and 14.14 amp.
(b) 1×10^{-2} sec and 7.07 amp.
(c) 5×10^{-3} sec and 7.07 amp.
(d) 5×10^{-3} sec and 14.14 amp.

28. There is a square wave of electric current whose values change from 0 to 5 A. What is the rms value of the current?

(a) 2 A (b) 2.5 A
(c) 3.5 A (d) 4 A

29. If E_0 is the peak emf of an AC current, the rms emf is given by

(a) $E_0/2$ (b) $\sqrt{E_0}$
(c) $E_0/\sqrt{2}$ (d) $E_0\sqrt{2}$

30. The root-mean square value of the alternating current is equal to

(a) twice the peak vlaue
(b) half the peak value
(c) $\frac{1}{\sqrt{2}}$ times the peak value
(d) equal to the peak value

31. The frequency of an alternating voltage is 50 cycles/sec and its amplitude is 120 V. What will be its r.m.s. value?

(a) 56.5 V (b) 70.7 V
(c) 84.8 V (d) 101.3 V

32. In an A.C. circuit, the rms value of current, I_{rms} is related to the peak current I_0 by the relation

(a) $I_{rms} = 1/\pi I_0$ (b) $I_{rms} = 1/\sqrt{2}\,I_0$
(c) $I_{rms} = \sqrt{2}\,I_0$ (d) $I_{rms} = \pi I_0$

33. The r.m.s. voltage of domestic electricity supply is 220 volt. Electrical appliances should be designed to withstand an instantaneous voltage of

(a) 220 V (b) 310 V
(c) 330 V (d) 440 V

34. The r.m.s. value of current $I = I_0 \sin(\omega t + \phi)$ depends on

(a) I_0 only (b) ω only
(c) I_0 and ω both (d) I_0 and ϕ both

35. If the instantaneous current in a circuit is given by $I = 4\cos(\omega t + \phi)$ in amperes, the root mean square value of the current, in ampere, is

(a) 2 (b) $\sqrt{2}$
(c) $2\sqrt{2}$ (d) 4

36. The voltage of an A.C. source varies with time according to the equation $W = 120 \sin 100\pi t \cos 100\pi t$. Then

(a) the peak voltage of source is 120 volts
(b) the peak voltage of source is 60 volts
(c) the peak voltage of the source is 120volts
(d) the frequency of the source is 50 hertz

37. In a circuit, the value of the alternating current is measured by hot wire ammeter as 10 ampere. Its peak value will be

(a) 10 ampere (b) 20 ampere
(c) 14.14 ampere (d) 7.07 ampere

38. An electric lamp is connected to 220 V, 50 Hz supply. The peak value of current is

(a) 210 V (b) 211 V
(c) 311 V (d) 320 V

39. Relation between the mean value I_m and the r.m.s. value $I_{r.m.s.}$ of a sinusoidal A.C. is

(a) $I_{r.m.s.} = 2\sqrt{2}/\pi\, I_m$
(b) $I_{r.m.s.} = I_m/\sqrt{2}$
(c) $I_{r.m.s.} = \sqrt{2}\, I_m$
(d) $I_m = 2\sqrt{2}/\pi\, I_{r.m.s.}$

40. The average value, over half a cycle, of alternating current $I = I_0 \sin \omega t$ is equal to

(a) zero (b) $I_0/2$
(c) $2I_0/\pi$ (d) $2I_0/\sqrt{2}$

41. An e.m.f. of 15 volt is applied in a circuit containing 5 henry inductance and 10 ohm resistance. The ratio of the currents at time $t = \infty$ and at t = 1 second is

(a) $\dfrac{e^{1/2}}{e^{1/2}-1}$ (b) $\dfrac{e^2}{e^2-1}$
(c) $1-e^{-1}$ (d) e^{-1}.

42. In L-R circuit, for the case of increasing current, the magnitude of current can be calculated by using the formula

(a) $I = I_0 e^{-Rt/L}$ (b) $I = I_0(1-e^{-Rt/L})$
(c) $I = I_0(1-e^{Rt/L})$ (d) $I = I_0 e^{Rt/L}$

43. A 50 volt potential difference is suddenly applied to a coil with $L = 5 \times 10^{-3}$ henry and $R = 180\ \Omega$. The rate of increase of current after 0.001 second is

(a) 27.3 amp/sec (b) 27.8 amp/sec
(c) 2.73 amp/sec (d) $10^4 \times e^{-36}$ amp/s

44. What is the dimension of the Inductive Time Constant (L/R)?

(a) $[MLT^{-2}I]$ (b) $[M^0L^0TI^0]$
(c) $[M^0LTI]$ (d) $[M^0L^0T^0I]$

45. A 50 mH coil carries a current of 2 amp. The energy stored in joule is

(a) 1 (b) 0.1
(c) 0.05 (d) 0.5

46. 5 cm long solenoid having 10 ohm resistance and 5 mH inductance is joined to a 10 volt battery. At steady state the current through the solenoid (in ampere) will be

(a) 5 (b) 1
(c) 2 (d) zero

47. An ideal coil of 10 Henry is joined in series with a resistance of 5 ohm and a battery of 5 volt 2 seconds after joining the current flowing (in ampere) in the circuit will be

(a) e^{-1} (b) $(1-e^{-1})$
(c) $(1-e)$ (d) e

48. In an L-R circuit, time constant is that time in which current grows from zero to the value; where I_0 is the steady state current

(a) $0.63\, I_0$ (b) $0.50\, I_0$
(c) $0.37\, I_0$ (d) I_0

49. A solenoid has an inductance of 60 henry and a resistance of 30 ohms. If it is connected to a 100 volt battery. How long will it take for the current to reach e–1/e ≈ 63.2% of its final value?

(a) 1 second (b) 2 seconds
(c) e seconds (d) 2e seconds

50. An electric bulb in series with a large inductor when connected across a D.C. source take a little time before reaching a stable glow. If an iron core is inserted into the inductor, the delay will

(a) increase
(b) decrease
(c) remain the same
(d) may change in either direction depending upon the values of inductance and resistance.

ANSWERS

1	2	3	4	5	6	7	8	9	10
(c)	(c)	(c)	(c)	(c)	(d)	(d)	(c)	(d)	(a)
11	**12**	**13**	**14**	**15**	**16**	**17**	**18**	**19**	**20**
(a)	(b)	(a)	(a)	(c)	(b)	(b)	(c)	(d)	(c)
21	**22**	**23**	**24**	**25**	**26**	**27**	**28**	**29**	**30**
(a)	(b)	(b)	(d)	(c)	(d)	(d)	(c)	(c)	(c)
31	**32**	**33**	**34**	**35**	**36**	**37**	**38**	**39**	**40**
(c)	(b)	(b)	(a)	(b)	(b)	(c)	(c)	(d)	(c)
41	**42**	**43**	**44**	**45**	**46**	**47**	**48**	**49**	**50**
(b)	(b)	(d)	(b)	(b)	(b)	(b)	(a)	(b)	(a)

HINTS / SOLUTIONS

2. Flux, $\phi = B \times A$ or $B = \phi/A$.

4. magnetic flux, $\phi = \vec{B}.\vec{A}$

10. According to Faraday's laws, an e.m.f. is induced in a conductor when the magnetic field surrounding its changes, and its magnitude is proportional to the rate of change of the field.

14. According to Faraday's laws, whenever the magnetic flux linked with a closed circuit changes, an e.m.f. (and hence a current) is induced in it. It lasts only as long as the change in flux is taking place.

15. Direction of induced current is opposite to direction of main current so in inner loop, current will be counter clockwise.

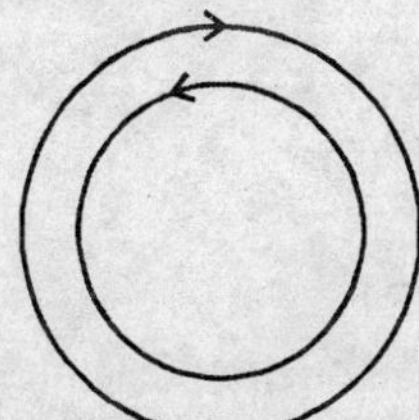

18. The induced current must oppose the cause which is inducing it.

22. The frequency of the electric current supplied in houses in India is 50 Hz.

25. As $E = E_0 \sin \omega t$ always, we get $\omega = 120$.

But $n = \omega/2\pi$. So $n = \dfrac{120}{2\pi} = 19$ Hz.

26. I_{eff} and E_{eff} are root mean square values.

27. Relation between i_{rms} and i_0 (peak value) is:

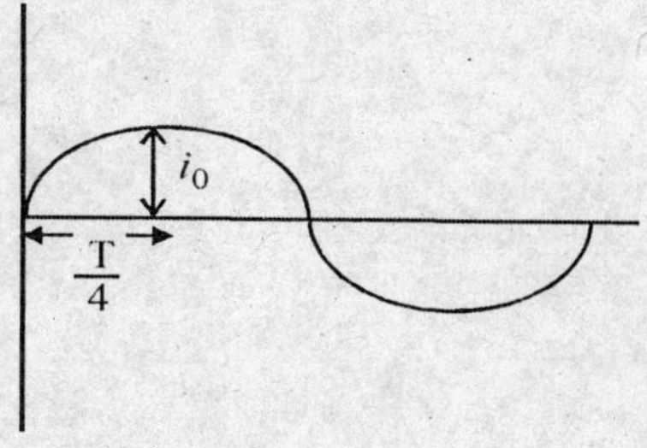

$$i_{rms} = \frac{i_0}{\sqrt{2}}$$

or $i_0 = \sqrt{2} i$ rms

Given : $i_{rms} = 10$ A

$\therefore i_0 = \sqrt{2} \times 10 = 14{\cdot}14$A.

From fig., it is clear that maximum value is reached

in time $= \dfrac{T}{4} = \dfrac{1}{4f}$. $\left(\because T = \dfrac{1}{f}\right)$

Given $f = 50$ Hz.

$\therefore$ Time $= \dfrac{1}{4 \times 50} = 5 \times 10^{-3}$ sec.

Other Similar concept

Similar question may be asked for E.M.F. instead of I.

28. rms value $= \sqrt{\dfrac{0^2 + 5^2}{2}} = 3.54$ A

29. If Peak value of e.m.f. is E_0

then r.m.s. value $E_{rms} = \dfrac{E_0}{\sqrt{2}}$

30. Root mean square value of current

$$I_{rms} = \frac{I_0}{\sqrt{2}}$$

or $I_{rms} = 0{\cdot}707\, I_0$

31. We know that the root mean square value of voltage (V_{rms})

$$= \frac{\text{Peak value of the voltage}}{\sqrt{2}} = \frac{V_0}{\sqrt{2}} = \frac{120}{\sqrt{2}}$$

$= 84{\cdot}8$ V.

37. Peak value of current $I_0 = \sqrt{2}\, I_{r.m.s.}$ Reading of hot wire ammeter gives $I_{r.m.s.}$ $\therefore I_{r.m.s} = 10$ amp. Therefore peak value $I_0 = \sqrt{2}\,(10) = 14.14$ amp.

41. Introduction of iron core will increase the inductive effect in the inductor coil.

UNIT-14

OPTICS

INTRODUCTION

Light falling on a surface, is divided into three parts : a part is reflected, a part is refracted and the remaining is absorbed.

Reflection. Depending on the nature of surface reflection is of two types.

(*I*) **Regular Reflection.** When the surface is smooth, the reflection is regular and follows the two laws :

(i) The incident ray, the reflected ray and normal to surface at the point of incidence all lie in the same plane.

(ii) The angle of incidence, *i* is equal to the angle of reflection, *r*

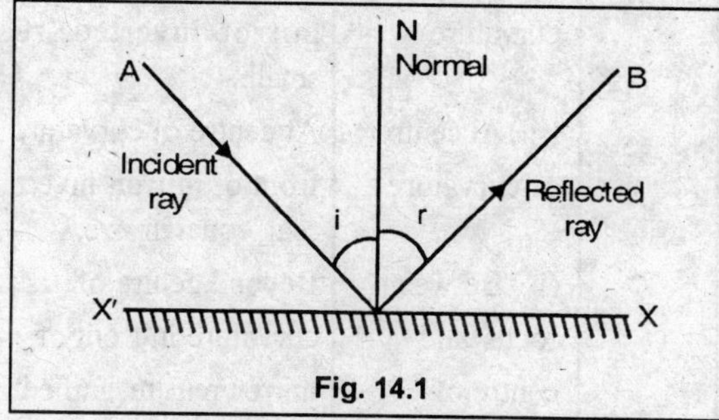

Fig. 14.1

Deviation produced by reflection

$$\delta = \pi - (i + r)$$

Since $i = r \quad \therefore \quad \delta = \pi - 2i = (180° - 2i)$

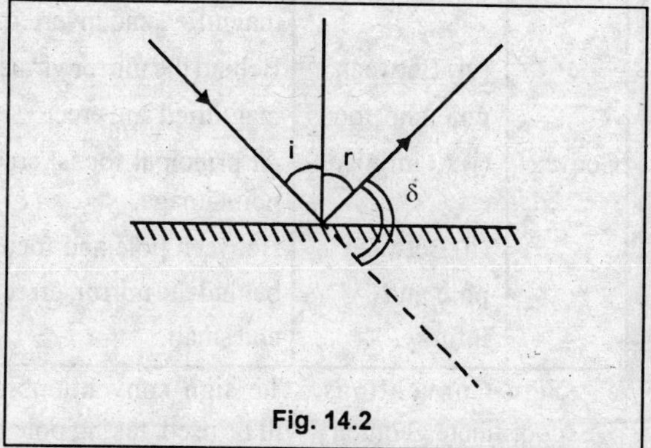

Fig. 14.2

(II) **Diffuse Reflection.** When the surface is rough, the irregularities of surface act as reflecting centres and reflect waves irregularly in any direction. This phenmenon is called diffuse reflection or scattering. The objects in a room are visible due to duffuse reflection.

Mirrors. Generally reflecting surface is called mirror. Mirrors are of three types

(i) Plane mirror

(ii) Concave mirror

(iii) Convex mirror

(i) Foundation of image by the plane mirror. The figure given below represents the formation of image of a point object *O* by a plane mirror. The image formed *I* has the following characteristics.

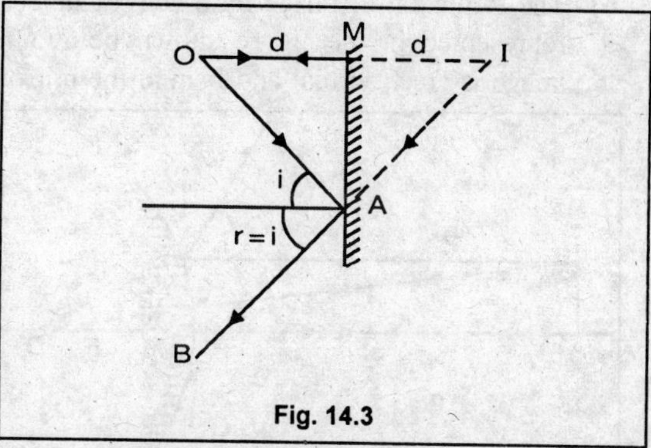

Fig. 14.3

(i) The size of image is equal to the size of object.

(ii) The separation of image from mirror formed behind the mirror is equal to the separation of object from the mirror i.e. $OM = MI$.

(iii) The image is virtual, erect and laterally reversed.

(II) Concave Mirror. The mirror at which the reflection takes place at inner surface and whose outer surface is polished is called a concave mirror.

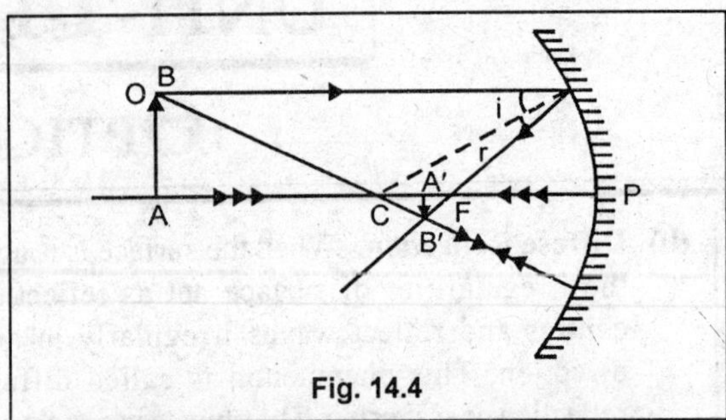

Fig. 14.4

The formation of image by a concave mirror is represented in the figure shown above. The ray starting from object parallel to principal axis is reflected from the mirror along the principal focus *F*. The ray directed towards centre of curvature *C* falls normally on the mirror and is reflected back to retrace its path. The two rays meet at *B′* which is real image of *B*. The image of *A* is formed at *A′*. Thus *I* is the image of object *O*.

(III) Convex Mirror. The mirror at which reflection takes place from outer surface and whose inner surface is polished is called a convex mirror. The formation of image by a convex mirror is represented in the figure shown below. The image is erect, virtual and behind the mirror.

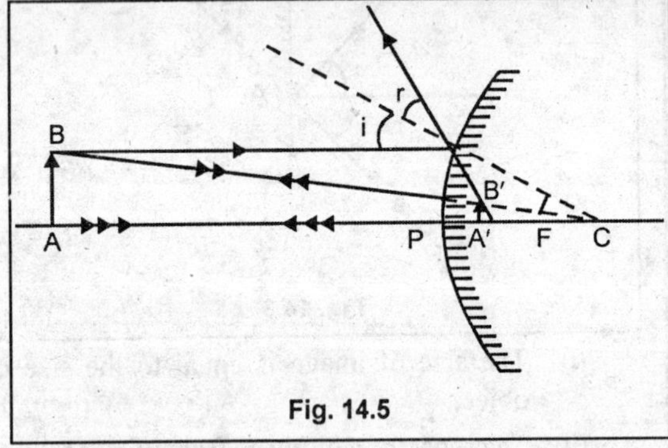

Fig. 14.5

Mirror Formula is

$$\frac{1}{f} = \frac{1}{v} + \frac{1}{u}$$

where u = distance of object from the pole of mirror

v = distance of image from the pole of mirror

$f = \frac{r}{2}$ focal length of mirror, r being radius of curvature of the mirror.

Lateral magnification produced by mirror,

$$m = \frac{I}{O} = -\frac{v}{u} = -\frac{f}{u-f}$$

where I = size of image and O = size of object.

Longitudinal magnification

$$mx = \frac{x_2}{x_1} = -\left(\frac{v}{u}\right)^2 = -\left(\frac{f}{u-f}\right)^2$$

The position and nature of image of an object placed at various positions from the mirror are given in the following table.

Mirror	*Position of Object*	*Position and Nature of image*
Concave	(i) At infinity	At principal focus in front of mirror, inverted, real very small.
	(ii) Beyond centre of curvature	Between focus and centre of curvature in front of mirror inverted, real, small.
	(iii) At centre of curvature	At centre of curvature in front of mirror, inverted, real, equal in size.
	(iv) Between focus and centre of curvature	Beyond centre of curvature in front of mirror, real, magnified and inverted.
	(*v*) At focus	At infinity in front of mirror, real highly magnified and inverted.
	(vi) Between pole and focus	Behind the mirror virtual, magnified and erect.
Convex	(i) At infinity	At principal focus, erect point image.
	(ii) Between pole and infinity	Between pole and focus behind the mirror, errect and small.

Sign Conventions. The sign conventions of coordinate geometry will be used, taking pole or mirror as origin. Accordingly the *focal length of* *concave mirror is negative and that of convex mirror is positive.* The distance of object placed in front of mirror on the left (u) (Negative X-axis) is negative and the distance of image from mirror (v) is negative for real image and positive for virtual image.

REFRACTION

There is a change in direction of ray when a ray of light falls on the boundary separating the two media. This penomenon is called *refraction.*

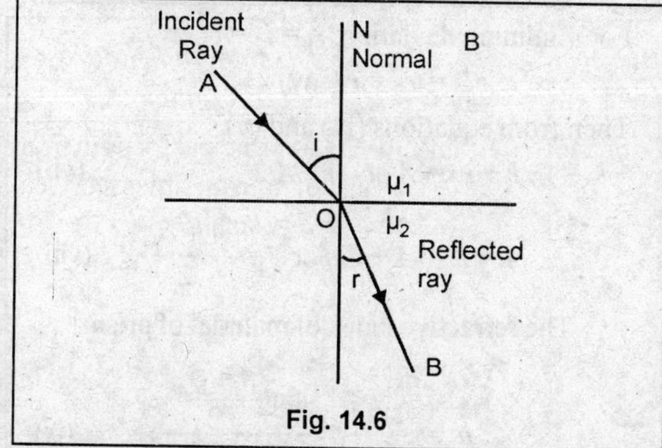

Fig. 14.6

LAWS OF REFRACTION

(i) The incident ray, the refracted ray and normal to the surface separating the two media all lie in the same plane.

(ii) **Snell's law.** For two media, the ratio of sine of angle of incidence of the sine of the angle of refraction is constant for a beam of particular wavelength i.e.

$$\frac{\sin i}{\sin r} = \text{Constant} = \frac{\mu_2}{\mu_1} = {}_1\mu_2$$

$$\Rightarrow \quad \mu_1 \sin i = \mu_2 \sin r \qquad \text{...(i)}$$

where μ_1 and μ_2 are absolute refractive indices of media I and II respectively and ${}_1\mu_2$ is the refractive index of second medium with respect to I medium.

As light follows reversible path, we have

$$\frac{\sin r}{\sin i} = {}_2\mu_1 \qquad \text{...(ii)}$$

Multiplying (i) and (ii), we get

$${}_2\mu_1 \times {}_1\mu_2 = 1 \text{ or } {}_2\mu_1 = \frac{1}{{}_1\mu_2} \qquad \text{...(iii)}$$

Also the frequency of light, v remains unchanged when passing from one medium to other and

$$\mu = \frac{c}{v} = \frac{\text{speed of light in vacuum or air}}{\text{Speed of light in air}}$$

$$= \frac{v\lambda_{\text{air}}}{v\lambda_{\text{medium}}} = \frac{\lambda_{\text{air}}}{\lambda_{\text{medium}}} \qquad \text{...(iv)}$$

Where λ_{air} and λ_{medium} are wavelength of light in air and medium respectively.

$$\therefore \quad \frac{\sin i}{\sin r} = \frac{\mu_2}{\mu_1} = \frac{c/V_2}{c/V_1} = \frac{V_1}{V_2} = \frac{\lambda_1}{\lambda_2} \qquad \text{...(v)}$$

TOTAL INTERNAL REFLECTION

When a ray of light passes from denser to a rarer medium it is deviated away from the normal. When the angle of incidence is increased, the angle of refraction increases. For a particular value of angle of incidence, the angle of refraction becomes 90°. The angle of incidence for which the angle of refraction is 90° is called the critical angle (C).

$$\frac{\sin i}{\sin r} = \frac{\mu_2}{\mu_1} \text{ gives } \frac{\sin C}{\sin 90°} = \frac{\mu_r}{\mu_d} = {}_d\mu_r,$$

where μ_r and μ_d are refractive indices for rarer and denser medium respectively.

$$\therefore \quad \sin C = \frac{1}{{}_r\mu_d} = \frac{1}{\mu},$$

where ${}_r\mu_d = \mu$ is the refractive index of denser medium with respect to rarer medium ${}_r\mu_d = \mu > 1$). When angle of incidence of the ray incident on rarer medium from denser medium is greater than the critical angle, the incident ray does not refract into rarer medium but is reflected back into denser medium. This phenomenon is called *total internal reflection.* The conditions for total internal reflection are

(i) The ray must travel from denser to rarer medium.

(ii) The angle of incidence (i) must be greater than the critical angle (C) i.e. $i > C$. The critical angles for water-air, glass-air and diamond air interfaces are 49°, 42°, and 24° respectively.

REFRACTION THROUGH A PRISM

Suppose a monochromatic ray EF is incident on the face PQ of prism PQR of refracting angle A at angle of incidence i_1. The ray is refracted along FG, r_1 being angle of refraction. The ray FG is incident on the face PR at angle of incidence r_2 and is refracted in air along GH. Thus, GH is the emergent ray and i_2 the angle of emergence. The angle between incident ray EF and emergent ray GH is called *angle of deviation* δ.

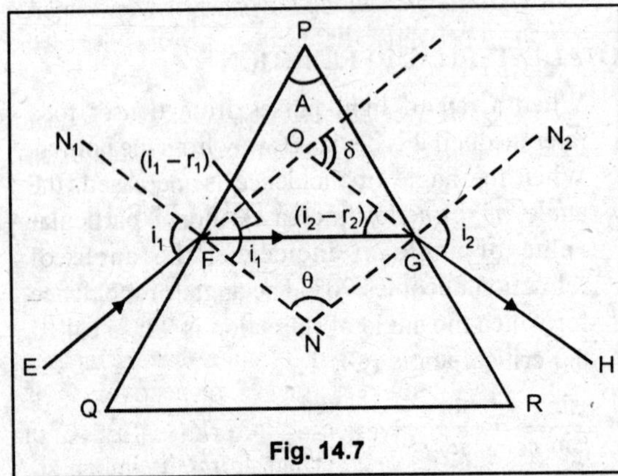

Fig. 14.7

From triangle OFG

$$\delta = (i_1 - r_1) + (i_2 - r_2) = (i_1 + i_2) - (r_1 + r_2) \quad ...(i)$$

In quadrilateral $PFNG$,

$$A + 90° + \theta + 90° = 360°$$

or
$$A + \theta = 180° \quad ...(ii)$$

In triangle FGN

$$r_1 + r_2 + \theta = 180° \quad ...(iii)$$

Comparing equations, (ii) and (iii)

$$A = r_1 + r_2. \quad ...(iv)$$

∴ From (i) $\delta = i_1 + i_2 - A$

or
$$i_1 + i_2 = A + \delta \quad ...(v)$$

Let μ be the refractive index of material of prism, then from Snell's law

$$\mu = \frac{\sin i_1}{\sin r_1} = \frac{\sin i_2}{\sin r_2}. \quad ...(vi)$$

If angle of incidence is changed, the angle of deviation δ changes as shown in Fig. below. For a particular angle of incidence the deviation is minimum and is called angle of minimum deviation δm.

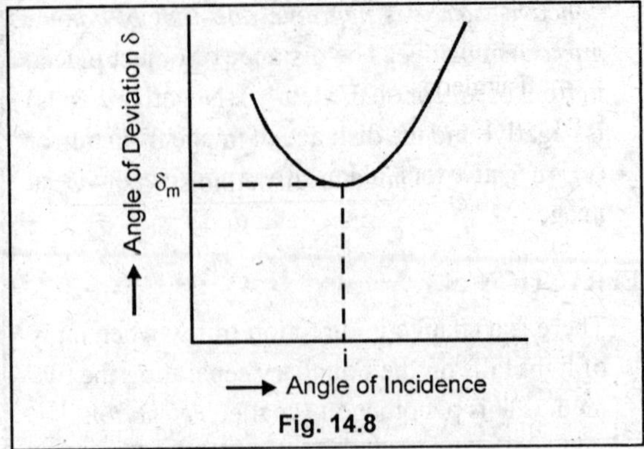

Fig. 14.8

For minimum deviation, $i_1 = i_2 = i$ (say).

∴ $r_1 = r_2 = r$ (say)

Then from equations (iv) and (v),

$$r + r = A \text{ or } r = A/2 \quad ...(vii)$$

$$i + i = A + \delta m \text{ or } i = \frac{A + \delta_m}{2} \quad ...(viii)$$

∴ The refractive index of material of prism

$$\mu = \frac{\sin i}{\sin r} = \frac{\sin \frac{A + \delta_m}{2}}{\sin A/2} \quad ...(ix)$$

Particular Case:

For a thin prism, viz. $A \leq 10°$, $\delta = (\mu - 1)A$.

At grazing incidence for a prism, $i_1 = 90°$, the $r_1 = C$ (the critical angle for material of the prism). Then $A = C + r_2$ or $r_2 = A - C$, then for refraction at PR

$$\mu = \frac{\sin i_2}{\sin r_2} \text{ or } \sin i_2 = \mu \sin r_2 = \mu \sin (A - C) \quad ...(x)$$

For maximum deviation produced by a prism either i_1 or $i_2 = 90°$.

DISPERSION

Dispersion is the splitting of white light into constituent colours (VIBGYOR). White light falling on a prism is broken into constituent colours within the prism. Hence the emergent light has a number of coloured beams, the violet being deviated most and red the least in the visible region.

Thus the prism causes deviation as well as dispersion. If δv, δ_r and δ_y are the deviation caused by prism in violet, red and mean yellow colour, then angular dispersion = $\delta_v - \delta_r = (\mu_v - \mu_r) A$ for small angled prism.

Dispersive power,

$$\omega = \frac{\text{angular dispersion}}{\text{mean deviation}} = \frac{\delta_v - \delta_r}{\delta_y}$$

$$= \frac{(\mu_v - \mu_r)A}{(\mu_y - 1)A} = \frac{(\mu_v - \mu_r)}{\mu_y - 1}.$$

SPECTRUM AND SPECTROMETER

The array of colours in a beam emerging from a prism is called the spectrum. These types :

(i) **Emission spectrum.** When the white light from a luminous body is directly incident on a prism, the light emerging from the prism forms the emission spectrum. It has bright colours or lines.

(ii) **Absorption spectrum.** When the white light from a luminous body is first passed through an unexcited substance and then transmitted light on a prism the light emerging from the prism forms absorption spectrum. It consists the absence of certain colours or lines.

The above two spectrum may be divided into three subgroups.

Emission Spectrum :

(i) **Continuous emission spectrum.** Continuous emission spectrum consists of continuous bright wavelengths in a definite wavelength range. It is produced by white hot solid and is independent of substance but depends on temperature only.

(ii) **Line emission spectrum.** Line emission spectrum consists of distinct bright lines and is produced by an excited source in atomic state e.g., helium, mercury vapours, etc.

(iii) **Band emission spectrum.** Band emission spectrum consists of distinct bright bands and is produced by an excited source in molecular state, e.g., HCl, NH_3, CO, etc.

Absorption Spectrum :

(i) **Continuous absorption spectrum.** Continuous absorption spectrum consists of the absence of continuous wavelengths or colours in a definite wavelength range and is produced when the substance between the luminous body and the prism is in unexcited bulk state.

(ii) **Line absorption spectrum.** Line absorption spectrum consists of the absence of distinct lines, (i.e. dark lines) and is produced, when the substance between luminous body and the prism is in unexcited atomic state.

(iii) **Band absorption spectrum.** Band absorption spectrum consists of the absence of certain distinct bands (i.e. dark bands) and is produced, when the substances between luminous body and the prism is in unexcited molecular state.

Spectrometer. Spectrometer consists of (i) collimator, (ii) prism table, (iii) telescope. The collimator renders the rays parallel from an extended source which fall on a prism and emerge in the form of parallel beam to be received by the telescope.

The use of spectrometer is to observe spectrum and measure the deviation caused by the prism.

REFRACTION THROUGH A THIN LENS

A transparent medium enclosed by two refracting surfaces, one of which at least must be spherical is called lens. The figure below shows a thin convex lens enclosed by spherical surfaces of radii of curvatures R_1 and R_2 respectively.

Let O be a point object on the principal axis of the lens, then the first surface forms its image at I' which acts as an object for the second surface and the final image is formed at I. Let P be the optical centre of the lens.

Then $\quad PO = u, PI' = v'$ and $PI = v$

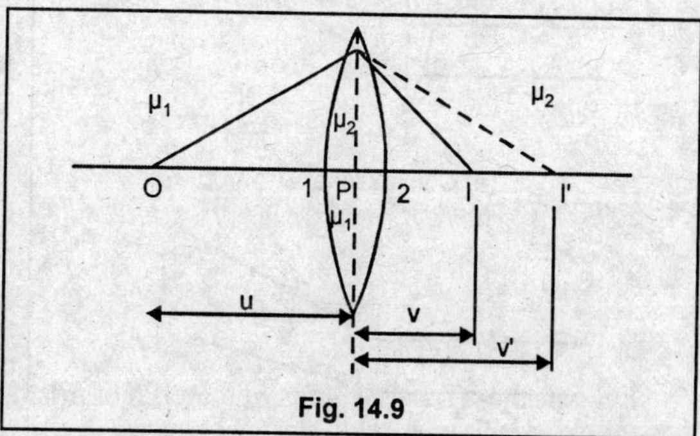

Fig. 14.9

Hence for refraction at I surface

$$\frac{\mu_2}{v'} - \frac{\mu_1}{u} = \frac{\mu_2 - \mu_1}{R_1} \qquad ...(i)$$

and for refraction at second surface

$$\frac{\mu_1}{v} - \frac{\mu_2}{v'} = \frac{\mu_1 - \mu_2}{R_2}$$

$$\frac{\mu_1}{v} - \frac{\mu_2}{v'} = -\frac{\mu_2 - \mu_1}{R_2} \quad \text{...(ii)}$$

Adding (i) and (ii), we get

$$\frac{\mu_1}{v} - \frac{\mu_1}{u} = (\mu_2 - \mu_1)\left(\frac{1}{R_1} - \frac{1}{R_2}\right)$$

or $$\frac{1}{v} - \frac{1}{u} = \left(\frac{\mu_2}{\mu_1} - 1\right)\left(\frac{1}{R_1} - \frac{1}{R_2}\right)$$

or $$\frac{1}{v} - \frac{1}{u} = ({}_1\mu_2 - 1)\left(\frac{1}{R_1} - \frac{1}{R_2}\right) \quad \text{...(iii)}$$

where ${}_1\mu_2 = \frac{\mu_2}{\mu_1}$ = refractive index of second medium with respect to first medium.

From definition of second focus of lens, if $u = \infty$, $v = f$, then equation (iii) gives

$$\frac{1}{f} = ({}_1\mu_2 - 1)\left(\frac{1}{R_1} - \frac{1}{R_2}\right) \quad \text{...(iv)}$$

This relation is called **Lens makers formula.**

Comparing (iii) and (iv), we get

$$\frac{1}{f} = \frac{1}{v} - \frac{1}{u} \quad \text{...(v)}$$

This is usual lens formula.

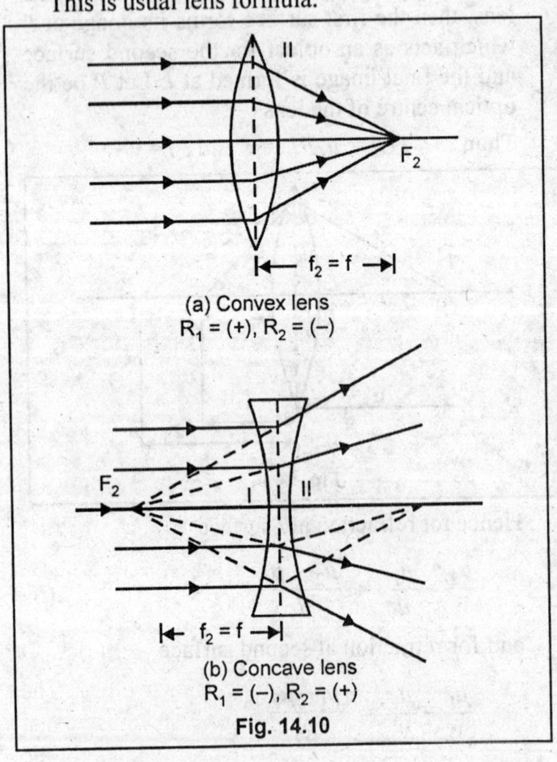

Fig. 14.10

According to sign conventions for convex lens R_1 is positive and R_2 is negative, hence focal length f is positive, while for a concave lens R_1 is positive, R_2 is negative, hence focal length f is negative. The convex lens is also called convergent or converging lens as it deviates (or converges) the rays towards the axis. The concave lens is also called divergent or diverging lens as it deviates (or diverges) the rays away from the axis.

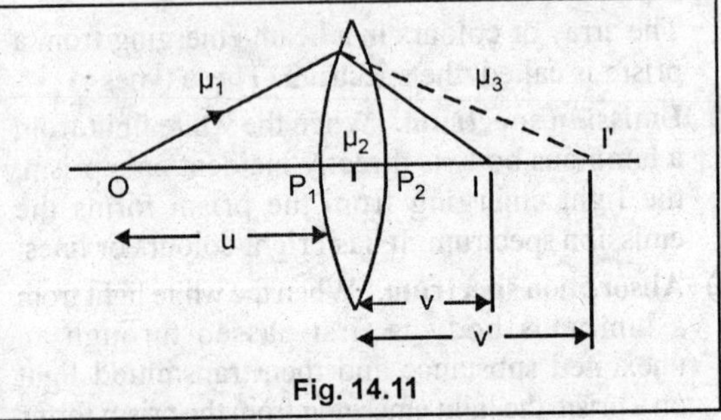

Fig. 14.11

For refraction at first surface

$$\frac{\mu_2}{v'} - \frac{\mu_1}{v} = \frac{\mu_2 - \mu_1}{R_1} \quad \text{...(i)}$$

For refraction at second surface

$$\frac{\mu_3}{v} - \frac{\mu_2}{(v' - t)} = \frac{\mu_3 - \mu_2}{R_2}$$

where t = thickness of lens. If lens is thin, then $t << v'$, so

$$\frac{\mu_3}{v} - \frac{\mu_2}{v'} = \frac{\mu_3 - \mu_2}{R_2} \quad \text{...(ii)}$$

Adding (i) and (ii), we get

$$\frac{\mu_3}{v} - \frac{\mu_1}{u} = \frac{\mu_2 - \mu_1}{R_1} + \frac{\mu_3 - \mu_2}{R_2} \quad \text{...(iii)}$$

For parallel incident rays, $u = \infty$, v = f (second focal length).

From equation (iii) we have

$$\frac{\mu_3}{f} = \frac{\mu_2 - \mu_1}{R_1} + \frac{\mu_3 - \mu_2}{R_2}$$

This is the general formula for a thin lens.

POWER OF LENS

The ability of a lens to deviate the rays towards the axis is called the power of a lens. Accordingly the power of a convex lens is positive and that of a concave lens is negative. Smaller is the focal length (f) of a lens, greater is the deviation produced by it and hence greater is its power (P) i.e.

$$P \propto \frac{1}{f}$$

If f is expressed in meters, then

$$\text{Power of a lens, } P = \frac{1}{f\text{ (in metres)}} \text{ Diopters.}$$

EQUIVALENT FOCAL LENGTH OF TWO LENSES IN CONTACT

The equivalent focal length F of two thin lenses of focal lengths f_1 and f_2 placed in contact is given by

$$\frac{1}{F} = \frac{1}{f_1} + \frac{1}{f_2}$$

Let P_1 and P_2 be the powers of two lenses in contact, then equivalent power P is given by

$$P = P_1 + P_2.$$

NEWTON'S FORMULA

If the distances of object and image are not measured from optical centre, but from first and second principal foci respectively, then Newton' formula states $f_1 f_2 = x_1 x_2$

where $x_1 = F_1O$ = distance of object from I principal focus F_1

$x_2 = F_2I$ = distance of image from II principal focus F_2

Let the medium on either side of the lens be same, then,

$$f_2 = -f_1 = f$$

Hence Newton's formula takes the form,

$$x_1 x_2 = -f^2.$$

MAGNIFICATION PRODUCED BY A LENS

The ratio of size of image formed by a lens to that of the object is called magnification and is given by

$$m = \frac{\text{size of image } (I)}{\text{size of object } (O)} = \frac{v}{u} = \frac{f}{f+u}$$

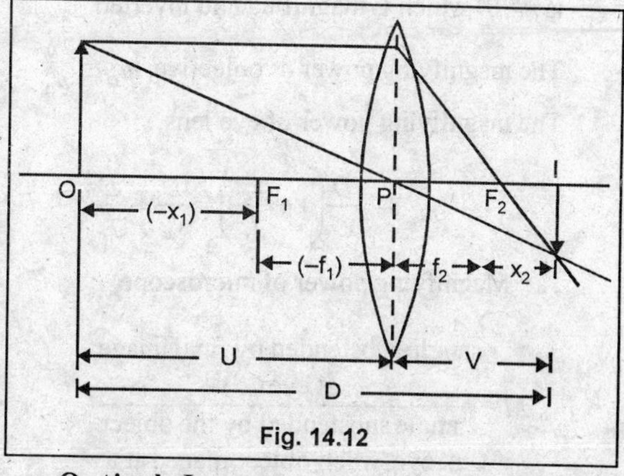

Fig. 14.12

Optical Instruments. Microscopes and Telescopes

I. Compound Microscope. To see distinct and magnified images of nearer tiny objects, not normally seen clearly by the eye a microscope is used. A compound microscope essentially consists of two coaxial convex lenses of small focal lengths. The lens facing the object is called objective while that towards eye is called eye lens. The focal lengths of objective and eye lenses are symbolized by f_o (o-objective) and f_e (e-eyelens) respectively. In a microscope $f_o < f_e$. The separation between both the lenses may be varied. The object (AB) is placed at a distance (u_o) slightly greater than the first focal point F'_o of objective.

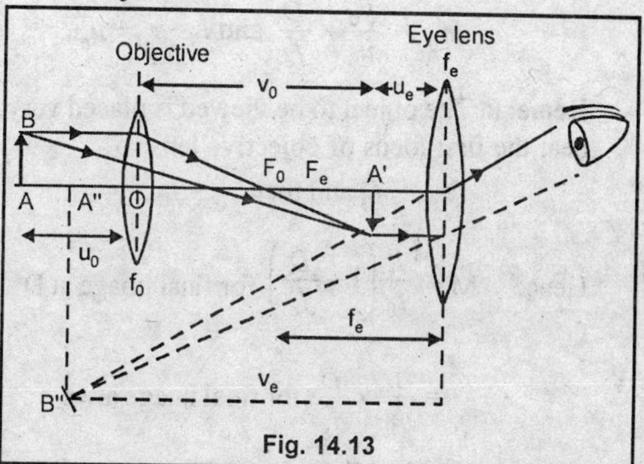

Fig. 14.13

The objective forms the real image $A'B'$ formed by objective acts as an object for eye lens. The separation between the lenses is so adjusted that the image lies within the first focal length of the eye lens. The final image formed by the eye lens is $A'' B''$ which is magnified and inverted.

The magnifying power of objective, $m_o = \frac{v_0}{u_0}$

The magnifying power of eye lens,

$$m_o = \frac{D}{v_e}\left(1+\frac{v_e}{f_e}\right) = \frac{D}{v_e} + \frac{D}{f_e}$$

∴ Magnifying power of microscope,

$$M = \frac{\text{angle substended by final image at eye } (\beta)}{\text{angle substended by the object at eye, when object placed at a distance of distinct vision } (\alpha)}$$

$$(= m_o \times m_e) = \frac{v_0}{u_0}\left(\frac{D}{v_e} + \frac{D}{f_e}\right)$$

The length of microscope,

L = separation between lenses = $v_0 + u_e$

Particular cases : (i) When final image is formed at distance of distinct vision, the $v_e = D$, Hence

$$M = \frac{v_0}{u_0}\left(1+\frac{D}{f_e}\right) \text{ and } L = v_0 + u_e$$

(i) When final image is formed at infinity, $v_e = \infty$, then

$$M_0 = \frac{v_0}{u_0} \times \frac{D}{f_e} \text{ and } L = v_0 + u_e.$$

Remark. The object to be viewed is placed very near the first focus of objective lens so

$$u_0 = f_0 \text{ and then } v_0 = L$$

Hence $\text{M} = \frac{L}{f_0}\left(1+\frac{D}{f_e}\right)$ for final image at D

$$= \frac{L}{f_0} \times \frac{D}{f_e} \text{ for final image at } \infty.$$

II. Astronomical Telescope. To see magnified images of distant objects an astronomical telescope used. An astronomical telescope essentially consists of two co-axial convex lenses. The lens facing the object has large focal length and large aperture and is called objective; while the lens towards eye has small focal length and small aperture and is called eye lens. The focal lengths of objective and eye lens are generally expressed by $F(= f_0)$ and $f(=f_e)$ respectively. The separation between the lenses may be varied. The object is at infinite distance from an astronomical telescope. The rays from distant object AB fall on the objective as a parallel beam at angle α. The real and inverted image $A'B'$ formed by the objective at its principal focus acts as an object for eye-lens. The separation between objective and eye lens is so adjusted that the image $A'B'$ lies within the first focal length of the eye lens. The eye lens forms the final image $A'' B''$ which is magnified, inverted and virtual.

The magnifying power of telescope is

$$M = \frac{\text{angle subtended by final image at eye}}{\text{angle subtended by object on eye}}$$

$$= \frac{\text{angle subtended by final image at eye}}{\text{angle subtended by object at objective}} = \frac{\beta}{\alpha}$$

$$= (m_0 \times m_e) = -\frac{F}{f}\left(1+\frac{f}{v}\right)$$

The length of telescope, $L = F + u$,

where v = distance of final image from eye lens,

u = distance of real image $A'B'$ from eye lens.

Particular cases. (i) When final image is formed at a distance of distinct vision then $v = D$. Hence,

$$M = -\frac{F}{f}\left(1+\frac{f}{D}\right) \text{ and } L = F + u$$

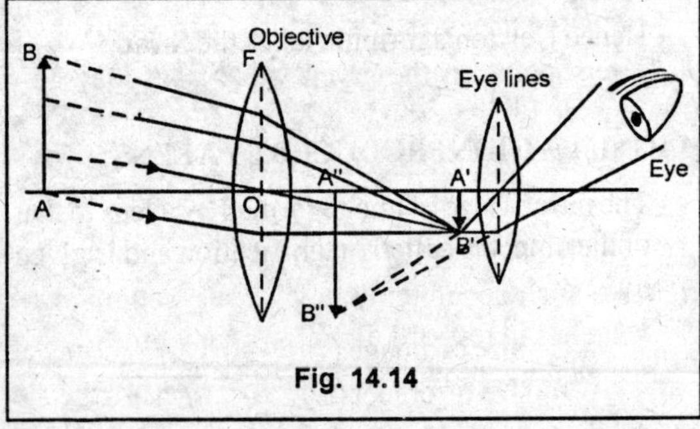

Fig. 14.14

(ii) When final image is formed at infinity, then $v = \infty$. Hence

$$M = -\frac{F}{f} \text{ and } L = F + f.$$

Obviously for greater magnification, the focal length of objective (F) should be large and that of eye lens (f) should be small.

Remark. To avoid aberrations, the objective is made of concave mirror in place of convex lens. Then the telescope is called reflecting telescope.

Galilean Telescope. Galilean telescope consists of a convex lens of large focal length as objective and concave lens of small focal length as eye-lens. It forms erect image. Separation between lenses,

$$d = F - u_e.$$

Magnifying power, $M = \beta / \alpha$.

WAVE OPTICS

INTRODUCTION

Newton's Corpuscular Theory could not explain the phenomenon of interference, diffraction and polarisation exhibited by light. Huygen's in 1678 suggested that light is propagated in the form of waves. Focault gave the first historic experiment in favour of wave theory, who in 1850 found experimentally that velocity of light in denser medium is less than that in the rarer medium which was contrary to Newton's Corpuscular Theory.

HUYGEN'S PRINCIPLE

Huygen's principle is useful for determining the position of a given wavefront at any time in future if its present position is known. This principle may be stated in three parts :

(i) Every point on the given wave-front may be regarded as the source of the new disturbance.

(ii) The new disturbances from each point spread out in all directions with the velocity of light and are called secondary wavelets.

(iii) The surface of tangency to the secondary wavelets in forward direction at any time gives the position of new wavefront at that time.

This principle explained successfully, the reflection, refraction, total internal reflection, interference and diffraction were successfully explained this principle but the rectilinear propagation of light couldn't be explained by this principle.

INTERFERENCE

When two waves of same frequency and constant initial phase difference travelling in the same direction along same straight line, superimpose in such a way that in the region of superposition, the intensity is maximum at some points and minimum at some other points. This modification in intensity in the region of superposition is called interference. The source having the same frequency and constant initial phase difference are called coherent sources. The phenomenon of interference is based on the conservation of energy.

Method of producing coherent sources. Coherent sources can be produced by following two methods :

(i) **Division of wave-front.** In this method the wave-front is divided into two parts by the use of mirrors, lenses and prism. The well known methods, are Young's double slit arrangement, Fresnel's biprism and Lloyd's single mirror etc.

(ii) **Division of amplitude.** In this method the amplitude of the incoming beam is divided into two parts by partial reflection or refraction. These divided parts travel different paths and finally brought together to produce interference. This class of interference requires broad sources of light. The common examples of such interference of light are the brilliant colours seen when a thin film of transparent material like soap bubble or thin film of kerosine oil spread on the surface of water is exposed to an extended source of light. There are two types of such interference.

(i) Interference of waves reflected from front and back surfaces of the film.

(ii) Interference of transmitted waves.

THEORY OF INTERFERENCE CONDITIONS OF MAXIMUM AND MINIMA

Suppose the two coherent waves be represented as

$y_1 = a_1 \sin \omega t$ and $y_2 = a_2 \sin (\omega t + \delta)$,

where a_1 and a_2 are amplitudes of individual waves, $\omega/2\pi$ is frequency and δ is the phase difference between waves at the point of observation.

According to Young's principle of superposition, we have

$$y = y_1 + y_2 = a_1 \sin \omega t + a_2 \sin (\omega t + \delta)$$
$$= a_1 \sin \omega t + a_2 (\sin \omega t \cos \delta + \cos \omega t \sin \delta)$$
$$= (a_1 + a_2 \cos \delta) \sin \omega t + a_2 \sin \delta \cos \omega t \quad ...(i)$$

Substituting,

$$a_1 + a_2 \cos \delta = A \cos \phi \quad ...(ii)$$

and $$a_2 \sin \delta = A \sin \phi \quad ...(iii)$$

we get, $$y = a \cos \phi \sin \omega t + A \sin \phi \cos \omega t.$$
$$= A \sin (\omega t + \phi).$$

This is the equation of the resultant wave. Thus the resultant wave has amplitude A determined by equation (ii) and (iii).

Squaring and adding equations (ii) and (iii), we get

$$A^2 = (a_1 + a_2 \cos \delta)^2 + (a_2 \sin \delta)^2$$
$$= (a_1^2 + a_2^2 + 2a_1a_2 \cos \delta)$$

$\therefore$ Amplitude

$$A = \sqrt{(a_1^2 + a_2^2 + 2a_1a_2 \cos \delta)} \quad ...(v)$$

The intensity is proportional to the square of amplitude and in arbitary units

$$I = A^2 = a_1^2 + a_2^2 + 2a_1a_2 \cos \delta \quad ...(vi)$$

Maxima. Intensity is maximum when

$$\cos \delta = +1$$

or $$\delta = 2n\pi (n = 0, 1, 2, ...)$$

$\therefore$ Path difference,

$$\Delta = \frac{\lambda}{2\pi} \times \text{Phase difference } (\delta)$$
$$= \frac{\lambda}{2\pi}(2n\pi) = (2n). \frac{\lambda}{2} = n\lambda.$$

Hence the intensity is maximum when the phase difference is even multiple π or the path difference is integral multiple of λ or even multiple of $\lambda/2$.

The maximum intensity is given by

$$I_{max} = a_1^2 + a_2^2 + 2a_1a_2 = (a_1 + a_2)^2.$$

Minima. Intensity is minimum when

$$\cos \delta = -1 \text{ or } \delta = (2n-1)\pi, (n = 1, 2, 3, ...)$$

$\therefore$ Path difference

$$\Delta = \frac{\lambda}{2\pi} \times (2n-1)\pi$$
$$= (2n-1)\frac{\lambda}{2}.$$

Hence intensity is minimum at points where phase difference is odd multiple of π or the path difference is odd multiple of $\lambda/2$.

The minimum intensity is given by

$$I_{min} = a_1^2 + a_2^2 - 2a_1a_2 = (a_1 - a_2)^2.$$

THEORY OF DIVISION OF WAVE-FRONT; YOUNG'S DOUBLE SLIT EXPERIMENT

In Young's double slit experiment, S is a monochromatic point source of light, S_1 and S_2 are two narrow close slits at separation d in a screen, MP is a screen at a distance D from the slits S_1 and S_2. The spherical wave-front originating from S is divided into two parts at slits S_1 and S_2, thus S_1 and S_2 act as coherent sources obtained by division of wavefront.

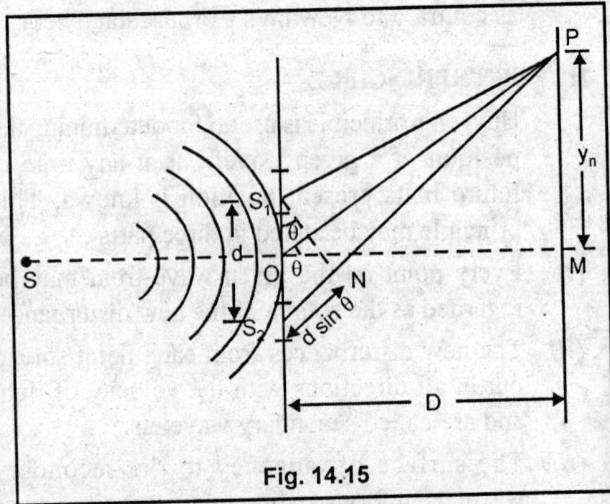

Fig. 14.15

The waves starting from S_1 and S_2 reach a point of observation P on the screen. The path difference between waves is

$$S_2P - S_1P = S_2N \text{ (if } \theta \text{ is small)}$$

$$= d \sin \theta = d\left(\frac{y_n}{D}\right)$$

$\because \sin \theta = \frac{y_n}{D}$, y_n being the distance of point P from M, a point on the screen, equidistant from S_1 and S_2.

POSITIONS OF MAXIMA

The condition of maxima is

Path difference $\Delta = n\lambda \therefore \frac{dy_n}{D} = n\lambda.$

$\therefore$ Position of nth maxima, $y_n = \frac{nD\lambda}{d}.$

Angular position of nth maxima,

$$\theta_n = \frac{y_n}{D} = \frac{n\lambda}{d}$$

POSITIONS OF MINIMA :

The condition of minima is

Path difference $\Delta = (2n-1)\frac{\lambda}{2}$

i.e., $\frac{dy_n}{D} = (2n-1)\frac{\lambda}{2}.$

$\therefore$ Position of nth minima,

$$y_n = \left(n - \frac{1}{2}\right)\frac{D\lambda}{d}.$$

Angular position of nth minima,

$$\theta_n = \frac{y_n}{D} = \left(n - \frac{1}{2}\right)\frac{\lambda}{d}.$$

DIFFRACTION

Departure of light from straight line path from the corners of small obstacle is called diffraction. Simple experiments illustrating this phenomenon are as follows :

(i) S is a point source and AB is narrow opaque obstacle (say a thin needle having thickness AB). CD is the shadow of AB on the screen XY as shown in the figure below. If light follows rectilinear path, then C and D must lie on the prolongation of straight lines SA and SB.

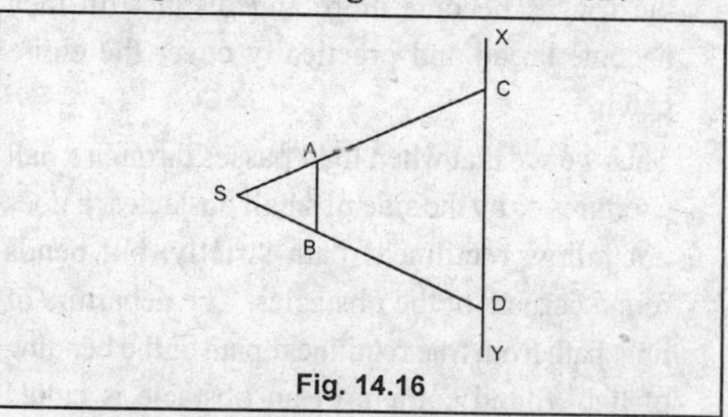

Fig. 14.16

Actually it is observed that the shadow is broader than CD and moreover, instead of being sharply defined, it is bordered by several coloured fringes. If the obstacle is very small and the bright source is sufficiently brilliant the dark and bright bands, resembling the interference bands, are also observed within the geometrical shadow.

(ii) In Fig. S is a point source of light AB is an aperture in the shutter and XY is a screen. CD represents the geometrical projection of AB on the screen a shown in the figure below.

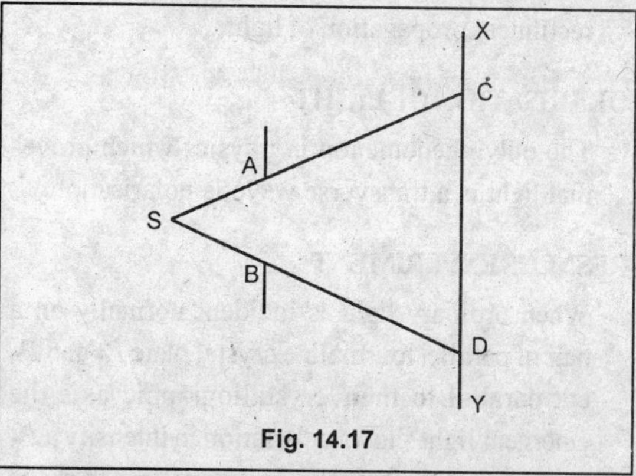

Fig. 14.17

If light follows rectilinear (straight line path strictly, the area CD should be uniformly illuminated; while on either side beyond CD, the intensity should be zero. But actually it is observed that outside the area CD the intensity does not fall to zero sharply; but gradually and near the edges the intensity is not uniform; but shows some fluctuations (i.e. fringes appear). If the aperture AB is diminished in width, the path of light on the screen becomes distinctly wider than given by the laws geometrical optics and the fringes become more and distinct till they become broad and practically cover the entire patch.

Thus we see that when light passes through small apertures or by the side of small obstacles, it does not follow rectilinear path strictly; but bends round corners of the obstacles. The departure of light path from true rectilinear path or the bending of light round corners of an obstacle is called diffraction.

The phenomenon of diffraction was satisfactorily explained by A.J. Fresnel who in 1815 combined in a striking manner, Huygen's wavelets with the principle of interference. Fresnel did not consider the diffraction and interference of two separate beams of light; but he considered that the diffraction phenomenon is caused by the unobstructed portions of the same wave-front. Fresnel not only explained satisfac orily the bending of light round corners; but also the rectilinear propagation of light.

POLARISATION OF LIGHT

The only phenomenon in physics which proves that light is a transverse wave is polarisation.

FRESNEL'S EXPERIMENT

When ordinary light is incident normally on a pair of parallel tourmaline crystal plate P_1 and P_2 cut parallel to their crystallographic axis the emergent light shows a variation in intensity a P_2 is rotated. The intensity is maximum when the axis of P_2 is parallel of that $f P_1$ (Fig. *a*), and minimum when at right angles (Fig. *b*). This shows that the light emerging from P_1 is not symmetrical about the direction of propagation of light but its vibrations are confined only to a single line in a plane perpendicular to the direction of propagation. Such light is called 'plane-polarised' or 'linearly-polarised' light.

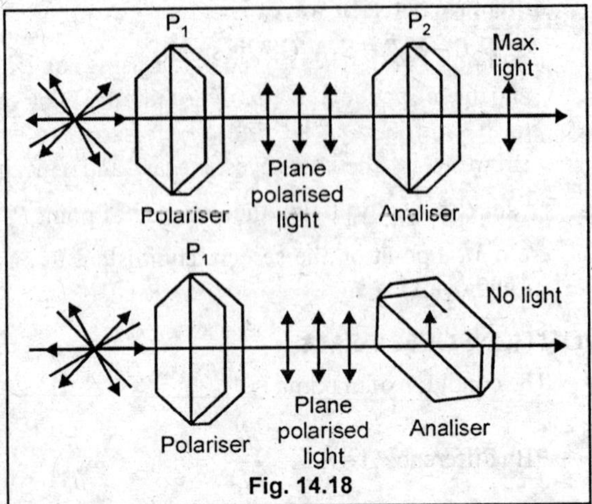

Fig. 14.18

In Fresnel's experiment the variation in intensity of the emergent light on rotation of P_2 shows that light waves are transverse. If the waves were longitudinal, i.e. having vibration along the direction of propagation of light, they would have passed through P_2 in all of its positions. Then there would have no variation in intensity of light during the rotation of P_2. i.e., the polarisation of light was not possible. Hence we conclude that 'polarisation proves transverse nature of light'.

PLANE OF VIBRATION

Plane of vibration is the plane containing the direction of vibration and the direction of propagation of light. *ABCD* is plane of vibration in the adjoining figure.

PLANE OF POLARISATION

Plane of polarisation is the plane passing through the direction of propagation and containing no vibration. *EFGH* is the plane of polarisation in the adjoining figure. The plane of polarisation is always at the right angles to the plane of vibration as shown in figure.

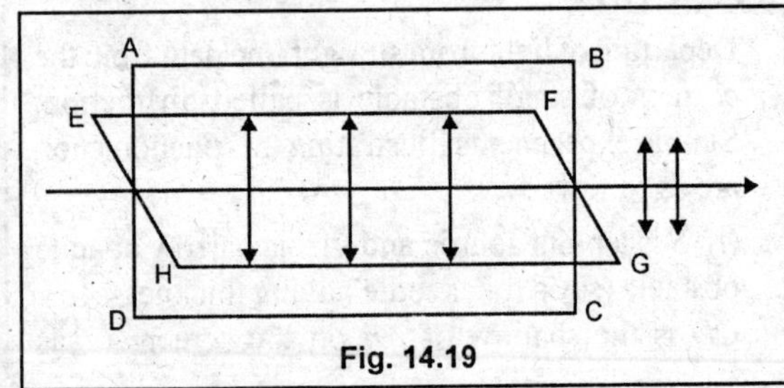

Fig. 14.19

BREWSTER'S LAW

A simple relation between the polarising angle i_p and the refractive index μ of the material relative to the surrounding medium was discovered by Brewester is called 'Breswester's law' and is given by

$$\mu = \tan i_p$$

The polarising angle for air-glass is 57°.

From Brewster law, we have

$$\mu = \tan i_p = \frac{\sin i_p}{\cos i_p} \quad \text{...(i)}$$

By Snell's law, we have

$$\mu = \frac{\sin i_p}{\sin r} \quad \text{...(ii)}$$

Comparing (i) and (ii), we get

$$\frac{\sin i_p}{\cos i_p} = \frac{\sin i_p}{\sin r}$$

or $\cos i_p = \sin r$

or $\sin (90° - i_p) = \sin r$

or $90° - i_p = r$

or $r + i_p = 90°$

Thus when light is incident at the polarising angle, the reflected beam is at right angles to the reflected beam.

POLAROID

Polaroid is a very big polarising film mounted between two glass plates, and is used to obtain plane-polarised light for commercial purposes. The film consists of a thin sheet of nitro-cellulose packed with ultra-microscopic crystals of an organic compound **iodosulphate quinone** (also known as **herapathite**) with their optic axis aligned parallel. These crystals are highly dichroic and absorb one of the doubly-refracted beams completely. Hence when a beam of unpolarised light passes through the polariod film, the emerging light is plane-polarised.

In recent polaroids have been made by stretching a film of polyvinyl alcohol. The stretching orients the complex molecules with their long axes in the direction of stress and makes them doubly-refracting. Then the film is impregnated with iodine which makes it dichroic. Such polaroids are called as H-polaroids. If, the stretched film is heated with a dehydrating agent, then it slightly darkens and becomes strongly dichroic which is called a K-polaroid.

USES OF POLAROIDS

1. Polaroids are used in the laboratory to produce and analyse plane polarised light. They are cheaper then the Nicols.
2. Polaroids are used in sun-glasses to cut off the light reflected from horizontal surfaces such as wet roads, cover glasses of paintings, polished tables, pavements, etc.
3. K-polaroids are used in head-lights and wind-screens of cars to cut off the dazzling light of a car approaching from the opposite direction.
4. Polaroids are used to control the intensity of light entering trains and aeroplanes. One polaroid is fixed outside the window while the other is fitted inside which can be rotated. The intensity of light can be adjusted by rotating the inner polaroid.
5. For viewing three dimensional picture polaroid glasses are used.

MULTIPLE CHOICE QUESTIONS

1. Ray optics is valid when the characteristic dimensions are
(a) much larger than wavelength of light
(b) much smaller than wavelength of light
(c) of the order of one millimetre
(d) of same order as wavelength of light

2. The rectilinear propagation of light in a medium is due to
(a) its short wavelength
(b) its high frequency
(c) its high velocity
(d) the refractive index of medium.

3. A man who is 1.40 m tall stands in front of a mirror and can just see himself from head to toe. Assuming that his eyes are 0.14 m below the top of his head, the minimum height of the mirror is
(a) 1.40 m (b) 1.26 m
(c) 0.70 m (d) 0.63 m

4. A man runs towards a mirror at a rate of 6 m/s. If we assume the mirror to be at rest, his image will have a velocity
(a) + 12 m/s (b) + 6 m/s
(c) – 6 m/s (d) – 12 m/s

5. To get three images of a single object, one should have two plane mirrors at an angle of
(a) 50° (b) 60°
(c) 30° (d) 90°

6. A clock shows hours with the help of numbers. If it shows 8–20 in the mirror placed in front of it, then the real time is
(a) 4 – 40 (b) 3 – 40
(c) 4 – 20 (d) 4 – 10

7. A man is 180 cm tall and his eyes are 10 cm below the top of his head. In order to see his entire height-right from toe to head he uses a plane mirror kept at a distance of 1 metre from him. The minimum height of the plane mirror required is
(a) 180 cm (b) 90 cm
(c) 85 cm (d) 170 cm

8. Plane mirrors A and B are kept at an angle θ with respect to each other. Light falls on A, is reflected, then falls on B and is reflected. The emergent ray is opposite to the incident direction. Then the angle θ is equal to
(a) 45° (b) 30°
(c) 60° (d) 90°

9. How many images will be formed if two mirrors are fitted on adjacent walls and one mirror on ceiling?
(a) 5 (b) 7
(c) 11 (d) 2

10. A thick mirror produces a number of images of an object. Which of the image is the brightest?
(a) first (b) second
(c) third (d) last one

11. Two plane mirrors are at right angle to each other. A man stands between them and combs his hair with his right hand. In how many the images will be seen using his right hand?
(a) none (b) 1
(c) 2 (d) 3

12. If an object is placed unsymmetrically between 2 plane mirrors, inclined at an angle of the 60°, then the total no. of images formed is
(a) 5 (b) 4
(c) 2 (d) infinite

13. A man moves towards a mirror with velocity 4 m/s. With what velocity its image moves towards him

(a) 8 m/s (b) 4 m/s
(c) 16 m/s (d) 2 m/s

14. Two mirrors are kept at 60° to each other and a body is placed at middle. The total number of images formed is
(a) six (b) four
(c) five (d) three

15. A pencil of light is incident on a plane mirror and after being reflected from it, forms a real image. Then the pencil, incident on the mirror is
(a) parallel (b) divergent
(c) convergent (d) statement is wrong

16. When a plane mirror is placed horizontally on level ground at a distance of 60 metres from the foot of a tower. The top of the tower and its image in the mirror subtend, at the eye close to mirror, an angle of 90°. The height of the tower is
(a) 30 m (b) 60 m
(c) 90 m (d) 120 m

17. Rays of light strike a horizontal plane mirror at an angle 45°. A second plane mirror is arranged at an angle θ with it. If the rays after reflection from the second mirror runs horizontally, i.e. parallel to the first mirror, then θ is
(a) 135° (b) 67° 30′
(c) 60° (d) 45° 30′

18. A plane mirror produces a magnification of
(a) – 1 (b) + 1
(c) zero (d) between 0 and + ∞

19. A man runs towards mirror with a speed of 5 m/s. What is the speed of his image?
(a) 5 m/s (b) 15 m/s
(c) 10 m/s (d) 20 m/s

20. A point source of light B is placed at a distance L in front of the centre of a mirror of width d hung vertically on a wall. A man walks in front of the mirror along a line parallel to the mirror at a distance 2L from it as shown. The greatest distance over which he can see the image of the light source in the mirror is

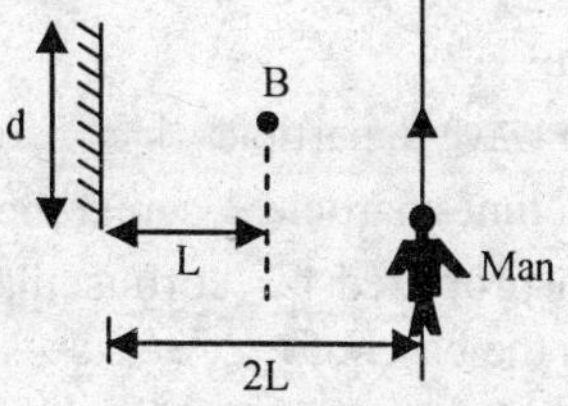

(a) d/2 (b) d
(c) 2d (d) 3d

21. The height of a man is 6 m. To see his full image the size of mirror is approximately
(a) 2.5 m (b) 3 m
(c) 6 m (d) 12 m

22. A light ray is incident normally on a plane mirror. The angle of reflection will be
(a) 135° (b) 90°
(c) 45° (d) 0°

23. A tall man of height 6 feet, want to see his full image. The required minimum length of the mirror will be
(a) 12 feet (b) 3 feet
(c) 6 feet (d) any length

24. A beam of light rays falls on a plane mirror and form a real image, so the incident rays are
(a) parallel (b) diverging
(c) converging (d) statement is false

25. A small object is placed 10 cm in front of a plane mirror. If you stand behind the object 30 cm from the mirror and look at its image, for what distance must you focus your eyes?

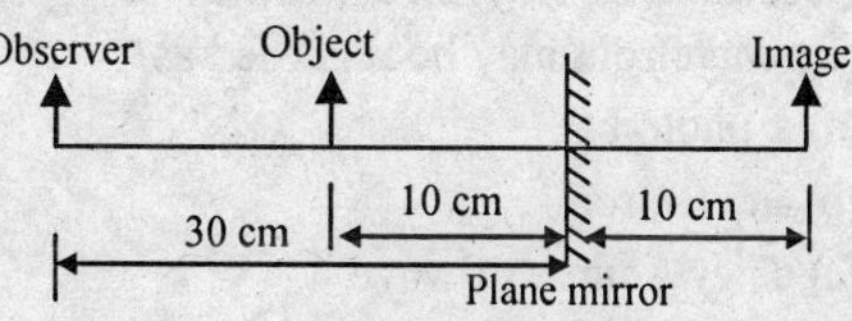

(a) 80 cm (b) 40 cm
(c) 20 cm (d) 60 cm

26. Evidence of the wave nature of light cannot be obtained from
(a) reflection (b) Doppler effect
(c) interference (d) diffraction

27. Light behave as
(a) particle

(b) wave
(c) both wave & particle
(d) sometimes particle & sometimes wave

28. Newton proposed his corpuscular theory of light on the basis of
(a) Planck's quantum theory
(b) rectilinear propagation of light
(c) refraction effect of photons
(d) dispersion effect of light

29. Which one of the following phenomena is not explained by Huygen's construction of wavefront?
(a) Refraction (b) Reflection
(c) Diffraction (d) Origin of spectra

30. Huygen's wave theory of light cannot explain
(a) diffraction (b) interference
(c) polarization (d) photoelectric effect.

31. According to Huygen's principle light is a form of
(a) particle (b) rays
(c) wave (d) none of these

32. Huygen's concept of secondary waves
(a) allows us to find the focal length of a thick lens
(b) is a geometrical method to find a wave front
(c) is used to determine the velocity of light
(d) is used to explain polarization.

33. According to Huygen's wave theory point on any wavefront may be regarded as
(a) a photon
(b) an electron
(c) a new source of wave
(d) neutron

34. Frequency of visible light is of the order of
(a) 10^{15} Hz (b) 10^{12} Hz
(c) 10^{8} Hz (d) 10^{5} Hz

35. Huygens's principle of secondary wavelets may be used to
(a) find the velocity of light in vacuum
(b) explain the particle behavior of light
(c) find the new position of the wavefront
(d) explain the photoelectric effect
(e) explain the scattering light

36. Light propagates rectilinearly because of its
(a) frequency (b) velocity
(c) wavelength (d) wave nature

37. The theory associated with secondary wavelets is
(a) Doppler's effect
(b) special theory of relativity
(c) Huygen's wave theory
(d) none of above

38. Huygen wave theory allows us to know
(a) the wavelength of the wave
(b) the velocity of the wave
(c) the amplitude of the wave
(d) the propagation of wave fronts

39. One important similarity between sound and light waves is that both
(a) can pass through even in the absence of any medium
(b) are transverse waves
(c) travel at the same speed in air
(d) can show interference effects

40. Two monochromatic light sources are said to be coherent if they have
(a) same frequency.
(b) constant relative phase difference.
(c) a phase difference changing with time.
(d) difference amplitude for their wave motion.

41. Interference is the redistribution of
(a) energy (b) intensity
(c) wavelength (d) speed.

42. Interference was observed in interference chamber when air was present now the chamber is evacuated and if the same light is used a careful observer will see
(a) no interference
(b) interference with bright bands
(c) interference with dark bands
(d) interference in which breadth of the fringe will be slightly increased.

43. Wave nature of light follows because
(a) light rays travel in a straight line
(b) light exhibits the phenomenon of reflection and refraction
(c) light exhibits the phenomenon of interference
(d) light causes the phenomenon of photoelectric effect

44. The interference phenomenon can take place
(a) in all waves
(b) in transverse waves only
(c) in longitudinal waves only
(d) in standing waves only

45. Pitch of sound depends upon the frequency of the sounding body. Similarly colour of light depends upon
(a) intensity (b) speed
(c) frequency (d) none of these

46. Two source of light are said to be coherent if wave produced by them have the same
(a) wavelength
(b) amplitude
(c) wavelength and constant phase difference
(d) amplitude and the same wavelength

47. Interference occurs in which of the following waves?
(a) Longitudinal
(b) Transverse
(c) Electro-magnetic
(d) All of these

48. The phenomenon of interference of light was discovered by
(a) Newton (b) Young
(c) Fresnel (d) Huygen

49. As a result of an interference of two coherent waves energy is
(a) increased
(b) decreased
(c) redistribution and distribution changes with time
(d) redistribution and distribution does not change with time

50. To demonstrate the phenomena of interference we require
(a) two sources which emit radiation of the same frequency
(b) two sources which emit radiation of nearly the same frequency
(c) two sources which emit radiation of the same frequency and have a definite phase relationship
(d) two sources which emit radiation of different wavelength

ANSWERS

1	**2**	**3**	**4**	**5**	**6**	**7**	**8**	**9**	**10**
(a)	(d)	(d)	(c)	(d)	(a)	(b)	(d)	(b)	(b)
11	**12**	**13**	**14**	**15**	**16**	**17**	**18**	**19**	**20**
(d)	(a)	(b)	(c)	(c)	(b)	(b)	(b)	(a)	(d)
21	**22**	**23**	**24**	**25**	**26**	**27**	**28**	**29**	**30**
(b)	(d)	(b)	(c)	(b)	(a)	(c)	(b)	(d)	(c)
31	**32**	**33**	**34**	**35**	**36**	**37**	**38**	**39**	**40**
(c)	(b)	(c)	(a)	(c)	(d)	(c)	(d)	(d)	(b)
41	**42**	**43**	**44**	**45**	**46**	**47**	**48**	**49**	**50**
(b)	(d)	(c)	(a)	(c)	(c)	(d)	(b)	(c)	(c)

HINTS / SOLUTIONS

1. We know that wave optics is valid, when the size of the objects is of the order of wavelength of light. And the ray optics is valid when the size of the object is much larger than the wavelength of light.

2. It is actually due to uniformity of refractive index of the medium. In case of a optically heterogenous medium, the light ray will not go straight.

3. Minimum size of the mirror = 1 / 2 × size of the man = 1. 26 / 2 = 0.63 m.

4. In one second, the man moves towards the mirror through a distance of 6 m, and his image moves in the opposite direction through an equal distance.

5. $n = (360/\theta) - 1; \quad \therefore \theta = 90°$

6. Plane mirror gives lateral inversion.

7. Length of mirror

$$A'C' = A'B' + B'C' = \frac{10}{2} + \frac{170}{2} = \frac{180}{2}$$

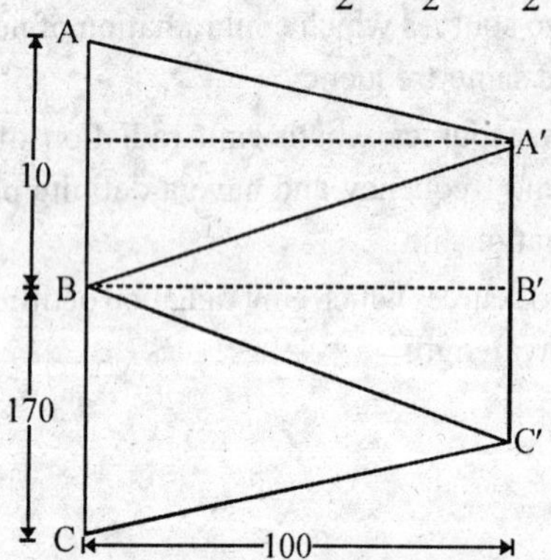

8. Ray is rotated through 90° at each reflection i.e. angle of incidence is 45°.

10. We know that first image is produced due to at the front surface and other images are produced due to multiple reflection at the front and rear surfaces. Since second image is produced due to reflection from rear and silvered point. Therefore it is brightest image.

12. No. of image = $\frac{2\pi}{\theta}$ or $\left(\frac{2\pi}{\theta} - 1\right)$, whichever is odd.

16.

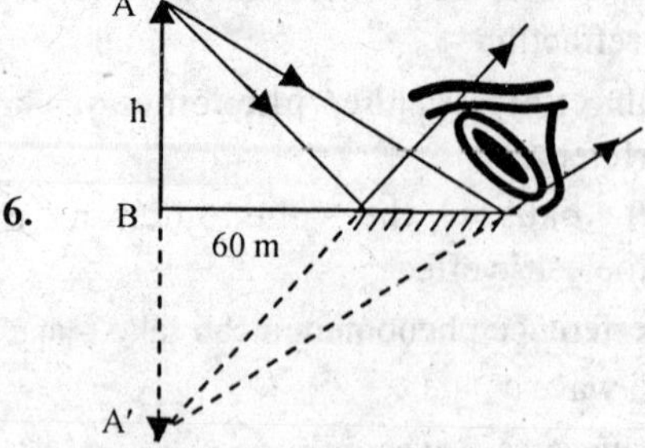

Angle subtended by AB = 90°/2 = 45°

$\tan\theta = h/60 = \tan 45° \Rightarrow h = 60$ m.

17.

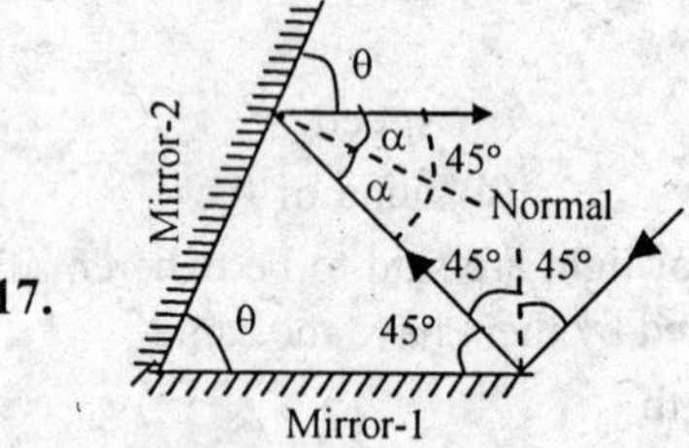

Let angle of incidence at mirror–2 be α.

So angle of reflection at mirror–2 is also α.

From the geometry of the figure

$\alpha + \alpha = 45° \Rightarrow \alpha = 22.5°$

Also $\alpha + \theta = 90° \Rightarrow \theta = 90° - \alpha$

$= 90° - 22.5° = 67.5° = 67°30'$.

19. In plane mirror, image distance = object distance

∴ Object speed = image speed

Speed of the image = 5 m/s.

23. The minimum mirror length should be half of the height of man.

25. Distance between the observer and the image = 30 + 10 = 40 cm.

26. Reflection is explained by ray optics.

28. On the basis of the rectilinear propagation of light Newton formulated his corpuscular theory of light because on its basis he could explain three things

(i) rectilinear propagation of light

(ii) reflection from a surface

(iii) refraction of light in an other medium.

30. According to Huygen's principle every point on a wavefront may itself be regarded as a source of secondary waves.

36. Light propagates rectilinearly. But it can take a slight turn at obstacles this property of light is due to its wave nature.

38. According to Huygen principle every point on primary wavefront acts as a source of spherical wavelets or secondary waves such that the primary wavefront at some later time is the envelope of these wavelets. The wavelets advance with a speed and frequency equal to those of primary wave at each point in space.

40. Coherent sources only can produce interference

42. Velocity of light in air is slightly less than that in vacuum and fringe-width is directly proportional to wavelength.

43. Wave nature of light is confirmed by interference of light because remaining all phenomenon are found in particles also.

44. Interfence phenomenon can take place in all waves. Therefore choice (a) is correct

48. Thomas Young discovered interference.

UNIT-15

Modern Physics

PHOTOELECTRIC EFFECT

(i) Hertz in 1887 observed that when ultraviolet rays are allowed to fall on negative plate of an electric discharge tube, then conduction takes place more easily. This shows that electrons are ejected from a metal surface when illuminated by light of suitable wavelength.

(ii) Hallwach confirmed Hertz observation through his following convincing experiment:

His apparatus consists of two zinc plates enclosed in an evacuated quartz tube. The plates are connected to a battery through a galvanometer (Fig. 15.1). He noted the following observations:

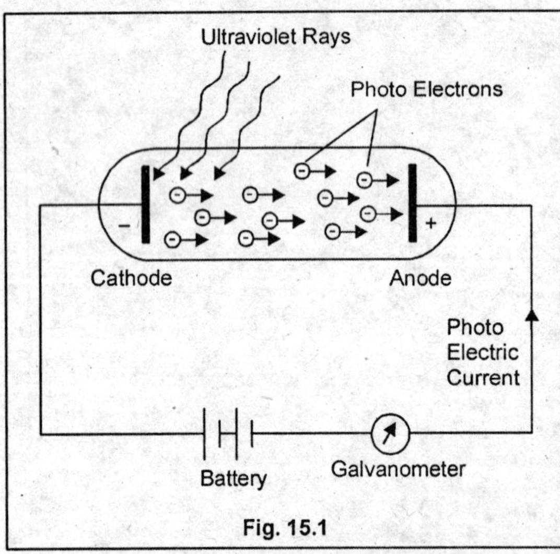

Fig. 15.1

(a) When U.V. rays are allowed to fall on the cathode, a deflection is produced in the galvanometer i.e. a current flows in the circuit.

(b) As soon as rays are stopped, the deflection in the galvanometer becomes zero or current stops.

(c) If rays arc made to fall on anode then either no current or a very small current flows in the circuit.

(iii) Lenard's explanation:

(a) He explained that when ultraviolet rays fall on cathode, electrons are ejected from it which are attracted towards anode or positively charged plate. Hence, the circuit which was incomplete till now, due to air gap between two plates in the tube, gets completed due to flow of electrons and a current starts flowing in the circuit.

(b) However, when rays fall on anode, the electrons are again emitted from the plate in the same way as earlier but due to being negatively charged do not reach the cathode i.e. circuit again remains incomplete and current does not flow.

(iv) This phenomenon of emission of electrons from a metallic surface when illuminated by light of appropriate wavelength or frequency is known as photoelectric effect. The electrons emitted in this process are called as photoelectrons and the current produced in the circuit is called as photoelectric current.

EXPERIMENTAL STUDY OF PHOTOELECTRIC EFFECT

(i) Lenard and Millikan studied the photoelectric effect experimentally. They used plates of different materials and illuminated them with light rays of different intensities and different frequencies and measured in each case.

(a) maximum kinetic energy of emitted photoelectrons, and

(b) the strength of photoelectric current. On the basis of the results of these experiments they found many interesting conclusions relating the phenomenon of photoelectric effect.

(ii) Experimental arrangement: It consists of two metallic plates P_1 and P_2, enclosed in an evacuated quartz tube as shown in the fig. 22.13. The plate P_1 is mounted in front of window W, through which light rays fall on it. The two plates are connected to an ammeter A and to a potential divider through a commutator C. With the help of potential divider, the value of potential difference applied between plates P_1 and P_2 can be altered while the commutator serves the purpose of changing the polarity of plates. A voltmeter is also connected in the circuit to measure the potential difference applied between plates P_1 and P_2.

(iii) Study of the dependence of maximum kinetic energy and photoelectric current on the intensity of incident light.

(a) When light rays of fixed intensity (I) and fixed frequency are made to fall on negative plate P_1, photoelectrons are ejected from it. If the plate P_2 is kept at a small positive potential with respect to plate P_1 (by inserting plugs in gaps 1, 1 in the commutator) then all the ejected electrons are attracted by it and a maximum photoelectric current flows in the circuit. If positive potential on plate P_2 is further increased, current does not increase further because all the emitted electrons are already reaching the plate P_2 (It is interesting

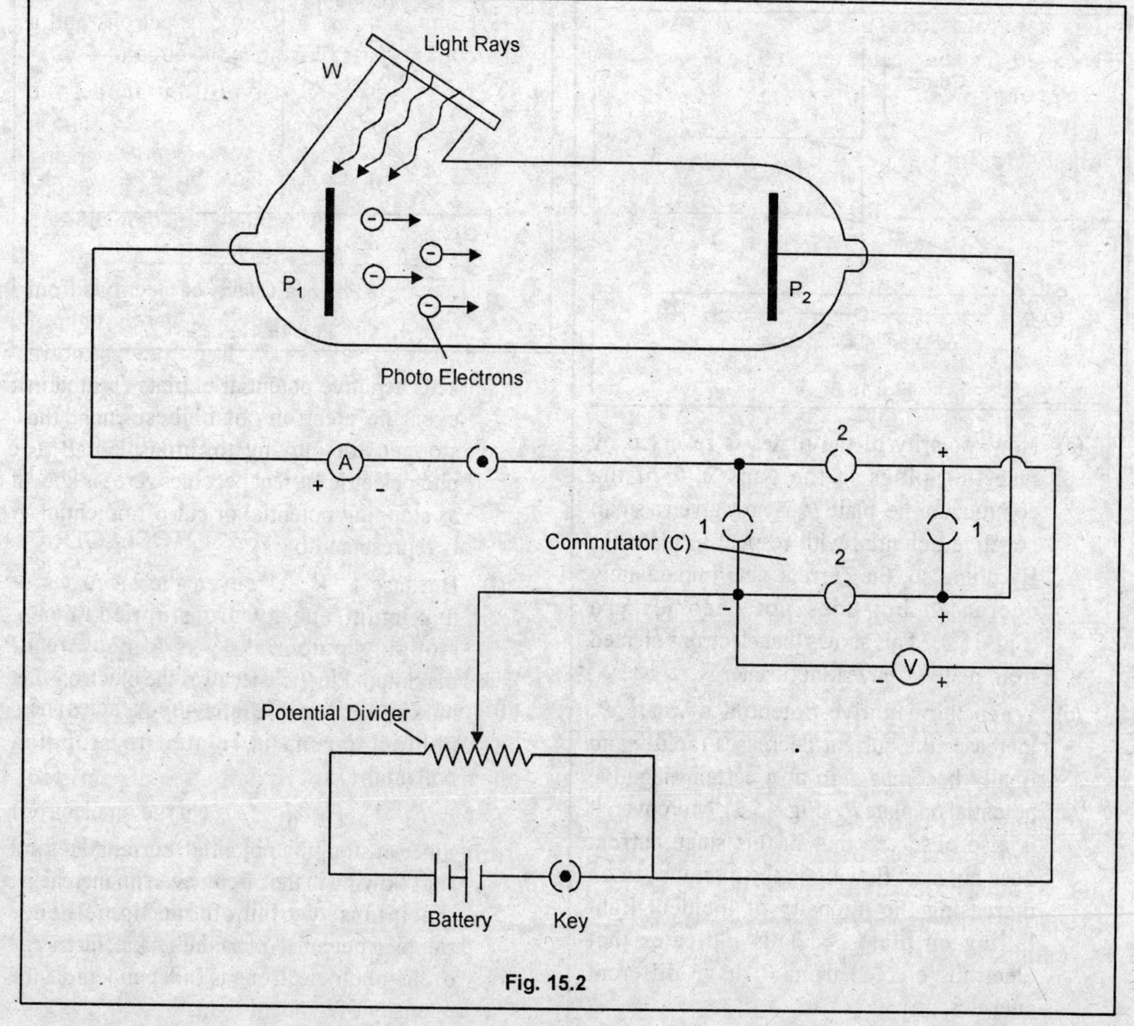

Fig. 15.2

to note here that photoelectrons emitted from plate P_1 are already of high kinetic energy, hence even a small positive potential on plate P_2 makes all of them enable to reach the plate P_2). This shows that current has acquired a saturation value.

(b) When intensity of incident light is just doubled (i.e. $2I$) without changing the frequency, the saturation of maximum photoelectric current also gets doubled (Fig. 15.3). This leads to the conclusion that saturation photoelectric current is directly proportional to the intensity of incident light.

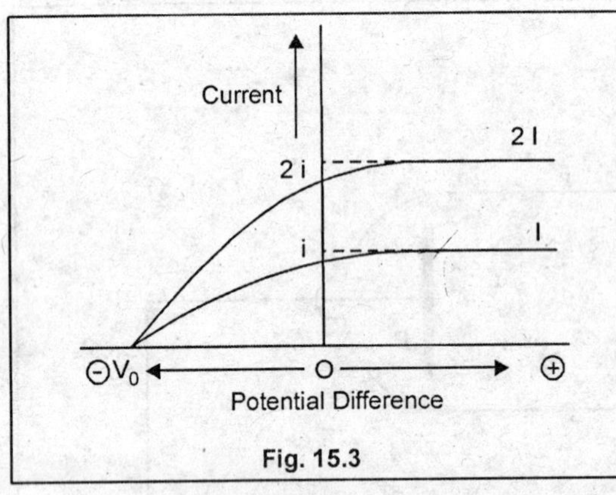

Fig. 15.3

(c) Now, polarity of the plates is reversed by inserting plugs in the gaps 2, 2 of the commutator i.e. plate P_2 is now given a small negative potential with respect to plate P_1. By doing so, the current gets immediately decreased but does not become zero (Fig. 15.3). This shows that electrons ejected from plate P_1 have kinetic energy.

(d) When the negative potential of plate P_2 increases the current decreases rapidly and finally becomes zero at a certain negative potential on plate P_2 (Fig. 15.3). Moreover, it is also observed that in this stage current does not start flowing in the circuit even on increasing the intensity of incident light falling on plate P_1. This indicates that electrons ejected from P_1 have different energies.

(e) Initially, when plate P_2 is kept at small negative potential with respect to plate P_1, it is able to repel only those electrons which have small kinetic energy but electrons of high energy are still reaching the plate P_2. Hence current gets decreased but does not become zero. As plate P_2 is given more and more –ve potential, the number of electrons reaching the plate P_2 goes on decreasing. Finally, at a certain fixed –ve potential even the electrons of highest energy are not able to reach plate P_2 and current becomes zero.

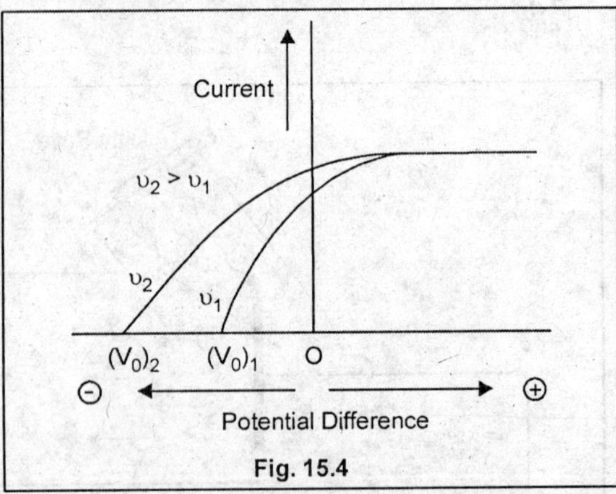

Fig. 15.4

This negative potential of plate P_2 at which even the electrons of highest energy are stopped for moving towards plate P_2 (or photoelectric current becomes zero) is known as stopping potential or cut-off potential. It is represented by V_0.

(f) Because at $V = V_0$ even the electrons of maximum energy are stopped, hence stopping potential V_0 is a measure of maximum kinetic energy of the electrons i.e. maximum kinetic energy E_k^{max} of the photoelectrons is related to stopping potential V_0 as:

$$E_k^{max} = eV_0 \quad (e = \text{charge on electron})$$

(g) Since at stopping potential, current does not start flowing in the circuit even on increasing the intensity of incident light, hence stopping potential or maximum kinetic energy of the photoelectrons is independent of the intensity of incident light.

(iv) Study of the dependence of maximum kinetic energy and photoelectric current on the frequency of the incident light:

(a) If, at the stopping potential, light of frequency higher than before is allowed to fall on plate P_1, then we find that current again starts flowing in the circuit. This current again reduces to zero on increasing further the negative potential on plate P_2. This leads to the conclusion that maximum kinetic energy of emitted photoelectrons or stopping potential increases with increase in the frequency of the incident light.

(b) On repeating above experiment by using light rays of different frequencies and plotting a graph between the measured values of maximum kinetic energies E_k^{max} $(= eV_0)$ of the photoelectrons and the frequencies of incident light (= V), a straight line is obtained (Fig. 15.5). This leads to the conclusion that the maximum kinetic energy of the photoelectrons increases linearly with increase in the frequency of the incident light.

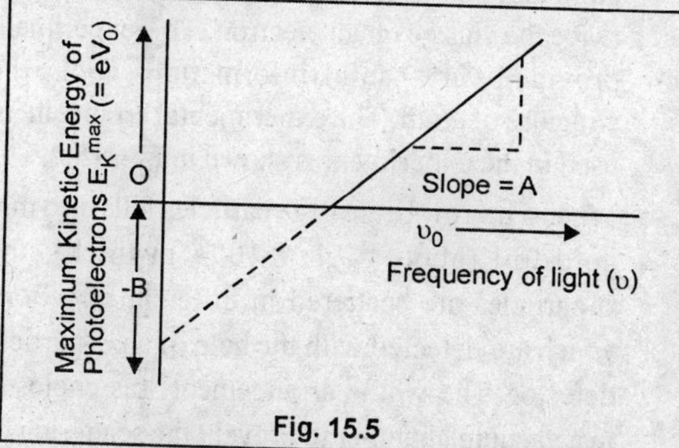

Fig. 15.5

(c) If the straight line graph obtained above is extended backwards, it cuts the frequency axis at a point ν_0 and gives an intercept – B on energy-axis (Fig. 15.5). This observation gives the conclusion that for the emission of photoelectrons from a given metal plate, the frequency of incident light must be higher than ν_0. If frequency is less than ν_0, no photoelectron will be emitted, whatever may be the intensity of incident light or for whatever time light is allowed to fall on the plate i.e. even a less intense light, having a frequency greater than ν_0, will be capable of emitting the photoelectrons. This minimum frequency of the incident light which can eject photoelectrons from a material is known as the threshold frequency or cut-off frequency of that material.

(d) Straight line graph shown in fig. 15.5, can be represented mathematically by the following equation:

$$E_m^{max} = A\nu - B$$

where A is the slope of straight line and $-B$ is the intercept on energy-axis. This is an equation written on the basis of experimental results. Any theory, developed to explain the phenomenon of photoelectric effect, must lead to a similar type of equation.

(v) Study of the effect of variation of the material of the plate P_1:

(a) If the experiment (study of the variation of E_k^{max} with respect to frequency) is repeated by using different metals 1, 2, 3 etc. for plate P_1, then the graph between E_k^{max} and ν is found to be a straight line in case of every metal (Fig. 15.6). Moreover, all these straight lines are found to be parallel to each other i.e. their slope A is same, whereas the values of ν_0 and B are different. This observation leads to the conclusion that in the experimental equation $E_k^{max} = A\nu - B$, A must be some universal constant (because its value is same for all the metals) while ν_0 and B must be some characteristic constants (because their values are fixed for a given metal but different for different metals).

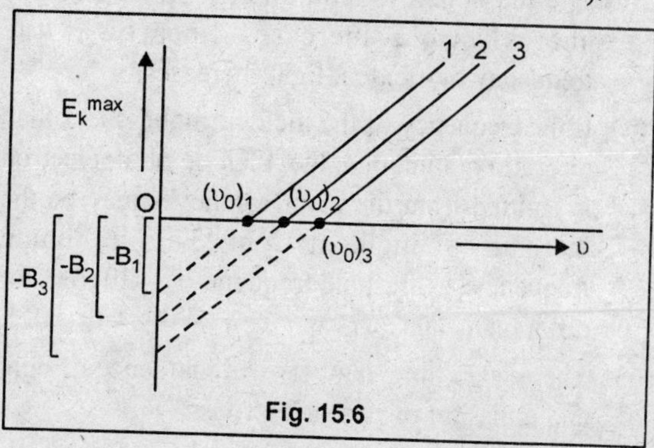

Fig. 15.6

(b) Further, it is also clear from the graph that when

$$\nu = \nu_0,\ E_k^{max} = 0$$

Hence from experimental equation, we get

$$0 = A\nu_0 - B$$

or $$B = A\nu_0$$

As ν_0 represents the minimum frequency required for the emission of photoelectron and B has got dimensions of energy, hence constant B represents the minimum energy necessary for emission of electrons from a metal. The minimum energy required for the emission of electrons from a metal is called as the work function of that metal. Hence B must represent the work function of metal. It is thus also clear that work function of a metal can be measured just by finding out the slope A of the straight line and the frequency ν_0 where the straight line cuts the frequency axis.

LAWS OF PHOTOELECTRIC EMISSION

Lenard and Millikan gave the following laws regarding photoelectric effect on the basis of above experiments.

(i) The number of photoelectrons emitted per second from the surface of metal is directly proportional to the intensity of the incident light falling on the metal plate.

(ii) The maximum kinetic energy of the emitted photoelectrons does not depend upon the intensity of incident light.

(iii) The maximum kinetic energy of the emitted photoelectrons increases linearly as the frequency of incident light increases.

(iv) If the frequency of the incident light is less than a certain minimum value, then no photoelectron is emitted from the metal whatever may be the intensity of incident light. This minimum frequency (= threshold frequency) is different for different metals.

(v) There is no time–lag between incidence of light and emission of photoelectrons.

ATOMS, MOLECULES AND NUCLEI

RUTHERFORD'S α-PARTICLE SCATTERING EXPERIMENT

(i) The first scientist to give a correct description of the distribution of positive and negative charges within the atom was Rutherford. Rutherford's atomic model was based on the α-particle scattering experiment. He bombarded a thin gold foil with highly energetic α-particles (emitted by a radioactive material) and studied the scattering of α-particles in order to investigate the structure of the atom. An α-particle is a positively charged particle having a mass equal to that of helium atom and positive charge in magnitude equal to twice the charge on an electron. This experiment provided very useful informations about the structure of atom. The experimental arrangement used in the experiment is shown in Fig. 15.7.

When a narrow beam of α-particles falls on a thin gold-foil (about 2.1×10^{-7} m thick), the α-particles are scattered in different directions which are detected with the help of an α-particle detector. The whole arrangement was enclosed in a vacuum chamber to prevent the scattering of α-particles from air molecules.

(ii) **Experimental observations:**

(a) Most of the α-particles were found to pass through the gold-foil without being deviated from their paths.

(b) Some α-particle were found to be deflected through small angles and their angular distribution is fixed (*e.g.* for particles 3, 4, 8 and 9 in Fig. 15.8, angle of scattering $\theta < 90°$).

(c) Few α-particle were found to be scattered at fairly large angles from their initial path and return back (*e.g.* for particles 5 and 7 in Fig. 15.8, the angle of scattering $\theta > 90°$).

(d) A very small number of α-particles about 1 in 8000 practically retraced their paths or suffered deflections of nearly 180° (*e.g.* particle 6 in Fig. 15.8).

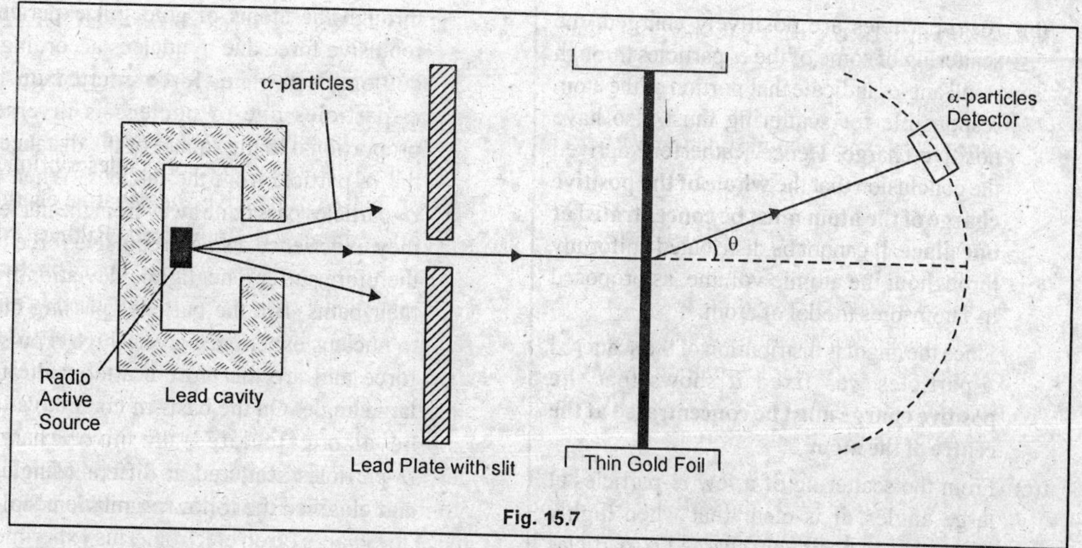

Fig. 15.7

The graph between the total number of α-particles (N) scattered and the scattering angles θ was found to be as shown in Fig. 15.9.

(iii) Conclusions:

(a) The large number of α-particles passing through the atom undeviated indicate that **Most of the portion of atom is hollow inside.** It can not be solid in any case, as proposed in Thomson's model of atom.

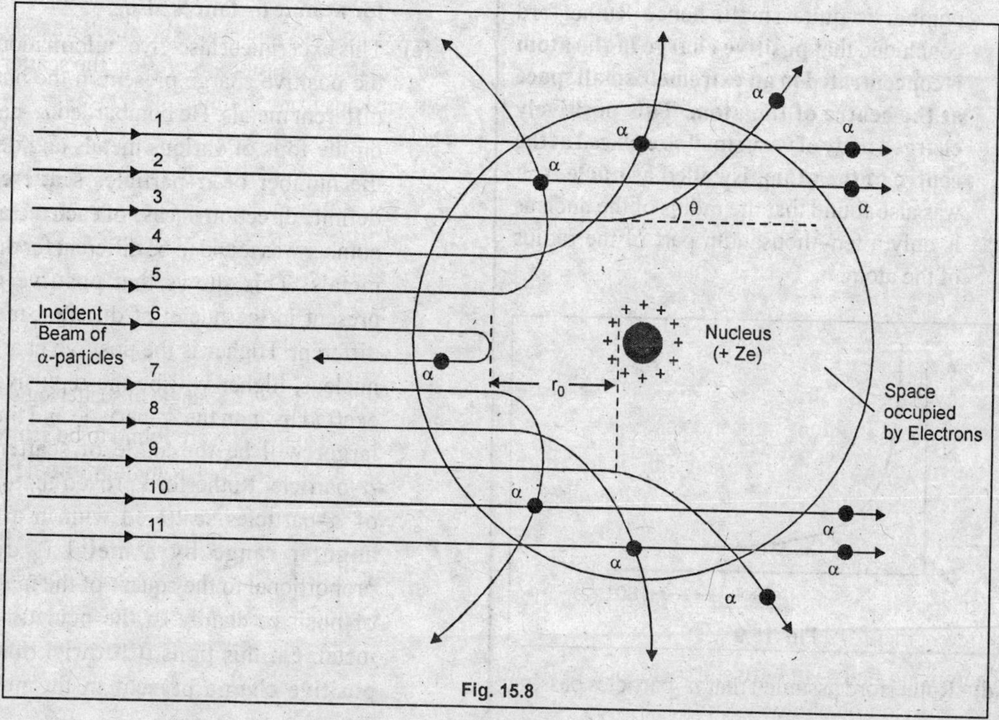

Fig. 15.8

(b) As α-particles are positively charged, the scattering of some of the α-particles through small angles indicate that portion of the atom responsible for scattering must also have positive charge. Hence Rutherford derived the conclusion that the **whole of the positive charge of the atom must be concentrated at one place.** It cannot be distributed uniformly throughout the atomic volume, as proposed in Thomson's model of atom.

Since the angular distribution of the scattered α-particles was fixed it shows that **the positive charge must be concentrated at the centre of the atom.**

(c) From the scattering of a few α–particles at large angles, it is clear that when highly energetic and positively charged α–particles pass through the atoms of the gold foil, then a few of them experience such a strong repulsive force so as to suffer large angled scattering in spite of having high energy. Naturally, these will be those α–particles which will be very close to positive charge of the atom. Since their number is quite small, hence Rutherford concluded that **positive charge in the atom is concentrated in an extremely small space at the centre of the atom. This positively charged body of very small size placed at the centre of the atom, is called as nucleus.** It was also found that the radius of the nucleus is only a ten–thousandth part of the radius of the atom.

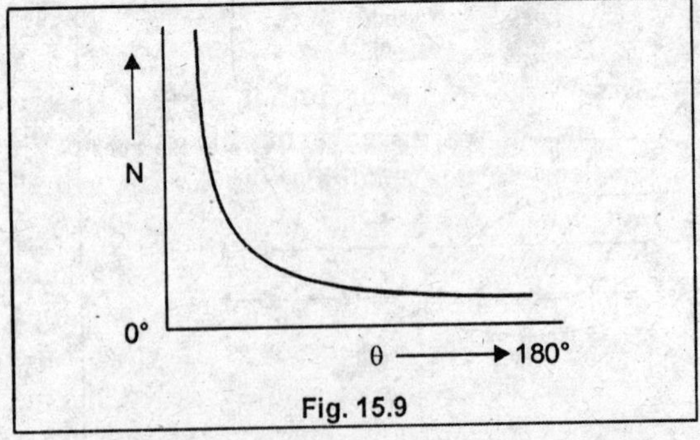

Fig. 15.9

(d) Rutherford assumed that α–particles passing through the atoms of gold foil experience repulsive force due to nucleus according to coulomb's law i.e. force exerted on the α–particles due to nucleus is inversely proportional to the square of the distance of the α–particle from the nucleus. When the α–particles pass quite away from the nucleus, they experience a small repulsive force and therefore suffer a negligible deviation from their paths. But the particles passing close to nucleus experience a very high repulsive force and are therefore scattered through large angle. On the basis of coulomb's law, he also calculated the number N of α–particles scattered at different angles θ and obtained the following relationship:

$$N \propto \frac{1}{\sin^4(\theta/2)}$$

Later on this relationship was also confirmed by the experiments of Geiger and Maesden. This confirms that **scattering of α–particles by the nucleus is in accordance with Coulomb's law and Coulomb's law is valid for atomic distances also.**

(e) This experiment also gives information about the positive charge present in the nuclei of different metals. He bombarded α–particles on the foils of various metals and detected the number of α–particles scattered in a definite direction in case of each metal. This number was found to be different for different metals. This shows that positive charge present in the nuclei of different metals is different. Higher is the positive charge in a nucleus, higher will be the repulsive force exerted by it on the α–particle and therefore larger will be the angle of scattering of α–particle. Rutherford proved that number of α–particles scattered with in a certain angular range by a metal is directly proportional to the square of the magnitude of positive charge in the nucleus of that metal. On this basis, Chadwick found the positive charge present in the nuclei of different metals and came to the conclusion that the **positive charge in the nucleus of a metal is equal to Ze,** where e is the charge on an electron and Z is a constant for the metal, known as atomic number.

RUTHERFORD'S MODEL OF ATOM

Rutherford proposed the following model for the structure of the atom on the basis of the results of his α–particle scattering experiment.

(i) Atom may be regarded as a sphere of the radius ~ 10^{-10}m, in which whole of the positive charge and almost the whole mass of the atom is concentrated in a very small region at the centre of the atom, called nucleus whose size is of the order of 10^{-14} m.

(ii) The nucleus is surrounded by the electrons in the remaining part of the atom. Rutherford assumed that electrons are revolving around the nucleus in circular orbits of all possible radii. The necessary centripetal force for circular motion of electrons around the nucleus is provided by electrostatic force of attraction between electrons and nucleus.

(iii) Since atom is electrically neutral, hence the total positive charge on the nucleus is equal to the total negative charge of the electrons in it.

DISTANCE OF CLOSEST APPROACH

(i) An α–particle which moves straight toward the nucleus in head –on direction reaches closest to the nucleus i.e. it moves close up to a distance r_0. As the α-particle approaches the nucleus, the electrostatic repulsive force due to the nucleus increases and kinetic energy of the alpha particle goes on converting into the electrostatic potential energy. When whole of the kinetic energy is converted into electrostatic potential energy, the α-particle cannot further move toward the nucleus but returns back on its initial path i.e. α-particle is scattered through an angle of 180°. The distance of α-particle from the nucleus in this stage is called as the distance of closest approach and is represented by r_0.

(ii) If m_a and v_a are the mass and velocity of the α-particle directed towards the centre of the nucleus, then kinetic energy of the α-particle

$$E_k = \left(\frac{1}{2}\right) m_\alpha v_a^2$$

Since the positive charge on the nucleus is Ze and that on the α-particle is $2e$, hence the electrostatic potential energy of the α-particle, when at a distance r_0 from the nucleus, is given by

$$E_P = \frac{1}{4\pi\varepsilon_0} \cdot \frac{(2e)(Ze)}{r_0}$$

Since at $r = r_0$, the kinetic energy of the α-particle appears as its potential energy, hence we get

$$E_P = E_K$$

$$\text{or} \quad \frac{1}{4\pi\varepsilon_0} \cdot \frac{(2e)(Ze)}{r_0} = E_k$$

$$\text{or} \quad r_0 = \frac{1}{4\pi\varepsilon_0} \cdot \frac{2Ze^2}{E_K}$$

$$= \frac{1}{4\pi\varepsilon_0} \frac{4Ze^2}{m_\alpha v_\alpha{}^2}$$

Above equation shows that for a given nucleus, the value of r_0 depends upon the initial kinetic energy of the α-particle.

(iii) As the initial kinetic energy of the alpha particle is increased more and more, α-particle will reach more and more close to the nucleus. At a certain very high value of initial kinetic energy, α-particle will reach extremely close to the nucleus. In this condition, the nucleus will no more be a point charge for the α-particle and Coulomb's law will no more be applicable. Moreover, the nuclear force (which is a strong attractive force) now becomes effective. As a result of this, α-particles now attracted into the nucleus and no more returns on its path. Thus **the distance of closest approach of the**

α-particles corresponding to that maximum value of kinetic energy for which the particle is not scattered back, will be a measure of the radius of the nucleus.

BOHR'S MODEL OF ATOM

Bohr's model of atom is based on the following three postulates:

First Postulate: The electrons revolve around the nucleus in certain allowed circular orbits only and while in these orbits they do not radiate energy i.e. electronic orbits are stable. The necessary centripetal force for their circular motion is provided by the electrostatic attractive force between the positively charged nucleus and negatively and charged electrons. If Z is the atomic number of the nucleus and r is the radius of any allowed electrons orbit, then

$$\frac{mv^2}{r} = \frac{Ze \times e}{4\pi\varepsilon_0 r^2} \qquad ...(1)$$

where m is the mass of electron and v, the velocity of electron in the allowed orbit.

Second Postulate: The allowed orbits in which electron can revolve are those in which the angular momentum of an electron is an integer multiple of $h/2\pi$, where h is Planck's constant having value 6.63×10^{-34} Js i.e. if m and v are the mass and velocity of the electron in a permitted orbit of radius r, then

$$mvr = \frac{nh}{2\pi} \qquad ...(2)$$

where n is called principal quantum number and has the integer values 1, 2, 3, ... The equation (2) is also called Bohr's quantisation condition.

Third Postulate: According to Bohr's model, the electrons do not radiate any energy till they revolve in their own orbits i.e. orbits of electrons are stable. The energy is radiated only and only when an electron jumps from higher energy orbit to lower energy orbit and the energy is absorbed, when it jumps from lower energy orbit to higher energy orbit. **Both the radiation and absorption of energy takes place in the form of photons.**

If E_i and E_f are the energies associated with the orbits of principal quantum numbers n_i and n_f respectively ($n_i > n_f$), then the frequency of the emitted radiation is given by

$$hn = E_i - E_f \qquad ...(3)$$

The equation (3) is called Bohr's frequency condition.

RADIOACTIVITY

(i) **Substance capable of emitting radiations are called radioactive substances and the phenomenon of spontaneous emission of radiations from the substance is called Radioactivity.**

(ii) After the discovery of radioactivity in uranium, it was found that some other elements like – thorium, polonium, actinium, etc. are also radioactive. In 1898, Piere Curie and Madame Curie discovered a new radioactive element called radium which is found to be 10^6 times more radioactive than uranium.

RADIATIONS EMITTED BY RADIOACTIVE ELEMENTS

A large number of experiments were conducted to determine the nature of radiations emitted by the radioactive substances immediate after the discovery of natural radioactivity. On the basis of these experiments, it was found that radiations emitted by a radioactive substance were of three different types namely; α, β and γ-rays. It should be noted here that all the radioactive elements do not necessarily emit all these three types of radiations.

LAWS OF RADIOACTIVE DECAY

(i) The following two laws are obeyed by radioactive decay.

(a) The radioactive decay is spontaneous with the emission of α, β and γ-rays. It is not influenced by external condition such as temperature, pressure, electric and magnetic field (The nuclear forces are extremely strong and hence nuclear disintegration is unaffected by normal changes in external conditions).

(b) The rate of disintegration (i.e. number of atoms that disintegrate per second) is directly proportional to the number of radioactive atoms present. This is known as decay law.

(ii) **Mathematical treatment of decay law:**

Let at the beginning of disintegration (i.e. at $t = 0$), the number of radioactive atoms present be N_0. As the time passes, the number of original radioactive atoms decreases due to continuous disintegration. Suppose after time t, the number of atoms left is N. Let us suppose that dN atoms now disintegrate in small time dt.

$\therefore$ Rate of disintegration $= \dfrac{dN}{dt}$

According to decay law, the rate of disintegration is directly proportional to the number of radioactive atoms present i.e.

$$\frac{dN}{dt} \propto N$$

or $$\frac{dN}{dt} = -\lambda N \qquad \text{...(1)}$$

When λ is a constant of proportionality and is called decay constant or disintegration constant. The minus sign indicates that N is decreasing with respect to time

Equation (1) can be written as

$$\frac{dN}{N} = -\lambda\, dt$$

Integrating on both sides, we get

$$\log_e N = -\lambda t + K \qquad \text{...(2)}$$

Where K is a constant of integration whose value can be found from the initial conditions.

When $t = 0, N = N_0$

Putting these values in equation (2), we get

$$\log_e N_0 = -\lambda \times 0 + K$$

$$\therefore \quad K = \log_e N_0$$

Hence equation (2) becomes

$$\log_e N = -\lambda t + \log_e N_0$$

or $\log_e N - \log_e N_0 = -\lambda t$

or $$\log_e \frac{N}{N_0} = -\lambda t$$

or $$\frac{N}{N_0} = e^{-\lambda t}$$

$$N = N_0 e^{-\lambda t} \qquad \text{...(3)}$$

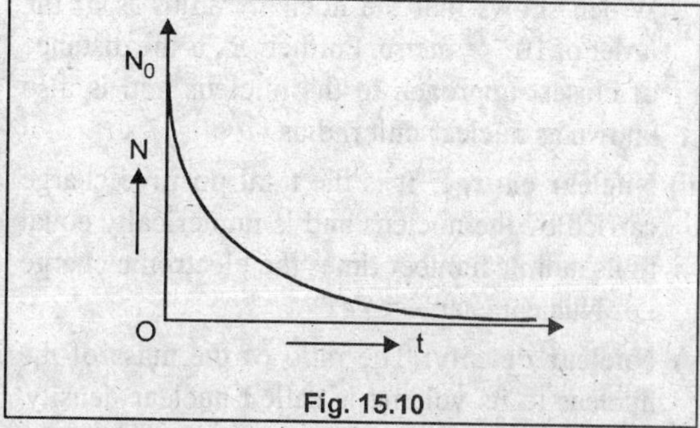

Fig. 15.10

Equation (3) follows exponential law and is known as decay equation. It can be used to find the number of radioactive atoms present at any time t if we know decay constant λ and the original number of radioactive atoms N_0. Fig. 15.10 shows the curve for the decay of a radioactive substance. The curve shows that the number of atoms of a given substance decrease exponentially with respect to time. Since N becomes zero only when t approaches infinite, therefore a radioactive substance will never disintegrate completely.

NUCLEAR CHARACTERISTICS

(i) **Nuclear mass:** From Rutherford's α–particle scattering experiment we have seen that the mass of an atom is concentrated within a very small, positively charged region at the centre, called as nucleus. The total mass of nucleons in the nucleus is called as **nuclear mass** i.e.

Nuclear mass,

A = mass of protons + mass of neutrons

Since the mass of a proton or neutron is very small, therefore, nuclear masses are extremely small.

(ii) **Size and Shape of the nucleus:** The nucleus is believed to be very nearly spherical. Hence, its size is usually given in terms of radius. The radius of nucleus was measured by Rutherford in his α–particle scattering experiment. It has been found that nuclear radius R is given by:

$$R = R_0 A^{1/3}$$

where $R_0 = 1.1$ fm (fermi) $= 1.1 \times 10^{-15}$ m and A is the mass number of the particular element.

Which shows that the nuclear radius is of the order of 10^{-15} metre. Further, R_0 is the distance of closest approach to the nucleus and is also known as nuclear unit radius.

(iii) Nuclear charge: It is the total positive charge carried by the nucleus and is numerically equal to its atomic number times the electronic charge i.e. Nuclear charge $= Ze$

(iv) Nuclear density: The ratio of the mass of the nucleus to its volume is called nuclear density. Consider the nucleus of an atom having mass number A. If we neglect the mass of the orbital electrons then mass of the nucleus of the atom $= A$. a. m. u. $= A \times 1.660565 \times 10^{-27}$Kg

If R is the radius of the nucleus then volume of the nucleus $= (4/3)\,\rho R^3 = (4/3)\,\rho R_0{}^3 A$.

$\therefore$ Density of the nucleus

$$\rho = \frac{\text{mass of nucleus}}{\text{Volume of nucleus}}$$

$$= \frac{A \times 1.660565 \times 10^{-27}\ \text{Kg}}{(4/3)\,\pi\,(1.1 \times 10^{-15})^3 \times \text{Am}^3}$$

$$= \mathbf{2.97 \times 10^{-17}\ Kg/m^3}$$

EINSTEIN'S MASS ENERGY EQUIVALENCE PRINCIPLE

(i) On the basis of his theory of Relativity, Einstein showed that the mass of a body is not constant but increases with velocity. In other words, when a body is given Kinetic energy, its mass is increased. This shows that mass depends upon energy and vice–versa. Therefore, mass and energy are inter–convertible i.e. they can be changed into each other. According to Einstein, if a substance loses an amount Δm of its mass, an equivalent amount ΔE of energy is produced, where

$$\Delta E = \Delta mc^2$$

where c, is the speed of light. This is called Einstein's mass-energy equivalence principle.

ATOMIC MASS UNIT (A.M.U.)

(i) The masses of atoms, nuclei, sub atomic particles are very small. Hence, a small unit is used to express these masses. This unit is called as atomic mass unit (a.m.u.) **1 a.m.u. is equal to one twelfth part of the mass of carbon ($_6C^{12}$) atom.** Mass of $_6C^{12}$ is 12.00 a.m.u.

(ii) Now, the mass of 1 gm-atom of carbon is 12 gm and according to Avogadro's Hypothesis it has N (Avogadro's Number) atoms. Thus, the mass of one atom of carbon is $(12/N)$ gms. According to the definition,

$$1\ \text{amu} = \frac{1}{12} \times \text{(mass of one carbon atom)}$$

$$= \frac{1}{12} \times \frac{12}{N}$$

$$= \frac{1}{N}\ \text{grams}$$

$$= \frac{1}{6.02 \times 10^{23}}\ \text{grams}$$

$$= 1.66 \times 10^{-24}\ \text{grams}$$

$$= 1.66 \times 10^{-27}\ \text{Kg}$$

(iii) We can now find energy equivalent to 1 a.m.u. mass with the help of Einstein's mass energy relation. If this energy be ΔE, then

$$\Delta E = \Delta mc^2$$

$$= (1.66 \times 10^{-27}) \times (3 \times 10^8)^2$$

$$= 1.49 \times 10^{-10}\ \text{Joules}$$

But 1.6×10^{-19} Joules $= 1$ eV

$$\therefore \quad \Delta E = \frac{1.46 \times 10^{-10}}{1.6 \times 10^{19}}$$

$$= 0.931 \times 10^9\ \text{eV}$$

$$= \mathbf{931\ MeV}$$

i.e. **1 a.m.u. of mass is equivalent of 931 MeV energy.**

MASS DEFECT

(i) Experimentally it has been observed that the rest mass of the nucleus of a stable atom is always less than the mass of the constituent nucleons in free state. The difference between the actual mass of the nucleus and the sum of the masses of the constituent nucleons is called mass defect.

(ii) Consider a nucleus having atomic number Z and mass number A. It consists of Z protons and $(A-Z)$ neutrons. If m_p and m_n are the masses of a proton and neutron respectively then, mass of constituent nucleons $= Zm_p + (A-Z)m_n$

Let M be the mass of nucleus, then mass defect of the nucleus of as atom is

$$\Delta m = Zm_p + (A-Z)m_n - M$$

BINDING ENERGY OF NUCLEUS

(i) Binding energy of nucleus is the total energy required to liberate all the nucleons from the nucleus (i.e. to disintegrate the nucleus completely into its constituent particles).

(ii) Obviously, this is the same energy with which the nucleons are held together within the nucleus. The origin of binding energy results from strong nuclear exchange forces. In other words, we may think of the existence of binding energy in other useful way also. A nucleus is made by the coming together of various nucleons. It has been observed experimentally that mass of the nucleus always less than the sum of the masses of its constituents then measured in free state. For example, Deutron ($_1H^2$) is composed of one proton and one neutron. The mass of $_1H^2$ nucleus is less than the sum of masses of 1 proton and 1 neutron. The question arises where the difference in mass has gone. The answer is that this decrease in mass has been converted into energy binding the nucleons together according to the following relation:

$$\Delta E = \Delta mc^2$$

Where, ΔE = Binding energy of nucleus, Δm = decrease in mass, called mass defect and c = velocity of light.

Hence in the formation of stable nucleus, the following equation holds good

Mass of protons + Mass of neutrons = Mass of Nucleus $+mc^2$ (B.E.)

Expression for binding energy per nucleon: We calculate binding energy per nucleon (BEN) in order to compare the stability of various nucleus. Higher is the binding energy per nucleon, more stable is the nucleus.

We have seen that mass defect during the formation of a nucleus

$$\Delta m = Zm_p + (A-Z)m_n - M$$

Total binding energy of nucleus

$$\Delta E = \Delta mc^2 = [Zmp + (A-Z)m_n - M] \times c^2$$

Mean binding energy per nucleon.

$$BEN = \frac{\Delta E}{A} = \frac{\Delta mc^2}{A} = \left[\frac{Z}{A}(m_p - m_n) + m_n - \frac{M}{A}\right] \times c^2$$

If the mass M of the nucleus is found experimentally, we can find the mean binding energy per nucleon since all other factors are known to us.

NUCLEAR FISSION

(i) Nuclear Fission is the phenomenon of breaking a heavy nucleus into two light nuclei of almost equal masses alongwith the release of huge amount of energy.

(ii) The process of nuclear fission was first discovered by German Scientists Otto Hahn and Strassman in 1939. They bombarded uranium nucleus ($_{92}U^{235}$) with slow neutrons and found that intermediate product ($_{92}U^{236}$) was split into two medium weight part with the release of enormous energy. These fragments had atomic numbers far less than the target nucleus ($_{92}U^{235}$). The nuclear fission of $_{92}U^{235}$ is given by the following nuclear reaction:

$$_{92}U^{235} + {_0n^1} \rightarrow [_{92}U^{236}]$$

$$\rightarrow {_{56}Ba^{144}} + {_{36}Kr^{89}} + 3\,{_0n^1} + \text{energy}$$

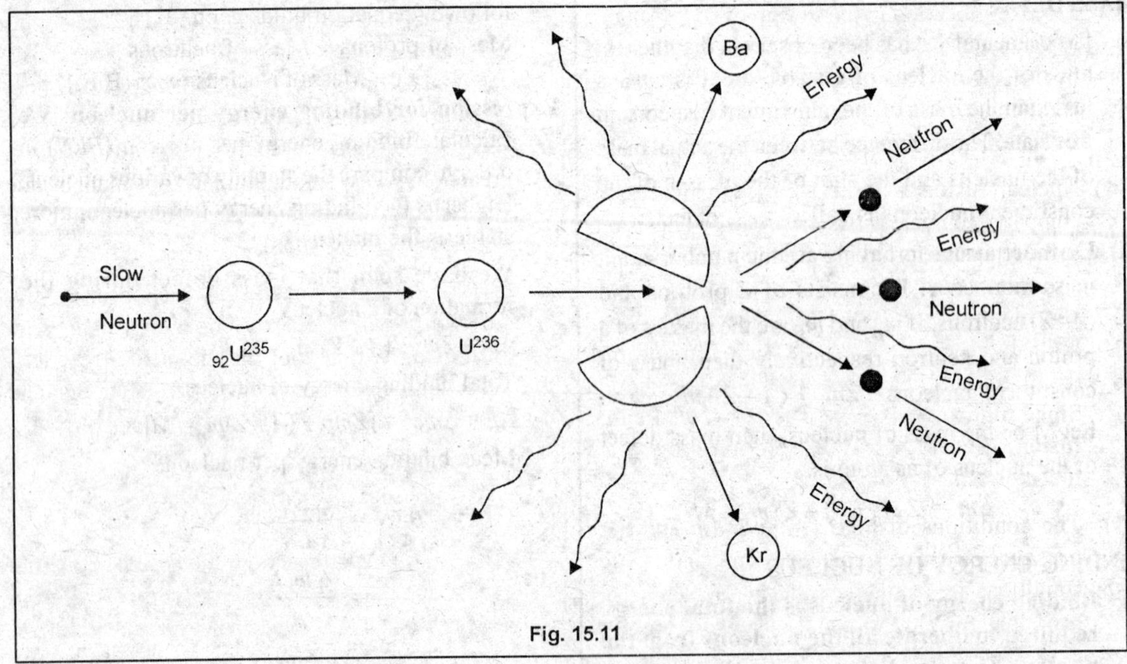

Fig. 15.11

(iii) Fig. 15.11 shows the fission of $_{92}U^{235}$ nucleus when bombarded with a neutron. When a neutron strikes $_{92}U^{235}$ nucleus, it is absorbed by it, producing a highly unstable $_{92}U^{236}$ nucleus is shown in figure. Instead of emitting α or β particles or γ-rays, this unstable nucleus is split into two middle weight parts viz $_{56}Ba^{144}$ and krypton ($_{36}Kr^{89}$). During this fission, three neutrons are given out and a mass defect occurs which is converted into enormous amount of energy.

NUCLEAR FUSION

(i) **Nuclear fusion is the process of combining two light nuclei to form a heavy nucleus. Clearly, the process of fusion is just the reverse of fission.** An important feature of fusion is that there is a release of huge amount of energy in the process. This can be easily understood. When two light nuclei are combined to form a heavy nucleus there occurs a small mass defect. In other words, the mass of the heavy nucleus turns out to be less than the sum of the masses of two light nuclei. This small mass defect results in the release of a huge amount of energy according to the relation

$$\Delta E = \Delta mc^2$$

(ii) ***Example:*** The following reaction is possible by the fusion of two nuclei of heavy hydrogen or deuterium ($_1H^2$).

$$_1H^2 + {_1H^2} \rightarrow {_1H^3} + {_1H^1} + 4.0 \text{ MeV}$$

The nucleus of tritium ($_1H^3$) so formed can again fuse with a deuterium nucleus

$$_1H^3 + {_1H^2} \rightarrow {_2He^4} + {_0n^1} + 17.6 \text{ MeV}$$

The net result of these two reactions is that then deuterium nuclei fuse together to form a helium nucleus and release 21.6 MeV energy which is obtained in the form of Kinetic energy of proton ($_1H^1$) and neutron ($_0n^1$).

Alternatively, following reactions are also possible for the fusion of three deuterium nuclei

$$_1H^2 + {_1H^2} \rightarrow {_2He^3} + {_0n^1} + 3.3 \text{ MeV}$$

$$_2He^3 + {_1H^2} \rightarrow {_2He^4} + {_1H^1} + 18.3 \text{ MeV}$$

(iii) The energy output in the process of Nuclear fusion (21.6 MeV) is quite less than the energy liberated in the fission of a U^{235} nucleus (200 MeV), but this does not imply that fusion is a weaker liberated in the fission of a U^{235} nuclei in 1 gram uranium. Therefore, **the energy liberated by the fusion of a certain mass of heavy hydrogen is much more than the energy released by the fission of equal mass of uranium.**

(iv) Nuclear fusion is quite a difficult process as compared to nuclear fission process. This is due to the repulsive force between them becomes very strong. For fusion against this force, they require very high energy ($\cong 0.1$ MeV). To provide so much high energy to them very high temperature ($\cong 10^8$ K) and very high pressure is required. **Since high temperature is required to cause fusion, therefore fusion is sometimes called thermonuclear reaction.**

(v) The conditions of high temperature and high pressure are not available on earth. Such conditions are available either in the sun or are produced when a nuclear - fission bomb is exploded. **Thus nuclear fusion is possible on earth only by the explosion of a nuclear fission bomb. Hydrogen bomb is a nuclear fusion bomb.**

(vi) **Source of Solar Energy :** We knows that hydrogen and helium constitute about 90% of the mass of the sun and the rest 10% are other elements. The sun has been radiating huge amount of energy for billions of years. Chemical reactions cannot possibly be the source of energy because the energy released in such a reaction is very small. Similarly, it cannot be due to fission as the amount of heavy elements present in the sun is very small.

It is now believed that fusion reactions in the sun are responsible for its enormous heat. The following two sets of thermonuclear reactions account for the energy produced in the Sun and Stars:

(a) Carbon – Nitrogen cycles,

(b) Proton – Proton cycle.

Both these fusion reactions take place in the sun. Although these two reactions have different sequence of intermediate reactions, the net effect is the combination of four hydrogen nuclei (proton, ${}_1H^1$) to form a helium nucleus and two positrons alongwith the release of energy.

$$4\,{}_1H^1 \rightarrow {}_2He^4 + 2\,{}_{+1}\beta^0 + \text{Energy} + 2\nu\,(\text{Neutrino})$$

(Positron)

MULTIPLE CHOICE QUESTIONS

1. A metallic surface has a threshold wavelength 5200 Å. This surface is irradiated by monochromatic light of wavelength 4500 Å. Which of the following statements is true?
   (a) the electrons are emitted from the surface having energy between 0 and infinity
   (b) the electrons are emitted from the surface having energy between 0 and certain finite maximum value
   (c) the electrons are emitted from the surface, all having certain finite energy
   (d) no electron is emitted from the surface

2. In photoelectric effect when photons of energy $h\nu$ fall on a photosensitive surface (work function $h\nu_0$) electrons are emitted from the metallic surface with a kinetic energy. It is possible to say that
   (a) all ejected electrons have same kinetic energy equal to $h\nu - h\nu_0$
   (b) the ejected electrons have a distribution of kinetic energy from zero to $(h\nu - h\nu_0)$
   (c) the most energetic electrons have kinetic energy equal to $h\nu_0$
   (d) all ejected electrons have kinetic energy $h\nu_0$

3. Photoelectric effect can be explained by assuming that light
   (a) is a form of transverse waves
   (b) is a form of longitudinal waves
   (c) can be polarised
   (d) consists of quanta

4. In photoelectric effect, the photoelectric current
   (a) does not depend on photon frequency, but only on intensity of incident beam
   (b) depends both on intensity and frequency of incident beam
   (c) increases when frequency of incident photons increases
   (d) decreases when frequency of incident photons increases

5. Photo electric effect supports the quantum nature of light because
   (a) there is minimum frequency of light below which no photoelectrons are emitted
   (b) the maximum kinetic energy of photoelectrons depends only on the frequency of light and not on intensity
   (c) even when a metal surface is faintly illuminated, the photoelectrons leave the surface immediately
   (d) electric charge of the photoelectrons is quantised

6. A photo cell is illuminated by a small bright source placed 1 m away. When the same source of light is placed 2 m away. Which of the following in true about the electrons emitted by the photo cathode?
   (a) each carry one quarter of their previous energy
   (b) each carry one quarter of their previous momenta
   (c) are half as numerous
   (d) are one-quarter as numerous

7. Which one of the following is incorrect statement about a photon?
   (a) photon's rest mass is zero
   (b) photon's momentum is $h\nu/c$
   (c) photon's energy is $h\nu$
   (d) photons exert no pressure

8. In photoelectric effect, the current
   (a) increases with increase of frequency of incident photon
   (b) decreases with increase of frequency of incident photon
   (c) does not depend on the frequency of photon but depends only on intensity of incident light
   (d) depends both on intensity and frequency of incident beam

9. If the distance of 100 watt lamp is increased from a photo cell, the saturation current 'i' in the photo cell varies with distance 'd' as
   (a) $i \propto d^2$ (b) $i \propto d$
   (c) $i \propto 1/d$ (d) $i \propto 1/d^2$

10. Blue light can cause photoelectric emission from a metal, but yellow light cannot. If red light is incident on the metal, then
(a) photoelectric current will increase
(b) rate of emission of photoelectrons will decrease
(c) no photoelectric emission will occur
(d) energy of the photoelectrons will increase

11. The graph between, which of the following two factors for photoelectric effect, is a straight line?
(a) intensity of radiation and photoelectric current
(b) potential of anode and photoelectric current
(c) threshold frequency and velocity of photoelectrons
(d) intensity of radiations and stopping potential

12. A photosensitive material would emit electrons if excited by photons beyond a threshold. To cross the threshold you would increase
(a) intensity of light
(b) wavelength of light
(c) frequency of light
(d) the voltage applied to light source

13. The study of photoelectric effect is useful in understanding
(a) quantization of energy
(b) quantization of charge
(c) conservation of charge
(d) conservation of kinetic energy

14. Which of the following is not property of the photons?
(a) momentum (b) energy
(c) frequency (d) rest mass

15. Photoelectrons are being obtained by irradiating zinc by a radiation of 3100 Å. In order to increase the kinetic energy of ejected photoelectrons
(a) the intensity of radiation should be increased
(b) the wavelength of radiation should be increased
(c) the wavelength of radiation should be decreased
(d) both wavelength and intensity of radiation should be increased

16. When a photon collides with an electron which of the following characteristic of the photon increases?
(a) energy (b) frequency
(c) wavelength (d) none of the above

17. A photon stimulates the emission of another photon of the same energy. The two are
(a) in phase and travel in the same direction
(b) in phase and travel in the opposite direction
(c) out of phase and travel in the same direction
(d) out of phase and travel in the opposite direction

18. Which of the following makes use of photoelectric effect?
(a) television receiver
(b) television camera
(c) cathode Ray oscillograph
(d) radar

19. The momentum of the photon is given by
(a) $\frac{h}{\lambda}$ (b) $\frac{h}{c\lambda}$
(c) $\frac{hc}{\lambda}$ (d) $\frac{h\lambda}{c}$

20. The dynamic mass of the photon is given by
(a) $\frac{h\nu}{c}$ (b) $\frac{h\lambda}{c}$
(c) $\frac{h}{c\lambda}$ (d) $\frac{h}{c\nu}$

21. Which of the following characteristics of photoelectric effect supports the particle nature of radiations.
(a) threshold frequency.
(b) dependence of the velocity of photoelectron on frequency.
(c) independence of velocity of photoelectrons on intensity of radiations.
(d) instantaneous photoelectric emission.

22. A photo sensitive metal is not emitting photoelectrons when irradiated. It will do so when threshold is crossed. To cross the threshold we need to increase
(a) intensity (b) frequency
(c) wavelength (d) none of the above

23. The frequency and intensity of the incident beam of light falling on the surface of photoelectric material is increased by a factor of two. This will

(a) increase the maximum kinetic energy of the photoelectrons as well as photoelectrons current by a factor of two
(b) increase the maximum kinetic energy of photoelectric and would increase the photoelectric current by a factor of two
(c) increase the maximum kinetic energy of photoelectrons by a factor of two and will have no effect on photo electric current
(d) increase the photoelectric current by a factor of two but will have no effect in kinetic energy of emitted electrons

24. The maximum energy of the electrons released in photocell is independent of
(a) frequency of incident light
(b) intensity of incident light
(c) nature of cathode surface
(d) none of these

25. Ultraviolet radiation of 6.2 eV falls on an aluminium surface (work function 4.2 eV). The kinetic energy in joule of the fastest electron emitted is approximately
(a) 3×10^{-21} (b) 3×10^{-19}
(c) 4×10^{-17} (d) 3×10^{-15}

26. The ionisation potential of hydrogen atom is 13.6 V. How much energy need to be supplied to ionise the hydrogen atom in the first excited state?
(a) 13.6 eV (b) 27.2 eV
(c) 3.4 eV (d) 6.8 eV

27. Ionisation energy for hydrogen atom in the ground state is E. What is the ionisation energy of Li^{++} atom in the 2nd excited state?
(a) E (b) $3E$
(c) $6E$ (d) $9E$

28. The energy difference between the first two levels of hydrogen atom is 10.2 eV. For another element of atomic number 10 and mass number 20, this will be
(a) 1020 eV (b) 2040 eV
(c) 0.51 eV (d) 0.102 eV

29. For the first member of Balmer series of hydrogen spectrum, the wavelength is λ. What is the wavelength of the second member?
(a) $\frac{5}{30}\lambda$ (b) $\frac{3}{16}\lambda$
(c) $\frac{4}{9}\lambda$ (d) $\frac{20}{27}\lambda$

30. If the ionisation energy for hydrogen atom is 13.6 eV. The energy required to excite it from the ground state to the next higher state is nearly
(a) 3.4 eV (b) 10.2 eV
(c) 12.1 eV (d) 1.5 eV

31. The ionisation energy of hydrogen atom is 13.6 eV. Hydrogen atoms in the ground state are excited by monochromatic radiation of photon energy 12.1 eV. The spectral lines emitted by hydrogen atom according to Bohr's theory will be
(a) one (b) two
(c) three (d) four

32. The transition of the electron takes place from $n = 2$ orbit to $n = 1$ orbit. Which of the following gives the shortest wavelength?
(a) Hydrogen atom
(b) Deutrium atom
(c) singly ionised Helium
(d) doubly ionised Helium

33. The wavelength of K_α-line in copper is 1.54 Å. The ionisation energy of K electron in copper in joule is
(a) 11.2×10^{-17} (b) 12.9×10^{-16}
(c) 17×10^{-15} (d) 10×10^{-16}

34. The following figure indicates the energy levels of a certain atom. When the system moves from $2E$ level to E, a photon of wavelength λ is emitted. The wavelength of photon produced during its transition from level $4E/3$ to level E is

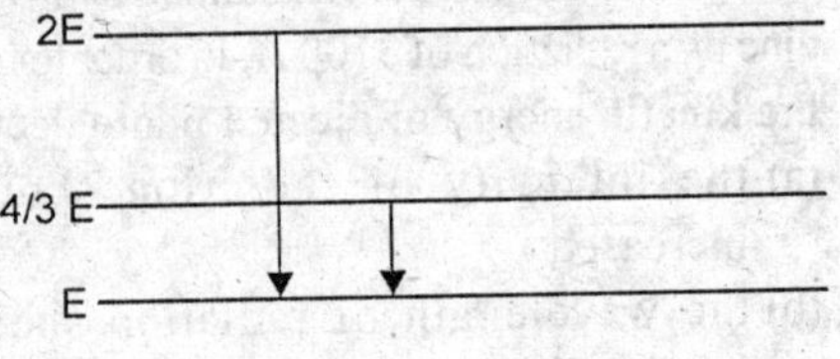

(a) $\frac{\lambda}{3}$ (b) $\frac{3\lambda}{4}$
(c) $\frac{4\lambda}{3}$ (d) 3λ

35. The ionisation energy of hydrogen atom is 13.6 eV. The ionisation energy of helium atom would be
(a) 1.6 eV (b) 27.2 eV
(c) 6.8 eV (d) 54.4 eV

36. The ionisation energy of 10 times ionised sodium atom is
(a) 13.6 eV (b) 13.6×11 eV
(c) $\frac{13.6}{11}$ (d) $13.6 \times (11)^2$ eV

37. The energy of hydrogen atom in its ground state is -13.6 eV. The energy of the level corresponding to $n = 5$ is
(a) -0.54 eV (b) -5.40 eV
(c) -0.85 eV (d) -2.72 eV

38. Which of the following sources give discrete emission spectrum?
(a) incandescent electric bulb
(b) sun
(c) mercury vapour lamp
(d) candle

39. Band spectrum is produced by
(a) H (b) He
(c) H_2 (d) Na

40. Energy levels A, B, C of a certain atom correspond to increasing values of energy i.e., $E_A < E_B < E_C$. If λ_1, λ_2, λ_3 are the wavelengths of radiation corresponding to the transitions C to B, B to A and C to A respectively, which of the following statement is correct?

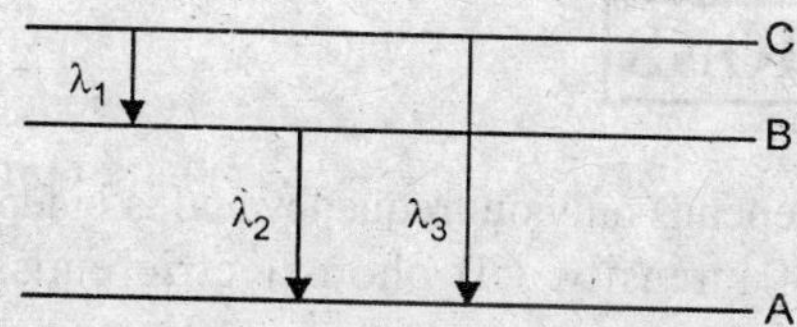

(a) $\lambda_3 = \lambda_1 + \lambda_2$
(b) $\lambda_3 = \frac{\lambda_1 \lambda_2}{\lambda_1 + \lambda_2}$
(c) $\lambda_1 + \lambda_2 + \lambda_3 = 0$
(d) $\lambda_3^2 = \lambda_1^2 + \lambda_2^2$

41. In the following figure the energy levels of hydrogen atom have been shown along with some transitions marked A, B, C, D and E. The transitions A, B and C respectively represent

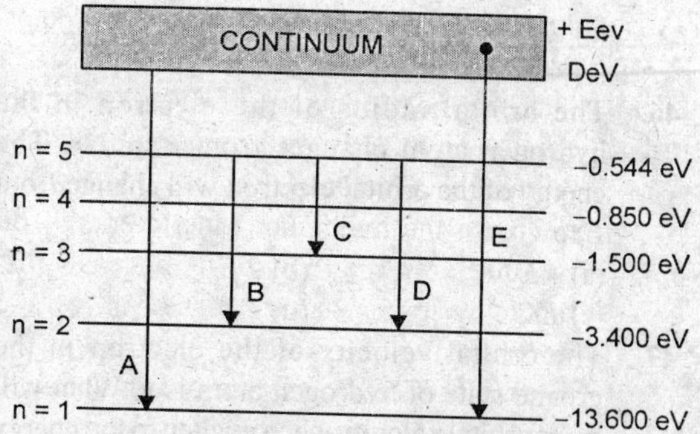

(a) the first member of Lyman series, third member of Balmer series and second member of Paschen series
(b) the ionisation potential of hydrogen, second member of Balmer series and third member of Paschen series
(c) the series limit of Lyman series, second member of Balmer series and second member of Paschen series
(d) the series limit of Lyman series, second member of Balmer series and third member of Paschen series

42. In an atom, the two electrons revolve around the nucleus. What is the ratio of their time periods in the first excited state and the ground state.
(a) 2 (b) 4
(c) 8 (d) 16

43. If the size of atom is enlarged such that the nucleus has a size of small seed (1 mm diameter) then the electron orbits will have the size of
(a) a big seed (1 cm diameter)
(b) a cricket ball (10 cm diameter)
(c) a cricket playground (100 m diameter)
(d) the earth

44. The radius of Bohr's first orbit is r. What is the radius of the first orbit in the singly ionised helium atom?
(a) $4r$ (b) $2r$
(c) $r/2$ (d) $r/4$

45. The orbital electron of the hydrogen atom jumps from the ground state to a higher energy state and its orbital velocity is reduced to one third of its initial value. If the radius of the orbit in the ground state is r, then what is the radius of the new orbit?

(a) $2r$ (b) $3r$
(c) $4r$ (d) $9r$

46. The orbital radius of the electron in the hydrogen atom changes from r to $4r$. The energy of the orbital electron will change from E to

(a) $4E$ (b) $2E$
(c) $E/2$ (d) $E/4$

47. The orbital velocity of the electron in the ground state of hydrogen atom is v. What will be its orbital velocity when excited to the energy state -1.51 eV?

(a) $v/9$ (b) $v/4$
(c) $v/3$ (d) $v/2$

48. Who proposed that the orbits of the electron in the atom are elliptical?

(a) Thomson (b) Bohr
(c) Rutherford (d) Sommerfield

49. Suppose the elements with principal quantum number $n > 4$ where not allowed in nature, what would have been the total number of elements in nature?

(a) 10 (b) 28
(c) 60 (d) 110

50. The distance of closest approach of an α-particle incident on a nucleus is r. If the velocity of the α-particle is doubled, the distance of closest approach will be

(a) $2r$ (b) $4r$
(c) $r/2$ (d) $r/4$

ANSWERS

1	2	3	4	5	6	7	8	9	10
(b)	(b)	(d)	(a)	(a,b,c)	(d)	(d)	(c)	(d)	(c)
11	**12**	**13**	**14**	**15**	**16**	**17**	**18**	**19**	**20**
(a)	(c)	(a)	(d)	(c)	(c)	(a)	(b)	(a)	(c)
21	**22**	**23**	**24**	**25**	**26**	**27**	**28**	**29**	**30**
(a)	(b)	(b)	(b)	(b)	(c)	(a)	(a)	(d)	(b)
31	**32**	**33**	**34**	**35**	**36**	**37**	**38**	**39**	**40**
(b)	(a)	(b)	(d)	(d)	(d)	(a)	(c)	(c)	(b)
41	**42**	**43**	**44**	**45**	**46**	**47**	**48**	**49**	**50**
(d)	(c)	(c)	(c)	(d)	(d)	(c)	(d)	(c)	(d)

HINTS / SOLUTIONS

1. Work function is the minimum amount of energy lost to get the electron ejected. More energy can also be lost due to the collision etc.

2. $h\nu_0$ is the minimum energy used to eject the electron. More energy of the electron can be lost due to collision etc.

3. Photoelectric effect, in fact, confirms the quantum nature of light.

4. Larger intensity means more incident photons which ejects larger number of electrons.

5. This shows that, there is a minimum amount of energy required to eject the electron. Also, according to quantum theory (i) max, KE depends only on frequency and is independent of intensity. (ii) photoelectric emission is instantaneous.

6. Intensity of light varies inversely as the square of the distance.

7. Photons exert pressure on the surface on which they fall.

8. It is the statement of fact.

9. The saturation current $\propto$ intensity $\propto (1/d^2)$.

10. Threshold wave length is less than that of yellow light. So, the red light cannot cause photoelectric emission.

12. $h\nu = h\nu_0 + E_k$. Here $\nu > \nu_0$.

14. Photons always travel with constant speed be decreased.

15. $\frac{hc}{\lambda} = \frac{hc}{\lambda_0} + E_k$.

To increase E_k, λ should be decreased.

20. $mc^2 = h\nu$, Hence $m = h\nu/c^2 = h/c\lambda$ and $p = h/\lambda$.

22. Current $\propto$ Intensity.

Kinetic energy increases with frequency.

24. $E_k = h\nu - h\nu_0$.

25. $E_k = 6.2 - 4.2 = 2$ eV
$= 2 \times 1.6 \times 10^{-19}$ J $= 3.2 \times 10^{-19}$ J.

26. Ionisation energy of nth state $= -E_n$.

For the first excited state $n = 2$ and energy in that state is $\frac{13.6}{2^2}$ eV $= 3.4$ eV.

27. $E_i = hcR_H Z^2$. Here $Z = 3$.

E_i (ground) for $Li^{++} = 9E$.

E_i (3rd ex. st.) $= 9E/(3)^2 = E$.

8. $\Delta E \propto Z^2$. Hence it will be $10.2 \times 10^2 = 1020$.

9. For Balmar series $\frac{1}{\lambda} = R_H\left[\frac{1}{2^2} - \frac{1}{n^2}\right]$

where $n = 3, 4, 5, 6$.

$\lambda_1 = 36/5\, R_H$ and $\lambda_2 = 16/3\, R_H$.

Hence $\lambda_2 = \frac{5 \times 16}{3 \times 36}\ \lambda_1 = \frac{20}{27}\lambda_1$

). Energy in the next higher orbit
$= 13.6/(2)^2 = 3.4$ eV

Excitation energy $= 13.6 - 3.4 = 10.2$ eV.

. Electron jumps to the energy level $13.6 - 12.1 = 1.5$ eV. It is the 3rd higher level. So, two lines corresponding to the transitions $3 \rightarrow 2$ and $3 \rightarrow 1$ will be obtained.

. $\lambda \propto (1/Z^2)$ for hydrogen like atoms.

. $E = \frac{hc}{\lambda}$.

$\frac{hc}{\lambda} = 2E - E = E$.

Hence $\frac{4}{3}E - E = \frac{1}{3}E$ that is $\lambda' = 3\lambda$.

35. $E \propto Z^2$ and Z for helium is 2.

36. It becomes hydrogen like atom with $Z = 11$.

37. $E_n = \frac{-13.6}{(5)^2} = -0.544$ eV.

38. Mercury vapours give line spectrum.

39. Molecules give band spectrum.

40. $\frac{1}{\lambda} = R\left[\frac{1}{n_i} - \frac{1}{n_0^2}\right]$

Here $\frac{1}{\lambda_1} = R\left[\frac{1}{n_2^2} - \frac{1}{n_3^2}\right]$, $\frac{1}{\lambda_2} = R\left[\frac{1}{n_1^2} - \frac{1}{n_2^2}\right]$

and $\frac{1}{\lambda_3} = R\left[\frac{1}{n_1^2} - \frac{1}{n_3^2}\right]$

Hence $\frac{1}{\lambda_3} = \frac{1}{\lambda_1} + \frac{1}{\lambda_2}$.

41. The electron jump to $n = 1$ level in the Lyman series, $n = 2$ in the Balmer series and $n = 3$ level in the Paschen series.

42. $T^2 \propto r^3$ and $r \propto n^2$.

Hence $r_2/r_1 = 2^2/1^2 = 4$.

Hence $T_2/T_1 = [4^3]^{1/2} = 8$.

43. The radius of electron orbit is about 10^5 times the size of nucleus. Hence 1 mm $\times 10^5 = 10^2$m.

44. $r \propto (1/Z)$.

45. $v \propto (1/n)$ and $r \propto n^2$.

46. $r \propto n^2$ and $E \propto (1/n^2)$.

47. Energy state -1.51 eV correspond to $n = 3$.

And $v \propto (1/n)$

48. Summerfield explained the elliptical nature of the electronic orbits.

49. Total number of elements
$= 2\,[1^2 + 2^2 + 3^2 + 4^2]$.

50. $r \propto \frac{2Ze^2}{\frac{1}{2}Mv^2}$.

UNIT-16

ELECTRONIC DEVICES

SEMICONDUCTORS

Substances whose conductivity lies between conductors and insulators are called semi-conductors.

The conductors, semiconductors and insulators can be distinguished on the basis of band theory.

The electrons revolving around the nucleus of an isolated atom possess discrete energy state 1s, 2s, 3p, ... and they occupy the quantum states available in those energy levels. Due to periodicity of lattice, each atom is in the electric field of neighboring atoms. Consequently the energy levels of an individual atom lose their validity. If the crystal contains N-atoms then due to interaction between the atom splits into N-close sub-levels. As N is very large the separation between sub-levels is very small so that these dense levels are almost continuous and are said to form an energy band. These energy bands are in general separated by regions called forbidden band or band gaps.

According to Pauli's exclusion principle, each energy level can be occupied by two electrons having opposite spins. Hence normally only lower energy bands will be filled with electrons. The highest energy band containing electrons is called the valence band and the next higher band is called the conduction band.

If the valence and conduction bands overlap, the substance is referred as *conductor*.

If the valence and conduction bands have a forbidden gap more than 3 eV, the substance is *insulator*.

If the valence and conduction bands have a forbidden gap less then 2 eV, the substance is a *semi-conductor*.

Germanium (Ge) and Silicon (Si) are well known examples of semiconductors. In germanium the forbidden gap E_g = 0.7 eV while in silicon E_g = 1.1. eV. The electrons can not gain this order of energy in the external field. Hence in such crystals the valence band is completely filled and conduction band is completely empty. At 0K semi-conductor is a perfect insulator.

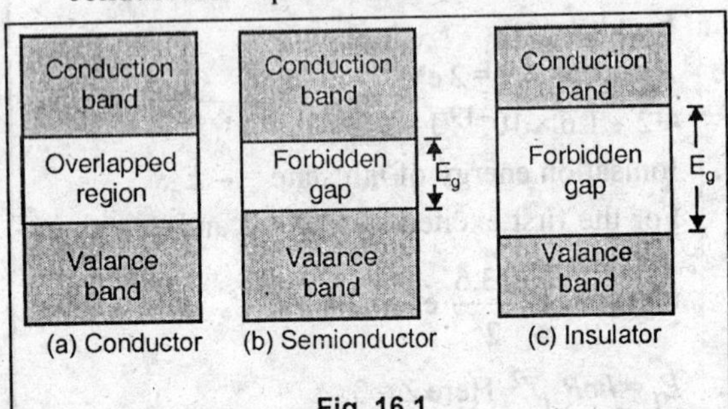

Fig. 16.1

Electric conduction in semi-conductors. The semi-conductors are of two types.

I. Instrinsic semi-conductor. The pure semi-conductors are called intrinsic semi-conductor. Their conductivity is due to their own (internal) charge carriers. Germanium (Ge), silicon (Si) are well known intrinsic semi-conductor. The valency of each of Ge and Si is 4. The four valence electrons are tightly bound with positive core of nucleus and remaining electrons. The charge of positive core is +ve. In Ge or Si crystal, the atoms are arranged regularly such that each atom lies at the corner of a regular tetrahedron. All the four electrons of an Ge-atom form covalent bonds with neighbouring electrons of other 4-Ge atoms; thereby leaving no free electron for conduction. When a semi-conductor is heated, some covalent bonds break due to thermal agitation and thus some electrons get free for conduction. As soon as one electron gets free, there is a deficiency of electron at its preceding position which acts as a positive charge and is called a hole. The number of holes is equal to number of free electrons. Thus in an intrinsic semi-conductor the conductivity is due to holes and electrons both which increases with rise of temperature. At normal temperature only 1 out by 10^9 covalent bonds breaks, hence the conductivity of intrinsic semiconductors is so small, that's why they can not be used for practical purpose.

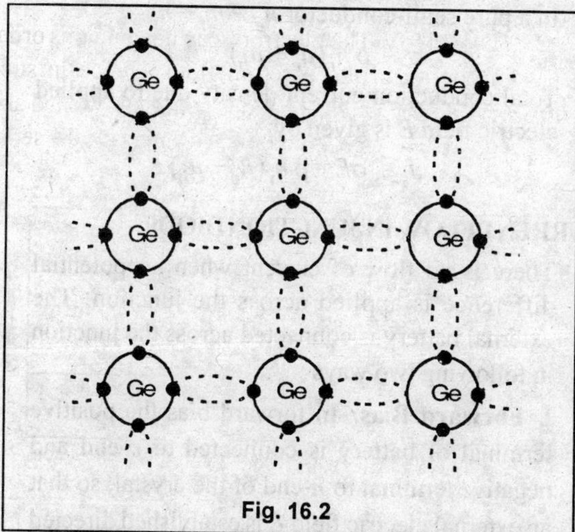

Fig. 16.2

II. Extrinsic semi-conductors. When a small amount of trivalent or pentavalent impurity is introduced into pure germanium (or silicon) crystal, the conductivity of the crystal increases appreciably. Such an impure semiconductor is called extrinsic semiconductor, the conductivity of an extrinsic semi-conductor is due to impurities. These are of two types

(i) n-type (ii) p-type

(i) **n-type semi-conductors.** When a pentavalent impurity like Phosphorus, Antimony, Arsenic is doped in pure germanium or silicon, then the conductivity of crystal increases due to surplus of electrons and such a crystal is said of be n-type semiconductor, while the impurity atoms are called *donors*.

Each impurity atom 5-valence electrons replaces a germanium (or Silicon) atom. Therefore the four valence electrons from covalent bonds with electrons of neighbouring germanium (or silicon) atoms while fifth electron becomes surplus. This electron is free to move to cause conduction. Therefore in n-type semi-conductors the charge carriers are negatively charged electrons.

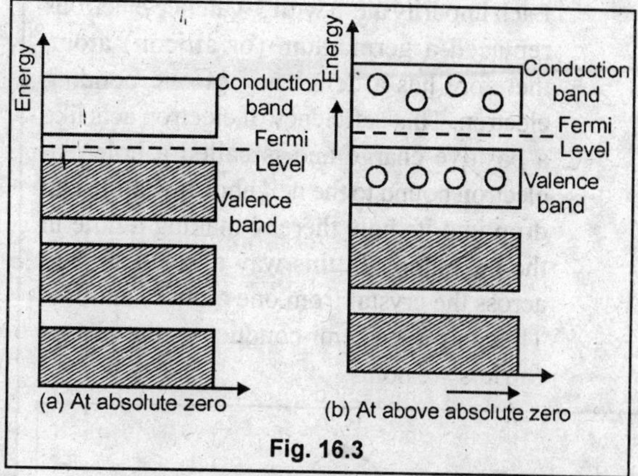

Fig. 16.3

In an n-type semi-conductor, the free electrons are called majority charge carriers and the holes are called minority charge carriers. In an n-type semi-conductor the donor level is near the conduction band.

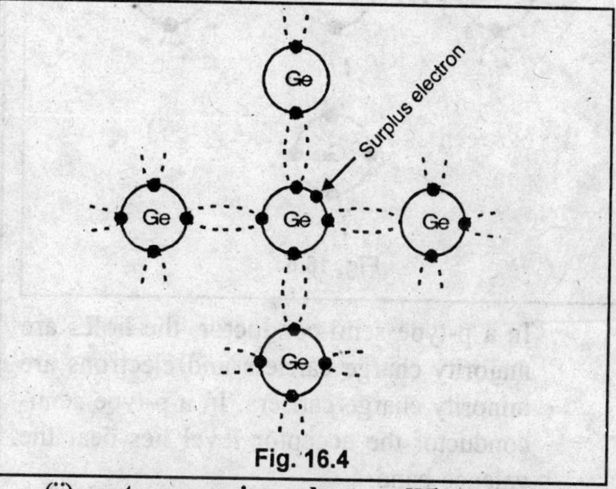

Fig. 16.4

(ii) **p-type semi-conductor.** When a trivalent impurity like Aluminium, Indium, Boron, Gallium etc. is doped in pure germanium (or silicon), then the conductivity of crystal increases due to deficiency of electrons i.e. holes and such a crystal is said to be p-type semi-conductor while the impurity atoms are called acceptors.

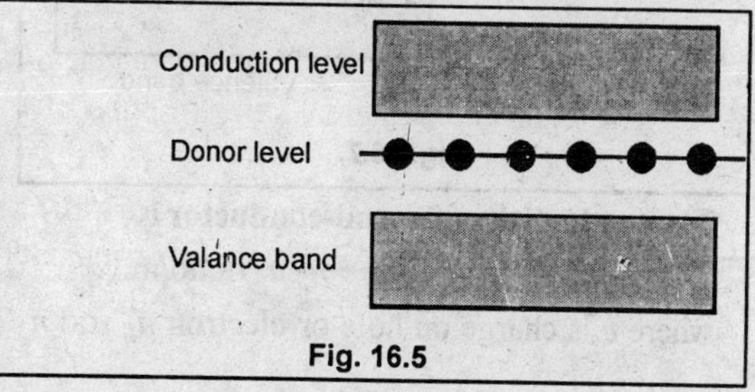

Fig. 16.5

Each impurity atom with 3-valence electrons replaced a germanium (or silicon) atom, therefore has a deficiency of one bonding electron. This deficiency of electron acts like a positive charge and is called a hole. An electron bound to the neighbouring atom can drop into its hole thereby making a hole in the next atom. In this way a hole can pass across the crystal from one atom to another. Thus in p-type semi-conductors the charge carriers are holes.

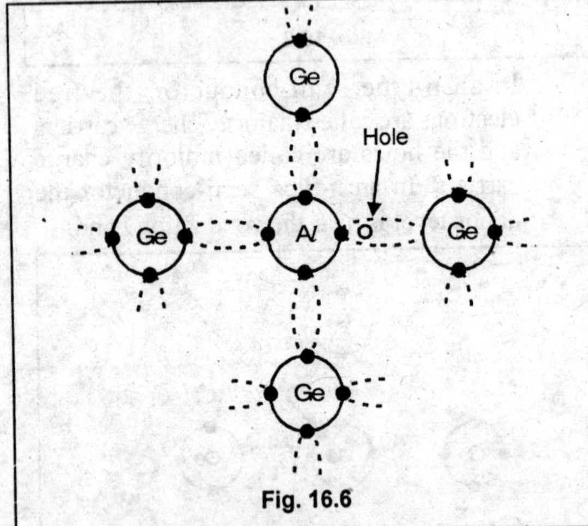

Fig. 16.6

In a p-type semi-conductor, the holes are majority charge carriers and electrons are minority charge carriers. In a p-type semi-conductor the acceptor level lies near the valence band.

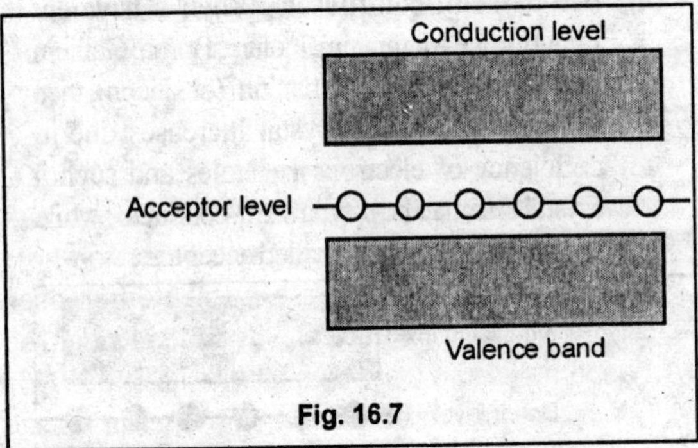

Fig. 16.7

The conductivity of a semi-conductor is

$$\rho = e(n_h \mu_h + n_e \mu_e) \text{ mho/m.}$$

where e is charge on hole or electron n_h and n_e are concentration of holes and electrons, μ_h and μ_e are mobilities of holes and electrons, Mobility means drift velocity per unit electric field.

Resistivity, $(\rho) = 1/\text{conductivity } (\sigma)$

In a pure semi-conductor $n_e = n_h = n_i$

$$\sigma = \rho\, n_i(\mu_e + \mu_h)$$

Total conduction current density due to applied electric field E is given by

$$J = \sigma E = \rho\, n_i(\mu_e + \mu_h) E$$

CURRENT FLOW IN JUNCTION DIODE

There is no flow of current when no potential difference is applied across the junction. The external battery is connected across the junction in following two ways :

I. Forward Bias. In forward bias the positive terminal of battery is connected to p-end and negative terminal to n-end of the crystal, so that an external electric field E is established directed from p to n-end to oppose the internal field E_i as shown in Fig. The external field E is much stronger than internal field E_i.

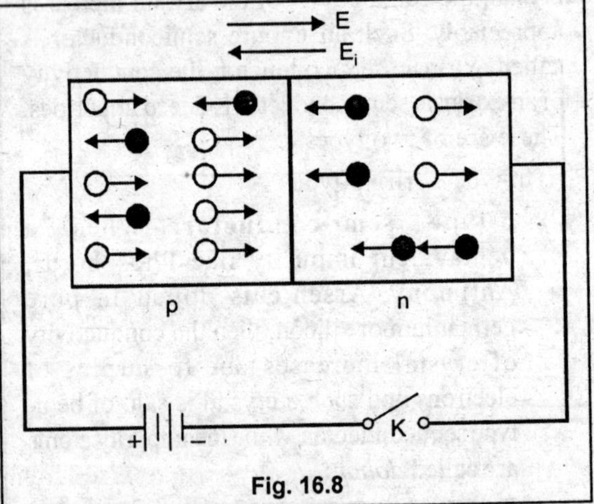

Fig. 16.8

Under this arrangement the holes move along the field E from p-region to n-region and electrons move opposite to field E from n-region to p-region; eliminating the depletion layer. A current is thus set up in the junction diode. The following are the basic features of forward biasing are as follows :

(i) Within the junction diode the current is due to both types of majority charge carriers but in external circuit it is due to electrons only.

(ii) The current is of the order of milliamperes.

(iii) The current increases with increase of external potential difference. The graph between potential difference V and current I is non-linear.

(iv) The forward current is due to diffusion of charge carriers.

II. Reverse Bias. In this bias the positive terminal of battery is connected to n-end and negative terminal to p-end of the crystal, so that the external field is established to help the internal field E_i as shown in Fig. Under this biasing the holes in p-region and the electrons in n-region are pushed away from the junction to widen the depletion layer and hence increase the potential barrier, the current flow stops.

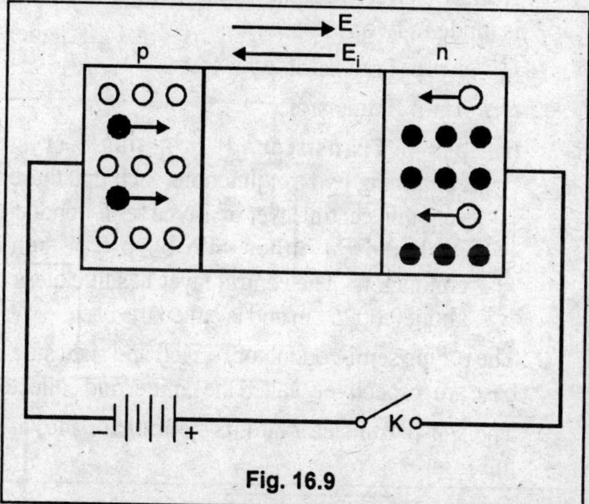

Fig. 16.9

When the potential difference across the junction is increased, a very small reverse current of the order of micro-amperes is found to flow. The reason is that due to thermal agitation there are few electrons in *p*-region and a few holes in *n*-region called the minority charge carriers. The reverse bias opposes the majority charge carriers but aids the minority charge carriers to move across the junction. Hence a very small current flows.

The basic characteristics of reverse bias as follows :

(i) Within the junction diode the current is due to both types of minority charge carriers but in external current it is due to electrons only.

(ii) The current is very small of the order of μA.

(iii) The graph of voltage V V/S current I is shown in the figure.

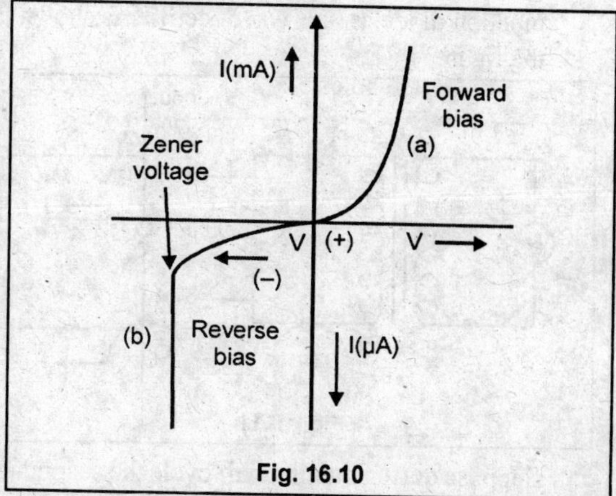

Fig. 16.10

(iv) The reverse current is due to drift of charge carriers.

DIODE RESISTANCE

$$R_{dc} = \frac{d}{I}$$

$$R_{ac} = \frac{dv}{dI} = \frac{26\,\eta}{I}$$

Hence the diode offers very small resistance in the forward bias while very large resistance in reverse bias.

AVALANCHE BREAKDOWN

When the reverse bias is made sufficiently high, the covalent bonds near the junction break down liberating a large number of electron-hole pairs. Then the reverse current increases abruptly to high value. This is called avalanche breakdown and may damage the junction. This phenomenon is used in Zener diode used in voltage regulators.

Current in a junction diode.

$$I = I_s\left(e^{eV/\eta kT} - 1\right)$$

or

$$I = I_s\left(e^{39/\eta}\right)$$

where I_s = reverse saturation current $\eta = 1$ for germanium and $\eta = 2$ for silicon.

V is positive, if junction is forward biased and negative, if the junction is reverse biased.

p-n JUNCTION DIODE AS A RECTIFIER

(i) **Half Wave Rectifier.** The circuit diagram of junction diode as half wave rectifier is shown in the figure

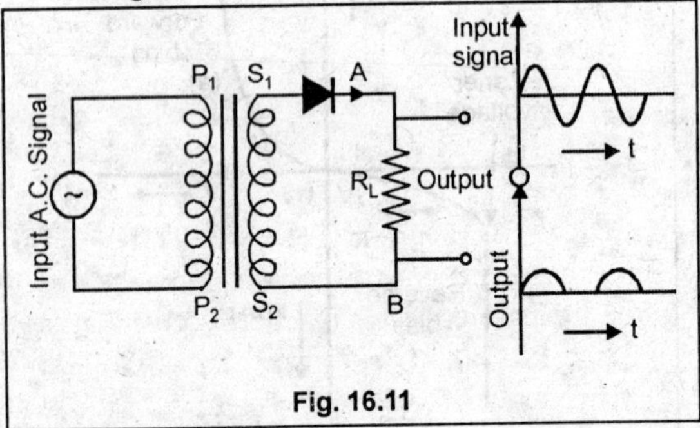

Fig. 16.11

Suppose during the first half cycle the secondary terminal S_1 of transformer is positive relative to S_2, then the junction diode is forward biased. Therefore the current flows and its direction in load resistance R_L is from A to B. In next half cycle the terminal S_1 is negative relative to S_2 then the diode is in reverse bias, therefore no current flows in diode and hence there is no potential difference across load R_L. Therefore the output current in load flows only when S_1 is positive relative to S_2. That is during first half cycles of input a.c. signal there is a current in circuit and hence a potential difference across load resistance R_L while no current flows for next half cycles. The direction of current in load is always from A to B. Thus a single *p-n* junction diode acts as a half wave rectifier.

(ii) **Full wave Rectifier.** We use two junction diodes for full wave rectifier. The circuit diagram for full wave rectifier using two junction diodes is shown in the figure below :

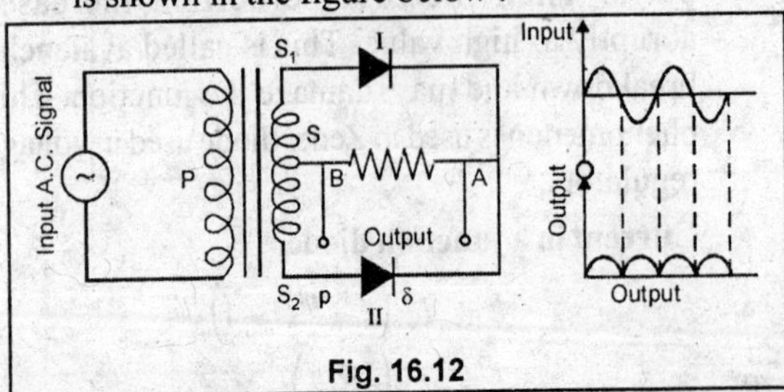

Fig. 16.12

Suppose during first half cycle of input A.C. signal the terminal S_1 is positive relative to S and S_2 is negative relative to S. Then diode I is forward biased and diode II is reverse biased. Hence current flows in diode I and not in diode II. The direction of current i_1 due to diode I in load resistance R_L is directed from A to B. In next half cycle, the terminal S_1 is negative relative to S and S_2 is positive relative to S. Then diode I is reverse biased and II is forward biased. Therefore current flows in diode II and there is no current in diode II in load resistance is again from A to B. Thus for input A.C. signal the output current is a continuous series of unidirectional pulses. This output current may be converted in fairly steady current by the use suitable filters.

TRANSISTOR

A semi-conductor electronic device which is used in place of a thermionic triode is called transistor. It was discovered by Willium Shockly in1951. It is made in two forms

(i) p-n-p Transistor

(ii) n-p-n Transistor

(i) **p-n-p Transistor.** It is a single crystal containing two p-n junctions such that there is very thin central layer of n-type semi-conductor enclosed on either side by p-type semi-conductors. The central layer has thickness of about 0.0025 cm and is called the base.

The p-type semi-conductors on left and right side of base are respectively called the emitter and collector. The p-n-p transistor and its symbol are shown in the figure

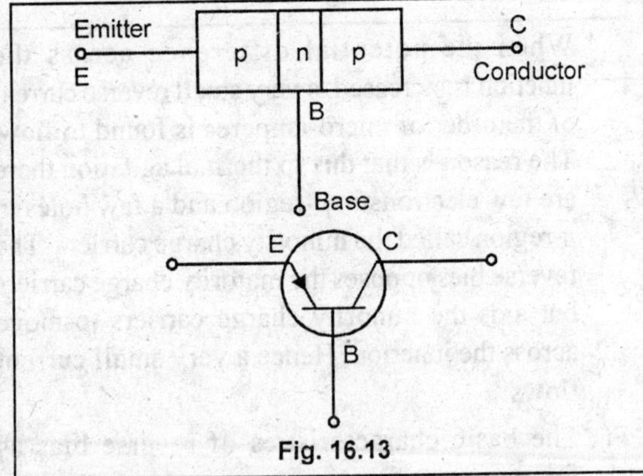

Fig. 16.13

WORKING OF p-n-p TRANSISTOR

The emitter-base junction is given a small forward bias, while base collector junction is given a large reverse bias.

Under the forward bias of emitter-base region, the positive holes of p-region move towards the base.

Due to thin base most of holes (about 98%) entering it pass on to the collector while a very few of them (nearly 2%) combine with the electron, a fresh electron leaves the negative terminal of battery V_{CC} and enters the base. This cause a very small base current i_b. The holes entering the collector move under the aiding reverse bias towards terminal C. As a hole reaches terminal C, an electron leaves the negative terminal of battery V_{CC} and neutralises the hole. This causes the collector current i_c. Both these currents i_b and i_c combine to form the emitter current i_e i.e.,

$$i_e = i_b + i_c$$

Obviously, the holes are the charge carriers within the p-n-p transistor while the electrons are charge carriers in external circuit.

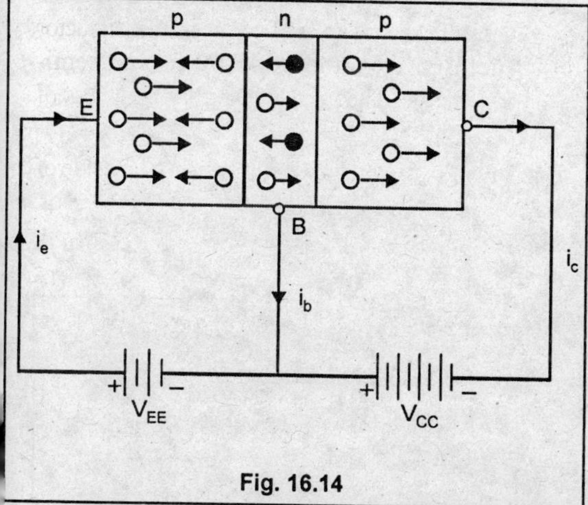

Fig. 16.14

(ii) n-p-n Transistor. It is a single crystal containing two p-n junctions such that there is a very thin central layer of p-type semi-conductor enclosed in either side by n-type semi-conductor. The *n*-p-n transistor and its symbol is shown in Fig.

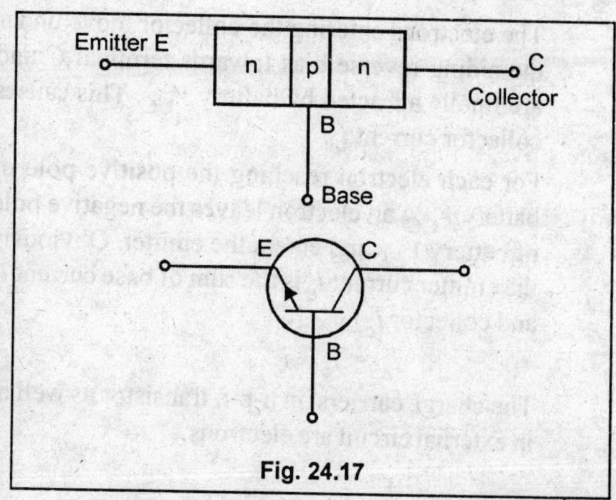

Fig. 24.17

WORKING OF n-p-n TRANSISTOR. The emitter base junction is given a small forward bias while the base collector junction is given large reverse bias. Under the forward bias of emitter base region the electrons of emitter region move toward the base.

Due to base being very thin most of electrons (about 98%) entering it pass into the collector while a very few of them (nearly 2%) combine with the holes of base. As soon as an electron combines with the hole, an electron leaves the negative terminal of the battery V_{EE} and enters to emitter through terminal E. At the same time the positive terminal of battery V_{EE} receives an electron from the base. This creates the base current i_b and also a new hole in the base.

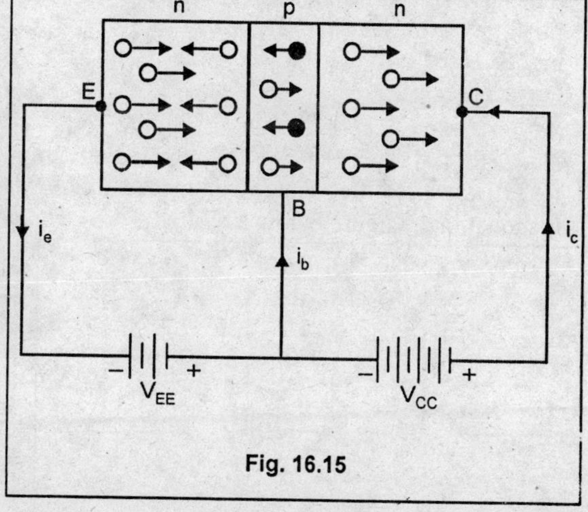

Fig. 16.15

The electrons entering the collector move under the aiding reverse bias towards terminal C and are finally attracted by battery V_{CC}. This causes collector current i_c.

For each electron reaching the positive pole of battery V_{CC}, an electron leaves the negative pole of battery V_{EE} and enters the emitter. Obviously the emitter current i_e is the sum of base current i_b and collector i_c i.e.,

$$i_e = i_b + i_c$$

The charge carriers in n-p-n transistor as well as in external circuit are electrons.

Characteristic curves of Transistor. There are three ways of using the transistor in a circuit.

(i) Common base configuration.

(ii) Common emitter configuration

(iii) Common collector configuration.

Out of these the first two are mostly used. In each configuration there are two types of characteristic curves.

(i) Input characteristic curves

(ii) Output characteristic curves

MULTIPLE CHOICE QUESTIONS

1. When the plate voltage of a triode is 150 V, its cut off voltage is –5V. On increasing the plate voltage to 200 V, the cut off voltage can be
(a) –4.5 V (b) –5.0 V
(c) –2.3 V (d) –6.66 V

2. A certain triode shows the following readings

V_p	V_g	I_p
150 V	–2 V	5 mA
150 V	–3.5 V	3.2 mA
195 V	–3.5 V	5 ma

The amplification factor of the triode is
(a) 22.5 (b) 45
(c) 30 (d) 60

3. If the amplification factor of a triode valve is 100, then at plate potential of 250 volt the cut off voltage of its grid will be
(a) 0 V (b) –0.4 V
(c) –2.5 V (d) –150 V

4. In the circuit of a triode valve, there is no change in the plate current, when the plate potential is increased from 200 V to 220 V and the grid potential is decreased from –0.5 V to –1.3 V. The amplification factor of this valve is
(a) 15 (b) 20
(c) 25 (d) 35

5. Using a triode as amplifier, the graph between its load resistance R_L and voltage gain A_v will be

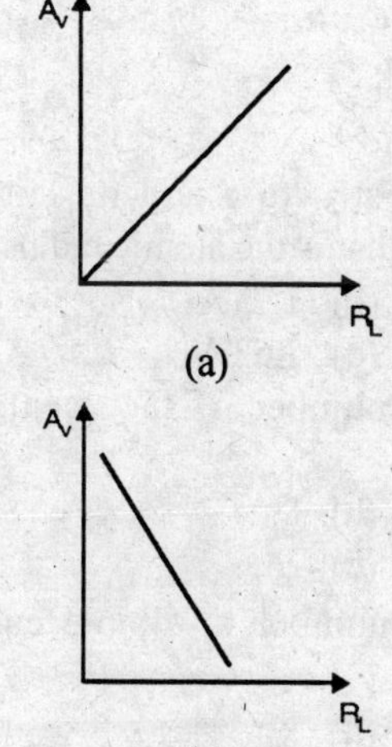

(a) (c)

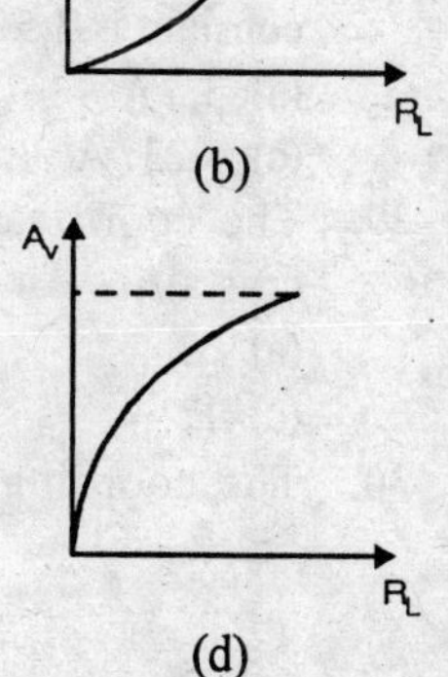

(b) (d)

6. Mutual conductance of a triode is 2 milli mho and the amplification factor is 50. Its anode is connected with a source of 250 volt and a resistance of 25 kΩ. The voltage gain of this amplifier is
(a) 12.5 (b) 10
(c) 25 (d) 50

7. In a triode amplifier, $\mu = 25$, $R_p = 10$ kΩ and load resistance $R_L = 40$ kΩ. If the input signal voltage is 0.5 V, then output signal voltage will be
(a) 1.25 V (b) 2.5 V
(c) 5 V (d) 10 V

8. In a triode valve, a change in anode voltage from 200 V to 240 V on a constant grid voltage produces an increase of anode current from 5 mA to 9.6 mA. The a.c. anode resistance is
(a) 870 Ω (b) 8700 Ω
(c) 87000 Ω (d) 870000 Ω

9. The value of current in a triode valve is given by $I_p = 0.004\ (V_p + 10\ V_g)^{3/2}$ mA. When plate potential and grid potential are 120 V and –2V respectively, then the value of mutual conductance will be
(a) 600 mho (b) 60 mho
(c) 6 mho (d) 6×10^{-4} mho

10. While using triode as an amplifier, we avoid making the grid positive because,
(a) the mutual characteristic is not straight
(b) it affects the amplification factor
(c) it decreases the plate current
(d) of some different reason

11. At a constant plate potential, if the grid is moved closer to the plate, the amplification factor of triode
(a) decreases
(b) increases
(c) remains unchanged
(d) may increase or decrease depending upon grid bias.

12. In vacuum diode for plate potential is graudally varied from –200 V to 200 V. How will the plate current vary ?
(a) first increase then decrease
(b) first decrease then increase
(c) first remain zero, then continuously increases and may cease to vary at higher potential
(d) the variation will be different than that described above.

13. In a cubic unit cell of *bcc* structure, the lattice points (i.e. number of atoms) are
(a) 2 (b) 6
(c) 8 (d) 12

14. According to Bravis, the number of possible space lattice is
(a) 18 (b) 16
(c) 14 (d) 10

15. Which of the following is a crystalline solid ?
(a) graphite (b) calcite
(c) gallium (d) oxygen.

16. In Q. No. 9, the value of plate resistance will be
(a) 20 kΩ (b) 16 kΩ
(c) 16.7 kΩ (d) 12.7 kΩ

17. The space lattice of diamond is
(a) fcc
(b) bcc with two atoms per unit cell
(c) bcc with 4 atoms per unit cell
(d) simple cubic

18. Which of the following is NOT the property of crystalline solid ?
(a) sharp melting point
(b) flat faces
(c) isotropic electrical conductivity
(d) long range order

19. If lattice parameter for a crystalline structure is 3.6 Å, then atomic radius in *fcc* crystal in Å is
(a) 7.20 (b) 1.80
(c) 1.27 (d) 2.90

20. Identify the system of crystal structure, if $a = b \neq c$ and $\alpha = \beta = 90°$ and $\gamma = 120°$.
(a) Monoclinic (b) Triclinic
(c) Hexagonal (d) Rhombohedral

21. A crystal has *bcc* structure and its lattice constant is 3.6 Å. What is the atomic radius ?
(a) 3.6 Å (b) 1.8 Å
(c) 1.27 Å (d) 1.56 Å

22. Diamond is very hard because
(a) it is covalent solid
(b) it has large cohesive energy
(c) high melting point
(d) insoluble in all solvents

23. Which one of the following is the weakest kind of bonding in solids
(a) ionic (b) metallic
(c) Van der Waals (d) covalent

24. What makes the crystalline solids have a sharp melting point ?
(a) anisotropic nature
(b) long range order of the constituent atoms/ions/molecules
(c) equal strength of all the interatomic bonds
(d) none of the these

25. The minimum number of parameters required, to describe three dimensional crystal system is
(a) 10 (b) 8
(c) 6 (d) 4

26. Sodium has body-centred packing. Distance between two nearest atoms is 3.7 Å. The lattice parameter is
(a) 4.8 Å (b) 4.3 Å
(c) 3.9 Å (d) 3.3 Å

27. If there are 4 atoms per unit cell in a solid, the crystal is
(a) simple cubic
(b) body centred cubic
(c) face-centred cubic
(d) end centred cubic

28. A crystal has *bcc* structure and its lattice constant is 3.5 Å. What is the atomic radius ?
(a) 3.5 Å (b) 1.75 Å
(c) 1.237 Å (d) 1.52 Å

29. The coordination number of face centred crystal is
(a) 6 (b) 8
(c) 12 (d) 16

30. The coordination number of simple cubic crystal is
(a) 6 (b) 8
(c) 12 (d) 16

31. The coordination number is the number of the
(a) closest neighbouring atoms in a crystal structure
(b) atoms per unit volume
(c) atoms per unit cell
(d) atoms per lattice

32. Which of the following has minimum portion of available volume, filled by hard spheres arranged in various structures ?
(a) simple cubic
(b) face centred cubic
(c) body centre cubic
(d) diamond.

33. If the physical properties of a solid depend upon the direction, the property of the crystal is called
(a) anisotropic (b) isotropic
(c) orthotropic (d) allotropic.

34. If the physical properties of solids do not depend on the direction, then solid is known as
(a) anisotropic (b) isotropic
(c) orthotropic (d) allotropic

35. The coordination number of body centred crystal is
(a) 6 (b) 8
(c) 12 (d) 16

36. The coordination number of hexagonal close-packing (hcp) is
(a) 6 (b) 8
(c) 12 (d) 16

37. The number of atoms per unit cell in a *sc*, *bcc*, and *fcc* system are
(a) 1, 2 and 4 respectively
(b) 8, 6 and 10 respectively
(c) 1, 4 and 2 respectively
(d) 2, 4 and 1 respectively

38. The unit cell of the shape of a match box is called
(a) cubic (b) tetragonal
(c) orthorhombic (d) rhombohedral

39. Which of the following is an example of polycrystal
(a) wood (b) metals
(c) ceramics (d) both b and c

40. Single crystals are also known as
(a) monocrystals (b) dual crystals
(c) polycrystals (d) all of the above

41. Atomic packing factor for a force centred cubic cell is
(a) $\frac{\pi}{6}$ (b) π
(c) $\frac{\sqrt{3}}{8}\pi$ (d) $\frac{\sqrt{2}}{6}\pi$

42. What makes the molecular crystals, solid at low temperature ?
(a) sharing of electrons
(b) transfer of electrons
(c) Van der Waal's force arising out of polarisation
(d) all of the above

43. Which of the following bonds produces a solid that reflects light in the visible region and whose electrical conductivity decreases with temperature and has high melting point.
(a) metallic bonding
(b) ionic bonding
(c) covalent bonding
(d) Van der Waal's bonding

44. Bonds in semiconductor are
(a) trivalent (b) covalent
(c) bivalent (d) monovalent

45. A solid which is not transparent to visible light and whose electrical condutivity increases with temperature is formed by
(a) ionic bonding
(b) metallic bonding
(c) covalent bonding
(d) Van der Waal bonding

46. A solid which is not transparent to visible light and whose electrical conductivity decreases with increase in temperature is formed by
(a) ionic bonding (b) metallic bonding
(c) covalent bonding (d) Van der Waal bonding

47. The density for an fcc lattice is (A = atomic wt, N = Avogadro's number, a = lattice parameter)
(a) $\frac{4A}{Na^3}$ (b) $\frac{2A}{Na^3}$
(c) $\frac{A}{Na^3}$ (d) $\frac{A}{Na^2}$

48. The density for simple cubic lattice is (where A is atomic weight, N Avogadro number and is a lattice parameter)

(a) $\frac{4A}{Na^3}$ (b) $\frac{2A}{Na^3}$

(c) $\frac{A}{Na^3}$ (d) $\frac{A}{Na^2}$

49. If copper and germanium are heated by 50 °C from room temperature, then

(a) resistance of copper increases while that of germanium decreases

(b) resistance of copper decreases while that of germanium increases

(c) resistance of both decreases

(d) resistance of both increases

50. The resistivity of a semiconductor at room temperature is in between

(a) 10^{-2} to 10^{-5} Ω cm

(b) 10^{-3} to 10^{6} Ω cm

(c) 10^{6} to 10^{8} Ω cm

(d) 10^{10} to 10^{12} Ω cm

ANSWERS

1	2	3	4	5	6	7	8	9	10
(d)	(c)	(c)	(c)	(d)	(c)	(d)	(b)	(d)	(a)
11	**12**	**13**	**14**	**15**	**16**	**17**	**18**	**19**	**20**
(a)	(c)	(a)	(c)	(b)	(c)	(a)	(c)	(c)	(c)
21	**22**	**23**	**24**	**25**	**26**	**27**	**28**	**29**	**30**
(d)	(b)	(c)	(c)	(c)	(b)	(c)	(b)	(c)	(a)
31	**32**	**33**	**34**	**35**	**36**	**37**	**38**	**39**	**40**
(a)	(b, d)	(a)	(b)	(b)	(c)	(a)	(c)	(d)	(a)
41	**42**	**43**	**44**	**45**	**46**	**47**	**48**	**49**	**50**
(d)	(c)	(b)	(b)	(c)	(b)	(a)	(c)	(a)	(b)

HINTS / SOLUTIONS

1. $V_{g_2} = V_{g_1} = \left(\frac{V_{p_2}}{V_{p_1}}\right) = -5\left(\frac{200}{150}\right) = -6.66$ V

2. $\mu = \left(\frac{\Delta V_p}{\Delta V_g}\right)_{\Delta I_p \text{ is constant}}$

$= \frac{195-150}{-2-(-3.5)} = \frac{45}{1.5} = 30.$

3. $V_g = \frac{V_p}{\mu} = -\frac{250}{100} = -2.5$ V

4. $\mu = \left(\frac{\Delta V_p}{\Delta V_g}\right)_{\Delta I_p \text{ is constant}}$

$= \frac{220-200}{-0.5-(-1.3)} = \frac{20}{0.8} = 25$

5. As, $A_v = \frac{\mu R_L}{R_a + R_L}$, so variation of A_v and R_L will be as given by Fig. (d).

6. $R_a = \frac{\mu}{g_m} = \frac{50}{2\times10^{-3}} = 25\times10^3$ Ω

$A_v = \frac{\mu R_L}{R_a + R_L} = \frac{50\times25\times10^3}{25\times10^3+25\times10^3} = 25$

7. $\frac{V_0}{V_i} = \frac{\mu R_L}{R_a + R_L}$

or $V_0 = \frac{V_i \mu R_L}{R_a + R_L} = \frac{0.5\times25\times40}{10+40} = 10$ V

8. $R_a = \frac{\Delta V_P}{\Delta I_P} = \frac{240-200}{(9.6-5)\times10^{-3}}$

$= \frac{40\times10^3}{4.6} = 8700$ Ω

9. & 16. $I_p = 0.004\,(V_p + 10\,V_g)^{3/2} \times 10^{-3}$ ...(i)

Differentiating it w.r.t V_g, keeping V_p constant, we have

$$\frac{\Delta I_p}{\Delta V_g} = 0.004 \times \frac{3}{2}(V_p + 10V_g)^{1/2} \times 10 \times 10^{-3}$$

or $$g_m = 0.004 \times \frac{3}{2}[120 + 10 \times (-2)]^{1/2} \times 10^{-2}$$

$= 6 \times 10^{-4}$ mho

Differentiating (i) w.r.t. V_p we have

$$\frac{\Delta I_p}{\Delta V_p} = 0.004 \times \frac{3}{2}(V_p + 10V_g)^{1/2} \times 10^{-3}$$

$$= 0.004 \times \frac{3}{2}[120 + 10 \times (-2)]^{1/2} \times 10^{-2}$$

$$= 6 \times 10^{-5}$$

$$r_p = \frac{\Delta V_p}{\Delta I_p} = \frac{1}{6 \times 10^{-5}} = 16.7 \times 10^3\ \Omega$$

$= 16.7\,\text{k}\Omega$.

10. For proper amplification of signal without distortion, we should use only straight proption of mutual characteristics.

1. When grid is moved closer to the plate, the separation between grid and cathode increases. Due to which the effect of grid potential on the flow of electron from cathode to plate decreases.

2. For negative plate potential, the plate current is zero.

3. No. of lattice points in a crystal structure will be

(a) $n = \frac{N_c}{8} + \frac{N_F}{2} + \frac{N_i}{1}$

In bcc crystal $N_C = 8$ and $N_F = 0$ and $N_i = 1$;

$$n = \frac{8}{8} + \frac{0}{2} + \frac{1}{1} = 2.$$

4. Number of possible space lattice according to Bravis is 14.

5. Calcite is a crystalline solid.

. The diamond is fcc structure.

. The crystalline substance have anisotropic electrical conductivity.

. Atomic radius for fcc crystal is

$$r = \frac{a}{2\sqrt{2}} = \frac{3.6\ \text{Å}}{2\sqrt{2}} = 1.27\ \text{Å}$$

20. For hexagonal crystal structure, $a = b \neq c$ and $\alpha = \beta = 90°$ but $\gamma = 120°$.

21. Atomic radius for bcc structure,

$$r = \frac{a\sqrt{3}}{4} = \frac{3.6\sqrt{3}}{4} = 1.56\ \text{Å}.$$

22. Diamond is very hard due to large cohesive energy.

23. Van derWaal's bonding is the weakest bonding in solids.

24. In a crystalline solid all the interatomic bonds are of equal strength.

25. The parameters required to describe three dimensional crystal system are six i.e. α, β, γ are a, b, c.

26. Atomic radius for bcc structure is

$$r = \frac{a\sqrt{3}}{4}$$

or $$a = \frac{4r}{\sqrt{3}} = \frac{4(3.7/2)}{\sqrt{3}}$$

$$= \frac{4 \times 1.75}{1.732} = 4.3\ \text{Å}$$

27. No. of atoms per unit cell,

$n = \frac{N_c}{8} + \frac{N_f}{2} + \frac{N_i}{1}$; for face centred cubic cell,

$N_c = 8$, $N_f = 6$ and $N_i = 0$

$$\therefore \quad n = \frac{8}{8} + \frac{6}{2} + \frac{0}{1} = 4.$$

28. Atomic radius for bcc structure,

$$r = \frac{a}{2} = \frac{3.5}{2} = 1.75\ \text{Å}$$

29. Each atom in face centred crystal is in contact with 4 atoms along X-axis, 4 atoms along Y-axis and 4 atoms along Z-axis, hence coordination number of fcc. crystal is 12.

30. The coordination number of simple cubic crystal is 6. As an atom at one corner of a simple cubic cell is in touch with two atoms along X-axis, 2 atoms along Y-axis and 2 atoms along Z-axis.

32. The minimum portion of available volume filled by hard spheres is for a very hard material. It is so in case of diamond.

35. In a body centred crystal each atom is in contact with eight atoms at the corners of the simple cubic cell, hence coordination number of bcc crystal is 8.

36. Hexagonal close packing is for face centred crystal.

37. Number of atoms per unit cell,

$$n = \frac{N_c}{8} + \frac{N_f}{2} + \frac{N_i}{1}$$

For s.c.c system, $N_c = 8, N_f = 0$

and $N_i = 0$

so $n = 1$

For b.c.c. system, $N_c = 8, N_f = 0$

and $N_i = 2$

so $n = 2$

For f.c.c. system, $N_c = 8, N_f = 0$

and $N_i = 4$

so $n = 4$

38. For orthorhombic unit cell, $a \neq b \neq c$ but $\alpha = \beta = \gamma$, which is of the shape of match box.

39. Examples of polycrystals are metals and ceramics.

40. Single crystals are also known as monocrystals.

41. Atomic packing factor

$$= \frac{\text{volume occupied by the atoms in a unit cell}}{\text{volume of the unit cell}}$$

For fcc structure, no. of atoms in a unit cell = 4

radius of each atom $r = \frac{a}{2\sqrt{2}}$.

where a is the lattice parameter.

42. Van der Waal's forces make the molecular crystals, solids at low temperature.

43. The given characteristics are of ionic bonding.

44. Bonds in semiconductors are covalent bonds.

45 and 46. A solid is not transparent to visible light if the value of wavelength of light is greater than the bond length between the atoms/molecules/ions of material. Conductivity depends upon the number of free charge carriers present in the substance at a given temperature or resistance of that material at that temperture.

47. In fcc lattice, the number of atoms per unit cell = 4

$$\text{Density} = \frac{\text{mass of unit cell}}{\text{volume of unit cell}}$$

$$= \frac{4A/N}{a^3} = \frac{4A}{Na^3}$$

48. In simple cubic lattice, volume, $V = a^3$

$$\text{density} = \frac{\text{mass of unit cell}}{\text{volume of unit cell}}$$

$$= \frac{A/N}{V} = \frac{A}{Na^3}$$

49. The temperature coefficient of resistance of copper is positive and that of germanium is negative.

50. Resistivity of a semiconductor at room temperture is in between 10^{-5} Ωm to 10^4 Ωm i.e. 10^{-3} to 10^6 Ωcm.

YOUR SPACE

YOUR SPACE